CHARLEY'S WAR

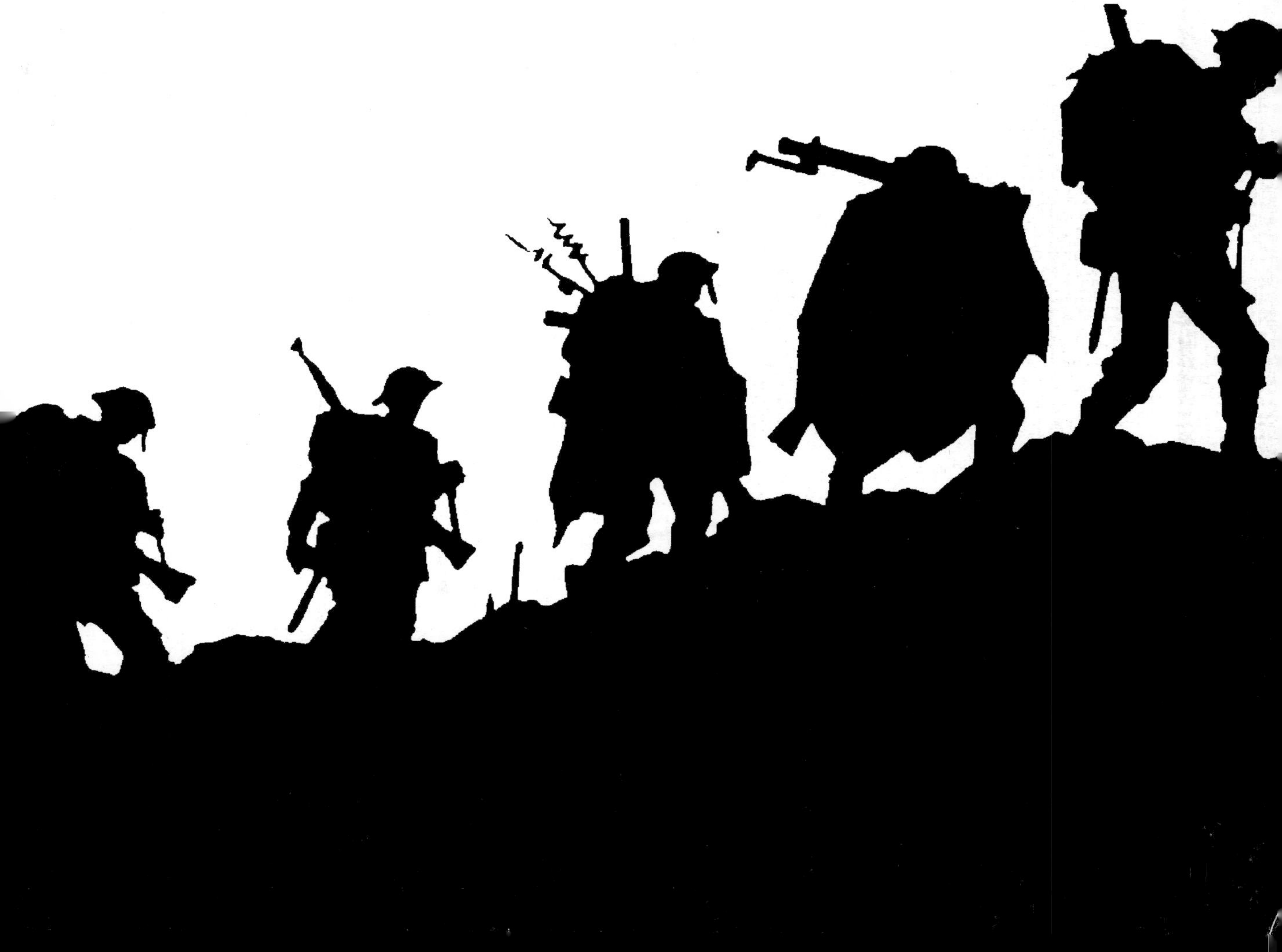

CHARLEY'S WAR: A BOY SOLDIER IN THE GREAT WAR
ISBN: 9781781169148

Published by
Titan Books
A division of Titan Publishing Group Ltd
144 Southwark Street
London SE1 0UP

A CIP catalogue record for this title is available from the British Library.

This edition first published: August 2014
2 4 6 8 10 9 7 5 3 1

Printed in Spain.

Cover photo used by permission of the Imperial War Museum, London (Q2756).
Poppy artwork © 2005 Trucie Henderson.
Page 12: Joe Colquhoun photograph © IPC.

'Into *Battle*' © 2004 Neil Emery
'Landships' © 2005 Steve White
Joe Colquhoun interview © 1982 Lew Stringer/*Fantasy Express*
Strip commentary © 2007 Pat Mills

What did you think of this book? We love to hear from our readers.
Please email us at: readerfeedback@titanemail.com, or write to us at the above address.

To receive advance information, news, competitions, and exclusive offers online, please sign up for the Titan newsletter on our website: **www.titanbooks.com**

This book is a collection of *Charley's War* strips, previously published by Titan Books as *Charley's War* volumes 1–4.

Much of the comic strip source material used by Titan Books in this edition is exceedingly rare. As such, we hope that readers appreciate that the quality of reproduction achievable can vary.

CHARLEY'S WAR

A BOY SOLDIER IN THE GREAT WAR

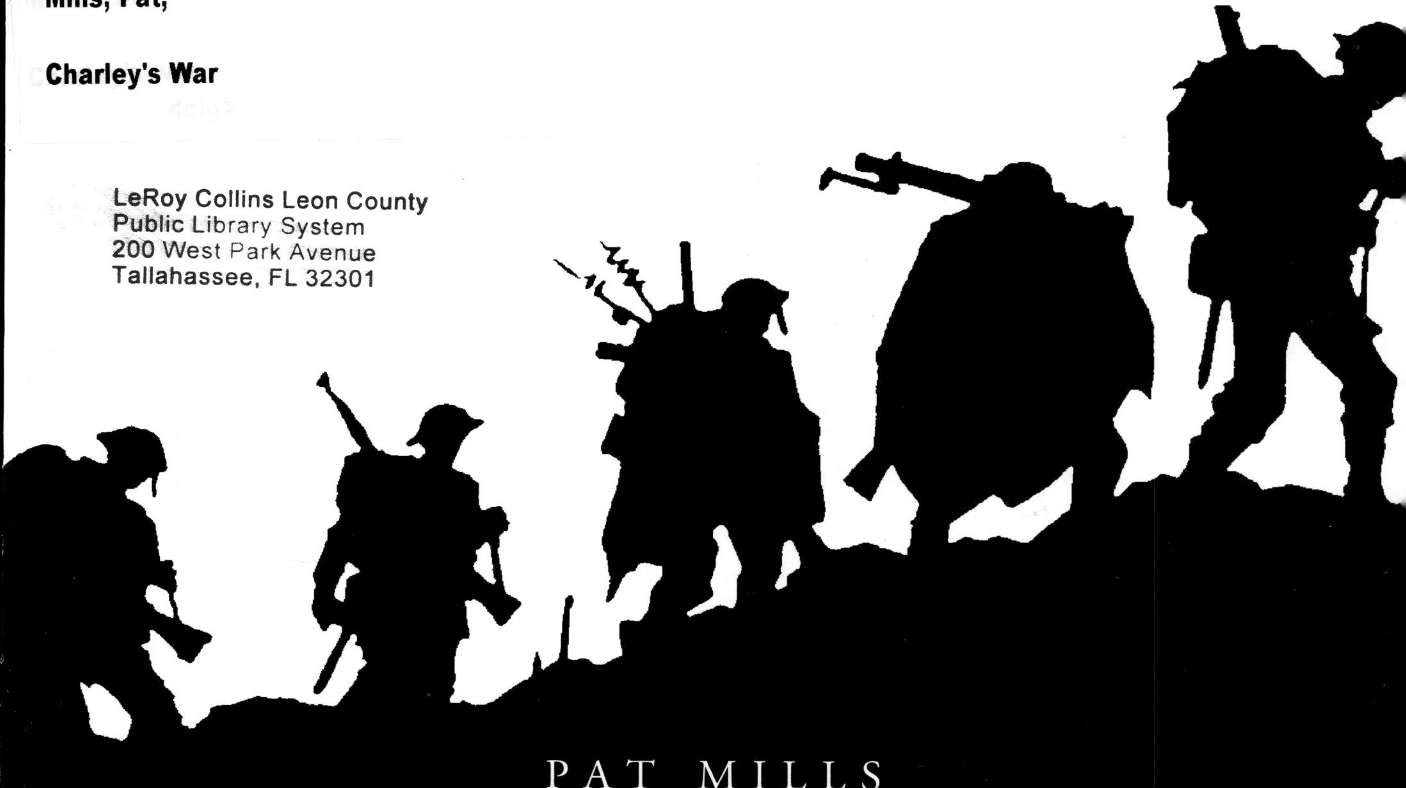

PAT MILLS
JOE COLQUHOUN

TITANBOOKS

INTO *BATTLE*

A Chronology of *Charley's War*

by Neil Emery

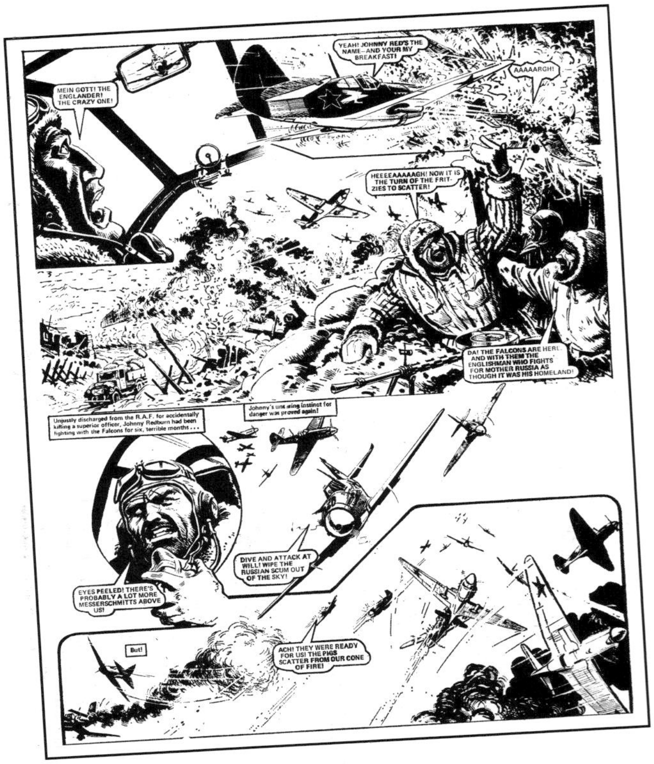
MEIN GOTT! THE ENGLANDER! THE CRAZY ONE!
YEAH! JOHNNY RED'S THE NAME—AND YOUR MY BREAKFAST!
AAAAARGH!
HEEEEAAAAAGH! NOW IT IS THE TURN OF THE FRIT-ZIES TO SCATTER!
DA! THE FALCONS ARE HERE. AND WITH THEM THE ENGLISHMAN WHO FIGHTS FOR MOTHER RUSSIA AS THOUGH IT WAS HIS HOMELAND!
Unjustly discharged from the R.A.F. for accidentally killing a superior officer, Johnny Redburn had been fighting with the Falcons for six, terrible months . . .
DIVE AND ATTACK AT WILL! WIPE THE RUSSIAN SCUM OUT OF THE SKY!
EYES PEELED! THERE'S PROBABLY A LOT MORE MESSERSCHMITTS ABOVE US!
But!
ACH! THEY WERE READY FOR US! THE PIGS SCATTER FROM OUR CONE OF FIRE!

ABOVE: A page of artwork from the much respected and very successful *Johnny Red*, written by Tom Tully and drawn by Joe Colquhoun.

Battle Picture Weekly (also known as *Battle Action*), published by IPC, débuted in the UK on 8 March 1975 to counter the successful new comic, *Warlord*, published by IPC's competitors, Thomson. Pat Mills and John Wagner were called in to produce the boys' war comic, and the first stories, whilst good, were somewhat predictable.

However, 29 January 1977 saw the start of one of the comic's more successful sagas, *Johnny Red*, written by Tom Tully, about an ex-RAF pilot who ends up fighting with the Soviet air force. Its artist was Joe Colquhoun, and with his help it quickly became one of the most popular strips in *Battle*, running longer than any other story.

It was Dave Hunt, editor of *Battle*, who in 1979 decided to gamble on the success of *Johnny Red* by taking Joe off the story and starting him on a new project with Pat Mills about the First World War. Joe said years later, 'When I was asked to take on a new story after *Johnny Red*, I said to the editor, 'God almighty, how are you going to make any subject matter out of something as static as trench warfare?' And the editor (Dave Hunt) said to me, 'We've got a damn good author — he'll be able to pull it through.' I was sceptical at the time because Pat Mills and his work were unknown to me. But as soon as we started I knew we were on to something. It seemed to catch on.'

The story was *Charley's War*, arguably the most important UK comics war story ever. An anti-war story in a pro-war comic, it never glorified or flinched from some of the harshest and most unpalatable aspects of the Great War. Pat Mills observed, 'In some ways *Charley's War* was my attempt to reverse the direction of my creation [*Battle*]. I wanted to counteract the danger of war comics helping to recruit cannon fodder for our country's appalling military attacks on other lands, which continue to this day.'

The strip was a big risk because, until then, First World War stories had consistently failed in boys' comics. The static nature of the subject made it difficult to hold the interest of readers more familiar with the fast paced adventures of heroes blazing their way across the many theatres of World War Two. If the strip was to be a success it would take an exceptional artist or an exceptional writer. It got both.

The very first episode of *Charley's War* appeared in a four-page wonderfully illustrated and archly written masterpiece on 6 January 1979 — the 200th issue of *Battle*. Dated 'June 2nd 1916', the story opens with the run-up to the British attack on the Somme, a tragedy in which 500,000 British troops perished.

Charley's transformation from idealistic, naïve recruit to hardened, war weary veteran took just ten episodes. His character took final shape in the 17 March 1979 episode covering the first terrible day of the Somme in which readers saw the senseless deaths of many of the characters whom they had come to know as Charley's friends. The tragedy of the Somme was also a difficult subject for Joe Colquhoun, who said at the time: 'You may find it hard to believe, but I find it hard to read them, especially the sequence at the end of the Somme. I was re-reading that in its printed form recently and I was actually close to tears… It's surprising how involved you can get.' The episode is as brilliant as it is harrowing, a benchmark in quality that the creators' peers would find hard to equal.

Those early strips are accompanied by poorly spelt, ink-stained letters and postcards sent home by Charley. They say nothing of the horrors of the trenches, focusing instead on more domestic matters, such as his thanks for the scarf his Auntie Mabel sent him, and his own simple impressions of his fellow characters. It is a brilliant narrative device that allows the reader to view another facet of Charley's personality.

The first year saw the introduction of such characters as 'Old Bill' Tozer, Charley's inimitable Platoon Sergeant, Ginger Jones, his deadpan pessimistic best friend, 'Weeper' Watkins, so called because he perpetually cries owing to the effects of poison gas on his eyes, and Captain Snell. Snell embodies the real enemy in the strip — those members of the upper classes who looked on the war as sport, retained servants and dined on hampers from Harrods in comfortable dugouts while their subordinates were exposed to the elements and enemy fire above. Charley's nemesis until the end of the story, Snell is a consistently brilliantly written character.

1979

September 1979 (August 1916 in Charley's world) saw the execution of the platoon's favourite commander, Lieutenant Thomas, who was court-martialled for cowardice after withdrawing his men from a situation that would have seen them needlessly massacred. Thomas' firing squad comes from his own platoon, but Charley and 'Weeper' Watkins refuse to take part. Thomas is shot anyway, and Charley and Watkins are given twenty-eight days of Number One field punishment — basically crucifixion on a gun wheel or fence — a form of discipline used by the British army until the late 1920s.

Shortly after, in the 13 October (September 1916) issue, Ginger was killed by a stray shell, and was subsequently buried by Charley after he had solemnly collected Ginger's remains in a sack. This graphic sudden death killed off the story's second principal supporting character. By killing Ginger, Mills hinted at the tone the script would take in the future: a quick turnover of characters echoing the transient nature of life in the trenches. Characters were introduced, told their own stories and then were taken suddenly in a meaningless death only to be replaced by new 'Tommies'. This difficult writing technique became Mills' signature on the story and adds to the realism of the piece.

1980

1980 saw *Charley's War* begin a plotline that would be one of its most enduring: 'The Judgment Troopers'. Although focusing on these elite German shock troops from the Eastern Front, the plot also tackled such topics as the execution of prisoners, the heartlessness of British doctors (the infamous 'Dr No') and the treachery of the Germans who feigned surrender. It contained some of Joe's best artwork so far, his bold dark inking capturing perfectly the rain-soaked, foreboding desolation of the trenches.

Charley is subsequently wounded and, by 9 August 1980 (Oct 1916), was in hospital with amnesia, allowing Mills and Colquhoun to explore the nature of 'shell shock'. These are brilliantly drawn episodes, full of the horrific swirling nightmares suffered by Charley as he is tormented by Ginger's death. Sergeant Tozer, also wounded, helps Charley eventually rediscover his identity. Both men are then returned to 'Blighty' to recover from their wounds, much to their delight.

Charley's spell of leave is set against the backdrop of the war on the home front, complete with Zeppelin raids and black-market dealing. His working-class family and background are revealed, set against Colquhoun's wonderfully detailed scenes of Edwardian London.

BELOW: The *Battle Action* cover for 19 May 1979. Note the Christmas tree in the background.

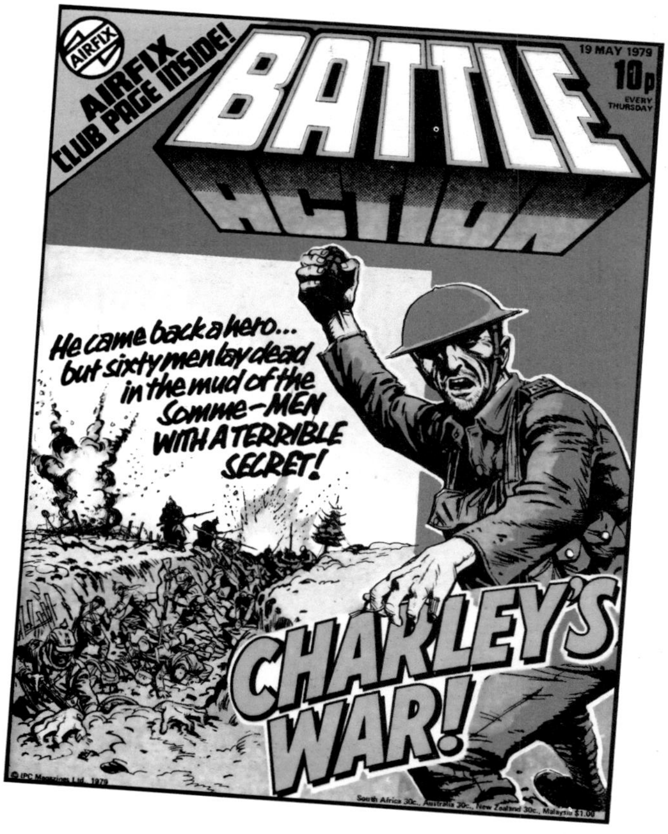
AIRFIX
AIRFIX CLUB PAGE INSIDE!
BATTLE
ACTION
19 MAY 1979
10p
EVERY THURSDAY
He came back a hero... but sixty men lay dead in the mud of the Somme–MEN WITH A TERRIBLE SECRET!
CHARLEY'S WAR!

Set during a Zeppelin raid, the 8 November 1980 episode introduced a character who was to reappear regularly over the next couple of years. Blue, a deserter on the run from the French Foreign Legion, plays a pivotal role in the narrative, establishing the person Charley would have been were it not for the instilled resignation to his fate and sense of duty that he could never shake. The two men become firm friends, sharing a hatred of the lives wasted in France and the apparent insanity gripping the High Command. In flashback, Blue describes to Charley the harshness of the Legion and the harrowing battles he has fought. This approach allows the story to shift its perspective to a new 'hero' and relate events that Charley couldn't possibly have experienced without turning the strip into fantasy — a device that would become Mills' forte throughout *Charley's War*. Blue's narrative formed the basis of *Charley's War* throughout 1980 and into 1981.

1981

1981 saw episodes shift from four pages to a more manageable three. A single episode of *Charley's War* would take Joe five full working days, and more complicated plots up to seven. The strip was his only commitment and therefore his earnings remained modest compared with others who would do two, sometimes three stories a week to boost their income. However, quality and accuracy were always paramount to Joe.

By October 1981 (May–June 1917), Charley and company had joined the 'Clay Kickers' — the navvies and coalminers who had been digging huge mines under the Messines Ridge for the last eighteen months. The trials and terror of working and fighting this poorly known underground war took up most of the year.

This long-running saga also introduced conscientious objector 'Budgie' Brown in a sub-plot that tells of the shameful treatment of pacifists at the hands of the British Army. Budgie proves himself to be braver in many ways than most by sticking to his ideals in the face of hatred from his peers, a hatred that ultimately leads to his abrupt and untimely death and brings Charley into violent conflict with Captain Snell.

By this time, letters in praise of *Charley's War* were regularly published in *Battle*. Many of them were from veterans of the Great War, acknowledging the strip's excellence after being shown it by grandsons and great-grandsons.

1982

For *Charley's War*, 1982 opened with a stunning colour cover that marked the beginning of the third battle of Ypres. The issue of self-inflicted wounds is touched upon when one of Charley's mates attempts to shoot himself in the foot to escape the battle. Charley's good intentioned efforts to stop him meet with a cruel and ironic twist.

February 1982 (August 1917) saw Charley and his platoon withdrawn from the line and sent to the notorious Etaples training camp, the scene of the British Army's only mutiny in modern times. As many as 100,000 soldiers were housed in the camp at any one time, where they were drilled constantly in the sand dunes of the notorious Bull Ring training area by 'canaries' — non-combatant military police instructors who were hand picked for their harsh methods. The mutiny storyline reintroduces 'Weeper' and Blue, who are part of a gang of deserters who live in the woods outside the town. It also allowed Mills to give greater depth to Charley, who is caught on the horns of a moral

BELOW: The cover from the 30 May 1981 edition of *Battle Action*. Joe used the classic photo seen below as the basis for his illustration.

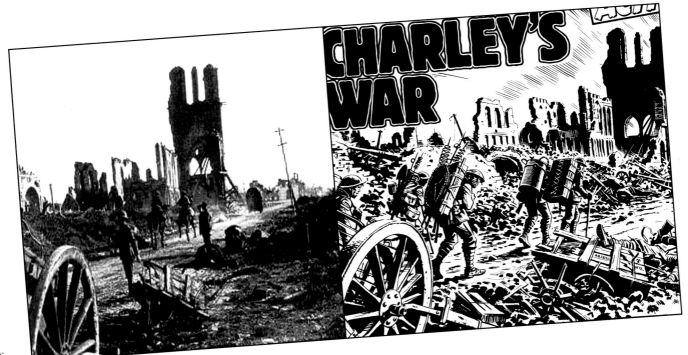

dilemma between his natural sympathies with the mutineers and his own sense of duty.

In July 1982, Charley's conscience got the better of him and, sick of the killing, he decided to hand in his rifle and become a stretcher bearer, a non-combatant. Unfortunately, as this plotline began Joe Colquhoun had a heart attack and was off work for three months (sadly, Joe died of a second heart attack in 1987).

He returned to work in October 1982 (October 1917), with Charley working as a stretcher bearer until the end of the year when, in a stroke of genius, Mills delivered a cliffhanger that takes the story into the present time. After Charley rescues a Flying Corps observer, Fred, at Passaendale, a shell burst catches the two men. The reader is then transported to 1982, where we join Fred as an old man visiting the same spot and wondering if Charley survived. The lifelong effects of the war on its survivors are shown as Fred vividly recalls the war seventy years later from the inside of a tour bus.

From February to May 1983, Charley, now a sniper after being sacked from the Medical Corps, took a back seat to the early life of Adolf Hitler, whose battalion finds itself in trenches opposite Charley's.

1983

The rest of '83 was a wild ride for Charley. He married a nurse called Kate, was court-martialled for cowardice after accidentally shooting himself through the foot, and his brother Wilf, a pilot, was killed over London attacking the first long-range bombers — the German Gotha.

1984

1984 began with Mills exploring the war at sea from the perspective of Charley's cousin, Jack. Jack tells the story of the first Battle of the Falklands where he is serving aboard *HMS Kent* and takes part in the sinking of the *Nuremburg*. Mills had wanted to broaden this story of the war at sea but, as he says, 'The readers didn't like it. The editor specifically rang me — the only time ever — to tell me to steer back to the trenches. I was disappointed because I had been hoping to do the battle of Jutland, an astonishing and hideous event that really needs to be chronicled, and the Falklands had been the warm-up.' So, Charley, now a lance corporal, returned to the front line just in time for the German Spring Offensive of March 1918.

June 1984 introduced Americans and the story of the African-American soldiers, which led to one of the few occasions when the strip was censored.

Then, on 15 September 1984, the First World War ended for *Charley's War* readers, but not before an eleventh-hour showdown with the insane Captain Snell. He sends Charley to participate in the little-known invasion of Russia in 1919 by, amongst others, Britain. The rest of 1984 followed this ill-fated campaign.

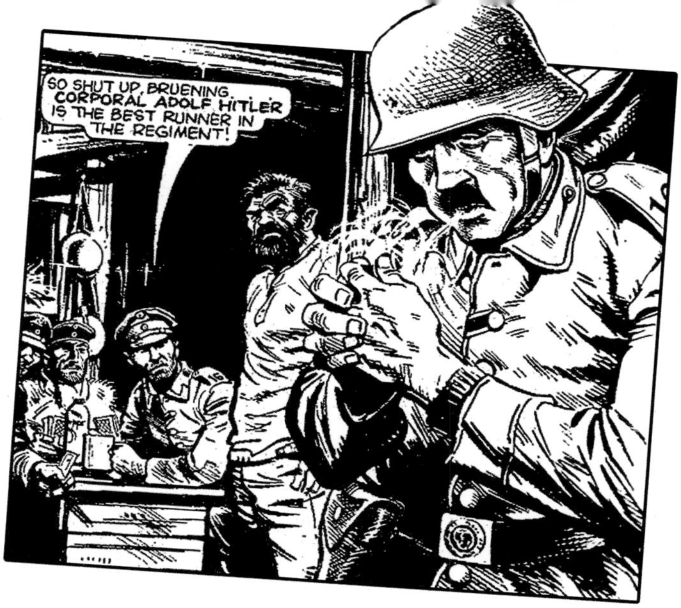
SO SHUT UP, BRUENING. CORPORAL ADOLF HITLER IS THE BEST RUNNER IN THE REGIMENT!

ABOVE: Adolf Hitler joins *Charley's War*.

1985

On 26 January 1985, Pat Mills wrote his last ever script for *Charley's War*, following a disagreement over his research budget. He says, 'My enduring memory and the true ending of *Charley's War* is in 1933, where Charley is on the dole and he's thinking, "Tomorrow is another day and things can only get better." He walks off into the grimy sunset of London's East End as a newspaper announces, "Adolf Hitler made Chancellor of Germany". That, to me, sums up Charley and the betrayal of his great, uncomplaining but tragic generation.'

Scott Goodall took up scripting chores and the story continued into the Second World War. Charley, now middle aged, is looking for his son Len, who joined up against his father's wishes and is somewhere in France. The last ten months of the story continued into 1986 and saw Charley thrown into the chaos of the British Army's 1940 defeat during Hitler's invasion of France. However, by now the story had sadly lost its edge, and although Joe Colquhoun's superlative artwork continued to impress, it could not change the fact that the best days of *Charley's War* were behind it. The series ended in October as Charley was reunited with Len on a ship leaving Dunkirk, where he concluded that his fighting days were now over. It was a rushed and somewhat lacklustre ending for such a classic story. A year later, Joe Colquhoun was dead. ✛

The Evolution of the Tank

by Steve White

Considering Pat Mills' zealous attention to detail and also the fact that the battle of the Somme provides the shattered backdrop to *Charley's War*, it was inevitable that young Charley would encounter tanks. An everyday occurrence on the modern battlefield, in September 1916 they were the British Army's soon-to-be-unleashed, war-ending secret weapon. It was therefore natural that Charley, never a mere observer of history within the story, would soon find himself at the helm of one of these steel monstrosities.

Armour is about as old as war itself – be it tightly thatched reeds, leather, iron, bronze or steel. But the idea of mechanised armour is somewhat newer, with the concept of a travelling fortress dating back to the invention of steam power and Stevenson's Rocket in the 18th century. Even Leonardo da Vinci sketched a cannon-armed design. But it was in the First World War that the tank as it is generally now seen came into being.

The battle of the Somme is remembered for many things. It immortalised forever the needless waste of young lives in the Great War, and the notion of an aristocratic high command squandering working-class cannon fodder before German machine guns. These sweeping generalisations have overshadowed one important and unassailable fact: the latter stages of the battle saw the first combat use of the tank.

The early stages in the evolution of the modern tank concept extend back to the end of the 19th century, when tractor builders in the US developed a working caterpillar track. The American Civil War had seen the development of steam-powered, metal-armoured warships, but it seemed something of a leap of faith and imagination to bring them ashore.

It was down to another mechanical enthusiast to take the next step. Frederick Simms designed a 'motor-war car' armed with two of the new machine guns, and powered by a Daimler engine. Simms offered it to the British Army but the Minister of War – Lord Kitchener – dismissed it, like the machine gun before it, as having little practical use. This shouldn't have come as any real surprise to Simms. The British Army's officer corps found it hard to look beyond its cavalry divisions.

BELOW: The first landships roll into action.

THEN, THROUGH THE MORNING MIST, THE "MOTHERS" OF DESTRUCTION APPEARED!

NEIN! THE DEVIL IS COMING! THE DEVIL IS COMING!

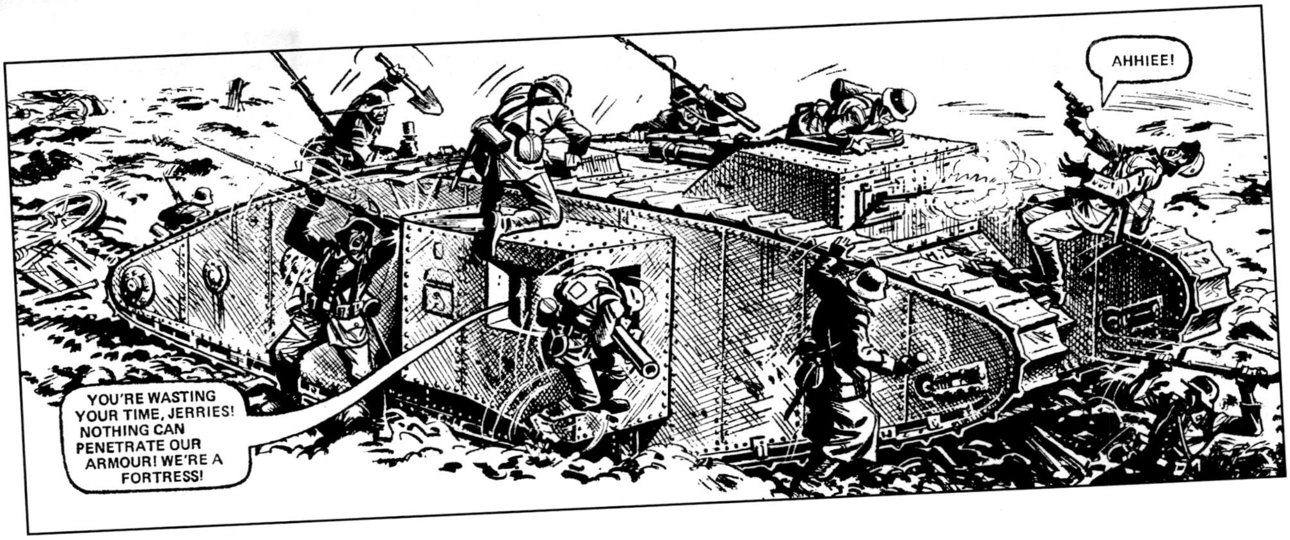
AHHIEE!
YOU'RE WASTING YOUR TIME, JERRIES! NOTHING CAN PENETRATE OUR ARMOUR! WE'RE A FORTRESS!

Lancers were still making charges at the outbreak of the First World War, even though these transpired to be the last huzzah of the cavalry, who now faced barbed wire and machine guns.

However, the concept of the tank had a champion in Colonel Ernest Swinton. He had been an officer with the British Army during the Boer War when, on 13 June 1900, he had a revelation and realised that there was a need for an armoured vehicle to withstand the growing power of artillery and the new automatic weapons.

He was joined in his enthusiasm by Maurice Hankey, Secretary of the Committee for Imperial Defence, and between them they arranged a demonstration of a Killen-Strait tractor in June 1915. The audience included David Lloyd George – at the time the Minister of Munitions but, by the end of the First World War, Prime Minister – and Winston Churchill, the First Lord of the Admiralty whose stock was at a low ebb after the disastrous landing at Gallipoli, which he had overseen.

Still, the demonstration went well. The vehicle cut a barbed-wire fence and both men were enthusiastic. Churchill went so far as to sponsor a study of the potential of what were known as 'landships' – a reflection of the belief that these armoured vehicles were just battleships on land.

This study led to an agreement to begin the design and construction of the first landships. Swinton was to work alongside Lieutenant Walter Wilson of the Naval Air Service and William Tritton of William Foster & Co. Whilst it may seem a little incongruous to have a member of the Royal Navy working on an ostensibly Army project, the Royal Navy were regular users of armoured cars, a popular vehicle on the Western Front in 1915, when the War was still one of mobility and firepower and had yet to be supplanted by the stultifying stagnation of trench warfare. The Royal Navy had been pioneers in the deployment of armoured cars, and in 1914 the Naval Brigade and the Royal Naval Air Squadron had sent theirs to Antwerp, in Belgium, to defend Allied airstrips. It was only natural, therefore, given the perceived nature of the tank, that the Royal Navy be involved from the start.

ABOVE: The tank crew enjoy the relative safety of their armour.

BELOW: But the protection of the armour also serves to trap the tank crew.

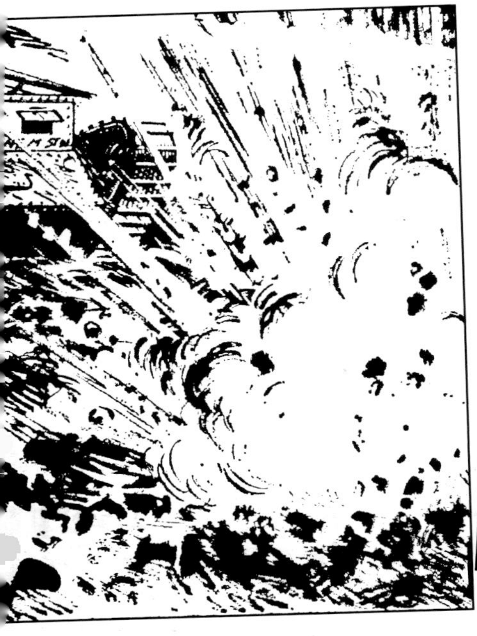

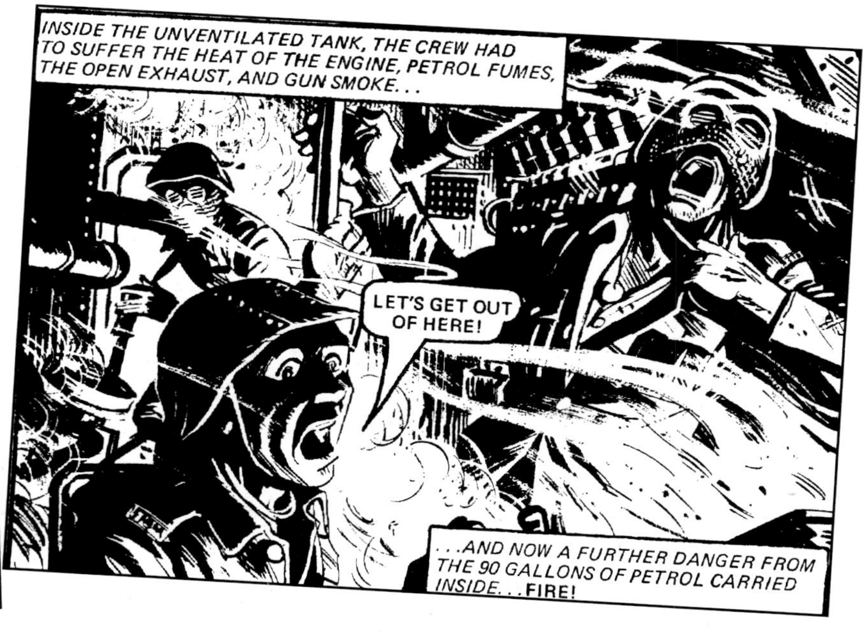
INSIDE THE UNVENTILATED TANK, THE CREW HAD TO SUFFER THE HEAT OF THE ENGINE, PETROL FUMES, THE OPEN EXHAUST, AND GUN SMOKE...
LET'S GET OUT OF HERE!
...AND NOW A FURTHER DANGER FROM THE 90 GALLONS OF PETROL CARRIED INSIDE...FIRE!

Due to the secret nature of the project, the vehicle was given a codename. Because it looked like a tracked water tank, it became known, as of December 1915, as a 'tank', and whilst 'landship' may be more evocative, the nickname stuck.

Swinton gave the builders several design criteria he felt had to be met. The tank had to be able to climb a five-foot obstacle; cross a five foot-wide trench; have a top speed of four miles an hour on a flat surface, two in battlefield conditions; withstand machine-gun bullets and have a crew of ten men, who were to man the two machine guns mounted on board.

Things got off to a bad start. The first prototype shed its tracks two days after leaving the production line on 8 September, then again on the 19th. Also, the first version, 'Little Willie', weighing fourteen tons and powered by a Daimler engine, did not meet the tough specifications laid down. It was not able to cross trenches and carried a crew of only three in very cramped conditions.

Fortunately, these were seen as mere teething troubles, and progress was such that by January 1916 a top-secret demonstration was arranged to put 'Big Willie' through its paces. The new tank was considerably larger, carried 10mm armour on the front and 8mm armour on its sides, had a crew of eight and was to be armed with 57mm naval guns in side turrets. In front on an audience of politicians and high-ranking military commanders, the tank was put through its paces. Lord Kitchener was amongst those watching and seemed unimpressed. He called it a 'pretty mechanical toy', but it's possible, according to those close to him, that he said this to goad the 'tank team' to greater effort in proving the worth of their creation.

More impressed was Lloyd George, who ordered a hundred of the tanks into production, which was now known as the heavy Mark I.

Driven by the enthusiasm and tenacity of Swinton, Wilson and Tritton, the teething troubles were beaten out of the prototypes and tactics were developed for their use. Swinton envisaged tanks and infantry operating in symphony, but knew the reality to be that the tanks would actually be supporting the soldiers on the ground as they attempted to break German defences.

In April, Sir Douglas Haig, Commander-in-Chief of the British Army in Europe, told Swinton he wanted tanks and their crews ready by 1 June in the hope that they would be ready to participate in the forthcoming battle of the Somme. This was easier said than done. There were no crews available and no tanks to train any on. It should be remembered as well that very few, except the very wealthy, had any experience in operating a mechanical vehicle. Horses were still the transport of choice.

In the end, crews were drawn from the Motor Machine Gun Service and Naval Armoured Car Squadrons. Also enlisted were civilians with experience in mechanical vehicles.

In an effort to disguise its true nature, the six companies formed were called the Armoured Car Section of the Motor Machine Gun Service. Despite the efforts of Swinton and his team, the tanks were not available to take part in the 'big push' on 1 July. The impact, if any, they would have had on the slaughter that took place that day can only be speculated on.

The tanks didn't get into action until 15 September. On that day, in a historical first, Captain H. W.

BELOW: Theoretically safer than footsoldiers, tank crews were still in great danger from flying shrapnel and debris.

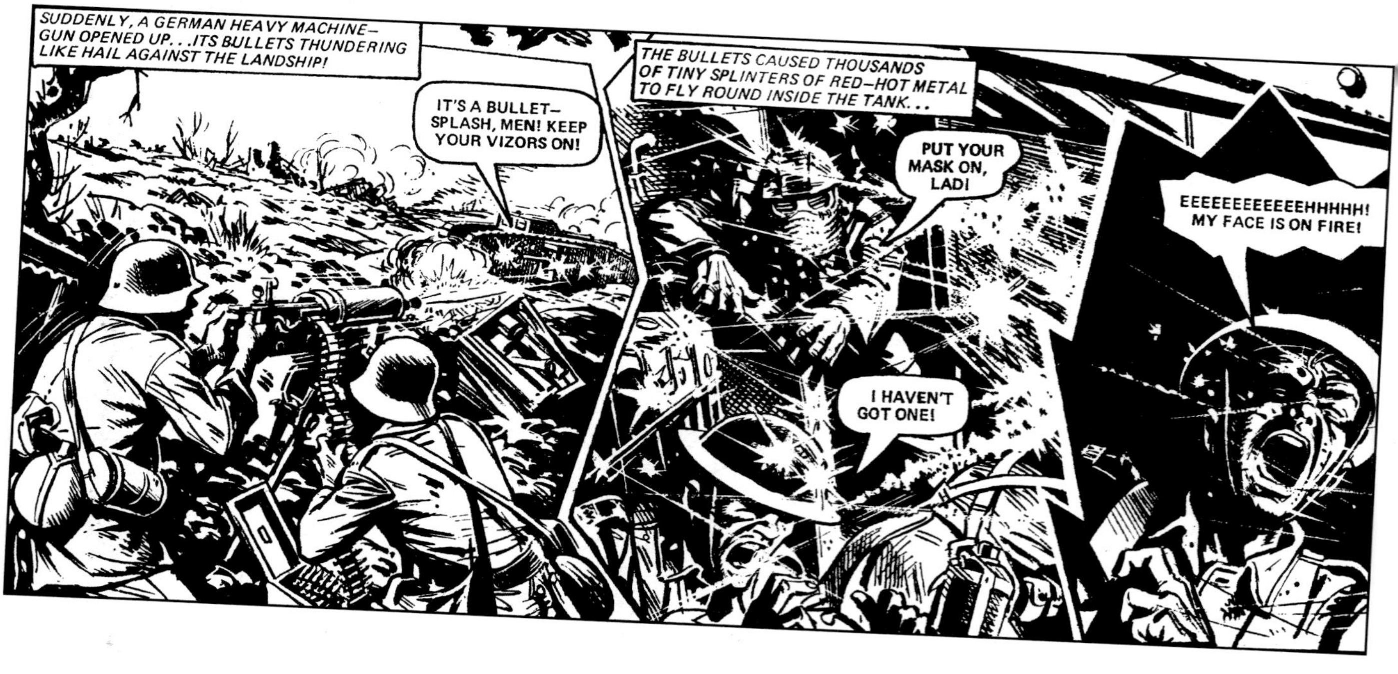
SUDDENLY, A GERMAN HEAVY MACHINE-GUN OPENED UP. . .ITS BULLETS THUNDERING LIKE HAIL AGAINST THE LANDSHIP!
IT'S A BULLET-SPLASH, MEN! KEEP YOUR VIZORS ON!
THE BULLETS CAUSED THOUSANDS OF TINY SPLINTERS OF RED-HOT METAL TO FLY ROUND INSIDE THE TANK. . .
PUT YOUR MASK ON, LAD!
I HAVEN'T GOT ONE!
EEEEEEEEEEEEHHHHH! MY FACE IS ON FIRE!

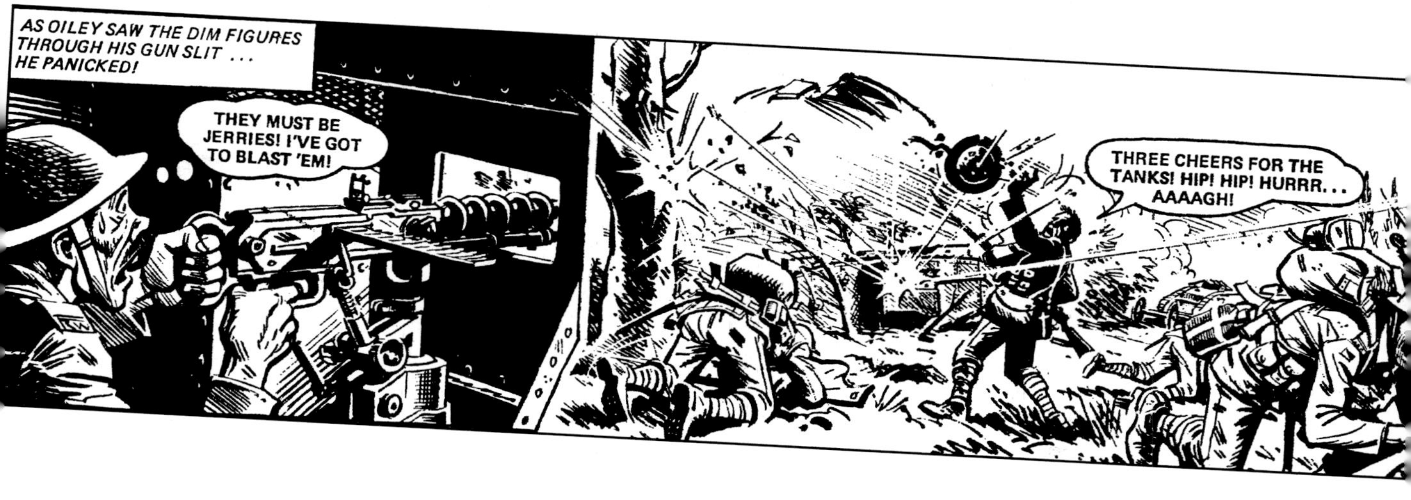
AS OILEY SAW THE DIM FIGURES THROUGH HIS GUN SLIT ... HE PANICKED!
THEY MUST BE JERRIES! I'VE GOT TO BLAST 'EM!
THREE CHEERS FOR THE TANKS! HIP! HIP! HURRR... AAAAGH!

Mortimore drove his tank into battle at the infamous Bois d'Elville (known as 'Devil's Wood' by the troops), where South African infantry had fought a gruelling battle against German defenders in what would be their most costly action on the Western Front. A single tank made little difference, and the South Africans were never able to overcome the Germans.

The tanks had a more positive impact in the fighting around the villages of Flers and Courcelette. In a subsidiary attack of the Somme offensive, the first massed tank assault took place when forty-nine tanks – the total available to the British Army – went into action on the same day, 15 September.

Conditions for the tank crews were at best uncomfortable, at worst infernal. They were stiflingly hot, cramped and noisy, and whilst able to shrug off machine-gun bullets, the impact of rounds would often send metal chips flying around the cabin. As protection, crews were expected to wear chain-mail visors, but in the blistering heat these were uncomfortable and seldom used.

There were other problems: visibility was poor, making navigation difficult and on occasion leading to friendly-fire incidents. The tanks were also reliability nightmares, breaking down with monotonous regularity. Of the forty-nine tanks that were scheduled to attack, seventeen failed to reach the start line. Seven more broke down before the attack began, leaving just fifteen to actually go into action.

Despite these problems, any misgivings about their impact on the battlefield were soon dispelled when the Germans fled at the approach of these mechanical monstrosities. The tanks' entry into Flers was witnessed by an aircraft overhead. The crew reported, 'A tank is walking down the main street of Flers with the British Army cheering behind it.'

It was a shaky start. Haig had had high hopes for the tanks, envisaging them breaking the deadlock gripping the Western Front. But the tanks and their crews had been ill prepared for the battle, and they had been too few in number to make a decisive difference. Stalwart supporter Winston Churchill feared that his 'poor little "land battleships" have been let off prematurely on a petty scale'.

Even so, the signs were all there, albeit on a local level, that the tank was going to have a bright future on the battlefield. In 1940, it was the Germans – who ironically had thought very little of tanks in 1916 – who proved just how far use of armour had come when the First World War battlefields rumbled once again to the approach of tanks as the blitzkrieg thundered into France and Belgium. ✢

ABOVE: 'Oiley' discovers the dangers of limited visibility when he accidentally fires on British troops.

BELOW: A British tank strikes terror into the hearts of the German army.

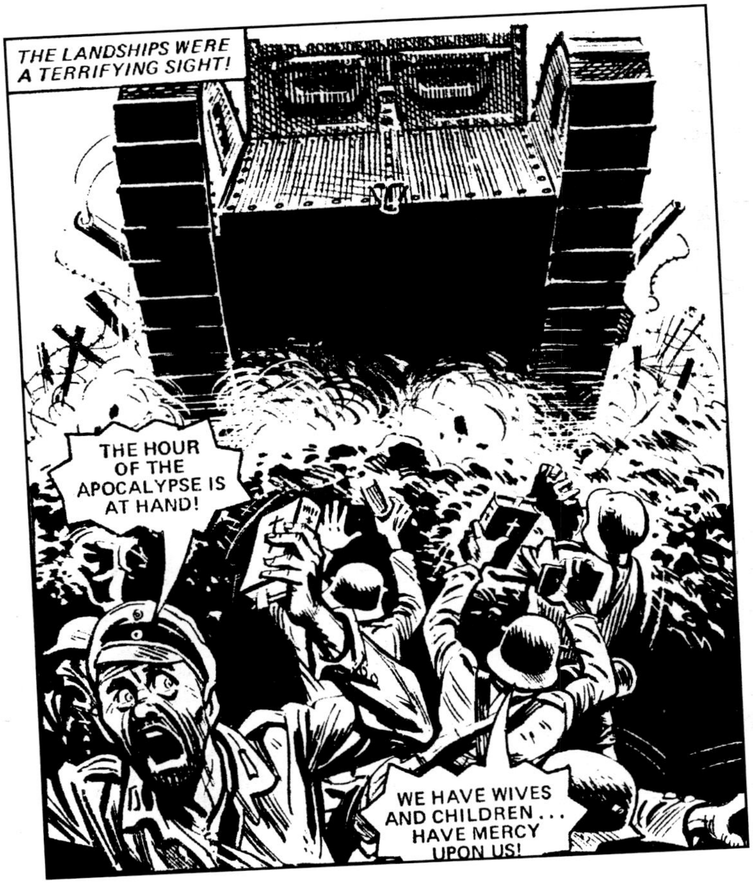
THE LANDSHIPS WERE A TERRIFYING SIGHT!
THE HOUR OF THE APOCALYPSE IS AT HAND!
WE HAVE WIVES AND CHILDREN... HAVE MERCY UPON US!

JOE COLQUHOUN IN CONVERSATION

by Stephen Oldman

The *Charley's War* artist was notoriously retiring, to the extent that it is believed that only one interview with him exists, conducted by Stephen Oldman in 1982 for the fanzine *Fantasy Express*. The following excerpt is drawn from that interview, with the kind permission of Lew Stringer.

How did you enter the comics field?

I'd always wanted to draw; even as a kid, I'd always wanted to be a comic artist – ever since I was old enough to pick up a pencil – so of course, I spent a lot of my early life drawing alone. I drew in an old ledger book; I would draw stories, just make them up, mainly in the adventure line – desert island stuff, war… I suppose it's stood me in good stead for what was to come! I was brought up on the usual diet – most kids were then: *Comic Cuts*; The 'Tu'penny Bloods'; *Magnet*; *Champion*; *Triumph*; *Wizard* and *Hotspur*, which were all prose stories – and well-written, for what you paid – with one-off illustrations. I always remember a chap called Simmons in *Champion* and *Triumph*, and a chap called Chapman, who stood out to me as very good artists.

Kids who could draw were often lionised at school and one got a false sense of one's capabilities at the time, because there was no competition. Though I was into comic strip in a minor form, it was never really my intention to be an artist. The war was on the horizon anyway, and we didn't think much about the future, to be honest. I got a place at Kingston-upon-Thames art school about halfway through the war; I did a stint there and then joined the navy, which I was in until 1947, when I went back to Kingston and did a more prolonged course in book illustration: this knocked the rough edges off my work.

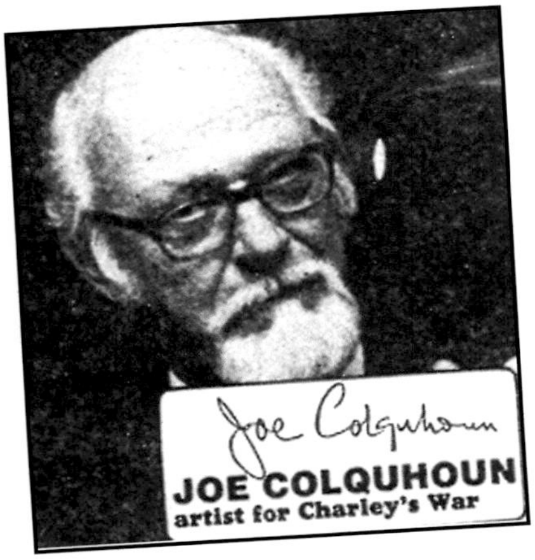
Joe Colquhoun
JOE COLQUHOUN
artist for Charley's War

I still had a hankering to work in the comic strip field, but it was very limited at the time. *Eagle* had just started publication, but at my present stage of development I knew I hadn't a hope of getting in there… then, suddenly, I saw an advert in a trade magazine, asking for samples for a new independent comics publishing project, and I jumped at this with alacrity! I met with a couple of ex-GIs who seemed pleased with the samples I had from art school, though, as I later found out from the fees they paid, they'd be lucky to get anybody. They paid the princely sum of £1.50 per page!

Our work was crude and rushed – it had to be; the printing was atrocious and although we had a foothold in the market, we'd rarely see our work in print. The very first publication I saw my own work in gave me the most euphoric feeling I ever had: it's like riding a bike, or having your first woman, I guess – never to be repeated. We were doing just one-off stories, covering war, space, sport – very American-orientated, very well written, and all done by the Yanks. I was there for seven or eight months and certainly never earned a fortune, though I did learn speed and a certain amount of slickness. However, the general consensus was that this outfit wasn't going anywhere, and I hadn't been paid for ages. I'd just got married and things were pretty grim.

I managed to get an interview with the editor of *Eagle*, and showed him what I could salvage from the Americans… and although he was very compassionate, it obviously wasn't quite what they were looking for. He said, 'Why don't you go across to Amalgamated Press? They've just started a comic called *Lion*.' *Lion* was a little more downmarket than *Eagle* but I saw a nice chap there, called Stan Boddington.

He mentioned something about artists writing scripts, and I said, 'Of course I do that as well' (though, in truth, I'd never done any in my life). His ears pricked up and he sent me away to write an adventure strip. Unfortunately – with me being influenced by the American writers I'd worked with – I wrote a story set in the Pacific, which had a very illogical beginning, rambling on and on into a very chaotic climax. AP were unimpressed, but we thrashed it out and they condensed it down to a half-decent four-page story.

AP then promptly relegated me to working on *Champion*, which still consisted mainly of illustrated prose stories, though they did have a two-page centre-spread. They got me to write and draw this two-pages-per-episode epic, called *Legionnaire Terry's Desert Quest*, which was all very much my own work, with very little interference from anyone. It became very much the basis for my scriptwriting experience.

Who were your artistic influences in those days?

The artist who most influenced me in those days was good old Alex Raymond, of *Rip Kirby* fame. His distinctive style; his ratio of black to white; his economy; his minimal use of cross-hatching – he was the

quintessence of what I would be happy to emulate, and his influence stayed with me for a very long time, until I eventually developed my own style. If his influence is still visible in my work, I'll be bloody happy!

Have the weekly schedules caused you many problems?
From the beginning, yes; serialisation is one of the world's worst ways to make a living. Deadlines and pressure can become pretty punitive from time to time. The worst is trying to get ahead for a holiday, and up comes bloody Easter, and the office are on the phone saying, 'You have to gain four days'. When you're working six to seven days a week, its nearly impossible, but you do it somehow. There were periods when I was a bit more ambitious, or needed to earn a bit more money, so I took on the Annual jobs as well, and even though you could be more slapdash, it was still very much a dash. I now try to take on as little work as possible and still remain solvent! I try to work Monday to Friday, 9am to 6pm, but it all depends. If there's a cast of thousands in Charley, or the 15th Ablutions are going over the top, it can take a hell of a lot longer.

Does your attitude to the work change with each job you do?
I can say – with a certain amount of satisfaction – that I've done my very best in every job I've done. You know there's a readership out there somewhere, so you want to do the best you can for your own personal pride, as well as to justify your wages. Of course, bad scripts have a very depressing effect; I feel happier if I know I have a rapport with the author, even if I have never met the guy. I was least interested in my own work when I was on *Buster*. I enjoyed 'Zarga' very much but it was relatively short-lived, and I was then relegated to childish material such as 'The Ski-Board Squad' and 'The Runaway Robinsons' – a *Little Orphan Annie*-type story which wasn't my thing. It wasn't the author's fault; it just wasn't my scene at all.

I think I've always put more into my work than my colleagues; they are wise, and have learnt the economy of line. Omission is always more difficult than overworking. I think my main failing is that I put in everything AND the kitchen sink. Most of it gets lost in the printing as well, so in effect it's a waste of time, and as time is money in this game, I'm a bit of a mug, really… but the leopard cannot change his spots.

In the '60s, your work was published alongside the greats – Eric Bradbury, Mike Western and Geoff Campion; were you aware of them?
No, because until very recently, IPC insisted on absolute anonymity – I mean even if you signed at the bottom of the page because of sheer pride in your work, they whited it out. We were anonymous until recently, when *Battle* put the credits up; I gradually got to know who the various artists were, if only by reputation, and formed a few opinions. I wasn't familiar with Western's work in the '60s, but I thought Bradbury, Lawrence and Campion were excellent.

You've worked on many scripts, but are there any you would have liked to have done more on?
That's easy – 'Football Family Robinson' was cut off in its prime; even though it was football, it was done with tongue-in-cheek, ribald humour,

and offered some good characterisations of the whole family. The saneness of it, really – plus it had a good author: Tom Tully. Another was 'Cap'n Codsmouth', my first ever slapstick comedy strip… that I was quite pleased with, actually. I also wrote the script, which was the first I'd done since I packed in *Roy of the Rovers*. Again, it was cut off in its prime, I think. The only other one is 'Zarga', and the rest, I think, had reached saturation point where I was happy to move on.

Obviously, you have a leaning toward humour. Do you have a favourite humour artist?
Yes – Nobby Clark, who drew in *Tiger*. I also believe he did 'Butlers Diary'. He had a smooth, clean, flowing line and drew amiable little characters – but also drew stunning little dolly birds when they were allowed! The other characters he did were 'Wild Bill Hiccup', and a World War Two pilot in the Luftwaffe called 'Messy Schmidt' – I thought he was an absolute scream! I would like to do more humour work; I like *Charley's War*, but it can be a sombre subject and doing it seven days a week can be a little depressing. It would be nice if I could find the time to do another 'Cap'n Codsmouth', or 'The Goodies', to relieve the tension once in a while.

***Charley's War* is considered by its fans – and professionals in the business – to be the best strip in Britain at the moment; how do you feel about that?**
First of all, let me say how flattered and surprised I am that its been talked about like that by so many upmarket intellectuals; I was astounded when one learned professor said, 'It stands equal with *All Quiet on the Western Front* as a social document'. That seems a bit high-flying for me, to be honest, but I'm beginning to understand it, in a way. I think that's due to the inspiration and dedication of Pat Mills, which I think has really rubbed off on me. I don't want to let him down, and again, I'm very interested in the subject, even though it can depress me and is very emotive. In particular – though you will find it hard to believe – re-reading the sequence at the end of the Somme left me almost in tears.

When I was first asked to take on *Charley's War*, I said, 'My God, how can you take something as static and non-moving as trench warfare and make any kind of subject matter for a script?' Dave Hunt, the editor at the time, said, 'Don't worry – we've got a great author! He'll pull it off!' I'd never met or even heard of Pat, so I was still very sceptical, but as the strip developed, I began to realise that we were really on to something – and it seemed to catch on. I've been very dedicated to the detail in the trenches and most of the stories are drawn from factual history, which leads to a certain amount of authenticity that's lacking in the more 'blood-and-guts' World War Two stories.

Finally – and this is only my own opinion – *Charley's War* illustrates a period that was already dying when we began the strip; a time when words like 'honour', 'duty' and 'patriotism' actually meant something. I believe that when reading this epic, kids today will have a sneaking – almost atavistic – feeling that in this sick and rather selfish world, where violence and amorality seem to pay dividends, they might actually be missing out on something. It sounds very pretentious… but just think about it. ✦

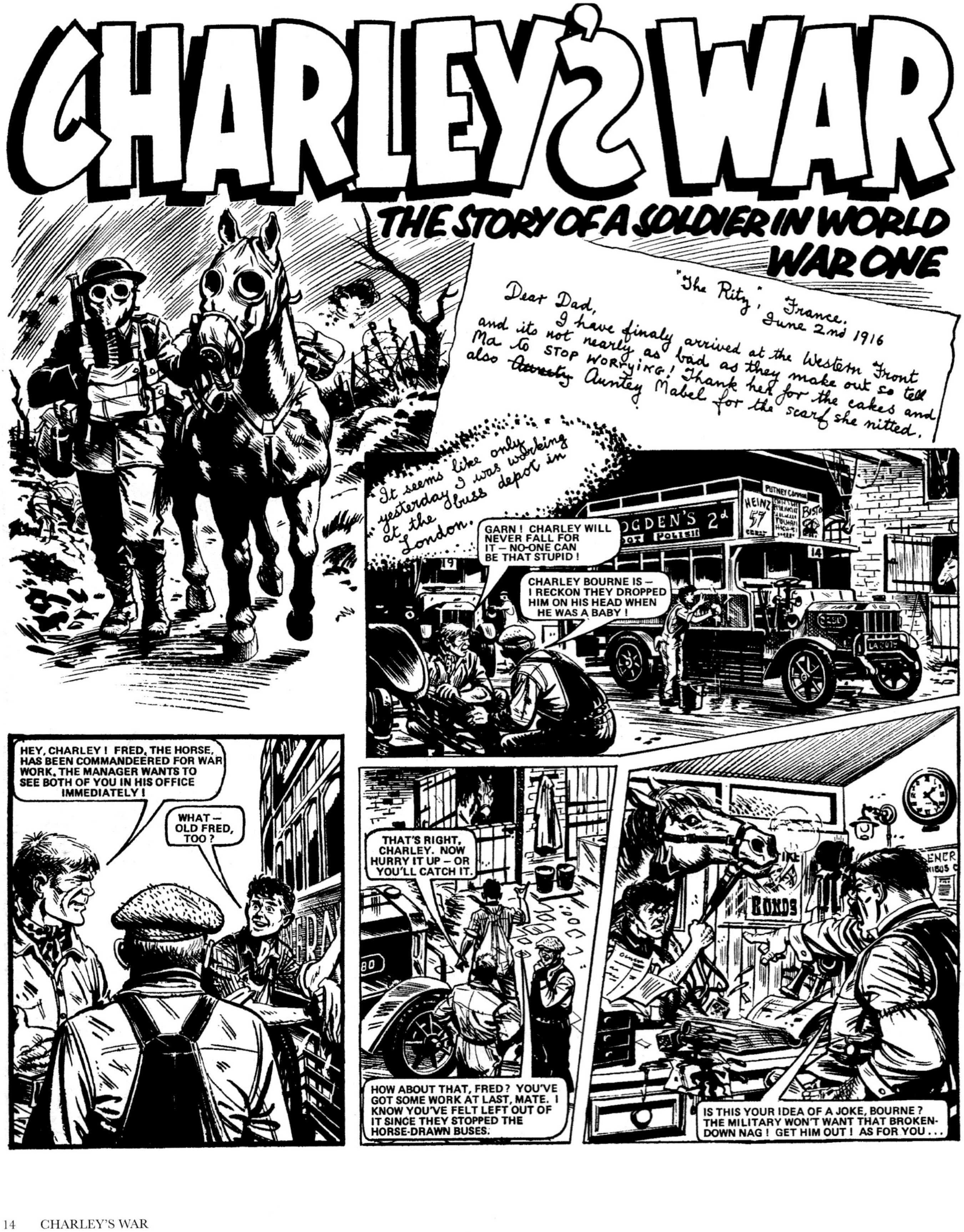
CHARLEY'S WAR
THE STORY OF A SOLDIER IN WORLD WAR ONE
"The Ritz", France. June 2nd 1916
Dear Dad,
I have finaly arrived at the Western Front and its not nearly as bad as they make out so tell Ma to STOP WORRYING! Thank her for the cakes and also Auntey Mabel for the scarf she nitted.
It seems like only yesterday I was working at the buss depot in London.
GARN! CHARLEY WILL NEVER FALL FOR IT – NO-ONE CAN BE THAT STUPID!
CHARLEY BOURNE IS – I RECKON THEY DROPPED HIM ON HIS HEAD WHEN HE WAS A BABY!
OGDEN'S 2d
HEINZ 57
PUTNEY COMMON
HEY, CHARLEY! FRED, THE HORSE, HAS BEEN COMMANDEERED FOR WAR WORK. THE MANAGER WANTS TO SEE BOTH OF YOU IN HIS OFFICE IMMEDIATELY!
WHAT – OLD FRED, TOO?
THAT'S RIGHT, CHARLEY. NOW HURRY IT UP – OR YOU'LL CATCH IT.
HOW ABOUT THAT, FRED? YOU'VE GOT SOME WORK AT LAST, MATE. I KNOW YOU'VE FELT LEFT OUT OF IT SINCE THEY STOPPED THE HORSE-DRAWN BUSES.
BONDS
IS THIS YOUR IDEA OF A JOKE, BOURNE? THE MILITARY WON'T WANT THAT BROKEN-DOWN NAG! GET HIM OUT! AS FOR YOU...

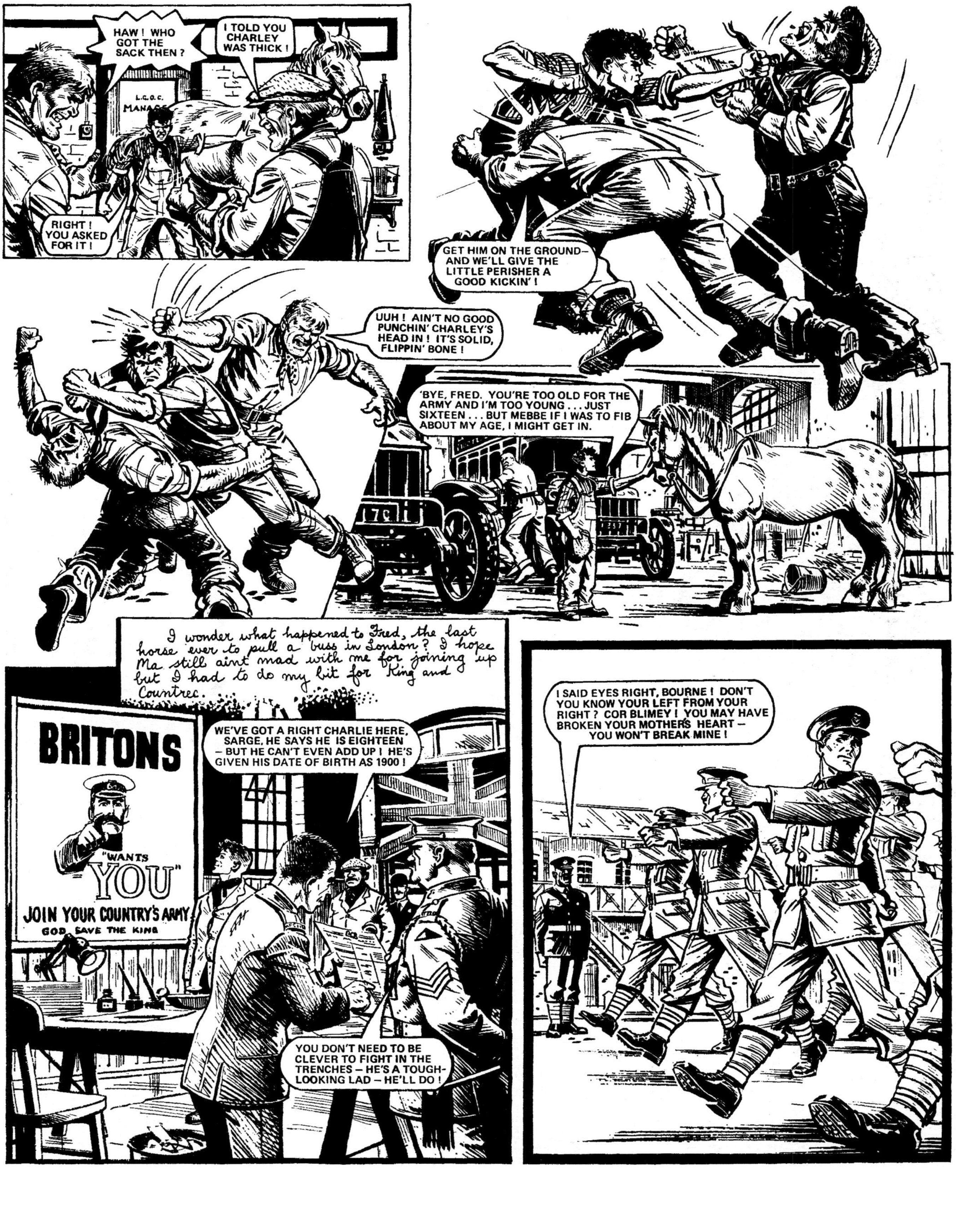
HAW! WHO GOT THE SACK THEN?
I TOLD YOU CHARLEY WAS THICK!
L.G.O.C. MANAGE
RIGHT! YOU ASKED FOR IT!
GET HIM ON THE GROUND— AND WE'LL GIVE THE LITTLE PERISHER A GOOD KICKIN'!
UUH! AIN'T NO GOOD PUNCHIN' CHARLEY'S HEAD IN! IT'S SOLID, FLIPPIN' BONE!
'BYE, FRED. YOU'RE TOO OLD FOR THE ARMY AND I'M TOO YOUNG . . . JUST SIXTEEN . . . BUT MEBBE IF I WAS TO FIB ABOUT MY AGE, I MIGHT GET IN.
I wonder what happened to Fred, the last horse ever to pull a buss in London? I hope Ma still aint mad with me for joining up but I had to do my bit for King and Countrec.
BRITONS
"WANTS YOU"
JOIN YOUR COUNTRY'S ARMY
GOD SAVE THE KING
WE'VE GOT A RIGHT CHARLIE HERE, SARGE, HE SAYS HE IS EIGHTEEN – BUT HE CAN'T EVEN ADD UP! HE'S GIVEN HIS DATE OF BIRTH AS 1900!
YOU DON'T NEED TO BE CLEVER TO FIGHT IN THE TRENCHES – HE'S A TOUGH-LOOKING LAD – HE'LL DO!
I SAID EYES RIGHT, BOURNE! DON'T YOU KNOW YOUR LEFT FROM YOUR RIGHT? COR BLIMEY! YOU MAY HAVE BROKEN YOUR MOTHERS HEART – YOU WON'T BREAK MINE!

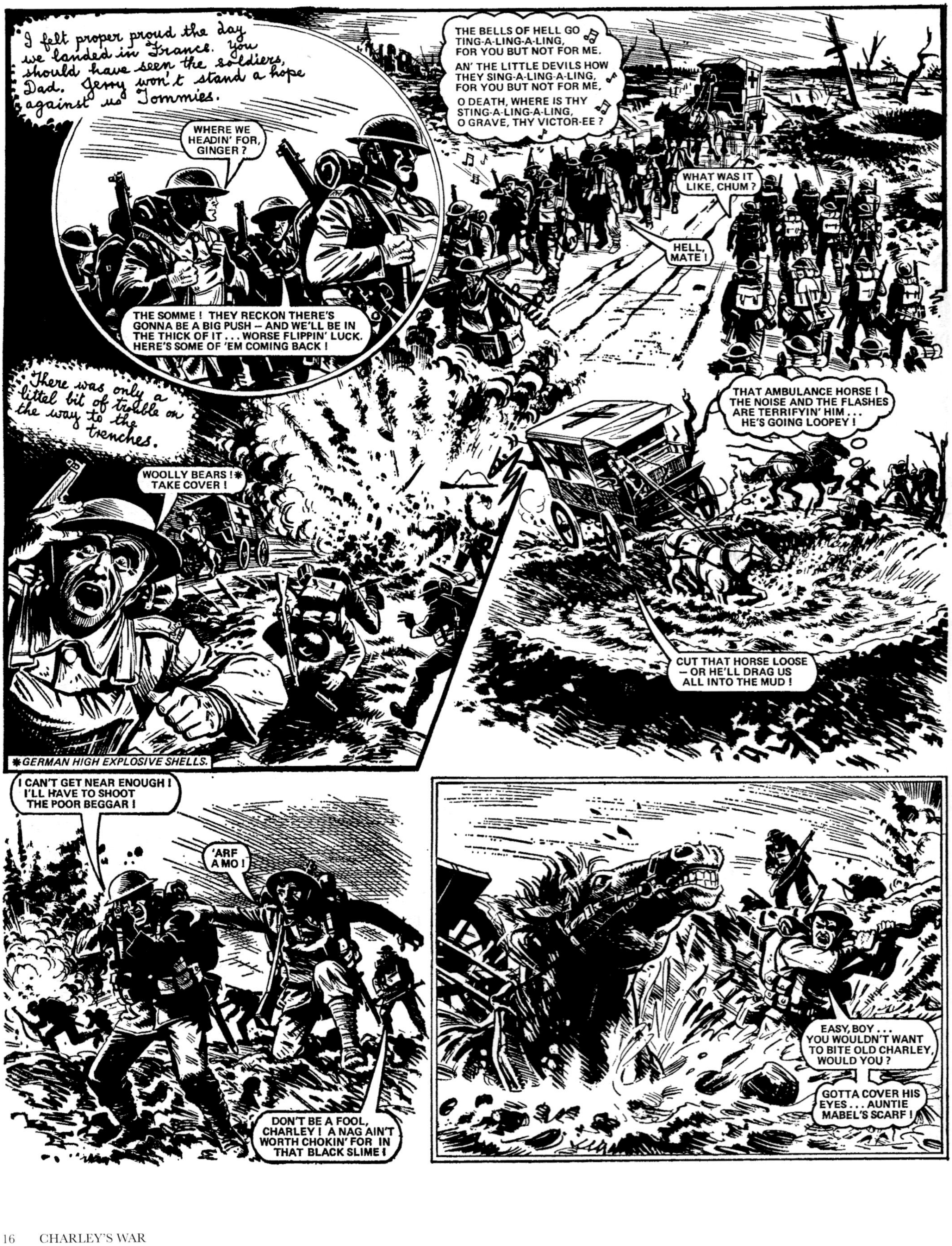

I felt proper proud the day we landed in France. You should have seen the soldiers, Dad. Jerry won't stand a hope against us Tommies.
WHERE WE HEADIN' FOR, GINGER?
THE SOMME! THEY RECKON THERE'S GONNA BE A BIG PUSH — AND WE'LL BE IN THE THICK OF IT ... WORSE FLIPPIN' LUCK. HERE'S SOME OF 'EM COMING BACK!
THE BELLS OF HELL GO TING-A-LING-A-LING, FOR YOU BUT NOT FOR ME, AN' THE LITTLE DEVILS HOW THEY SING-A-LING-A-LING, FOR YOU BUT NOT FOR ME, O DEATH, WHERE IS THY STING-A-LING-A-LING, O GRAVE, THY VICTOR-EE?
WHAT WAS IT LIKE, CHUM?
HELL, MATE!
There was only a littel bit of trouble on the way to the trenches.
WOOLLY BEARS!* TAKE COVER!
*GERMAN HIGH EXPLOSIVE SHELLS.
THAT AMBULANCE HORSE! THE NOISE AND THE FLASHES ARE TERRIFYIN' HIM ... HE'S GOING LOOPEY!
CUT THAT HORSE LOOSE — OR HE'LL DRAG US ALL INTO THE MUD!
I CAN'T GET NEAR ENOUGH! I'LL HAVE TO SHOOT THE POOR BEGGAR!
'ARF A MO!
DON'T BE A FOOL, CHARLEY! A NAG AIN'T WORTH CHOKIN' FOR IN THAT BLACK SLIME!
EASY, BOY ... YOU WOULDN'T WANT TO BITE OLD CHARLEY, WOULD YOU?
GOTTA COVER HIS EYES ... AUNTIE MABEL'S SCARF!

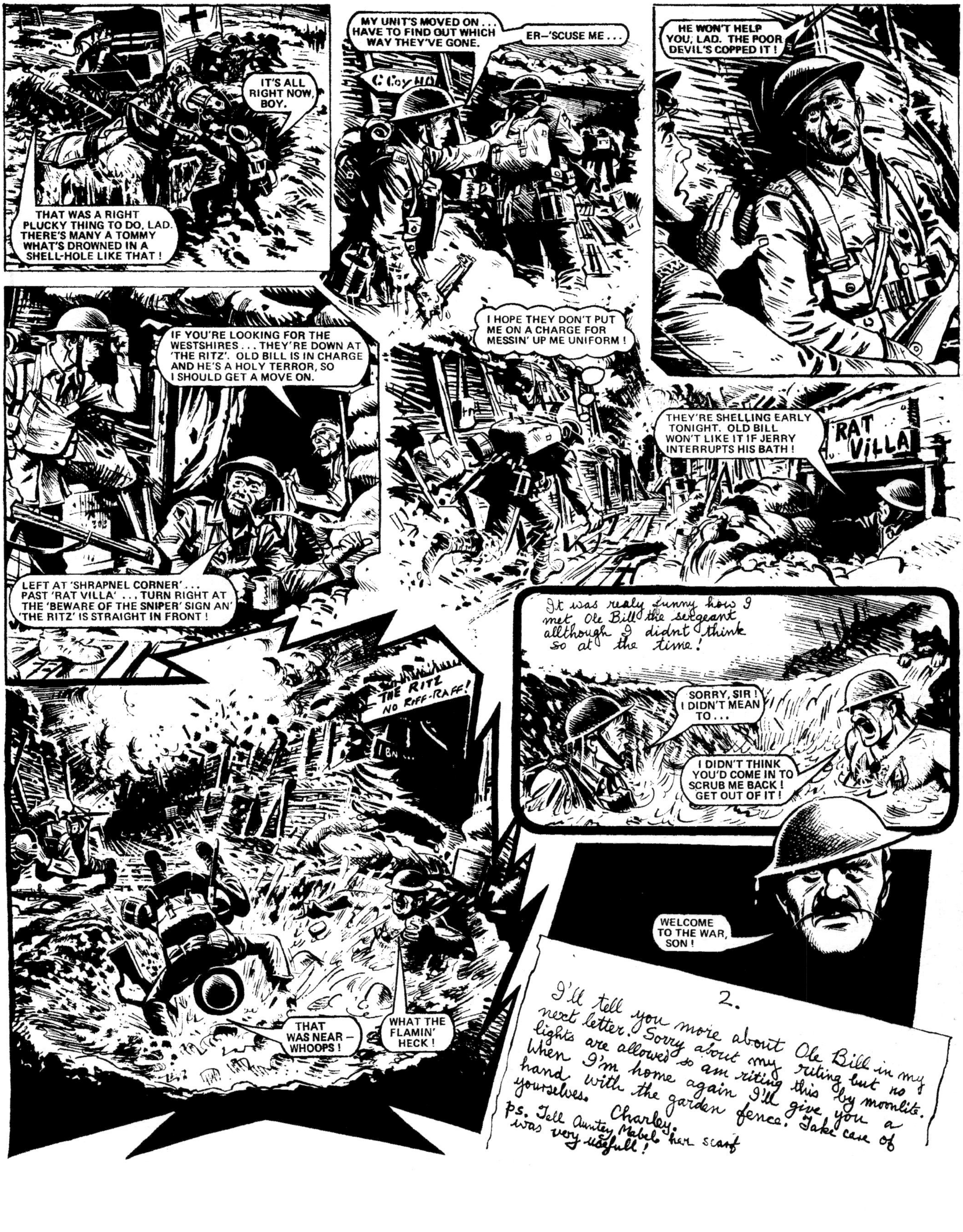
IT'S ALL RIGHT NOW, BOY.
THAT WAS A RIGHT PLUCKY THING TO DO, LAD. THERE'S MANY A TOMMY WHAT'S DROWNED IN A SHELL-HOLE LIKE THAT!
MY UNIT'S MOVED ON... HAVE TO FIND OUT WHICH WAY THEY'VE GONE.
ER–'SCUSE ME...
HE WON'T HELP YOU, LAD. THE POOR DEVIL'S COPPED IT!
IF YOU'RE LOOKING FOR THE WESTSHIRES... THEY'RE DOWN AT 'THE RITZ'. OLD BILL IS IN CHARGE AND HE'S A HOLY TERROR, SO I SHOULD GET A MOVE ON.
LEFT AT 'SHRAPNEL CORNER'... PAST 'RAT VILLA'... TURN RIGHT AT THE 'BEWARE OF THE SNIPER' SIGN AN' 'THE RITZ' IS STRAIGHT IN FRONT!
I HOPE THEY DON'T PUT ME ON A CHARGE FOR MESSIN' UP ME UNIFORM!
THEY'RE SHELLING EARLY TONIGHT. OLD BILL WON'T LIKE IT IF JERRY INTERRUPTS HIS BATH!
RAT VILLA
THE RITZ NO RIFF-RAFF!
THAT WAS NEAR – WHOOPS!
WHAT THE FLAMIN' HECK!
It was realy funny how I met Ole Bill the sergeant allthough I didnt think so at the time!
SORRY, SIR! I DIDN'T MEAN TO...
I DIDN'T THINK YOU'D COME IN TO SCRUB ME BACK! GET OUT OF IT!
WELCOME TO THE WAR, SON!
2.
I'll tell you more about Ole Bill in my next letter. Sorry about my riting but no lights are allowed so am riting this by moonlite. When I'm home again I'll give you a hand with the garden fence. Take care of yourselves.
Charley.
ps. Tell Auntey Mabel her scarf was very usefull!

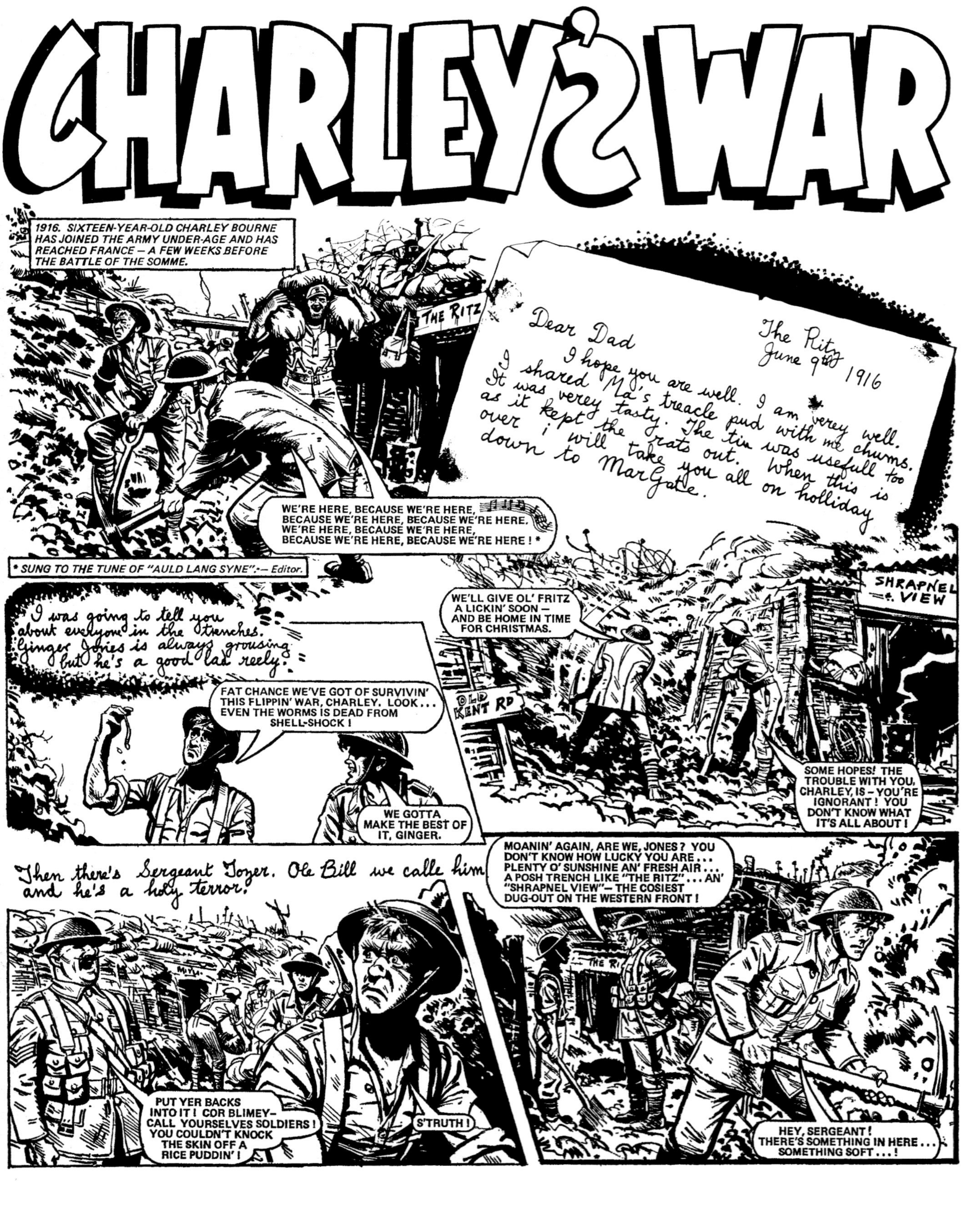

CHARLEY'S WAR
1916. SIXTEEN-YEAR-OLD CHARLEY BOURNE HAS JOINED THE ARMY UNDER-AGE AND HAS REACHED FRANCE – A FEW WEEKS BEFORE THE BATTLE OF THE SOMME.
THE RITZ
Dear Dad
The Ritz
June 9th 1916
I hope you are well. I am verey well.
I shared Ma's treacle pud with me chums.
It was verey tasty. The tin was usefull too
as it kept the rats out. When this is
over i will take you all on holliday
down to MarGate.
WE'RE HERE, BECAUSE WE'RE HERE, BECAUSE WE'RE HERE, BECAUSE WE'RE HERE. WE'RE HERE, BECAUSE WE'RE HERE, BECAUSE WE'RE HERE, BECAUSE WE'RE HERE! *
* SUNG TO THE TUNE OF "AULD LANG SYNE".– Editor.
I was going to tell you about everyone in the trenches. Ginger Jones is always grousing but he's a good lad reely.
FAT CHANCE WE'VE GOT OF SURVIVIN' THIS FLIPPIN' WAR, CHARLEY. LOOK... EVEN THE WORMS IS DEAD FROM SHELL-SHOCK!
WE GOTTA MAKE THE BEST OF IT, GINGER.
SHRAPNEL VIEW
OLD KENT RD
WE'LL GIVE OL' FRITZ A LICKIN' SOON – AND BE HOME IN TIME FOR CHRISTMAS.
SOME HOPES! THE TROUBLE WITH YOU, CHARLEY, IS – YOU'RE IGNORANT! YOU DON'T KNOW WHAT IT'S ALL ABOUT!
Then there's Sergeant Tozer. Ole Bill we calle him and he's a holy terror.
PUT YER BACKS INTO IT! COR BLIMEY– CALL YOURSELVES SOLDIERS! YOU COULDN'T KNOCK THE SKIN OFF A RICE PUDDIN'!
S'TRUTH!
MOANIN' AGAIN, ARE WE, JONES? YOU DON'T KNOW HOW LUCKY YOU ARE... PLENTY O' SUNSHINE AN' FRESH AIR... A POSH TRENCH LIKE "THE RITZ"... AN' "SHRAPNEL VIEW" – THE COSIEST DUG-OUT ON THE WESTERN FRONT!
HEY, SERGEANT! THERE'S SOMETHING IN HERE... SOMETHING SOFT...!

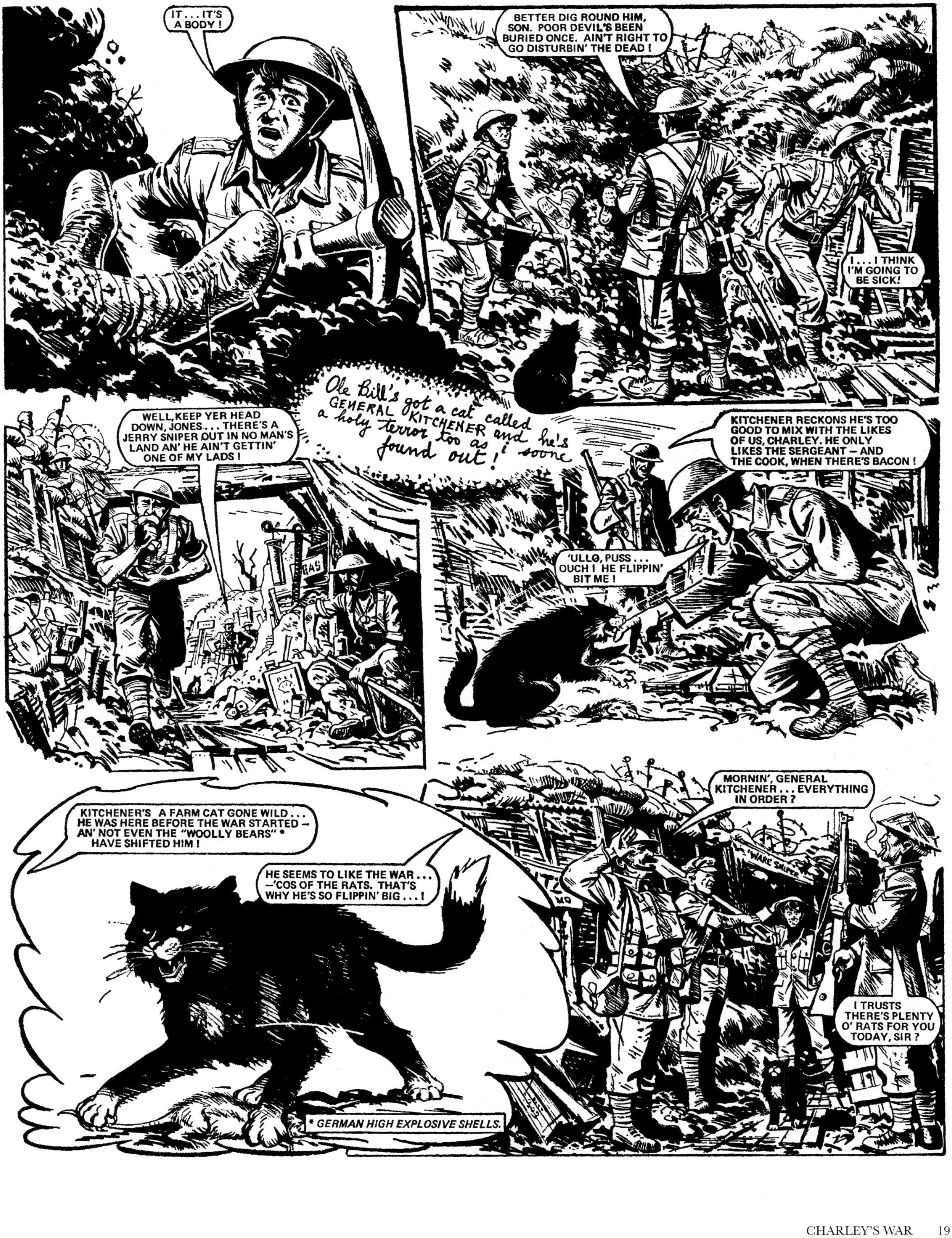
IT . . . IT'S A BODY !
BETTER DIG ROUND HIM, SON. POOR DEVIL'S BEEN BURIED ONCE. AIN'T RIGHT TO GO DISTURBIN' THE DEAD !
I . . . I THINK I'M GOING TO BE SICK!
Ole Bill's got a cat called GENERAL KITCHENER and he's a holy terror too as I soon found out!
WELL, KEEP YER HEAD DOWN, JONES . . . THERE'S A JERRY SNIPER OUT IN NO MAN'S LAND AN' HE AIN'T GETTIN' ONE OF MY LADS !
KITCHENER RECKONS HE'S TOO GOOD TO MIX WITH THE LIKES OF US, CHARLEY. HE ONLY LIKES THE SERGEANT – AND THE COOK, WHEN THERE'S BACON !
'ULLO, PUSS . . . OUCH ! HE FLIPPIN' BIT ME !
KITCHENER'S A FARM CAT GONE WILD . . . HE WAS HERE BEFORE THE WAR STARTED – AN' NOT EVEN THE "WOOLLY BEARS" * HAVE SHIFTED HIM !
HE SEEMS TO LIKE THE WAR . . . –'COS OF THE RATS. THAT'S WHY HE'S SO FLIPPIN' BIG . . . !
* GERMAN HIGH EXPLOSIVE SHELLS.
MORNIN', GENERAL KITCHENER . . . EVERYTHING IN ORDER ?
'WARE SNIPER
I TRUSTS THERE'S PLENTY O' RATS FOR YOU TODAY, SIR ?

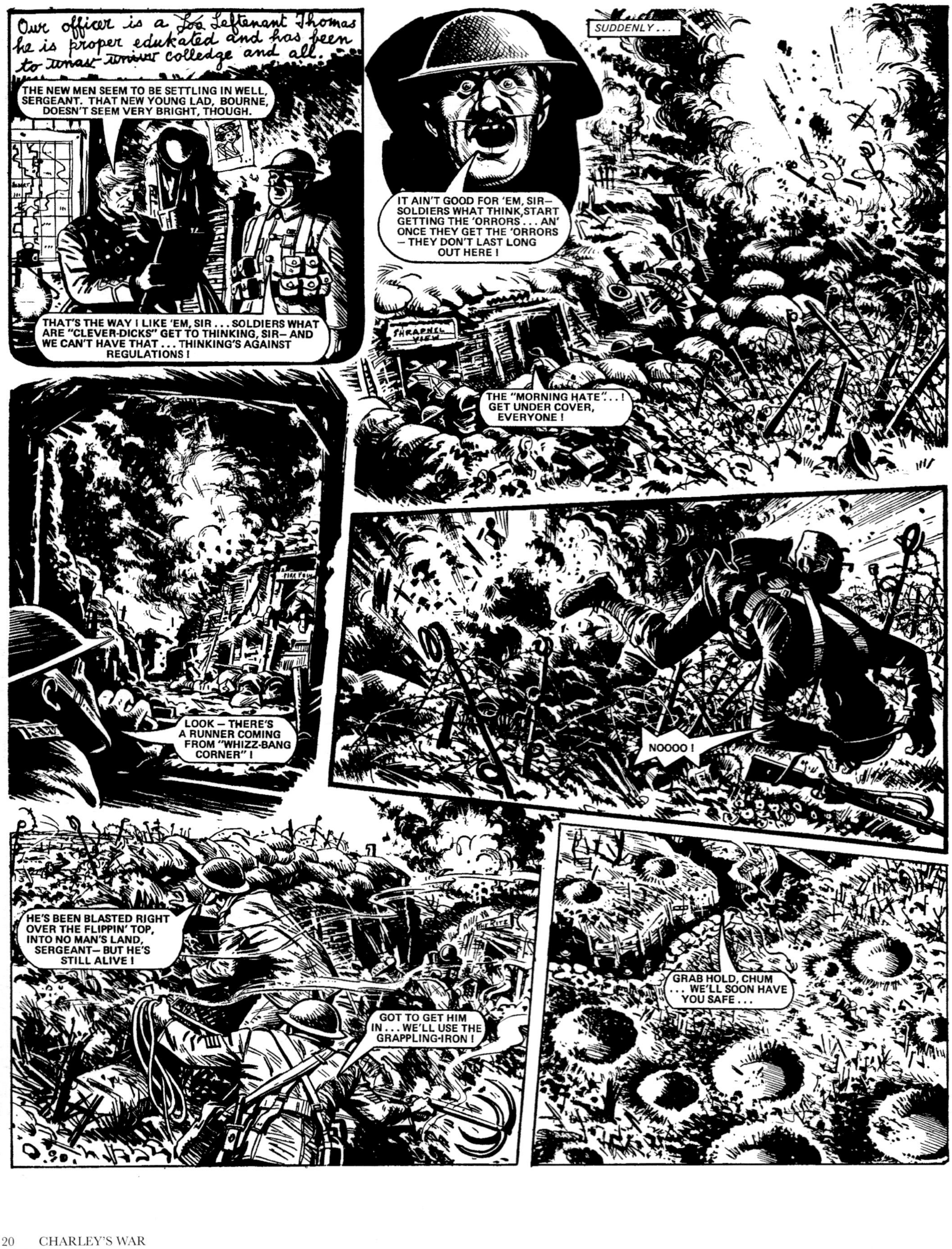
Our officer is a ~~Los~~ Leftenant Thomas he is proper edukated and has been to ~~unav univer~~ colledge and all.
THE NEW MEN SEEM TO BE SETTLING IN WELL, SERGEANT. THAT NEW YOUNG LAD, BOURNE, DOESN'T SEEM VERY BRIGHT, THOUGH.
THAT'S THE WAY I LIKE 'EM, SIR . . . SOLDIERS WHAT ARE "CLEVER-DICKS" GET TO THINKING, SIR– AND WE CAN'T HAVE THAT . . . THINKING'S AGAINST REGULATIONS !
IT AIN'T GOOD FOR 'EM, SIR– SOLDIERS WHAT THINK, START GETTING THE 'ORRORS . . . AN' ONCE THEY GET THE 'ORRORS – THEY DON'T LAST LONG OUT HERE !
SUDDENLY . . .
SHRAPNEL VIEW
THE "MORNING HATE" . . ! GET UNDER COVER, EVERYONE !
LOOK – THERE'S A RUNNER COMING FROM "WHIZZ-BANG CORNER" !
NOOOO !
HE'S BEEN BLASTED RIGHT OVER THE FLIPPIN' TOP, INTO NO MAN'S LAND, SERGEANT– BUT HE'S STILL ALIVE !
GOT TO GET HIM IN . . . WE'LL USE THE GRAPPLING-IRON !
GRAB HOLD, CHUM . . . WE'LL SOON HAVE YOU SAFE . . .

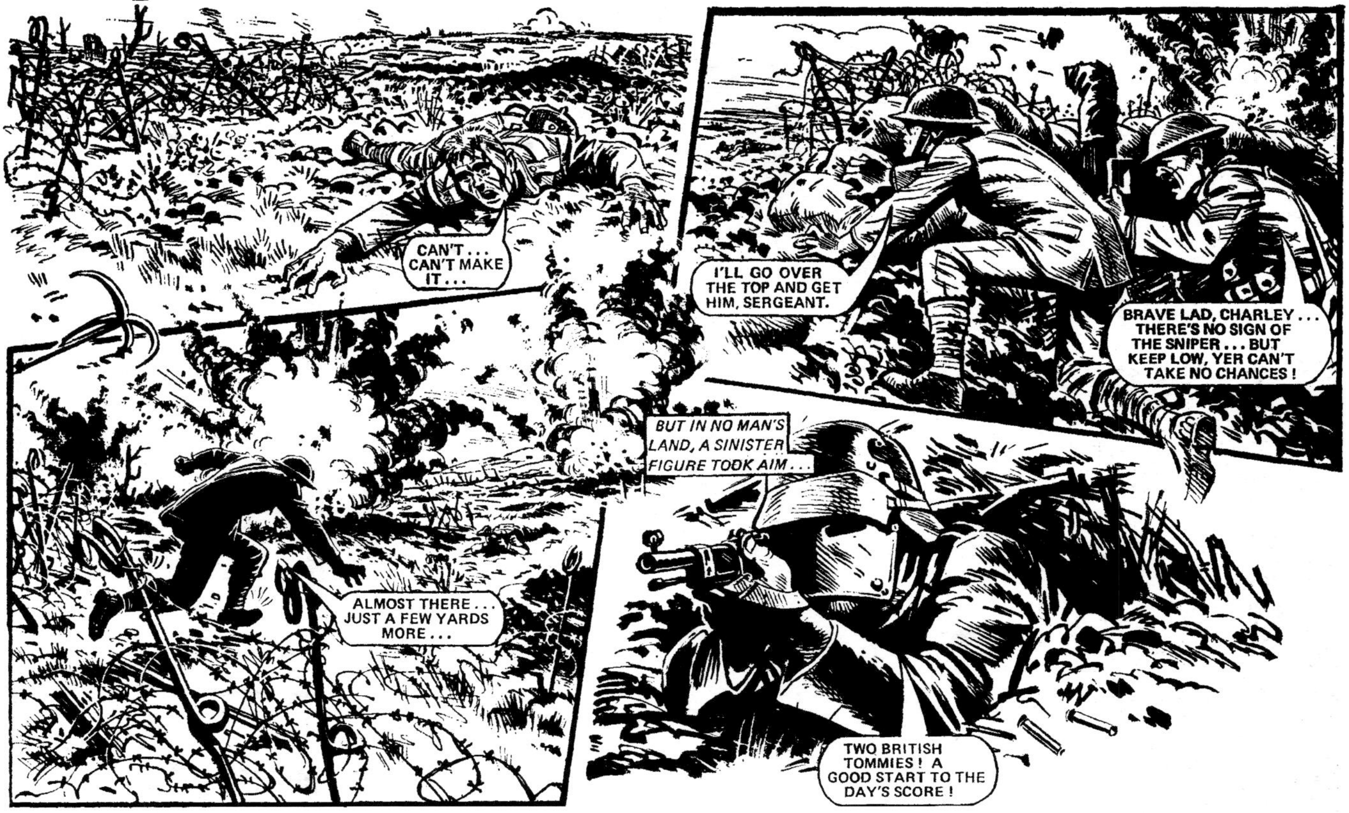
CAN'T . . . CAN'T MAKE IT . . .
I'LL GO OVER THE TOP AND GET HIM, SERGEANT.
BRAVE LAD, CHARLEY . . . THERE'S NO SIGN OF THE SNIPER . . . BUT KEEP LOW, YER CAN'T TAKE NO CHANCES !
ALMOST THERE . . . JUST A FEW YARDS MORE . . .
BUT IN NO MAN'S LAND, A SINISTER FIGURE TOOK AIM . . .
TWO BRITISH TOMMIES ! A GOOD START TO THE DAY'S SCORE !

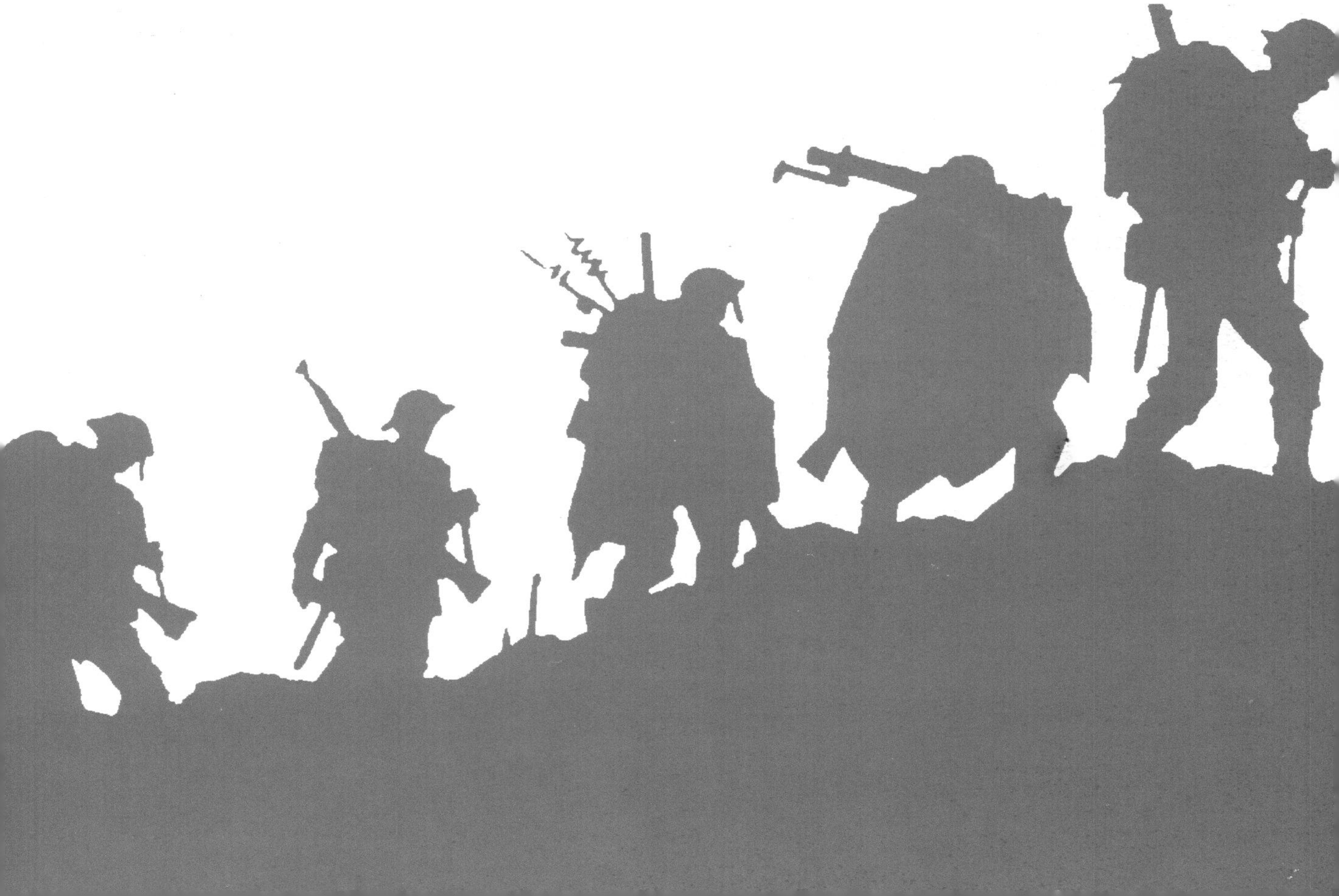

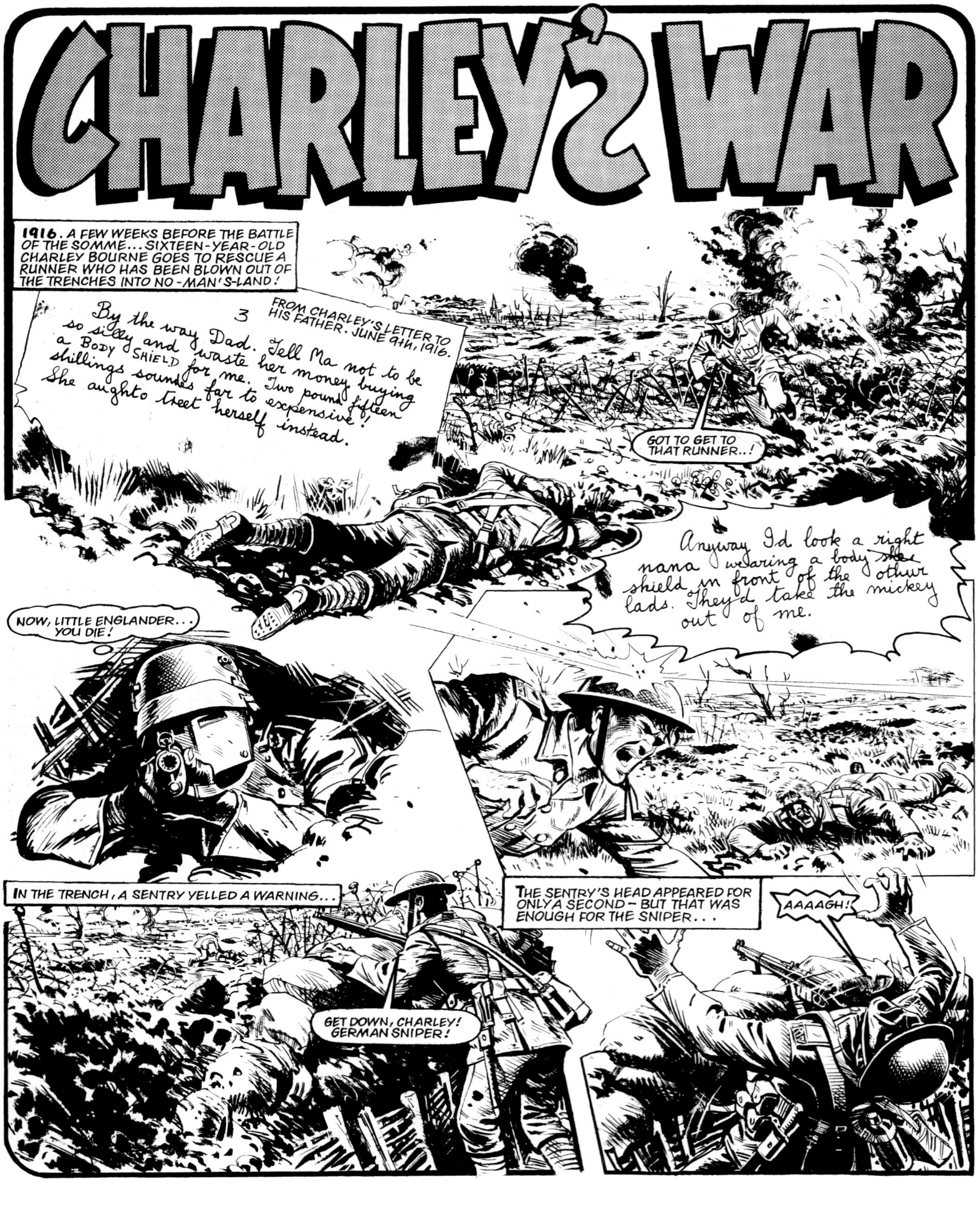
CHARLEY'S WAR
1916. A FEW WEEKS BEFORE THE BATTLE OF THE SOMME... SIXTEEN-YEAR-OLD CHARLEY BOURNE GOES TO RESCUE A RUNNER WHO HAS BEEN BLOWN OUT OF THE TRENCHES INTO NO-MAN'S-LAND!
FROM CHARLEY'S LETTER TO HIS FATHER. JUNE 9th, 1916.
3
By the way Dad. Tell Ma not to be so silly and waste her money buying a BODY SHIELD for me. Two pound fifteen shillings soundes far to expensive! She aughto treet herself instead.
GOT TO GET TO THAT RUNNER..!
Anyway I'd look a right nana wearing a body shield in front of the other lads. They'd take the mickey out of me.
NOW, LITTLE ENGLANDER... YOU DIE!
IN THE TRENCH, A SENTRY YELLED A WARNING...
GET DOWN, CHARLEY! GERMAN SNIPER!
THE SENTRY'S HEAD APPEARED FOR ONLY A SECOND – BUT THAT WAS ENOUGH FOR THE SNIPER...
AAAAGH!

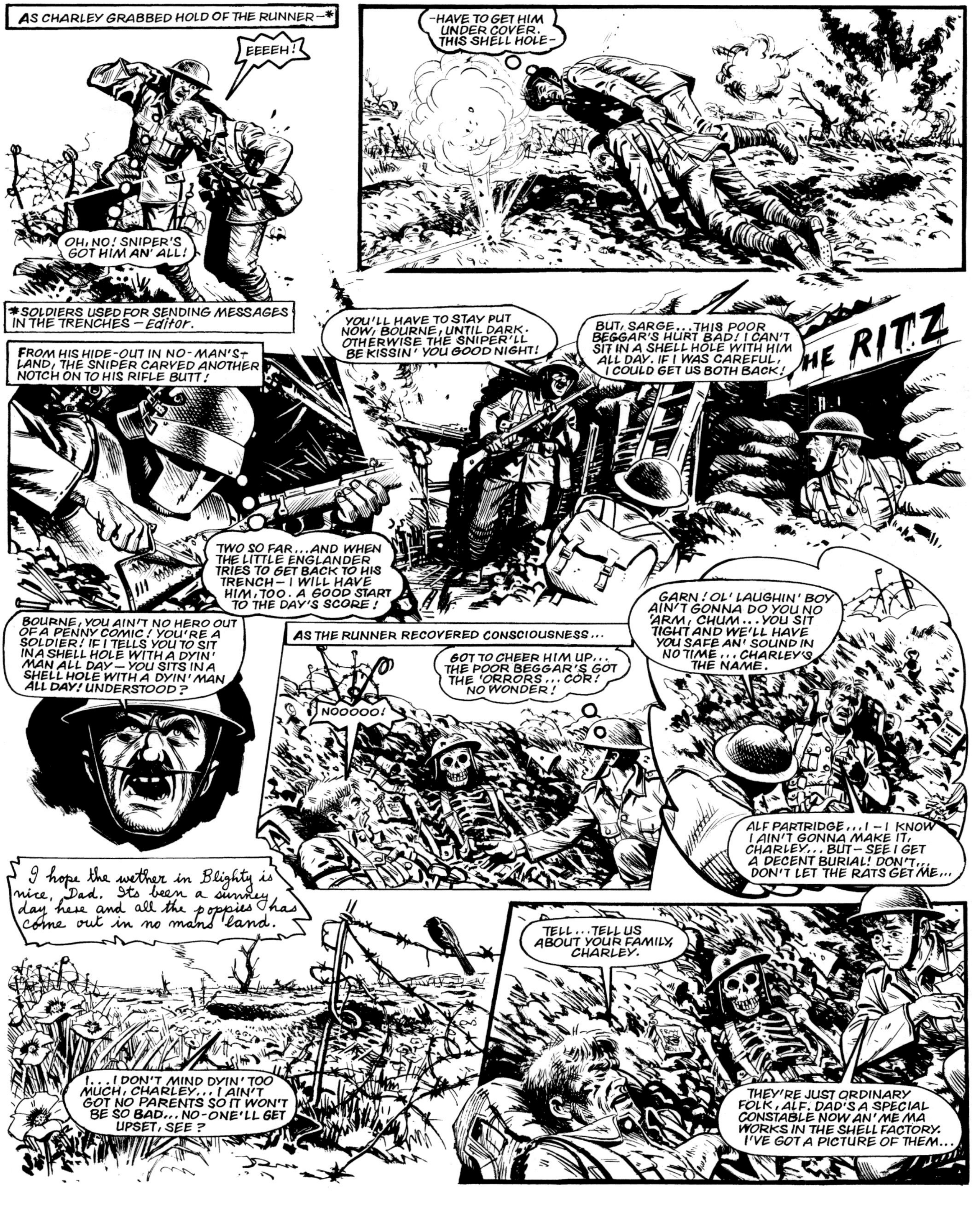

AS CHARLEY GRABBED HOLD OF THE RUNNER—*
EEEEH!
OH, NO! SNIPER'S GOT HIM AN' ALL!
*SOLDIERS USED FOR SENDING MESSAGES IN THE TRENCHES — Editor.
—HAVE TO GET HIM UNDER COVER. THIS SHELL HOLE—
FROM HIS HIDE-OUT IN NO-MAN'S-LAND, THE SNIPER CARVED ANOTHER NOTCH ON TO HIS RIFLE BUTT!
TWO SO FAR... AND WHEN THE LITTLE ENGLANDER TRIES TO GET BACK TO HIS TRENCH — I WILL HAVE HIM, TOO. A GOOD START TO THE DAY'S SCORE!
YOU'LL HAVE TO STAY PUT NOW, BOURNE, UNTIL DARK. OTHERWISE THE SNIPER'LL BE KISSIN' YOU GOOD NIGHT!
BUT, SARGE... THIS POOR BEGGAR'S HURT BAD! I CAN'T SIT IN A SHELL HOLE WITH HIM ALL DAY. IF I WAS CAREFUL, I COULD GET US BOTH BACK!
HE RITZ
BOURNE, YOU AIN'T NO HERO OUT OF A PENNY COMIC! YOU'RE A SOLDIER! IF I TELLS YOU TO SIT IN A SHELL HOLE WITH A DYIN' MAN ALL DAY — YOU SITS IN A SHELL HOLE WITH A DYIN' MAN ALL DAY! UNDERSTOOD?
AS THE RUNNER RECOVERED CONSCIOUSNESS...
NOOOOO!
GOT TO CHEER HIM UP... THE POOR BEGGAR'S GOT THE 'ORRORS... COR! NO WONDER!
GARN! OL' LAUGHIN' BOY AIN'T GONNA DO YOU NO 'ARM, CHUM... YOU SIT TIGHT AND WE'LL HAVE YOU SAFE AN' SOUND IN NO TIME... CHARLEY'S THE NAME.
ALF PARTRIDGE... I — I KNOW I AIN'T GONNA MAKE IT, CHARLEY... BUT — SEE I GET A DECENT BURIAL! DON'T... DON'T LET THE RATS GET ME...
I hope the wether in Blighty is nice, Dad. Its been a sunney day here and all the poppies has come out in no mans land.
I... I DON'T MIND DYIN' TOO MUCH, CHARLEY... I AIN'T GOT NO PARENTS SO IT WON'T BE SO BAD... NO-ONE'LL GET UPSET, SEE?
TELL... TELL US ABOUT YOUR FAMILY, CHARLEY.
THEY'RE JUST ORDINARY FOLK, ALF. DAD'S A SPECIAL CONSTABLE NOW AN' ME MA WORKS IN THE SHELL FACTORY. I'VE GOT A PICTURE OF THEM...

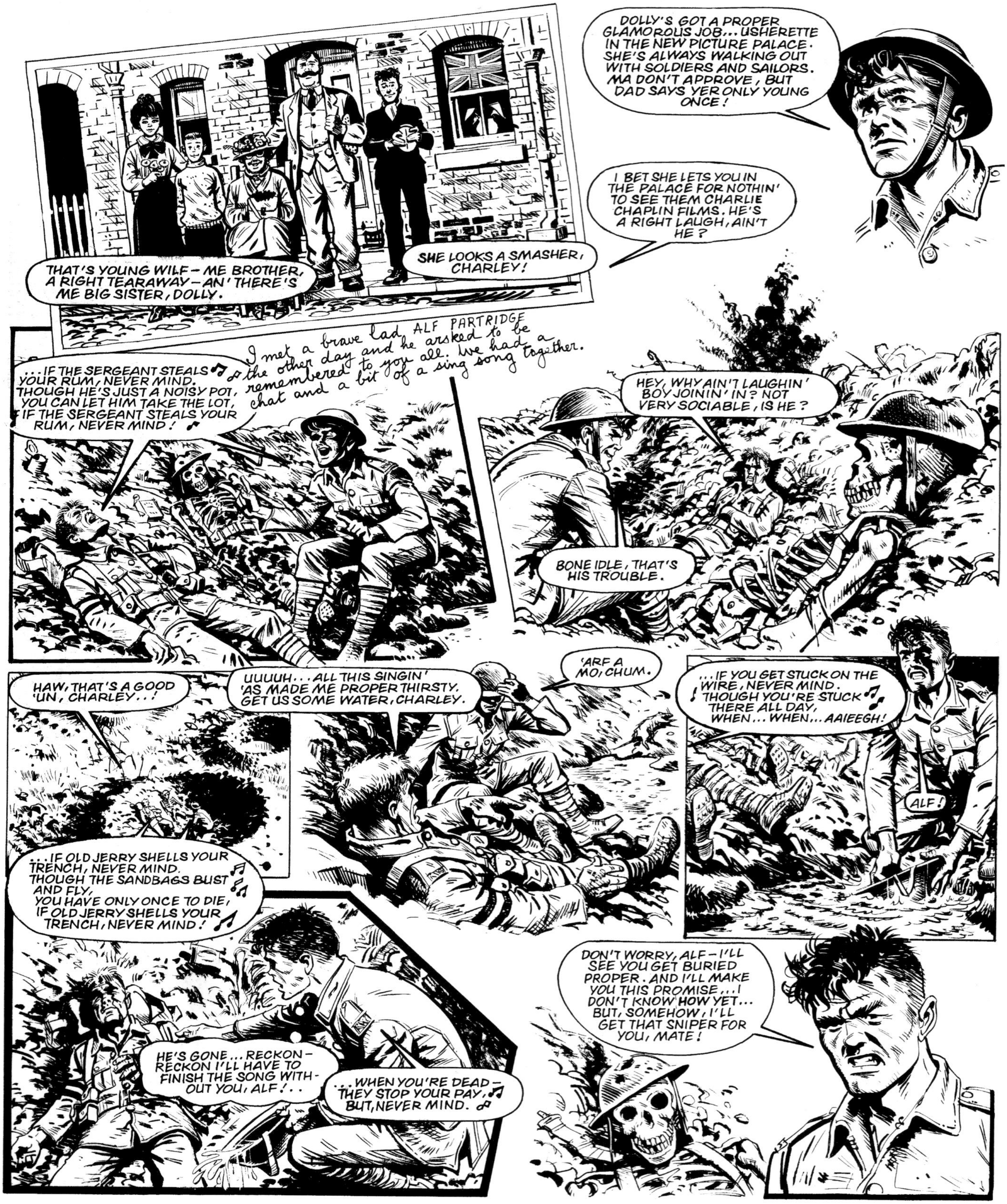
THAT'S YOUNG WILF – ME BROTHER, A RIGHT TEARAWAY – AN' THERE'S ME BIG SISTER, DOLLY.
SHE LOOKS A SMASHER, CHARLEY!
DOLLY'S GOT A PROPER GLAMOROUS JOB... USHERETTE IN THE NEW PICTURE PALACE. SHE'S ALWAYS WALKING OUT WITH SOLDIERS AND SAILORS. MA DON'T APPROVE, BUT DAD SAYS YER ONLY YOUNG ONCE!
I BET SHE LETS YOU IN THE PALACE FOR NOTHIN' TO SEE THEM CHARLIE CHAPLIN FILMS. HE'S A RIGHT LAUGH, AIN'T HE?
I met a brave lad ALF PARTRIDGE the other day and he arsked to be remembered to you all. We had a chat and a bit of a sing song together.
...IF THE SERGEANT STEALS YOUR RUM, NEVER MIND. THOUGH HE'S JUST A NOISY POT, YOU CAN LET HIM TAKE THE LOT, IF THE SERGEANT STEALS YOUR RUM, NEVER MIND!
HEY, WHY AIN'T LAUGHIN' BOY JOININ' IN? NOT VERY SOCIABLE, IS HE?
BONE IDLE, THAT'S HIS TROUBLE.
HAW, THAT'S A GOOD 'UN, CHARLEY...!
UUUUH... ALL THIS SINGIN' 'AS MADE ME PROPER THIRSTY. GET US SOME WATER, CHARLEY.
'ARF A MO, CHUM.
...IF YOU GET STUCK ON THE WIRE, NEVER MIND. THOUGH YOU'RE STUCK THERE ALL DAY, WHEN... WHEN... AAIEEGH!
ALF!
...IF OLD JERRY SHELLS YOUR TRENCH, NEVER MIND. THOUGH THE SANDBAGS BUST AND FLY, YOU HAVE ONLY ONCE TO DIE, IF OLD JERRY SHELLS YOUR TRENCH, NEVER MIND!
HE'S GONE... RECKON– RECKON I'LL HAVE TO FINISH THE SONG WITHOUT YOU, ALF!..
...WHEN YOU'RE DEAD– THEY STOP YOUR PAY, BUT, NEVER MIND.
DON'T WORRY, ALF – I'LL SEE YOU GET BURIED PROPER. AND I'LL MAKE YOU THIS PROMISE... I DON'T KNOW HOW YET... BUT, SOMEHOW, I'LL GET THAT SNIPER FOR YOU, MATE!

CHARLEY'S WAR

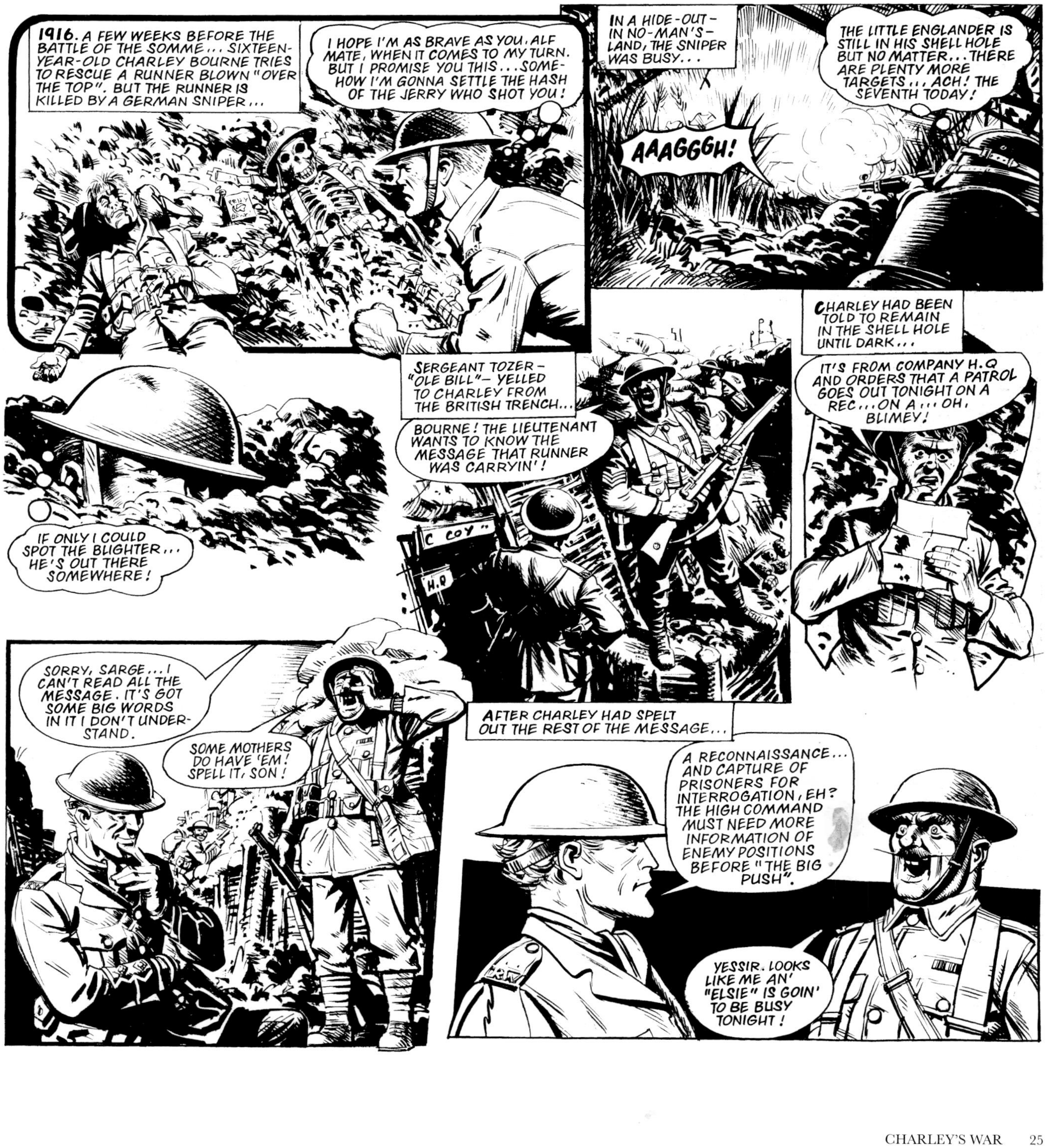
1916. A FEW WEEKS BEFORE THE BATTLE OF THE SOMME... SIXTEEN-YEAR-OLD CHARLEY BOURNE TRIES TO RESCUE A RUNNER BLOWN "OVER THE TOP". BUT THE RUNNER IS KILLED BY A GERMAN SNIPER...
I HOPE I'M AS BRAVE AS YOU, ALF MATE, WHEN IT COMES TO MY TURN. BUT I PROMISE YOU THIS... SOMEHOW I'M GONNA SETTLE THE HASH OF THE JERRY WHO SHOT YOU!
IN A HIDE-OUT – IN NO-MAN'S-LAND, THE SNIPER WAS BUSY...
THE LITTLE ENGLANDER IS STILL IN HIS SHELL HOLE BUT NO MATTER... THERE ARE PLENTY MORE TARGETS... ACH! THE SEVENTH TODAY!
AAAGGGH!
IF ONLY I COULD SPOT THE BLIGHTER... HE'S OUT THERE SOMEWHERE!
SERGEANT TOZER – "OLE BILL" – YELLED TO CHARLEY FROM THE BRITISH TRENCH...
BOURNE! THE LIEUTENANT WANTS TO KNOW THE MESSAGE THAT RUNNER WAS CARRYIN'!
C COY.
H.Q
CHARLEY HAD BEEN TOLD TO REMAIN IN THE SHELL HOLE UNTIL DARK...
IT'S FROM COMPANY H.Q AND ORDERS THAT A PATROL GOES OUT TONIGHT ON A REC... ON A... OH, BLIMEY!
SORRY, SARGE... I CAN'T READ ALL THE MESSAGE. IT'S GOT SOME BIG WORDS IN IT I DON'T UNDERSTAND.
SOME MOTHERS DO HAVE 'EM! SPELL IT, SON!
AFTER CHARLEY HAD SPELT OUT THE REST OF THE MESSAGE...
A RECONNAISSANCE... AND CAPTURE OF PRISONERS FOR INTERROGATION, EH? THE HIGH COMMAND MUST NEED MORE INFORMATION OF ENEMY POSITIONS BEFORE "THE BIG PUSH".
YESSIR. LOOKS LIKE ME AN' "ELSIE" IS GOIN' TO BE BUSY TONIGHT!

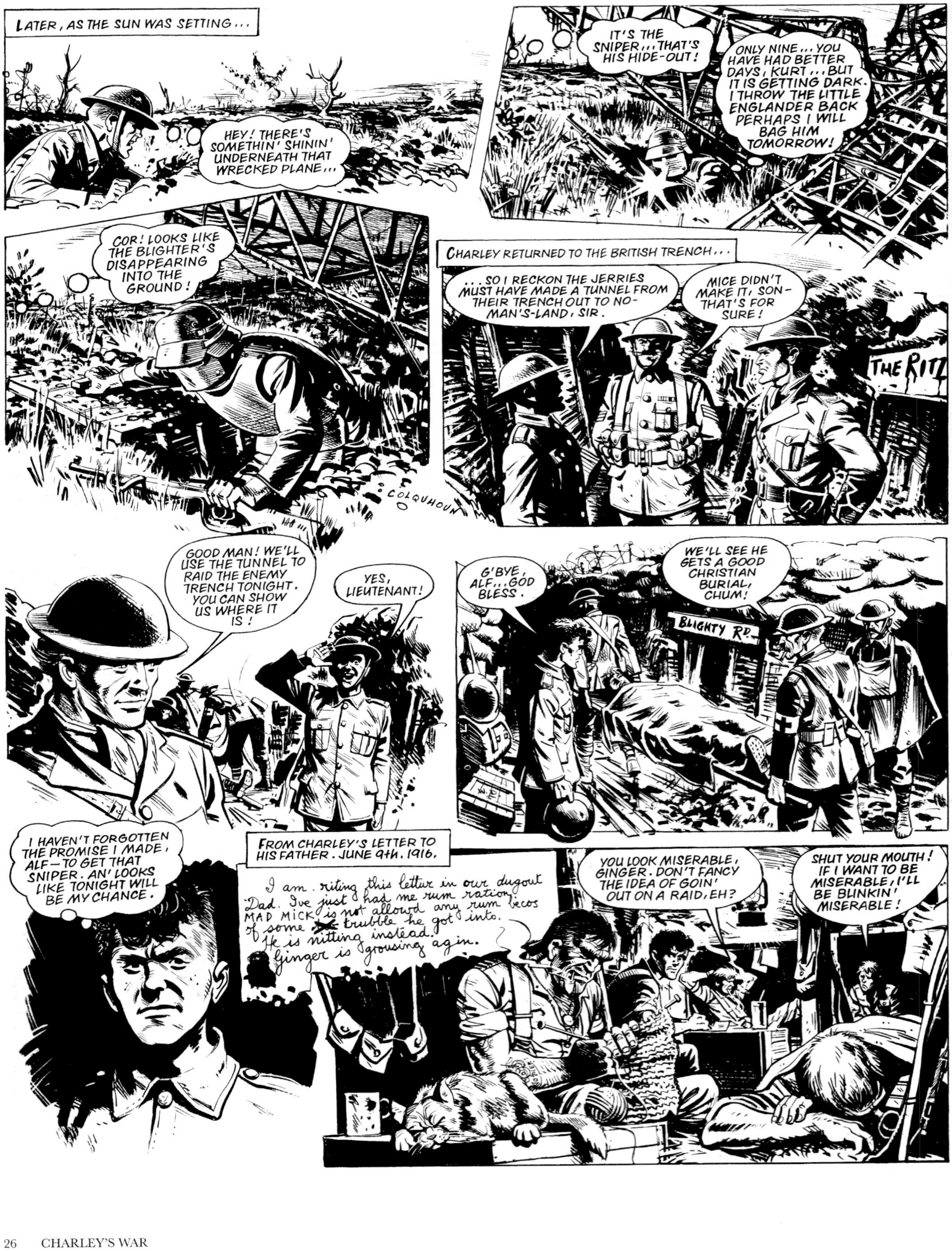

LATER, AS THE SUN WAS SETTING...
HEY! THERE'S SOMETHIN' SHININ' UNDERNEATH THAT WRECKED PLANE...
IT'S THE SNIPER... THAT'S HIS HIDE-OUT!
ONLY NINE... YOU HAVE HAD BETTER DAYS, KURT... BUT IT IS GETTING DARK. I THROW THE LITTLE ENGLANDER BACK PERHAPS I WILL BAG HIM TOMORROW!
COR! LOOKS LIKE THE BLIGHTER'S DISAPPEARING INTO THE GROUND!
COLQUHOUN
CHARLEY RETURNED TO THE BRITISH TRENCH...
...SO I RECKON THE JERRIES MUST HAVE MADE A TUNNEL FROM THEIR TRENCH OUT TO NO-MAN'S-LAND, SIR.
MICE DIDN'T MAKE IT, SON— THAT'S FOR SURE!
THE RITZ
GOOD MAN! WE'LL USE THE TUNNEL TO RAID THE ENEMY TRENCH TONIGHT. YOU CAN SHOW US WHERE IT IS!
YES, LIEUTENANT!
G'BYE, ALF... GOD BLESS.
WE'LL SEE HE GETS A GOOD CHRISTIAN BURIAL, CHUM!
BLIGHTY RD.
I HAVEN'T FORGOTTEN THE PROMISE I MADE, ALF— TO GET THAT SNIPER. AN' LOOKS LIKE TONIGHT WILL BE MY CHANCE.
FROM CHARLEY'S LETTER TO HIS FATHER. JUNE 9th. 1916.
I am riting this letter in our dugout Dad. Ive just had me rum ration. MAD MICK is not allowd any rum becos of some trubble he got into. He is nitting instead. Ginger is grousing agin.
YOU LOOK MISERABLE, GINGER. DON'T FANCY THE IDEA OF GOIN' OUT ON A RAID, EH?
SHUT YOUR MOUTH! IF I WANT TO BE MISERABLE, I'LL BE BLINKIN' MISERABLE!

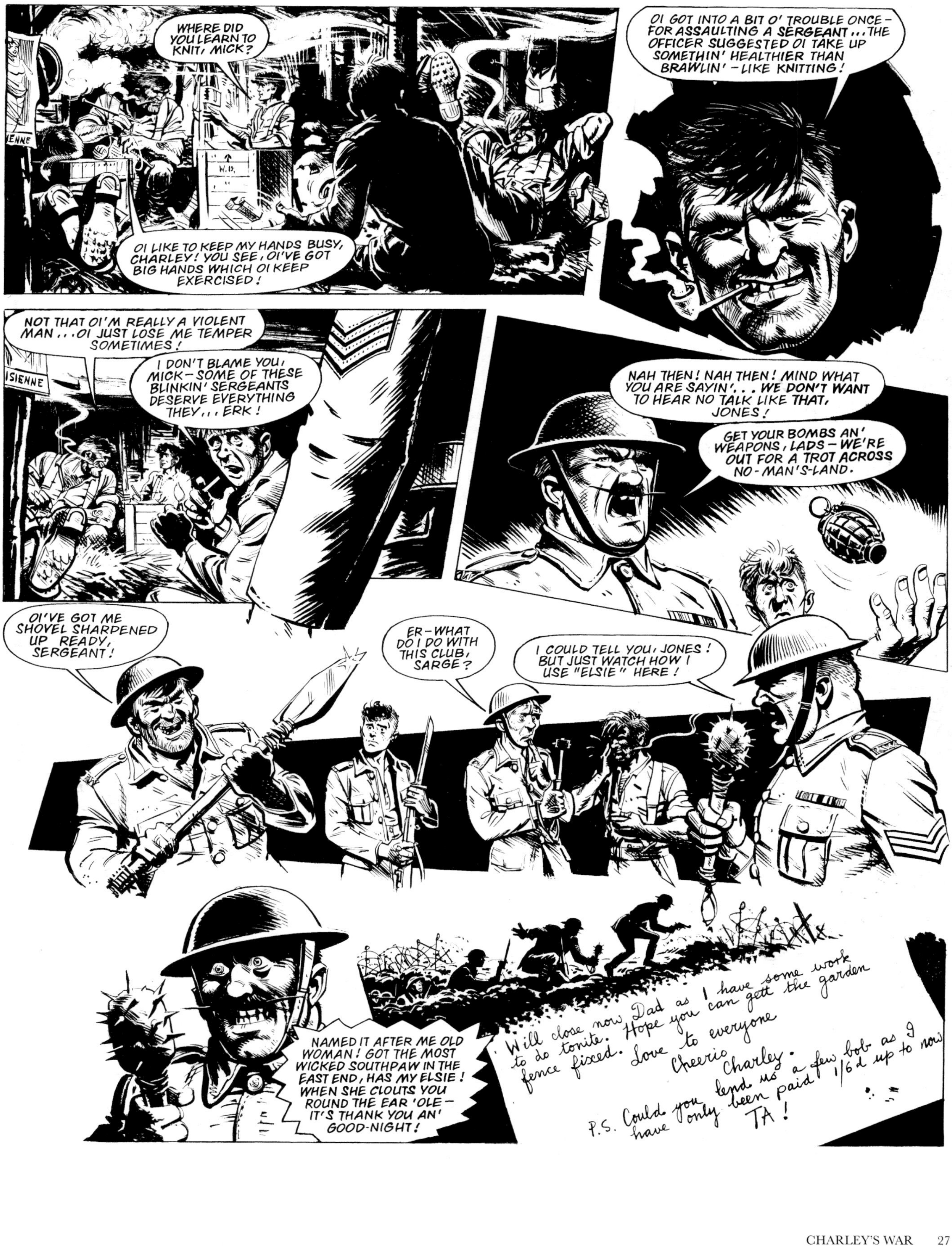
WHERE DID YOU LEARN TO KNIT, MICK?
OI LIKE TO KEEP MY HANDS BUSY, CHARLEY! YOU SEE, OI'VE GOT BIG HANDS WHICH OI KEEP EXERCISED!
OI GOT INTO A BIT O' TROUBLE ONCE – FOR ASSAULTING A SERGEANT... THE OFFICER SUGGESTED OI TAKE UP SOMETHIN' HEALTHIER THAN BRAWLIN' – LIKE KNITTING!
NOT THAT OI'M REALLY A VIOLENT MAN... OI JUST LOSE ME TEMPER SOMETIMES!
I DON'T BLAME YOU, MICK – SOME OF THESE BLINKIN' SERGEANTS DESERVE EVERYTHING THEY... ERK!
NAH THEN! NAH THEN! MIND WHAT YOU ARE SAYIN'... WE DON'T WANT TO HEAR NO TALK LIKE THAT, JONES!
GET YOUR BOMBS AN' WEAPONS, LADS – WE'RE OUT FOR A TROT ACROSS NO-MAN'S-LAND.
OI'VE GOT ME SHOVEL SHARPENED UP READY, SERGEANT!
ER – WHAT DO I DO WITH THIS CLUB, SARGE?
I COULD TELL YOU, JONES! BUT JUST WATCH HOW I USE "ELSIE" HERE!
NAMED IT AFTER ME OLD WOMAN! GOT THE MOST WICKED SOUTHPAW IN THE EAST END, HAS MY ELSIE! WHEN SHE CLOUTS YOU ROUND THE EAR 'OLE – IT'S THANK YOU AN' GOOD-NIGHT!
Will close now Dad as I have some work to do tonite. Hope you can get the garden fence fixed. Love to everyone
Cheerio
Charley.
P.S. Could you lend me a few bob as I have only been paid 1/6d up to now
TA!

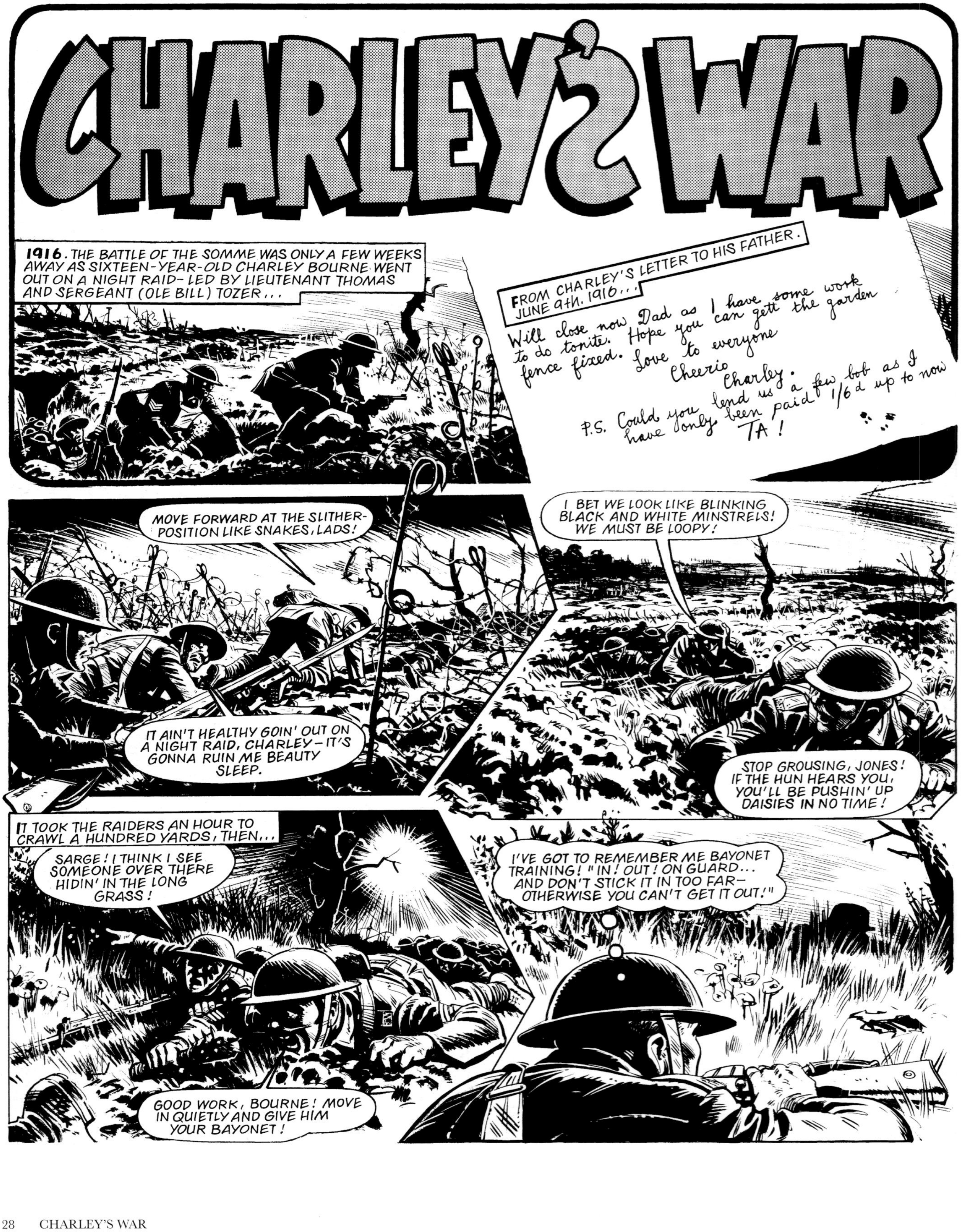
CHARLEY'S WAR
1916. THE BATTLE OF THE SOMME WAS ONLY A FEW WEEKS AWAY AS SIXTEEN-YEAR-OLD CHARLEY BOURNE WENT OUT ON A NIGHT RAID- LED BY LIEUTENANT THOMAS AND SERGEANT (OLE BILL) TOZER...
FROM CHARLEY'S LETTER TO HIS FATHER. JUNE 9th. 1916...
Will close now Dad as I have some work to do tonite. Hope you can gett the garden fence fixed. Love to everyone
Cheerio
Charley.
P.S. Could you lend us a few bob as I have only been paid 1/6d up to now
TA!
MOVE FORWARD AT THE SLITHER-POSITION LIKE SNAKES, LADS!
IT AIN'T HEALTHY GOIN' OUT ON A NIGHT RAID, CHARLEY—IT'S GONNA RUIN ME BEAUTY SLEEP.
I BET WE LOOK LIKE BLINKING BLACK AND WHITE MINSTRELS! WE MUST BE LOOPY!
STOP GROUSING, JONES! IF THE HUN HEARS YOU, YOU'LL BE PUSHIN' UP DAISIES IN NO TIME!
IT TOOK THE RAIDERS AN HOUR TO CRAWL A HUNDRED YARDS, THEN...
SARGE! I THINK I SEE SOMEONE OVER THERE HIDIN' IN THE LONG GRASS!
GOOD WORK, BOURNE! MOVE IN QUIETLY AND GIVE HIM YOUR BAYONET!
I'VE GOT TO REMEMBER ME BAYONET TRAINING! "IN! OUT! ON GUARD... AND DON'T STICK IT IN TOO FAR—OTHERWISE YOU CAN'T GET IT OUT!"

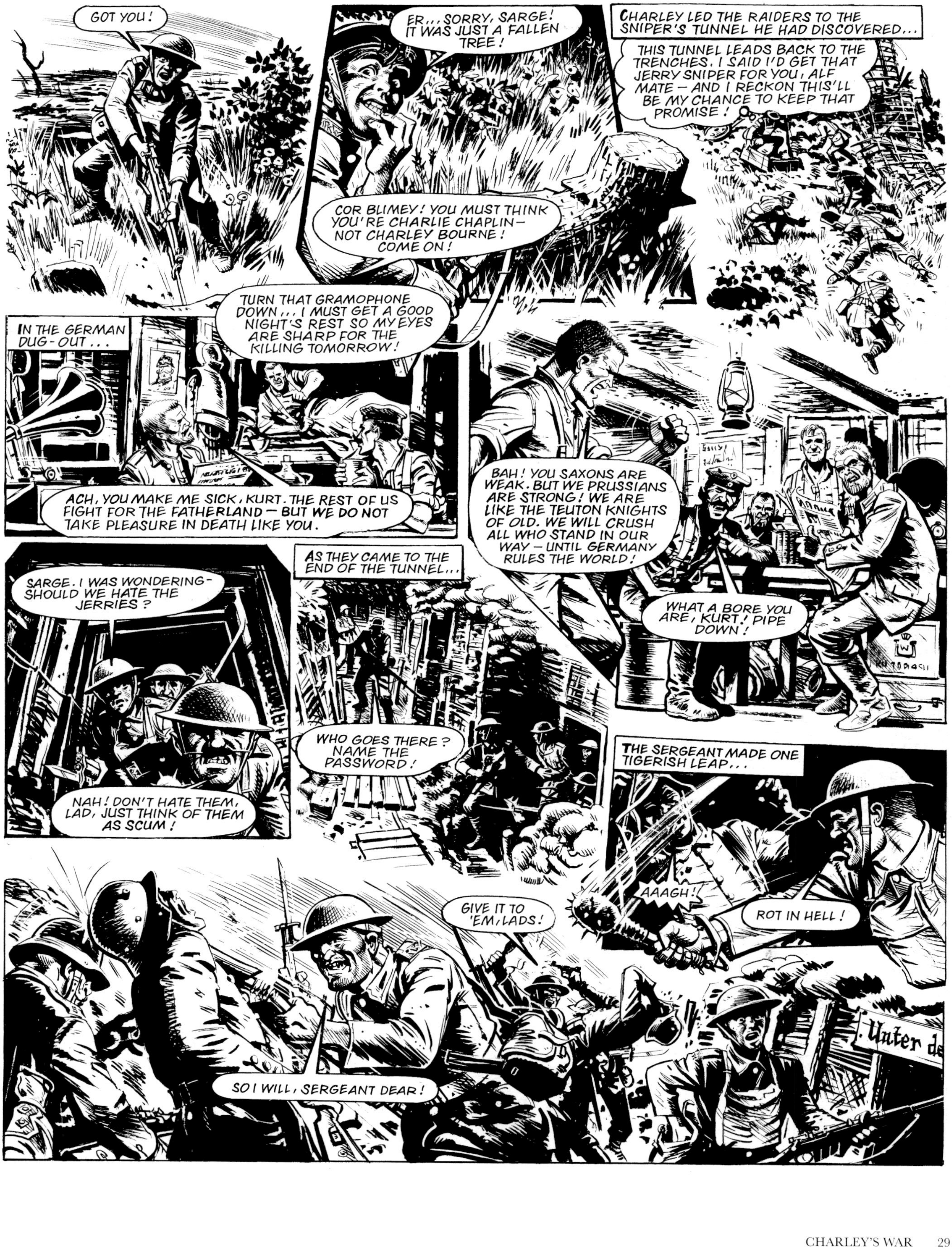
GOT YOU!
ER... SORRY, SARGE! IT WAS JUST A FALLEN TREE!
COR BLIMEY! YOU MUST THINK YOU'RE CHARLIE CHAPLIN - NOT CHARLEY BOURNE! COME ON!
CHARLEY LED THE RAIDERS TO THE SNIPER'S TUNNEL HE HAD DISCOVERED...
THIS TUNNEL LEADS BACK TO THE TRENCHES. I SAID I'D GET THAT JERRY SNIPER FOR YOU, ALF MATE - AND I RECKON THIS'LL BE MY CHANCE TO KEEP THAT PROMISE!
IN THE GERMAN DUG-OUT...
TURN THAT GRAMOPHONE DOWN... I MUST GET A GOOD NIGHT'S REST SO MY EYES ARE SHARP FOR THE KILLING TOMORROW!
ACH, YOU MAKE ME SICK, KURT. THE REST OF US FIGHT FOR THE FATHERLAND - BUT WE DO NOT TAKE PLEASURE IN DEATH LIKE YOU.
BAH! YOU SAXONS ARE WEAK. BUT WE PRUSSIANS ARE STRONG! WE ARE LIKE THE TEUTON KNIGHTS OF OLD. WE WILL CRUSH ALL WHO STAND IN OUR WAY - UNTIL GERMANY RULES THE WORLD!
WHAT A BORE YOU ARE, KURT! PIPE DOWN!
SARGE. I WAS WONDERING - SHOULD WE HATE THE JERRIES?
NAH! DON'T HATE THEM, LAD, JUST THINK OF THEM AS SCUM!
AS THEY CAME TO THE END OF THE TUNNEL...
WHO GOES THERE? NAME THE PASSWORD!
THE SERGEANT MADE ONE TIGERISH LEAP...
AAAGH!
ROT IN HELL!
GIVE IT TO 'EM, LADS!
SO I WILL, SERGEANT DEAR!
Unter de

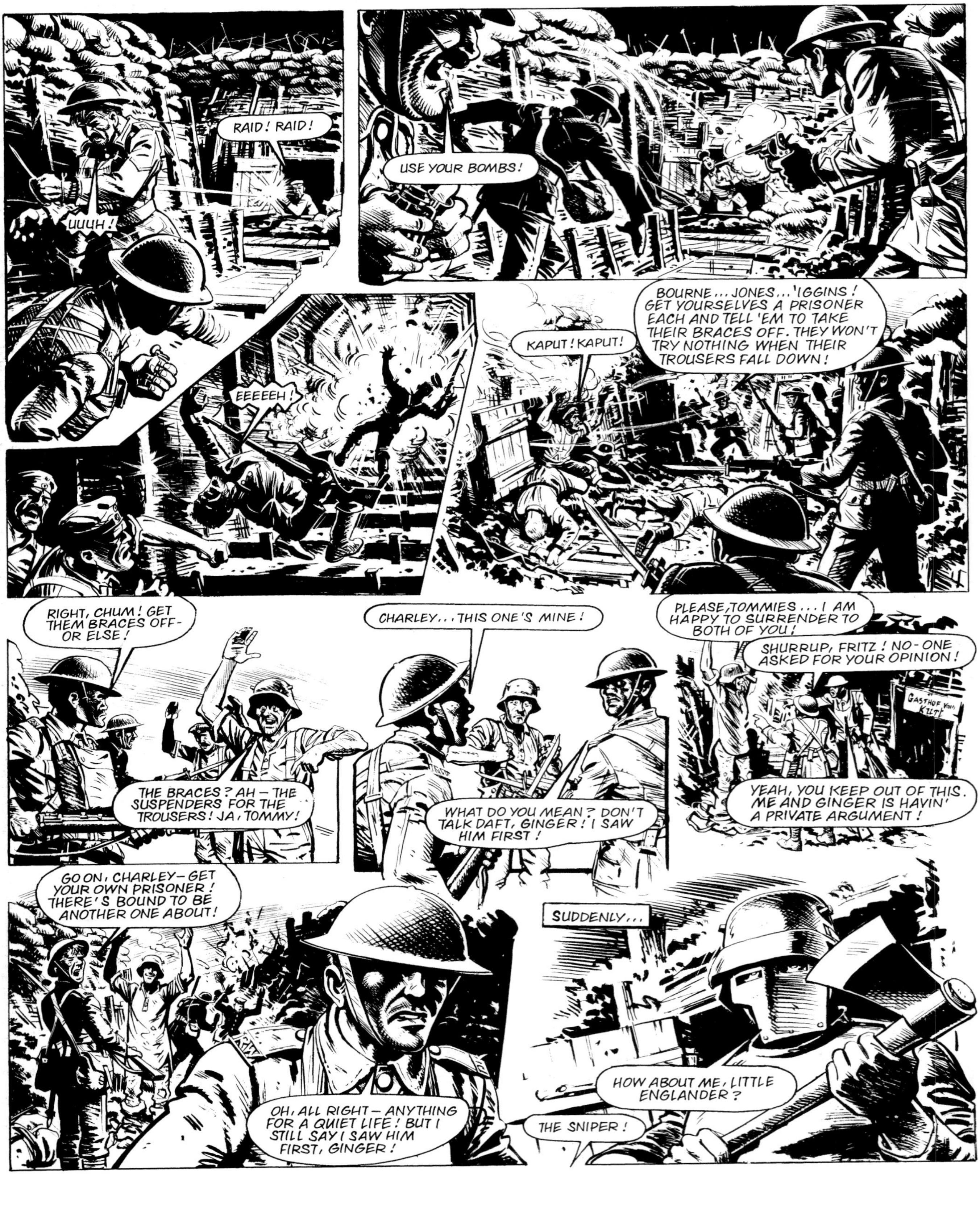
RAID! RAID!
UUUH!
USE YOUR BOMBS!
EEEEEH!
KAPUT! KAPUT!
BOURNE... JONES... 'IGGINS! GET YOURSELVES A PRISONER EACH AND TELL 'EM TO TAKE THEIR BRACES OFF. THEY WON'T TRY NOTHING WHEN THEIR TROUSERS FALL DOWN!
RIGHT, CHUM! GET THEM BRACES OFF-OR ELSE!
THE BRACES? AH – THE SUSPENDERS FOR THE TROUSERS! JA, TOMMY!
CHARLEY... THIS ONE'S MINE!
WHAT DO YOU MEAN? DON'T TALK DAFT, GINGER! I SAW HIM FIRST!
PLEASE, TOMMIES... I AM HAPPY TO SURRENDER TO BOTH OF YOU!
SHURRUP, FRITZ! NO-ONE ASKED FOR YOUR OPINION!
YEAH, YOU KEEP OUT OF THIS. ME AND GINGER IS HAVIN' A PRIVATE ARGUMENT!
GO ON, CHARLEY– GET YOUR OWN PRISONER! THERE'S BOUND TO BE ANOTHER ONE ABOUT!
OH, ALL RIGHT – ANYTHING FOR A QUIET LIFE! BUT I STILL SAY I SAW HIM FIRST, GINGER!
SUDDENLY...
HOW ABOUT ME, LITTLE ENGLANDER?
THE SNIPER!

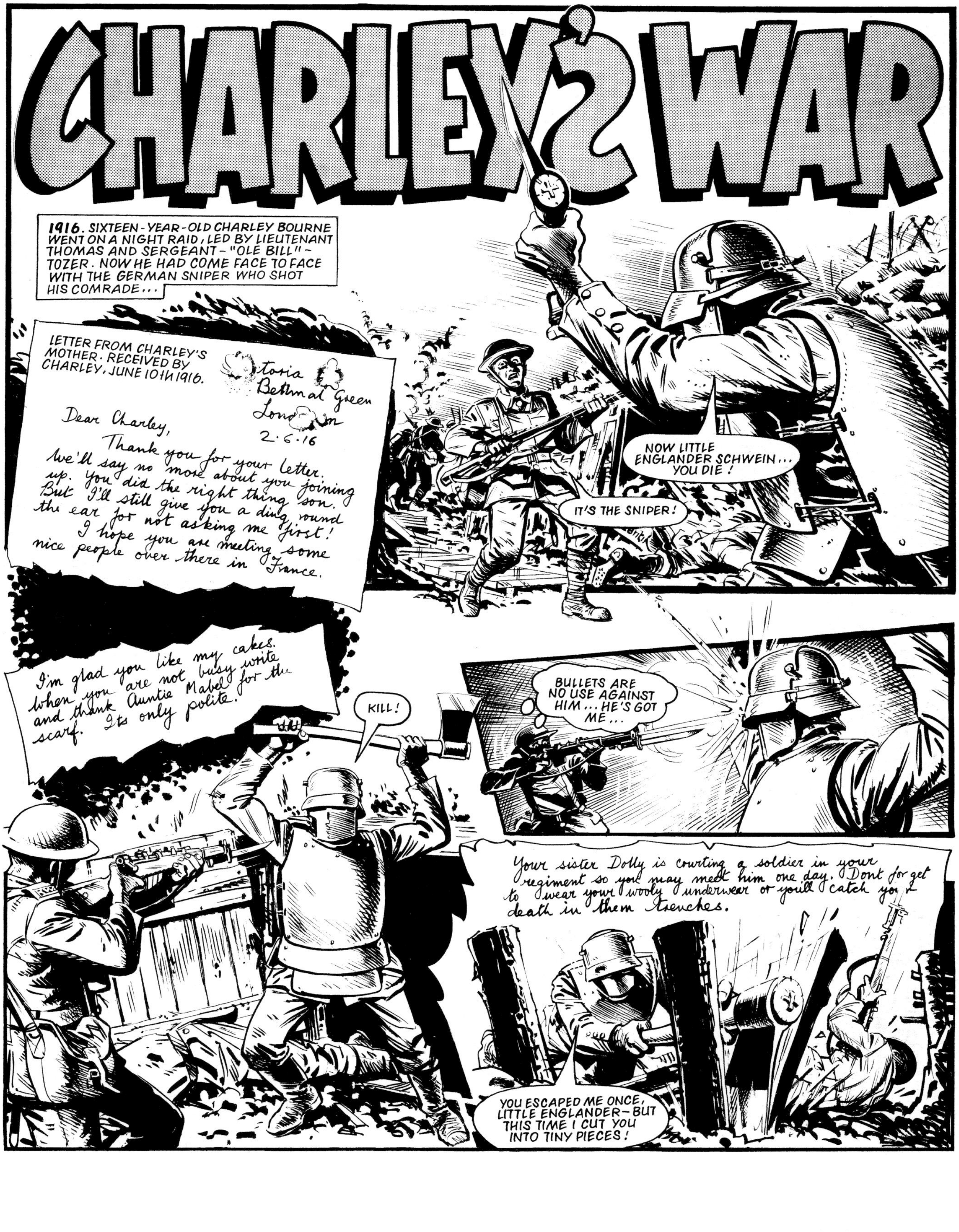
CHARLEY'S WAR
1916. SIXTEEN-YEAR-OLD CHARLEY BOURNE WENT ON A NIGHT RAID, LED BY LIEUTENANT THOMAS AND SERGEANT - "OLE BILL" - TOZER. NOW HE HAD COME FACE TO FACE WITH THE GERMAN SNIPER WHO SHOT HIS COMRADE...
LETTER FROM CHARLEY'S MOTHER. RECEIVED BY CHARLEY, JUNE 10th 1916.
toria
Bethnal Green
Lond n
2.6.16
Dear Charley,
Thank you for your letter. We'll say no more about you joining up. You did the right thing son. But I'll still give you a ding round the ear for not asking me first! I hope you are meeting some nice people over there in France.
NOW LITTLE ENGLANDER SCHWEIN... YOU DIE!
IT'S THE SNIPER!
BULLETS ARE NO USE AGAINST HIM... HE'S GOT ME...
I'm glad you like my cakes. When you are not busy write and thank Auntie Mabel for the scarf. Its only polite.
KILL!
Your sister Dolly is courting a soldier in your regiment so you may meet him one day. Dont for get to wear your wooly underwear or you'll catch your death in them trenches.
YOU ESCAPED ME ONCE, LITTLE ENGLANDER - BUT THIS TIME I CUT YOU INTO TINY PIECES!

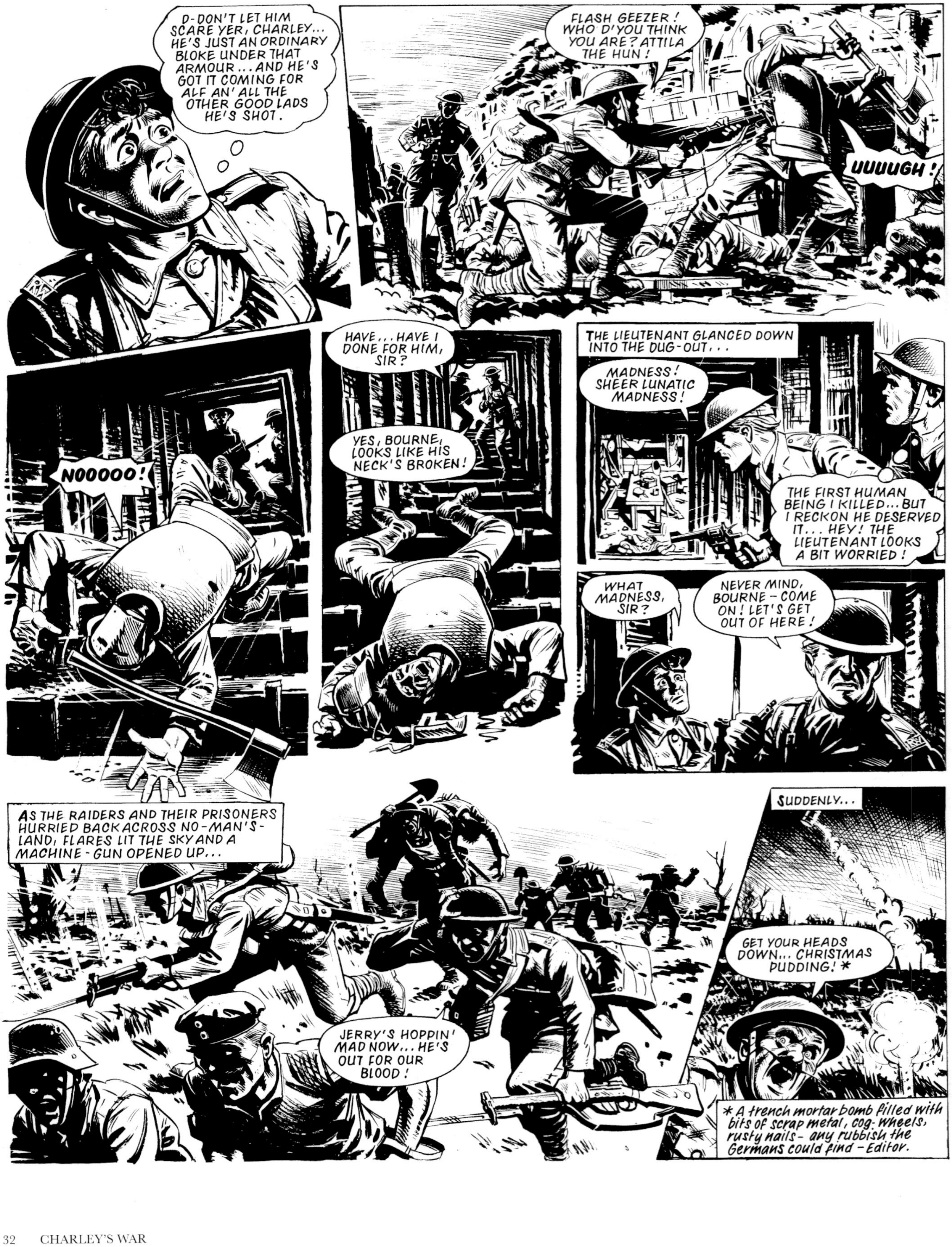
D-DON'T LET HIM SCARE YER, CHARLEY... HE'S JUST AN ORDINARY BLOKE UNDER THAT ARMOUR... AND HE'S GOT IT COMING FOR ALF AN' ALL THE OTHER GOOD LADS HE'S SHOT.
FLASH GEEZER! WHO D'YOU THINK YOU ARE? ATTILA THE HUN!
UUUUGH!
NOOOOO!
HAVE... HAVE I DONE FOR HIM, SIR?
YES, BOURNE, LOOKS LIKE HIS NECK'S BROKEN!
THE LIEUTENANT GLANCED DOWN INTO THE DUG-OUT...
MADNESS! SHEER LUNATIC MADNESS!
THE FIRST HUMAN BEING I KILLED... BUT I RECKON HE DESERVED IT... HEY! THE LIEUTENANT LOOKS A BIT WORRIED!
WHAT MADNESS, SIR?
NEVER MIND, BOURNE - COME ON! LET'S GET OUT OF HERE!
AS THE RAIDERS AND THEIR PRISONERS HURRIED BACK ACROSS NO-MAN'S-LAND, FLARES LIT THE SKY AND A MACHINE-GUN OPENED UP...
JERRY'S HOPPIN' MAD NOW... HE'S OUT FOR OUR BLOOD!
SUDDENLY...
GET YOUR HEADS DOWN... CHRISTMAS PUDDING! *
* A trench mortar bomb filled with bits of scrap metal, cog-wheels, rusty nails - any rubbish the Germans could find - Editor.

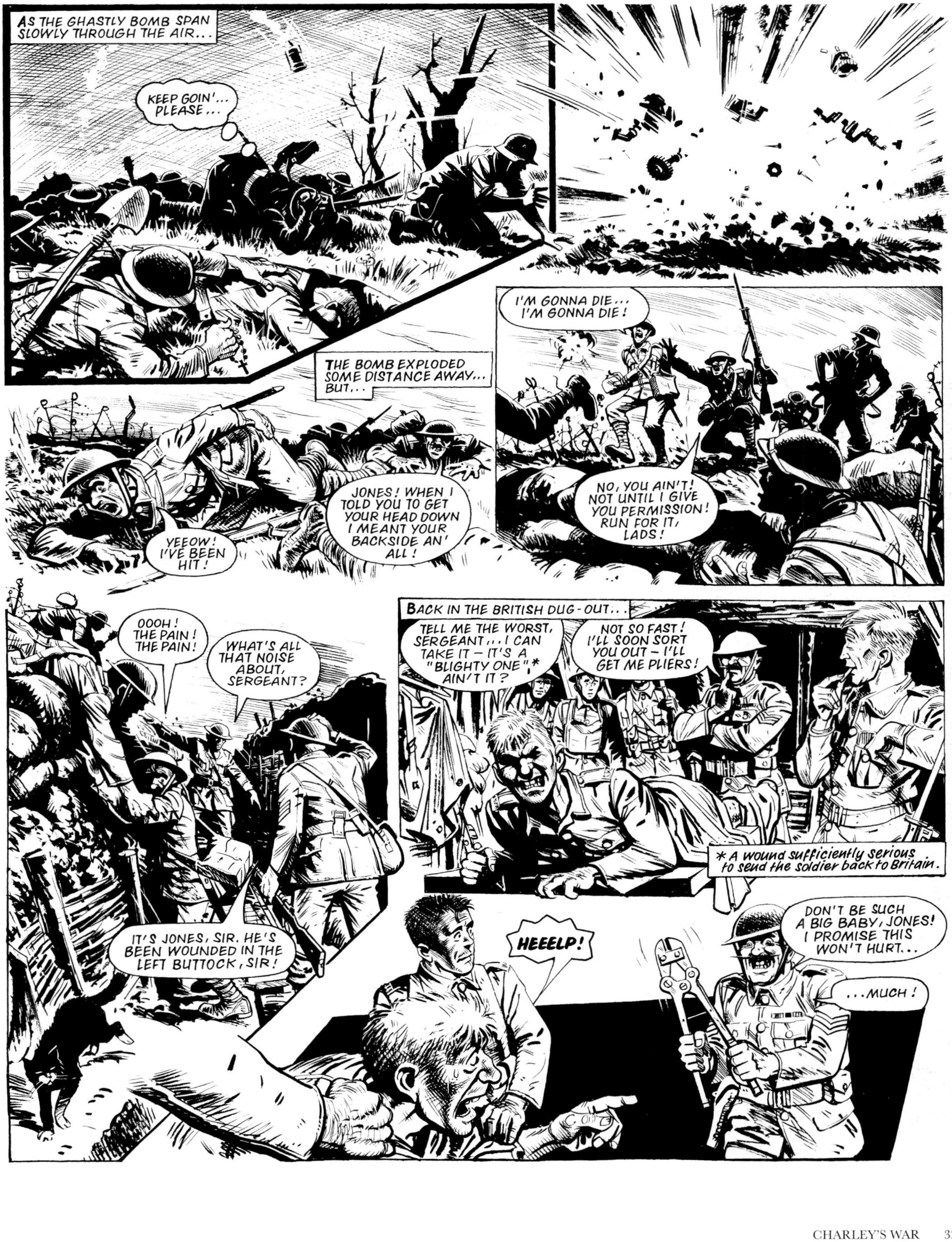
AS THE GHASTLY BOMB SPAN SLOWLY THROUGH THE AIR...
KEEP GOIN'... PLEASE...
THE BOMB EXPLODED SOME DISTANCE AWAY... BUT...
YEEOW! I'VE BEEN HIT!
JONES! WHEN I TOLD YOU TO GET YOUR HEAD DOWN I MEANT YOUR BACKSIDE AN' ALL!
I'M GONNA DIE... I'M GONNA DIE!
NO, YOU AIN'T! NOT UNTIL I GIVE YOU PERMISSION! RUN FOR IT, LADS!
OOOH! THE PAIN! THE PAIN!
WHAT'S ALL THAT NOISE ABOUT, SERGEANT?
IT'S JONES, SIR. HE'S BEEN WOUNDED IN THE LEFT BUTTOCK, SIR!
BACK IN THE BRITISH DUG-OUT...
TELL ME THE WORST, SERGEANT... I CAN TAKE IT – IT'S A "BLIGHTY ONE",* AIN'T IT?
NOT SO FAST! I'LL SOON SORT YOU OUT – I'LL GET ME PLIERS!
* A wound sufficiently serious to send the soldier back to Britain.
HEEELP!
DON'T BE SUCH A BIG BABY, JONES! I PROMISE THIS WON'T HURT...
...MUCH!

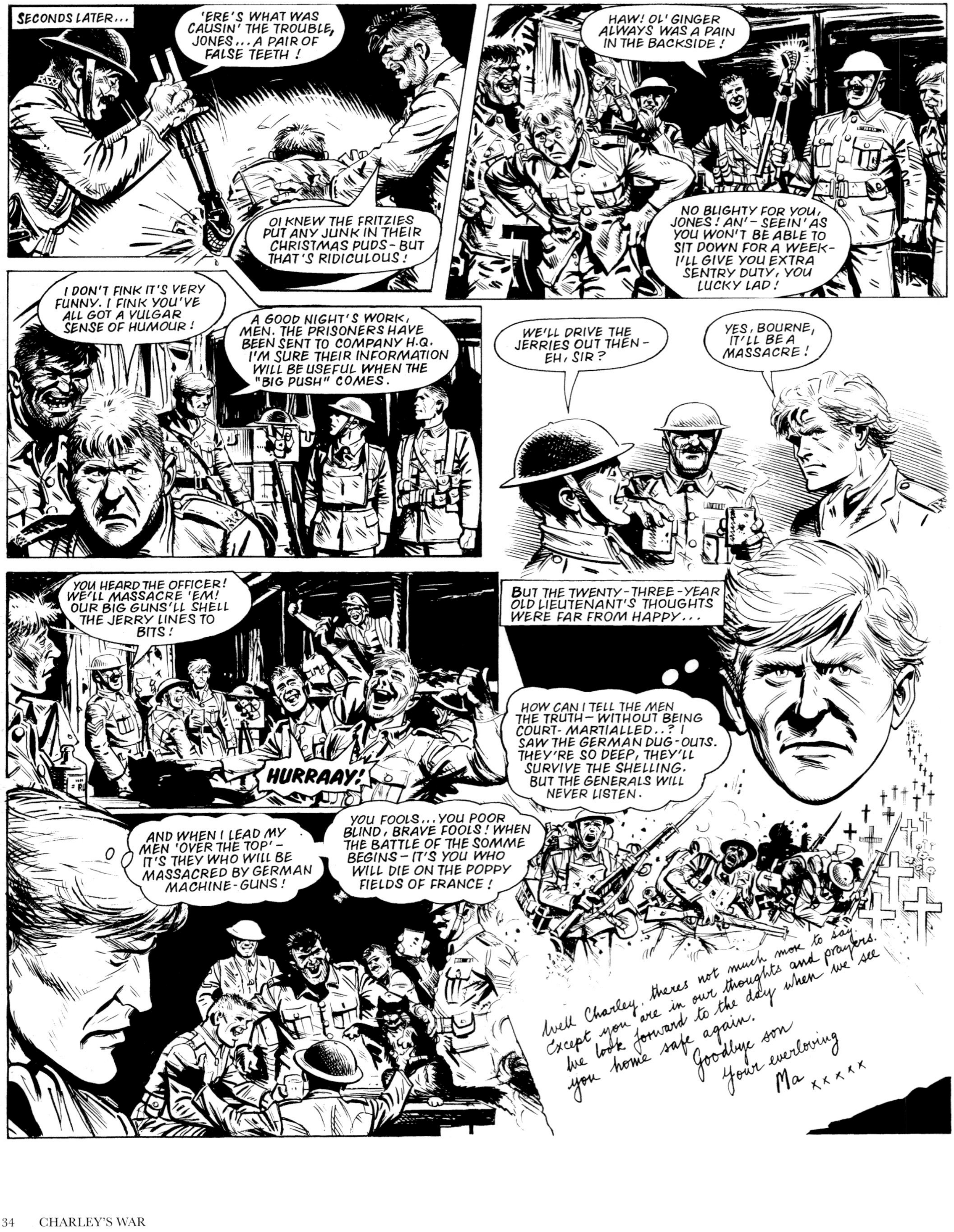
SECONDS LATER...
'ERE'S WHAT WAS CAUSIN' THE TROUBLE, JONES... A PAIR OF FALSE TEETH !
OI KNEW THE FRITZIES PUT ANY JUNK IN THEIR CHRISTMAS PUDS - BUT THAT'S RIDICULOUS !
HAW! OL' GINGER ALWAYS WAS A PAIN IN THE BACKSIDE !
NO BLIGHTY FOR YOU, JONES! AN' - SEEIN' AS YOU WON'T BE ABLE TO SIT DOWN FOR A WEEK - I'LL GIVE YOU EXTRA SENTRY DUTY, YOU LUCKY LAD !
I DON'T FINK IT'S VERY FUNNY. I FINK YOU'VE ALL GOT A VULGAR SENSE OF HUMOUR !
A GOOD NIGHT'S WORK, MEN. THE PRISONERS HAVE BEEN SENT TO COMPANY H.Q. I'M SURE THEIR INFORMATION WILL BE USEFUL WHEN THE "BIG PUSH" COMES.
WE'LL DRIVE THE JERRIES OUT THEN - EH, SIR ?
YES, BOURNE, IT'LL BE A MASSACRE !
YOU HEARD THE OFFICER! WE'LL MASSACRE 'EM! OUR BIG GUNS'LL SHELL THE JERRY LINES TO BITS !
HURRAAY!
BUT THE TWENTY-THREE-YEAR OLD LIEUTENANT'S THOUGHTS WERE FAR FROM HAPPY...
HOW CAN I TELL THE MEN THE TRUTH - WITHOUT BEING COURT-MARTIALLED..? I SAW THE GERMAN DUG-OUTS. THEY'RE SO DEEP, THEY'LL SURVIVE THE SHELLING. BUT THE GENERALS WILL NEVER LISTEN.
AND WHEN I LEAD MY MEN 'OVER THE TOP' - IT'S THEY WHO WILL BE MASSACRED BY GERMAN MACHINE-GUNS !
YOU FOOLS... YOU POOR BLIND, BRAVE FOOLS! WHEN THE BATTLE OF THE SOMME BEGINS - IT'S YOU WHO WILL DIE ON THE POPPY FIELDS OF FRANCE !
Well Charley, theres not much more to say
Except you are in our thoughts and prayers.
We look forward to the day when we see
you home safe again.
Goodbye son
Your everloving
Ma xxxxx

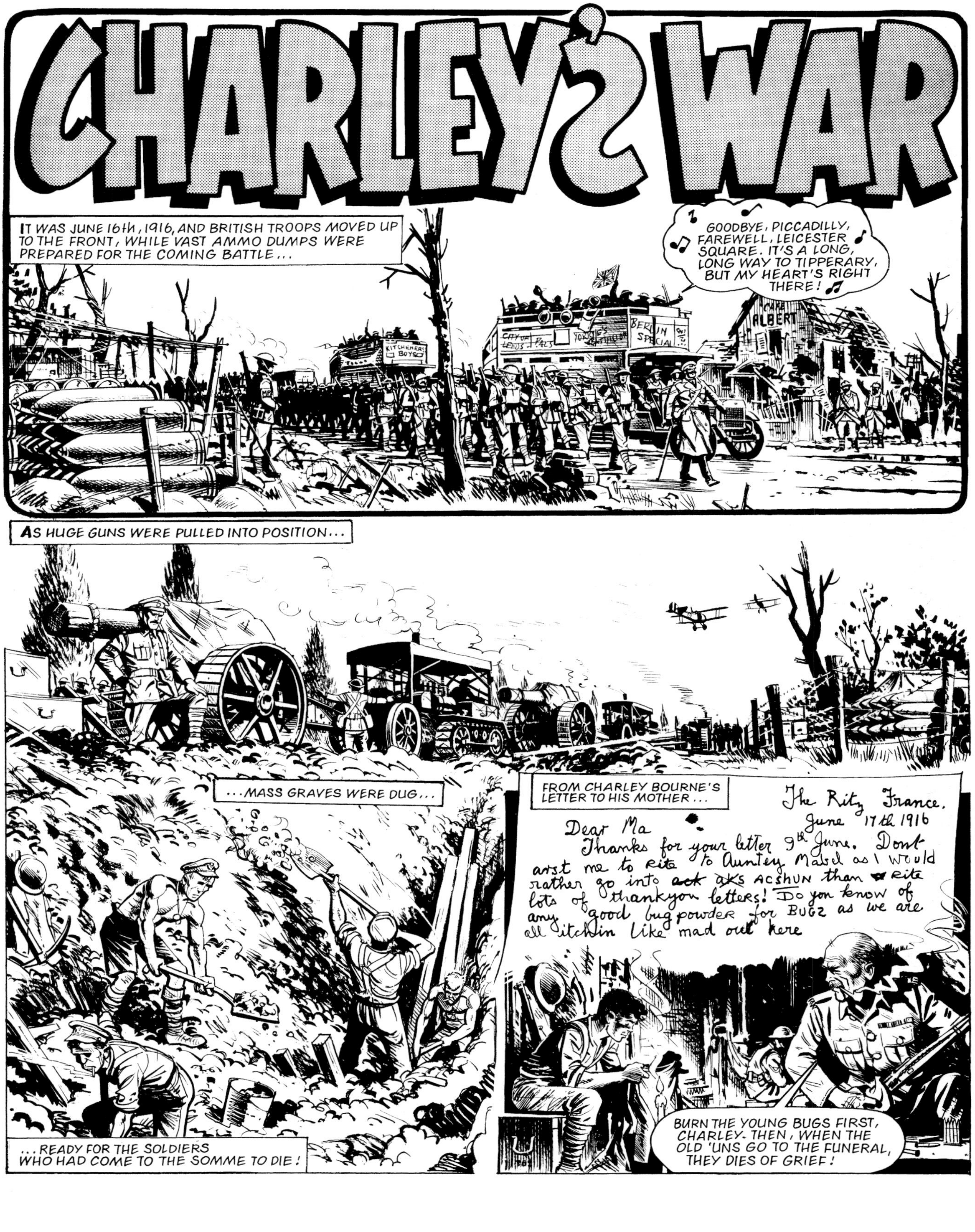
CHARLEY'S WAR
IT WAS JUNE 16th, 1916, AND BRITISH TROOPS MOVED UP TO THE FRONT, WHILE VAST AMMO DUMPS WERE PREPARED FOR THE COMING BATTLE...
GOODBYE, PICCADILLY, FAREWELL, LEICESTER SQUARE. IT'S A LONG, LONG WAY TO TIPPERARY, BUT MY HEART'S RIGHT THERE!
KITCHENER'S BOYS
BERLIN SPECIAL
CAFE ALBERT
AS HUGE GUNS WERE PULLED INTO POSITION...
...MASS GRAVES WERE DUG...
...READY FOR THE SOLDIERS WHO HAD COME TO THE SOMME TO DIE!
FROM CHARLEY BOURNE'S LETTER TO HIS MOTHER...
The Ritz France. June 17th 1916
Dear Ma
Thanks for your letter 9th June. Dont arst me to rite to Auntey Mabel as I would rather go into ack AKS ACSHUN than rite lots of thankyou letters! Do you know of any good bug powder for BUGZ as we are all itchin like mad out here
BURN THE YOUNG BUGS FIRST, CHARLEY- THEN, WHEN THE OLD 'UNS GO TO THE FUNERAL, THEY DIES OF GRIEF!

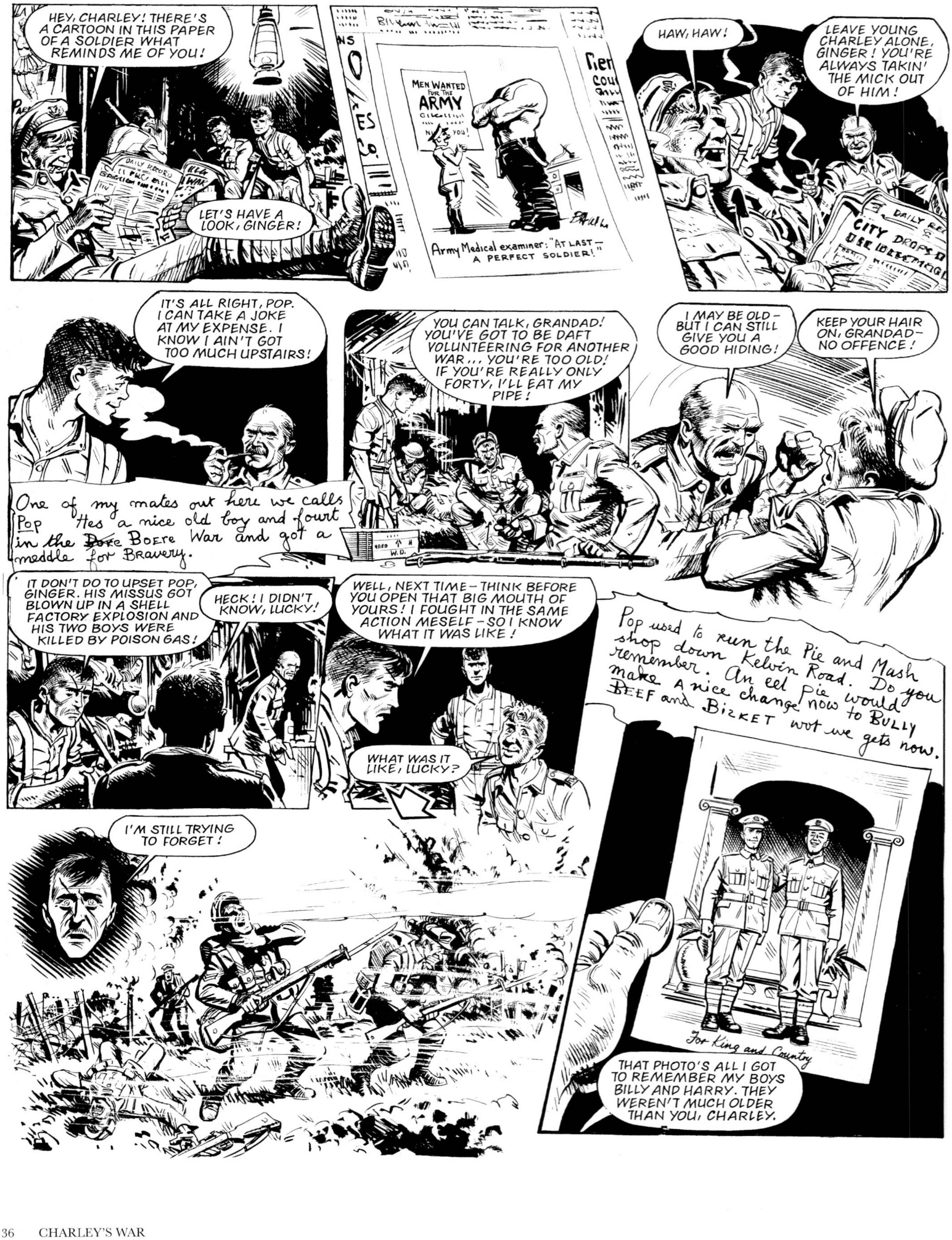
HEY, CHARLEY! THERE'S A CARTOON IN THIS PAPER OF A SOLDIER WHAT REMINDS ME OF YOU!
LET'S HAVE A LOOK, GINGER!
MEN WANTED FOR THE ARMY
Army Medical examiner: "AT LAST — A PERFECT SOLDIER!"
HAW, HAW!
LEAVE YOUNG CHARLEY ALONE, GINGER! YOU'RE ALWAYS TAKIN' THE MICK OUT OF HIM!
DAILY RECORD
CITY DROPS
IT'S ALL RIGHT, POP. I CAN TAKE A JOKE AT MY EXPENSE. I KNOW I AIN'T GOT TOO MUCH UPSTAIRS!
One of my mates out here we calls Pop Hes a nice old boy and fourt in the Doer Boere War and got a meddle for Bravery.
YOU CAN TALK, GRANDAD! YOU'VE GOT TO BE DAFT VOLUNTEERING FOR ANOTHER WAR... YOU'RE TOO OLD! IF YOU'RE REALLY ONLY FORTY, I'LL EAT MY PIPE!
W.D.
I MAY BE OLD — BUT I CAN STILL GIVE YOU A GOOD HIDING!
KEEP YOUR HAIR ON, GRANDAD — NO OFFENCE!
IT DON'T DO TO UPSET POP, GINGER. HIS MISSUS GOT BLOWN UP IN A SHELL FACTORY EXPLOSION AND HIS TWO BOYS WERE KILLED BY POISON GAS!
HECK! I DIDN'T KNOW, LUCKY!
WELL, NEXT TIME — THINK BEFORE YOU OPEN THAT BIG MOUTH OF YOURS! I FOUGHT IN THE SAME ACTION MESELF — SO I KNOW WHAT IT WAS LIKE!
WHAT WAS IT LIKE, LUCKY?
Pop used to run the Pie and Mash shop down Kelvin Road. Do you remember. An eel pie would make a nice change now to Bully Beef and Bizket wot we gets now.
I'M STILL TRYING TO FORGET!
For King and Country
THAT PHOTO'S ALL I GOT TO REMEMBER MY BOYS BILLY AND HARRY. THEY WEREN'T MUCH OLDER THAN YOU, CHARLEY.

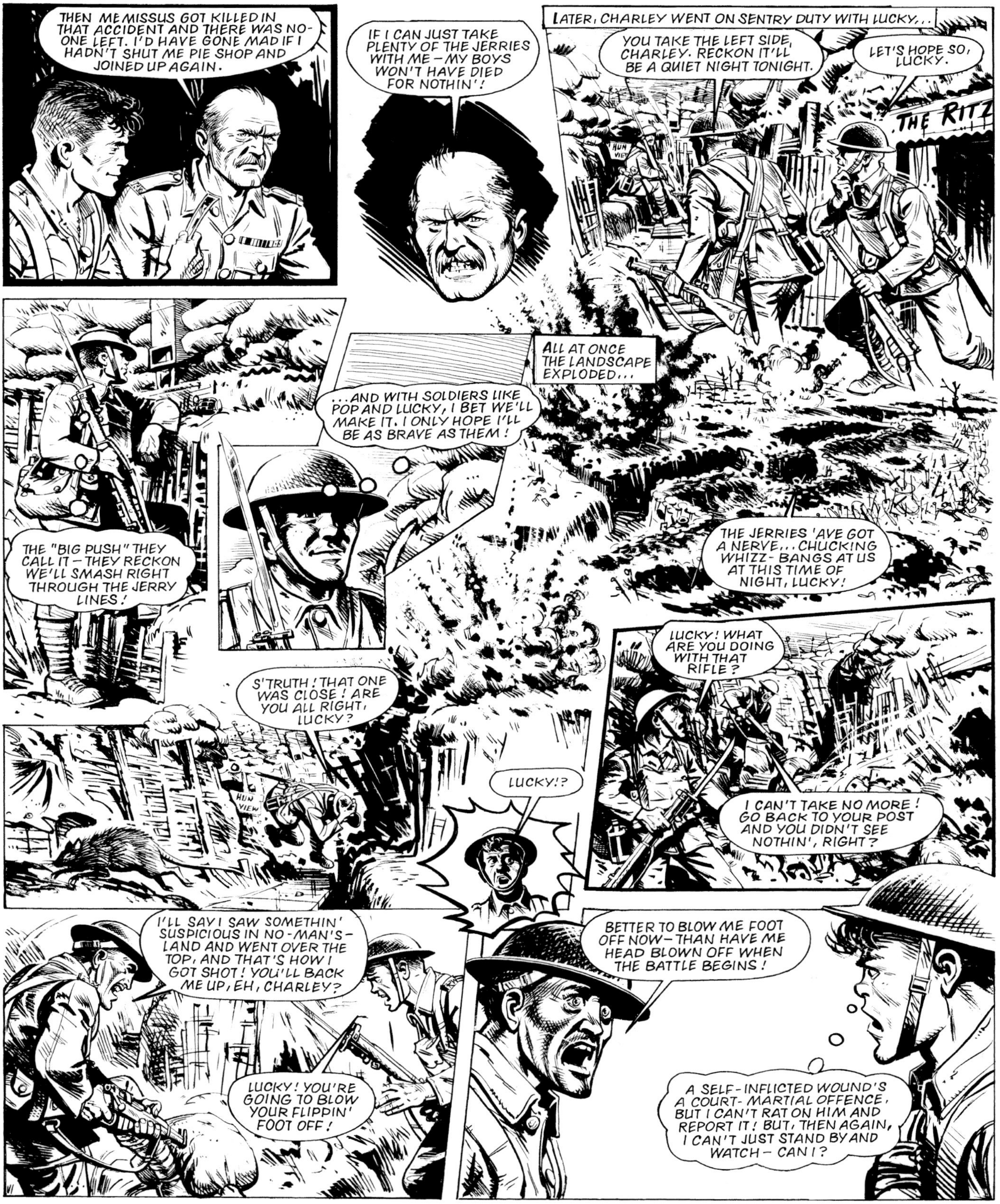
THEN ME MISSUS GOT KILLED IN THAT ACCIDENT AND THERE WAS NO-ONE LEFT. I'D HAVE GONE MAD IF I HADN'T SHUT ME PIE SHOP AND JOINED UP AGAIN.
IF I CAN JUST TAKE PLENTY OF THE JERRIES WITH ME – MY BOYS WON'T HAVE DIED FOR NOTHIN'!
LATER, CHARLEY WENT ON SENTRY DUTY WITH LUCKY...
YOU TAKE THE LEFT SIDE, CHARLEY. RECKON IT'LL BE A QUIET NIGHT TONIGHT.
LET'S HOPE SO, LUCKY.
THE RITZ
HUN VIEW
THE "BIG PUSH" THEY CALL IT – THEY RECKON WE'LL SMASH RIGHT THROUGH THE JERRY LINES!
...AND WITH SOLDIERS LIKE POP AND LUCKY, I BET WE'LL MAKE IT. I ONLY HOPE I'LL BE AS BRAVE AS THEM!
ALL AT ONCE THE LANDSCAPE EXPLODED...
THE JERRIES 'AVE GOT A NERVE... CHUCKING WHIZZ-BANGS AT US AT THIS TIME OF NIGHT, LUCKY!
S'TRUTH! THAT ONE WAS CLOSE! ARE YOU ALL RIGHT, LUCKY?
HUN VIEW
LUCKY!?
LUCKY! WHAT ARE YOU DOING WITH THAT RIFLE?
I CAN'T TAKE NO MORE! GO BACK TO YOUR POST AND YOU DIDN'T SEE NOTHIN', RIGHT?
I'LL SAY I SAW SOMETHIN' SUSPICIOUS IN NO-MAN'S-LAND AND WENT OVER THE TOP, AND THAT'S HOW I GOT SHOT! YOU'LL BACK ME UP, EH, CHARLEY?
LUCKY! YOU'RE GOING TO BLOW YOUR FLIPPIN' FOOT OFF!
BETTER TO BLOW ME FOOT OFF NOW – THAN HAVE ME HEAD BLOWN OFF WHEN THE BATTLE BEGINS!
A SELF-INFLICTED WOUND'S A COURT-MARTIAL OFFENCE, BUT I CAN'T RAT ON HIM AND REPORT IT! BUT, THEN AGAIN, I CAN'T JUST STAND BY AND WATCH – CAN I?

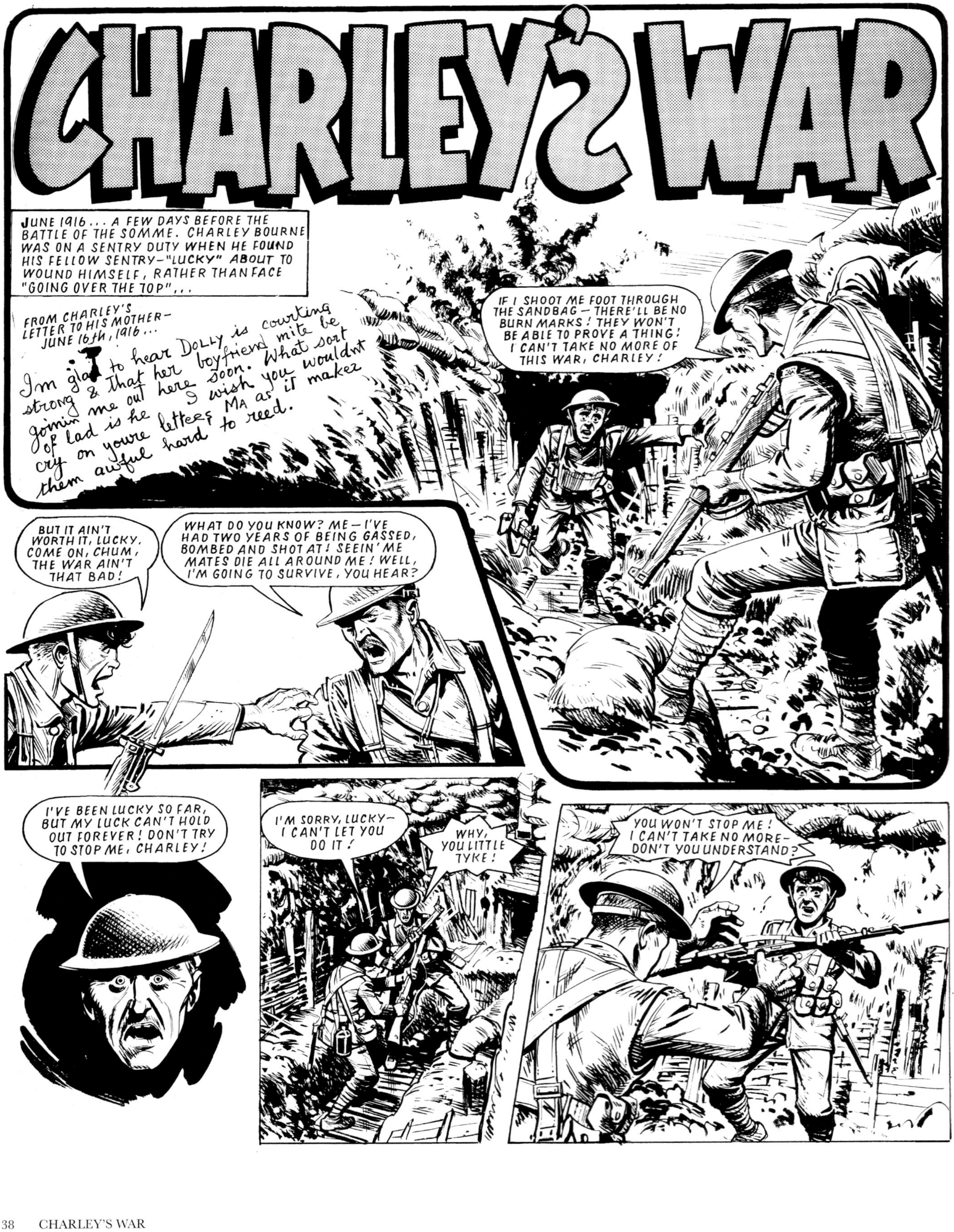
CHARLEY'S WAR
JUNE 1916... A FEW DAYS BEFORE THE BATTLE OF THE SOMME. CHARLEY BOURNE WAS ON A SENTRY DUTY WHEN HE FOUND HIS FELLOW SENTRY—"LUCKY" ABOUT TO WOUND HIMSELF, RATHER THAN FACE "GOING OVER THE TOP"...
FROM CHARLEY'S LETTER TO HIS MOTHER— JUNE 16th, 1916...
I'm glad to hear Dolly is courting strong & that her boyfriend mite be joinin me out here soon. What sort of lad is he I wish you wouldnt cry on youre letters Ma as it makes them awful hard to reed.
IF I SHOOT ME FOOT THROUGH THE SANDBAG — THERE'LL BE NO BURN MARKS! THEY WON'T BE ABLE TO PROVE A THING! I CAN'T TAKE NO MORE OF THIS WAR, CHARLEY!
BUT IT AIN'T WORTH IT, LUCKY. COME ON, CHUM, THE WAR AIN'T THAT BAD!
WHAT DO YOU KNOW? ME — I'VE HAD TWO YEARS OF BEING GASSED, BOMBED AND SHOT AT! SEEIN' ME MATES DIE ALL AROUND ME! WELL, I'M GOING TO SURVIVE, YOU HEAR?
I'VE BEEN LUCKY SO FAR, BUT MY LUCK CAN'T HOLD OUT FOREVER! DON'T TRY TO STOP ME, CHARLEY!
I'M SORRY, LUCKY— I CAN'T LET YOU DO IT!
WHY, YOU LITTLE TYKE!
YOU WON'T STOP ME! I CAN'T TAKE NO MORE— DON'T YOU UNDERSTAND?

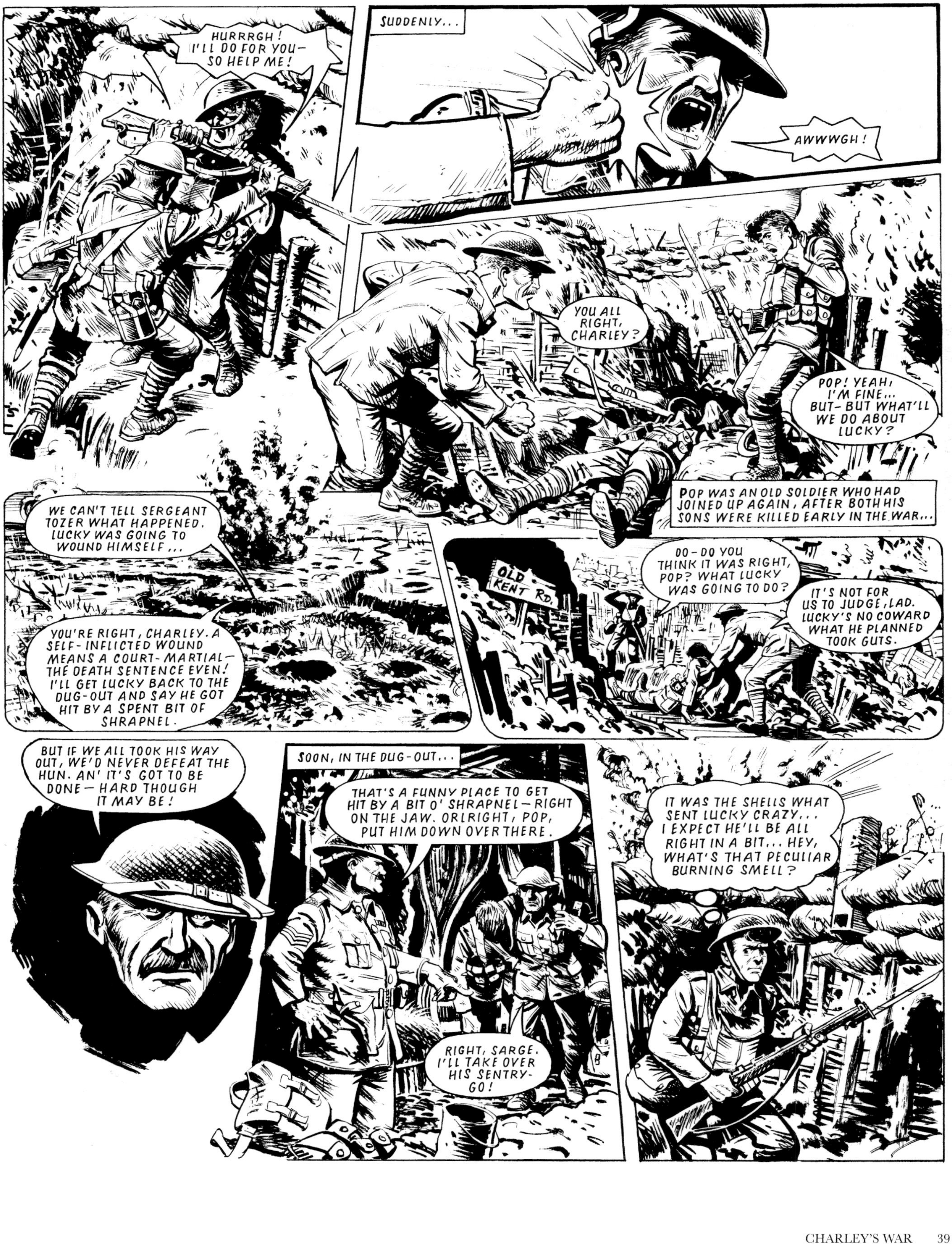
HURRRGH! I'LL DO FOR YOU— SO HELP ME!
SUDDENLY...
AWWWGH!
YOU ALL RIGHT, CHARLEY?
POP! YEAH, I'M FINE... BUT— BUT WHAT'LL WE DO ABOUT LUCKY?
POP WAS AN OLD SOLDIER WHO HAD JOINED UP AGAIN, AFTER BOTH HIS SONS WERE KILLED EARLY IN THE WAR...
WE CAN'T TELL SERGEANT TOZER WHAT HAPPENED. LUCKY WAS GOING TO WOUND HIMSELF...
YOU'RE RIGHT, CHARLEY. A SELF-INFLICTED WOUND MEANS A COURT-MARTIAL— THE DEATH SENTENCE EVEN! I'LL GET LUCKY BACK TO THE DUG-OUT AND SAY HE GOT HIT BY A SPENT BIT OF SHRAPNEL.
OLD KENT RD.
DO-DO YOU THINK IT WAS RIGHT, POP? WHAT LUCKY WAS GOING TO DO?
IT'S NOT FOR US TO JUDGE, LAD. LUCKY'S NO COWARD WHAT HE PLANNED TOOK GUTS.
BUT IF WE ALL TOOK HIS WAY OUT, WE'D NEVER DEFEAT THE HUN. AN' IT'S GOT TO BE DONE— HARD THOUGH IT MAY BE!
SOON, IN THE DUG-OUT...
THAT'S A FUNNY PLACE TO GET HIT BY A BIT O' SHRAPNEL— RIGHT ON THE JAW. ORLRIGHT, POP, PUT HIM DOWN OVER THERE.
RIGHT, SARGE. I'LL TAKE OVER HIS SENTRY-GO!
IT WAS THE SHELLS WHAT SENT LUCKY CRAZY... I EXPECT HE'LL BE ALL RIGHT IN A BIT... HEY, WHAT'S THAT PECULIAR BURNING SMELL?

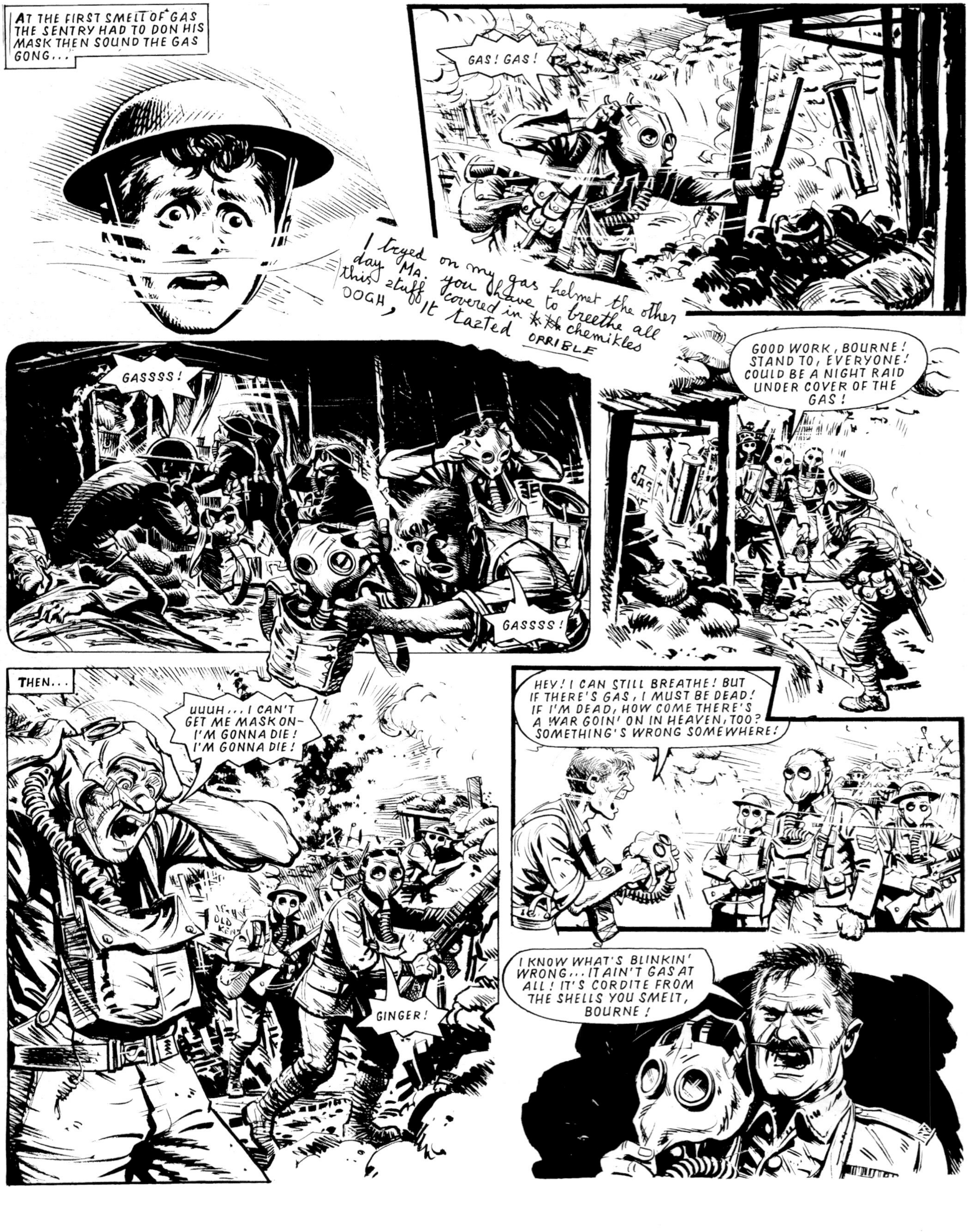
AT THE FIRST SMELT OF GAS THE SENTRY HAD TO DON HIS MASK THEN SOUND THE GAS GONG...
GAS! GAS!
I tryed on my gas helmet the other day MA, you have to breethe all this stuff covered in *** chemikles OOGH, It tazted ORRIBLE
GASSSS!
GASSSS!
GOOD WORK, BOURNE! STAND TO, EVERYONE! COULD BE A NIGHT RAID UNDER COVER OF THE GAS!
GAS
THEN...
UUUH... I CAN'T GET ME MASK ON-I'M GONNA DIE! I'M GONNA DIE!
GINGER!
HEY! I CAN STILL BREATHE! BUT IF THERE'S GAS, I MUST BE DEAD! IF I'M DEAD, HOW COME THERE'S A WAR GOIN' ON IN HEAVEN, TOO? SOMETHING'S WRONG SOMEWHERE!
I KNOW WHAT'S BLINKIN' WRONG... IT AIN'T GAS AT ALL! IT'S CORDITE FROM THE SHELLS YOU SMELT, BOURNE!

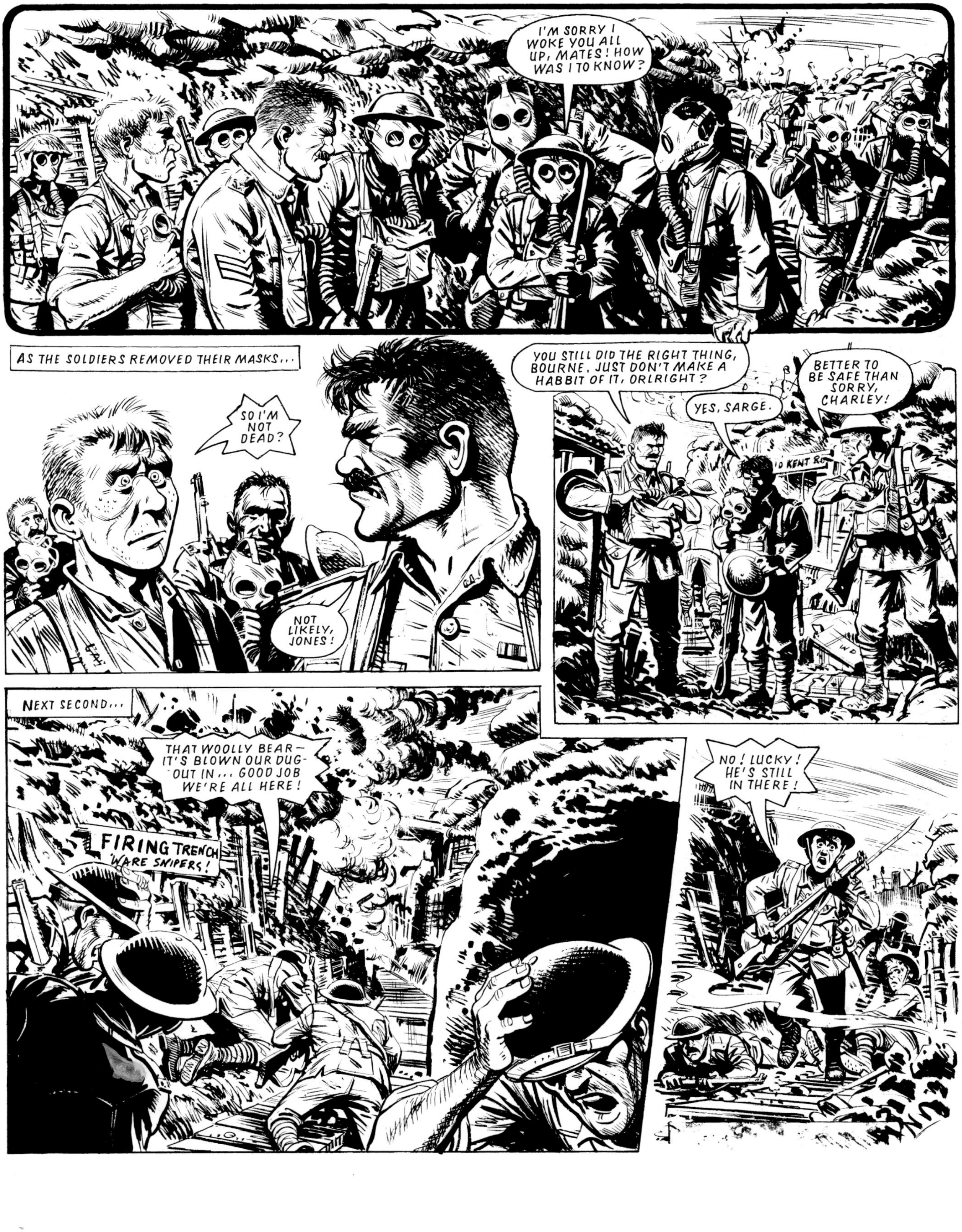

I'M SORRY I WOKE YOU ALL UP, MATES! HOW WAS I TO KNOW?
AS THE SOLDIERS REMOVED THEIR MASKS...
SO I'M NOT DEAD?
NOT LIKELY, JONES!
YOU STILL DID THE RIGHT THING, BOURNE. JUST DON'T MAKE A HABBIT OF IT, ORLRIGHT?
YES, SARGE.
BETTER TO BE SAFE THAN SORRY, CHARLEY!
NEXT SECOND...
THAT WOOLLY BEAR — IT'S BLOWN OUR DUG-OUT IN... GOOD JOB WE'RE ALL HERE!
FIRING TRENCH 'WARE SNIPERS!
NO! LUCKY! HE'S STILL IN THERE!

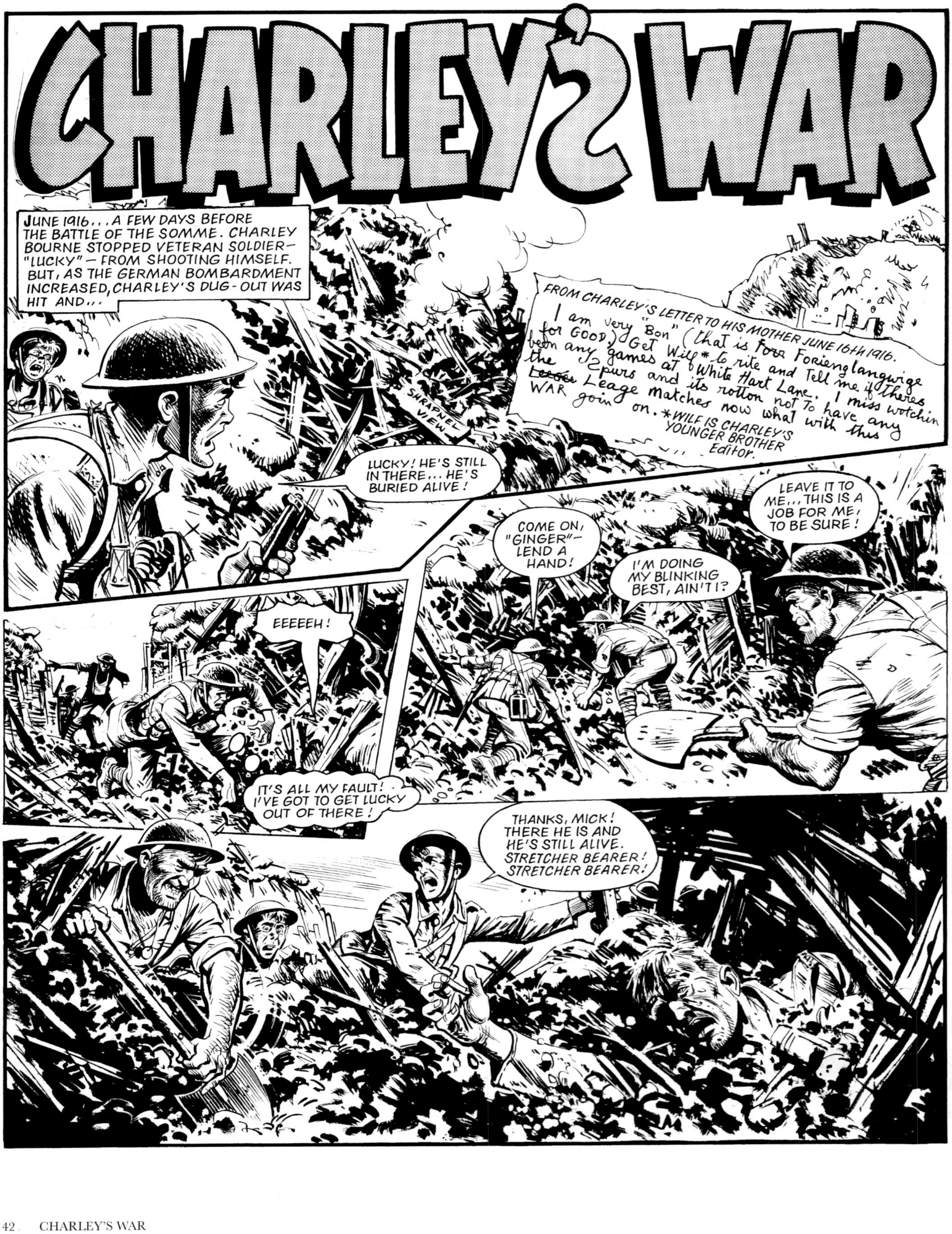
CHARLEY'S WAR
JUNE 1916... A FEW DAYS BEFORE THE BATTLE OF THE SOMME. CHARLEY BOURNE STOPPED VETERAN SOLDIER— "LUCKY" — FROM SHOOTING HIMSELF. BUT, AS THE GERMAN BOMBARDMENT INCREASED, CHARLEY'S DUG-OUT WAS HIT AND...
FROM CHARLEY'S LETTER TO HIS MOTHER JUNE 16th 1916.
I am very "Bon" (that is ~~Foor~~ Forienglangwige for GOOD.) Get Wilf* to rite and Tell me if theres been any games at White Hart Lane. I miss wotchin the Spurs and its rotton not to have any ~~Leage~~ Leage matches now what with this WAR goin on.
*WILF IS CHARLEY'S YOUNGER BROTHER Editor.
SHRAPNEL VIEW
LUCKY! HE'S STILL IN THERE... HE'S BURIED ALIVE!
COME ON, "GINGER"— LEND A HAND!
I'M DOING MY BLINKING BEST, AIN'T I?
LEAVE IT TO ME... THIS IS A JOB FOR ME, TO BE SURE!
EEEEEH!
IT'S ALL MY FAULT! I'VE GOT TO GET LUCKY OUT OF THERE!
THANKS, MICK! THERE HE IS AND HE'S STILL ALIVE. STRETCHER BEARER! STRETCHER BEARER!

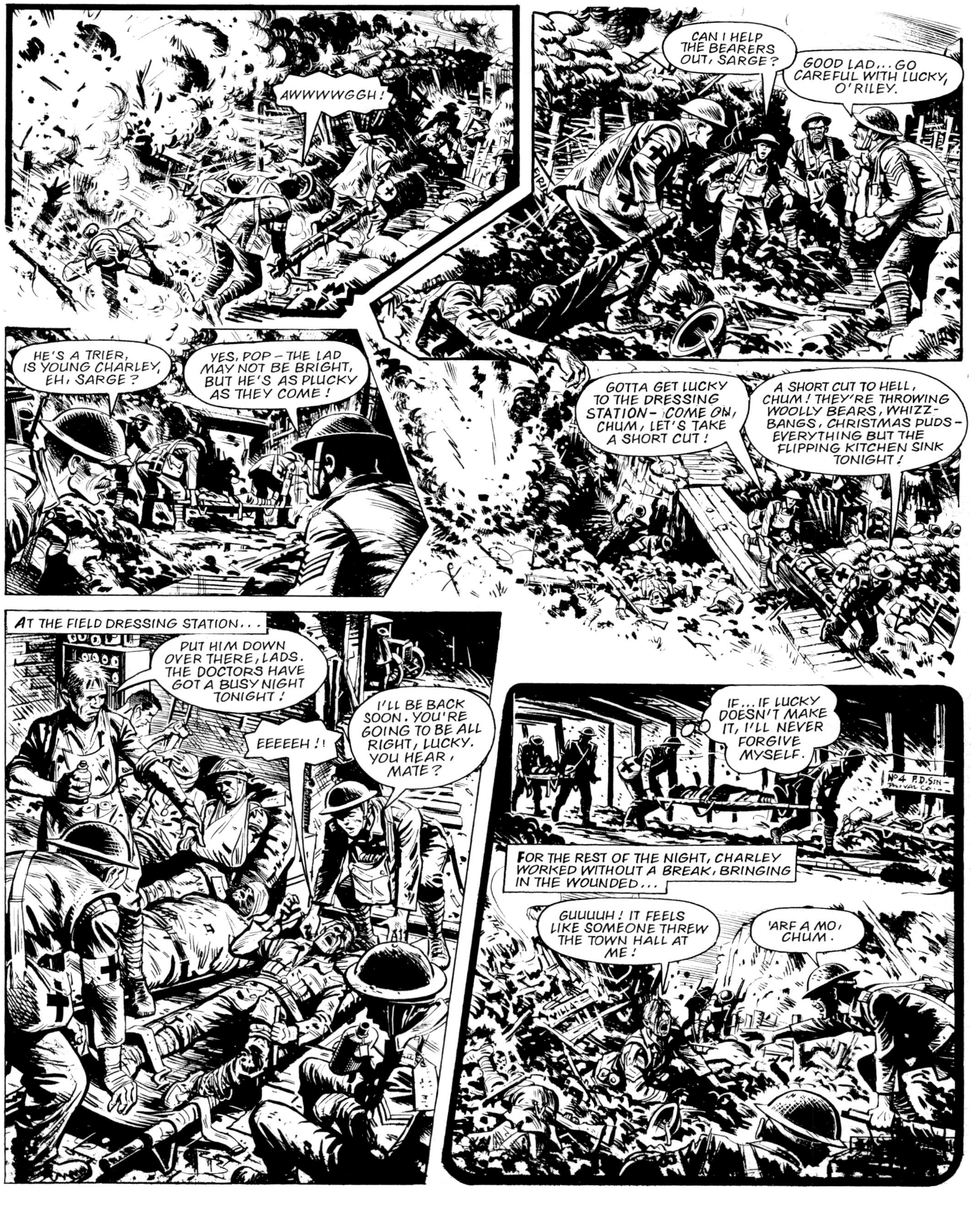
AWWWWGGH!
CAN I HELP THE BEARERS OUT, SARGE?
GOOD LAD... GO CAREFUL WITH LUCKY, O'RILEY.
HE'S A TRIER, IS YOUNG CHARLEY, EH, SARGE?
YES, POP - THE LAD MAY NOT BE BRIGHT, BUT HE'S AS PLUCKY AS THEY COME!
GOTTA GET LUCKY TO THE DRESSING STATION - COME ON, CHUM, LET'S TAKE A SHORT CUT!
A SHORT CUT TO HELL, CHUM! THEY'RE THROWING WOOLLY BEARS, WHIZZ-BANGS, CHRISTMAS PUDS - EVERYTHING BUT THE FLIPPING KITCHEN SINK TONIGHT!
AT THE FIELD DRESSING STATION...
PUT HIM DOWN OVER THERE, LADS. THE DOCTORS HAVE GOT A BUSY NIGHT TONIGHT!
EEEEEH!!
I'LL BE BACK SOON. YOU'RE GOING TO BE ALL RIGHT, LUCKY. YOU HEAR, MATE?
IF... IF LUCKY DOESN'T MAKE IT, I'LL NEVER FORGIVE MYSELF.
FOR THE REST OF THE NIGHT, CHARLEY WORKED WITHOUT A BREAK, BRINGING IN THE WOUNDED...
GUUUUH! IT FEELS LIKE SOMEONE THREW THE TOWN HALL AT ME!
'ARF A MO, CHUM.

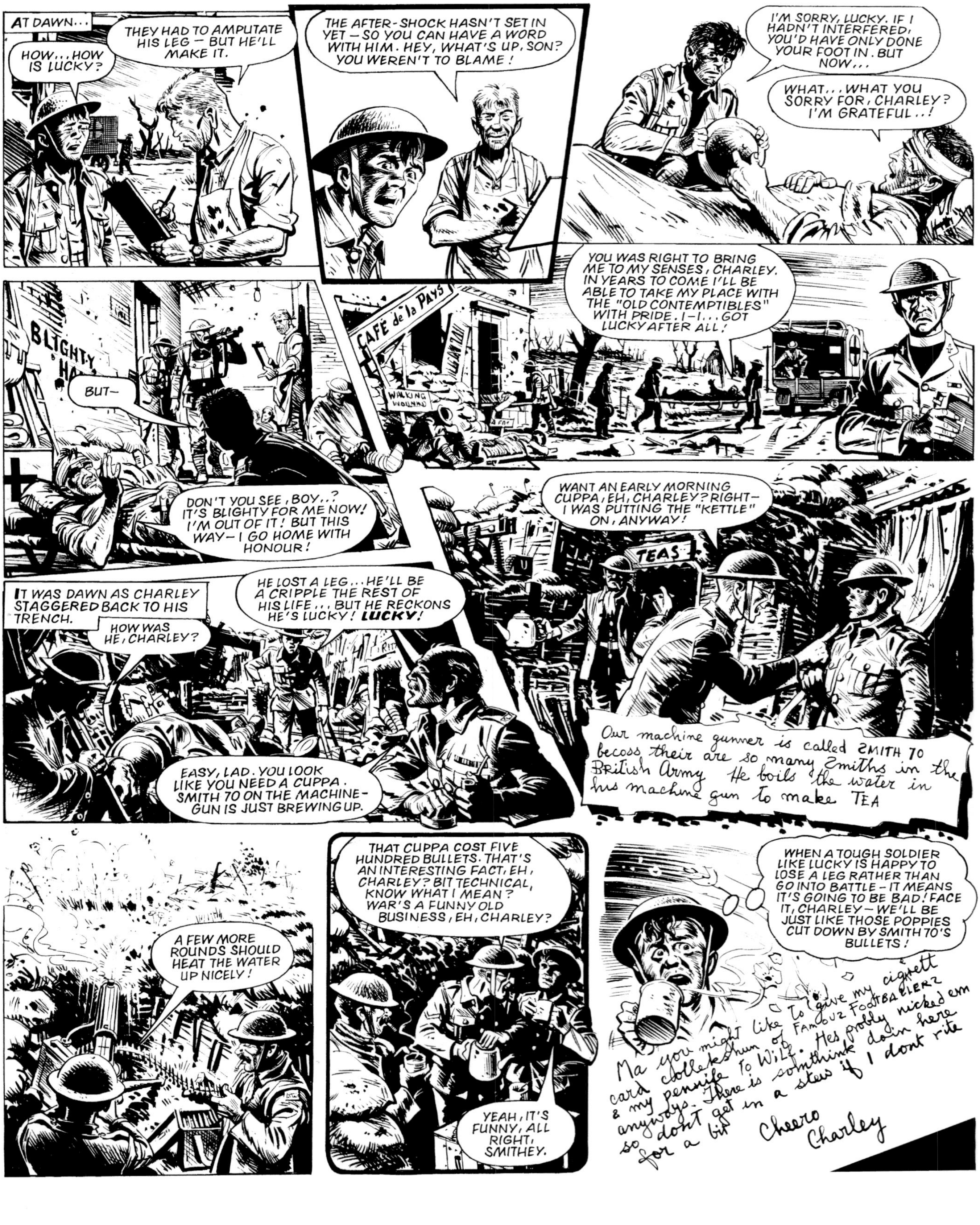

AT DAWN...
HOW...HOW IS LUCKY?
THEY HAD TO AMPUTATE HIS LEG — BUT HE'LL MAKE IT.
THE AFTER-SHOCK HASN'T SET IN YET — SO YOU CAN HAVE A WORD WITH HIM. HEY, WHAT'S UP, SON? YOU WEREN'T TO BLAME!
I'M SORRY, LUCKY. IF I HADN'T INTERFERED, YOU'D HAVE ONLY DONE YOUR FOOT IN. BUT NOW...
WHAT...WHAT YOU SORRY FOR, CHARLEY? I'M GRATEFUL..!
BLIGHTY
BUT—
DON'T YOU SEE, BOY..? IT'S BLIGHTY FOR ME NOW! I'M OUT OF IT! BUT THIS WAY — I GO HOME WITH HONOUR!
CAFÉ de la PAYS
WALKING WOUNDED
YOU WAS RIGHT TO BRING ME TO MY SENSES, CHARLEY. IN YEARS TO COME I'LL BE ABLE TO TAKE MY PLACE WITH THE "OLD CONTEMPTIBLES" WITH PRIDE. I-I... GOT LUCKY AFTER ALL!
IT WAS DAWN AS CHARLEY STAGGERED BACK TO HIS TRENCH.
HOW WAS HE, CHARLEY?
HE LOST A LEG...HE'LL BE A CRIPPLE THE REST OF HIS LIFE...BUT HE RECKONS HE'S LUCKY! LUCKY!
EASY, LAD. YOU LOOK LIKE YOU NEED A CUPPA. SMITH 70 ON THE MACHINE-GUN IS JUST BREWING UP.
WANT AN EARLY MORNING CUPPA, EH, CHARLEY? RIGHT — I WAS PUTTING THE "KETTLE" ON, ANYWAY!
TEAS
Our machine gunner is called SMITH 70 becoss their are so many Smiths in the British Army. He boils the water in the his machine gun to make TEA
A FEW MORE ROUNDS SHOULD HEAT THE WATER UP NICELY!
THAT CUPPA COST FIVE HUNDRED BULLETS. THAT'S AN INTERESTING FACT, EH, CHARLEY? BIT TECHNICAL, KNOW WHAT I MEAN? WAR'S A FUNNY OLD BUSINESS, EH, CHARLEY?
YEAH, IT'S FUNNY, ALL RIGHT, SMITHEY.
WHEN A TOUGH SOLDIER LIKE LUCKY IS HAPPY TO LOSE A LEG RATHER THAN GO INTO BATTLE — IT MEANS IT'S GOING TO BE BAD! FACE IT, CHARLEY — WE'LL BE JUST LIKE THOSE POPPIES CUT DOWN BY SMITH 70'S BULLETS!
Ma you might like to give my cigrett card collekshun of FAMOUZ FOOTBALLERZ & my pennife to WILF. Hes probly nicked em anyways. There is somthink doin here so dont get in a stew if I dont rite for a bit
Cheero Charley

CHARLEY'S WAR

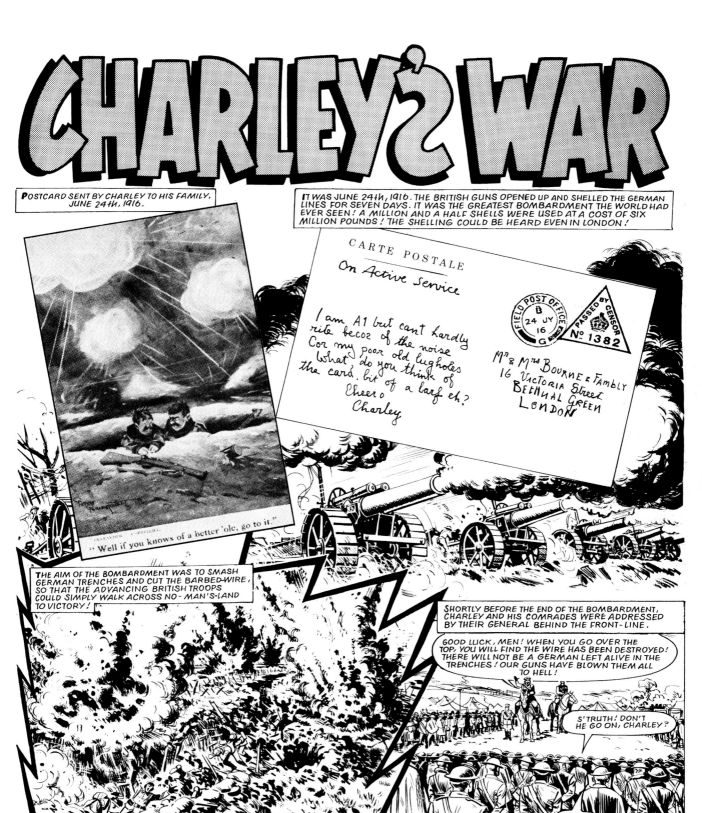

POSTCARD SENT BY CHARLEY TO HIS FAMILY, JUNE 24th, 1916.

IT WAS JUNE 24th, 1916. THE BRITISH GUNS OPENED UP AND SHELLED THE GERMAN LINES FOR SEVEN DAYS. IT WAS THE GREATEST BOMBARDMENT THE WORLD HAD EVER SEEN! A MILLION AND A HALF SHELLS WERE USED AT A COST OF SIX MILLION POUNDS! THE SHELLING COULD BE HEARD EVEN IN LONDON!

"Well if you knows of a better 'ole, go to it."

CARTE POSTALE

On Active Service

I am A1 but can't hardly rite becoz of the noise Cor my poor old lugholes what do you think of the card. bit of a larf eh? Cheero Charley

FIELD POST OFFICE 24 JY 16

PASSED BY CENSOR No. 1382

Mr & Mrs BOURNE & FAMBLY 16 Victoria Street BETHNAL GREEN LONDON

THE AIM OF THE BOMBARDMENT WAS TO SMASH GERMAN TRENCHES AND CUT THE BARBED-WIRE, SO THAT THE ADVANCING BRITISH TROOPS COULD SIMPLY WALK ACROSS NO-MAN'S-LAND TO VICTORY!

SHORTLY BEFORE THE END OF THE BOMBARDMENT, CHARLEY AND HIS COMRADES WERE ADDRESSED BY THEIR GENERAL BEHIND THE FRONT-LINE.

GOOD LUCK, MEN! WHEN YOU GO OVER THE TOP, YOU WILL FIND THE WIRE HAS BEEN DESTROYED! THERE WILL NOT BE A GERMAN LEFT ALIVE IN THE TRENCHES! OUR GUNS HAVE BLOWN THEM ALL TO HELL!

S'TRUTH! DON'T HE GO ON, CHARLEY?

SHUT UP, GINGER!

BUT THE WIRE WAS NOT DESTROYED COMPLETELY AND THE DEEP GERMAN DUG-OUTS SURVIVED!

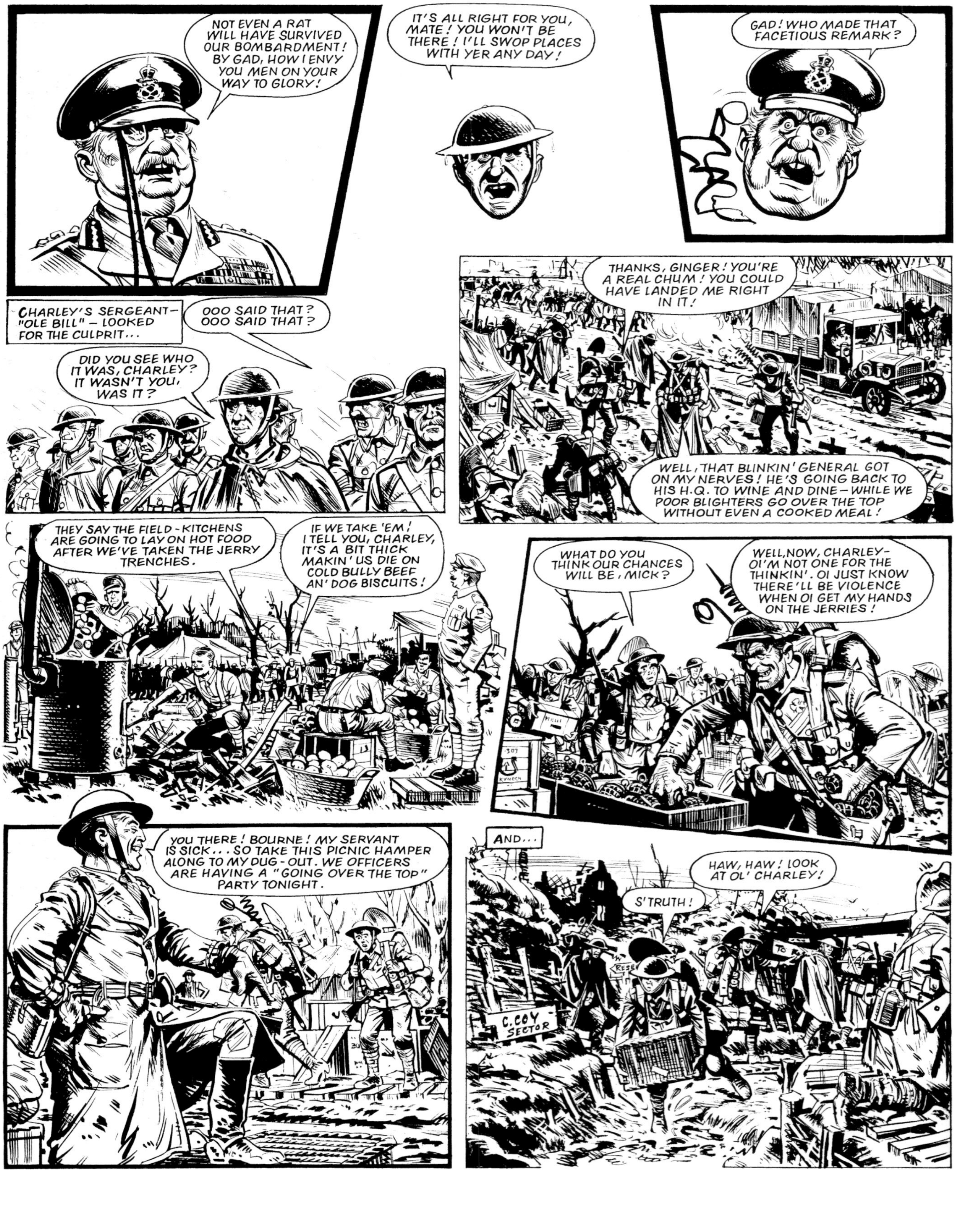
NOT EVEN A RAT WILL HAVE SURVIVED OUR BOMBARDMENT! BY GAD, HOW I ENVY YOU MEN ON YOUR WAY TO GLORY!
IT'S ALL RIGHT FOR YOU, MATE! YOU WON'T BE THERE! I'LL SWOP PLACES WITH YER ANY DAY!
GAD! WHO MADE THAT FACETIOUS REMARK?
CHARLEY'S SERGEANT– "OLE BILL" – LOOKED FOR THE CULPRIT...
OOO SAID THAT? OOO SAID THAT?
DID YOU SEE WHO IT WAS, CHARLEY? IT WASN'T YOU, WAS IT?
THANKS, GINGER! YOU'RE A REAL CHUM! YOU COULD HAVE LANDED ME RIGHT IN IT!
WELL, THAT BLINKIN' GENERAL GOT ON MY NERVES! HE'S GOING BACK TO HIS H.Q. TO WINE AND DINE – WHILE WE POOR BLIGHTERS GO OVER THE TOP WITHOUT EVEN A COOKED MEAL!
THEY SAY THE FIELD-KITCHENS ARE GOING TO LAY ON HOT FOOD AFTER WE'VE TAKEN THE JERRY TRENCHES.
IF WE TAKE 'EM! I TELL YOU, CHARLEY, IT'S A BIT THICK MAKIN' US DIE ON COLD BULLY BEEF AN' DOG BISCUITS!
WHAT DO YOU THINK OUR CHANCES WILL BE, MICK?
WELL, NOW, CHARLEY– OI'M NOT ONE FOR THE THINKIN'. OI JUST KNOW THERE'LL BE VIOLENCE WHEN OI GET MY HANDS ON THE JERRIES!
YOU THERE! BOURNE! MY SERVANT IS SICK... SO TAKE THIS PICNIC HAMPER ALONG TO MY DUG-OUT. WE OFFICERS ARE HAVING A "GOING OVER THE TOP" PARTY TONIGHT.
AND...
HAW, HAW! LOOK AT OL' CHARLEY!
S'TRUTH!
C. COY SECTOR

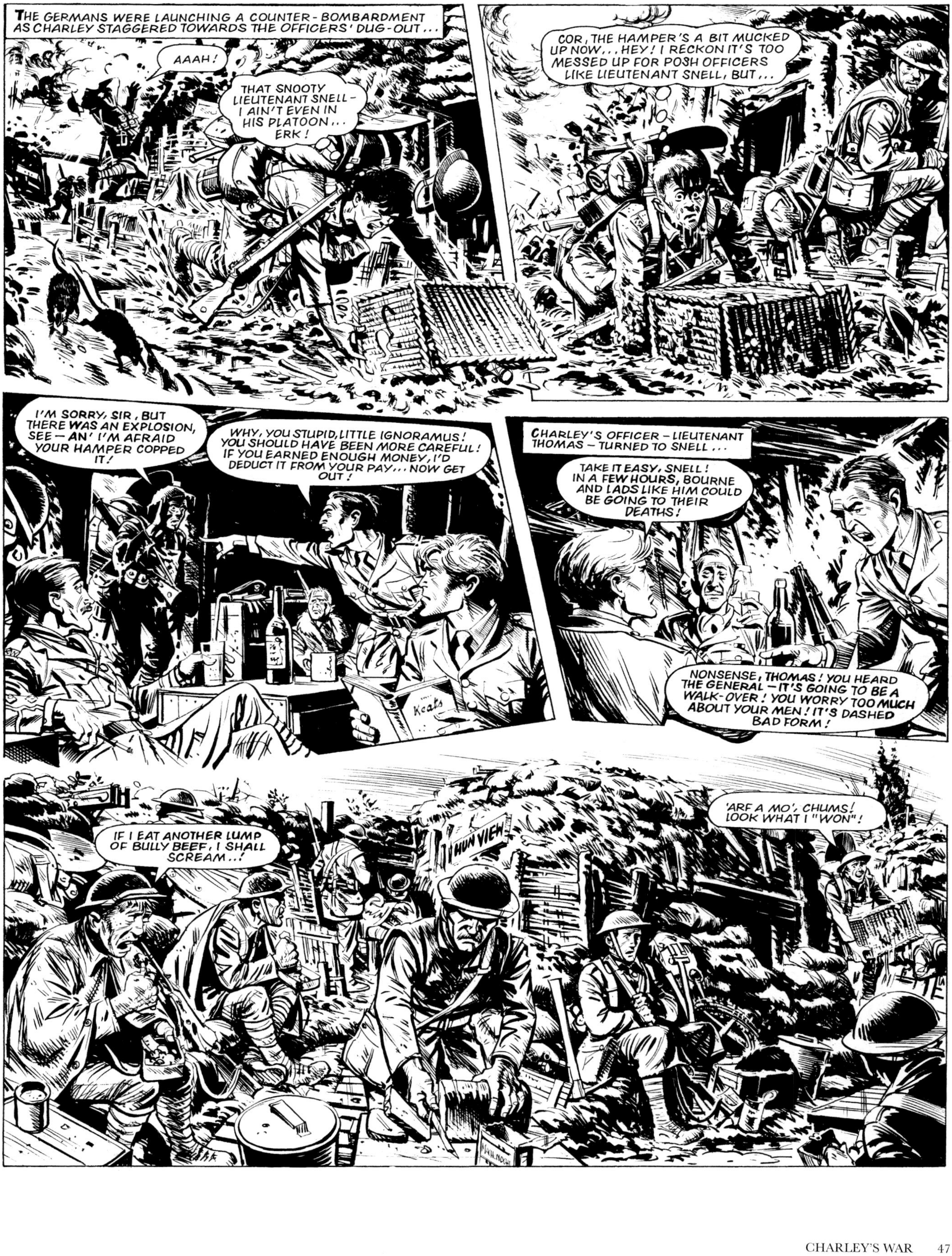
THE GERMANS WERE LAUNCHING A COUNTER-BOMBARDMENT AS CHARLEY STAGGERED TOWARDS THE OFFICERS' DUG-OUT...
AAAH!
THAT SNOOTY LIEUTENANT SNELL - I AIN'T EVEN IN HIS PLATOON... ERK!
COR, THE HAMPER'S A BIT MUCKED UP NOW... HEY! I RECKON IT'S TOO MESSED UP FOR POSH OFFICERS LIKE LIEUTENANT SNELL, BUT...
I'M SORRY, SIR, BUT THERE WAS AN EXPLOSION, SEE - AN' I'M AFRAID YOUR HAMPER COPPED IT!
WHY, YOU STUPID, LITTLE IGNORAMUS! YOU SHOULD HAVE BEEN MORE CAREFUL! IF YOU EARNED ENOUGH MONEY, I'D DEDUCT IT FROM YOUR PAY... NOW GET OUT!
Keats
CHARLEY'S OFFICER - LIEUTENANT THOMAS - TURNED TO SNELL...
TAKE IT EASY, SNELL! IN A FEW HOURS, BOURNE AND LADS LIKE HIM COULD BE GOING TO THEIR DEATHS!
NONSENSE, THOMAS! YOU HEARD THE GENERAL - IT'S GOING TO BE A WALK-OVER! YOU WORRY TOO MUCH ABOUT YOUR MEN! IT'S DASHED BAD FORM!
IF I EAT ANOTHER LUMP OF BULLY BEEF, I SHALL SCREAM...!
HUN VIEW
'ARF A MO', CHUMS! LOOK WHAT I "WON"!

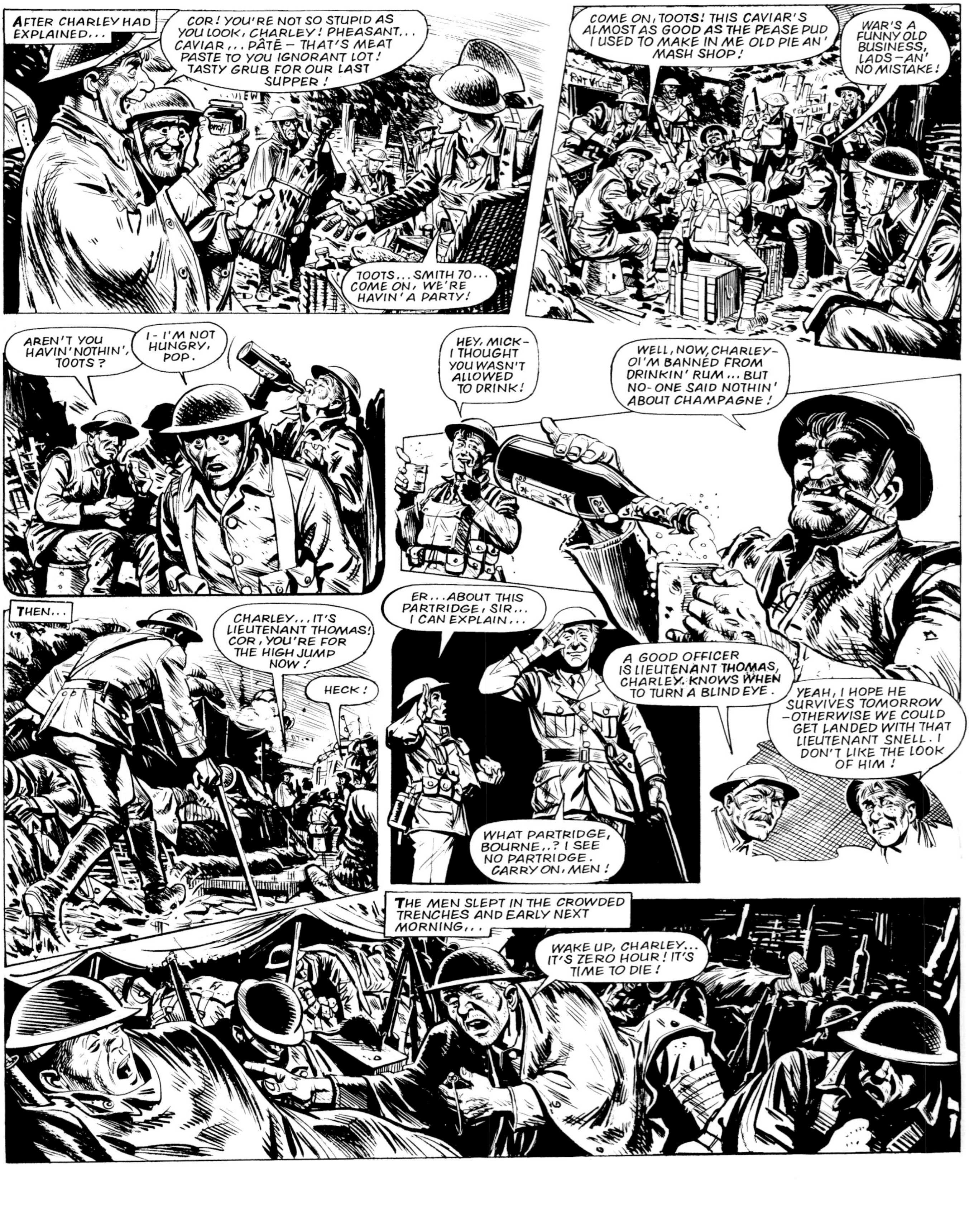

AFTER CHARLEY HAD EXPLAINED...
COR! YOU'RE NOT SO STUPID AS YOU LOOK, CHARLEY! PHEASANT... CAVIAR... PÂTÉ – THAT'S MEAT PASTE TO YOU IGNORANT LOT! TASTY GRUB FOR OUR LAST SUPPER!
TOOTS... SMITH 70... COME ON, WE'RE HAVIN' A PARTY!
COME ON, TOOTS! THIS CAVIAR'S ALMOST AS GOOD AS THE PEASE PUD I USED TO MAKE IN ME OLD PIE AN' MASH SHOP!
WAR'S A FUNNY OLD BUSINESS, LADS – AN' NO MISTAKE!
AREN'T YOU HAVIN' NOTHIN', TOOTS?
I- I'M NOT HUNGRY, POP.
HEY, MICK- I THOUGHT YOU WASN'T ALLOWED TO DRINK!
WELL, NOW, CHARLEY- OI'M BANNED FROM DRINKIN' RUM... BUT NO-ONE SAID NOTHIN' ABOUT CHAMPAGNE!
THEN...
CHARLEY... IT'S LIEUTENANT THOMAS! COR, YOU'RE FOR THE HIGH JUMP NOW!
HECK!
ER... ABOUT THIS PARTRIDGE, SIR... I CAN EXPLAIN...
WHAT PARTRIDGE, BOURNE..? I SEE NO PARTRIDGE. CARRY ON, MEN!
A GOOD OFFICER IS LIEUTENANT THOMAS, CHARLEY. KNOWS WHEN TO TURN A BLIND EYE.
YEAH, I HOPE HE SURVIVES TOMORROW – OTHERWISE WE COULD GET LANDED WITH THAT LIEUTENANT SNELL. I DON'T LIKE THE LOOK OF HIM!
THE MEN SLEPT IN THE CROWDED TRENCHES AND EARLY NEXT MORNING...
WAKE UP, CHARLEY... IT'S ZERO HOUR! IT'S TIME TO DIE!

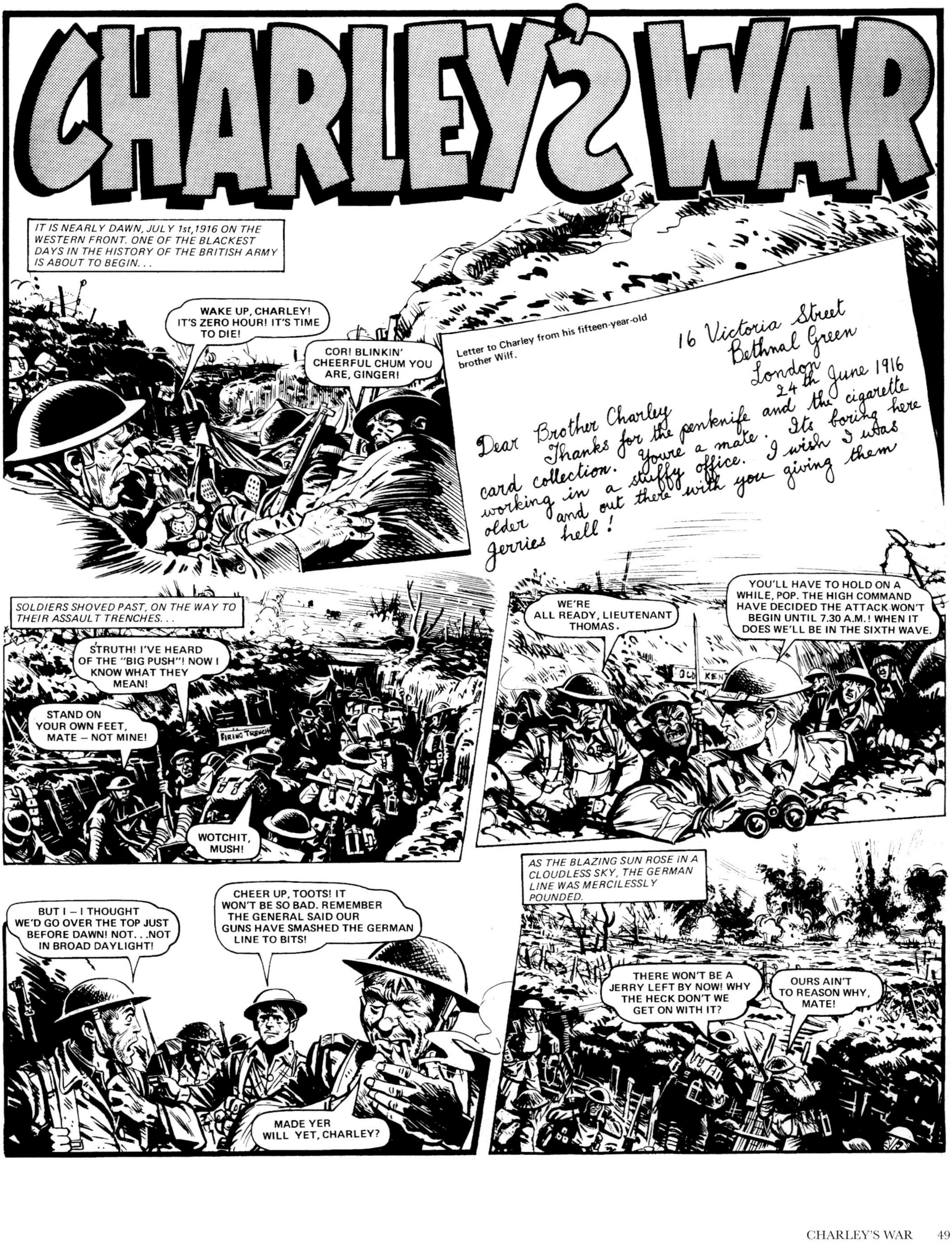
CHARLEY'S WAR
IT IS NEARLY DAWN, JULY 1st,1916 ON THE WESTERN FRONT. ONE OF THE BLACKEST DAYS IN THE HISTORY OF THE BRITISH ARMY IS ABOUT TO BEGIN. . .
WAKE UP, CHARLEY! IT'S ZERO HOUR! IT'S TIME TO DIE!
COR! BLINKIN' CHEERFUL CHUM YOU ARE, GINGER!
Letter to Charley from his fifteen-year-old brother Wilf.
16 Victoria Street
Bethnal Green
London
24 th June 1916
Dear Brother Charley
Thanks for the penknife and the cigarette card collection. Youre a mate. Its boring here working in a stuffy office. I wish I was older and out there with you giving them Jerries hell!
SOLDIERS SHOVED PAST, ON THE WAY TO THEIR ASSAULT TRENCHES. . .
STRUTH! I'VE HEARD OF THE "BIG PUSH"! NOW I KNOW WHAT THEY MEAN!
STAND ON YOUR OWN FEET, MATE – NOT MINE!
FIRING TRENCH
WOTCHIT, MUSH!
WE'RE ALL READY, LIEUTENANT THOMAS.
YOU'LL HAVE TO HOLD ON A WHILE, POP. THE HIGH COMMAND HAVE DECIDED THE ATTACK WON'T BEGIN UNTIL 7.30 A.M.! WHEN IT DOES WE'LL BE IN THE SIXTH WAVE.
OLD KENT
BUT I – I THOUGHT WE'D GO OVER THE TOP JUST BEFORE DAWN! NOT. . .NOT IN BROAD DAYLIGHT!
CHEER UP, TOOTS! IT WON'T BE SO BAD. REMEMBER THE GENERAL SAID OUR GUNS HAVE SMASHED THE GERMAN LINE TO BITS!
MADE YER WILL YET, CHARLEY?
AS THE BLAZING SUN ROSE IN A CLOUDLESS SKY, THE GERMAN LINE WAS MERCILESSLY POUNDED.
THERE WON'T BE A JERRY LEFT BY NOW! WHY THE HECK DON'T WE GET ON WITH IT?
OURS AIN'T TO REASON WHY, MATE!

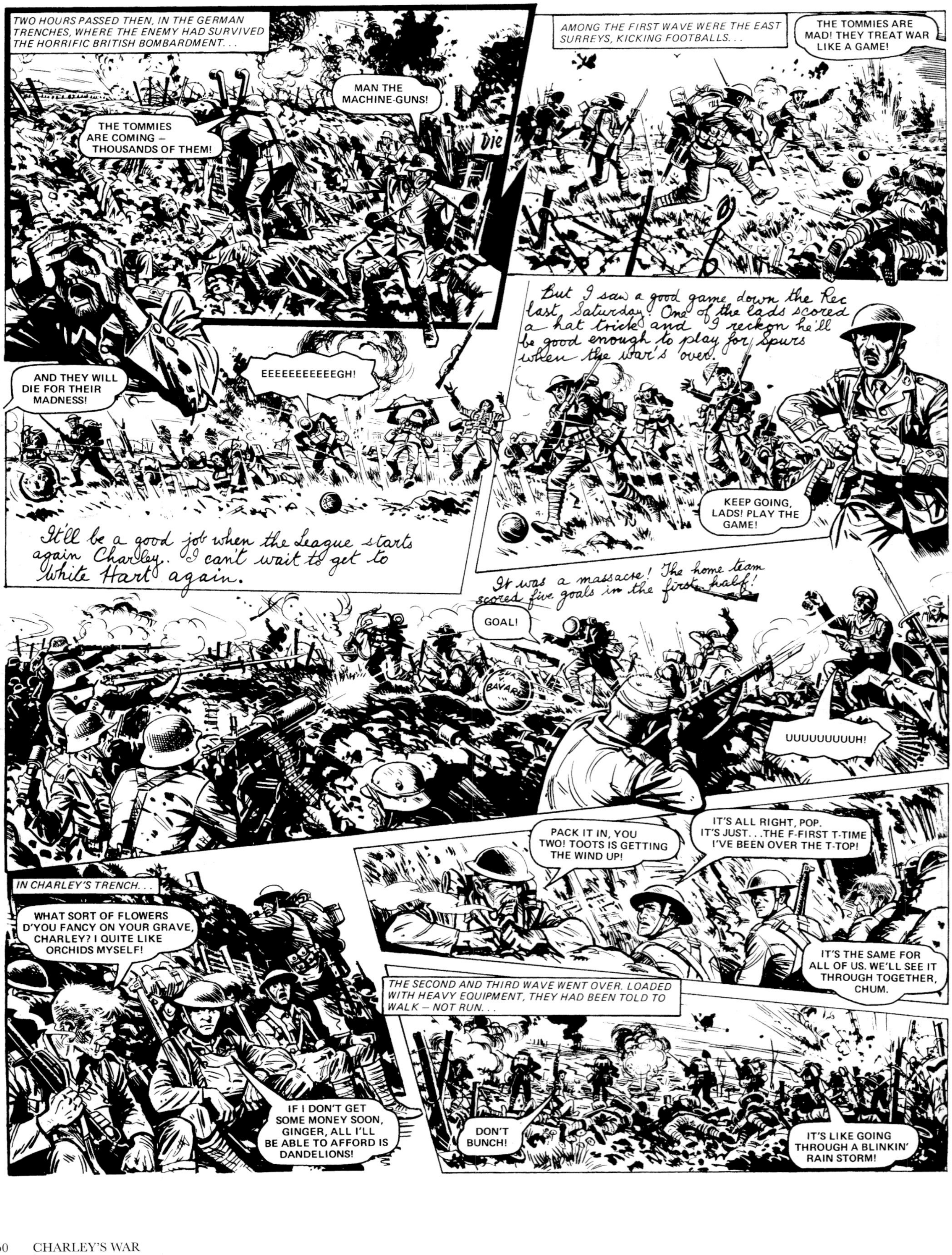
TWO HOURS PASSED THEN, IN THE GERMAN TRENCHES, WHERE THE ENEMY HAD SURVIVED THE HORRIFIC BRITISH BOMBARDMENT. . .
THE TOMMIES ARE COMING – THOUSANDS OF THEM!
MAN THE MACHINE-GUNS!
AMONG THE FIRST WAVE WERE THE EAST SURREYS, KICKING FOOTBALLS. . .
THE TOMMIES ARE MAD! THEY TREAT WAR LIKE A GAME!
AND THEY WILL DIE FOR THEIR MADNESS!
EEEEEEEEEEEGH!
It'll be a good job when the League starts again Charley. I can't wait to get to White Hart again.
But I saw a good game down the Rec last Saturday. One of the lads scored a hat trick and I reckon he'll be good enough to play for Spurs when the war's over.
KEEP GOING, LADS! PLAY THE GAME!
It was a massacre! The home team scored five goals in the first half!
GOAL!
UUUUUUUUUH!
IN CHARLEY'S TRENCH. . .
WHAT SORT OF FLOWERS D'YOU FANCY ON YOUR GRAVE, CHARLEY? I QUITE LIKE ORCHIDS MYSELF!
IF I DON'T GET SOME MONEY SOON, GINGER, ALL I'LL BE ABLE TO AFFORD IS DANDELIONS!
PACK IT IN, YOU TWO! TOOTS IS GETTING THE WIND UP!
IT'S ALL RIGHT, POP. IT'S JUST. . .THE F-FIRST T-TIME I'VE BEEN OVER THE T-TOP!
IT'S THE SAME FOR ALL OF US. WE'LL SEE IT THROUGH TOGETHER, CHUM.
THE SECOND AND THIRD WAVE WENT OVER. LOADED WITH HEAVY EQUIPMENT, THEY HAD BEEN TOLD TO WALK – NOT RUN. . .
DON'T BUNCH!
IT'S LIKE GOING THROUGH A BLINKIN' RAIN STORM!

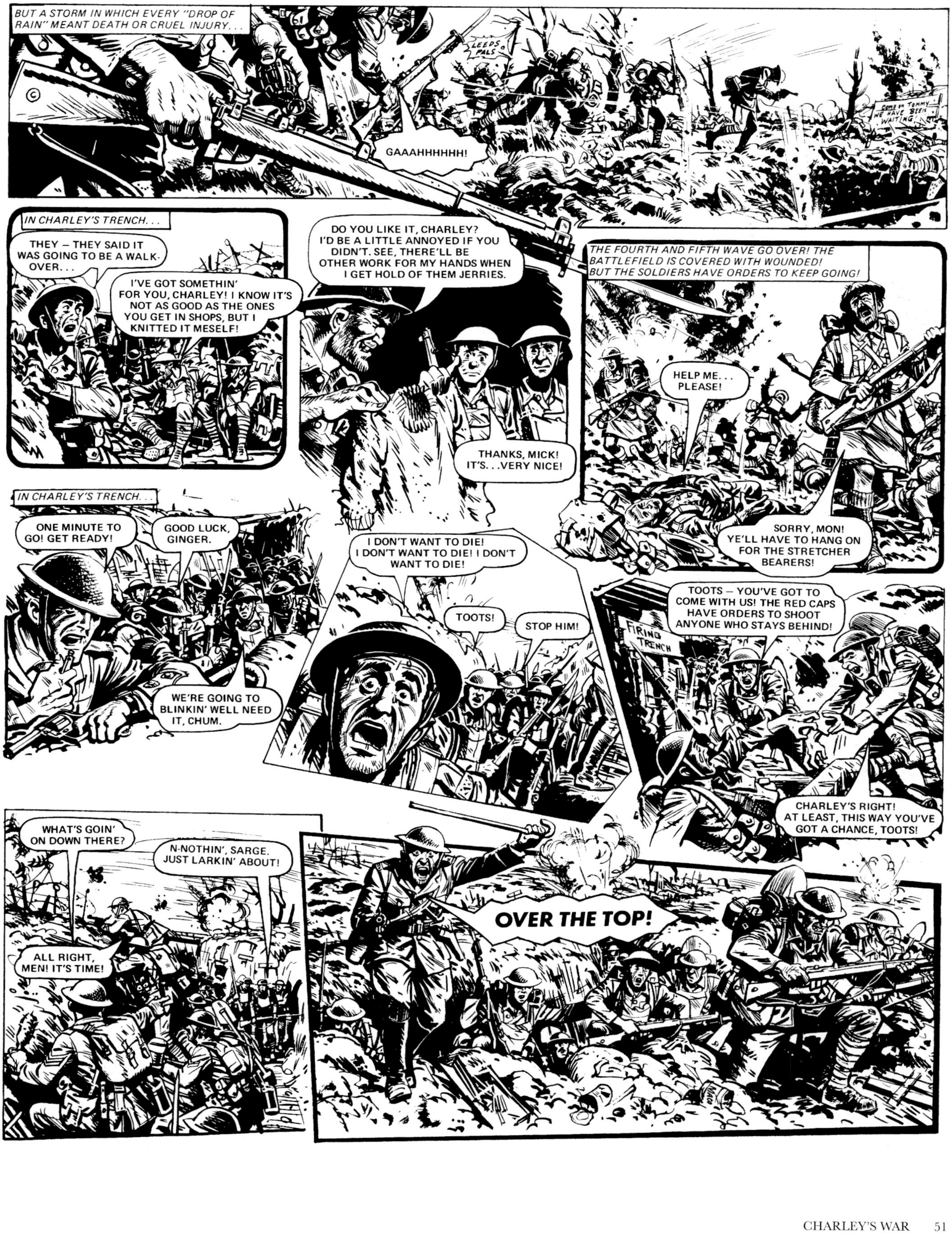
BUT A STORM IN WHICH EVERY "DROP OF RAIN" MEANT DEATH OR CRUEL INJURY...
LEEDS PALS
GAAAHHHHHH!
IN CHARLEY'S TRENCH...
THEY – THEY SAID IT WAS GOING TO BE A WALK-OVER...
I'VE GOT SOMETHIN' FOR YOU, CHARLEY! I KNOW IT'S NOT AS GOOD AS THE ONES YOU GET IN SHOPS, BUT I KNITTED IT MESELF!
DO YOU LIKE IT, CHARLEY? I'D BE A LITTLE ANNOYED IF YOU DIDN'T. SEE, THERE'LL BE OTHER WORK FOR MY HANDS WHEN I GET HOLD OF THEM JERRIES.
THANKS, MICK! IT'S...VERY NICE!
THE FOURTH AND FIFTH WAVE GO OVER! THE BATTLEFIELD IS COVERED WITH WOUNDED! BUT THE SOLDIERS HAVE ORDERS TO KEEP GOING!
HELP ME... PLEASE!
SORRY, MON! YE'LL HAVE TO HANG ON FOR THE STRETCHER BEARERS!
IN CHARLEY'S TRENCH...
ONE MINUTE TO GO! GET READY!
GOOD LUCK, GINGER.
WE'RE GOING TO BLINKIN' WELL NEED IT, CHUM.
I DON'T WANT TO DIE! I DON'T WANT TO DIE! I DON'T WANT TO DIE!
TOOTS!
STOP HIM!
FIRING TRENCH
TOOTS – YOU'VE GOT TO COME WITH US! THE RED CAPS HAVE ORDERS TO SHOOT ANYONE WHO STAYS BEHIND!
CHARLEY'S RIGHT! AT LEAST, THIS WAY YOU'VE GOT A CHANCE, TOOTS!
WHAT'S GOIN' ON DOWN THERE?
N-NOTHIN', SARGE. JUST LARKIN' ABOUT!
ALL RIGHT, MEN! IT'S TIME!
OVER THE TOP!

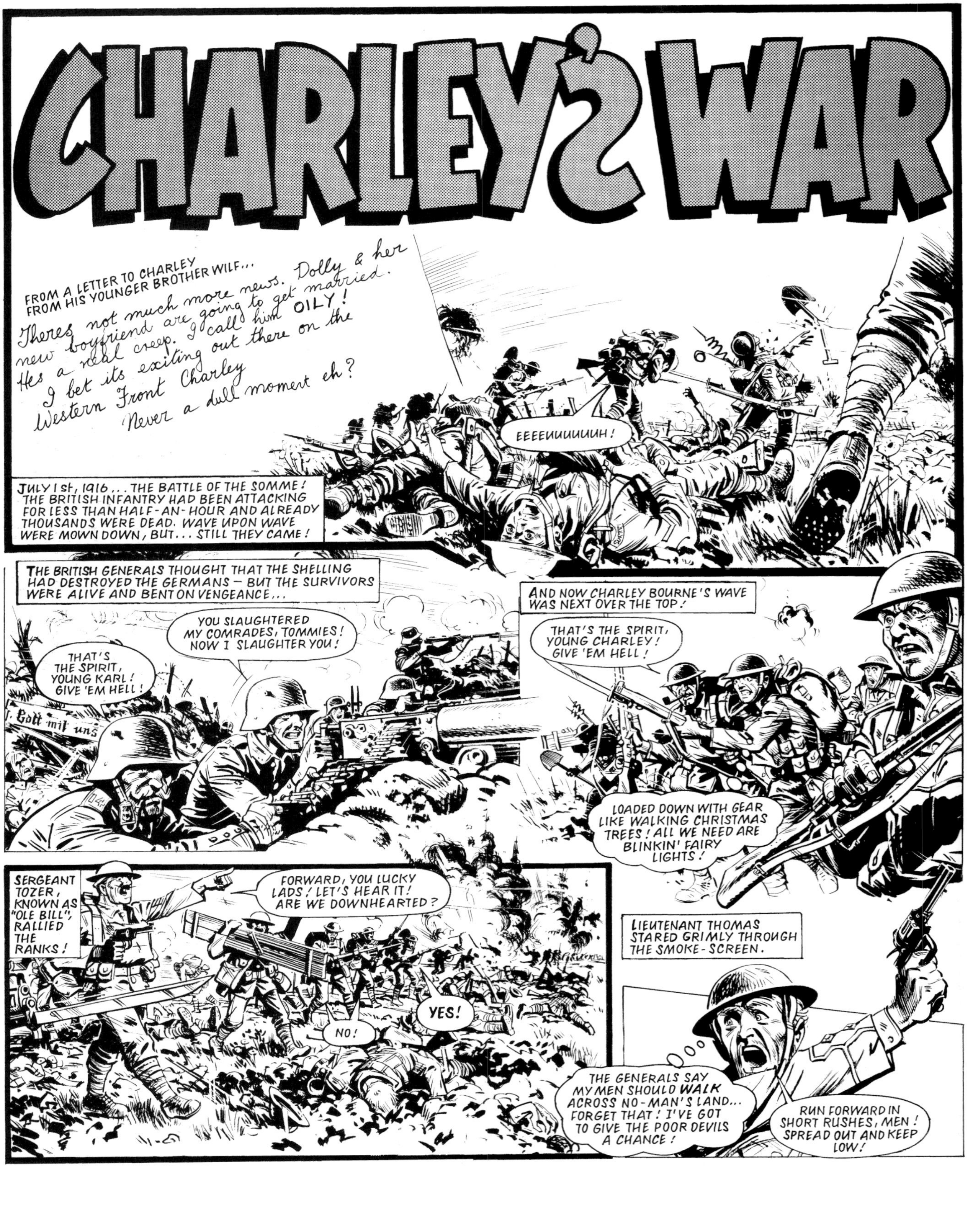
CHARLEY'S WAR
FROM A LETTER TO CHARLEY FROM HIS YOUNGER BROTHER WILF...
Theres not much more news. Dolly & her new boyfriend are going to get married. Hes a real creep. I call him OILY! I bet its exciting out there on the Western Front Charley Never a dull moment eh?
EEEEUUUUUUH!
JULY 1st, 1916... THE BATTLE OF THE SOMME! THE BRITISH INFANTRY HAD BEEN ATTACKING FOR LESS THAN HALF-AN-HOUR AND ALREADY THOUSANDS WERE DEAD. WAVE UPON WAVE WERE MOWN DOWN, BUT... STILL THEY CAME!
THE BRITISH GENERALS THOUGHT THAT THE SHELLING HAD DESTROYED THE GERMANS — BUT THE SURVIVORS WERE ALIVE AND BENT ON VENGEANCE...
YOU SLAUGHTERED MY COMRADES, TOMMIES! NOW I SLAUGHTER YOU!
THAT'S THE SPIRIT, YOUNG KARL! GIVE 'EM HELL!
Gott mit uns
AND NOW CHARLEY BOURNE'S WAVE WAS NEXT OVER THE TOP!
THAT'S THE SPIRIT, YOUNG CHARLEY! GIVE 'EM HELL!
LOADED DOWN WITH GEAR LIKE WALKING CHRISTMAS TREES! ALL WE NEED ARE BLINKIN' FAIRY LIGHTS!
SERGEANT TOZER, KNOWN AS "OLE BILL", RALLIED THE RANKS!
FORWARD, YOU LUCKY LADS! LET'S HEAR IT! ARE WE DOWNHEARTED?
YES!
NO!
LIEUTENANT THOMAS STARED GRIMLY THROUGH THE SMOKE-SCREEN.
THE GENERALS SAY MY MEN SHOULD WALK ACROSS NO-MAN'S LAND... FORGET THAT! I'VE GOT TO GIVE THE POOR DEVILS A CHANCE!
RUN FORWARD IN SHORT RUSHES, MEN! SPREAD OUT AND KEEP LOW!

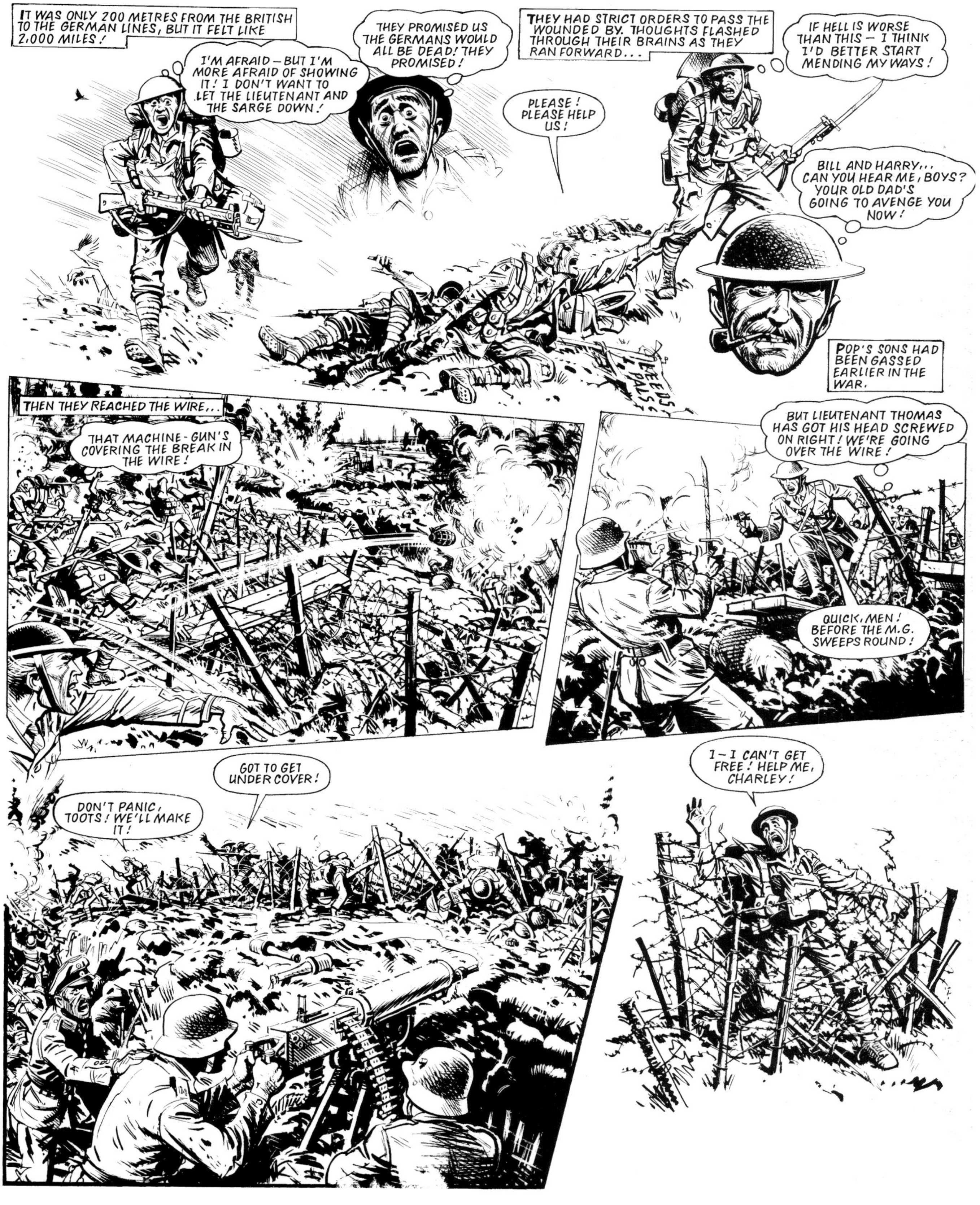
IT WAS ONLY 200 METRES FROM THE BRITISH TO THE GERMAN LINES, BUT IT FELT LIKE 2,000 MILES!
I'M AFRAID – BUT I'M MORE AFRAID OF SHOWING IT! I DON'T WANT TO LET THE LIEUTENANT AND THE SARGE DOWN!
THEY PROMISED US THE GERMANS WOULD ALL BE DEAD! THEY PROMISED!
THEY HAD STRICT ORDERS TO PASS THE WOUNDED BY. THOUGHTS FLASHED THROUGH THEIR BRAINS AS THEY RAN FORWARD...
PLEASE! PLEASE HELP US!
IF HELL IS WORSE THAN THIS – I THINK I'D BETTER START MENDING MY WAYS!
BILL AND HARRY... CAN YOU HEAR ME, BOYS? YOUR OLD DAD'S GOING TO AVENGE YOU NOW!
POP'S SONS HAD BEEN GASSED EARLIER IN THE WAR.
THEN THEY REACHED THE WIRE...
THAT MACHINE-GUN'S COVERING THE BREAK IN THE WIRE!
BUT LIEUTENANT THOMAS HAS GOT HIS HEAD SCREWED ON RIGHT! WE'RE GOING OVER THE WIRE!
QUICK, MEN! BEFORE THE M.G. SWEEPS ROUND!
DON'T PANIC, TOOTS! WE'LL MAKE IT!
GOT TO GET UNDER COVER!
I – I CAN'T GET FREE! HELP ME, CHARLEY!

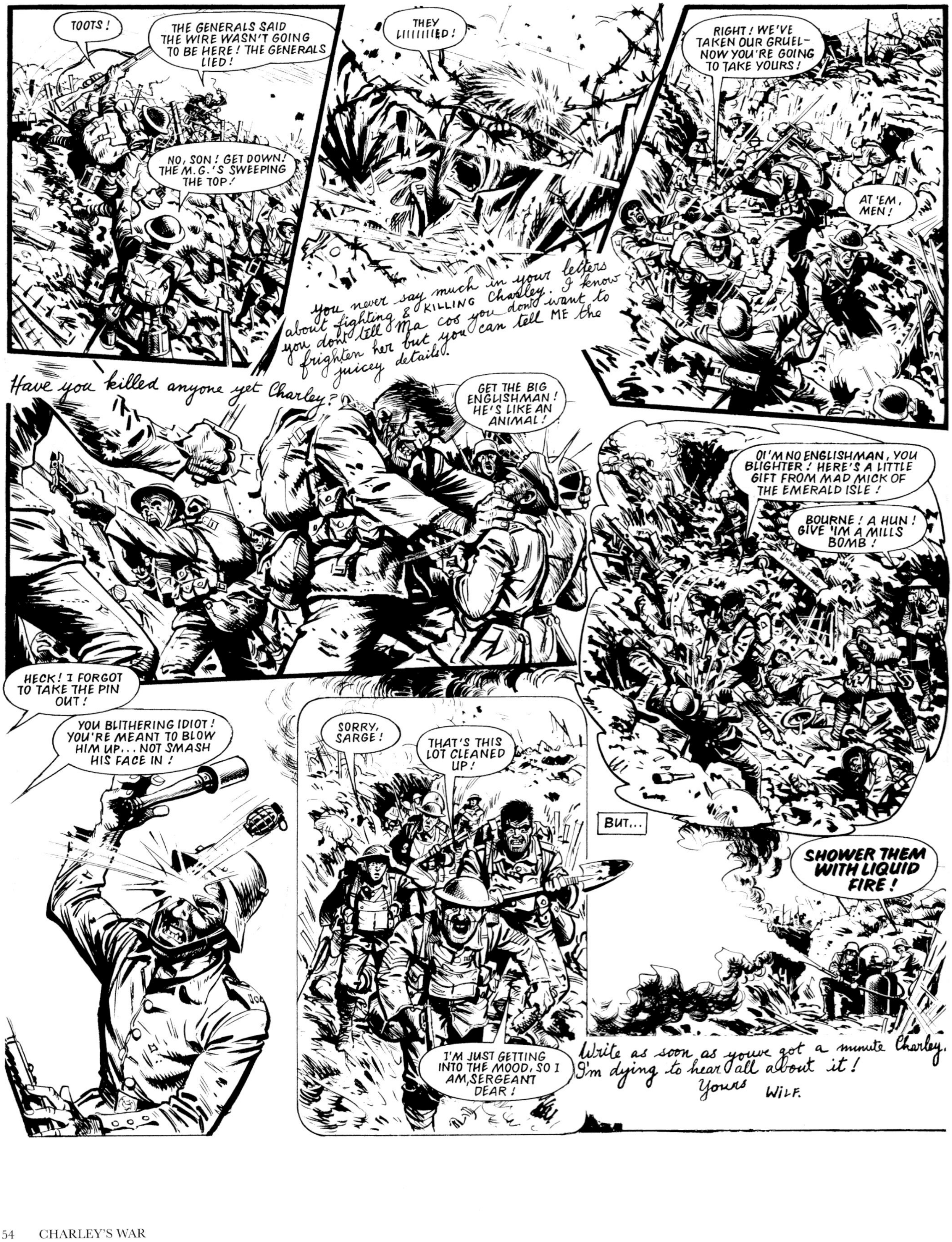

TOOTS!
THE GENERALS SAID THE WIRE WASN'T GOING TO BE HERE! THE GENERALS LIED!
NO, SON! GET DOWN! THE M.G.'S SWEEPING THE TOP!
THEY LIIIIIIIED!
RIGHT! WE'VE TAKEN OUR GRUEL- NOW YOU'RE GOING TO TAKE YOURS!
AT 'EM, MEN!
You never say much in your letters about fighting & KILLING Charley. I know you don't tell Ma cos you don't want to frighten her but you can tell ME the juicey details.
Have you killed anyone yet Charley?
GET THE BIG ENGLISHMAN! HE'S LIKE AN ANIMAL!
OI'M NO ENGLISHMAN, YOU BLIGHTER! HERE'S A LITTLE GIFT FROM MAD MICK OF THE EMERALD ISLE!
BOURNE! A HUN! GIVE 'IM A MILLS BOMB!
HECK! I FORGOT TO TAKE THE PIN OUT!
YOU BLITHERING IDIOT! YOU'RE MEANT TO BLOW HIM UP... NOT SMASH HIS FACE IN!
SORRY, SARGE!
THAT'S THIS LOT CLEANED UP!
I'M JUST GETTING INTO THE MOOD, SO I AM, SERGEANT DEAR!
BUT...
SHOWER THEM WITH LIQUID FIRE!
Write as soon as you've got a minute Charley. I'm dying to hear all about it!
Yours
WILF.

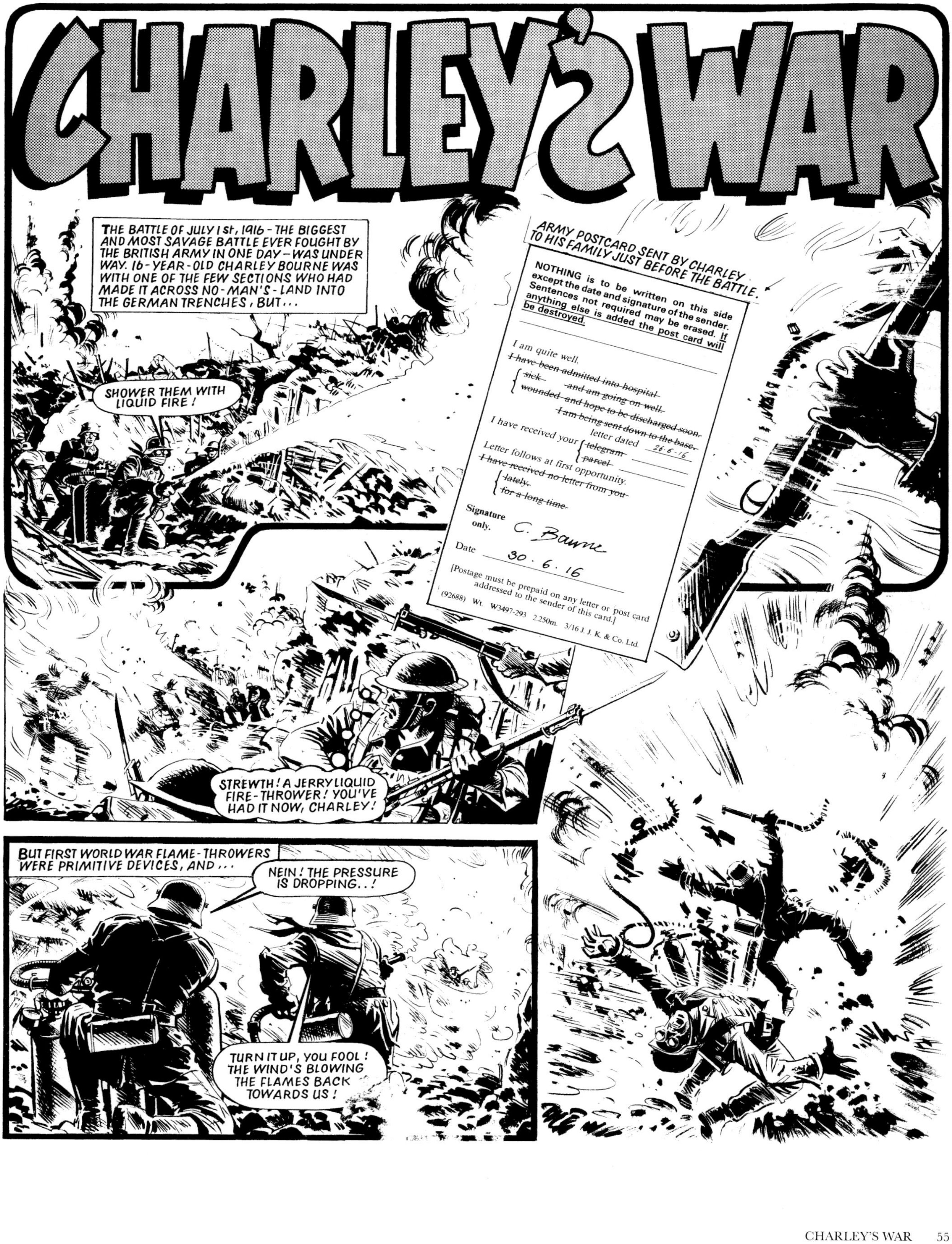
CHARLEY'S WAR
THE BATTLE OF JULY 1st, 1916 - THE BIGGEST AND MOST SAVAGE BATTLE EVER FOUGHT BY THE BRITISH ARMY IN ONE DAY - WAS UNDER WAY. 16-YEAR-OLD CHARLEY BOURNE WAS WITH ONE OF THE FEW SECTIONS WHO HAD MADE IT ACROSS NO-MAN'S-LAND INTO THE GERMAN TRENCHES, BUT...
ARMY POSTCARD SENT BY CHARLEY TO HIS FAMILY JUST BEFORE THE BATTLE.
NOTHING is to be written on this side except the date and signature of the sender. Sentences not required may be erased. If anything else is added the post card will be destroyed.
I am quite well.
~~I have been admitted into hospital~~
~~sick and am going on well.~~
~~wounded and hope to be discharged soon.~~
~~I am being sent down to the base.~~
I have received your letter dated 26.6.16 ~~telegram~~ ~~parcel~~
Letter follows at first opportunity.
~~I have received no letter from you~~
~~lately.~~
~~for a long time.~~
Signature only. C. Bourne
Date 30.6.16
[Postage must be prepaid on any letter or post card addressed to the sender of this card.]
(92688) Wt. W3497-293 2.250m. 3/16 J. J. K. & Co. Ltd.
SHOWER THEM WITH LIQUID FIRE!
STREWTH! A JERRY LIQUID FIRE-THROWER! YOU'VE HAD IT NOW, CHARLEY!
BUT FIRST WORLD WAR FLAME-THROWERS WERE PRIMITIVE DEVICES, AND...
NEIN! THE PRESSURE IS DROPPING..!
TURN IT UP, YOU FOOL! THE WIND'S BLOWING THE FLAMES BACK TOWARDS US!

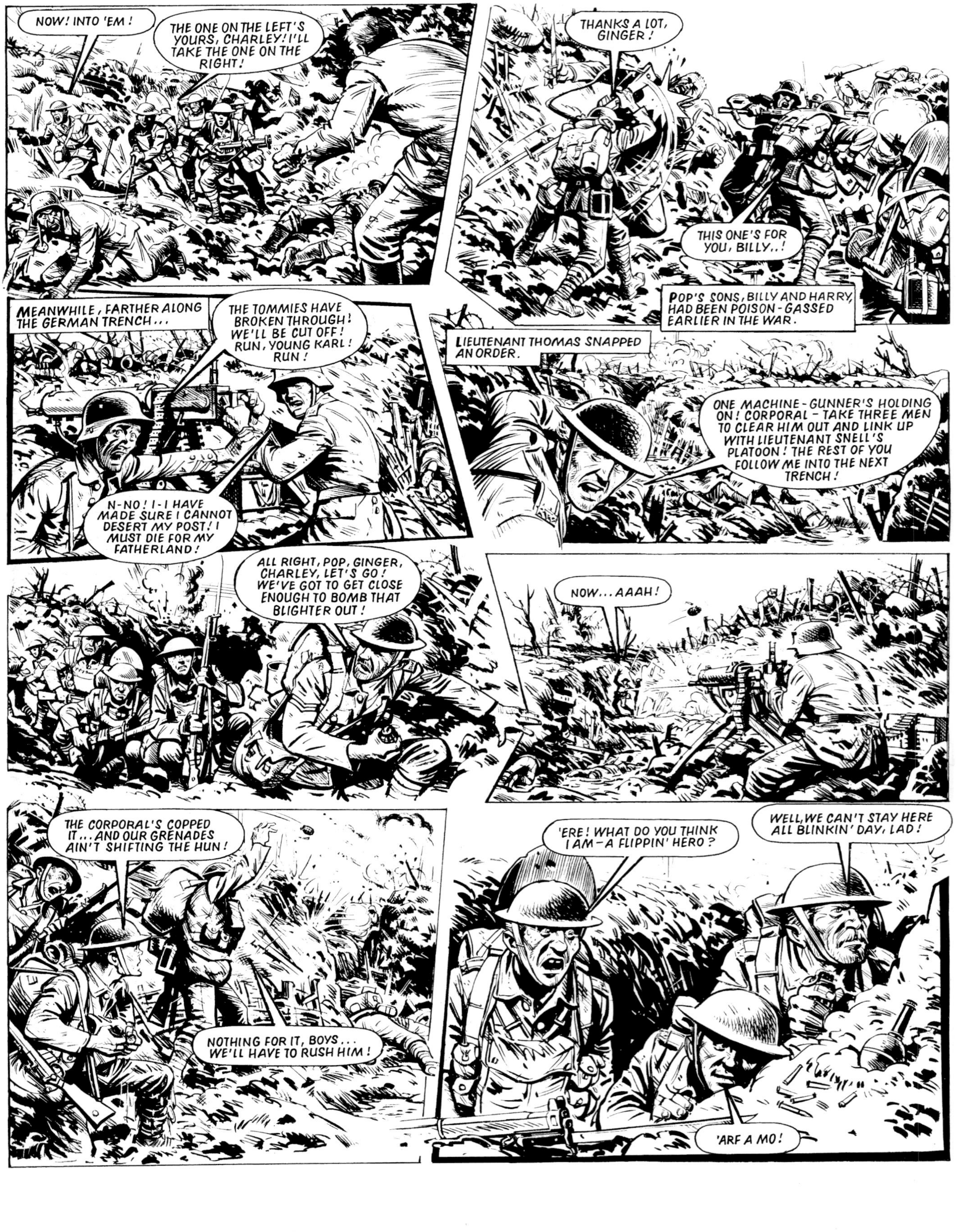
NOW! INTO 'EM!
THE ONE ON THE LEFT'S YOURS, CHARLEY! I'LL TAKE THE ONE ON THE RIGHT!
THANKS A LOT, GINGER!
THIS ONE'S FOR YOU, BILLY..!
POP'S SONS, BILLY AND HARRY, HAD BEEN POISON-GASSED EARLIER IN THE WAR.
MEANWHILE, FARTHER ALONG THE GERMAN TRENCH...
THE TOMMIES HAVE BROKEN THROUGH! WE'LL BE CUT OFF! RUN, YOUNG KARL! RUN!
N-NO! I-I HAVE MADE SURE I CANNOT DESERT MY POST! I MUST DIE FOR MY FATHERLAND!
LIEUTENANT THOMAS SNAPPED AN ORDER.
ONE MACHINE-GUNNER'S HOLDING ON! CORPORAL - TAKE THREE MEN TO CLEAR HIM OUT AND LINK UP WITH LIEUTENANT SNELL'S PLATOON! THE REST OF YOU FOLLOW ME INTO THE NEXT TRENCH!
ALL RIGHT, POP, GINGER, CHARLEY, LET'S GO! WE'VE GOT TO GET CLOSE ENOUGH TO BOMB THAT BLIGHTER OUT!
NOW... AAAH!
THE CORPORAL'S COPPED IT... AND OUR GRENADES AIN'T SHIFTING THE HUN!
NOTHING FOR IT, BOYS... WE'LL HAVE TO RUSH HIM!
'ERE! WHAT DO YOU THINK I AM - A FLIPPIN' HERO?
WELL, WE CAN'T STAY HERE ALL BLINKIN' DAY, LAD!
'ARF A MO!

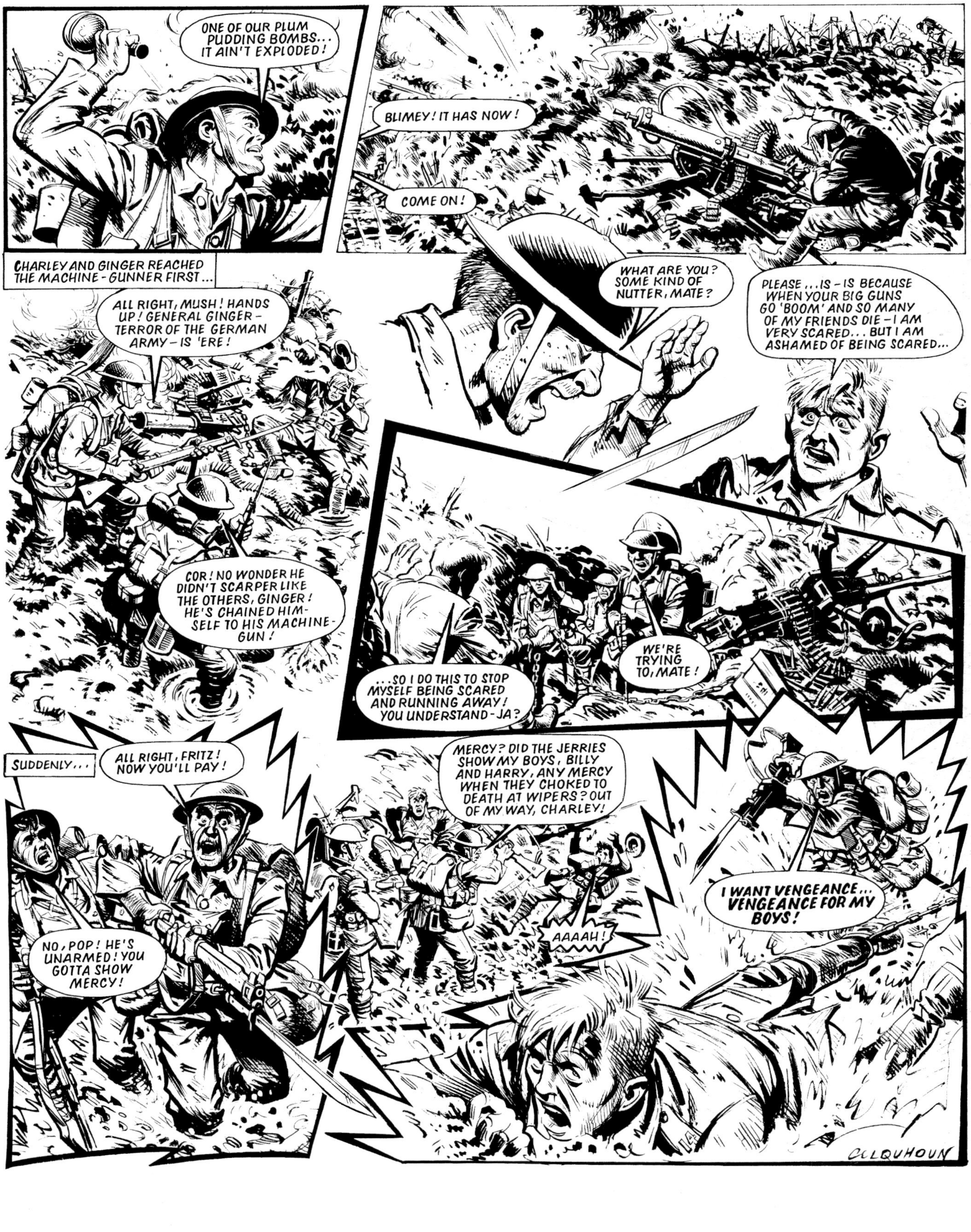
ONE OF OUR PLUM PUDDING BOMBS... IT AIN'T EXPLODED!
BLIMEY! IT HAS NOW!
COME ON!
CHARLEY AND GINGER REACHED THE MACHINE-GUNNER FIRST...
ALL RIGHT, MUSH! HANDS UP! GENERAL GINGER - TERROR OF THE GERMAN ARMY - IS 'ERE!
COR! NO WONDER HE DIDN'T SCARPER LIKE THE OTHERS, GINGER! HE'S CHAINED HIMSELF TO HIS MACHINE-GUN!
WHAT ARE YOU? SOME KIND OF NUTTER, MATE?
PLEASE... IS - IS BECAUSE WHEN YOUR BIG GUNS GO 'BOOM' AND SO MANY OF MY FRIENDS DIE - I AM VERY SCARED... BUT I AM ASHAMED OF BEING SCARED...
...SO I DO THIS TO STOP MYSELF BEING SCARED AND RUNNING AWAY! YOU UNDERSTAND - JA?
WE'RE TRYING TO, MATE!
SUDDENLY...
ALL RIGHT, FRITZ! NOW YOU'LL PAY!
NO, POP! HE'S UNARMED! YOU GOTTA SHOW MERCY!
MERCY? DID THE JERRIES SHOW MY BOYS, BILLY AND HARRY, ANY MERCY WHEN THEY CHOKED TO DEATH AT WIPERS? OUT OF MY WAY, CHARLEY!
AAAAH!
I WANT VENGEANCE... VENGEANCE FOR MY BOYS!
COLQUHOUN

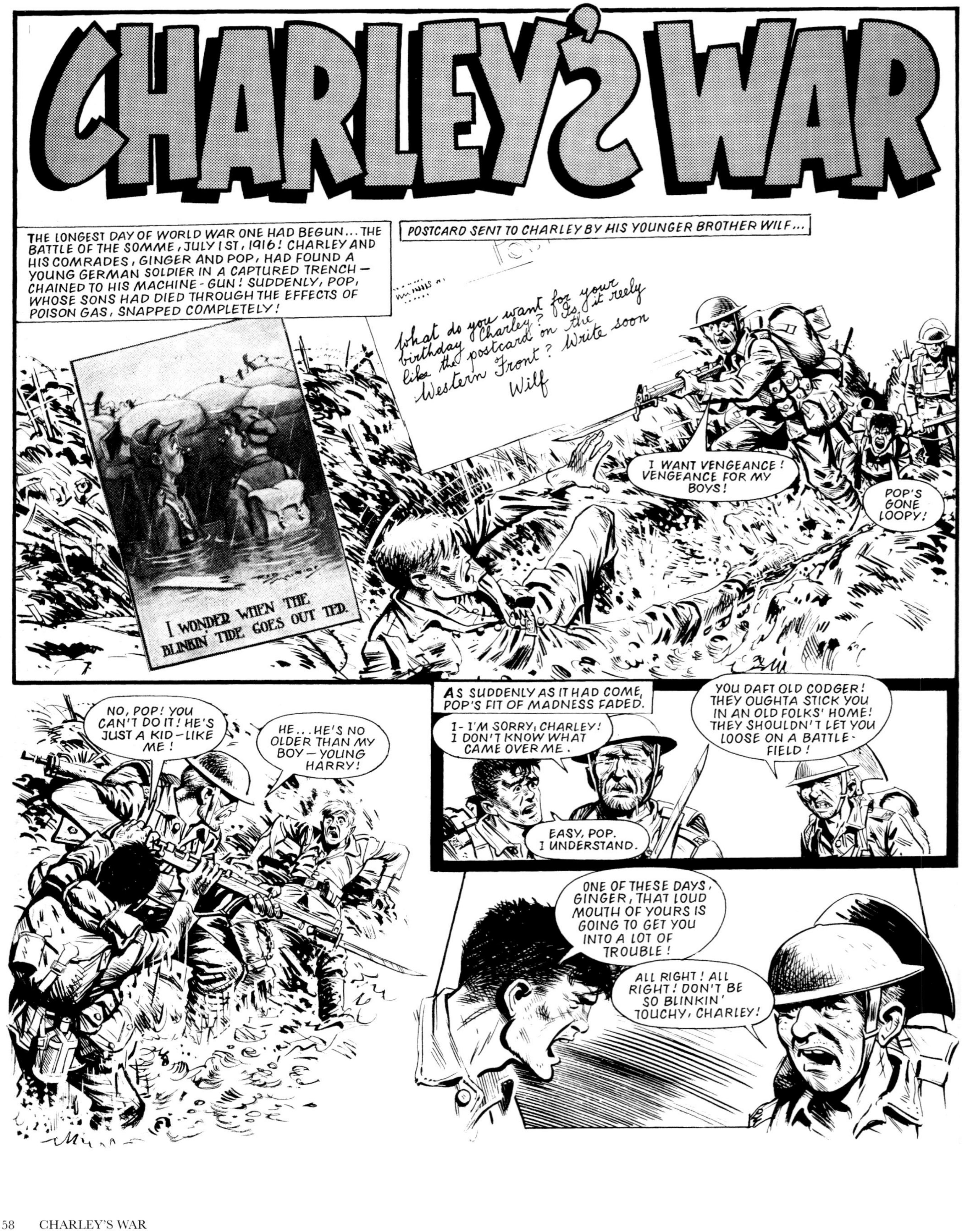

CHARLEY'S WAR
THE LONGEST DAY OF WORLD WAR ONE HAD BEGUN... THE BATTLE OF THE SOMME, JULY 1ST, 1916! CHARLEY AND HIS COMRADES, GINGER AND POP, HAD FOUND A YOUNG GERMAN SOLDIER IN A CAPTURED TRENCH — CHAINED TO HIS MACHINE-GUN! SUDDENLY, POP, WHOSE SONS HAD DIED THROUGH THE EFFECTS OF POISON GAS, SNAPPED COMPLETELY!
POSTCARD SENT TO CHARLEY BY HIS YOUNGER BROTHER WILF...
What do you want for your birthday Charley? Is it reely like the postcard on the Western Front? Write soon Wilf
I WONDER WHEN THE BLINKIN' TIDE GOES OUT TED.
I WANT VENGEANCE! VENGEANCE FOR MY BOYS!
POP'S GONE LOOPY!
NO, POP! YOU CAN'T DO IT! HE'S JUST A KID—LIKE ME!
HE...HE'S NO OLDER THAN MY BOY—YOUNG HARRY!
AS SUDDENLY AS IT HAD COME, POP'S FIT OF MADNESS FADED.
I-I'M SORRY, CHARLEY! I DON'T KNOW WHAT CAME OVER ME.
EASY, POP. I UNDERSTAND.
YOU DAFT OLD CODGER! THEY OUGHTA STICK YOU IN AN OLD FOLKS' HOME! THEY SHOULDN'T LET YOU LOOSE ON A BATTLE-FIELD!
ONE OF THESE DAYS, GINGER, THAT LOUD MOUTH OF YOURS IS GOING TO GET YOU INTO A LOT OF TROUBLE!
ALL RIGHT! ALL RIGHT! DON'T BE SO BLINKIN' TOUCHY, CHARLEY!

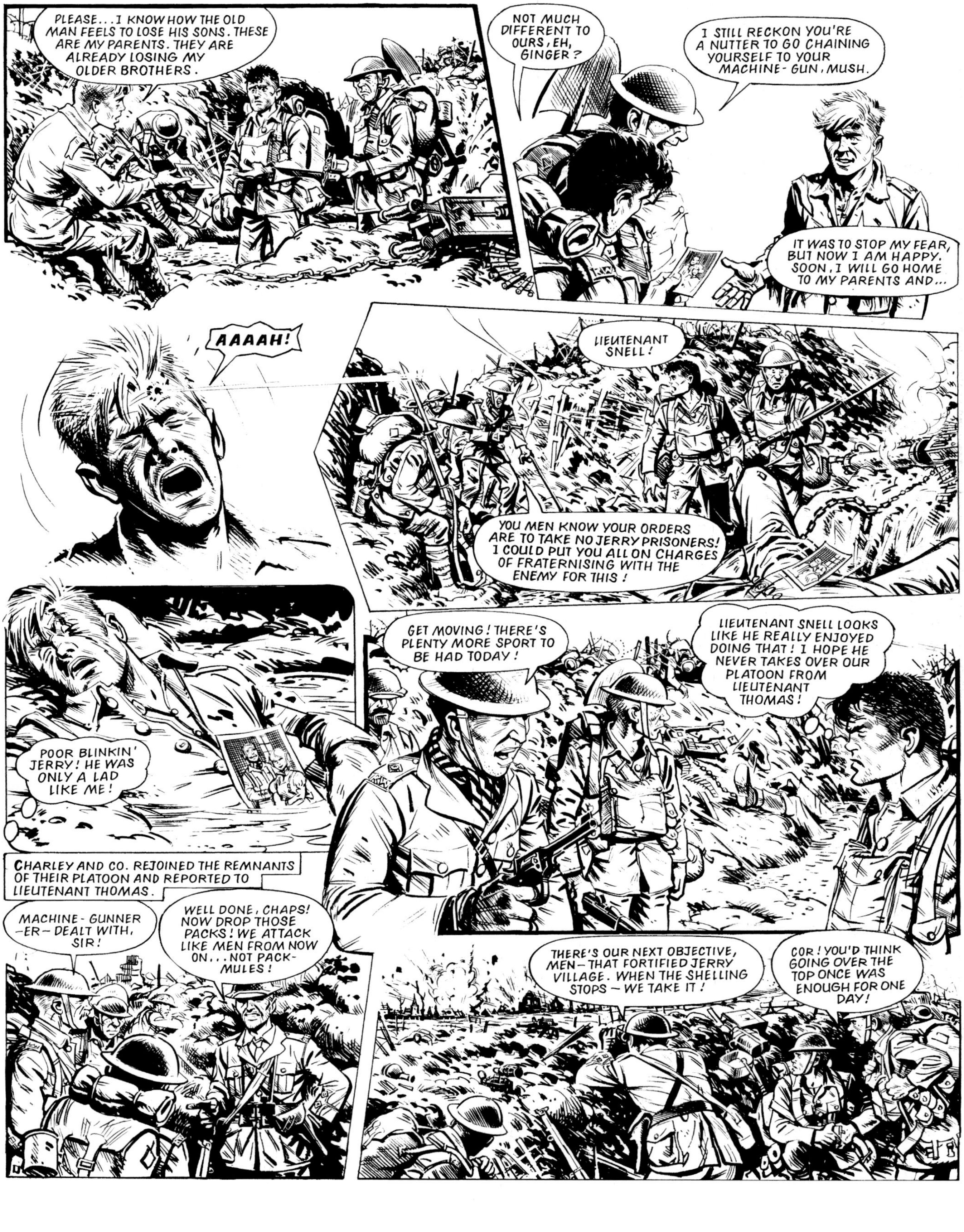
PLEASE... I KNOW HOW THE OLD MAN FEELS TO LOSE HIS SONS. THESE ARE MY PARENTS. THEY ARE ALREADY LOSING MY OLDER BROTHERS.
NOT MUCH DIFFERENT TO OURS, EH, GINGER?
I STILL RECKON YOU'RE A NUTTER TO GO CHAINING YOURSELF TO YOUR MACHINE-GUN, MUSH.
IT WAS TO STOP MY FEAR, BUT NOW I AM HAPPY. SOON, I WILL GO HOME TO MY PARENTS AND...
AAAAH!
LIEUTENANT SNELL!
YOU MEN KNOW YOUR ORDERS ARE TO TAKE NO JERRY PRISONERS! I COULD PUT YOU ALL ON CHARGES OF FRATERNISING WITH THE ENEMY FOR THIS!
POOR BLINKIN' JERRY! HE WAS ONLY A LAD LIKE ME!
GET MOVING! THERE'S PLENTY MORE SPORT TO BE HAD TODAY!
LIEUTENANT SNELL LOOKS LIKE HE REALLY ENJOYED DOING THAT! I HOPE HE NEVER TAKES OVER OUR PLATOON FROM LIEUTENANT THOMAS!
CHARLEY AND CO. REJOINED THE REMNANTS OF THEIR PLATOON AND REPORTED TO LIEUTENANT THOMAS.
MACHINE-GUNNER -ER- DEALT WITH, SIR!
WELL DONE, CHAPS! NOW DROP THOSE PACKS! WE ATTACK LIKE MEN FROM NOW ON... NOT PACK-MULES!
THERE'S OUR NEXT OBJECTIVE, MEN-THAT FORTIFIED JERRY VILLAGE. WHEN THE SHELLING STOPS-WE TAKE IT!
COR! YOU'D THINK GOING OVER THE TOP ONCE WAS ENOUGH FOR ONE DAY!

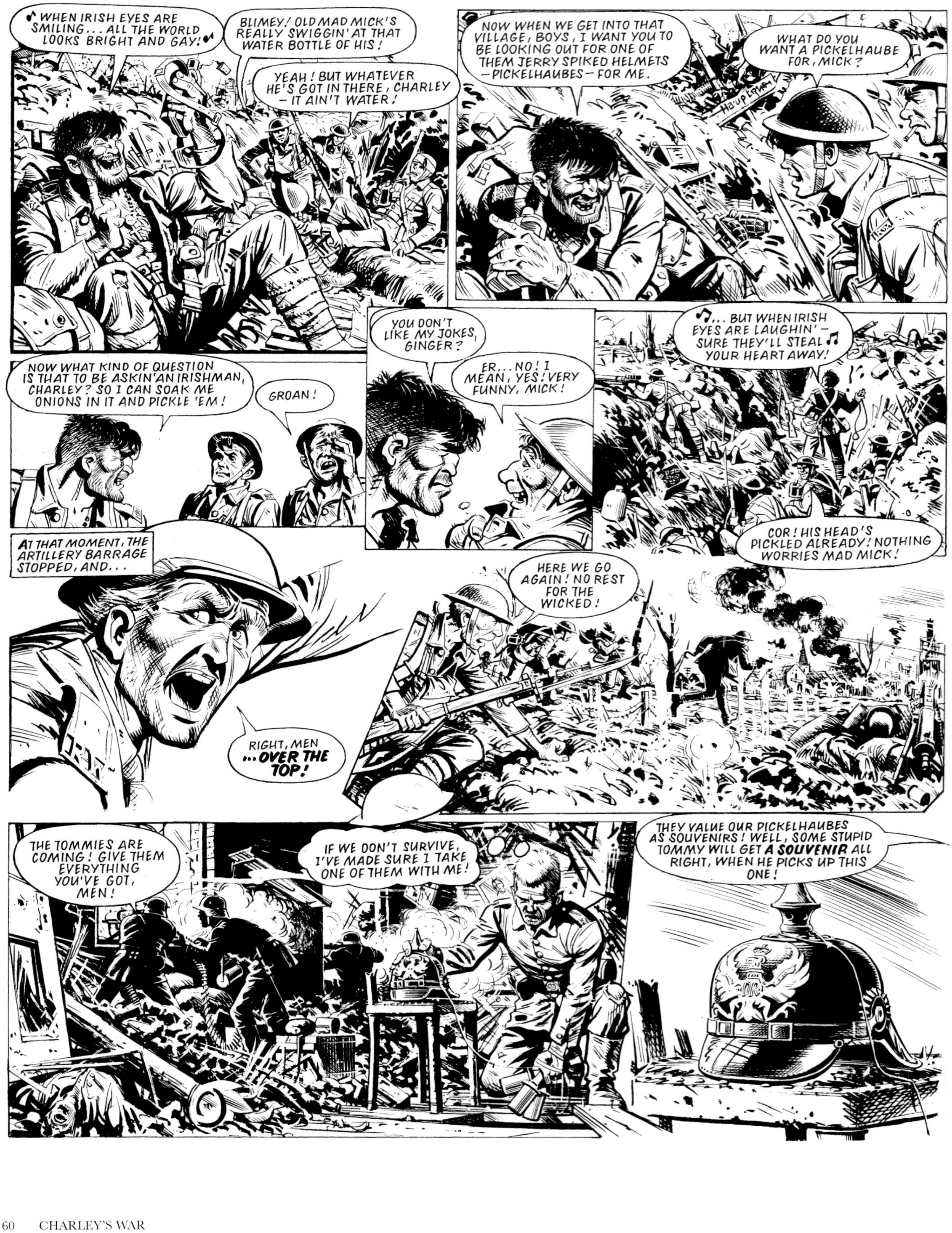

WHEN IRISH EYES ARE SMILING... ALL THE WORLD LOOKS BRIGHT AND GAY!
BLIMEY! OLD MAD MICK'S REALLY SWIGGIN' AT THAT WATER BOTTLE OF HIS!
YEAH! BUT WHATEVER HE'S GOT IN THERE, CHARLEY — IT AIN'T WATER!
NOW WHEN WE GET INTO THAT VILLAGE, BOYS, I WANT YOU TO BE LOOKING OUT FOR ONE OF THEM JERRY SPIKED HELMETS — PICKELHAUBES — FOR ME.
WHAT DO YOU WANT A PICKELHAUBE FOR, MICK?
NOW WHAT KIND OF QUESTION IS THAT TO BE ASKIN' AN IRISHMAN, CHARLEY? SO I CAN SOAK ME ONIONS IN IT AND PICKLE 'EM!
GROAN!
YOU DON'T LIKE MY JOKES, GINGER?
ER... NO! I MEAN, YES! VERY FUNNY, MICK!
... BUT WHEN IRISH EYES ARE LAUGHIN' — SURE THEY'LL STEAL YOUR HEART AWAY!
COR! HIS HEAD'S PICKLED ALREADY! NOTHING WORRIES MAD MICK!
AT THAT MOMENT, THE ARTILLERY BARRAGE STOPPED, AND...
RIGHT, MEN ... OVER THE TOP!
HERE WE GO AGAIN! NO REST FOR THE WICKED!
THE TOMMIES ARE COMING! GIVE THEM EVERYTHING YOU'VE GOT, MEN!
IF WE DON'T SURVIVE, I'VE MADE SURE I TAKE ONE OF THEM WITH ME!
THEY VALUE OUR PICKELHAUBES AS SOUVENIRS! WELL, SOME STUPID TOMMY WILL GET A SOUVENIR ALL RIGHT, WHEN HE PICKS UP THIS ONE!

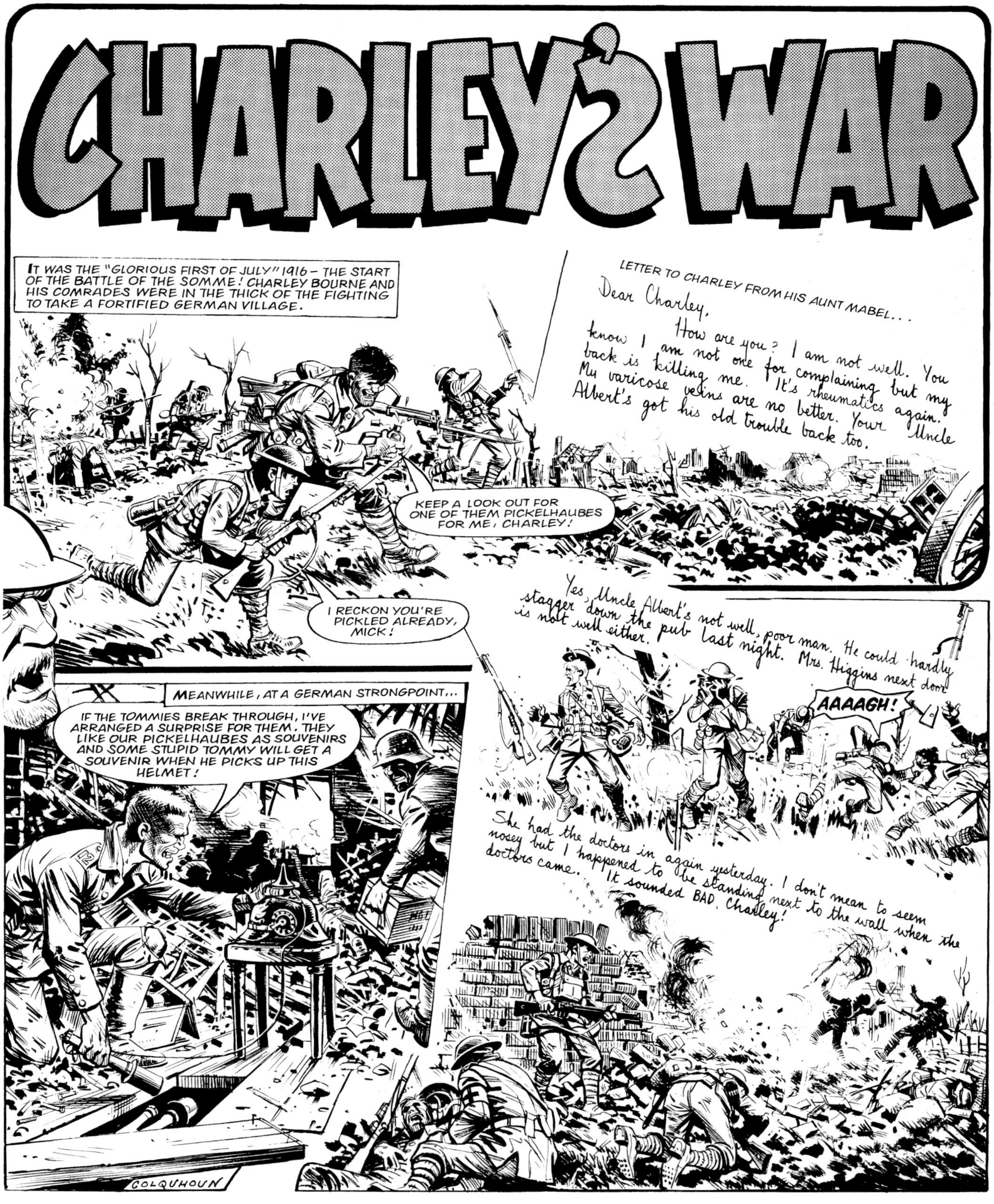
CHARLEY'S WAR
IT WAS THE "GLORIOUS FIRST OF JULY" 1916 – THE START OF THE BATTLE OF THE SOMME! CHARLEY BOURNE AND HIS COMRADES WERE IN THE THICK OF THE FIGHTING TO TAKE A FORTIFIED GERMAN VILLAGE.
LETTER TO CHARLEY FROM HIS AUNT MABEL...
Dear Charley,
How are you? I am not well. You know I am not one for complaining but my back is killing me. It's rheumatics again. My varicose veins are no better. Your Uncle Albert's got his old trouble back too.
KEEP A LOOK OUT FOR ONE OF THEM PICKELHAUBES FOR ME, CHARLEY!
I RECKON YOU'RE PICKLED ALREADY, MICK!
Yes, Uncle Albert's not well, poor man. He could hardly stagger down the pub last night. Mrs. Higgins next door is not well either.
AAAAGH!
MEANWHILE, AT A GERMAN STRONGPOINT...
IF THE TOMMIES BREAK THROUGH, I'VE ARRANGED A SURPRISE FOR THEM. THEY LIKE OUR PICKELHAUBES AS SOUVENIRS AND SOME STUPID TOMMY WILL GET A SOUVENIR WHEN HE PICKS UP THIS HELMET!
She had the doctors in again yesterday. I don't mean to seem nosey but I happened to be standing next to the wall when the doctors came. It sounded BAD, Charley!
COLQUHOUN

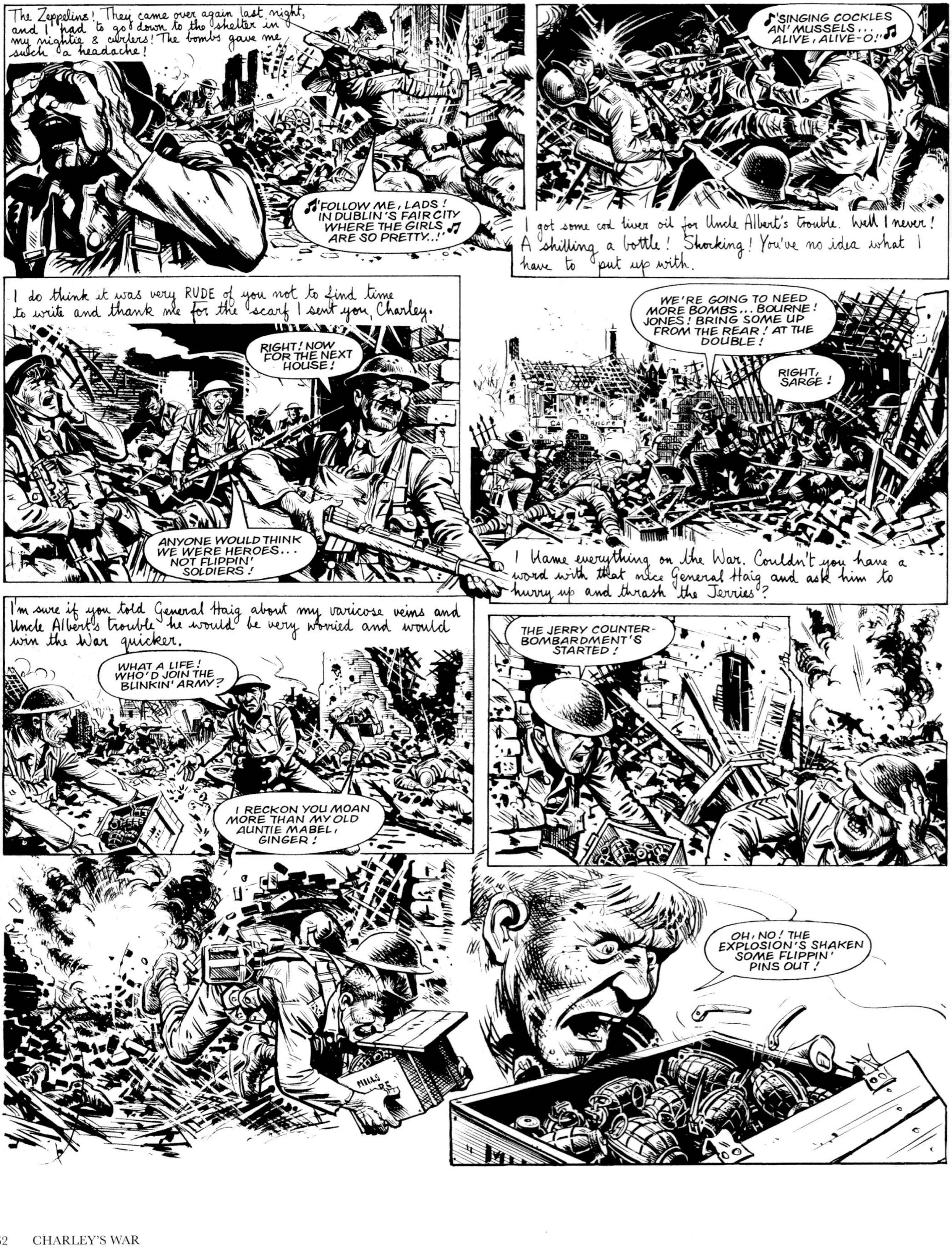
The Zeppelins! They came over again last night, and I had to go down to the shelter in my nightie & curlers! The bombs gave me such a headache!
'FOLLOW ME, LADS! IN DUBLIN'S FAIR CITY WHERE THE GIRLS ARE SO PRETTY..!'
'SINGING COCKLES AN' MUSSELS... ALIVE, ALIVE-O!'
I got some cod liver oil for Uncle Albert's trouble. Well I never! A shilling a bottle! Shocking! You've no idea what I have to put up with.
I do think it was very RUDE of you not to find time to write and thank me for the scarf I sent you, Charley.
RIGHT! NOW FOR THE NEXT HOUSE!
ANYONE WOULD THINK WE WERE HEROES... NOT FLIPPIN' SOLDIERS!
WE'RE GOING TO NEED MORE BOMBS... BOURNE! JONES! BRING SOME UP FROM THE REAR! AT THE DOUBLE!
RIGHT, SARGE!
I blame everything on the War. Couldn't you have a word with that nice General Haig and ask him to hurry up and thrash the Jerries?
I'm sure if you told General Haig about my varicose veins and Uncle Albert's trouble he would be very worried and would win the War quicker.
WHAT A LIFE! WHO'D JOIN THE BLINKIN' ARMY?
I RECKON YOU MOAN MORE THAN MY OLD AUNTIE MABEL, GINGER!
THE JERRY COUNTER-BOMBARDMENT'S STARTED!
OH, NO! THE EXPLOSION'S SHAKEN SOME FLIPPIN' PINS OUT!

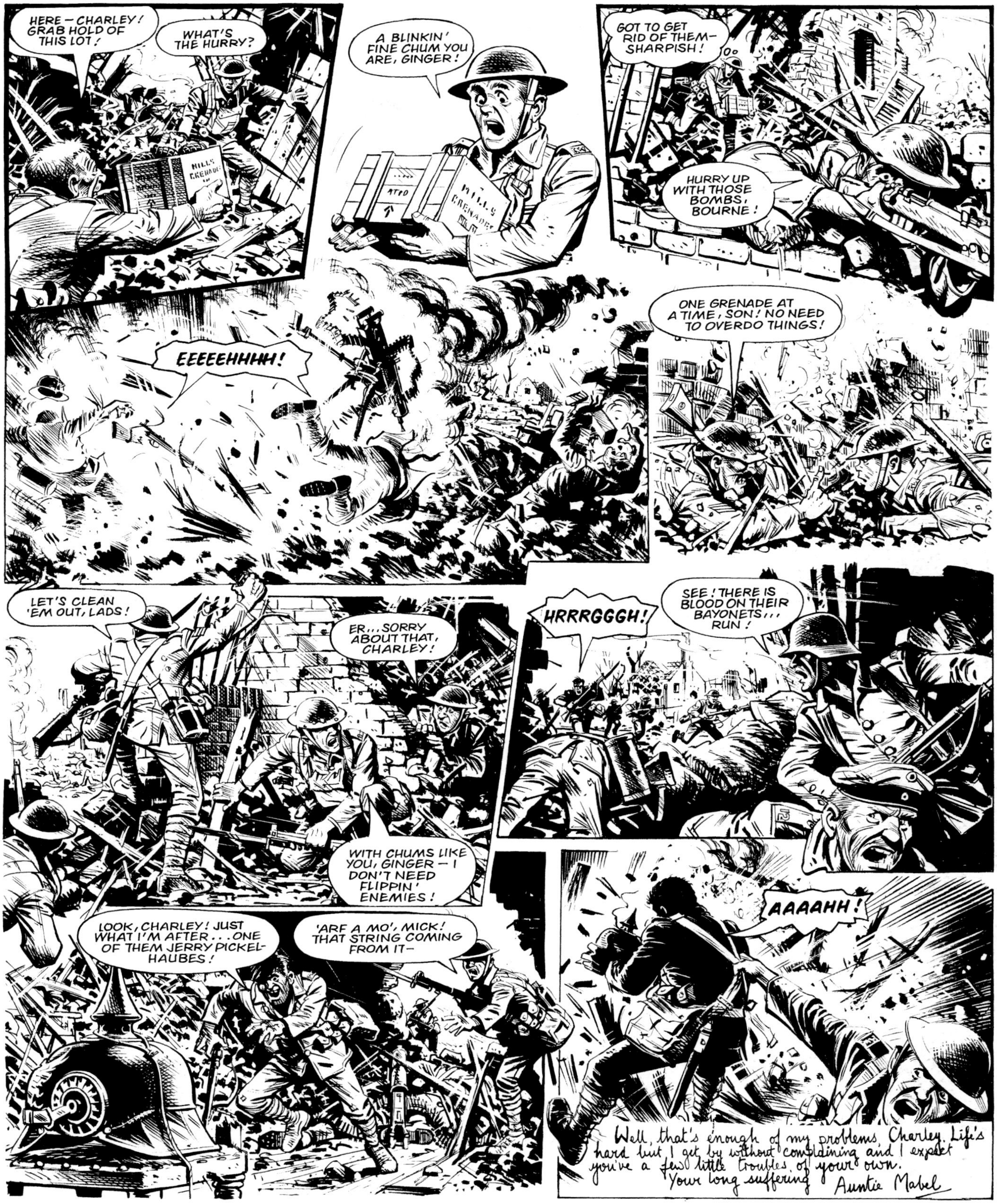
HERE – CHARLEY! GRAB HOLD OF THIS LOT!
WHAT'S THE HURRY?
A BLINKIN' FINE CHUM YOU ARE, GINGER!
GOT TO GET RID OF THEM – SHARPISH!
HURRY UP WITH THOSE BOMBS, BOURNE!
EEEEEHHHH!
ONE GRENADE AT A TIME, SON! NO NEED TO OVERDO THINGS!
LET'S CLEAN 'EM OUT, LADS!
ER... SORRY ABOUT THAT, CHARLEY!
WITH CHUMS LIKE YOU, GINGER – I DON'T NEED FLIPPIN' ENEMIES!
HRRRGGGH!
SEE! THERE IS BLOOD ON THEIR BAYONETS... RUN!
LOOK, CHARLEY! JUST WHAT I'M AFTER... ONE OF THEM JERRY PICKEL-HAUBES!
'ARF A MO', MICK! THAT STRING COMING FROM IT–
AAAAHH!
Well, that's enough of my problems, Charley. Life's hard but I get by without complaining and I expect you've a few little troubles of your own.
Your long suffering Auntie Mabel

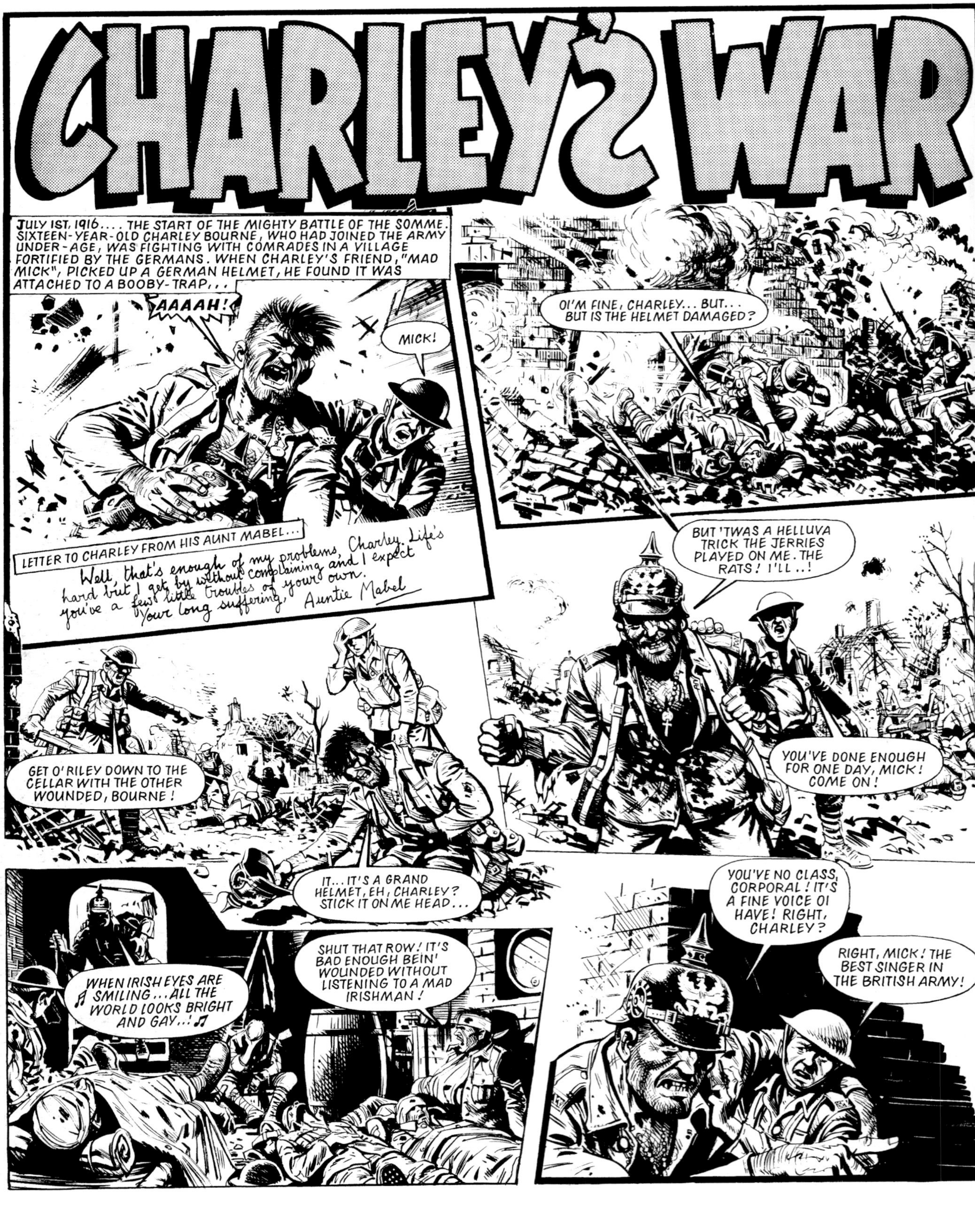
CHARLEY'S WAR
JULY 1ST, 1916... THE START OF THE MIGHTY BATTLE OF THE SOMME. SIXTEEN-YEAR-OLD CHARLEY BOURNE, WHO HAD JOINED THE ARMY UNDER-AGE, WAS FIGHTING WITH COMRADES IN A VILLAGE FORTIFIED BY THE GERMANS. WHEN CHARLEY'S FRIEND, "MAD MICK", PICKED UP A GERMAN HELMET, HE FOUND IT WAS ATTACHED TO A BOOBY-TRAP...
AAAAH!
MICK!
OI'M FINE, CHARLEY... BUT... BUT IS THE HELMET DAMAGED?
LETTER TO CHARLEY FROM HIS AUNT MABEL...
Well, that's enough of my problems, Charley. Life's hard but I get by without complaining and I expect you've a few little troubles of your own. Your long suffering, Auntie Mabel
BUT 'TWAS A HELLUVA TRICK THE JERRIES PLAYED ON ME. THE RATS! I'LL..!
GET O'RILEY DOWN TO THE CELLAR WITH THE OTHER WOUNDED, BOURNE!
YOU'VE DONE ENOUGH FOR ONE DAY, MICK! COME ON!
IT... IT'S A GRAND HELMET, EH, CHARLEY? STICK IT ON ME HEAD...
WHEN IRISH EYES ARE SMILING... ALL THE WORLD LOOKS BRIGHT AND GAY..!
SHUT THAT ROW! IT'S BAD ENOUGH BEIN' WOUNDED WITHOUT LISTENING TO A MAD IRISHMAN!
YOU'VE NO CLASS, CORPORAL! IT'S A FINE VOICE OI HAVE! RIGHT, CHARLEY?
RIGHT, MICK! THE BEST SINGER IN THE BRITISH ARMY!

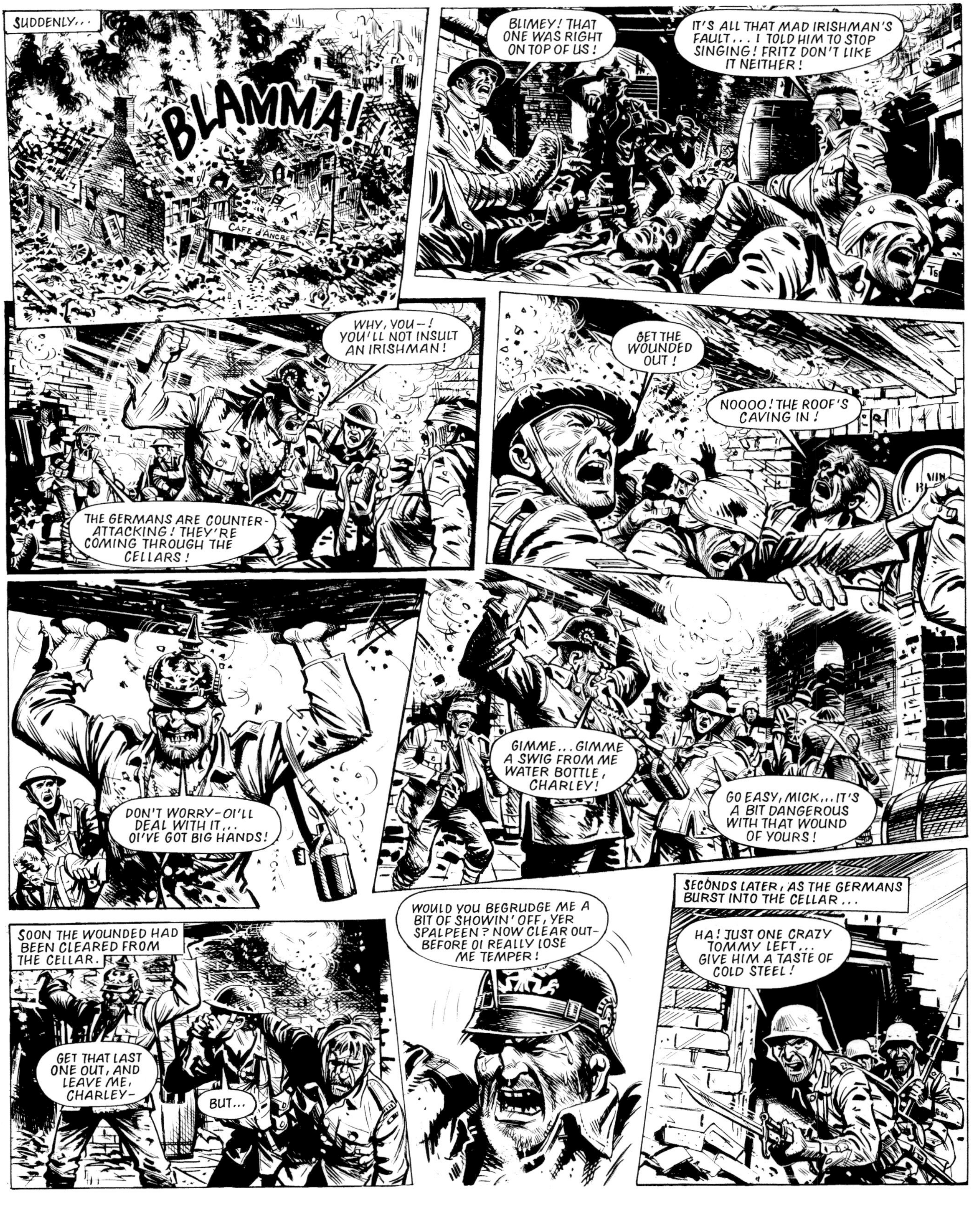
SUDDENLY...
BLAMMA!
CAFE d'ANCRE
BLIMEY! THAT ONE WAS RIGHT ON TOP OF US!
IT'S ALL THAT MAD IRISHMAN'S FAULT... I TOLD HIM TO STOP SINGING! FRITZ DON'T LIKE IT NEITHER!
WHY, YOU-! YOU'LL NOT INSULT AN IRISHMAN!
THE GERMANS ARE COUNTER-ATTACKING! THEY'RE COMING THROUGH THE CELLARS!
GET THE WOUNDED OUT!
NOOOO! THE ROOF'S CAVING IN!
DON'T WORRY-OI'LL DEAL WITH IT... OI'VE GOT BIG HANDS!
GIMME... GIMME A SWIG FROM ME WATER BOTTLE, CHARLEY!
GO EASY, MICK... IT'S A BIT DANGEROUS WITH THAT WOUND OF YOURS!
SOON THE WOUNDED HAD BEEN CLEARED FROM THE CELLAR.
GET THAT LAST ONE OUT, AND LEAVE ME, CHARLEY-
BUT...
WOULD YOU BEGRUDGE ME A BIT OF SHOWIN' OFF, YER SPALPEEN? NOW CLEAR OUT-BEFORE OI REALLY LOSE ME TEMPER!
SECONDS LATER, AS THE GERMANS BURST INTO THE CELLAR...
HA! JUST ONE CRAZY TOMMY LEFT... GIVE HIM A TASTE OF COLD STEEL!

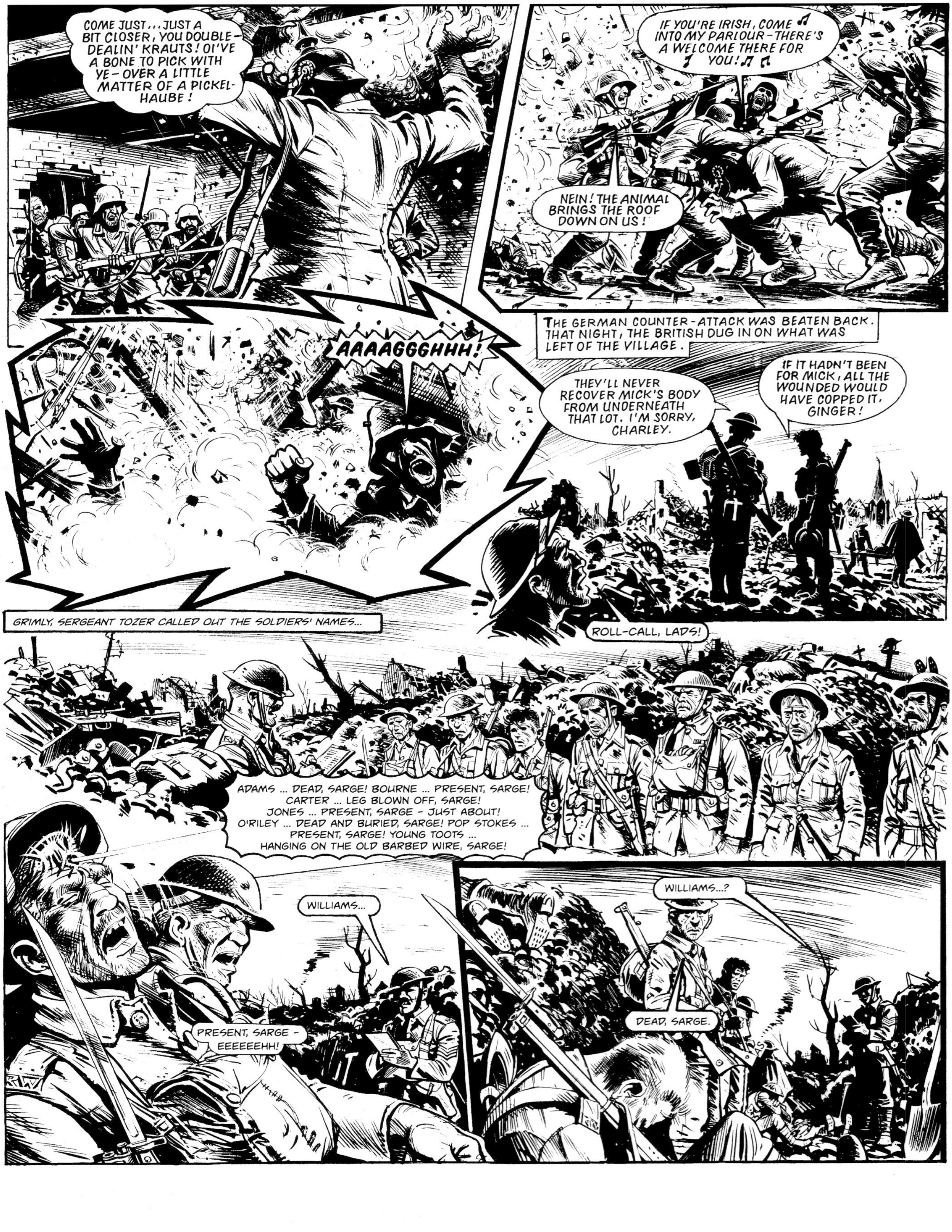

COME JUST... JUST A BIT CLOSER, YOU DOUBLE-DEALIN' KRAUTS! OI'VE A BONE TO PICK WITH YE – OVER A LITTLE MATTER OF A PICKEL-HAUBE!
IF YOU'RE IRISH, COME INTO MY PARLOUR – THERE'S A WELCOME THERE FOR YOU! ♫ ♫
NEIN! THE ANIMAL BRINGS THE ROOF DOWN ON US!
AAAAGGGHHH!
THE GERMAN COUNTER-ATTACK WAS BEATEN BACK. THAT NIGHT, THE BRITISH DUG IN ON WHAT WAS LEFT OF THE VILLAGE.
THEY'LL NEVER RECOVER MICK'S BODY FROM UNDERNEATH THAT LOT. I'M SORRY, CHARLEY.
IF IT HADN'T BEEN FOR MICK, ALL THE WOUNDED WOULD HAVE COPPED IT, GINGER!
GRIMLY, SERGEANT TOZER CALLED OUT THE SOLDIERS' NAMES...
ROLL-CALL, LADS!
ADAMS ... DEAD, SARGE! BOURNE ... PRESENT, SARGE! CARTER ... LEG BLOWN OFF, SARGE! JONES ... PRESENT, SARGE – JUST ABOUT! O'RILEY ... DEAD AND BURIED, SARGE! POP STOKES ... PRESENT, SARGE! YOUNG TOOTS ... HANGING ON THE OLD BARBED WIRE, SARGE!
WILLIAMS...
PRESENT, SARGE – EEEEEEHH!
WILLIAMS...?
DEAD, SARGE.

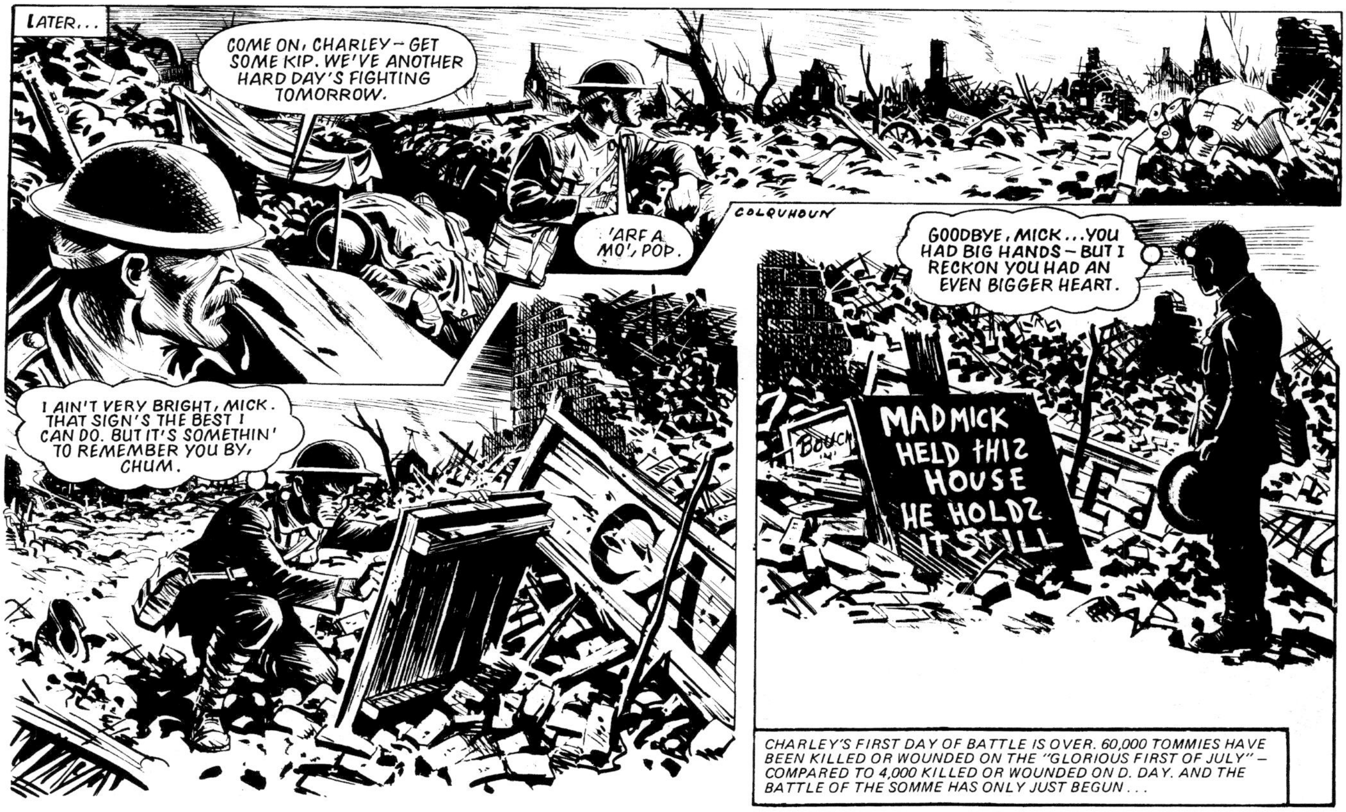
LATER...
COME ON, CHARLEY – GET SOME KIP. WE'VE ANOTHER HARD DAY'S FIGHTING TOMORROW.
'ARF A MO', POP.
COLQUHOUN
I AIN'T VERY BRIGHT, MICK. THAT SIGN'S THE BEST I CAN DO. BUT IT'S SOMETHIN' TO REMEMBER YOU BY, CHUM.
GOODBYE, MICK... YOU HAD BIG HANDS – BUT I RECKON YOU HAD AN EVEN BIGGER HEART.
MADMICK HELD THIZ HOUSE HE HOLDZ IT STILL
CHARLEY'S FIRST DAY OF BATTLE IS OVER. 60,000 TOMMIES HAVE BEEN KILLED OR WOUNDED ON THE "GLORIOUS FIRST OF JULY" – COMPARED TO 4,000 KILLED OR WOUNDED ON D. DAY. AND THE BATTLE OF THE SOMME HAS ONLY JUST BEGUN...

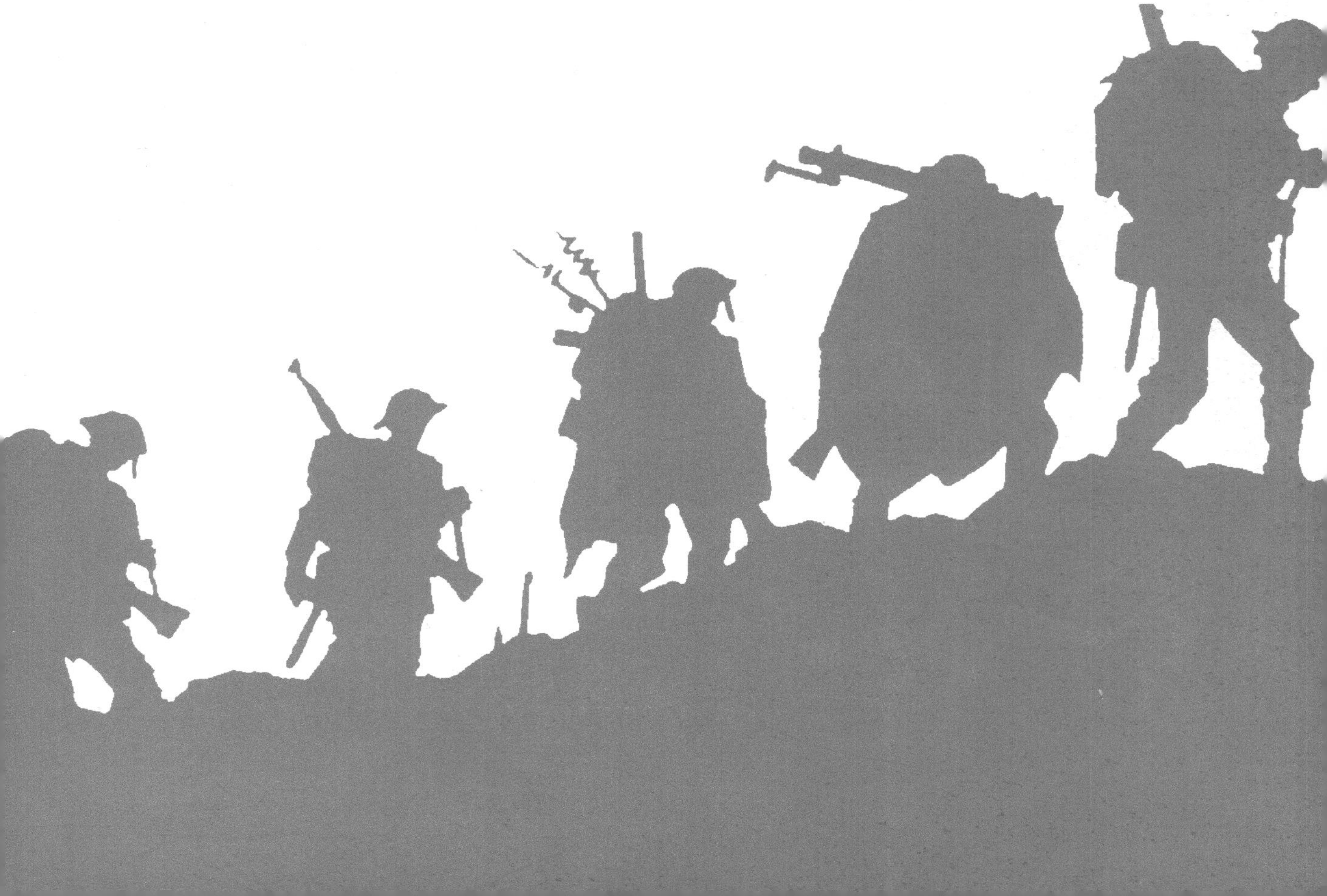

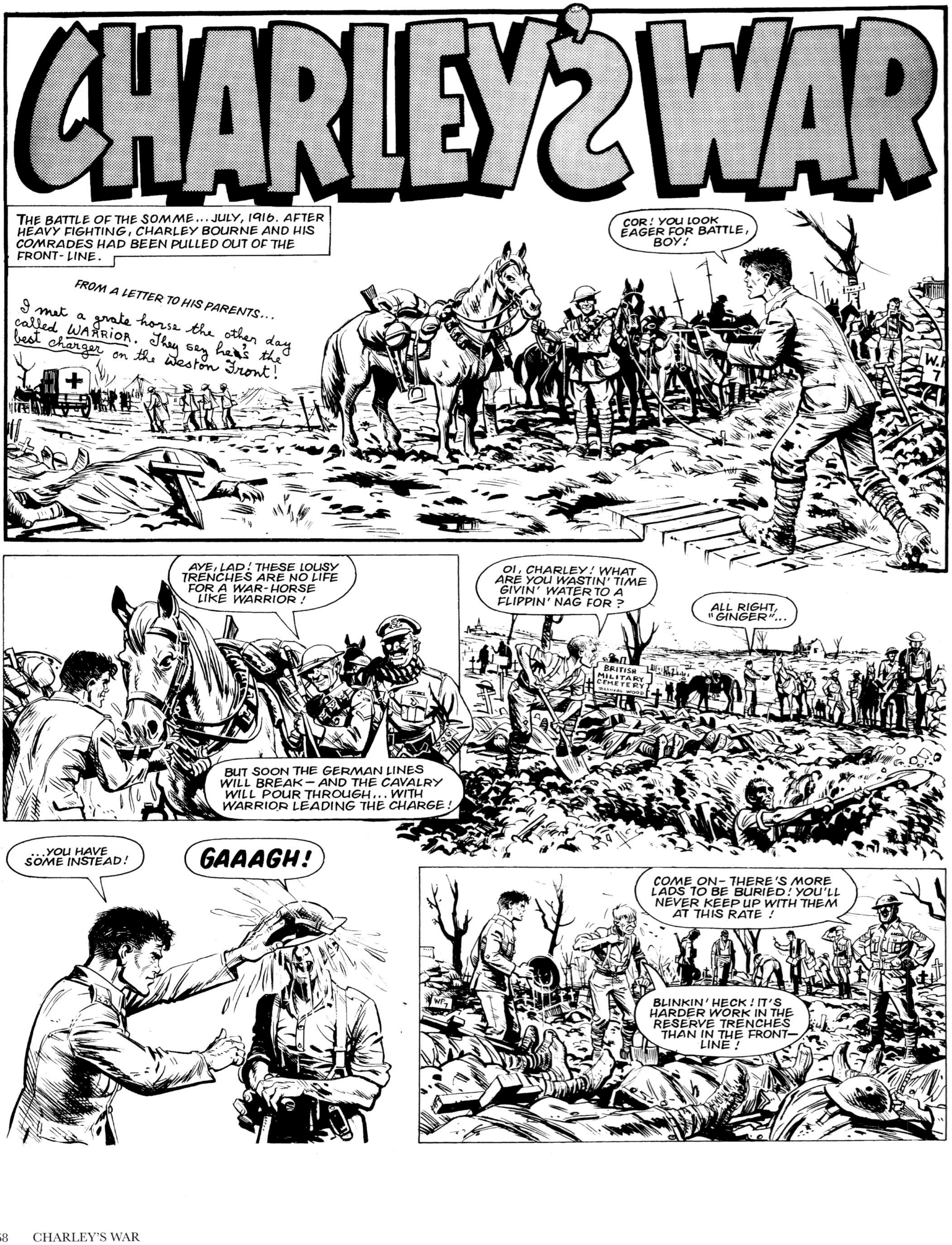
CHARLEY'S WAR
THE BATTLE OF THE SOMME... JULY, 1916. AFTER HEAVY FIGHTING, CHARLEY BOURNE AND HIS COMRADES HAD BEEN PULLED OUT OF THE FRONT-LINE.
FROM A LETTER TO HIS PARENTS...
I met a grate horse the other day called WARRIOR. They say he's the best charger on the Weston Front!
COR! YOU LOOK EAGER FOR BATTLE, BOY!
AYE, LAD! THESE LOUSY TRENCHES ARE NO LIFE FOR A WAR-HORSE LIKE WARRIOR!
BUT SOON THE GERMAN LINES WILL BREAK – AND THE CAVALRY WILL POUR THROUGH... WITH WARRIOR LEADING THE CHARGE!
OI, CHARLEY! WHAT ARE YOU WASTIN' TIME GIVIN' WATER TO A FLIPPIN' NAG FOR?
ALL RIGHT, "GINGER"...
BRITISH MILITARY CEMETERY
...YOU HAVE SOME INSTEAD!
GAAAGH!
COME ON– THERE'S MORE LADS TO BE BURIED! YOU'LL NEVER KEEP UP WITH THEM AT THIS RATE!
BLINKIN' HECK! IT'S HARDER WORK IN THE RESERVE TRENCHES THAN IN THE FRONT-LINE!

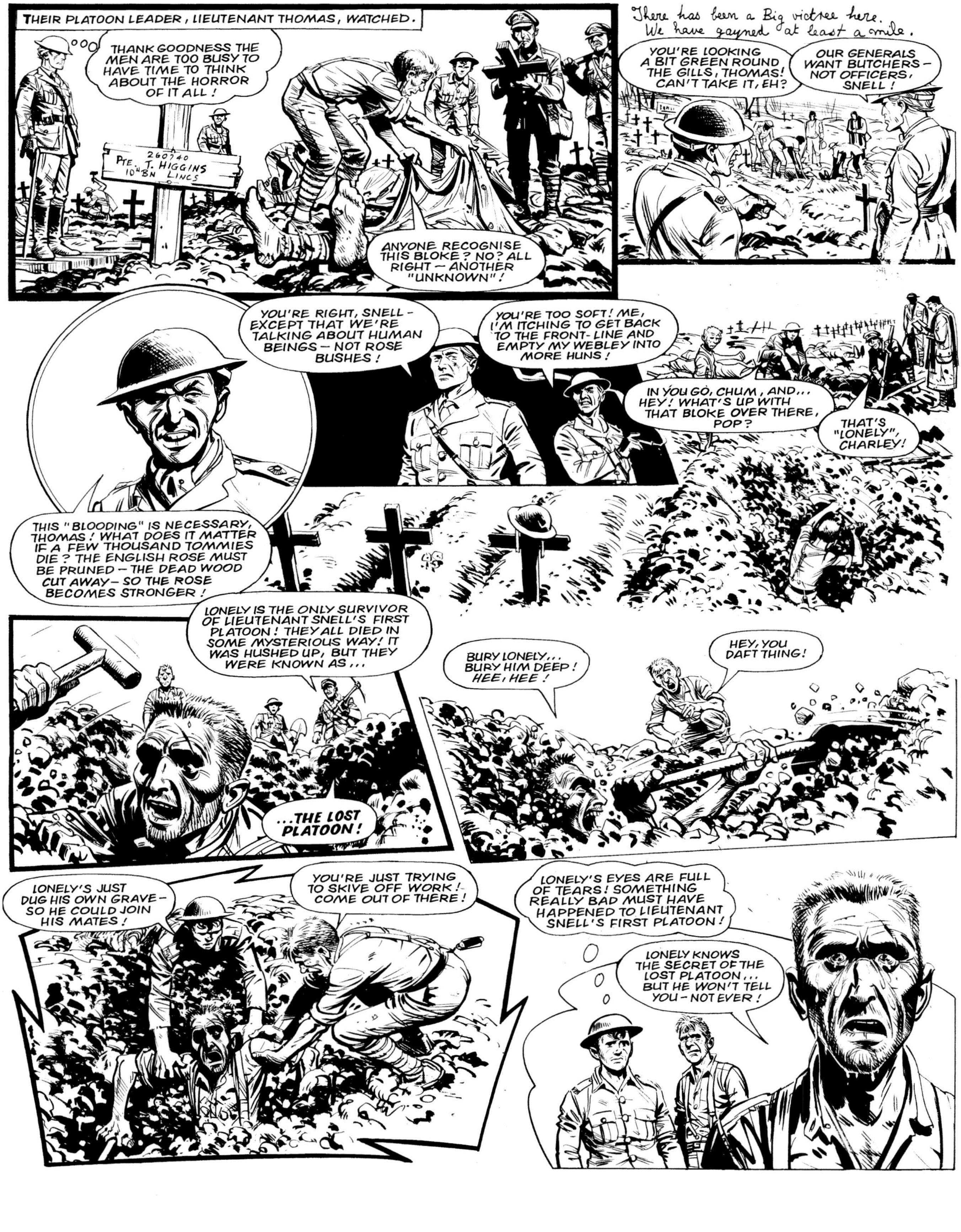

THEIR PLATOON LEADER, LIEUTENANT THOMAS, WATCHED.
THANK GOODNESS THE MEN ARE TOO BUSY TO HAVE TIME TO THINK ABOUT THE HORROR OF IT ALL!
260740 PTE. T. HIGGINS 10th BN LINCS
ANYONE RECOGNISE THIS BLOKE? NO? ALL RIGHT — ANOTHER "UNKNOWN"!
There has been a Big victree here. We have gayned at least a mile.
YOU'RE LOOKING A BIT GREEN ROUND THE GILLS, THOMAS! CAN'T TAKE IT, EH?
OUR GENERALS WANT BUTCHERS — NOT OFFICERS, SNELL!
THIS "BLOODING" IS NECESSARY, THOMAS! WHAT DOES IT MATTER IF A FEW THOUSAND TOMMIES DIE? THE ENGLISH ROSE MUST BE PRUNED — THE DEAD WOOD CUT AWAY — SO THE ROSE BECOMES STRONGER!
YOU'RE RIGHT, SNELL - EXCEPT THAT WE'RE TALKING ABOUT HUMAN BEINGS — NOT ROSE BUSHES!
YOU'RE TOO SOFT! ME, I'M ITCHING TO GET BACK TO THE FRONT-LINE AND EMPTY MY WEBLEY INTO MORE HUNS!
IN YOU GO, CHUM, AND... HEY! WHAT'S UP WITH THAT BLOKE OVER THERE, POP?
THAT'S "LONELY", CHARLEY!
LONELY IS THE ONLY SURVIVOR OF LIEUTENANT SNELL'S FIRST PLATOON! THEY ALL DIED IN SOME MYSTERIOUS WAY! IT WAS HUSHED UP, BUT THEY WERE KNOWN AS...
...THE LOST PLATOON!
BURY LONELY... BURY HIM DEEP! HEE, HEE!
HEY, YOU DAFT THING!
LONELY'S JUST DUG HIS OWN GRAVE - SO HE COULD JOIN HIS MATES!
YOU'RE JUST TRYING TO SKIVE OFF WORK! COME OUT OF THERE!
LONELY'S EYES ARE FULL OF TEARS! SOMETHING REALLY BAD MUST HAVE HAPPENED TO LIEUTENANT SNELL'S FIRST PLATOON!
LONELY KNOWS THE SECRET OF THE LOST PLATOON... BUT HE WON'T TELL YOU - NOT EVER!

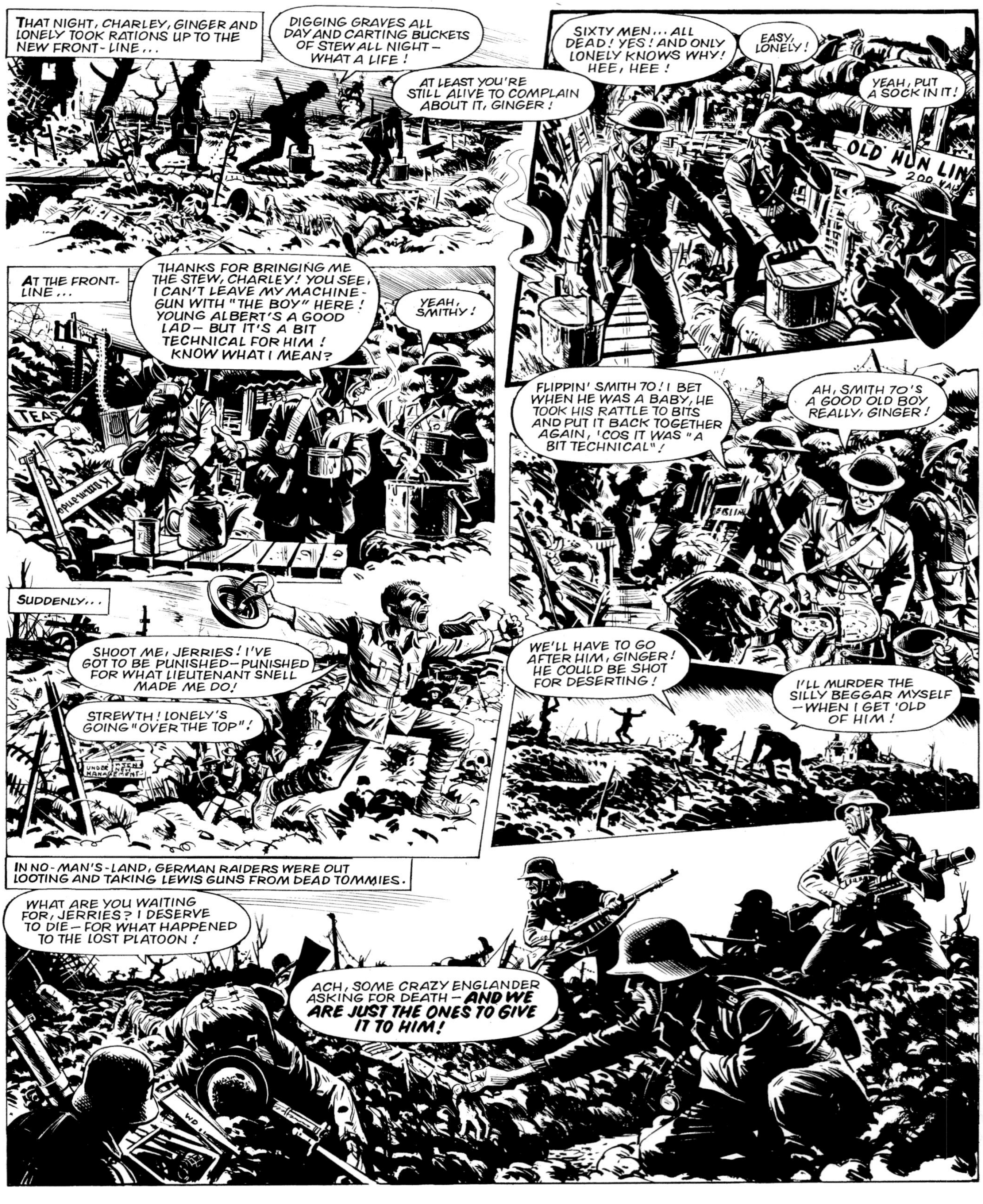
THAT NIGHT, CHARLEY, GINGER AND LONELY TOOK RATIONS UP TO THE NEW FRONT-LINE...
DIGGING GRAVES ALL DAY AND CARTING BUCKETS OF STEW ALL NIGHT – WHAT A LIFE!
AT LEAST YOU'RE STILL ALIVE TO COMPLAIN ABOUT IT, GINGER!
SIXTY MEN... ALL DEAD! YES! AND ONLY LONELY KNOWS WHY! HEE, HEE!
EASY, LONELY!
YEAH, PUT A SOCK IN IT!
AT THE FRONT-LINE...
THANKS FOR BRINGING ME THE STEW, CHARLEY! YOU SEE, I CAN'T LEAVE MY MACHINE-GUN WITH "THE BOY" HERE! YOUNG ALBERT'S A GOOD LAD – BUT IT'S A BIT TECHNICAL FOR HIM! KNOW WHAT I MEAN?
YEAH, SMITHY!
FLIPPIN' SMITH 70! I BET WHEN HE WAS A BABY, HE TOOK HIS RATTLE TO BITS AND PUT IT BACK TOGETHER AGAIN, 'COS IT WAS "A BIT TECHNICAL"!
AH, SMITH 70'S A GOOD OLD BOY REALLY, GINGER!
SUDDENLY...
SHOOT ME, JERRIES! I'VE GOT TO BE PUNISHED – PUNISHED FOR WHAT LIEUTENANT SNELL MADE ME DO!
STREWTH! LONELY'S GOING "OVER THE TOP"!
WE'LL HAVE TO GO AFTER HIM, GINGER! HE COULD BE SHOT FOR DESERTING!
I'LL MURDER THE SILLY BEGGAR MYSELF – WHEN I GET 'OLD OF HIM!
IN NO-MAN'S-LAND, GERMAN RAIDERS WERE OUT LOOTING AND TAKING LEWIS GUNS FROM DEAD TOMMIES.
WHAT ARE YOU WAITING FOR, JERRIES? I DESERVE TO DIE – FOR WHAT HAPPENED TO THE LOST PLATOON!
ACH, SOME CRAZY ENGLANDER ASKING FOR DEATH – AND WE ARE JUST THE ONES TO GIVE IT TO HIM!

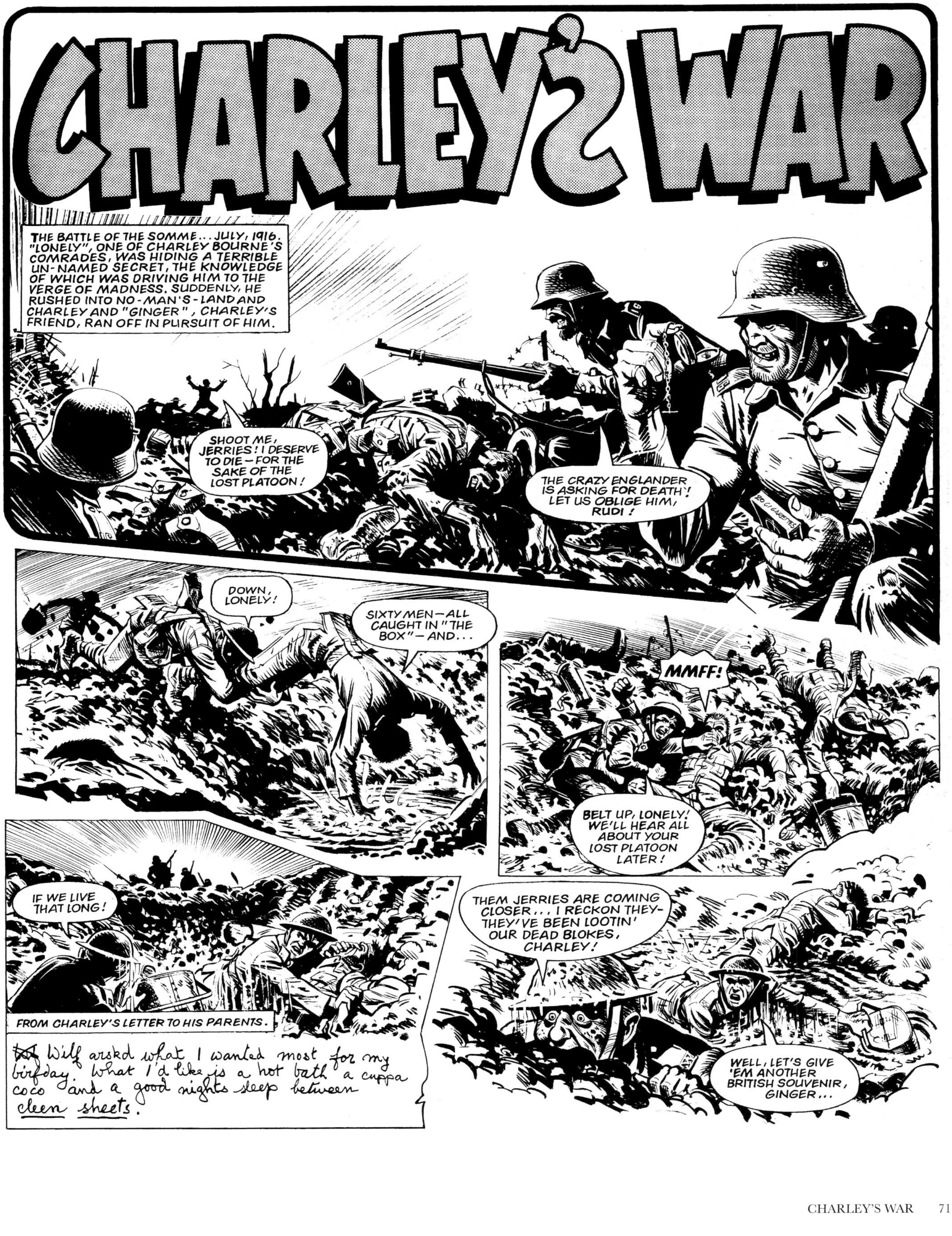
CHARLEY'S WAR
THE BATTLE OF THE SOMME... JULY, 1916. "LONELY", ONE OF CHARLEY BOURNE'S COMRADES, WAS HIDING A TERRIBLE UN-NAMED SECRET, THE KNOWLEDGE OF WHICH WAS DRIVING HIM TO THE VERGE OF MADNESS. SUDDENLY, HE RUSHED INTO NO-MAN'S-LAND AND CHARLEY AND "GINGER", CHARLEY'S FRIEND, RAN OFF IN PURSUIT OF HIM.
SHOOT ME, JERRIES! I DESERVE TO DIE—FOR THE SAKE OF THE LOST PLATOON!
THE CRAZY ENGLANDER IS ASKING FOR DEATH! LET US OBLIGE HIM, RUDI!
DOWN, LONELY!
SIXTY MEN—ALL CAUGHT IN "THE BOX"—AND...
MMFF!
BELT UP, LONELY! WE'LL HEAR ALL ABOUT YOUR LOST PLATOON LATER!
IF WE LIVE THAT LONG!
THEM JERRIES ARE COMING CLOSER... I RECKON THEY- THEY'VE BEEN LOOTIN' OUR DEAD BLOKES, CHARLEY!
WELL, LET'S GIVE 'EM ANOTHER BRITISH SOUVENIR, GINGER...
FROM CHARLEY'S LETTER TO HIS PARENTS.
Wilf arskd what I wanted most for my birfday. What I'd like is a hot bath a cuppa coco and a good nights sleep between cleen sheets.

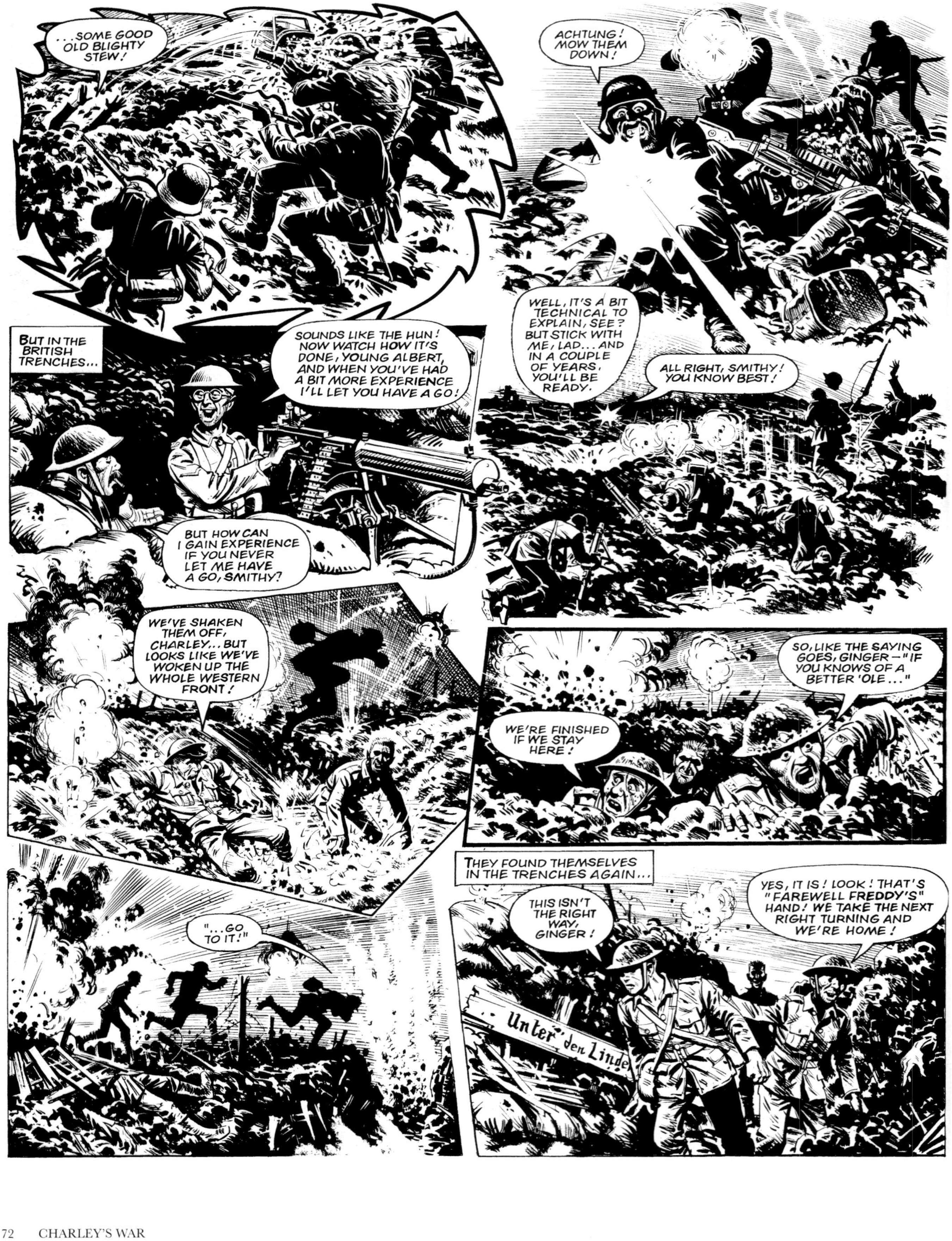

"...SOME GOOD OLD BLIGHTY STEW!"
ACHTUNG! MOW THEM DOWN!
BUT IN THE BRITISH TRENCHES...
SOUNDS LIKE THE HUN! NOW WATCH HOW IT'S DONE, YOUNG ALBERT, AND WHEN YOU'VE HAD A BIT MORE EXPERIENCE I'LL LET YOU HAVE A GO!
BUT HOW CAN I GAIN EXPERIENCE IF YOU NEVER LET ME HAVE A GO, SMITHY?
WELL, IT'S A BIT TECHNICAL TO EXPLAIN, SEE? BUT STICK WITH ME, LAD... AND IN A COUPLE OF YEARS, YOU'LL BE READY.
ALL RIGHT, SMITHY! YOU KNOW BEST!
WE'VE SHAKEN THEM OFF, CHARLEY... BUT LOOKS LIKE WE'VE WOKEN UP THE WHOLE WESTERN FRONT!
WE'RE FINISHED IF WE STAY HERE!
SO, LIKE THE SAYING GOES, GINGER – "IF YOU KNOWS OF A BETTER 'OLE..."
"...GO TO IT!"
THEY FOUND THEMSELVES IN THE TRENCHES AGAIN...
THIS ISN'T THE RIGHT WAY, GINGER!
YES, IT IS! LOOK! THAT'S "FAREWELL FREDDY'S" HAND! WE TAKE THE NEXT RIGHT TURNING AND WE'RE HOME!
Unter den Linde

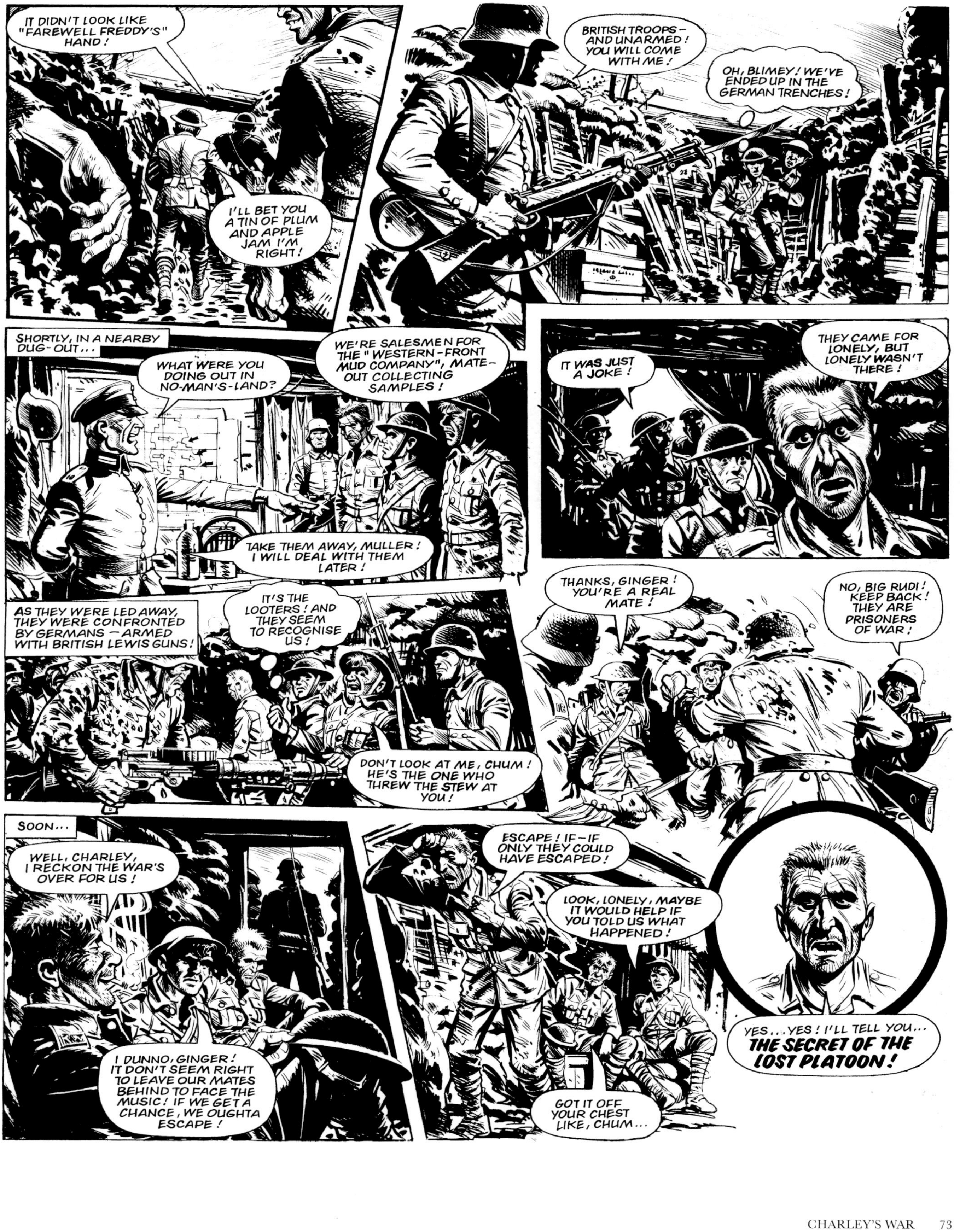
IT DIDN'T LOOK LIKE "FAREWELL FREDDY'S" HAND!
I'LL BET YOU A TIN OF PLUM AND APPLE JAM I'M RIGHT!
BRITISH TROOPS – AND UNARMED! YOU WILL COME WITH ME!
OH, BLIMEY! WE'VE ENDED UP IN THE GERMAN TRENCHES!
SHORTLY, IN A NEARBY DUG-OUT...
WHAT WERE YOU DOING OUT IN NO-MAN'S-LAND?
WE'RE SALESMEN FOR THE "WESTERN-FRONT MUD COMPANY", MATE – OUT COLLECTING SAMPLES!
TAKE THEM AWAY, MULLER! I WILL DEAL WITH THEM LATER!
IT WAS JUST A JOKE!
THEY CAME FOR LONELY, BUT LONELY WASN'T THERE!
AS THEY WERE LED AWAY, THEY WERE CONFRONTED BY GERMANS – ARMED WITH BRITISH LEWIS GUNS!
IT'S THE LOOTERS! AND THEY SEEM TO RECOGNISE US!
DON'T LOOK AT ME, CHUM! HE'S THE ONE WHO THREW THE STEW AT YOU!
THANKS, GINGER! YOU'RE A REAL MATE!
NO, BIG RUDI! KEEP BACK! THEY ARE PRISONERS OF WAR!
SOON...
WELL, CHARLEY, I RECKON THE WAR'S OVER FOR US!
I DUNNO, GINGER! IT DON'T SEEM RIGHT TO LEAVE OUR MATES BEHIND TO FACE THE MUSIC! IF WE GET A CHANCE, WE OUGHTA ESCAPE!
ESCAPE! IF – IF ONLY THEY COULD HAVE ESCAPED!
LOOK, LONELY, MAYBE IT WOULD HELP IF YOU TOLD US WHAT HAPPENED!
GOT IT OFF YOUR CHEST LIKE, CHUM...
YES...YES! I'LL TELL YOU... THE SECRET OF THE LOST PLATOON!

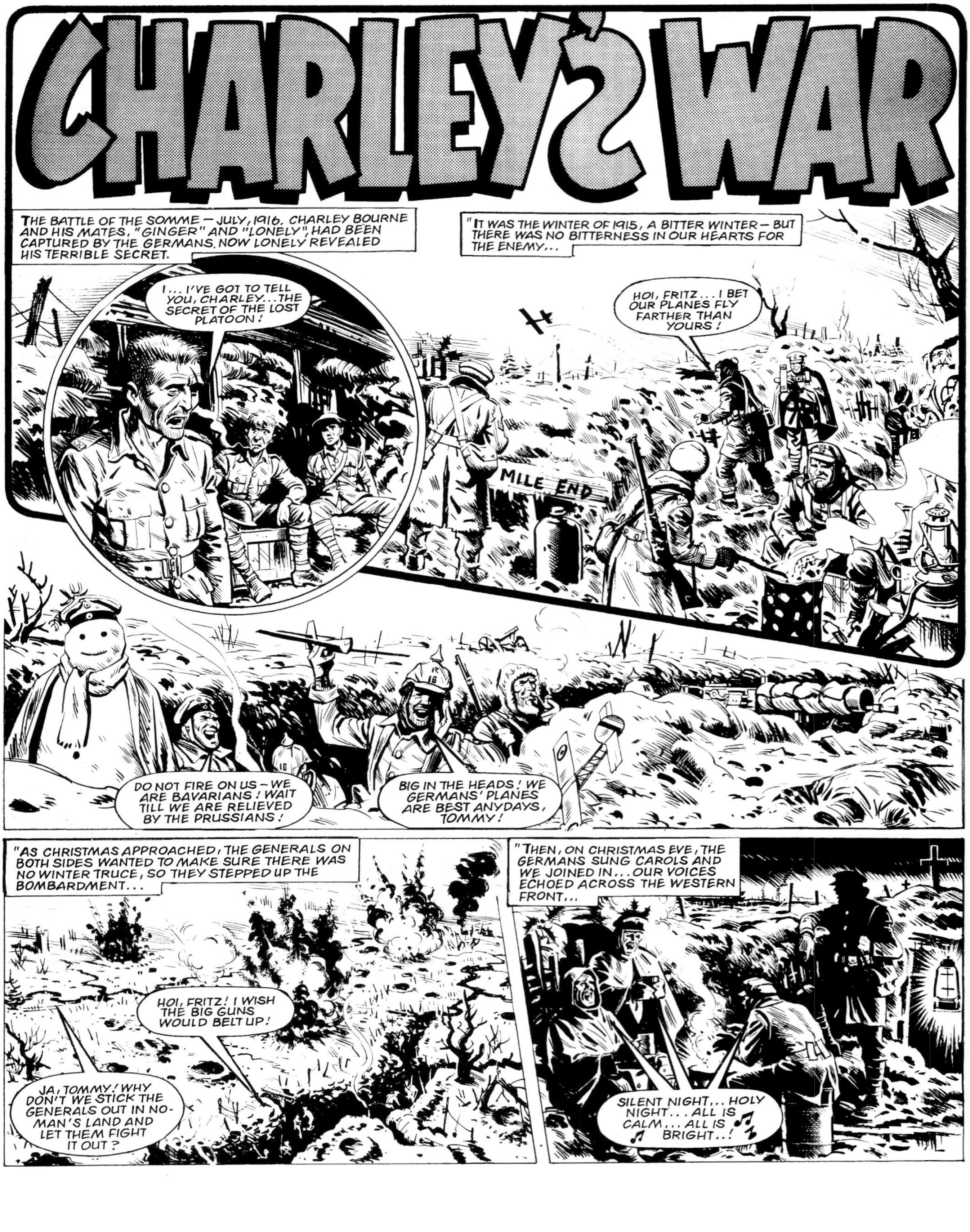
CHARLEY'S WAR
THE BATTLE OF THE SOMME – JULY, 1916. CHARLEY BOURNE AND HIS MATES, "GINGER" AND "LONELY", HAD BEEN CAPTURED BY THE GERMANS. NOW LONELY REVEALED HIS TERRIBLE SECRET.
I... I'VE GOT TO TELL YOU, CHARLEY... THE SECRET OF THE LOST PLATOON!
"IT WAS THE WINTER OF 1915, A BITTER WINTER – BUT THERE WAS NO BITTERNESS IN OUR HEARTS FOR THE ENEMY...
HOI, FRITZ... I BET OUR PLANES FLY FARTHER THAN YOURS!
MILE END
DO NOT FIRE ON US – WE ARE BAVARIANS! WAIT TILL WE ARE RELIEVED BY THE PRUSSIANS!
BIG IN THE HEADS! WE GERMANS' PLANES ARE BEST ANYDAYS, TOMMY!
"AS CHRISTMAS APPROACHED, THE GENERALS ON BOTH SIDES WANTED TO MAKE SURE THERE WAS NO WINTER TRUCE, SO THEY STEPPED UP THE BOMBARDMENT...
HOI, FRITZ! I WISH THE BIG GUNS WOULD BELT UP!
JA, TOMMY! WHY DON'T WE STICK THE GENERALS OUT IN NO-MAN'S LAND AND LET THEM FIGHT IT OUT?
"THEN, ON CHRISTMAS EVE, THE GERMANS SUNG CAROLS AND WE JOINED IN... OUR VOICES ECHOED ACROSS THE WESTERN FRONT...
SILENT NIGHT... HOLY NIGHT... ALL IS CALM... ALL IS BRIGHT...!

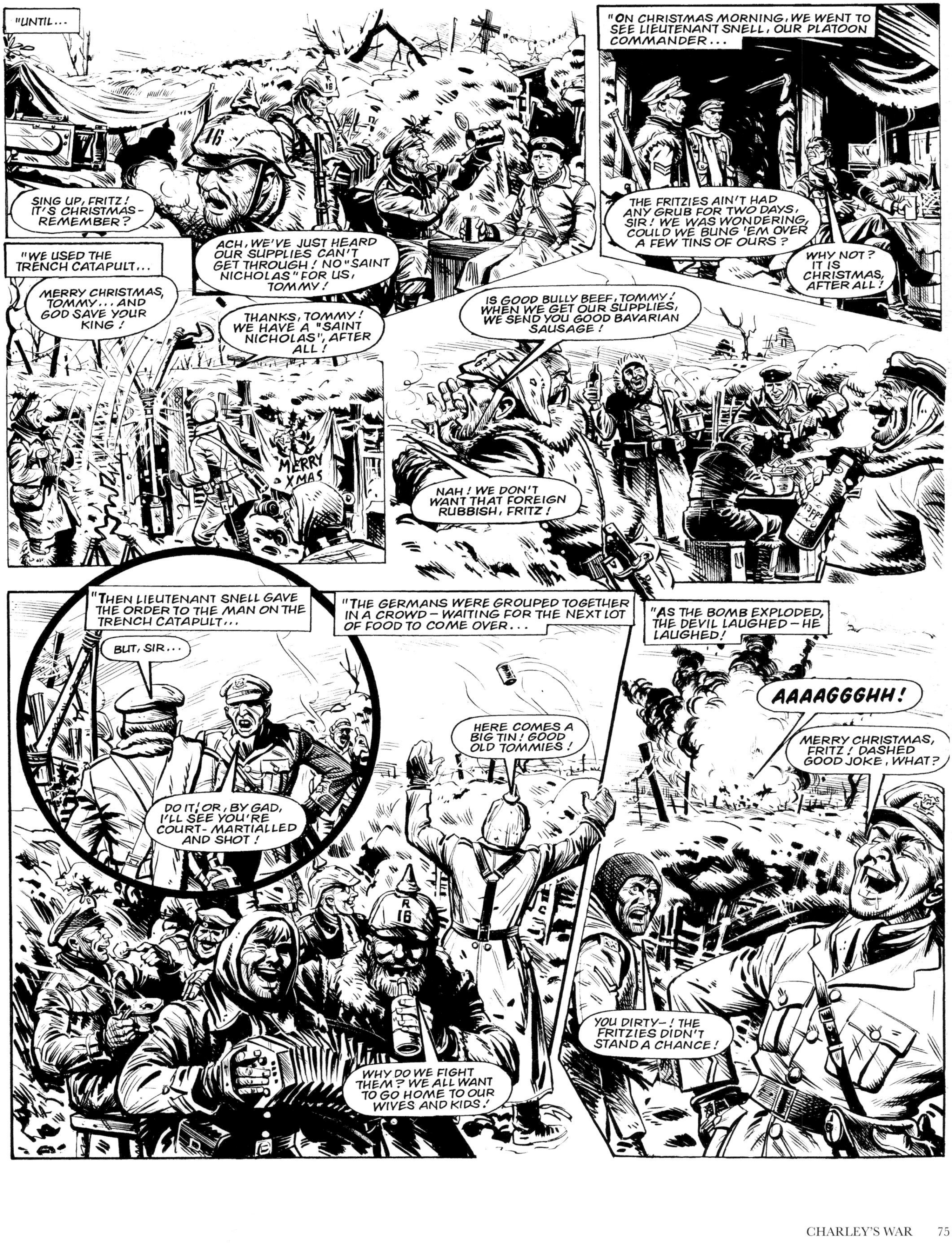
"UNTIL...
SING UP, FRITZ! IT'S CHRISTMAS - REMEMBER?
ACH, WE'VE JUST HEARD OUR SUPPLIES CAN'T GET THROUGH! NO "SAINT NICHOLAS" FOR US, TOMMY!
"ON CHRISTMAS MORNING, WE WENT TO SEE LIEUTENANT SNELL, OUR PLATOON COMMANDER...
THE FRITZIES AIN'T HAD ANY GRUB FOR TWO DAYS, SIR! WE WAS WONDERING, COULD WE BUNG 'EM OVER A FEW TINS OF OURS?
WHY NOT? IT IS CHRISTMAS, AFTER ALL!
"WE USED THE TRENCH CATAPULT...
MERRY CHRISTMAS, TOMMY... AND GOD SAVE YOUR KING!
THANKS, TOMMY! WE HAVE A "SAINT NICHOLAS", AFTER ALL!
MERRY XMAS
IS GOOD BULLY BEEF, TOMMY! WHEN WE GET OUR SUPPLIES, WE SEND YOU GOOD BAVARIAN SAUSAGE!
NAH! WE DON'T WANT THAT FOREIGN RUBBISH, FRITZ!
"THEN LIEUTENANT SNELL GAVE THE ORDER TO THE MAN ON THE TRENCH CATAPULT...
BUT, SIR...
DO IT, OR, BY GAD, I'LL SEE YOU'RE COURT-MARTIALLED AND SHOT!
"THE GERMANS WERE GROUPED TOGETHER IN A CROWD - WAITING FOR THE NEXT LOT OF FOOD TO COME OVER...
HERE COMES A BIG TIN! GOOD OLD TOMMIES!
WHY DO WE FIGHT THEM? WE ALL WANT TO GO HOME TO OUR WIVES AND KIDS!
"AS THE BOMB EXPLODED, THE DEVIL LAUGHED - HE LAUGHED!
AAAAGGGHH!
MERRY CHRISTMAS, FRITZ! DASHED GOOD JOKE, WHAT?
YOU DIRTY-! THE FRITZIES DIDN'T STAND A CHANCE!

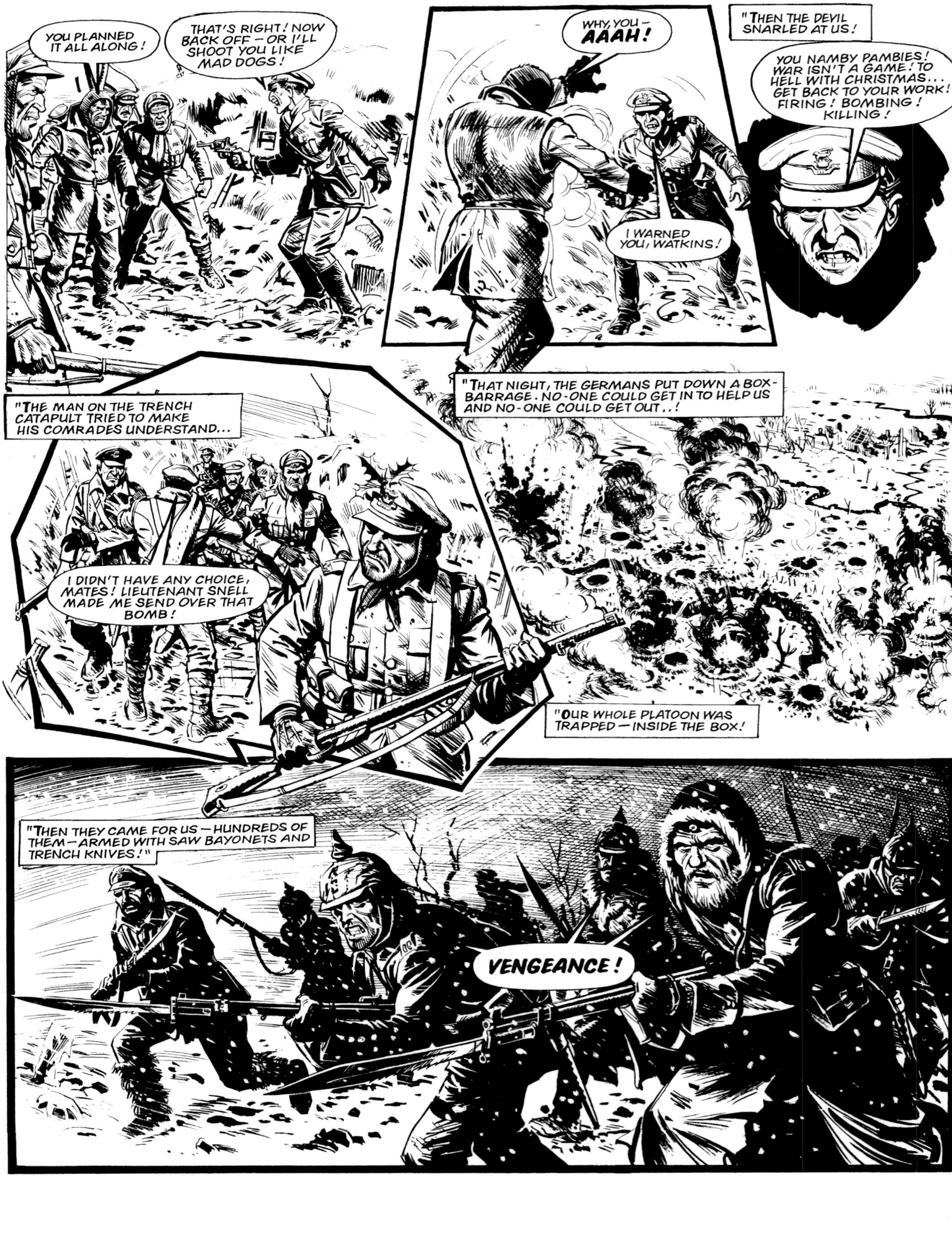
YOU PLANNED IT ALL ALONG!
THAT'S RIGHT! NOW BACK OFF - OR I'LL SHOOT YOU LIKE MAD DOGS!
WHY, YOU - AAAH!
I WARNED YOU, WATKINS!
"THEN THE DEVIL SNARLED AT US!
YOU NAMBY PAMBIES! WAR ISN'T A GAME! TO HELL WITH CHRISTMAS... GET BACK TO YOUR WORK! FIRING! BOMBING! KILLING!
"THE MAN ON THE TRENCH CATAPULT TRIED TO MAKE HIS COMRADES UNDERSTAND...
I DIDN'T HAVE ANY CHOICE, MATES! LIEUTENANT SNELL MADE ME SEND OVER THAT BOMB!
"THAT NIGHT, THE GERMANS PUT DOWN A BOX-BARRAGE. NO-ONE COULD GET IN TO HELP US AND NO-ONE COULD GET OUT..!
"OUR WHOLE PLATOON WAS TRAPPED - INSIDE THE BOX!
"THEN THEY CAME FOR US - HUNDREDS OF THEM - ARMED WITH SAW BAYONETS AND TRENCH KNIVES!"
VENGEANCE!

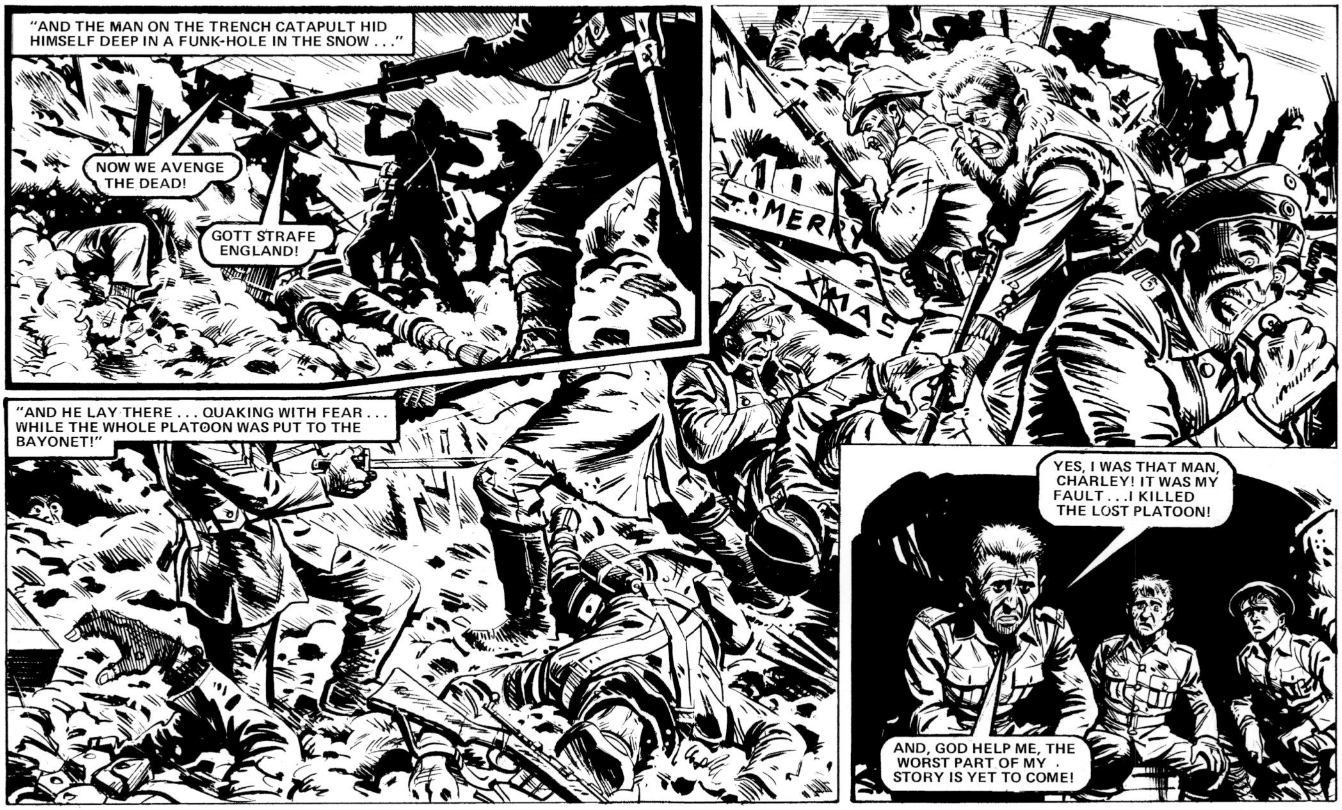
"AND THE MAN ON THE TRENCH CATAPULT HID HIMSELF DEEP IN A FUNK-HOLE IN THE SNOW . . ."
NOW WE AVENGE THE DEAD!
GOTT STRAFE ENGLAND!
MERRY
XMAS
"AND HE LAY THERE . . . QUAKING WITH FEAR . . . WHILE THE WHOLE PLATOON WAS PUT TO THE BAYONET!"
YES, I WAS THAT MAN, CHARLEY! IT WAS MY FAULT . . . I KILLED THE LOST PLATOON!
AND, GOD HELP ME, THE WORST PART OF MY STORY IS YET TO COME!

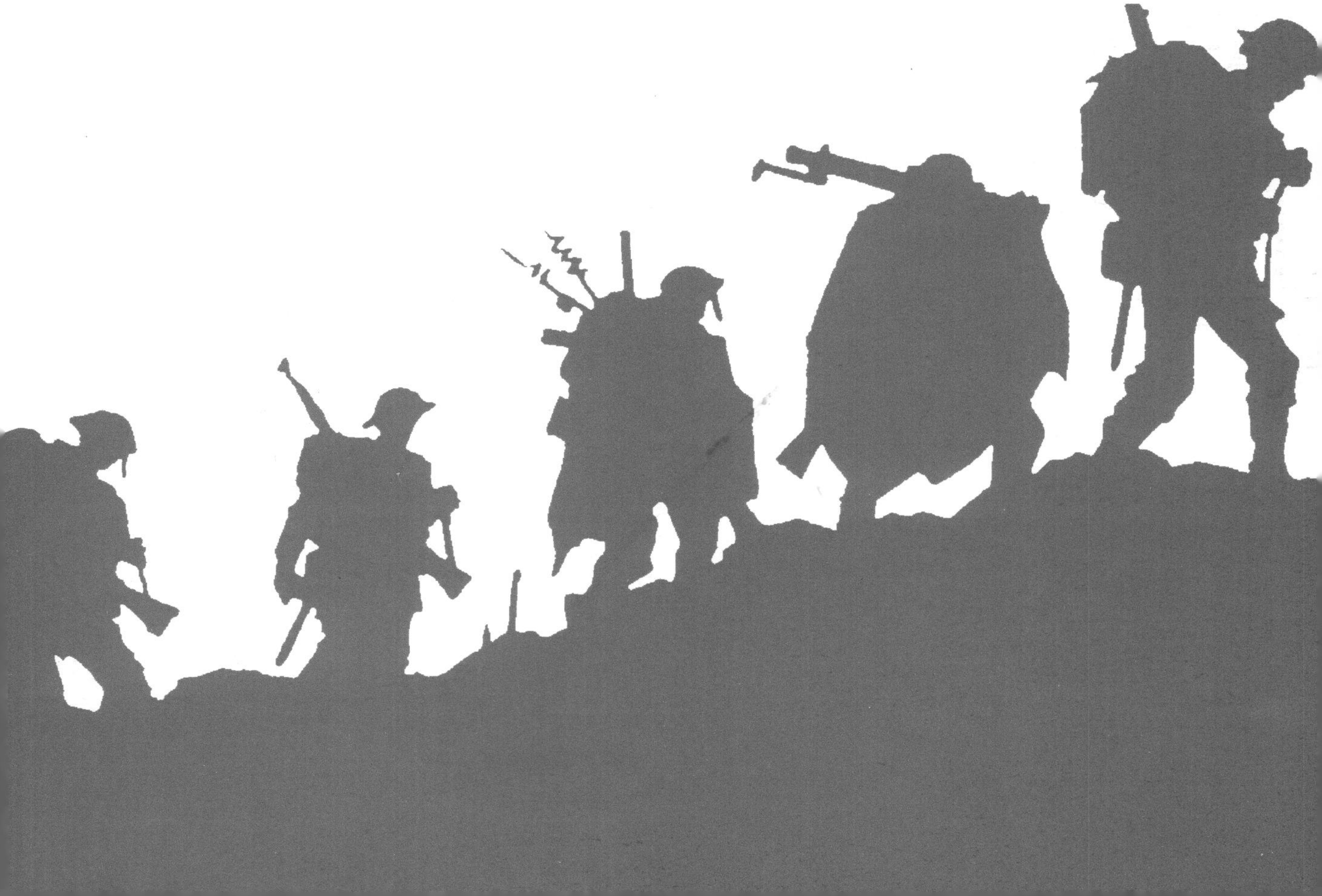

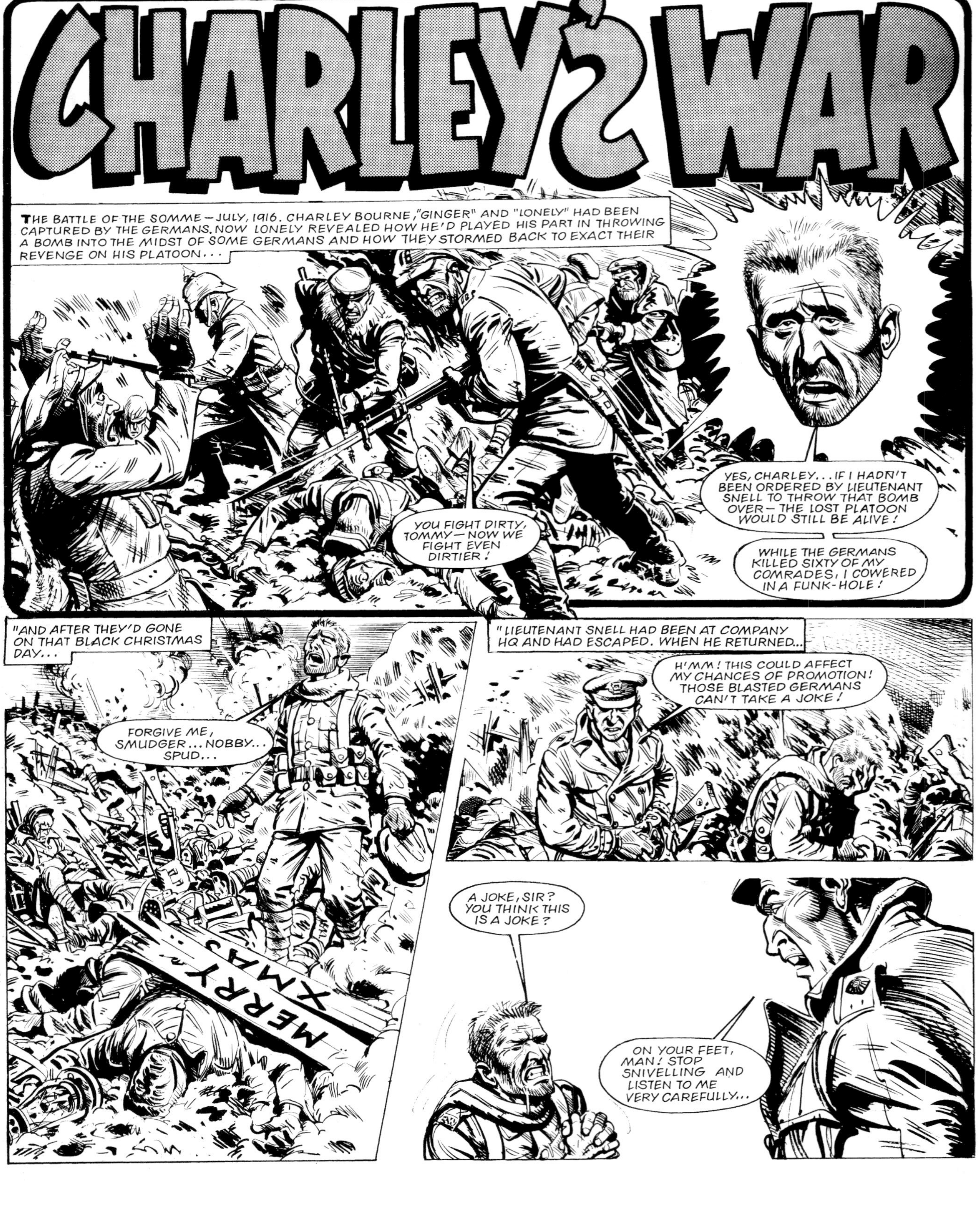
CHARLEY'S WAR
THE BATTLE OF THE SOMME – JULY, 1916. CHARLEY BOURNE, "GINGER" AND "LONELY" HAD BEEN CAPTURED BY THE GERMANS. NOW LONELY REVEALED HOW HE'D PLAYED HIS PART IN THROWING A BOMB INTO THE MIDST OF SOME GERMANS AND HOW THEY STORMED BACK TO EXACT THEIR REVENGE ON HIS PLATOON...
YOU FIGHT DIRTY, TOMMY – NOW WE FIGHT EVEN DIRTIER!
YES, CHARLEY... IF I HADN'T BEEN ORDERED BY LIEUTENANT SNELL TO THROW THAT BOMB OVER – THE LOST PLATOON WOULD STILL BE ALIVE!
WHILE THE GERMANS KILLED SIXTY OF MY COMRADES, I COWERED IN A FUNK-HOLE!
"AND AFTER THEY'D GONE ON THAT BLACK CHRISTMAS DAY...
FORGIVE ME, SMUDGER... NOBBY... SPUD...
MERRY XMAS
"LIEUTENANT SNELL HAD BEEN AT COMPANY HQ AND HAD ESCAPED. WHEN HE RETURNED...
H'MM! THIS COULD AFFECT MY CHANCES OF PROMOTION! THOSE BLASTED GERMANS CAN'T TAKE A JOKE!
A JOKE, SIR? YOU THINK THIS IS A JOKE?
ON YOUR FEET, MAN! STOP SNIVELLING AND LISTEN TO ME VERY CAREFULLY...

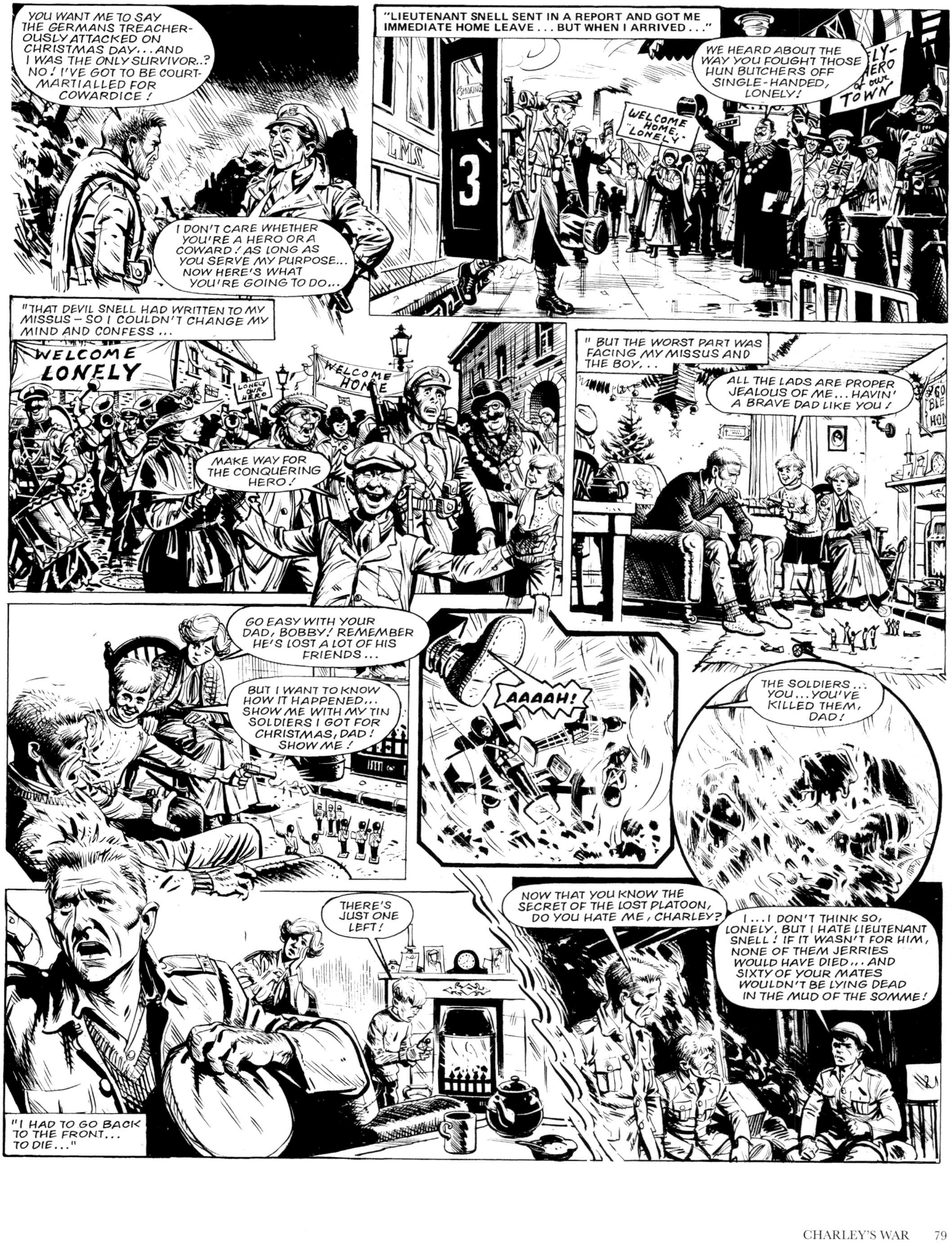

YOU WANT ME TO SAY THE GERMANS TREACHEROUSLY ATTACKED ON CHRISTMAS DAY... AND I WAS THE ONLY SURVIVOR..? NO! I'VE GOT TO BE COURT-MARTIALLED FOR COWARDICE!
I DON'T CARE WHETHER YOU'RE A HERO OR A COWARD! AS LONG AS YOU SERVE MY PURPOSE... NOW HERE'S WHAT YOU'RE GOING TO DO...
"LIEUTENANT SNELL SENT IN A REPORT AND GOT ME IMMEDIATE HOME LEAVE . . . BUT WHEN I ARRIVED . . ."
L.M.S.
3
WE HEARD ABOUT THE WAY YOU FOUGHT THOSE HUN BUTCHERS OFF SINGLE-HANDED, LONELY!
WELCOME HOME "LONELY"
HERO of our TOWN
"THAT DEVIL SNELL HAD WRITTEN TO MY MISSUS – SO I COULDN'T CHANGE MY MIND AND CONFESS ...
WELCOME LONELY
WELCOME HOME
LONELY OUR HERO
MAKE WAY FOR THE CONQUERING HERO!
" BUT THE WORST PART WAS FACING MY MISSUS AND THE BOY. . .
ALL THE LADS ARE PROPER JEALOUS OF ME... HAVIN' A BRAVE DAD LIKE YOU!
GO EASY WITH YOUR DAD, BOBBY! REMEMBER HE'S LOST A LOT OF HIS FRIENDS...
BUT I WANT TO KNOW HOW IT HAPPENED... SHOW ME WITH MY TIN SOLDIERS I GOT FOR CHRISTMAS, DAD! SHOW ME!
AAAAH!
THE SOLDIERS... YOU... YOU'VE KILLED THEM, DAD!
THERE'S JUST ONE LEFT!
NOW THAT YOU KNOW THE SECRET OF THE LOST PLATOON, DO YOU HATE ME, CHARLEY?
I... I DON'T THINK SO, LONELY. BUT I HATE LIEUTENANT SNELL! IF IT WASN'T FOR HIM, NONE OF THEM JERRIES WOULD HAVE DIED... AND SIXTY OF YOUR MATES WOULDN'T BE LYING DEAD IN THE MUD OF THE SOMME!
"I HAD TO GO BACK TO THE FRONT... TO DIE..."

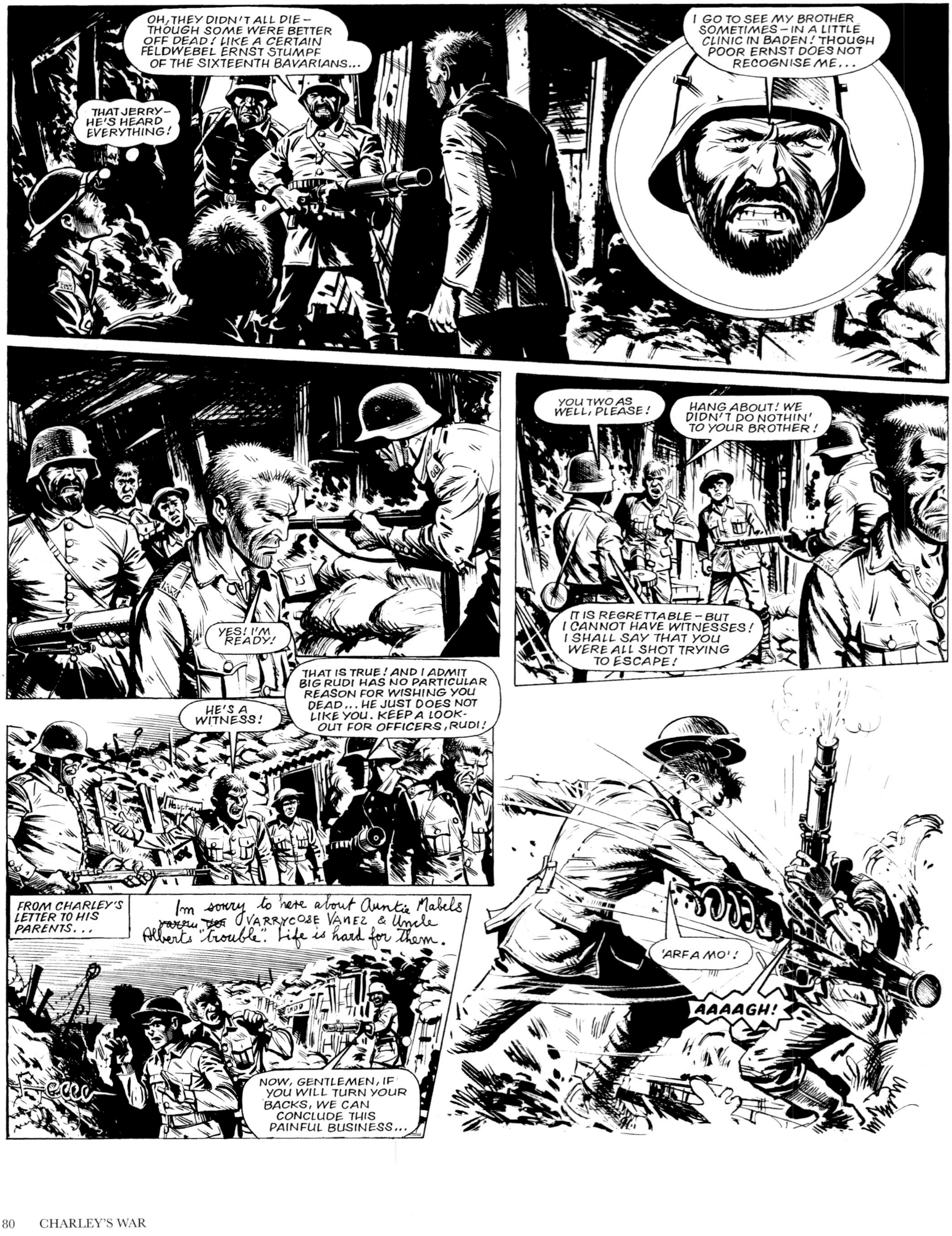
OH, THEY DIDN'T ALL DIE – THOUGH SOME WERE BETTER OFF DEAD! LIKE A CERTAIN FELDWEBEL ERNST STUMPF OF THE SIXTEENTH BAVARIANS...
THAT JERRY – HE'S HEARD EVERYTHING!
I GO TO SEE MY BROTHER SOMETIMES – IN A LITTLE CLINIC IN BADEN! THOUGH POOR ERNST DOES NOT RECOGNISE ME...
YES! I'M READY!
YOU TWO AS WELL, PLEASE!
HANG ABOUT! WE DIDN'T DO NOTHIN' TO YOUR BROTHER!
IT IS REGRETTABLE – BUT I CANNOT HAVE WITNESSES! I SHALL SAY THAT YOU WERE ALL SHOT TRYING TO ESCAPE!
HE'S A WITNESS!
THAT IS TRUE! AND I ADMIT BIG RUDI HAS NO PARTICULAR REASON FOR WISHING YOU DEAD... HE JUST DOES NOT LIKE YOU. KEEP A LOOK-OUT FOR OFFICERS, RUDI!
FROM CHARLEY'S LETTER TO HIS PARENTS...
I'm sorry to here about Auntie Mabels VARRYCOSE VANEZ & Uncle Alberts "trouble". Life is hard for them.
NOW, GENTLEMEN, IF YOU WILL TURN YOUR BACKS, WE CAN CONCLUDE THIS PAINFUL BUSINESS...
'ARF A MO'!
AAAAGH!

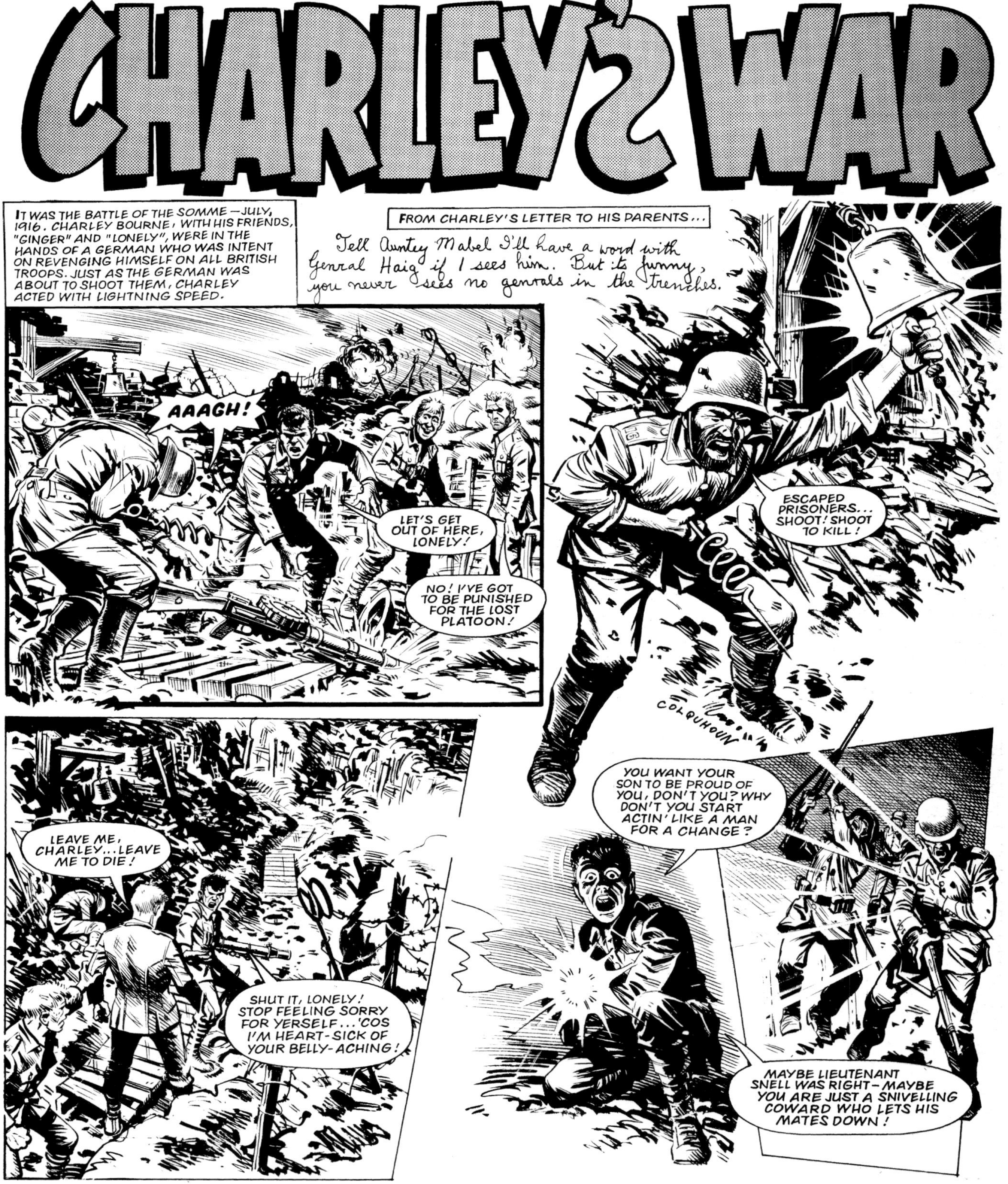
CHARLEY'S WAR
IT WAS THE BATTLE OF THE SOMME — JULY, 1916. CHARLEY BOURNE, WITH HIS FRIENDS, "GINGER" AND "LONELY", WERE IN THE HANDS OF A GERMAN WHO WAS INTENT ON REVENGING HIMSELF ON ALL BRITISH TROOPS. JUST AS THE GERMAN WAS ABOUT TO SHOOT THEM, CHARLEY ACTED WITH LIGHTNING SPEED.
FROM CHARLEY'S LETTER TO HIS PARENTS...
Tell Auntey Mabel I'll have a word with Genral Haig if I sees him. But its funny, you never sees no genrals in the trenches.
AAAGH!
LET'S GET OUT OF HERE, LONELY!
NO! I'VE GOT TO BE PUNISHED FOR THE LOST PLATOON!
ESCAPED PRISONERS... SHOOT! SHOOT TO KILL!
COLQUHOUN
LEAVE ME, CHARLEY... LEAVE ME TO DIE!
SHUT IT, LONELY! STOP FEELING SORRY FOR YERSELF... 'COS I'M HEART-SICK OF YOUR BELLY-ACHING!
YOU WANT YOUR SON TO BE PROUD OF YOU, DON'T YOU? WHY DON'T YOU START ACTIN' LIKE A MAN FOR A CHANGE?
MAYBE LIEUTENANT SNELL WAS RIGHT — MAYBE YOU ARE JUST A SNIVELLING COWARD WHO LETS HIS MATES DOWN!

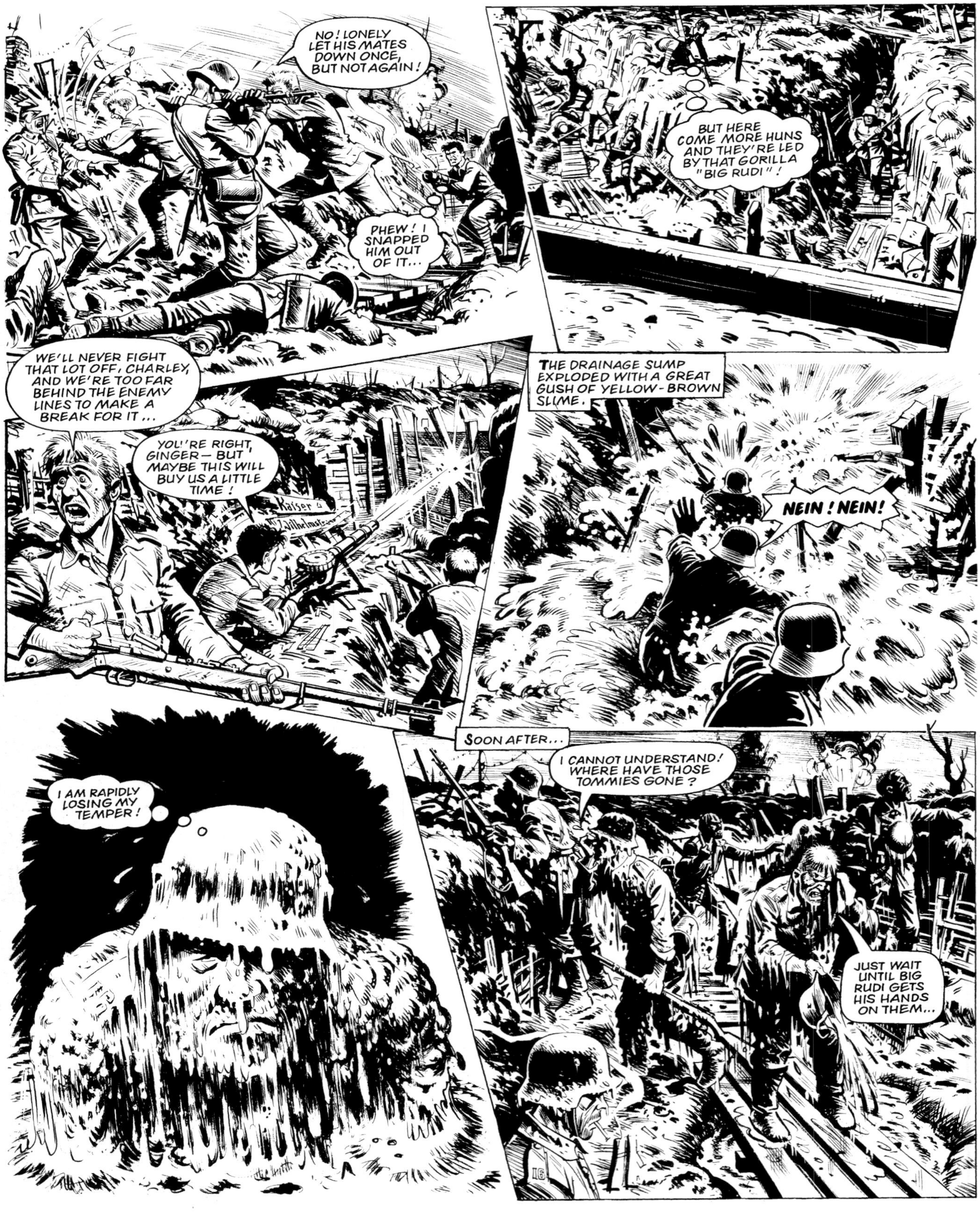
NO! LONELY LET HIS MATES DOWN ONCE, BUT NOT AGAIN!
PHEW! I SNAPPED HIM OUT OF IT...
BUT HERE COME MORE HUNS AND THEY'RE LED BY THAT GORILLA "BIG RUDI"!
WE'LL NEVER FIGHT THAT LOT OFF, CHARLEY, AND WE'RE TOO FAR BEHIND THE ENEMY LINES TO MAKE A BREAK FOR IT...
YOU'RE RIGHT, GINGER — BUT MAYBE THIS WILL BUY US A LITTLE TIME!
Kaiser
THE DRAINAGE SUMP EXPLODED WITH A GREAT GUSH OF YELLOW-BROWN SLIME.
NEIN! NEIN!
I AM RAPIDLY LOSING MY TEMPER!
SOON AFTER...
I CANNOT UNDERSTAND! WHERE HAVE THOSE TOMMIES GONE?
JUST WAIT UNTIL BIG RUDI GETS HIS HANDS ON THEM...

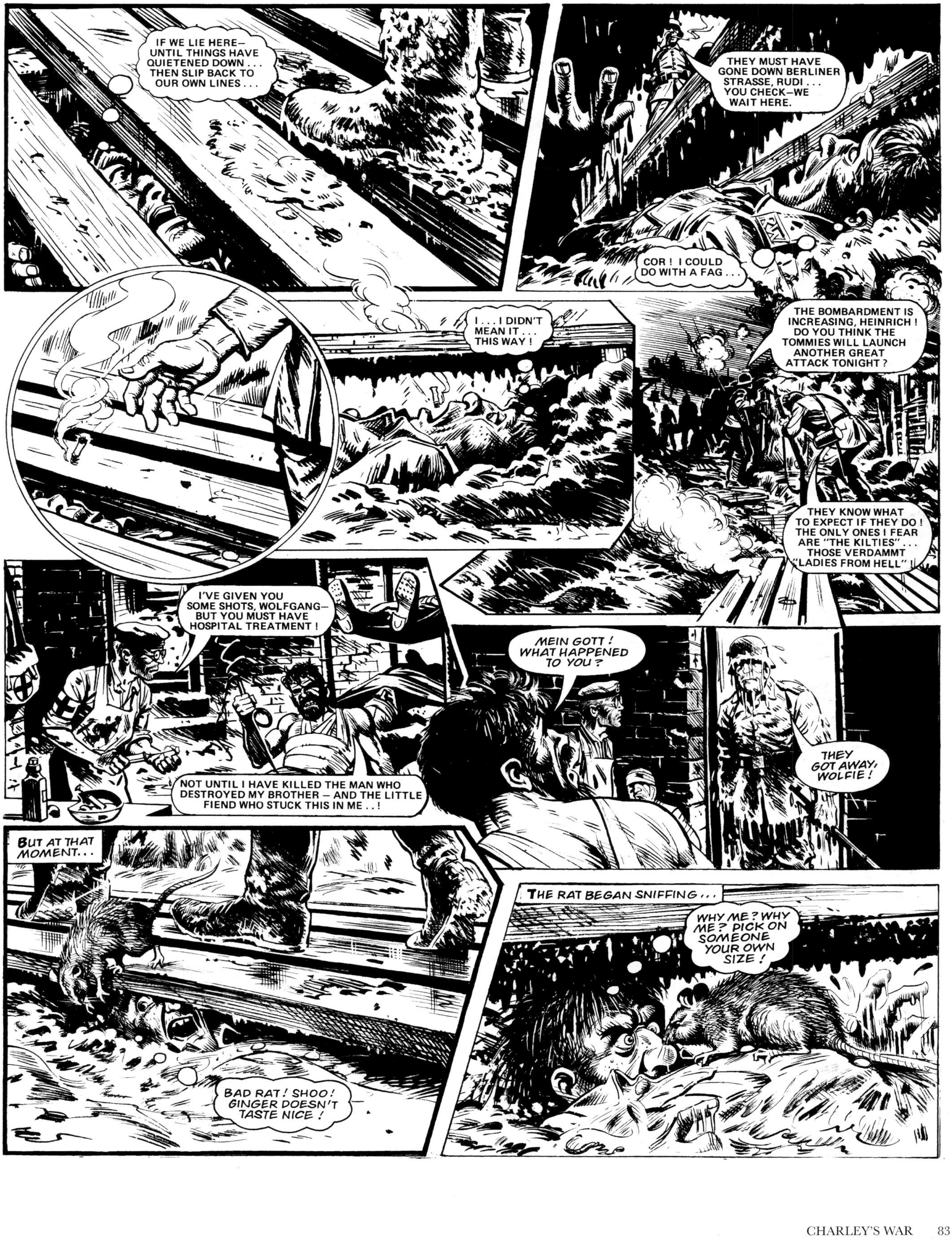
IF WE LIE HERE– UNTIL THINGS HAVE QUIETENED DOWN . . . THEN SLIP BACK TO OUR OWN LINES . . .
THEY MUST HAVE GONE DOWN BERLINER STRASSE, RUDI . . . YOU CHECK–WE WAIT HERE.
COR ! I COULD DO WITH A FAG . . .
I . . . I DIDN'T MEAN IT . . . THIS WAY !
THE BOMBARDMENT IS INCREASING, HEINRICH ! DO YOU THINK THE TOMMIES WILL LAUNCH ANOTHER GREAT ATTACK TONIGHT ?
THEY KNOW WHAT TO EXPECT IF THEY DO ! THE ONLY ONES I FEAR ARE "THE KILTIES" . . . THOSE VERDAMMT "LADIES FROM HELL"
I'VE GIVEN YOU SOME SHOTS, WOLFGANG– BUT YOU MUST HAVE HOSPITAL TREATMENT !
NOT UNTIL I HAVE KILLED THE MAN WHO DESTROYED MY BROTHER – AND THE LITTLE FIEND WHO STUCK THIS IN ME . . !
MEIN GOTT ! WHAT HAPPENED TO YOU ?
THEY GOT AWAY, WOLFIE !
BUT AT THAT MOMENT . . .
BAD RAT ! SHOO ! GINGER DOESN'T TASTE NICE !
THE RAT BEGAN SNIFFING . . .
WHY ME ? WHY ME ? PICK ON SOMEONE YOUR OWN SIZE !

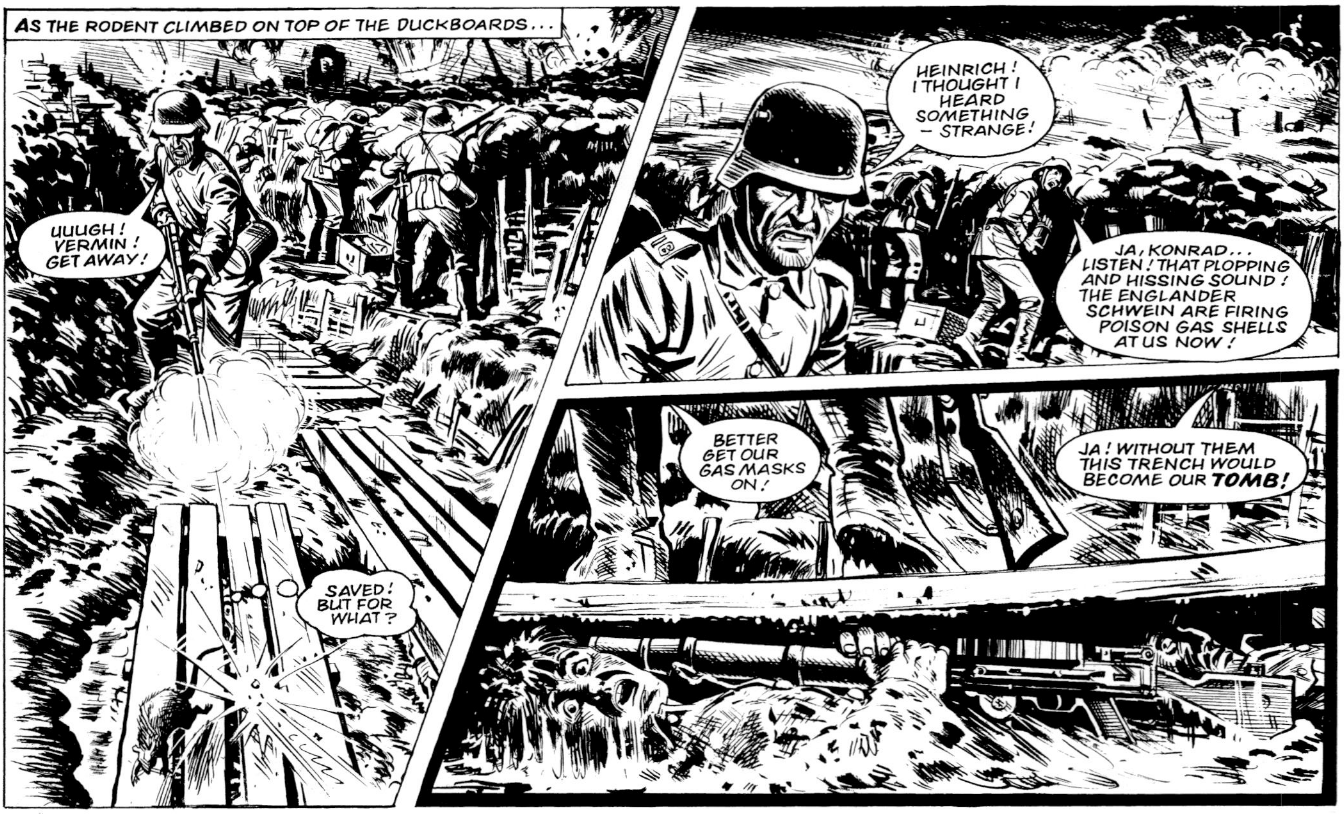
AS THE RODENT CLIMBED ON TOP OF THE DUCKBOARDS...
UUUGH! VERMIN! GET AWAY!
SAVED! BUT FOR WHAT?
HEINRICH! I THOUGHT I HEARD SOMETHING – STRANGE!
JA, KONRAD... LISTEN! THAT PLOPPING AND HISSING SOUND! THE ENGLANDER SCHWEIN ARE FIRING POISON GAS SHELLS AT US NOW!
BETTER GET OUR GAS MASKS ON!
JA! WITHOUT THEM THIS TRENCH WOULD BECOME OUR TOMB!

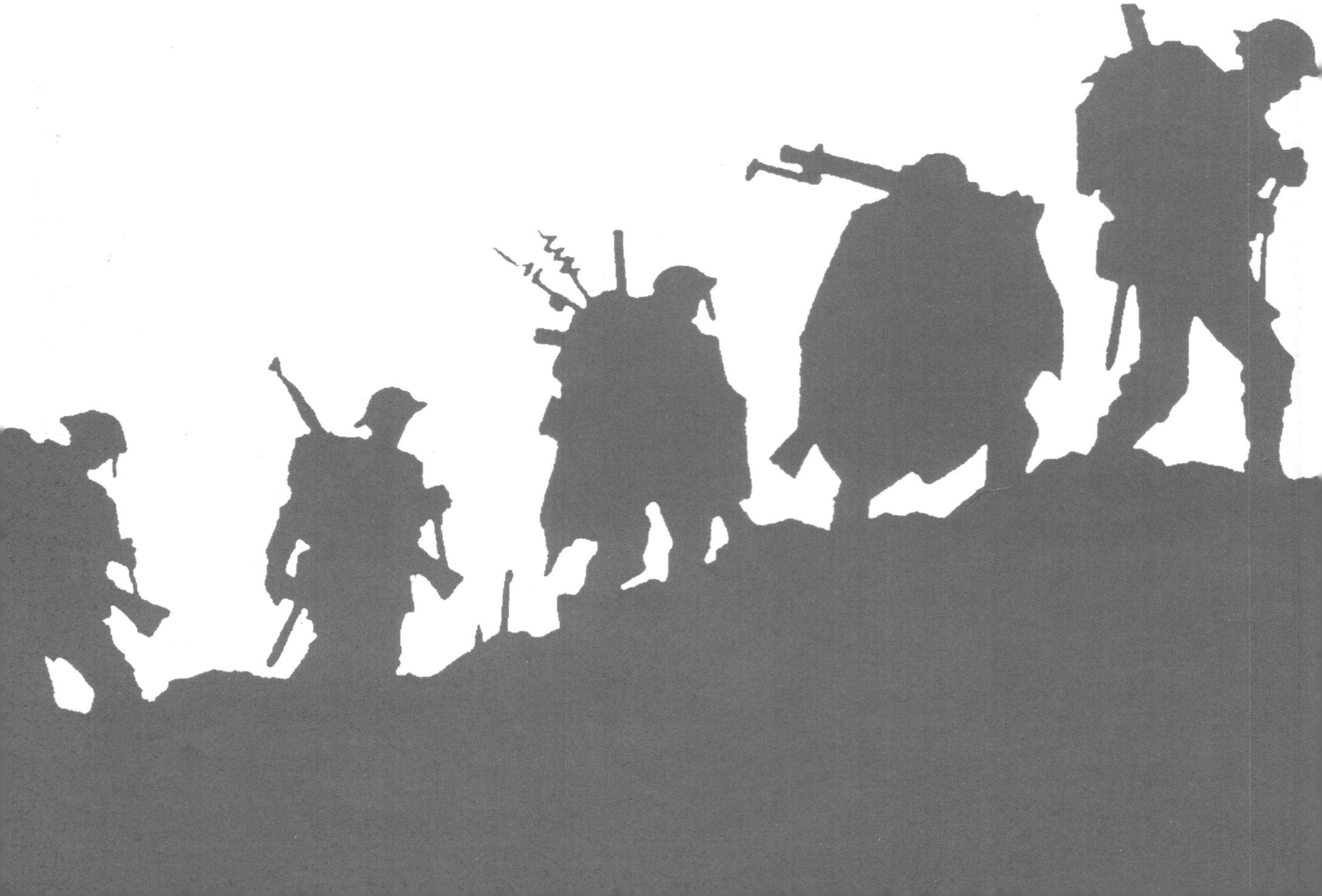

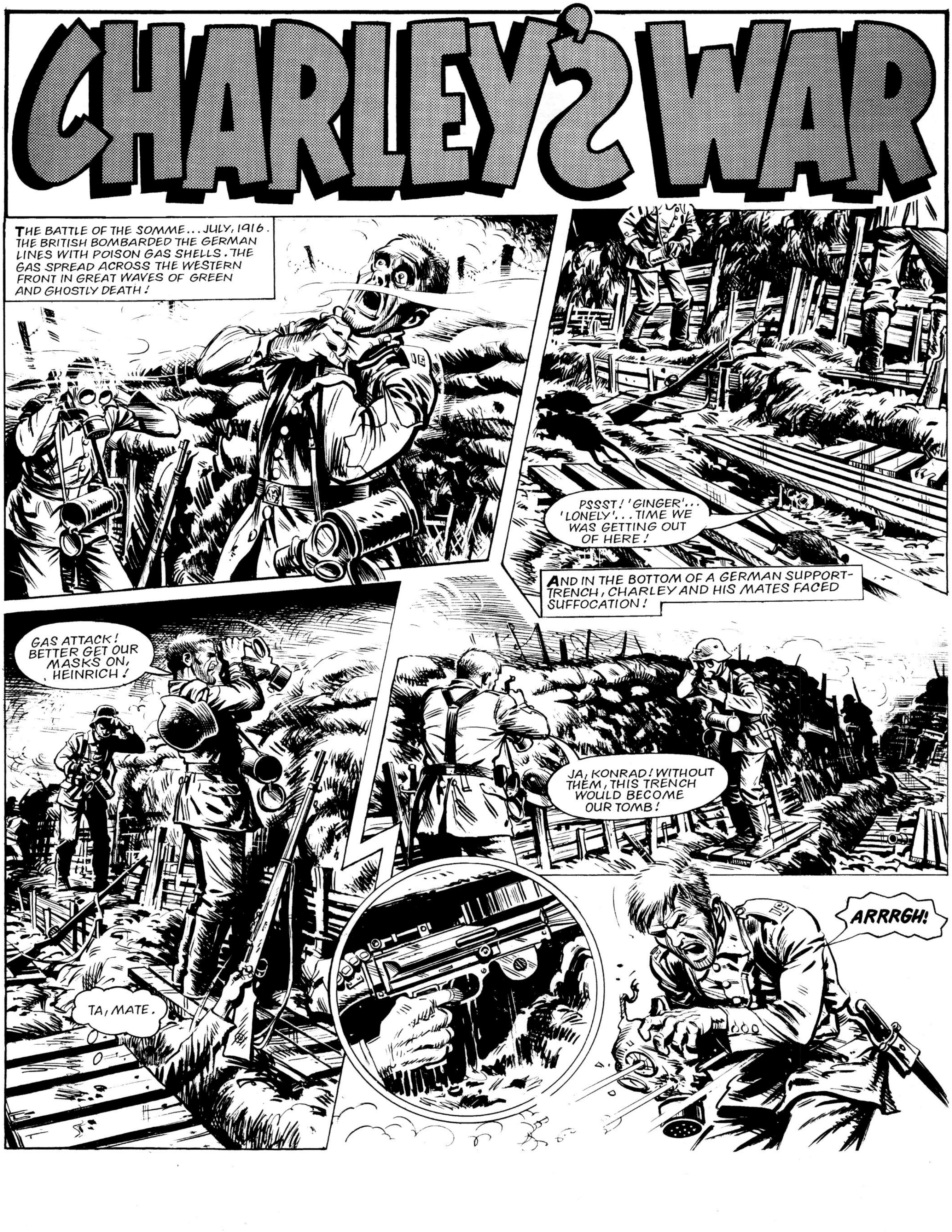
CHARLEY'S WAR
THE BATTLE OF THE SOMME... JULY, 1916. THE BRITISH BOMBARDED THE GERMAN LINES WITH POISON GAS SHELLS. THE GAS SPREAD ACROSS THE WESTERN FRONT IN GREAT WAVES OF GREEN AND GHOSTLY DEATH!
PSSST! 'GINGER'... 'LONELY'... TIME WE WAS GETTING OUT OF HERE!
AND IN THE BOTTOM OF A GERMAN SUPPORT-TRENCH, CHARLEY AND HIS MATES FACED SUFFOCATION!
GAS ATTACK! BETTER GET OUR MASKS ON, HEINRICH!
JA, KONRAD! WITHOUT THEM, THIS TRENCH WOULD BECOME OUR TOMB!
TA, MATE.
ARRRGH!

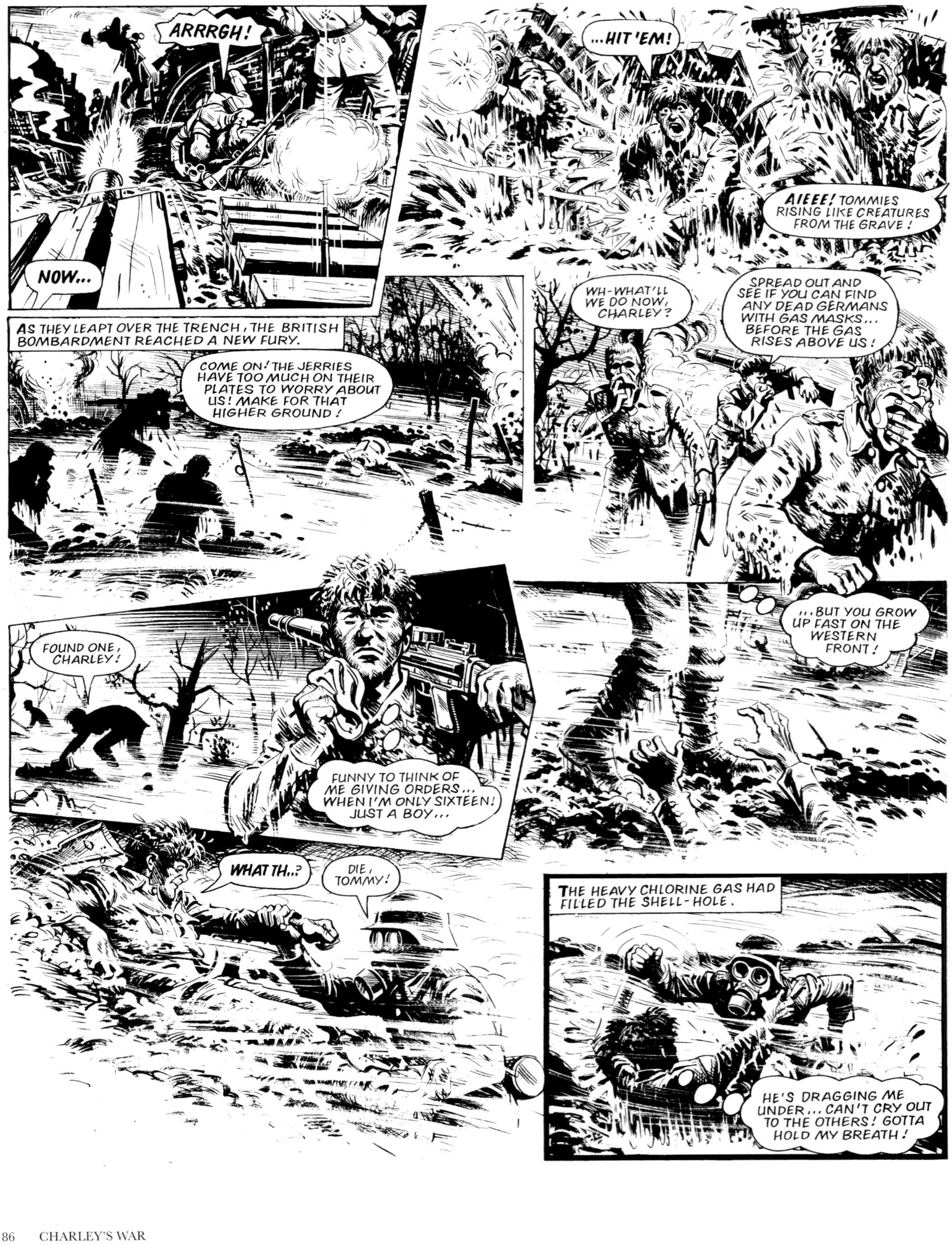
ARRRGH!
NOW...
...HIT 'EM!
AIEEE! TOMMIES RISING LIKE CREATURES FROM THE GRAVE!
AS THEY LEAPT OVER THE TRENCH, THE BRITISH BOMBARDMENT REACHED A NEW FURY.
COME ON! THE JERRIES HAVE TOO MUCH ON THEIR PLATES TO WORRY ABOUT US! MAKE FOR THAT HIGHER GROUND!
WH-WHAT'LL WE DO NOW, CHARLEY?
SPREAD OUT AND SEE IF YOU CAN FIND ANY DEAD GERMANS WITH GAS MASKS... BEFORE THE GAS RISES ABOVE US!
FOUND ONE, CHARLEY!
FUNNY TO THINK OF ME GIVING ORDERS... WHEN I'M ONLY SIXTEEN! JUST A BOY...
...BUT YOU GROW UP FAST ON THE WESTERN FRONT!
WHAT TH..?
DIE, TOMMY!
THE HEAVY CHLORINE GAS HAD FILLED THE SHELL-HOLE.
HE'S DRAGGING ME UNDER... CAN'T CRY OUT TO THE OTHERS! GOTTA HOLD MY BREATH!

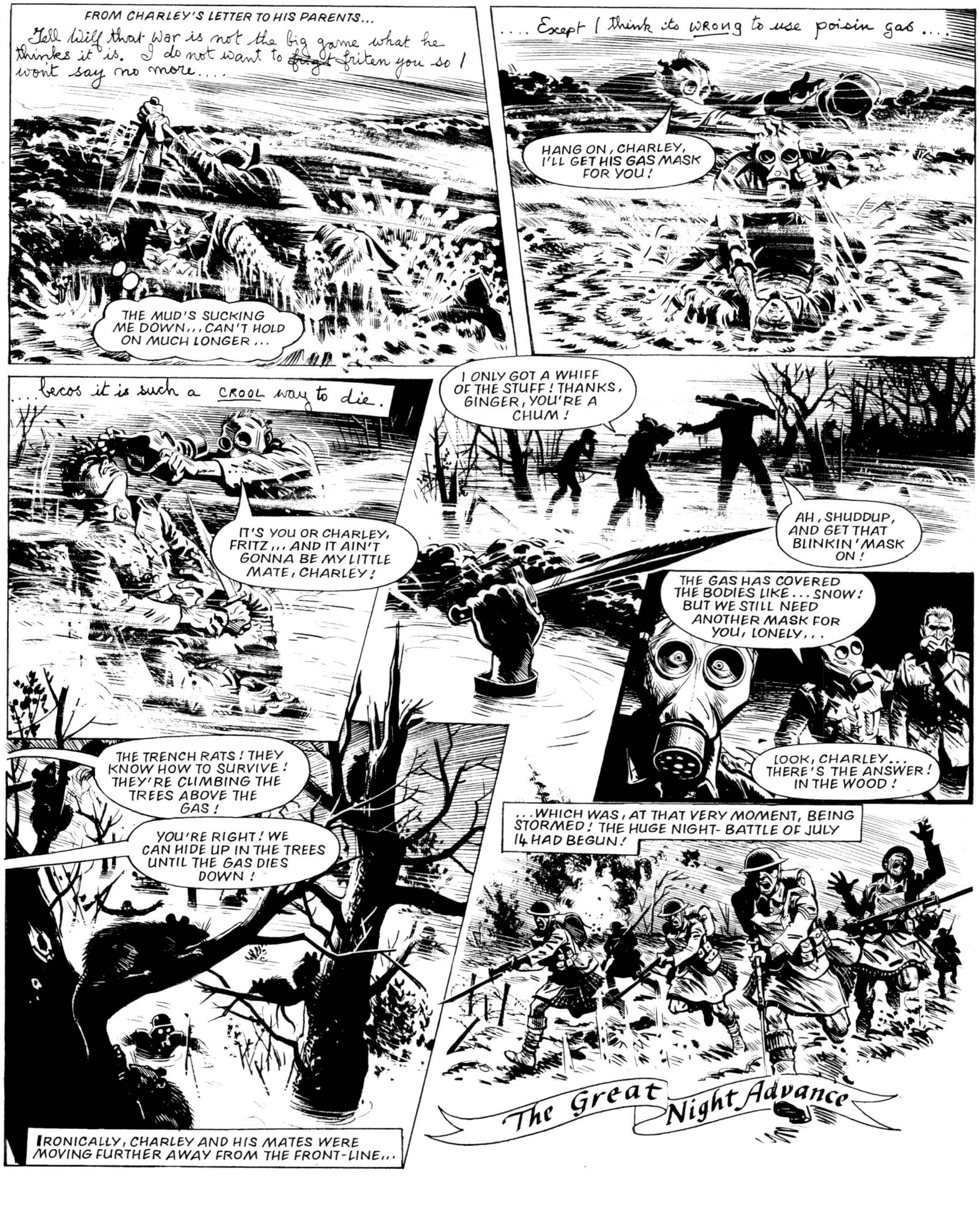
FROM CHARLEY'S LETTER TO HIS PARENTS...
Tell Wilf that War is not the big game what he thinks it is. I do not want to friten you so I wont say no more....
THE MUD'S SUCKING ME DOWN,,, CAN'T HOLD ON MUCH LONGER...
.... Exept I think its WRONG to use poisin gas ....
HANG ON, CHARLEY, I'LL GET HIS GAS MASK FOR YOU!
... becos it is such a CROOL way to die.
IT'S YOU OR CHARLEY, FRITZ,,, AND IT AIN'T GONNA BE MY LITTLE MATE, CHARLEY!
I ONLY GOT A WHIFF OF THE STUFF! THANKS, GINGER, YOU'RE A CHUM!
AH, SHUDDUP, AND GET THAT BLINKIN' MASK ON!
THE GAS HAS COVERED THE BODIES LIKE... SNOW! BUT WE STILL NEED ANOTHER MASK FOR YOU, LONELY...
LOOK, CHARLEY... THERE'S THE ANSWER! IN THE WOOD!
THE TRENCH RATS! THEY KNOW HOW TO SURVIVE! THEY'RE CLIMBING THE TREES ABOVE THE GAS!
YOU'RE RIGHT! WE CAN HIDE UP IN THE TREES UNTIL THE GAS DIES DOWN!
IRONICALLY, CHARLEY AND HIS MATES WERE MOVING FURTHER AWAY FROM THE FRONT-LINE...
...WHICH WAS, AT THAT VERY MOMENT, BEING STORMED! THE HUGE NIGHT-BATTLE OF JULY 14 HAD BEGUN!
The Great Night Advance

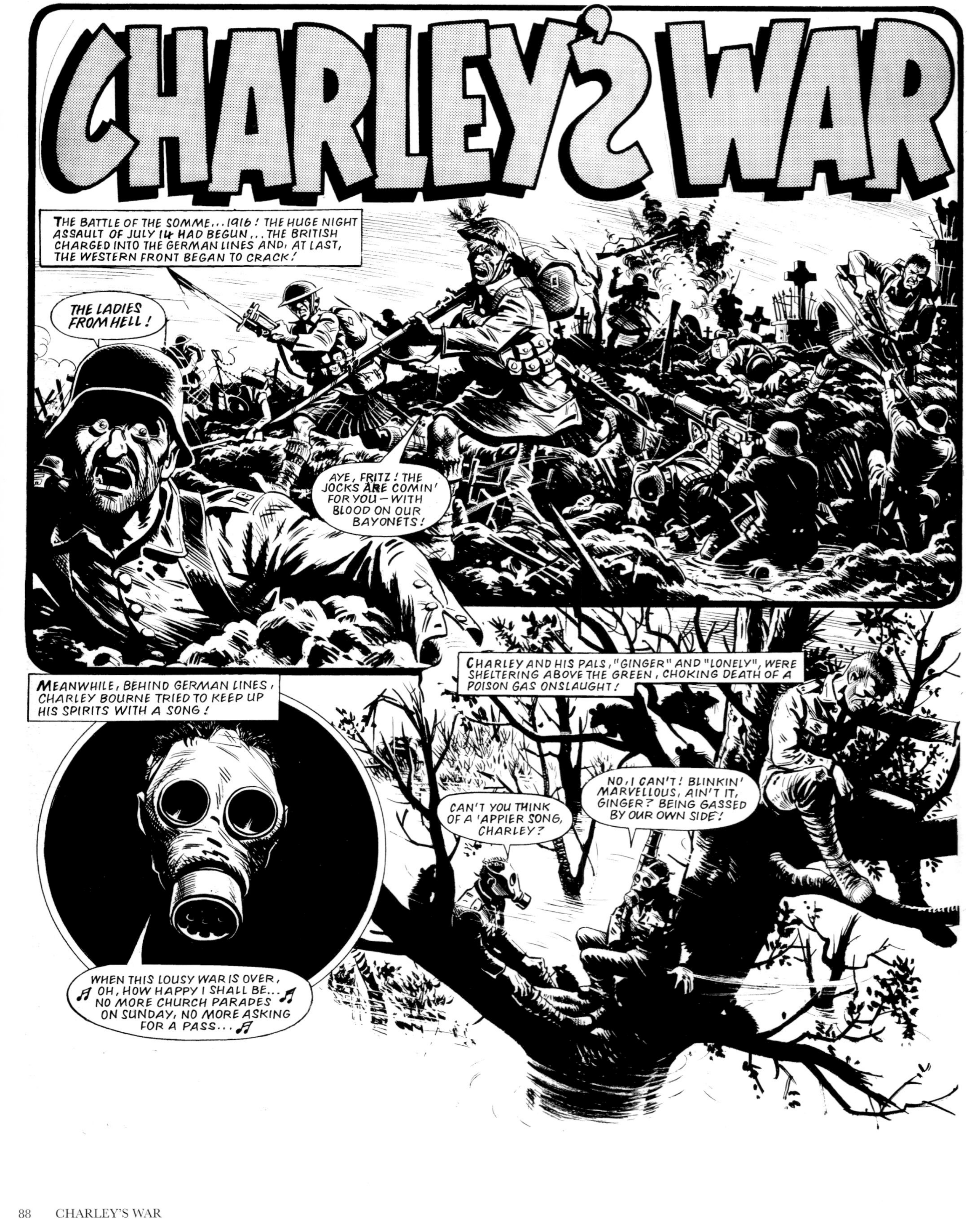
CHARLEY'S WAR
THE BATTLE OF THE SOMME... 1916! THE HUGE NIGHT ASSAULT OF JULY 14 HAD BEGUN... THE BRITISH CHARGED INTO THE GERMAN LINES AND, AT LAST, THE WESTERN FRONT BEGAN TO CRACK!
THE LADIES FROM HELL!
AYE, FRITZ! THE JOCKS ARE COMIN' FOR YOU — WITH BLOOD ON OUR BAYONETS!
MEANWHILE, BEHIND GERMAN LINES, CHARLEY BOURNE TRIED TO KEEP UP HIS SPIRITS WITH A SONG!
WHEN THIS LOUSY WAR IS OVER, OH, HOW HAPPY I SHALL BE... NO MORE CHURCH PARADES ON SUNDAY, NO MORE ASKING FOR A PASS...
CHARLEY AND HIS PALS, "GINGER" AND "LONELY", WERE SHELTERING ABOVE THE GREEN, CHOKING DEATH OF A POISON GAS ONSLAUGHT!
CAN'T YOU THINK OF A 'APPIER SONG, CHARLEY?
NO, I CAN'T! BLINKIN' MARVELLOUS, AIN'T IT, GINGER? BEING GASSED BY OUR OWN SIDE!

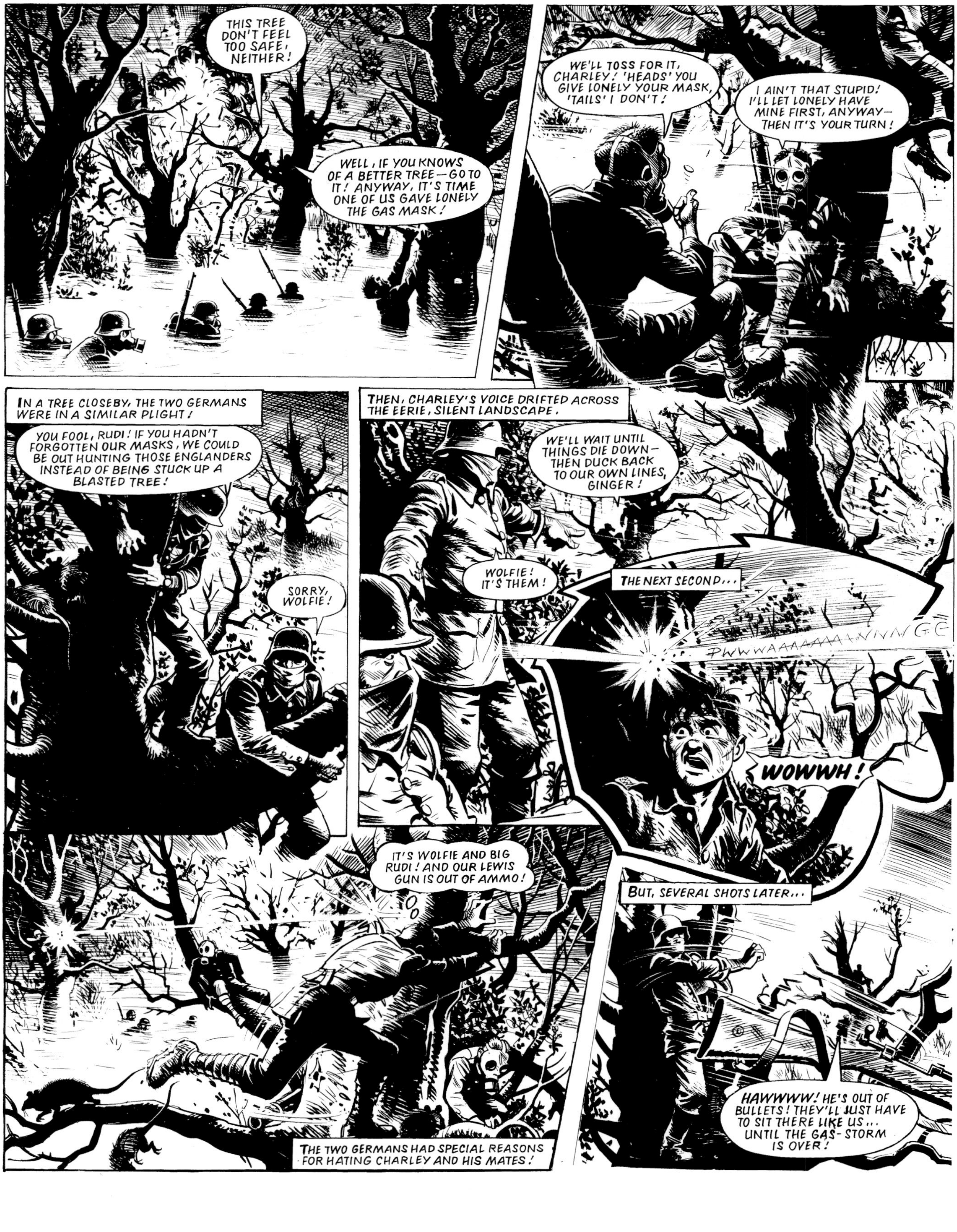
THIS TREE DON'T FEEL TOO SAFE, NEITHER!
WELL, IF YOU KNOWS OF A BETTER TREE—GO TO IT! ANYWAY, IT'S TIME ONE OF US GAVE LONELY THE GAS MASK!
WE'LL TOSS FOR IT, CHARLEY! 'HEADS' YOU GIVE LONELY YOUR MASK, 'TAILS' I DON'T!
I AIN'T THAT STUPID! I'LL LET LONELY HAVE MINE FIRST, ANYWAY— THEN IT'S YOUR TURN!
IN A TREE CLOSEBY, THE TWO GERMANS WERE IN A SIMILAR PLIGHT!
YOU FOOL, RUDI! IF YOU HADN'T FORGOTTEN OUR MASKS, WE COULD BE OUT HUNTING THOSE ENGLANDERS INSTEAD OF BEING STUCK UP A BLASTED TREE!
SORRY, WOLFIE!
THEN, CHARLEY'S VOICE DRIFTED ACROSS THE EERIE, SILENT LANDSCAPE.
WE'LL WAIT UNTIL THINGS DIE DOWN— THEN DUCK BACK TO OUR OWN LINES, GINGER!
WOLFIE! IT'S THEM!
THE NEXT SECOND...
PWWWAAAAAAAAAWNNNGEE
WOWWH!
IT'S WOLFIE AND BIG RUDI! AND OUR LEWIS GUN IS OUT OF AMMO!
THE TWO GERMANS HAD SPECIAL REASONS FOR HATING CHARLEY AND HIS MATES!
BUT, SEVERAL SHOTS LATER...
HAWWWW! HE'S OUT OF BULLETS! THEY'LL JUST HAVE TO SIT THERE LIKE US... UNTIL THE GAS-STORM IS OVER!

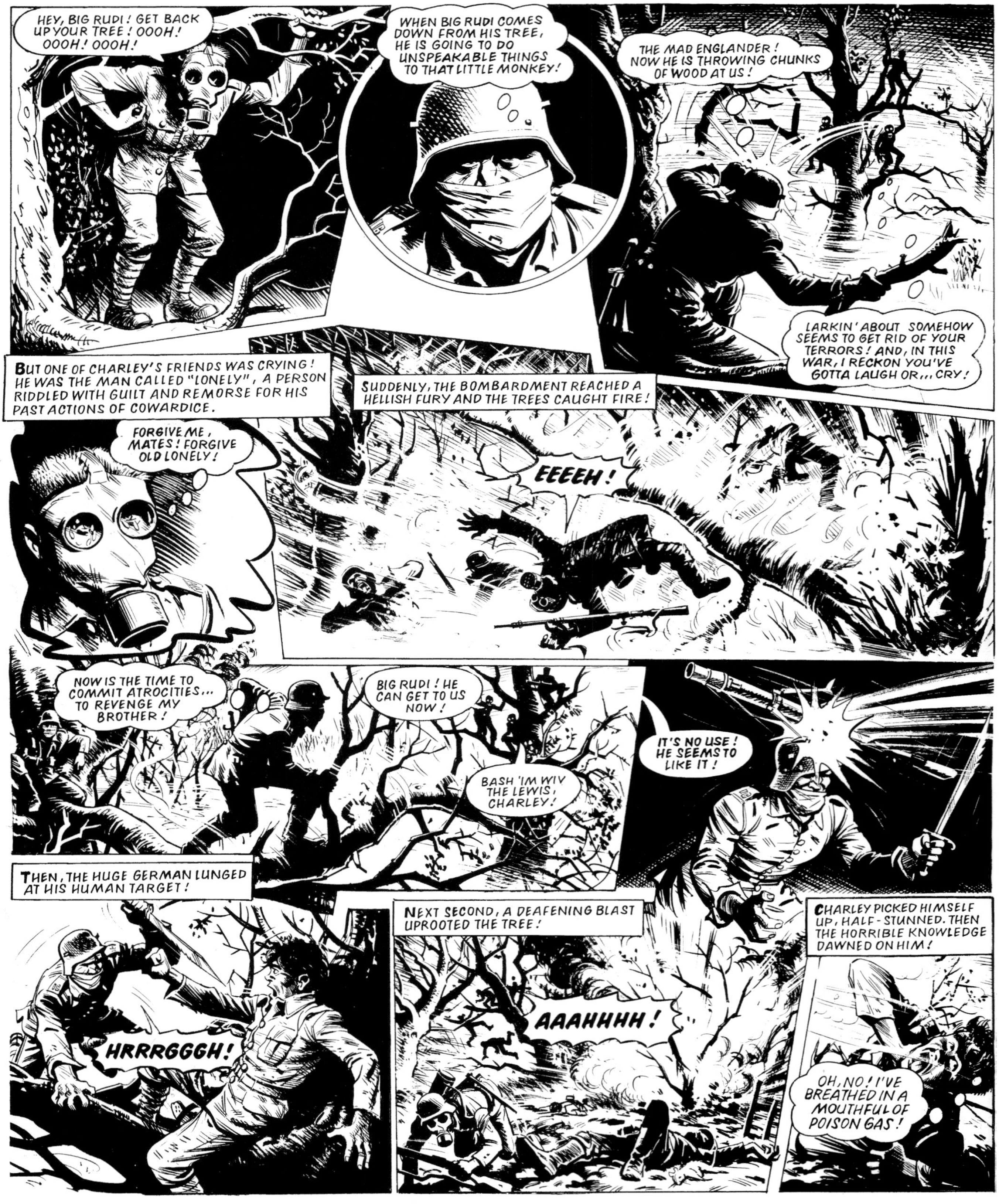
HEY, BIG RUDI! GET BACK UP YOUR TREE! OOOH! OOOH! OOOH!
WHEN BIG RUDI COMES DOWN FROM HIS TREE, HE IS GOING TO DO UNSPEAKABLE THINGS TO THAT LITTLE MONKEY!
THE MAD ENGLANDER! NOW HE IS THROWING CHUNKS OF WOOD AT US!
LARKIN' ABOUT SOMEHOW SEEMS TO GET RID OF YOUR TERRORS! AND, IN THIS WAR, I RECKON YOU'VE GOTTA LAUGH OR... CRY!
BUT ONE OF CHARLEY'S FRIENDS WAS CRYING! HE WAS THE MAN CALLED "LONELY", A PERSON RIDDLED WITH GUILT AND REMORSE FOR HIS PAST ACTIONS OF COWARDICE.
FORGIVE ME, MATES! FORGIVE OLD LONELY!
SUDDENLY, THE BOMBARDMENT REACHED A HELLISH FURY AND THE TREES CAUGHT FIRE!
EEEEH!
NOW IS THE TIME TO COMMIT ATROCITIES... TO REVENGE MY BROTHER!
BIG RUDI! HE CAN GET TO US NOW!
BASH 'IM WIV THE LEWIS, CHARLEY!
IT'S NO USE! HE SEEMS TO LIKE IT!
THEN, THE HUGE GERMAN LUNGED AT HIS HUMAN TARGET!
HRRRGGGH!
NEXT SECOND, A DEAFENING BLAST UPROOTED THE TREE!
AAAHHHH!
CHARLEY PICKED HIMSELF UP, HALF-STUNNED. THEN THE HORRIBLE KNOWLEDGE DAWNED ON HIM!
OH, NO! I'VE BREATHED IN A MOUTHFUL OF POISON GAS!

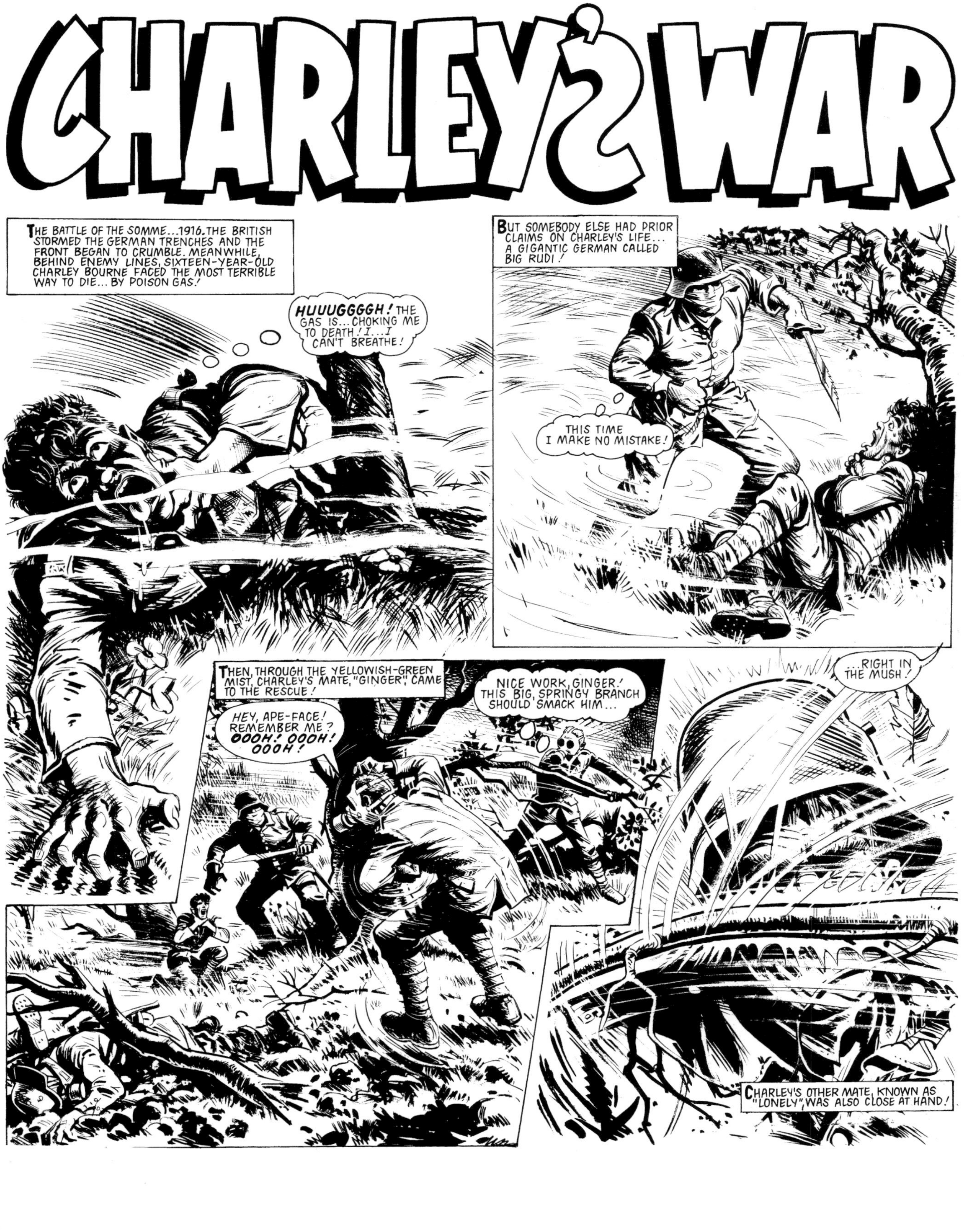
CHARLEY'S WAR
THE BATTLE OF THE SOMME...1916. THE BRITISH STORMED THE GERMAN TRENCHES AND THE FRONT BEGAN TO CRUMBLE. MEANWHILE, BEHIND ENEMY LINES, SIXTEEN-YEAR-OLD CHARLEY BOURNE FACED THE MOST TERRIBLE WAY TO DIE... BY POISON GAS!
HUUUGGGGH! THE GAS IS... CHOKING ME TO DEATH! I...I CAN'T BREATHE!
BUT SOMEBODY ELSE HAD PRIOR CLAIMS ON CHARLEY'S LIFE... A GIGANTIC GERMAN CALLED BIG RUDI!
THIS TIME I MAKE NO MISTAKE!
THEN, THROUGH THE YELLOWISH-GREEN MIST, CHARLEY'S MATE, "GINGER", CAME TO THE RESCUE!
HEY, APE-FACE! REMEMBER ME? OOOH! OOOH! OOOH!
NICE WORK, GINGER! THIS BIG, SPRINGY BRANCH SHOULD SMACK HIM...
...RIGHT IN THE MUSH!
CHARLEY'S OTHER MATE, KNOWN AS "LONELY", WAS ALSO CLOSE AT HAND!

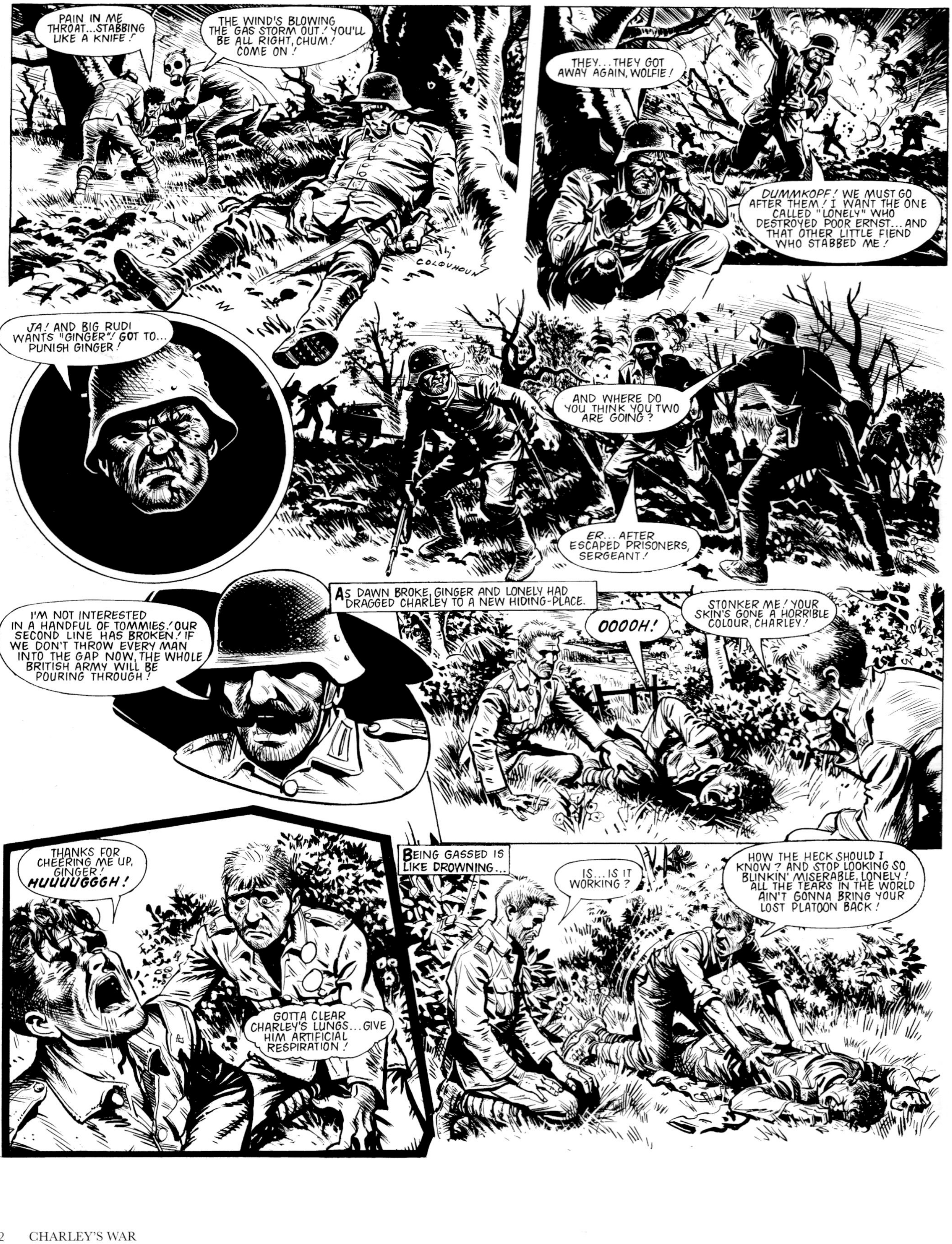
PAIN IN ME THROAT... STABBING LIKE A KNIFE!
THE WIND'S BLOWING THE GAS STORM OUT! YOU'LL BE ALL RIGHT, CHUM! COME ON!
COLQUHOUN
THEY... THEY GOT AWAY AGAIN, WOLFIE!
DUMMKOPF! WE MUST GO AFTER THEM! I WANT THE ONE CALLED "LONELY" WHO DESTROYED POOR ERNST... AND THAT OTHER LITTLE FIEND WHO STABBED ME!
JA! AND BIG RUDI WANTS "GINGER"! GOT TO... PUNISH GINGER!
AND WHERE DO YOU THINK YOU TWO ARE GOING?
ER... AFTER ESCAPED PRISONERS, SERGEANT!
I'M NOT INTERESTED IN A HANDFUL OF TOMMIES! OUR SECOND LINE HAS BROKEN! IF WE DON'T THROW EVERY MAN INTO THE GAP NOW, THE WHOLE BRITISH ARMY WILL BE POURING THROUGH!
AS DAWN BROKE GINGER AND LONELY HAD DRAGGED CHARLEY TO A NEW HIDING-PLACE.
OOOOH!
STONKER ME! YOUR SKIN'S GONE A HORRIBLE COLOUR, CHARLEY!
THANKS FOR CHEERING ME UP, GINGER! HUUUUGGGH!
GOTTA CLEAR CHARLEY'S LUNGS... GIVE HIM ARTIFICIAL RESPIRATION!
BEING GASSED IS LIKE DROWNING...
IS... IS IT WORKING?
HOW THE HECK SHOULD I KNOW? AND STOP LOOKING SO BLINKIN' MISERABLE, LONELY! ALL THE TEARS IN THE WORLD AIN'T GONNA BRING YOUR LOST PLATOON BACK!

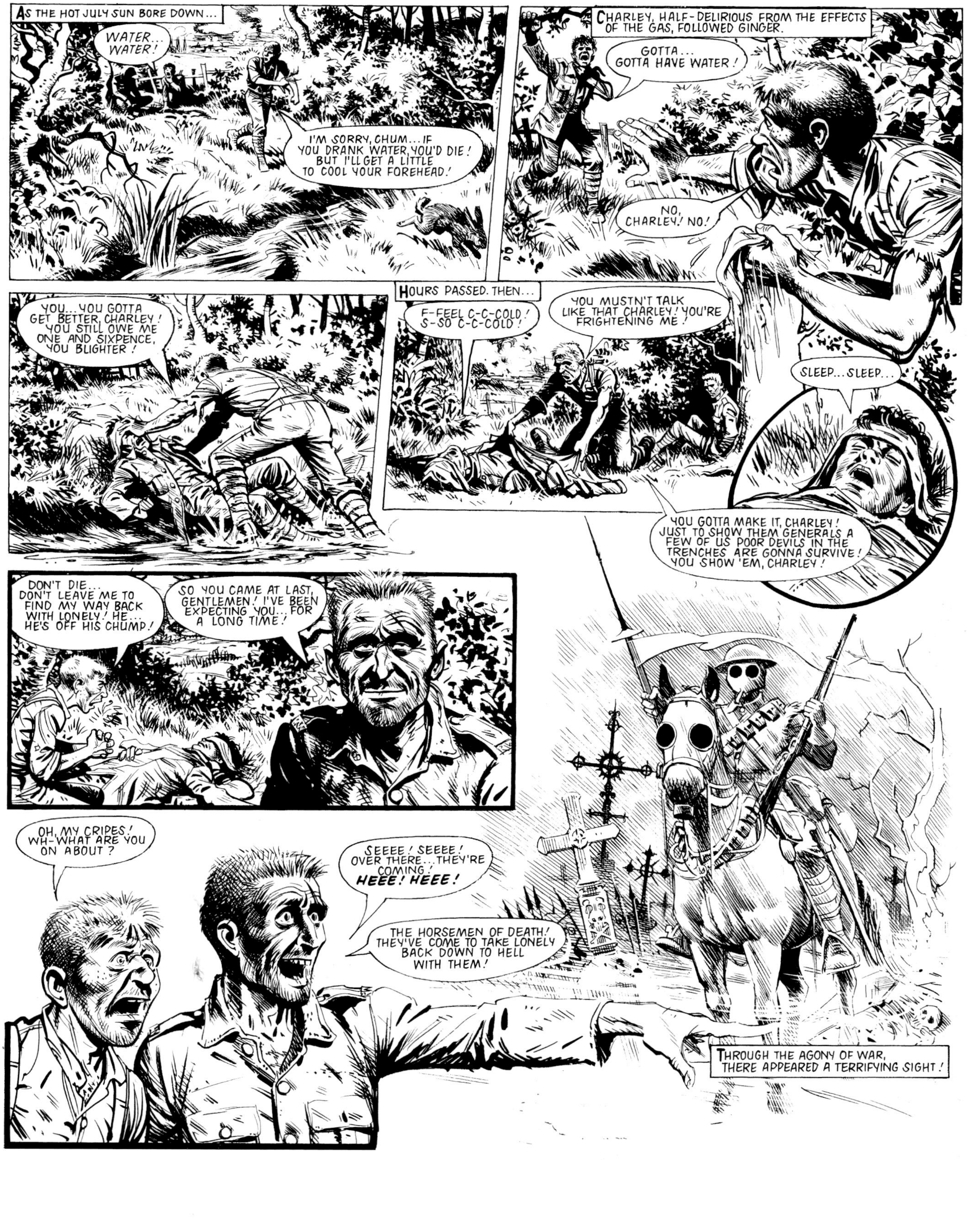
AS THE HOT JULY SUN BORE DOWN...
WATER... WATER!
I'M SORRY, CHUM... IF YOU DRANK WATER YOU'D DIE! BUT I'LL GET A LITTLE TO COOL YOUR FOREHEAD!
CHARLEY, HALF-DELIRIOUS FROM THE EFFECTS OF THE GAS, FOLLOWED GINGER.
GOTTA... GOTTA HAVE WATER!
NO, CHARLEY! NO!
YOU... YOU GOTTA GET BETTER, CHARLEY! YOU STILL OWE ME ONE AND SIXPENCE, YOU BLIGHTER!
HOURS PASSED. THEN...
F-FEEL C-C-COLD! S-SO C-C-COLD!
YOU MUSTN'T TALK LIKE THAT CHARLEY! YOU'RE FRIGHTENING ME!
SLEEP... SLEEP...
YOU GOTTA MAKE IT, CHARLEY! JUST TO SHOW THEM GENERALS A FEW OF US POOR DEVILS IN THE TRENCHES ARE GONNA SURVIVE! YOU SHOW 'EM, CHARLEY!
DON'T DIE... DON'T LEAVE ME TO FIND MY WAY BACK WITH LONELY! HE... HE'S OFF HIS CHUMP!
SO YOU CAME AT LAST, GENTLEMEN! I'VE BEEN EXPECTING YOU... FOR A LONG TIME!
OH, MY CRIPES! WH-WHAT ARE YOU ON ABOUT?
SEEEE! SEEEE! OVER THERE... THEY'RE COMING! HEEE! HEEE!
THE HORSEMEN OF DEATH! THEY'VE COME TO TAKE LONELY BACK DOWN TO HELL WITH THEM!
THROUGH THE AGONY OF WAR, THERE APPEARED A TERRIFYING SIGHT!

CHARLEY'S WAR

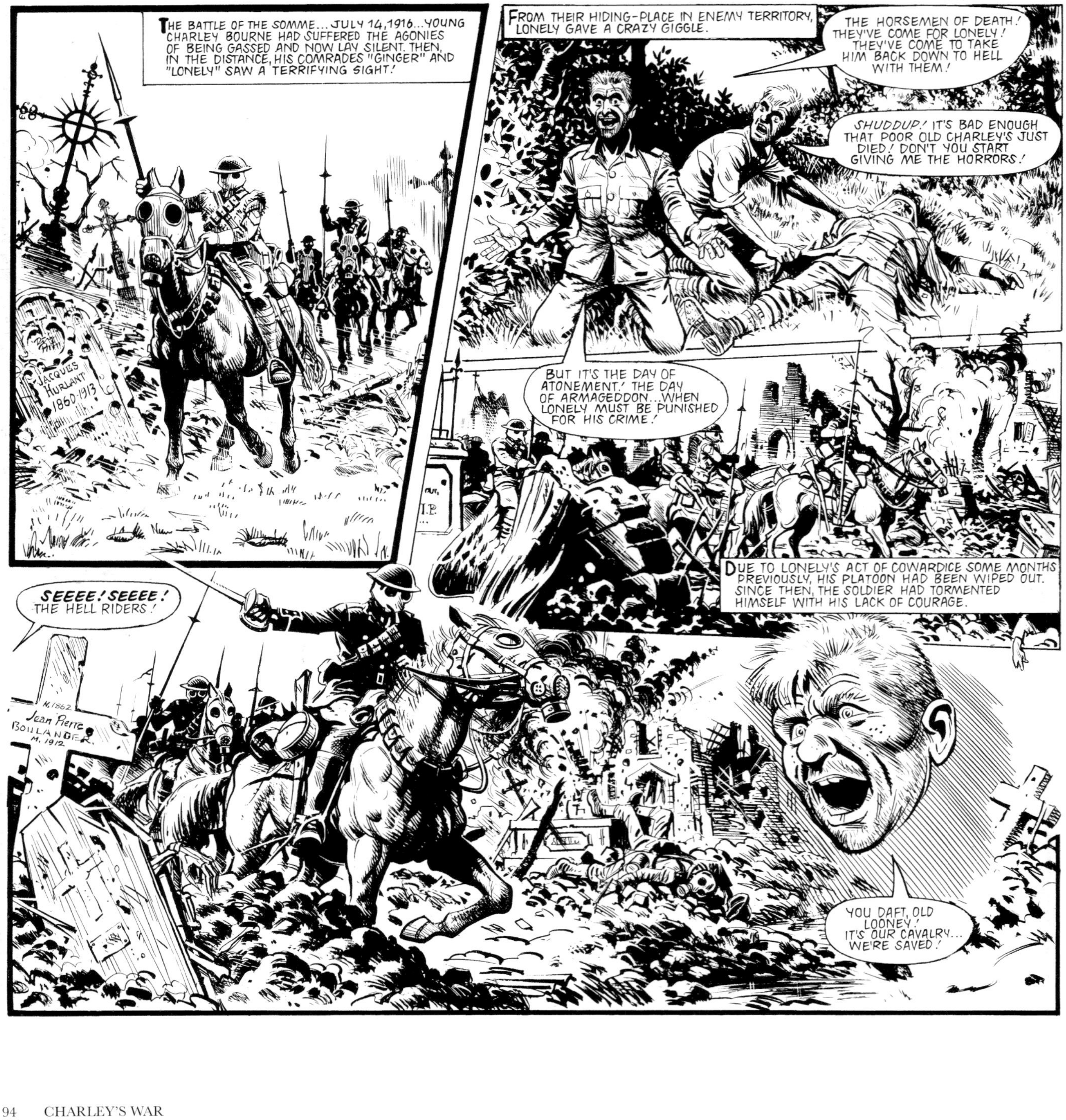

THE BATTLE OF THE SOMME... JULY 14, 1916... YOUNG CHARLEY BOURNE HAD SUFFERED THE AGONIES OF BEING GASSED AND NOW LAY SILENT. THEN, IN THE DISTANCE, HIS COMRADES "GINGER" AND "LONELY" SAW A TERRIFYING SIGHT!
JACQUES HURLANT 1860-1913
FROM THEIR HIDING-PLACE IN ENEMY TERRITORY, LONELY GAVE A CRAZY GIGGLE.
THE HORSEMEN OF DEATH! THEY'VE COME FOR LONELY! THEY'VE COME TO TAKE HIM BACK DOWN TO HELL WITH THEM!
SHUDDUP! IT'S BAD ENOUGH THAT POOR OLD CHARLEY'S JUST DIED! DON'T YOU START GIVING ME THE HORRORS!
BUT IT'S THE DAY OF ATONEMENT! THE DAY OF ARMAGEDDON... WHEN LONELY MUST BE PUNISHED FOR HIS CRIME!
DUE TO LONELY'S ACT OF COWARDICE SOME MONTHS PREVIOUSLY, HIS PLATOON HAD BEEN WIPED OUT. SINCE THEN, THE SOLDIER HAD TORMENTED HIMSELF WITH HIS LACK OF COURAGE.
SEEEE! SEEEE! THE HELL RIDERS!
N. 1862 Jean Pierre BOULANGER M. 1912
YOU DAFT, OLD LOONEY! IT'S OUR CAVALRY... WE'RE SAVED!

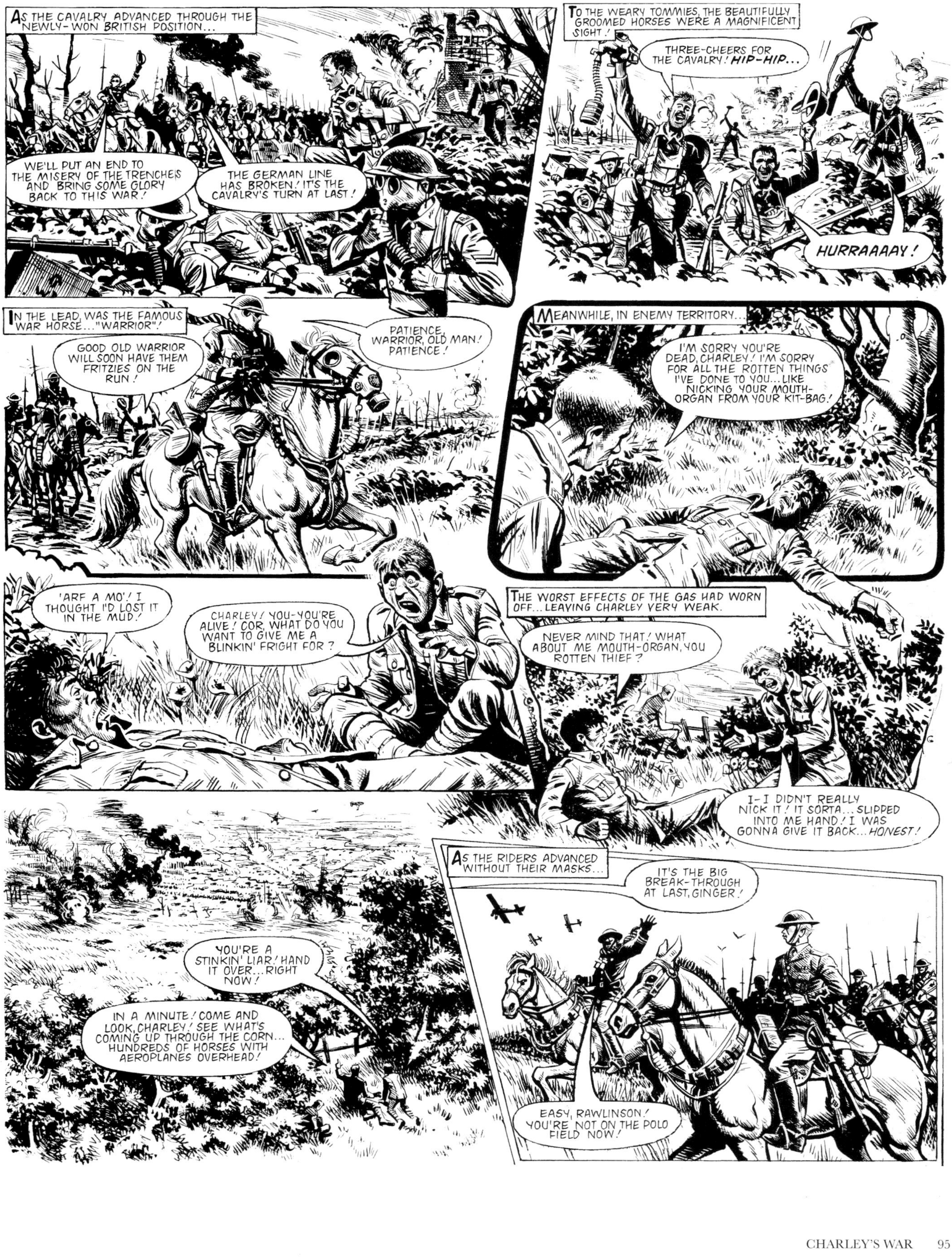
AS THE CAVALRY ADVANCED THROUGH THE NEWLY-WON BRITISH POSITION...
WE'LL PUT AN END TO THE MISERY OF THE TRENCHES AND BRING SOME GLORY BACK TO THIS WAR!
THE GERMAN LINE HAS BROKEN! IT'S THE CAVALRY'S TURN AT LAST!
TO THE WEARY TOMMIES, THE BEAUTIFULLY GROOMED HORSES WERE A MAGNIFICENT SIGHT!
THREE-CHEERS FOR THE CAVALRY! HIP-HIP...
HURRAAAAY!
IN THE LEAD, WAS THE FAMOUS WAR HORSE..."WARRIOR"!
GOOD OLD WARRIOR WILL SOON HAVE THEM FRITZIES ON THE RUN!
PATIENCE, WARRIOR, OLD MAN! PATIENCE!
MEANWHILE, IN ENEMY TERRITORY...
I'M SORRY YOU'RE DEAD, CHARLEY! I'M SORRY FOR ALL THE ROTTEN THINGS I'VE DONE TO YOU... LIKE NICKING YOUR MOUTH-ORGAN FROM YOUR KIT-BAG!
'ARF A MO'! I THOUGHT I'D LOST IT IN THE MUD!
CHARLEY! YOU-YOU'RE ALIVE! COR, WHAT DO YOU WANT TO GIVE ME A BLINKIN' FRIGHT FOR?
THE WORST EFFECTS OF THE GAS HAD WORN OFF... LEAVING CHARLEY VERY WEAK.
NEVER MIND THAT! WHAT ABOUT ME MOUTH-ORGAN, YOU ROTTEN THIEF?
I-I DIDN'T REALLY NICK IT! IT SORTA... SLIPPED INTO ME HAND! I WAS GONNA GIVE IT BACK... HONEST!
YOU'RE A STINKIN' LIAR! HAND IT OVER... RIGHT NOW!
IN A MINUTE! COME AND LOOK, CHARLEY! SEE WHAT'S COMING UP THROUGH THE CORN... HUNDREDS OF HORSES WITH AEROPLANES OVERHEAD!
AS THE RIDERS ADVANCED WITHOUT THEIR MASKS...
IT'S THE BIG BREAK-THROUGH AT LAST, GINGER!
EASY, RAWLINSON! YOU'RE NOT ON THE POLO FIELD NOW!

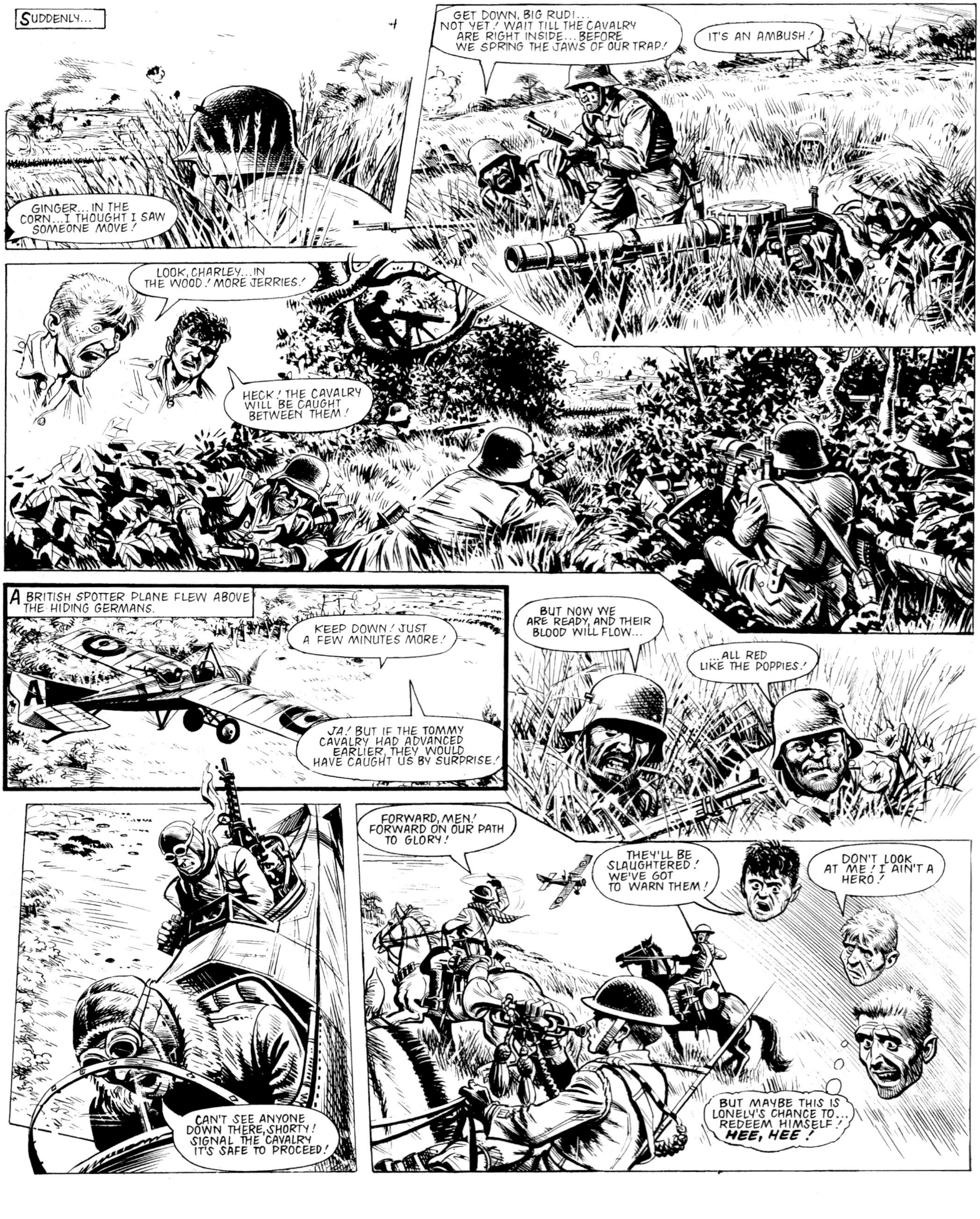
SUDDENLY...
GINGER... IN THE CORN... I THOUGHT I SAW SOMEONE MOVE!
GET DOWN, BIG RUDI... NOT YET! WAIT TILL THE CAVALRY ARE RIGHT INSIDE... BEFORE WE SPRING THE JAWS OF OUR TRAP!
IT'S AN AMBUSH!
LOOK, CHARLEY... IN THE WOOD! MORE JERRIES!
HECK! THE CAVALRY WILL BE CAUGHT BETWEEN THEM!
A BRITISH SPOTTER PLANE FLEW ABOVE THE HIDING GERMANS.
KEEP DOWN! JUST A FEW MINUTES MORE!
JA! BUT IF THE TOMMY CAVALRY HAD ADVANCED EARLIER, THEY WOULD HAVE CAUGHT US BY SURPRISE!
BUT NOW WE ARE READY, AND THEIR BLOOD WILL FLOW...
...ALL RED LIKE THE POPPIES!
CAN'T SEE ANYONE DOWN THERE, SHORTY! SIGNAL THE CAVALRY IT'S SAFE TO PROCEED!
FORWARD, MEN! FORWARD ON OUR PATH TO GLORY!
THEY'LL BE SLAUGHTERED! WE'VE GOT TO WARN THEM!
DON'T LOOK AT ME! I AIN'T A HERO!
BUT MAYBE THIS IS LONELY'S CHANCE TO... REDEEM HIMSELF! HEE, HEE!

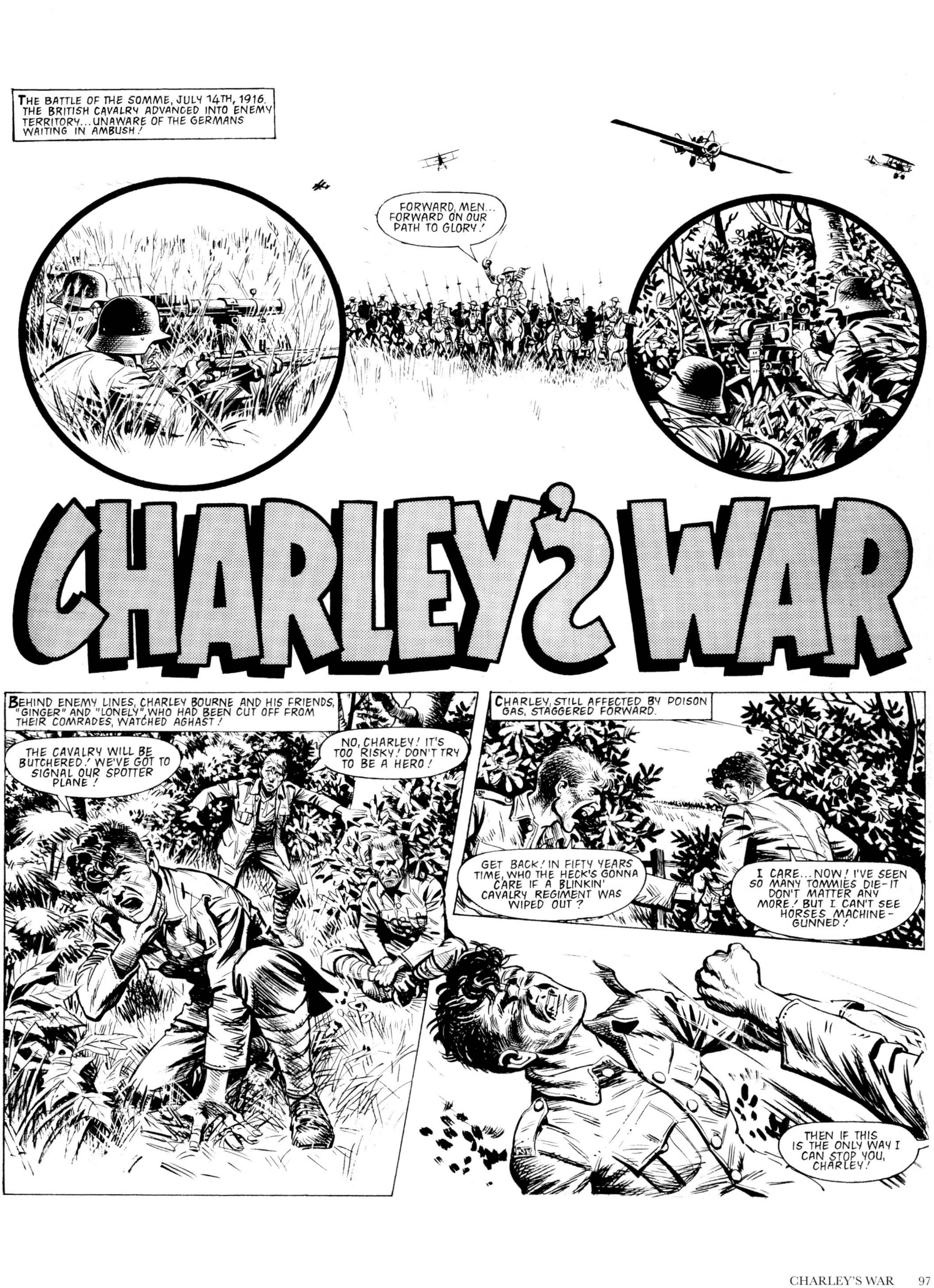
THE BATTLE OF THE SOMME, JULY 14TH, 1916. THE BRITISH CAVALRY ADVANCED INTO ENEMY TERRITORY... UNAWARE OF THE GERMANS WAITING IN AMBUSH!
FORWARD, MEN... FORWARD ON OUR PATH TO GLORY!
CHARLEY'S WAR
BEHIND ENEMY LINES, CHARLEY BOURNE AND HIS FRIENDS, "GINGER" AND "LONELY", WHO HAD BEEN CUT OFF FROM THEIR COMRADES, WATCHED AGHAST!
THE CAVALRY WILL BE BUTCHERED! WE'VE GOT TO SIGNAL OUR SPOTTER PLANE!
NO, CHARLEY! IT'S TOO RISKY! DON'T TRY TO BE A HERO!
CHARLEY, STILL AFFECTED BY POISON GAS, STAGGERED FORWARD.
GET BACK! IN FIFTY YEARS TIME, WHO THE HECK'S GONNA CARE IF A BLINKIN' CAVALRY REGIMENT WAS WIPED OUT?
I CARE... NOW! I'VE SEEN SO MANY TOMMIES DIE-IT DON'T MATTER ANY MORE! BUT I CAN'T SEE HORSES MACHINE-GUNNED!
THEN IF THIS IS THE ONLY WAY I CAN STOP YOU, CHARLEY!

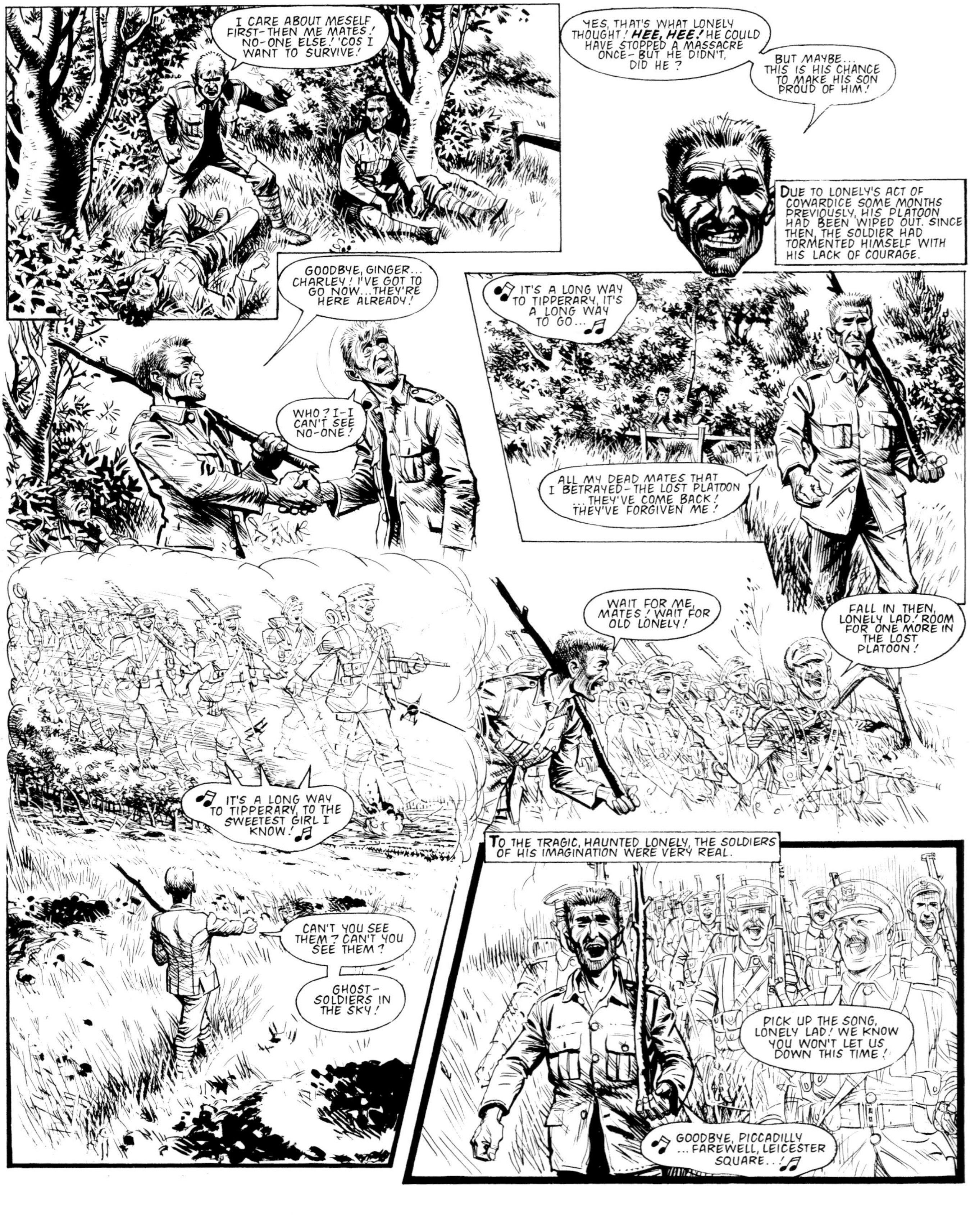
I CARE ABOUT MESELF FIRST- THEN ME MATES! NO-ONE ELSE! 'COS I WANT TO SURVIVE!
YES, THAT'S WHAT LONELY THOUGHT! HEE, HEE! HE COULD HAVE STOPPED A MASSACRE ONCE- BUT HE DIDN'T, DID HE?
BUT MAYBE... THIS IS HIS CHANCE TO MAKE HIS SON PROUD OF HIM!
DUE TO LONELY'S ACT OF COWARDICE SOME MONTHS PREVIOUSLY, HIS PLATOON HAD BEEN WIPED OUT. SINCE THEN, THE SOLDIER HAD TORMENTED HIMSELF WITH HIS LACK OF COURAGE.
GOODBYE, GINGER... CHARLEY! I'VE GOT TO GO NOW... THEY'RE HERE ALREADY!
WHO? I-I CAN'T SEE NO-ONE!
IT'S A LONG WAY TO TIPPERARY, IT'S A LONG WAY TO GO...
ALL MY DEAD MATES THAT I BETRAYED- THE LOST PLATOON ...THEY'VE COME BACK! THEY'VE FORGIVEN ME!
WAIT FOR ME, MATES! WAIT FOR OLD LONELY!
FALL IN THEN, LONELY LAD! ROOM FOR ONE MORE IN THE LOST PLATOON!
IT'S A LONG WAY TO TIPPERARY, TO THE SWEETEST GIRL I KNOW!
CAN'T YOU SEE THEM? CAN'T YOU SEE THEM?
GHOST-SOLDIERS IN THE SKY!
TO THE TRAGIC, HAUNTED LONELY, THE SOLDIERS OF HIS IMAGINATION WERE VERY REAL.
PICK UP THE SONG, LONELY LAD! WE KNOW YOU WON'T LET US DOWN THIS TIME!
GOODBYE, PICCADILLY ... FAREWELL, LEICESTER SQUARE..!

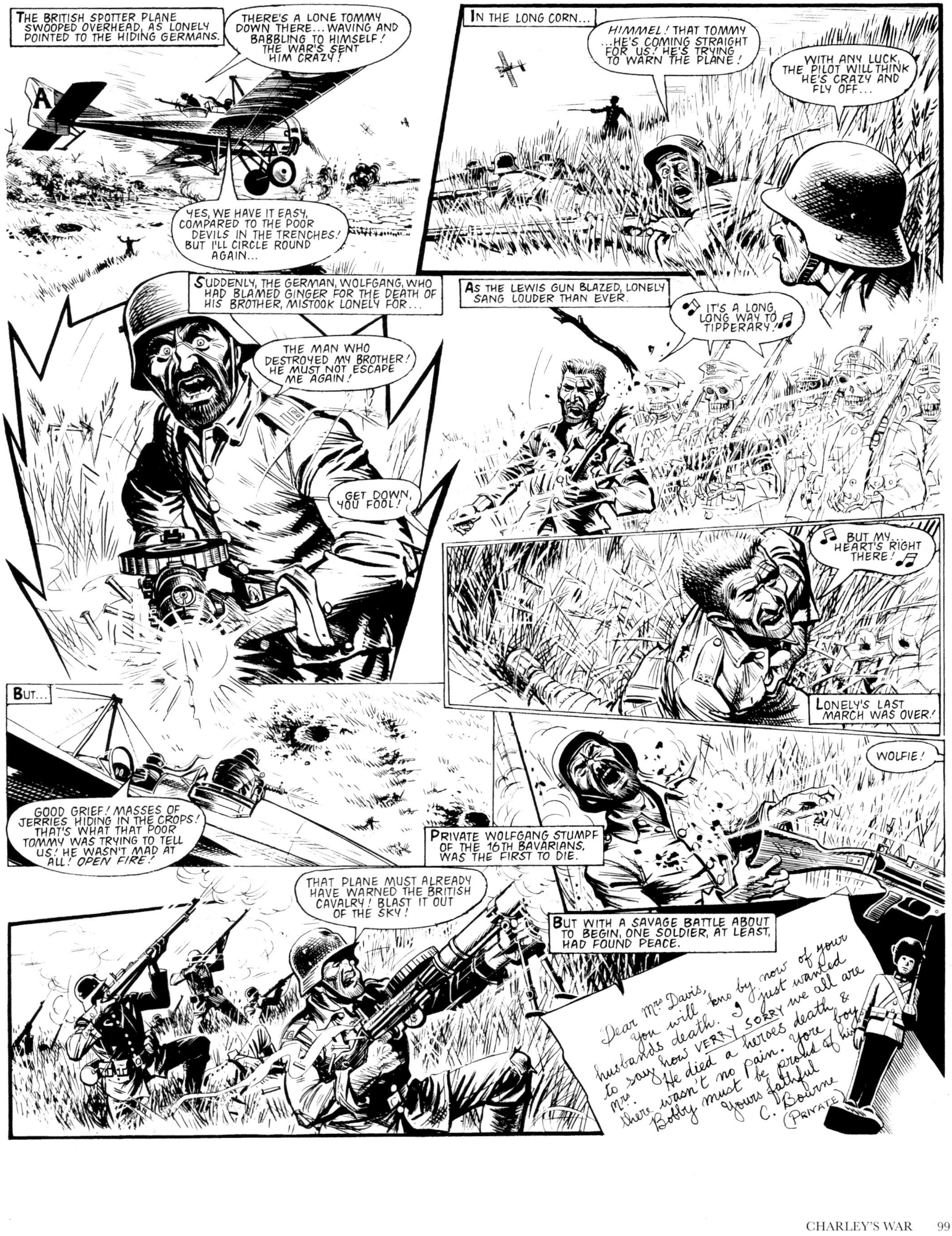

THE BRITISH SPOTTER PLANE SWOOPED OVERHEAD, AS LONELY POINTED TO THE HIDING GERMANS.
THERE'S A LONE TOMMY DOWN THERE... WAVING AND BABBLING TO HIMSELF! THE WAR'S SENT HIM CRAZY!
YES, WE HAVE IT EASY, COMPARED TO THE POOR DEVILS IN THE TRENCHES! BUT I'LL CIRCLE ROUND AGAIN...
IN THE LONG CORN...
HIMMEL! THAT TOMMY ...HE'S COMING STRAIGHT FOR US! HE'S TRYING TO WARN THE PLANE!
WITH ANY LUCK, THE PILOT WILL THINK HE'S CRAZY AND FLY OFF...
SUDDENLY, THE GERMAN, WOLFGANG, WHO HAD BLAMED GINGER FOR THE DEATH OF HIS BROTHER, MISTOOK LONELY FOR...
THE MAN WHO DESTROYED MY BROTHER! HE MUST NOT ESCAPE ME AGAIN!
GET DOWN, YOU FOOL!
AS THE LEWIS GUN BLAZED, LONELY SANG LOUDER THAN EVER.
IT'S A LONG, LONG WAY TO TIPPERARY!
BUT MY... HEART'S RIGHT THERE!
LONELY'S LAST MARCH WAS OVER!
BUT...
GOOD GRIEF! MASSES OF JERRIES HIDING IN THE CROPS! THAT'S WHAT THAT POOR TOMMY WAS TRYING TO TELL US! HE WASN'T MAD AT ALL! OPEN FIRE!
WOLFIE!
PRIVATE WOLFGANG STUMPF OF THE 16TH BAVARIANS, WAS THE FIRST TO DIE.
THAT PLANE MUST ALREADY HAVE WARNED THE BRITISH CAVALRY! BLAST IT OUT OF THE SKY!
BUT WITH A SAVAGE BATTLE ABOUT TO BEGIN, ONE SOLDIER, AT LEAST, HAD FOUND PEACE.
Dear Mrs Davis,
You will kno by now of your
husbands death. I just wanted
to say how VERRY SORRY we all are
Mrs. He died a heroes death &
there wasn't no pain. Yore boy
Bobby must be proud of him
Yours faithful
C. Bourne
(PRIVATE)

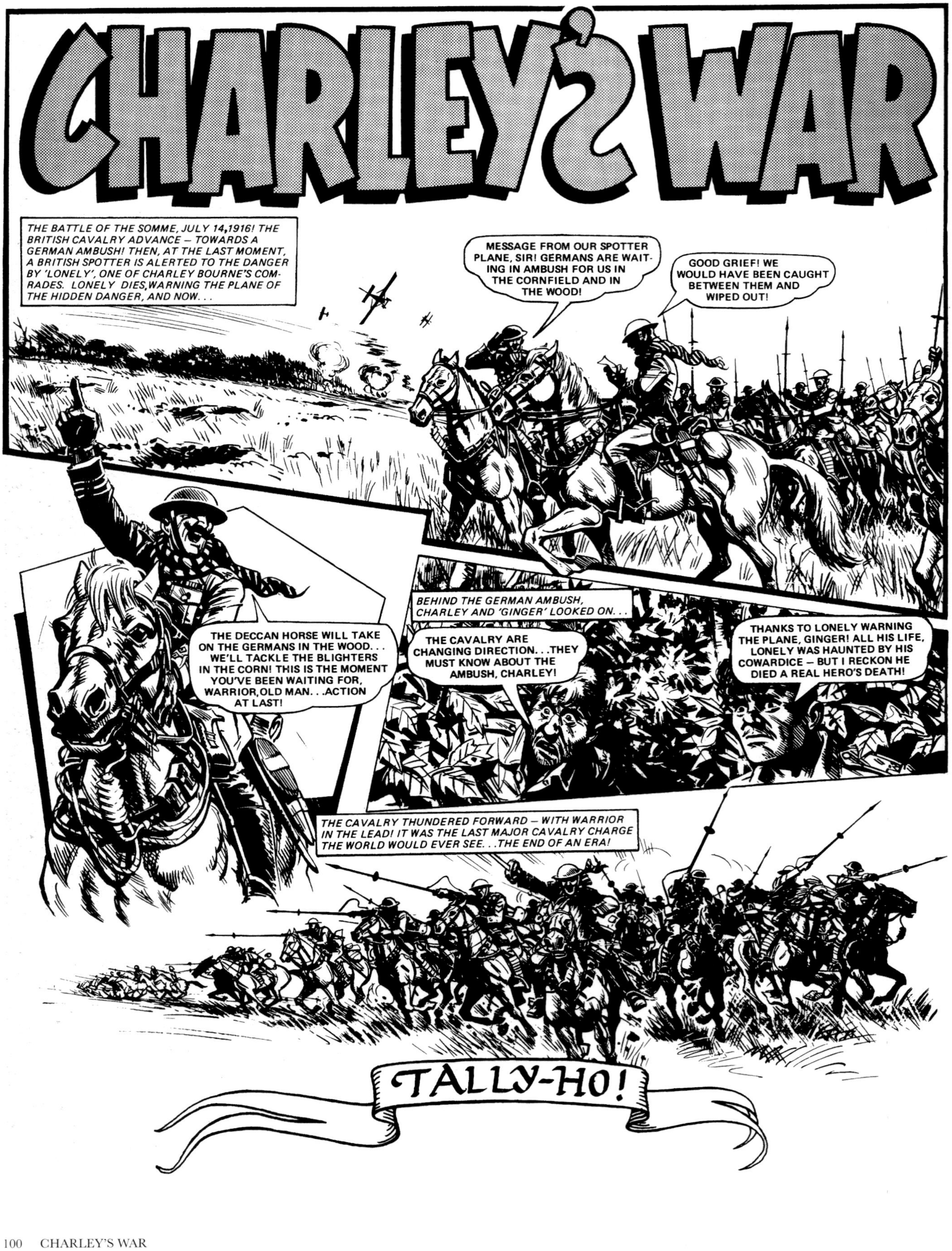
CHARLEY'S WAR
THE BATTLE OF THE SOMME, JULY 14,1916! THE BRITISH CAVALRY ADVANCE – TOWARDS A GERMAN AMBUSH! THEN, AT THE LAST MOMENT, A BRITISH SPOTTER IS ALERTED TO THE DANGER BY 'LONELY', ONE OF CHARLEY BOURNE'S COMRADES. LONELY DIES,WARNING THE PLANE OF THE HIDDEN DANGER, AND NOW. . .
MESSAGE FROM OUR SPOTTER PLANE, SIR! GERMANS ARE WAITING IN AMBUSH FOR US IN THE CORNFIELD AND IN THE WOOD!
GOOD GRIEF! WE WOULD HAVE BEEN CAUGHT BETWEEN THEM AND WIPED OUT!
THE DECCAN HORSE WILL TAKE ON THE GERMANS IN THE WOOD. . . WE'LL TACKLE THE BLIGHTERS IN THE CORN! THIS IS THE MOMENT YOU'VE BEEN WAITING FOR, WARRIOR,OLD MAN. . .ACTION AT LAST!
BEHIND THE GERMAN AMBUSH, CHARLEY AND 'GINGER' LOOKED ON. . .
THE CAVALRY ARE CHANGING DIRECTION. . .THEY MUST KNOW ABOUT THE AMBUSH, CHARLEY!
THANKS TO LONELY WARNING THE PLANE, GINGER! ALL HIS LIFE, LONELY WAS HAUNTED BY HIS COWARDICE – BUT I RECKON HE DIED A REAL HERO'S DEATH!
THE CAVALRY THUNDERED FORWARD – WITH WARRIOR IN THE LEAD! IT WAS THE LAST MAJOR CAVALRY CHARGE THE WORLD WOULD EVER SEE. . .THE END OF AN ERA!
TALLY-HO!

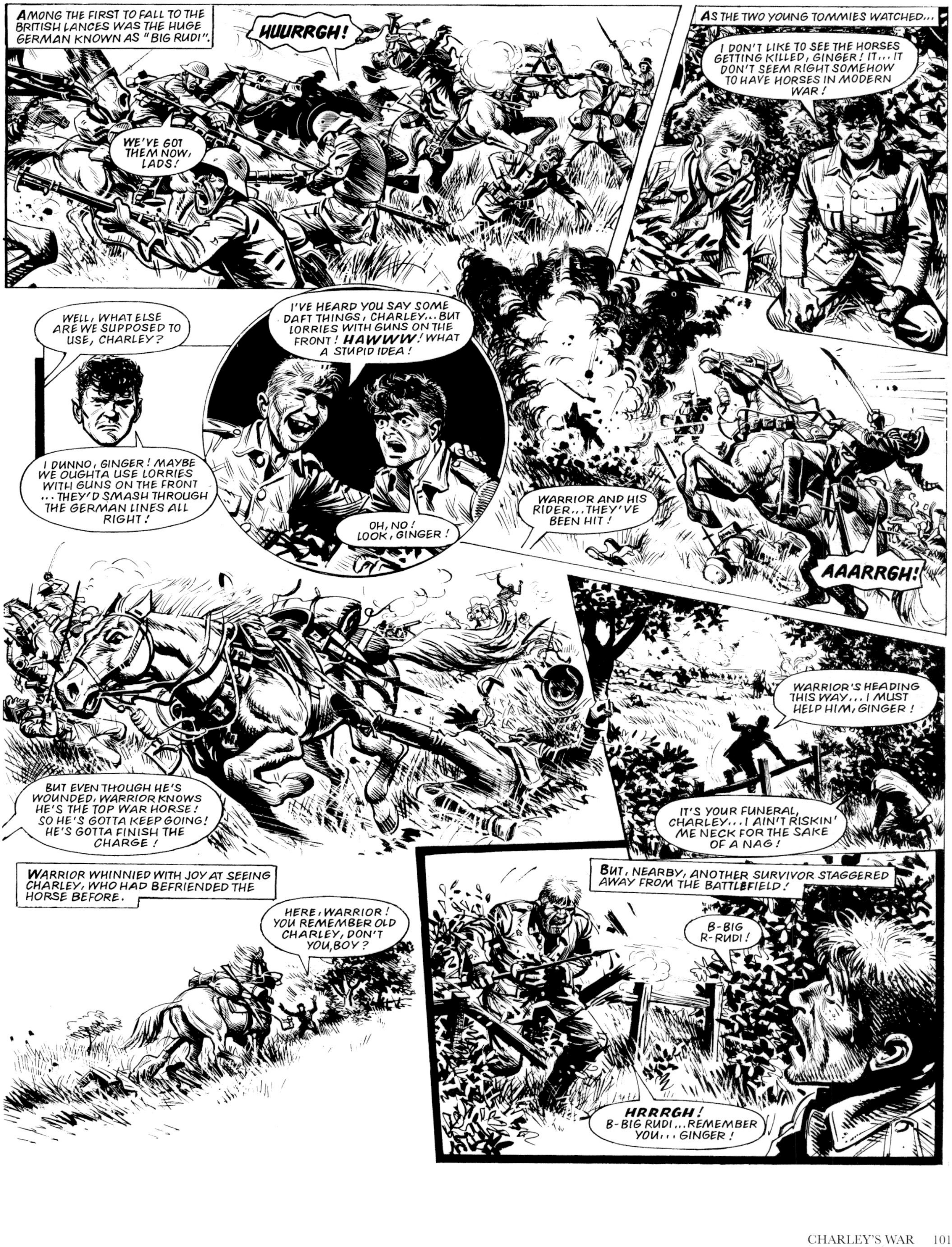
AMONG THE FIRST TO FALL TO THE BRITISH LANCES WAS THE HUGE GERMAN KNOWN AS "BIG RUDI".
HUURRGH!
WE'VE GOT THEM NOW, LADS!
AS THE TWO YOUNG TOMMIES WATCHED...
I DON'T LIKE TO SEE THE HORSES GETTING KILLED, GINGER! IT... IT DON'T SEEM RIGHT SOMEHOW TO HAVE HORSES IN MODERN WAR!
WELL, WHAT ELSE ARE WE SUPPOSED TO USE, CHARLEY?
I DUNNO, GINGER! MAYBE WE OUGHTA USE LORRIES WITH GUNS ON THE FRONT ... THEY'D SMASH THROUGH THE GERMAN LINES ALL RIGHT!
I'VE HEARD YOU SAY SOME DAFT THINGS, CHARLEY... BUT LORRIES WITH GUNS ON THE FRONT! HAWWW! WHAT A STUPID IDEA!
OH, NO! LOOK, GINGER!
WARRIOR AND HIS RIDER... THEY'VE BEEN HIT!
AAARRGH!
BUT EVEN THOUGH HE'S WOUNDED, WARRIOR KNOWS HE'S THE TOP WAR HORSE! SO HE'S GOTTA KEEP GOING! HE'S GOTTA FINISH THE CHARGE!
WARRIOR'S HEADING THIS WAY... I MUST HELP HIM, GINGER!
IT'S YOUR FUNERAL, CHARLEY... I AIN'T RISKIN' ME NECK FOR THE SAKE OF A NAG!
WARRIOR WHINNIED WITH JOY AT SEEING CHARLEY, WHO HAD BEFRIENDED THE HORSE BEFORE.
HERE, WARRIOR! YOU REMEMBER OLD CHARLEY, DON'T YOU, BOY?
BUT, NEARBY, ANOTHER SURVIVOR STAGGERED AWAY FROM THE BATTLEFIELD!
B-BIG R-RUDI!
HRRRGH! B-BIG RUDI... REMEMBER YOU... GINGER!

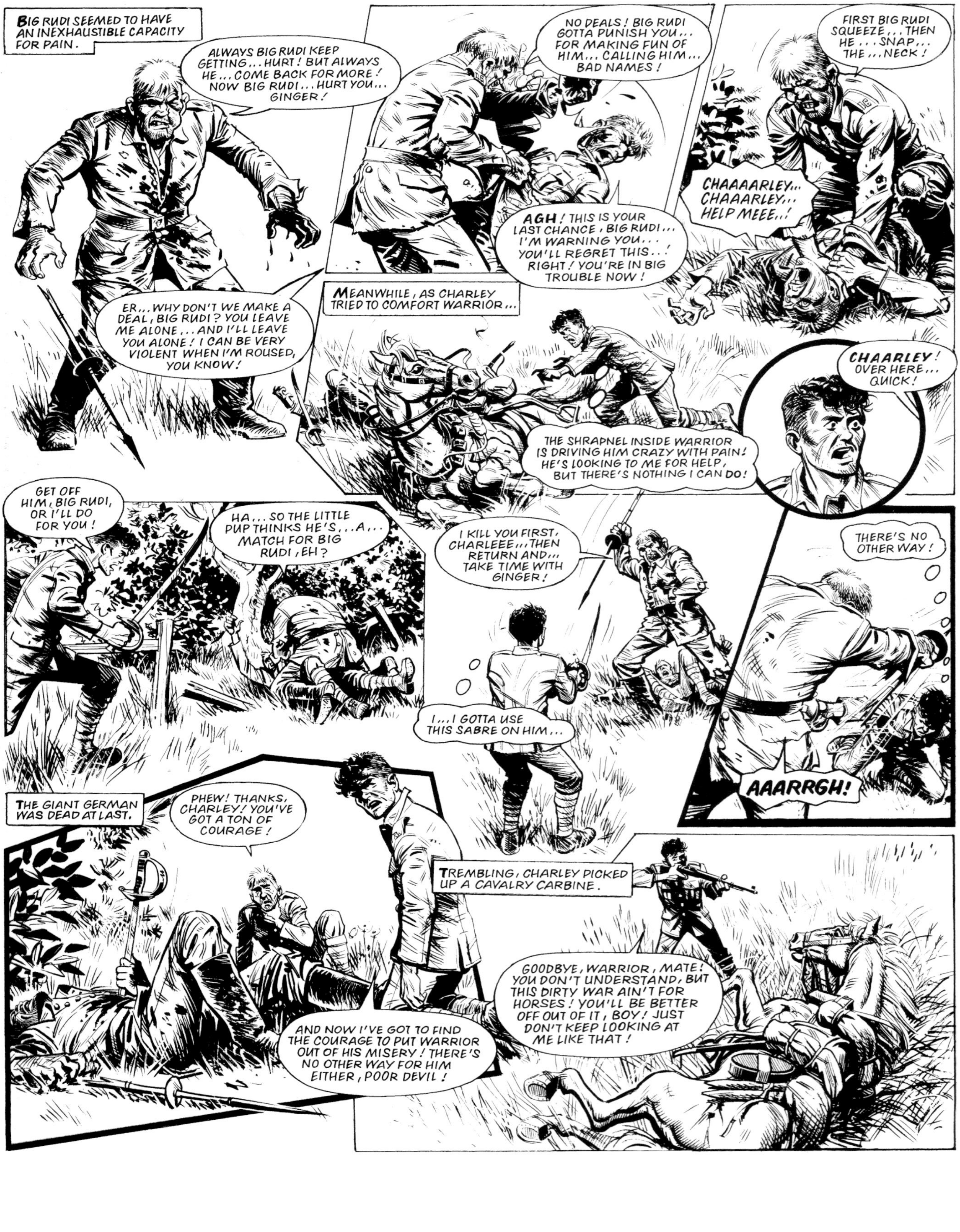
BIG RUDI SEEMED TO HAVE AN INEXHAUSTIBLE CAPACITY FOR PAIN.
ALWAYS BIG RUDI KEEP GETTING... HURT! BUT ALWAYS HE... COME BACK FOR MORE! NOW BIG RUDI... HURT YOU... GINGER!
ER... WHY DON'T WE MAKE A DEAL, BIG RUDI? YOU LEAVE ME ALONE... AND I'LL LEAVE YOU ALONE! I CAN BE VERY VIOLENT WHEN I'M ROUSED, YOU KNOW!
NO DEALS! BIG RUDI GOTTA PUNISH YOU... FOR MAKING FUN OF HIM... CALLING HIM... BAD NAMES!
AGH! THIS IS YOUR LAST CHANCE, BIG RUDI... I'M WARNING YOU... YOU'LL REGRET THIS...! RIGHT! YOU'RE IN BIG TROUBLE NOW!
FIRST BIG RUDI SQUEEZE... THEN HE... SNAP... THE... NECK!
CHAAAARLEY... CHAAARLEY... HELP MEEE...!
MEANWHILE, AS CHARLEY TRIED TO COMFORT WARRIOR...
THE SHRAPNEL INSIDE WARRIOR IS DRIVING HIM CRAZY WITH PAIN! HE'S LOOKING TO ME FOR HELP, BUT THERE'S NOTHING I CAN DO!
CHAARLEY! OVER HERE... QUICK!
GET OFF HIM, BIG RUDI, OR I'LL DO FOR YOU!
HA... SO THE LITTLE PUP THINKS HE'S... A... MATCH FOR BIG RUDI, EH?
I KILL YOU FIRST, CHARLEEE... THEN RETURN AND... TAKE TIME WITH GINGER!
I... I GOTTA USE THIS SABRE ON HIM...
THERE'S NO OTHER WAY!
AAARRGH!
THE GIANT GERMAN WAS DEAD AT LAST.
PHEW! THANKS, CHARLEY! YOU'VE GOT A TON OF COURAGE!
AND NOW I'VE GOT TO FIND THE COURAGE TO PUT WARRIOR OUT OF HIS MISERY! THERE'S NO OTHER WAY FOR HIM EITHER, POOR DEVIL!
TREMBLING, CHARLEY PICKED UP A CAVALRY CARBINE.
GOODBYE, WARRIOR, MATE! YOU DON'T UNDERSTAND, BUT THIS DIRTY WAR AIN'T FOR HORSES! YOU'LL BE BETTER OFF OUT OF IT, BOY! JUST DON'T KEEP LOOKING AT ME LIKE THAT!

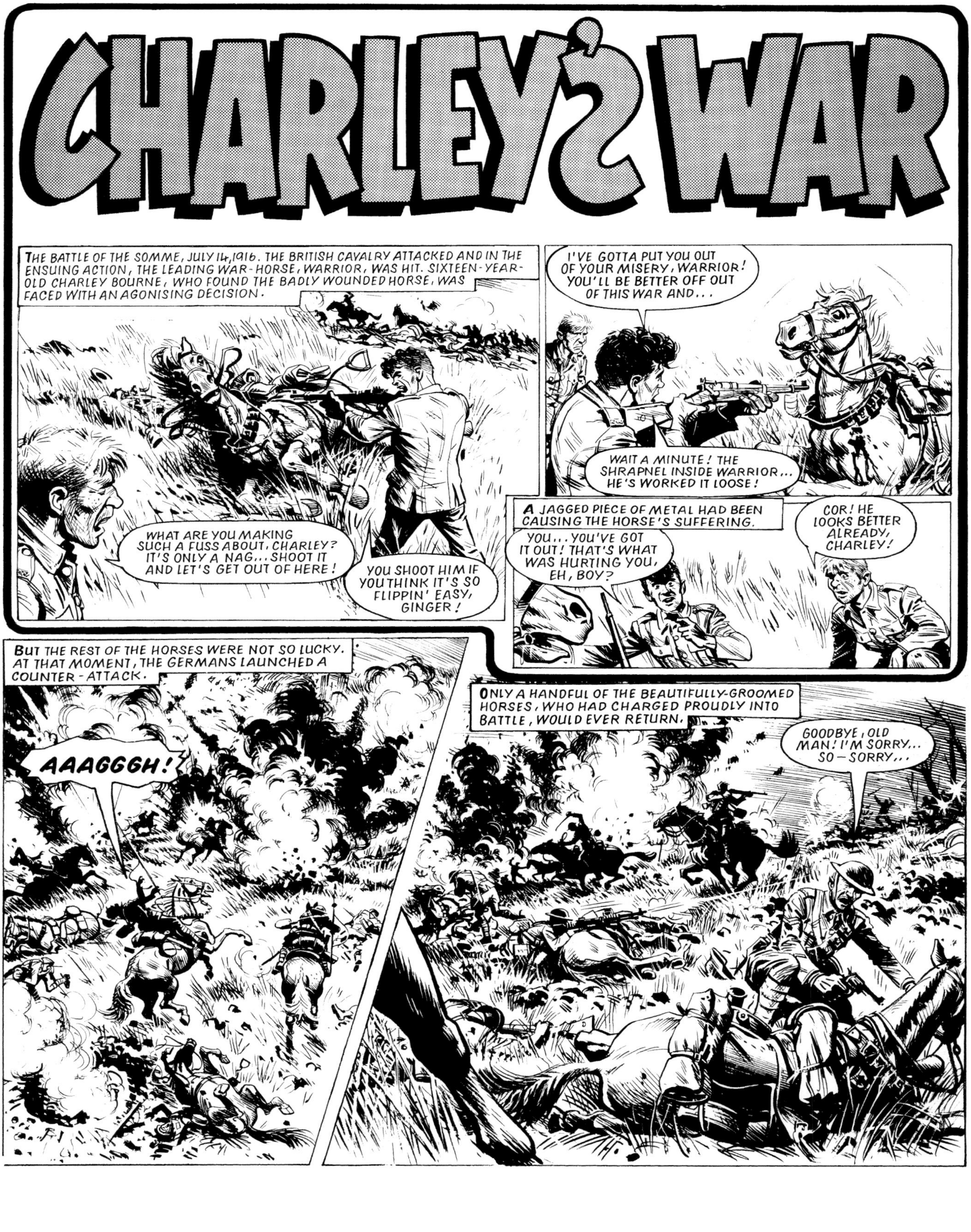

CHARLEY'S WAR
THE BATTLE OF THE SOMME, JULY 14, 1916. THE BRITISH CAVALRY ATTACKED AND IN THE ENSUING ACTION, THE LEADING WAR-HORSE, WARRIOR, WAS HIT. SIXTEEN-YEAR-OLD CHARLEY BOURNE, WHO FOUND THE BADLY WOUNDED HORSE, WAS FACED WITH AN AGONISING DECISION.
WHAT ARE YOU MAKING SUCH A FUSS ABOUT, CHARLEY? IT'S ONLY A NAG... SHOOT IT AND LET'S GET OUT OF HERE!
YOU SHOOT HIM IF YOU THINK IT'S SO FLIPPIN' EASY, GINGER!
I'VE GOTTA PUT YOU OUT OF YOUR MISERY, WARRIOR! YOU'LL BE BETTER OFF OUT OF THIS WAR AND...
WAIT A MINUTE! THE SHRAPNEL INSIDE WARRIOR... HE'S WORKED IT LOOSE!
A JAGGED PIECE OF METAL HAD BEEN CAUSING THE HORSE'S SUFFERING.
YOU... YOU'VE GOT IT OUT! THAT'S WHAT WAS HURTING YOU, EH, BOY?
COR! HE LOOKS BETTER ALREADY, CHARLEY!
BUT THE REST OF THE HORSES WERE NOT SO LUCKY. AT THAT MOMENT, THE GERMANS LAUNCHED A COUNTER-ATTACK.
AAAGGGH!
ONLY A HANDFUL OF THE BEAUTIFULLY-GROOMED HORSES, WHO HAD CHARGED PROUDLY INTO BATTLE, WOULD EVER RETURN.
GOODBYE, OLD MAN! I'M SORRY... SO—SORRY...

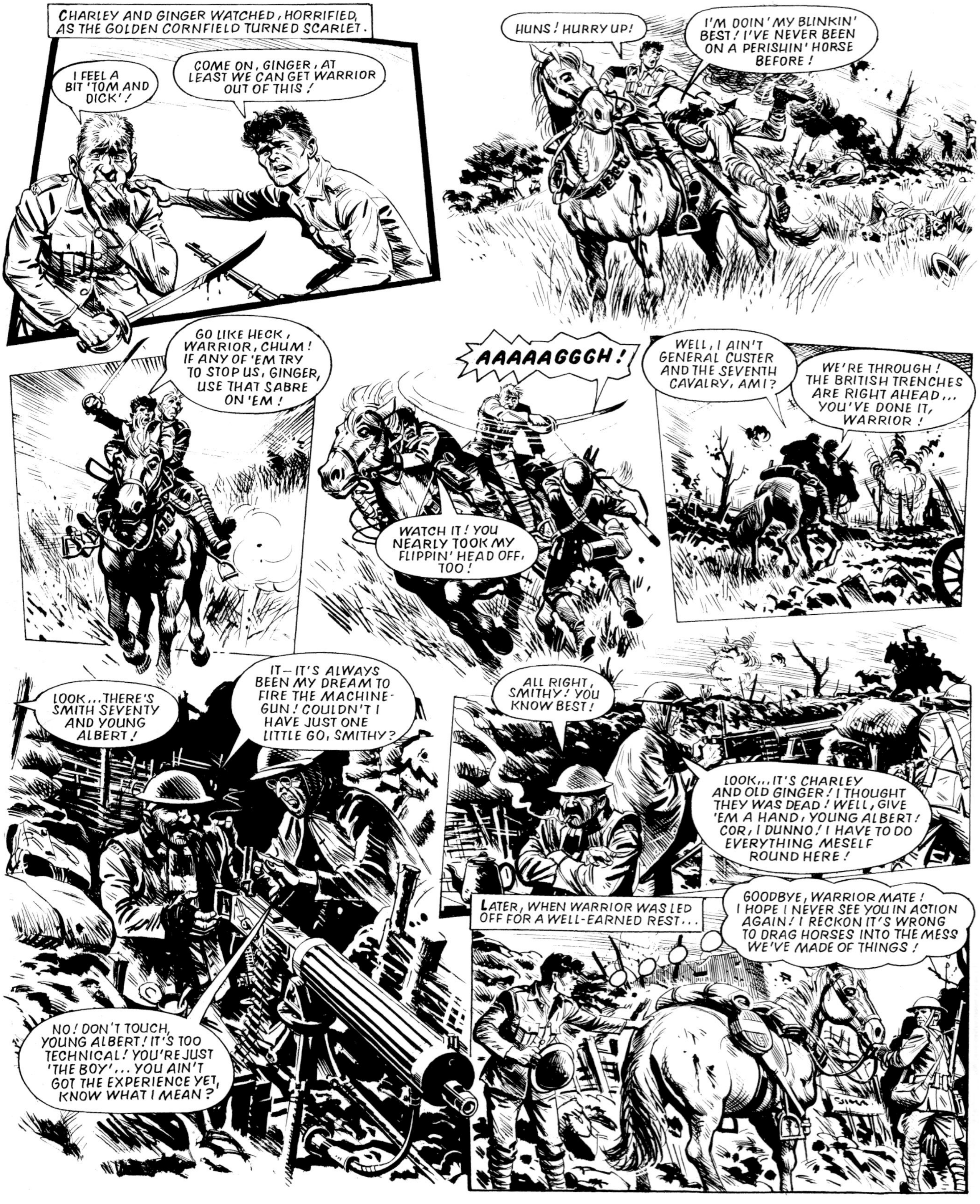
CHARLEY AND GINGER WATCHED, HORRIFIED, AS THE GOLDEN CORNFIELD TURNED SCARLET.
I FEEL A BIT 'TOM AND DICK'!
COME ON, GINGER, AT LEAST WE CAN GET WARRIOR OUT OF THIS!
HUNS! HURRY UP!
I'M DOIN' MY BLINKIN' BEST! I'VE NEVER BEEN ON A PERISHIN' HORSE BEFORE!
GO LIKE HECK, WARRIOR, CHUM! IF ANY OF 'EM TRY TO STOP US, GINGER, USE THAT SABRE ON 'EM!
AAAAAGGGH!
WATCH IT! YOU NEARLY TOOK MY FLIPPIN' HEAD OFF, TOO!
WELL, I AIN'T GENERAL CUSTER AND THE SEVENTH CAVALRY, AM I?
WE'RE THROUGH! THE BRITISH TRENCHES ARE RIGHT AHEAD... YOU'VE DONE IT, WARRIOR!
LOOK... THERE'S SMITH SEVENTY AND YOUNG ALBERT!
IT—IT'S ALWAYS BEEN MY DREAM TO FIRE THE MACHINE-GUN! COULDN'T I HAVE JUST ONE LITTLE GO, SMITHY?
NO! DON'T TOUCH, YOUNG ALBERT! IT'S TOO TECHNICAL! YOU'RE JUST 'THE BOY'... YOU AIN'T GOT THE EXPERIENCE YET, KNOW WHAT I MEAN?
ALL RIGHT, SMITHY! YOU KNOW BEST!
LOOK... IT'S CHARLEY AND OLD GINGER! I THOUGHT THEY WAS DEAD! WELL, GIVE 'EM A HAND, YOUNG ALBERT! COR, I DUNNO! I HAVE TO DO EVERYTHING MESELF ROUND HERE!
LATER, WHEN WARRIOR WAS LED OFF FOR A WELL-EARNED REST...
GOODBYE, WARRIOR MATE! I HOPE I NEVER SEE YOU IN ACTION AGAIN! I RECKON IT'S WRONG TO DRAG HORSES INTO THE MESS WE'VE MADE OF THINGS!

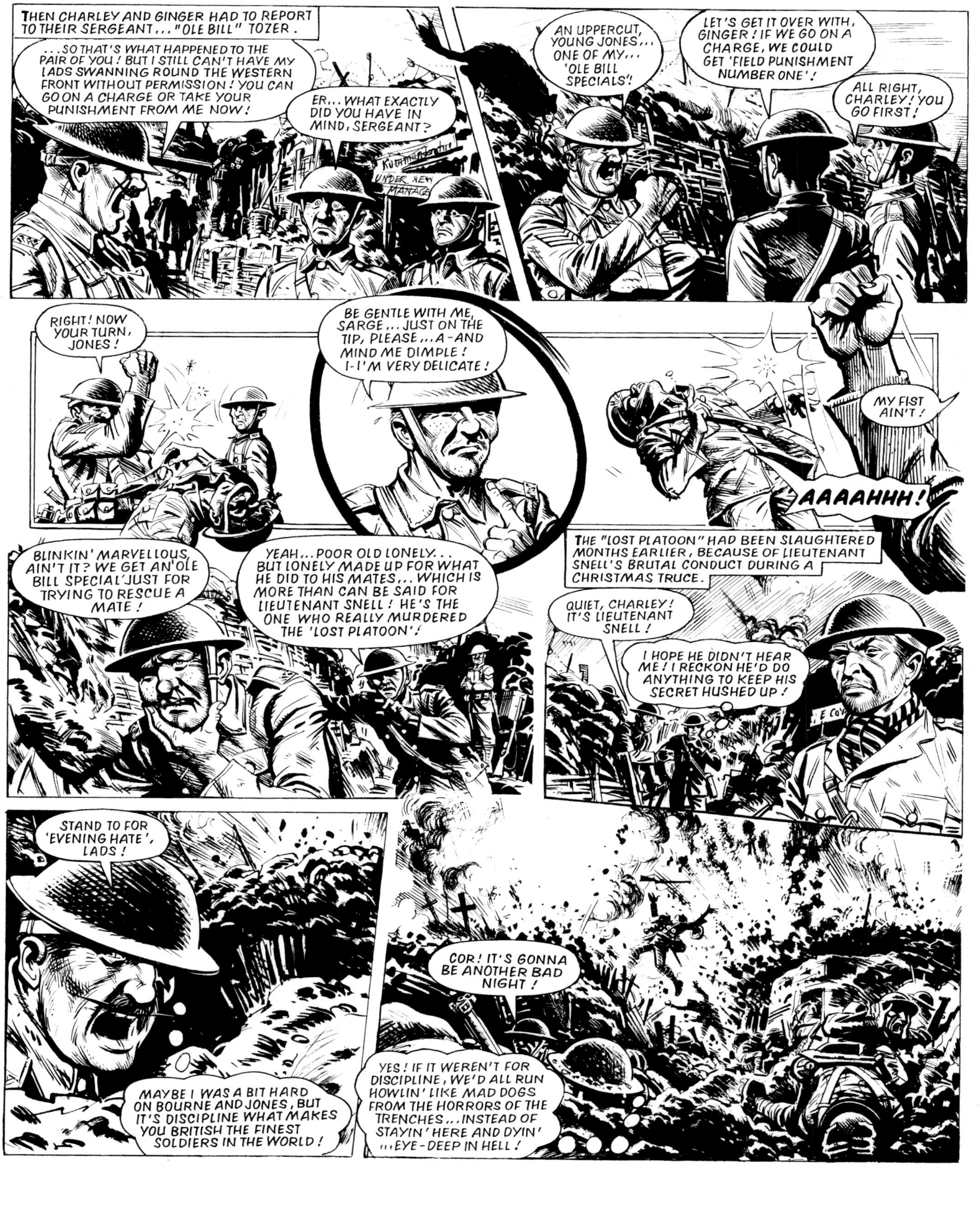
THEN CHARLEY AND GINGER HAD TO REPORT TO THEIR SERGEANT... "OLE BILL" TOZER.
...SO THAT'S WHAT HAPPENED TO THE PAIR OF YOU! BUT I STILL CAN'T HAVE MY LADS SWANNING ROUND THE WESTERN FRONT WITHOUT PERMISSION! YOU CAN GO ON A CHARGE OR TAKE YOUR PUNISHMENT FROM ME NOW!
ER... WHAT EXACTLY DID YOU HAVE IN MIND, SERGEANT?
UNDER NEW MANAGE
AN UPPERCUT, YOUNG JONES... ONE OF MY... 'OLE BILL SPECIALS'!
LET'S GET IT OVER WITH, GINGER! IF WE GO ON A CHARGE, WE COULD GET 'FIELD PUNISHMENT NUMBER ONE'!
ALL RIGHT, CHARLEY! YOU GO FIRST!
RIGHT! NOW YOUR TURN, JONES!
BE GENTLE WITH ME, SARGE... JUST ON THE TIP, PLEASE... A-AND MIND ME DIMPLE! I-I'M VERY DELICATE!
MY FIST AIN'T!
AAAAAHHH!
BLINKIN' MARVELLOUS, AIN'T IT? WE GET AN 'OLE BILL SPECIAL' JUST FOR TRYING TO RESCUE A MATE!
YEAH... POOR OLD LONELY... BUT LONELY MADE UP FOR WHAT HE DID TO HIS MATES... WHICH IS MORE THAN CAN BE SAID FOR LIEUTENANT SNELL! HE'S THE ONE WHO REALLY MURDERED THE 'LOST PLATOON'!
THE "LOST PLATOON" HAD BEEN SLAUGHTERED MONTHS EARLIER, BECAUSE OF LIEUTENANT SNELL'S BRUTAL CONDUCT DURING A CHRISTMAS TRUCE.
QUIET, CHARLEY! IT'S LIEUTENANT SNELL!
I HOPE HE DIDN'T HEAR ME! I RECKON HE'D DO ANYTHING TO KEEP HIS SECRET HUSHED UP!
STAND TO FOR 'EVENING HATE', LADS!
MAYBE I WAS A BIT HARD ON BOURNE AND JONES, BUT IT'S DISCIPLINE WHAT MAKES YOU BRITISH THE FINEST SOLDIERS IN THE WORLD!
COR! IT'S GONNA BE ANOTHER BAD NIGHT!
YES! IF IT WEREN'T FOR DISCIPLINE, WE'D ALL RUN HOWLIN' LIKE MAD DOGS FROM THE HORRORS OF THE TRENCHES... INSTEAD OF STAYIN' HERE AND DYIN' ...EYE-DEEP IN HELL!

CHARLEY'S WAR

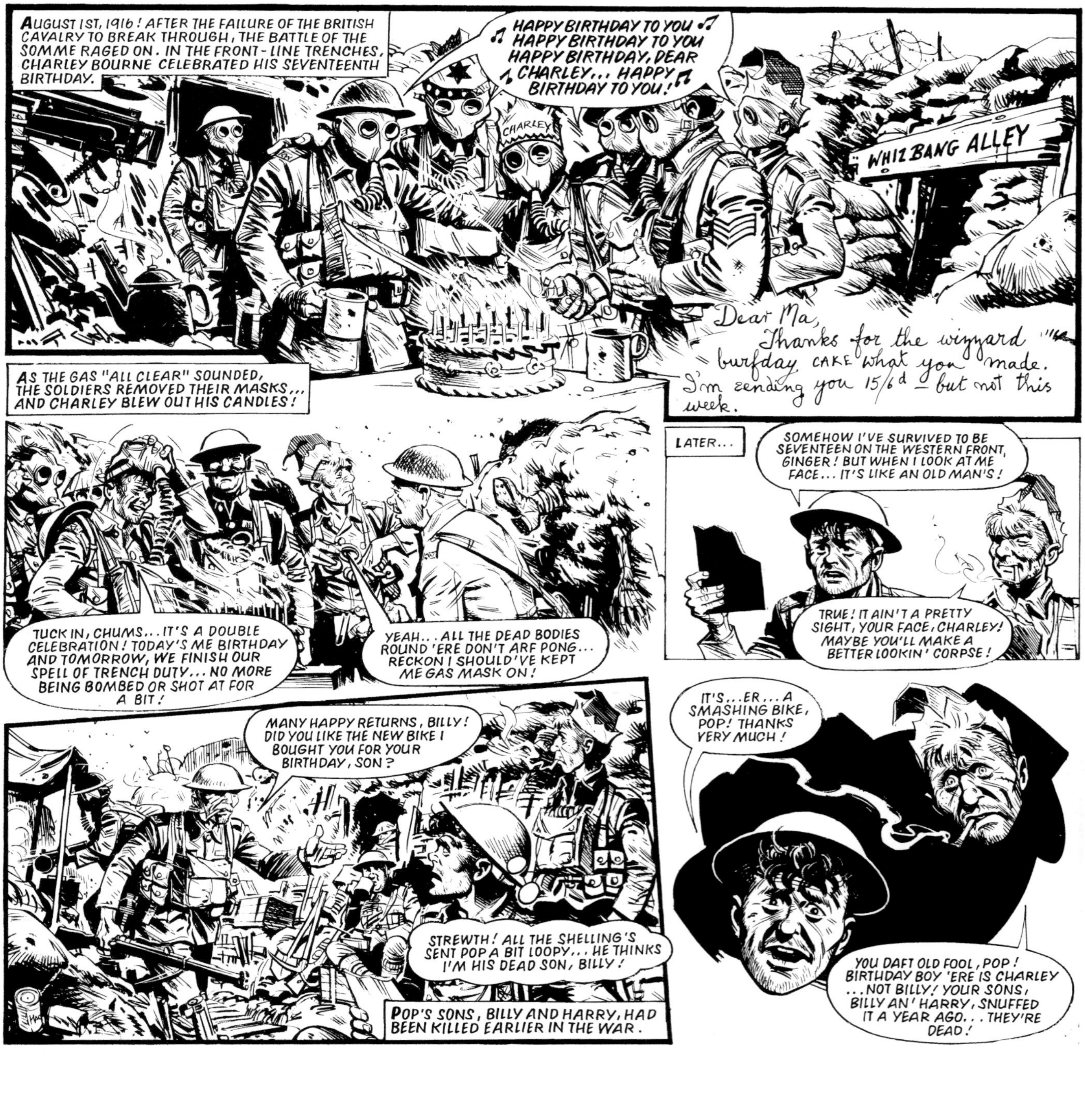

AUGUST 1ST, 1916! AFTER THE FAILURE OF THE BRITISH CAVALRY TO BREAK THROUGH, THE BATTLE OF THE SOMME RAGED ON. IN THE FRONT-LINE TRENCHES, CHARLEY BOURNE CELEBRATED HIS SEVENTEENTH BIRTHDAY.
HAPPY BIRTHDAY TO YOU HAPPY BIRTHDAY TO YOU HAPPY BIRTHDAY, DEAR CHARLEY... HAPPY BIRTHDAY TO YOU!
CHARLEY
WHIZ BANG ALLEY
Dear Ma, Thanks for the wizzard burfday CAKE what you made. I'm sending you 15/6d – but not this week.
AS THE GAS "ALL CLEAR" SOUNDED, THE SOLDIERS REMOVED THEIR MASKS... AND CHARLEY BLEW OUT HIS CANDLES!
TUCK IN, CHUMS... IT'S A DOUBLE CELEBRATION! TODAY'S ME BIRTHDAY AND TOMORROW, WE FINISH OUR SPELL OF TRENCH DUTY... NO MORE BEING BOMBED OR SHOT AT FOR A BIT!
YEAH... ALL THE DEAD BODIES ROUND 'ERE DON'T ARF PONG... RECKON I SHOULD'VE KEPT ME GAS MASK ON!
LATER...
SOMEHOW I'VE SURVIVED TO BE SEVENTEEN ON THE WESTERN FRONT, GINGER! BUT WHEN I LOOK AT ME FACE... IT'S LIKE AN OLD MAN'S!
TRUE! IT AIN'T A PRETTY SIGHT, YOUR FACE, CHARLEY! MAYBE YOU'LL MAKE A BETTER LOOKIN' CORPSE!
MANY HAPPY RETURNS, BILLY! DID YOU LIKE THE NEW BIKE I BOUGHT YOU FOR YOUR BIRTHDAY, SON?
STREWTH! ALL THE SHELLING'S SENT POP A BIT LOOPY... HE THINKS I'M HIS DEAD SON, BILLY!
POP'S SONS, BILLY AND HARRY, HAD BEEN KILLED EARLIER IN THE WAR.
IT'S... ER... A SMASHING BIKE, POP! THANKS VERY MUCH!
YOU DAFT OLD FOOL, POP! BIRTHDAY BOY 'ERE IS CHARLEY ...NOT BILLY! YOUR SONS, BILLY AN' HARRY, SNUFFED IT A YEAR AGO... THEY'RE DEAD!

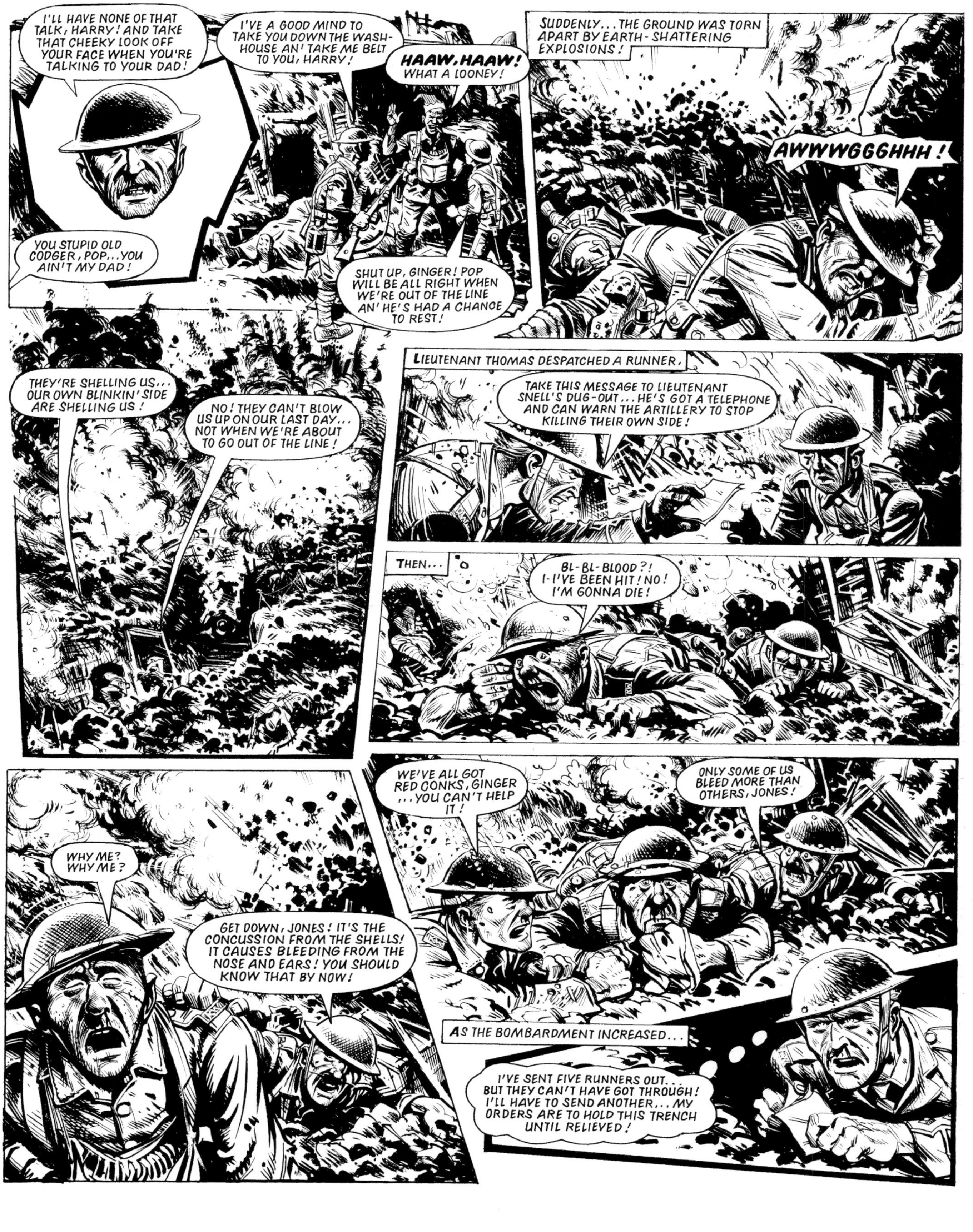
I'LL HAVE NONE OF THAT TALK, HARRY! AND TAKE THAT CHEEKY LOOK OFF YOUR FACE WHEN YOU'RE TALKING TO YOUR DAD!
YOU STUPID OLD CODGER, POP... YOU AIN'T MY DAD!
I'VE A GOOD MIND TO TAKE YOU DOWN THE WASH-HOUSE AN' TAKE ME BELT TO YOU, HARRY!
HAAW, HAAW! WHAT A LOONEY!
SHUT UP, GINGER! POP WILL BE ALL RIGHT WHEN WE'RE OUT OF THE LINE AN' HE'S HAD A CHANCE TO REST!
SUDDENLY... THE GROUND WAS TORN APART BY EARTH-SHATTERING EXPLOSIONS!
AWWWGGGHHH!
THEY'RE SHELLING US... OUR OWN BLINKIN' SIDE ARE SHELLING US!
NO! THEY CAN'T BLOW US UP ON OUR LAST DAY... NOT WHEN WE'RE ABOUT TO GO OUT OF THE LINE!
LIEUTENANT THOMAS DESPATCHED A RUNNER.
TAKE THIS MESSAGE TO LIEUTENANT SNELL'S DUG-OUT... HE'S GOT A TELEPHONE AND CAN WARN THE ARTILLERY TO STOP KILLING THEIR OWN SIDE!
THEN...
BL-BL-BLOOD?! I-I'VE BEEN HIT! NO! I'M GONNA DIE!
WHY ME? WHY ME?
GET DOWN, JONES! IT'S THE CONCUSSION FROM THE SHELLS! IT CAUSES BLEEDING FROM THE NOSE AND EARS! YOU SHOULD KNOW THAT BY NOW!
WE'VE ALL GOT RED CONKS, GINGER ... YOU CAN'T HELP IT!
ONLY SOME OF US BLEED MORE THAN OTHERS, JONES!
AS THE BOMBARDMENT INCREASED...
I'VE SENT FIVE RUNNERS OUT... BUT THEY CAN'T HAVE GOT THROUGH! I'LL HAVE TO SEND ANOTHER... MY ORDERS ARE TO HOLD THIS TRENCH UNTIL RELIEVED!

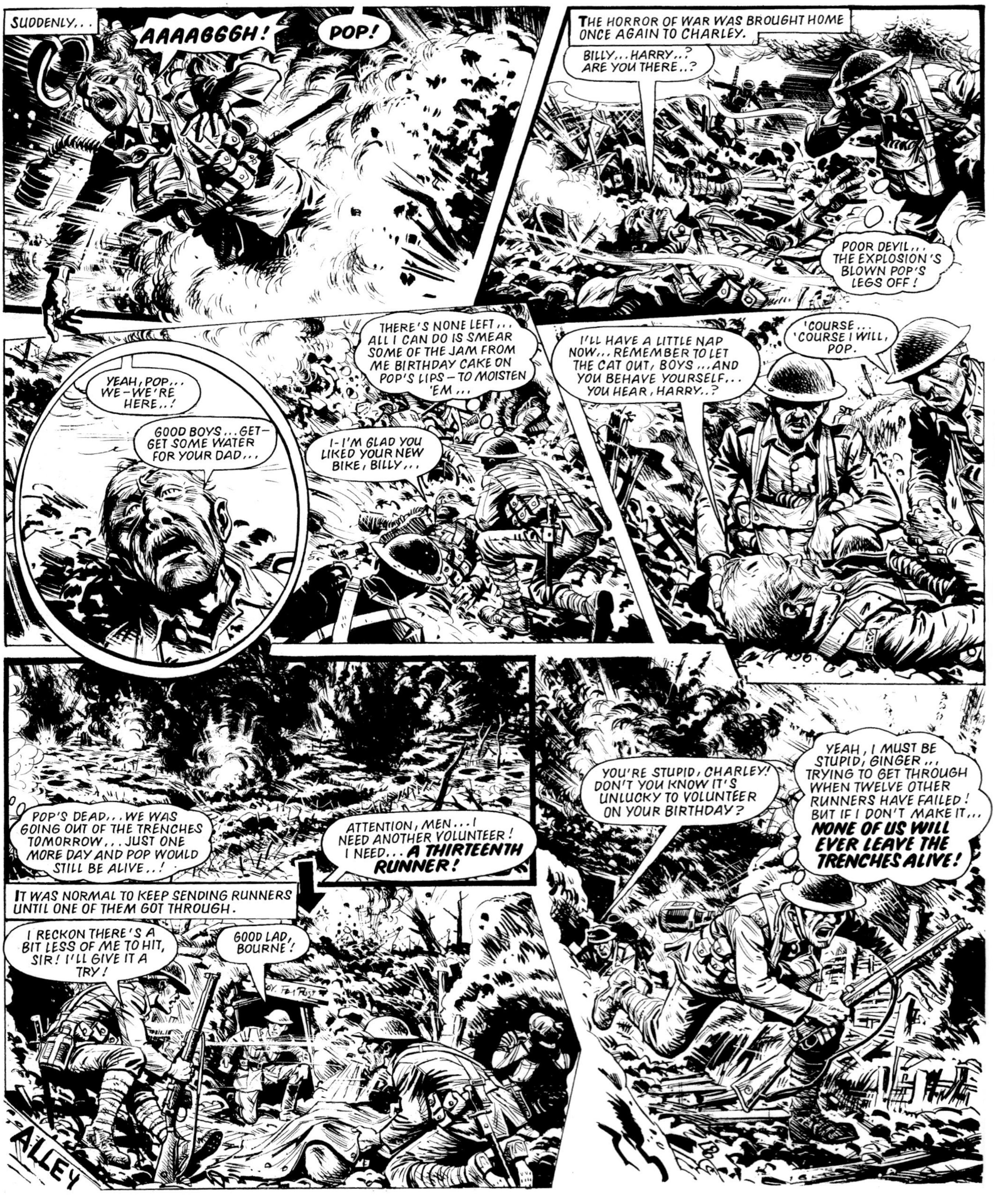

SUDDENLY...
AAAABGGH!
POP!
THE HORROR OF WAR WAS BROUGHT HOME ONCE AGAIN TO CHARLEY.
BILLY... HARRY..? ARE YOU THERE..?
POOR DEVIL... THE EXPLOSION'S BLOWN POP'S LEGS OFF!
YEAH, POP... WE-WE'RE HERE..!
GOOD BOYS... GET-GET SOME WATER FOR YOUR DAD...
THERE'S NONE LEFT... ALL I CAN DO IS SMEAR SOME OF THE JAM FROM ME BIRTHDAY CAKE ON POP'S LIPS—TO MOISTEN 'EM...
I-I'M GLAD YOU LIKED YOUR NEW BIKE, BILLY...
I'LL HAVE A LITTLE NAP NOW... REMEMBER TO LET THE CAT OUT, BOYS... AND YOU BEHAVE YOURSELF... YOU HEAR, HARRY..?
'COURSE... 'COURSE I WILL, POP.
POP'S DEAD... WE WAS GOING OUT OF THE TRENCHES TOMORROW... JUST ONE MORE DAY AND POP WOULD STILL BE ALIVE..!
ATTENTION, MEN... I NEED ANOTHER VOLUNTEER! I NEED... A THIRTEENTH RUNNER!
IT WAS NORMAL TO KEEP SENDING RUNNERS UNTIL ONE OF THEM GOT THROUGH.
I RECKON THERE'S A BIT LESS OF ME TO HIT, SIR! I'LL GIVE IT A TRY!
GOOD LAD, BOURNE!
YOU'RE STUPID, CHARLEY! DON'T YOU KNOW IT'S UNLUCKY TO VOLUNTEER ON YOUR BIRTHDAY?
YEAH, I MUST BE STUPID, GINGER... TRYING TO GET THROUGH WHEN TWELVE OTHER RUNNERS HAVE FAILED! BUT IF I DON'T MAKE IT... NONE OF US WILL EVER LEAVE THE TRENCHES ALIVE!
ALLEY

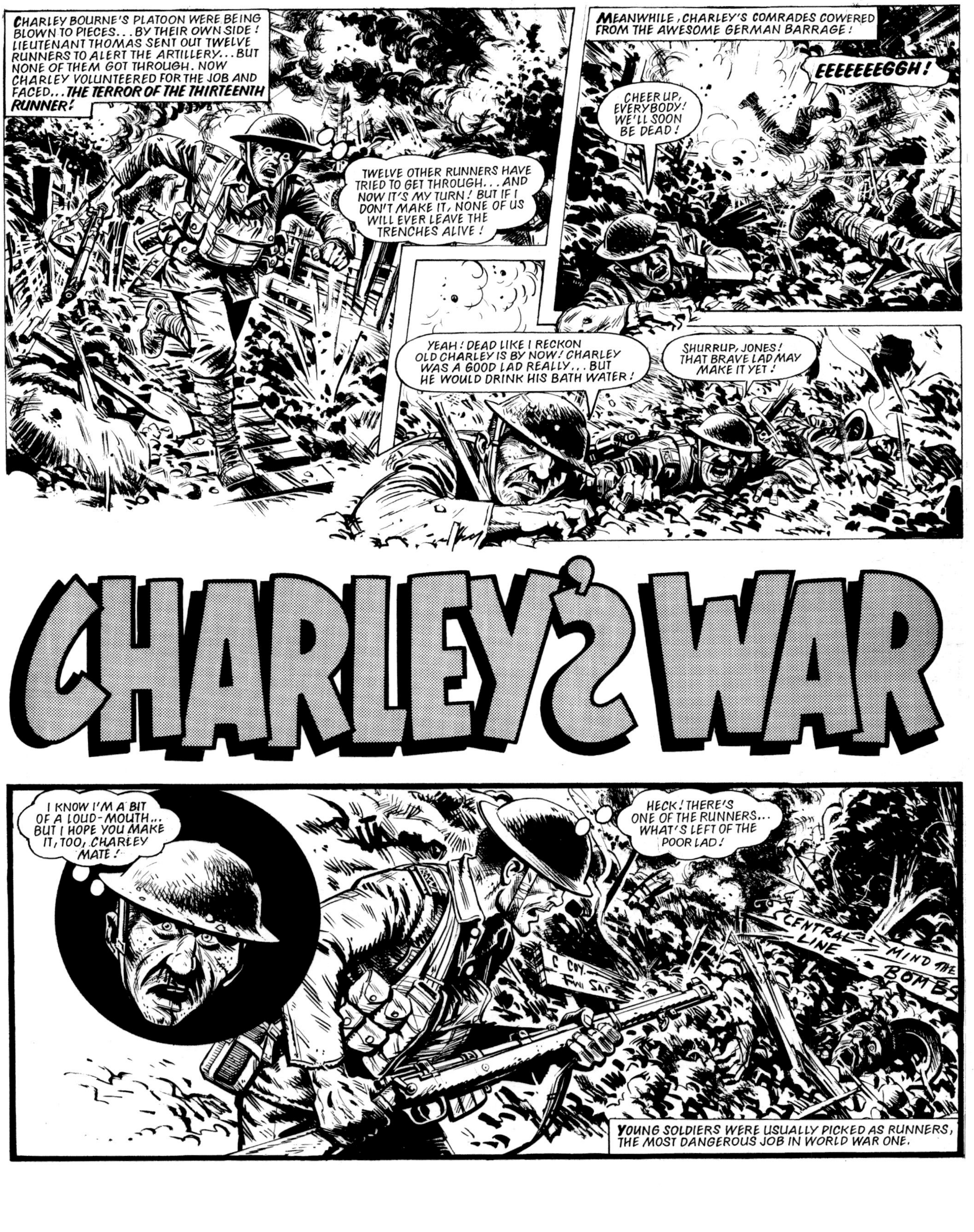
CHARLEY BOURNE'S PLATOON WERE BEING BLOWN TO PIECES... BY THEIR OWN SIDE! LIEUTENANT THOMAS SENT OUT TWELVE RUNNERS TO ALERT THE ARTILLERY... BUT NONE OF THEM GOT THROUGH. NOW CHARLEY VOLUNTEERED FOR THE JOB AND FACED... THE TERROR OF THE THIRTEENTH RUNNER!
TWELVE OTHER RUNNERS HAVE TRIED TO GET THROUGH... AND NOW IT'S MY TURN! BUT IF I DON'T MAKE IT, NONE OF US WILL EVER LEAVE THE TRENCHES ALIVE!
MEANWHILE, CHARLEY'S COMRADES COWERED FROM THE AWESOME GERMAN BARRAGE!
EEEEEEEGGH!
CHEER UP, EVERYBODY! WE'LL SOON BE DEAD!
YEAH! DEAD LIKE I RECKON OLD CHARLEY IS BY NOW! CHARLEY WAS A GOOD LAD REALLY... BUT HE WOULD DRINK HIS BATH WATER!
SHURRUP, JONES! THAT BRAVE LAD MAY MAKE IT YET!
CHARLEY'S WAR
I KNOW I'M A BIT OF A LOUD-MOUTH... BUT I HOPE YOU MAKE IT, TOO, CHARLEY MATE!
HECK! THERE'S ONE OF THE RUNNERS... WHAT'S LEFT OF THE POOR LAD!
C COY.
CENTRAL LINE
MIND THE BOMBS
YOUNG SOLDIERS WERE USUALLY PICKED AS RUNNERS, THE MOST DANGEROUS JOB IN WORLD WAR ONE.

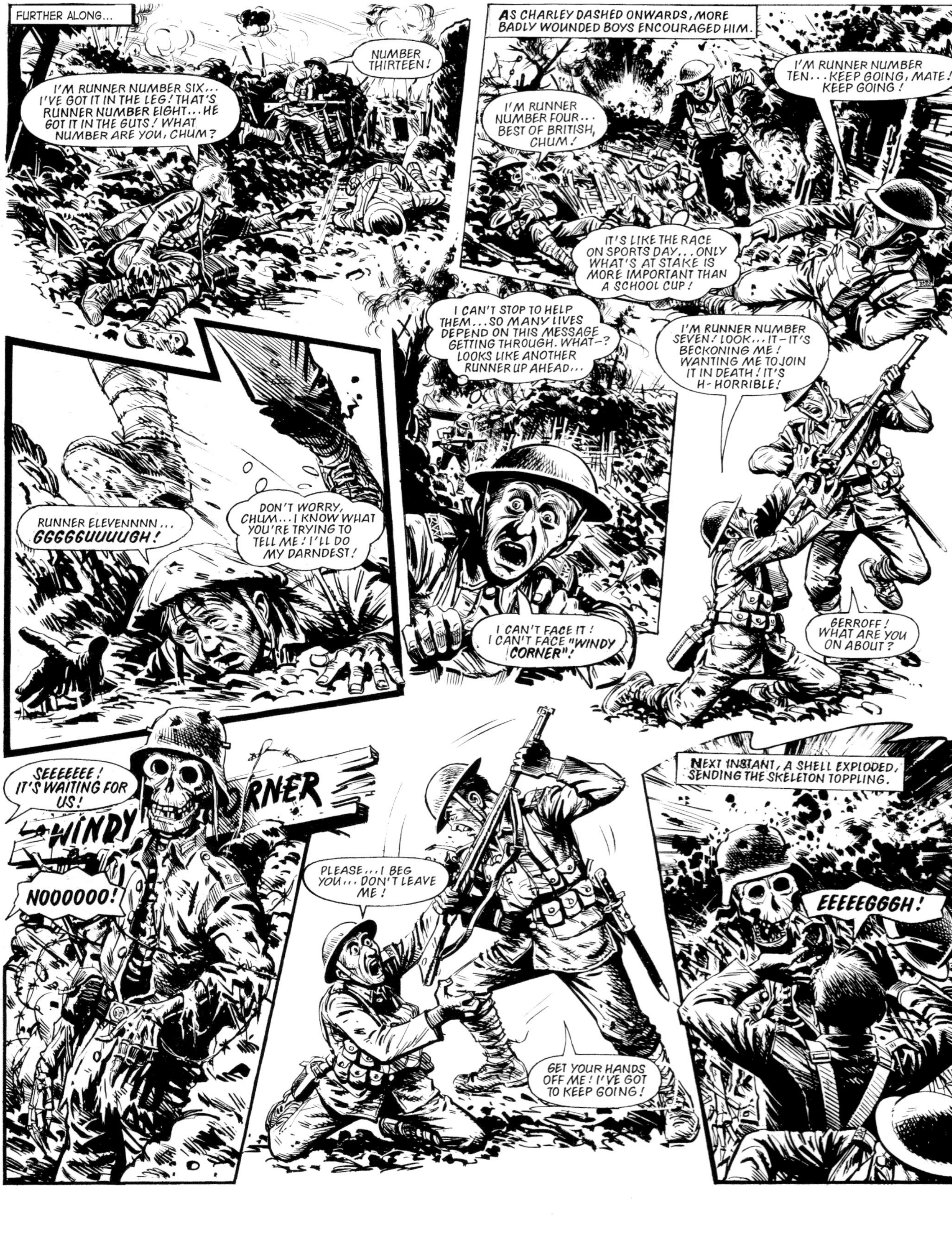
FURTHER ALONG...
I'M RUNNER NUMBER SIX... I'VE GOT IT IN THE LEG! THAT'S RUNNER NUMBER EIGHT... HE GOT IT IN THE GUTS! WHAT NUMBER ARE YOU, CHUM?
NUMBER THIRTEEN!
AS CHARLEY DASHED ONWARDS, MORE BADLY WOUNDED BOYS ENCOURAGED HIM.
I'M RUNNER NUMBER FOUR... BEST OF BRITISH, CHUM!
I'M RUNNER NUMBER TEN... KEEP GOING, MATE! KEEP GOING!
IT'S LIKE THE RACE ON SPORTS DAY... ONLY WHAT'S AT STAKE IS MORE IMPORTANT THAN A SCHOOL CUP!
RUNNER ELEVENNNN... GGGGGUUUUGH!
DON'T WORRY, CHUM... I KNOW WHAT YOU'RE TRYING TO TELL ME! I'LL DO MY DARNDEST!
I CAN'T STOP TO HELP THEM... SO MANY LIVES DEPEND ON THIS MESSAGE GETTING THROUGH. WHAT-? LOOKS LIKE ANOTHER RUNNER UP AHEAD...
I'M RUNNER NUMBER SEVEN! LOOK... IT-IT'S BECKONING ME! WANTING ME TO JOIN IT IN DEATH! IT'S H-HORRIBLE!
I CAN'T FACE IT! I CAN'T FACE "WINDY CORNER"!
GERROFF! WHAT ARE YOU ON ABOUT?
SEEEEEEE! IT'S WAITING FOR US!
WINDY CORNER
NOOOOOO!
PLEASE... I BEG YOU... DON'T LEAVE ME!
GET YOUR HANDS OFF ME! I'VE GOT TO KEEP GOING!
NEXT INSTANT, A SHELL EXPLODED, SENDING THE SKELETON TOPPLING.
EEEEEGGGH!

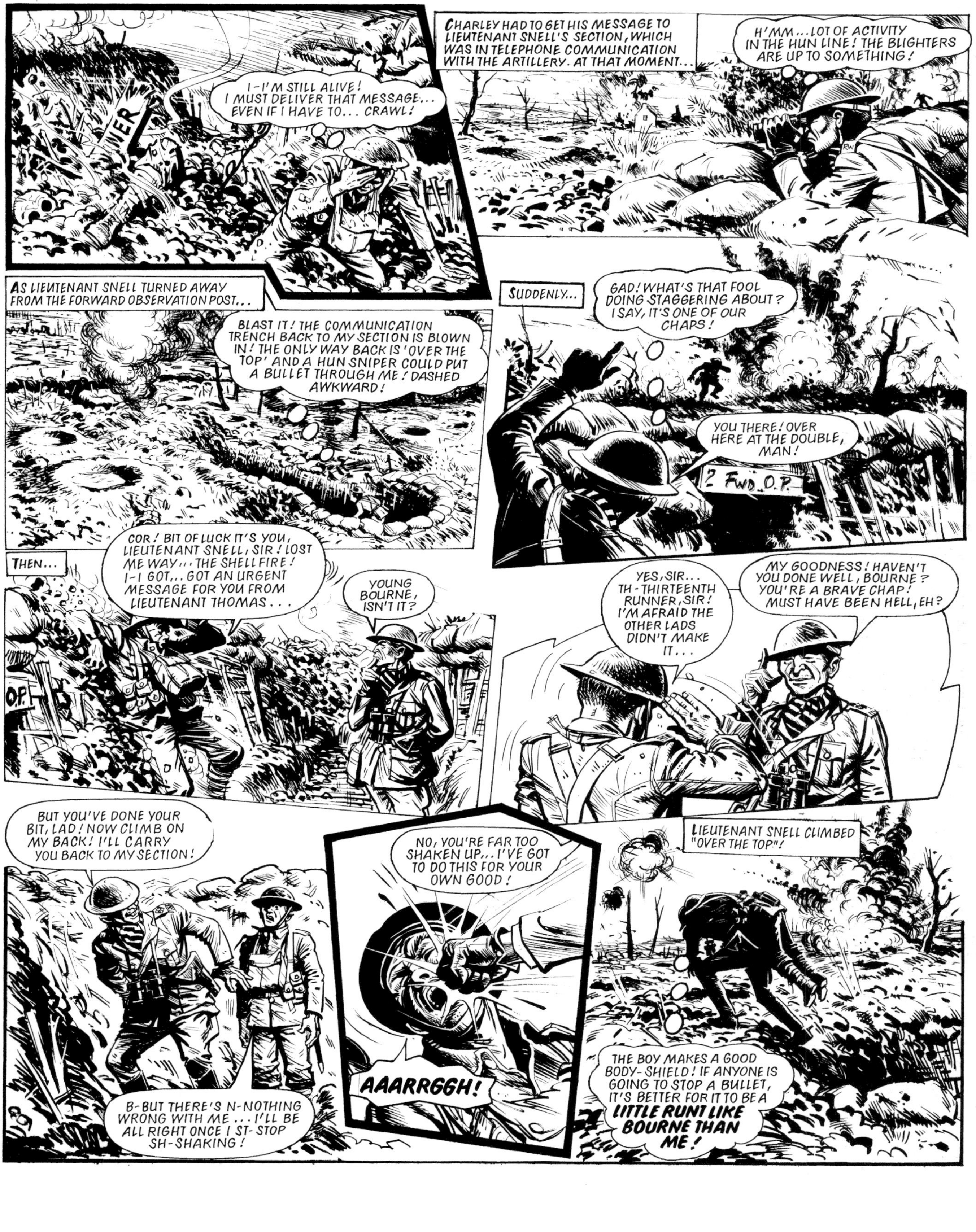
I-I'M STILL ALIVE! I MUST DELIVER THAT MESSAGE... EVEN IF I HAVE TO... CRAWL!
CHARLEY HAD TO GET HIS MESSAGE TO LIEUTENANT SNELL'S SECTION, WHICH WAS IN TELEPHONE COMMUNICATION WITH THE ARTILLERY. AT THAT MOMENT...
H'MM... LOT OF ACTIVITY IN THE HUN LINE! THE BLIGHTERS ARE UP TO SOMETHING!
AS LIEUTENANT SNELL TURNED AWAY FROM THE FORWARD OBSERVATION POST...
BLAST IT! THE COMMUNICATION TRENCH BACK TO MY SECTION IS BLOWN IN! THE ONLY WAY BACK IS 'OVER THE TOP' AND A HUN SNIPER COULD PUT A BULLET THROUGH ME! DASHED AWKWARD!
SUDDENLY...
GAD! WHAT'S THAT FOOL DOING STAGGERING ABOUT? I SAY, IT'S ONE OF OUR CHAPS!
YOU THERE! OVER HERE AT THE DOUBLE, MAN!
2 FWD. O.P.
THEN...
COR! BIT OF LUCK IT'S YOU, LIEUTENANT SNELL, SIR! LOST ME WAY... THE SHELLFIRE! I-I GOT... GOT AN URGENT MESSAGE FOR YOU FROM LIEUTENANT THOMAS...
YOUNG BOURNE, ISN'T IT?
O.P.
YES, SIR... TH-THIRTEENTH RUNNER, SIR! I'M AFRAID THE OTHER LADS DIDN'T MAKE IT...
MY GOODNESS! HAVEN'T YOU DONE WELL, BOURNE? YOU'RE A BRAVE CHAP! MUST HAVE BEEN HELL, EH?
BUT YOU'VE DONE YOUR BIT, LAD! NOW CLIMB ON MY BACK! I'LL CARRY YOU BACK TO MY SECTION!
B-BUT THERE'S N-NOTHING WRONG WITH ME... I'LL BE ALL RIGHT ONCE I ST-STOP SH-SHAKING!
NO, YOU'RE FAR TOO SHAKEN UP... I'VE GOT TO DO THIS FOR YOUR OWN GOOD!
AAARRGGH!
LIEUTENANT SNELL CLIMBED "OVER THE TOP"!
THE BOY MAKES A GOOD BODY-SHIELD! IF ANYONE IS GOING TO STOP A BULLET, IT'S BETTER FOR IT TO BE A LITTLE RUNT LIKE BOURNE THAN ME!

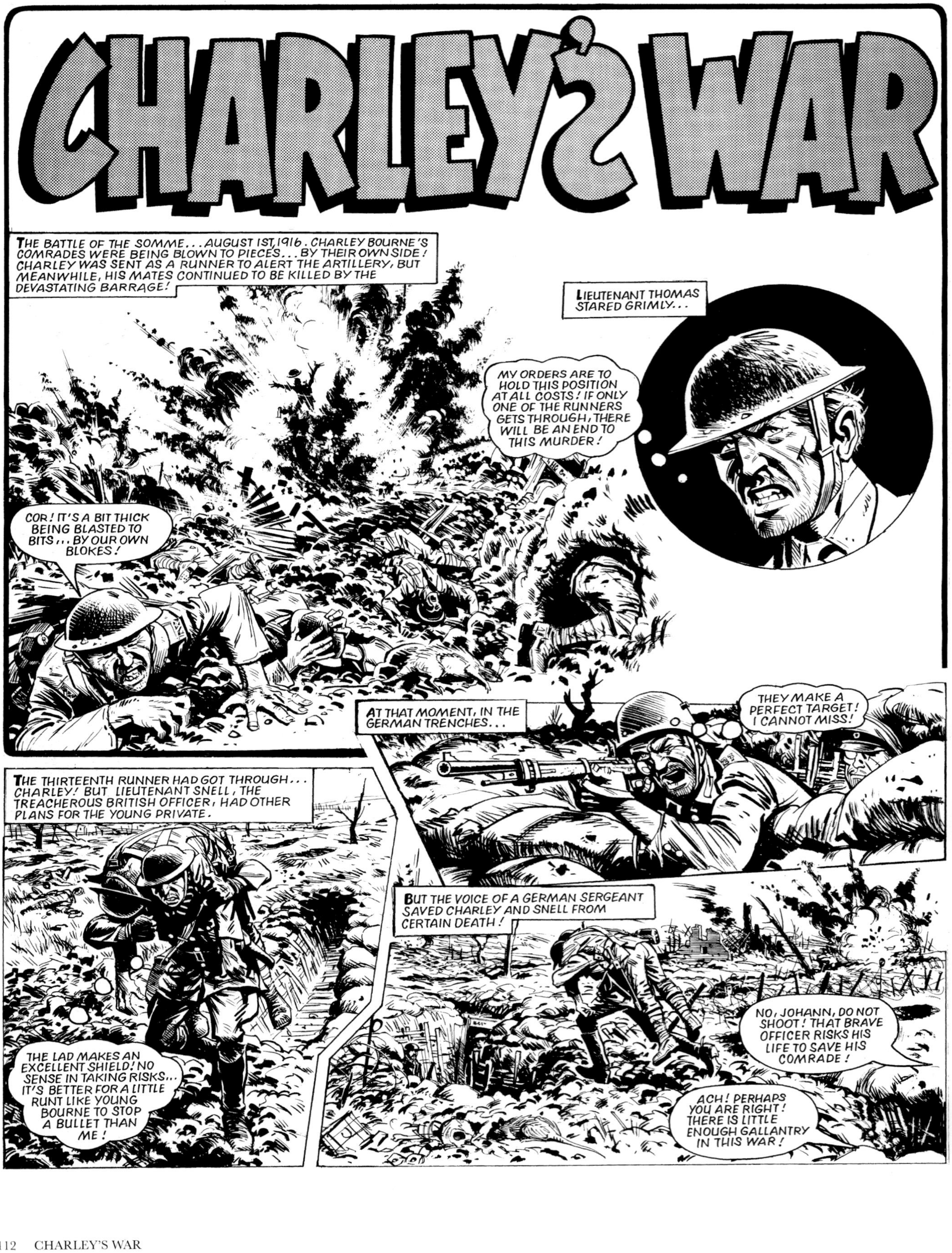
CHARLEY'S WAR
THE BATTLE OF THE SOMME... AUGUST 1ST, 1916. CHARLEY BOURNE'S COMRADES WERE BEING BLOWN TO PIECES... BY THEIR OWN SIDE! CHARLEY WAS SENT AS A RUNNER TO ALERT THE ARTILLERY, BUT MEANWHILE, HIS MATES CONTINUED TO BE KILLED BY THE DEVASTATING BARRAGE!
COR! IT'S A BIT THICK BEING BLASTED TO BITS... BY OUR OWN BLOKES!
LIEUTENANT THOMAS STARED GRIMLY...
MY ORDERS ARE TO HOLD THIS POSITION AT ALL COSTS! IF ONLY ONE OF THE RUNNERS GETS THROUGH, THERE WILL BE AN END TO THIS MURDER!
THE THIRTEENTH RUNNER HAD GOT THROUGH... CHARLEY! BUT LIEUTENANT SNELL, THE TREACHEROUS BRITISH OFFICER, HAD OTHER PLANS FOR THE YOUNG PRIVATE.
THE LAD MAKES AN EXCELLENT SHIELD! NO SENSE IN TAKING RISKS... IT'S BETTER FOR A LITTLE RUNT LIKE YOUNG BOURNE TO STOP A BULLET THAN ME!
AT THAT MOMENT, IN THE GERMAN TRENCHES...
THEY MAKE A PERFECT TARGET! I CANNOT MISS!
BUT THE VOICE OF A GERMAN SERGEANT SAVED CHARLEY AND SNELL FROM CERTAIN DEATH!
NO, JOHANN, DO NOT SHOOT! THAT BRAVE OFFICER RISKS HIS LIFE TO SAVE HIS COMRADE!
ACH! PERHAPS YOU ARE RIGHT! THERE IS LITTLE ENOUGH GALLANTRY IN THIS WAR!

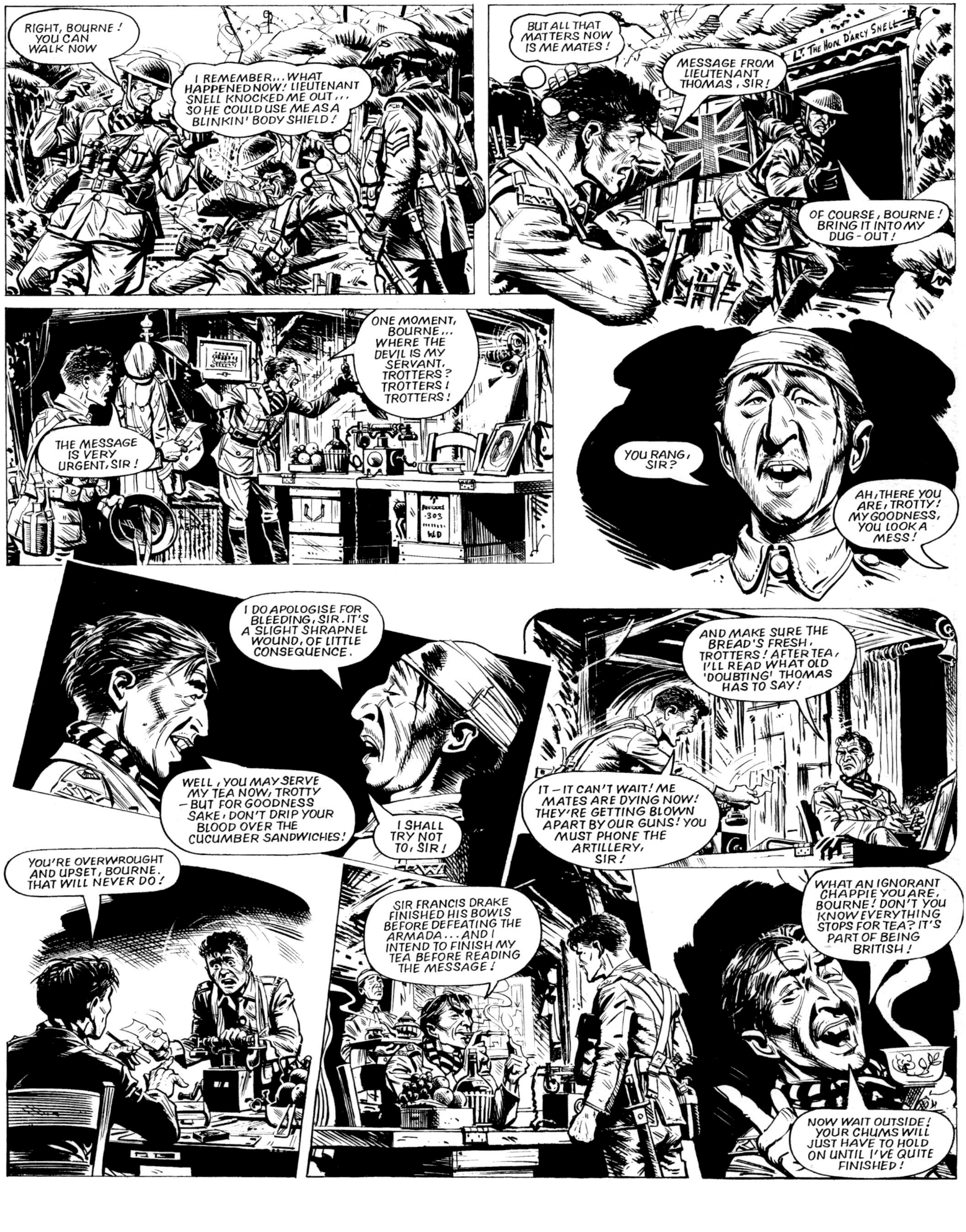
RIGHT, BOURNE! YOU CAN WALK NOW
I REMEMBER... WHAT HAPPENED NOW! LIEUTENANT SNELL KNOCKED ME OUT,,, SO HE COULD USE ME AS A BLINKIN' BODY SHIELD!
BUT ALL THAT MATTERS NOW IS ME MATES!
LT. THE HON. D'ARCY SNELL
MESSAGE FROM LIEUTENANT THOMAS, SIR!
OF COURSE, BOURNE! BRING IT INTO MY DUG-OUT!
ONE MOMENT, BOURNE... WHERE THE DEVIL IS MY SERVANT, TROTTERS? TROTTERS! TROTTERS!
THE MESSAGE IS VERY URGENT, SIR!
YOU RANG, SIR?
AH, THERE YOU ARE, TROTTY! MY GOODNESS, YOU LOOK A MESS!
I DO APOLOGISE FOR BLEEDING, SIR. IT'S A SLIGHT SHRAPNEL WOUND, OF LITTLE CONSEQUENCE.
WELL, YOU MAY SERVE MY TEA NOW, TROTTY — BUT FOR GOODNESS SAKE, DON'T DRIP YOUR BLOOD OVER THE CUCUMBER SANDWICHES!
I SHALL TRY NOT TO, SIR!
AND MAKE SURE THE BREAD'S FRESH, TROTTERS! AFTER TEA, I'LL READ WHAT OLD 'DOUBTING' THOMAS HAS TO SAY!
IT — IT CAN'T WAIT! ME MATES ARE DYING NOW! THEY'RE GETTING BLOWN APART BY OUR GUNS! YOU MUST PHONE THE ARTILLERY, SIR!
YOU'RE OVERWROUGHT AND UPSET, BOURNE. THAT WILL NEVER DO!
SIR FRANCIS DRAKE FINISHED HIS BOWLS BEFORE DEFEATING THE ARMADA... AND I INTEND TO FINISH MY TEA BEFORE READING THE MESSAGE!
WHAT AN IGNORANT CHAPPIE YOU ARE, BOURNE! DON'T YOU KNOW EVERYTHING STOPS FOR TEA? IT'S PART OF BEING BRITISH!
NOW WAIT OUTSIDE! YOUR CHUMS WILL JUST HAVE TO HOLD ON UNTIL I'VE QUITE FINISHED!

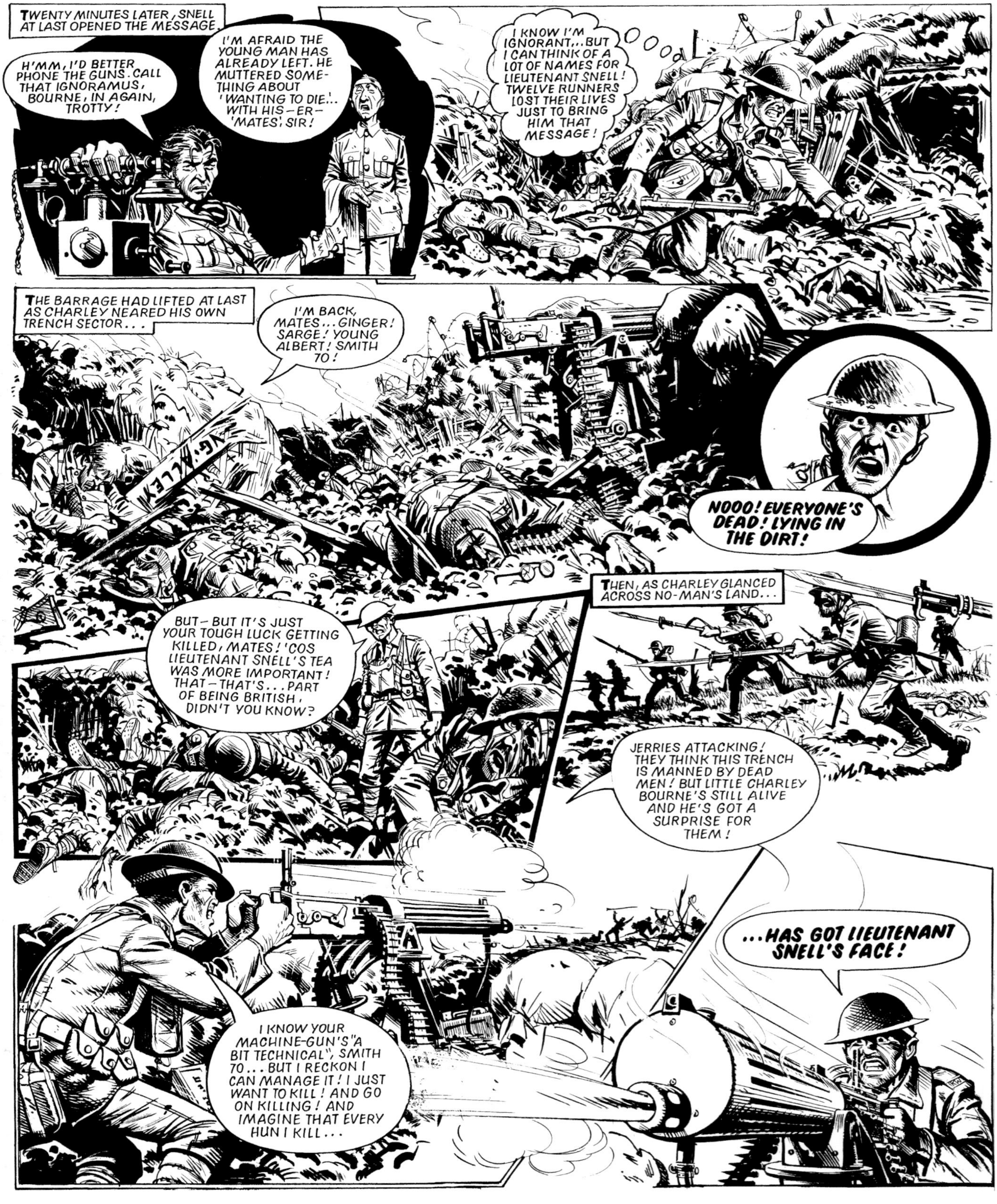

TWENTY MINUTES LATER, SNELL AT LAST OPENED THE MESSAGE.
H'MM, I'D BETTER PHONE THE GUNS. CALL THAT IGNORAMUS, BOURNE, IN AGAIN, TROTTY!
I'M AFRAID THE YOUNG MAN HAS ALREADY LEFT. HE MUTTERED SOMETHING ABOUT 'WANTING TO DIE'... WITH HIS-ER- 'MATES', SIR!
I KNOW I'M IGNORANT... BUT I CAN THINK OF A LOT OF NAMES FOR LIEUTENANT SNELL! TWELVE RUNNERS LOST THEIR LIVES JUST TO BRING HIM THAT MESSAGE!
THE BARRAGE HAD LIFTED AT LAST AS CHARLEY NEARED HIS OWN TRENCH SECTOR...
I'M BACK, MATES... GINGER! SARGE! YOUNG ALBERT! SMITH 70!
NOOO! EVERYONE'S DEAD! LYING IN THE DIRT!
BUT- BUT IT'S JUST YOUR TOUGH LUCK GETTING KILLED, MATES! 'COS LIEUTENANT SNELL'S TEA WAS MORE IMPORTANT! THAT- THAT'S... PART OF BEING BRITISH, DIDN'T YOU KNOW?
THEN, AS CHARLEY GLANCED ACROSS NO-MAN'S LAND...
JERRIES ATTACKING! THEY THINK THIS TRENCH IS MANNED BY DEAD MEN! BUT LITTLE CHARLEY BOURNE'S STILL ALIVE AND HE'S GOT A SURPRISE FOR THEM!
I KNOW YOUR MACHINE-GUN'S "A BIT TECHNICAL", SMITH 70... BUT I RECKON I CAN MANAGE IT! I JUST WANT TO KILL! AND GO ON KILLING! AND IMAGINE THAT EVERY HUN I KILL...
...HAS GOT LIEUTENANT SNELL'S FACE!

CHARLEY'S WAR

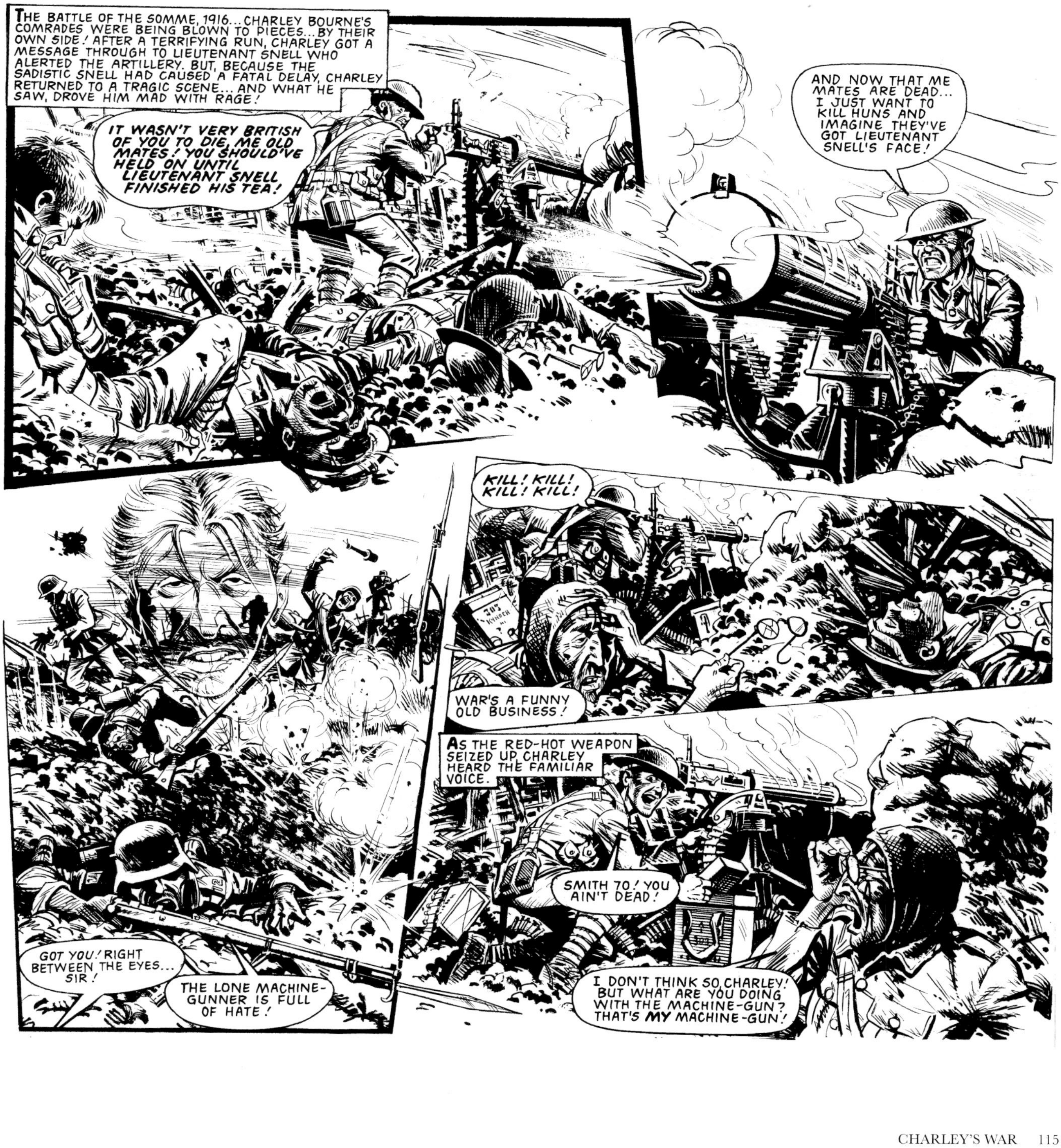

THE BATTLE OF THE SOMME, 1916... CHARLEY BOURNE'S COMRADES WERE BEING BLOWN TO PIECES... BY THEIR OWN SIDE! AFTER A TERRIFYING RUN, CHARLEY GOT A MESSAGE THROUGH TO LIEUTENANT SNELL WHO ALERTED THE ARTILLERY. BUT, BECAUSE THE SADISTIC SNELL HAD CAUSED A FATAL DELAY, CHARLEY RETURNED TO A TRAGIC SCENE... AND WHAT HE SAW, DROVE HIM MAD WITH RAGE!
IT WASN'T VERY BRITISH OF YOU TO DIE, ME OLD MATES! YOU SHOULD'VE HELD ON UNTIL LIEUTENANT SNELL FINISHED HIS TEA!
AND NOW THAT ME MATES ARE DEAD... I JUST WANT TO KILL HUNS AND IMAGINE THEY'VE GOT LIEUTENANT SNELL'S FACE!
GOT YOU! RIGHT BETWEEN THE EYES... SIR!
THE LONE MACHINE-GUNNER IS FULL OF HATE!
KILL! KILL! KILL! KILL!
WAR'S A FUNNY OLD BUSINESS!
AS THE RED-HOT WEAPON SEIZED UP, CHARLEY HEARD THE FAMILIAR VOICE.
SMITH 70! YOU AIN'T DEAD!
I DON'T THINK SO, CHARLEY! BUT WHAT ARE YOU DOING WITH THE MACHINE-GUN? THAT'S MY MACHINE-GUN!

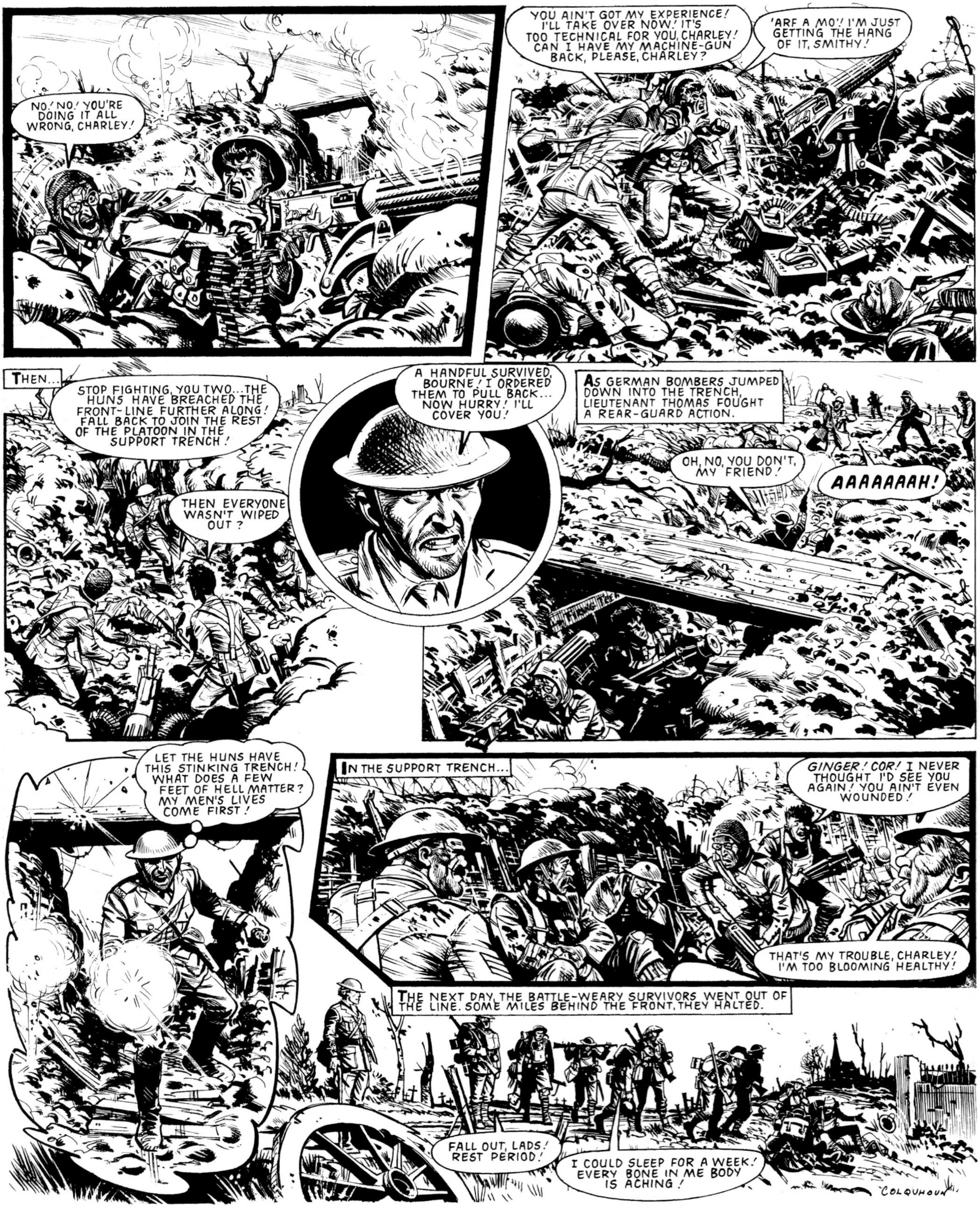
NO! NO! YOU'RE DOING IT ALL WRONG, CHARLEY!
YOU AIN'T GOT MY EXPERIENCE! I'LL TAKE OVER NOW! IT'S TOO TECHNICAL FOR YOU, CHARLEY! CAN I HAVE MY MACHINE-GUN BACK, PLEASE, CHARLEY?
'ARF A MO'! I'M JUST GETTING THE HANG OF IT, SMITHY!
THEN...
STOP FIGHTING, YOU TWO... THE HUNS HAVE BREACHED THE FRONT-LINE FURTHER ALONG! FALL BACK TO JOIN THE REST OF THE PLATOON IN THE SUPPORT TRENCH!
THEN EVERYONE WASN'T WIPED OUT?
A HANDFUL SURVIVED, BOURNE! I ORDERED THEM TO PULL BACK... NOW HURRY! I'LL COVER YOU!
AS GERMAN BOMBERS JUMPED DOWN INTO THE TRENCH, LIEUTENANT THOMAS FOUGHT A REAR-GUARD ACTION.
OH, NO, YOU DON'T, MY FRIEND!
AAAAAAAH!
LET THE HUNS HAVE THIS STINKING TRENCH! WHAT DOES A FEW FEET OF HELL MATTER? MY MEN'S LIVES COME FIRST!
IN THE SUPPORT TRENCH...
GINGER! COR! I NEVER THOUGHT I'D SEE YOU AGAIN! YOU AIN'T EVEN WOUNDED!
THAT'S MY TROUBLE, CHARLEY! I'M TOO BLOOMING HEALTHY!
THE NEXT DAY, THE BATTLE-WEARY SURVIVORS WENT OUT OF THE LINE. SOME MILES BEHIND THE FRONT, THEY HALTED.
FALL OUT, LADS! REST PERIOD!
I COULD SLEEP FOR A WEEK! EVERY BONE IN ME BODY IS ACHING!
COLQUHOUN

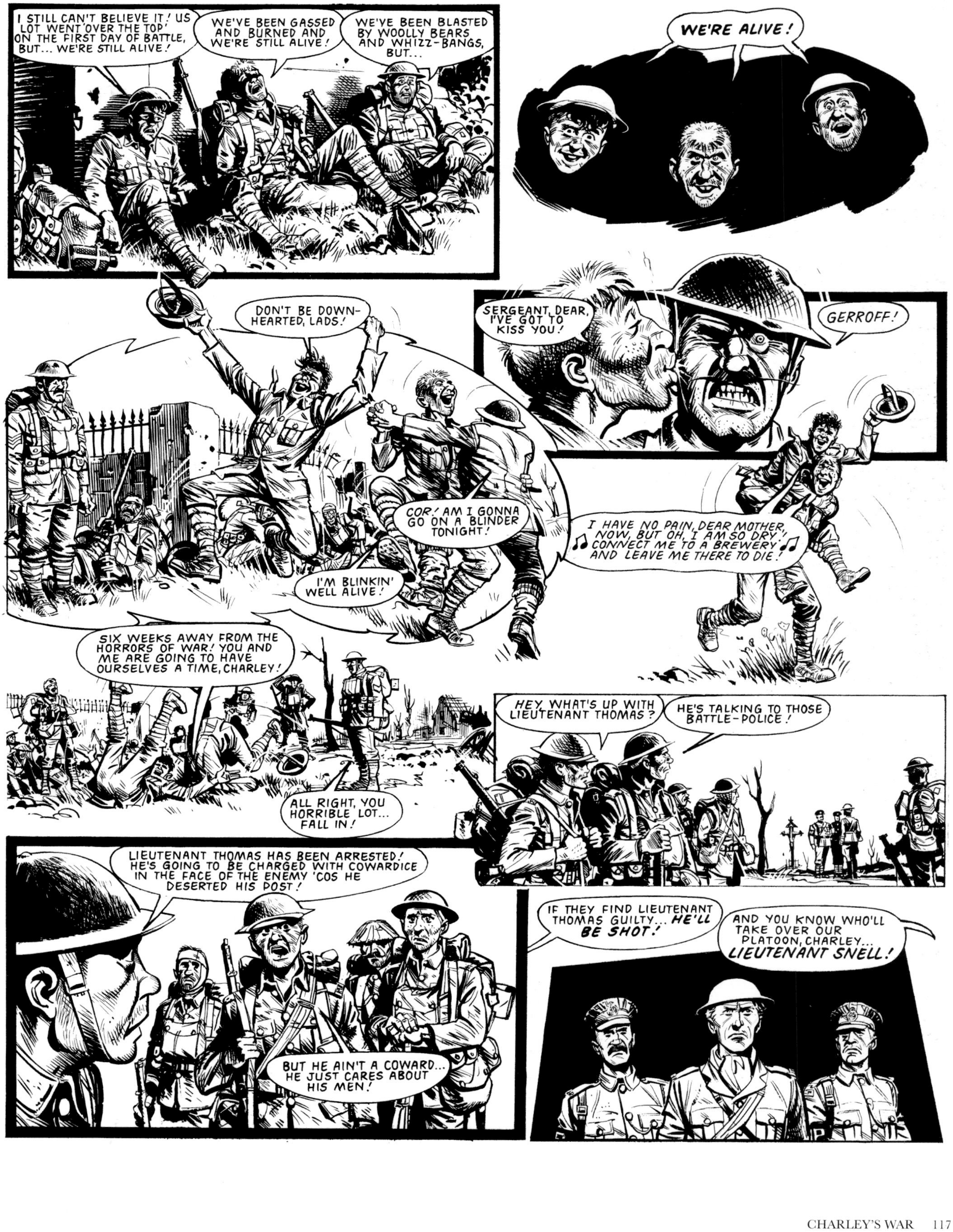

I STILL CAN'T BELIEVE IT! US LOT WENT 'OVER THE TOP' ON THE FIRST DAY OF BATTLE, BUT... WE'RE STILL ALIVE!
WE'VE BEEN GASSED AND BURNED AND WE'RE STILL ALIVE!
WE'VE BEEN BLASTED BY WOOLLY BEARS AND WHIZZ-BANGS, BUT...
WE'RE ALIVE!
DON'T BE DOWN-HEARTED, LADS!
SERGEANT, DEAR, I'VE GOT TO KISS YOU!
GERROFF!
COR! AM I GONNA GO ON A BLINDER TONIGHT!
I'M BLINKIN' WELL ALIVE!
I HAVE NO PAIN, DEAR MOTHER, NOW, BUT OH, I AM SO DRY! CONNECT ME TO A BREWERY AND LEAVE ME THERE TO DIE!
SIX WEEKS AWAY FROM THE HORRORS OF WAR! YOU AND ME ARE GOING TO HAVE OURSELVES A TIME, CHARLEY!
ALL RIGHT, YOU HORRIBLE LOT... FALL IN!
HEY, WHAT'S UP WITH LIEUTENANT THOMAS?
HE'S TALKING TO THOSE BATTLE-POLICE!
LIEUTENANT THOMAS HAS BEEN ARRESTED! HE'S GOING TO BE CHARGED WITH COWARDICE IN THE FACE OF THE ENEMY 'COS HE DESERTED HIS POST!
BUT HE AIN'T A COWARD... HE JUST CARES ABOUT HIS MEN!
IF THEY FIND LIEUTENANT THOMAS GUILTY... HE'LL BE SHOT!
AND YOU KNOW WHO'LL TAKE OVER OUR PLATOON, CHARLEY... LIEUTENANT SNELL!

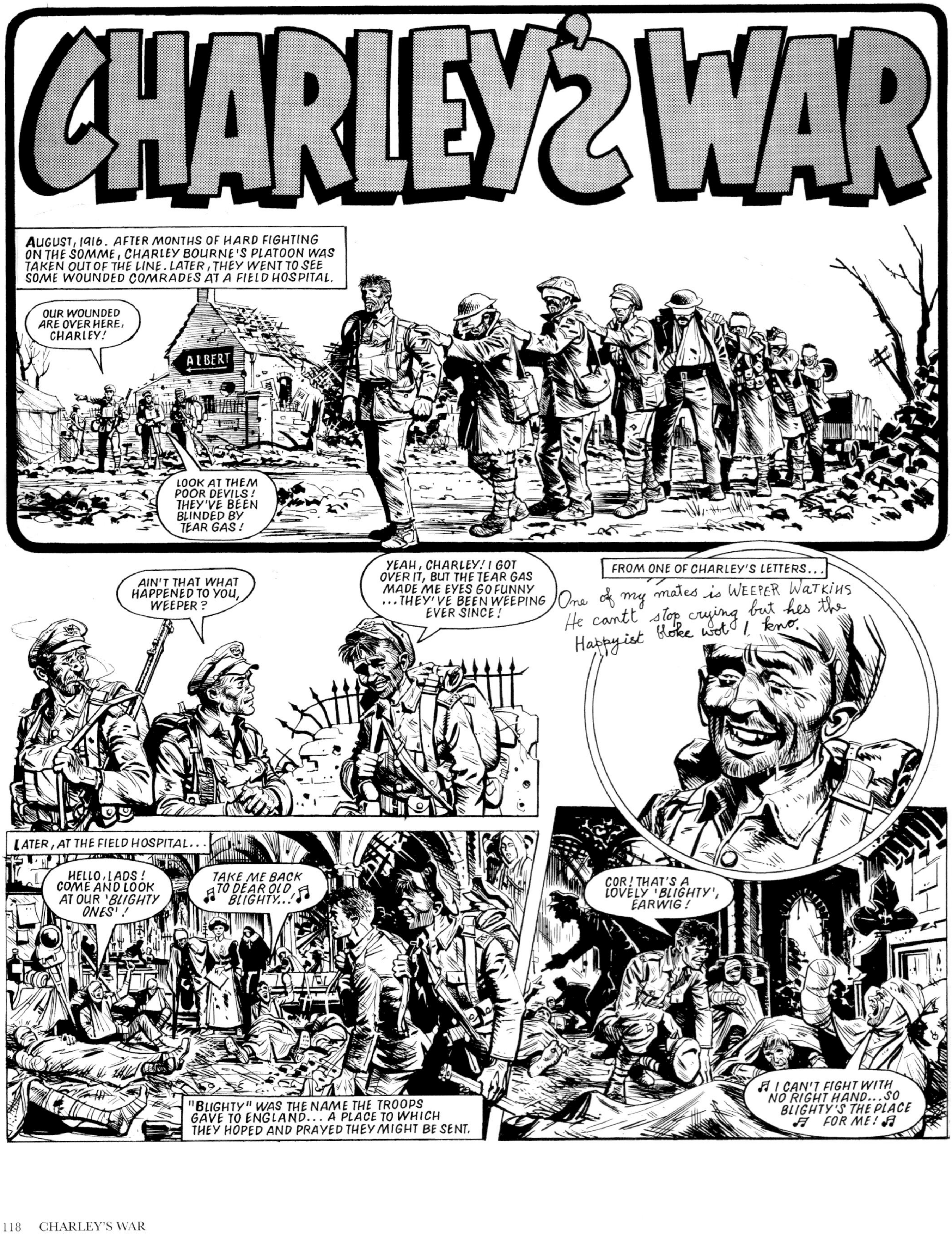
CHARLEY'S WAR
AUGUST, 1916. AFTER MONTHS OF HARD FIGHTING ON THE SOMME, CHARLEY BOURNE'S PLATOON WAS TAKEN OUT OF THE LINE. LATER, THEY WENT TO SEE SOME WOUNDED COMRADES AT A FIELD HOSPITAL.
OUR WOUNDED ARE OVER HERE, CHARLEY!
ALBERT
LOOK AT THEM POOR DEVILS! THEY'VE BEEN BLINDED BY TEAR GAS!
AIN'T THAT WHAT HAPPENED TO YOU, WEEPER?
YEAH, CHARLEY! I GOT OVER IT, BUT THE TEAR GAS MADE ME EYES GO FUNNY ... THEY'VE BEEN WEEPING EVER SINCE!
FROM ONE OF CHARLEY'S LETTERS...
One of my mates is WEEPER WATKINS He cantt stop crying but hes the Happyist bloke wot I kno.
LATER, AT THE FIELD HOSPITAL...
HELLO, LADS! COME AND LOOK AT OUR 'BLIGHTY ONES'!
TAKE ME BACK TO DEAR OLD BLIGHTY..!
"BLIGHTY" WAS THE NAME THE TROOPS GAVE TO ENGLAND... A PLACE TO WHICH THEY HOPED AND PRAYED THEY MIGHT BE SENT.
COR! THAT'S A LOVELY 'BLIGHTY', EARWIG!
I CAN'T FIGHT WITH NO RIGHT HAND... SO BLIGHTY'S THE PLACE FOR ME!

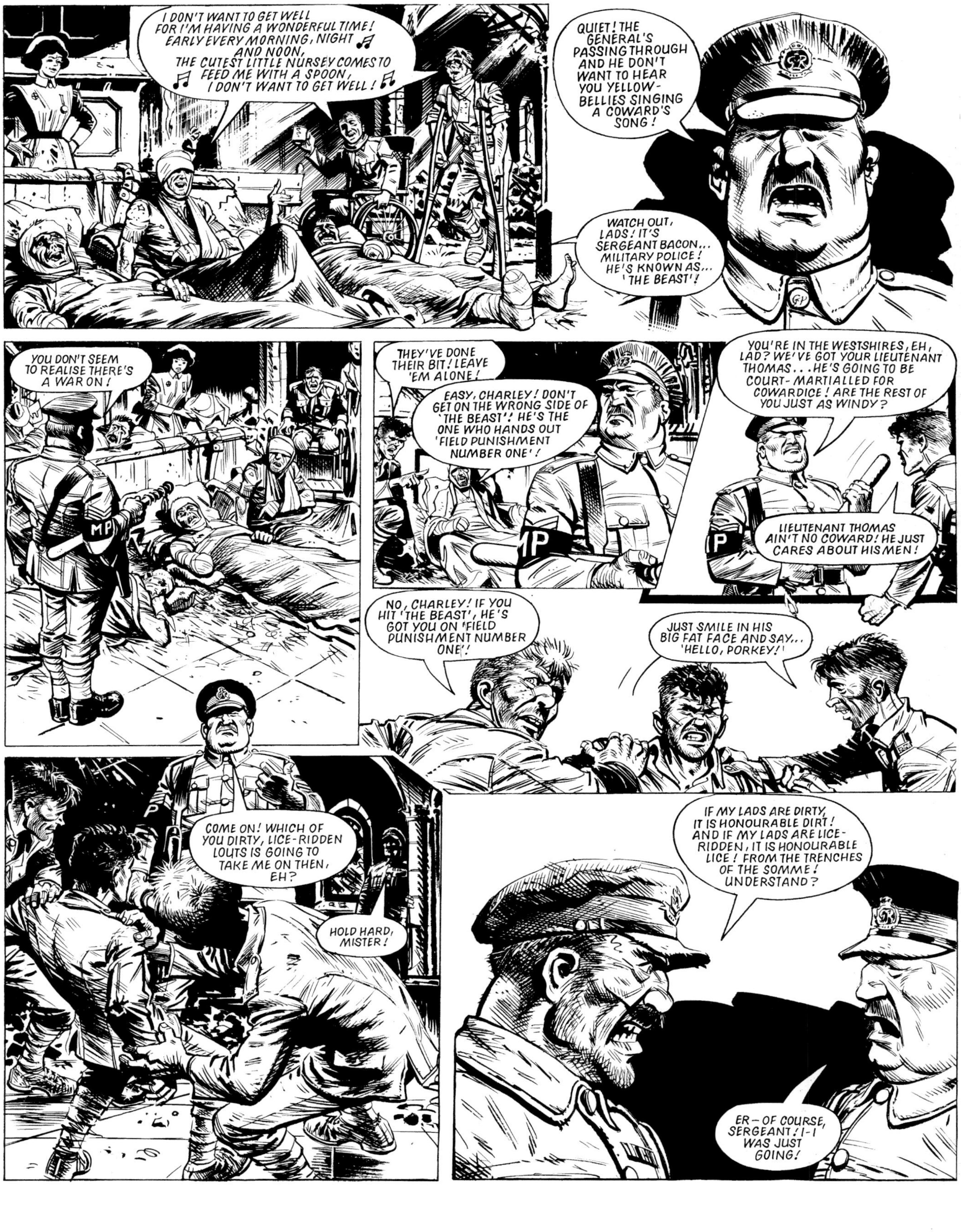

I DON'T WANT TO GET WELL FOR I'M HAVING A WONDERFUL TIME! EARLY EVERY MORNING, NIGHT AND NOON, THE CUTEST LITTLE NURSEY COMES TO FEED ME WITH A SPOON, I DON'T WANT TO GET WELL!
QUIET! THE GENERAL'S PASSING THROUGH AND HE DON'T WANT TO HEAR YOU YELLOW-BELLIES SINGING A COWARD'S SONG!
WATCH OUT, LADS! IT'S SERGEANT BACON... MILITARY POLICE! HE'S KNOWN AS... 'THE BEAST'!
YOU DON'T SEEM TO REALISE THERE'S A WAR ON!
MP
THEY'VE DONE THEIR BIT! LEAVE 'EM ALONE!
EASY, CHARLEY! DON'T GET ON THE WRONG SIDE OF 'THE BEAST'! HE'S THE ONE WHO HANDS OUT 'FIELD PUNISHMENT NUMBER ONE'!
MP
YOU'RE IN THE WESTSHIRES, EH, LAD? WE'VE GOT YOUR LIEUTENANT THOMAS... HE'S GOING TO BE COURT-MARTIALLED FOR COWARDICE! ARE THE REST OF YOU JUST AS WINDY?
LIEUTENANT THOMAS AIN'T NO COWARD! HE JUST CARES ABOUT HIS MEN!
NO, CHARLEY! IF YOU HIT 'THE BEAST', HE'S GOT YOU ON 'FIELD PUNISHMENT NUMBER ONE'!
JUST SMILE IN HIS BIG FAT FACE AND SAY... 'HELLO, PORKEY!'
COME ON! WHICH OF YOU DIRTY, LICE-RIDDEN LOUTS IS GOING TO TAKE ME ON THEN, EH?
HOLD HARD, MISTER!
IF MY LADS ARE DIRTY, IT IS HONOURABLE DIRT! AND IF MY LADS ARE LICE-RIDDEN, IT IS HONOURABLE LICE! FROM THE TRENCHES OF THE SOMME! UNDERSTAND?
ER–OF COURSE, SERGEANT! I-I WAS JUST GOING!

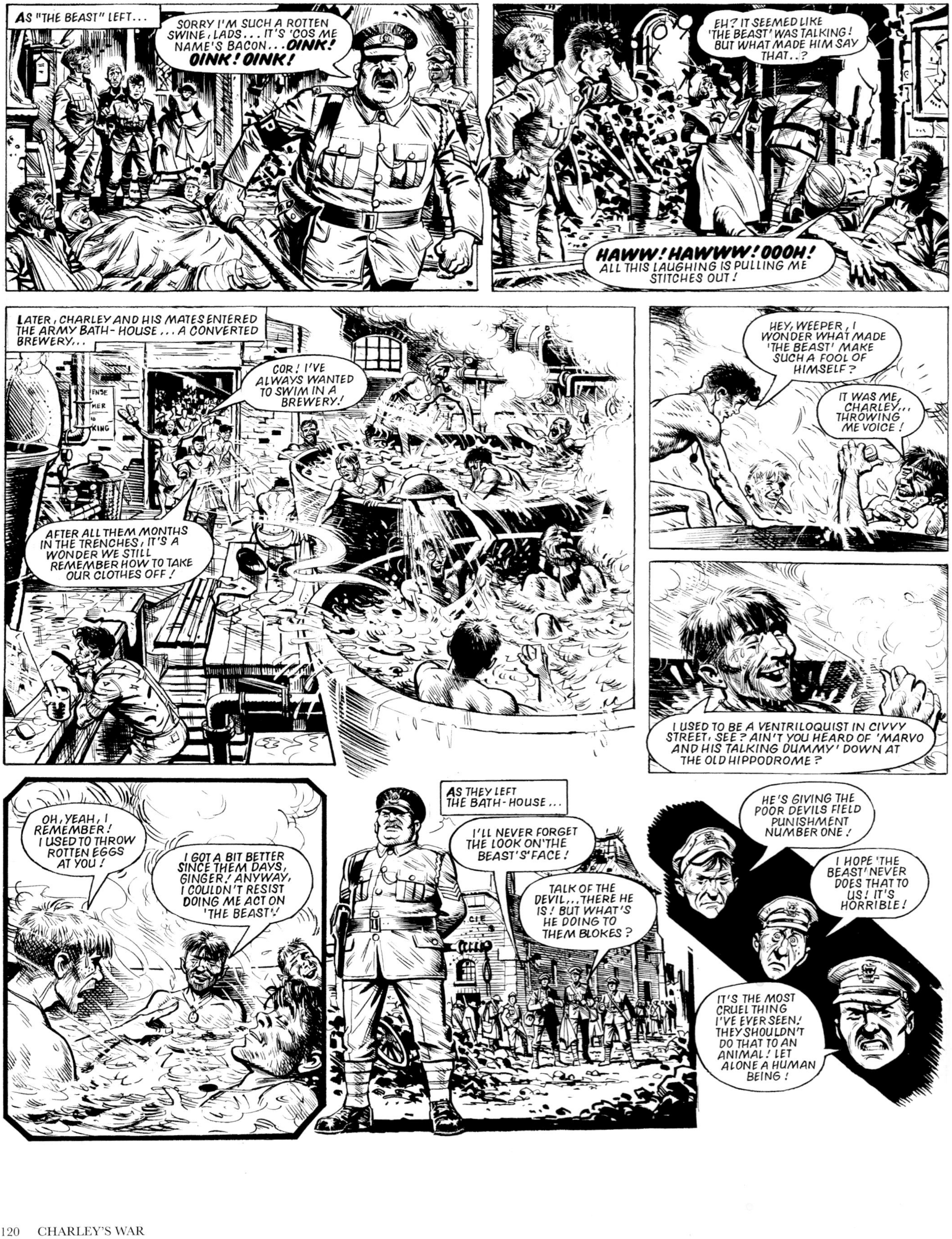

AS "THE BEAST" LEFT...
SORRY I'M SUCH A ROTTEN SWINE, LADS... IT'S 'COS ME NAME'S BACON... OINK! OINK! OINK!
EH? IT SEEMED LIKE 'THE BEAST' WAS TALKING! BUT WHAT MADE HIM SAY THAT..?
HAWW! HAWWW! OOOH! ALL THIS LAUGHING IS PULLING ME STITCHES OUT!
LATER, CHARLEY AND HIS MATES ENTERED THE ARMY BATH-HOUSE... A CONVERTED BREWERY...
COR! I'VE ALWAYS WANTED TO SWIM IN A BREWERY!
AFTER ALL THEM MONTHS IN THE TRENCHES, IT'S A WONDER WE STILL REMEMBER HOW TO TAKE OUR CLOTHES OFF!
HEY, WEEPER, I WONDER WHAT MADE 'THE BEAST' MAKE SUCH A FOOL OF HIMSELF?
IT WAS ME, CHARLEY... THROWING ME VOICE!
I USED TO BE A VENTRILOQUIST IN CIVVY STREET, SEE? AIN'T YOU HEARD OF 'MARVO AND HIS TALKING DUMMY' DOWN AT THE OLD HIPPODROME?
OH, YEAH, I REMEMBER! I USED TO THROW ROTTEN EGGS AT YOU!
I GOT A BIT BETTER SINCE THEM DAYS, GINGER! ANYWAY, I COULDN'T RESIST DOING ME ACT ON 'THE BEAST'!
AS THEY LEFT THE BATH-HOUSE...
I'LL NEVER FORGET THE LOOK ON 'THE BEAST'S' FACE!
TALK OF THE DEVIL... THERE HE IS! BUT WHAT'S HE DOING TO THEM BLOKES?
HE'S GIVING THE POOR DEVILS FIELD PUNISHMENT NUMBER ONE!
I HOPE 'THE BEAST' NEVER DOES THAT TO US! IT'S HORRIBLE!
IT'S THE MOST CRUEL THING I'VE EVER SEEN! THEY SHOULDN'T DO THAT TO AN ANIMAL! LET ALONE A HUMAN BEING!

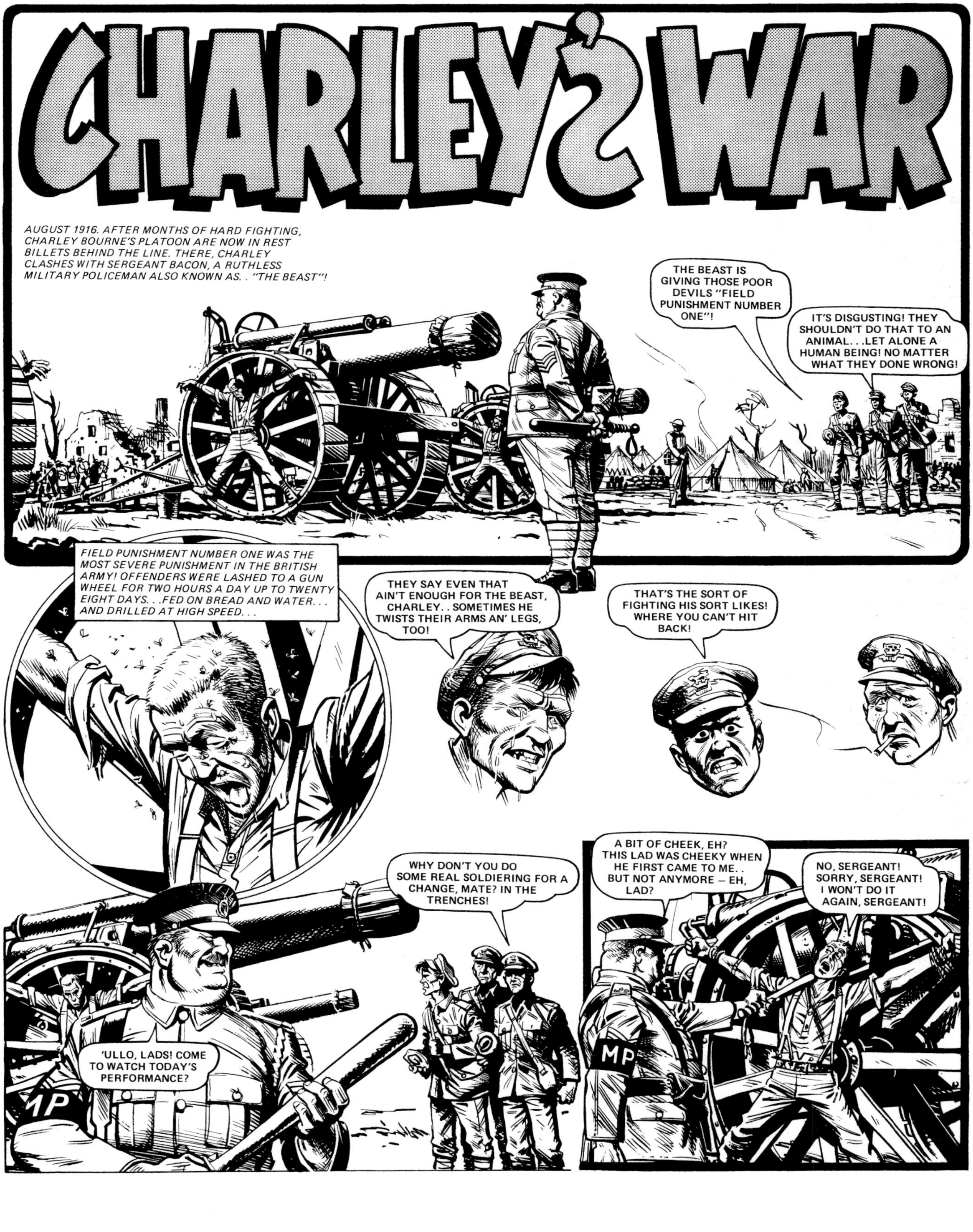
CHARLEY'S WAR
AUGUST 1916. AFTER MONTHS OF HARD FIGHTING, CHARLEY BOURNE'S PLATOON ARE NOW IN REST BILLETS BEHIND THE LINE. THERE, CHARLEY CLASHES WITH SERGEANT BACON, A RUTHLESS MILITARY POLICEMAN ALSO KNOWN AS. . "THE BEAST"!
THE BEAST IS GIVING THOSE POOR DEVILS "FIELD PUNISHMENT NUMBER ONE"!
IT'S DISGUSTING! THEY SHOULDN'T DO THAT TO AN ANIMAL. . .LET ALONE A HUMAN BEING! NO MATTER WHAT THEY DONE WRONG!
FIELD PUNISHMENT NUMBER ONE WAS THE MOST SEVERE PUNISHMENT IN THE BRITISH ARMY! OFFENDERS WERE LASHED TO A GUN WHEEL FOR TWO HOURS A DAY UP TO TWENTY EIGHT DAYS. . .FED ON BREAD AND WATER. . . AND DRILLED AT HIGH SPEED. . .
THEY SAY EVEN THAT AIN'T ENOUGH FOR THE BEAST, CHARLEY. . SOMETIMES HE TWISTS THEIR ARMS AN' LEGS, TOO!
THAT'S THE SORT OF FIGHTING HIS SORT LIKES! WHERE YOU CAN'T HIT BACK!
'ULLO, LADS! COME TO WATCH TODAY'S PERFORMANCE?
WHY DON'T YOU DO SOME REAL SOLDIERING FOR A CHANGE, MATE? IN THE TRENCHES!
A BIT OF CHEEK, EH? THIS LAD WAS CHEEKY WHEN HE FIRST CAME TO ME. . BUT NOT ANYMORE – EH, LAD?
NO, SERGEANT! SORRY, SERGEANT! I WON'T DO IT AGAIN, SERGEANT!
MP
MP
MP

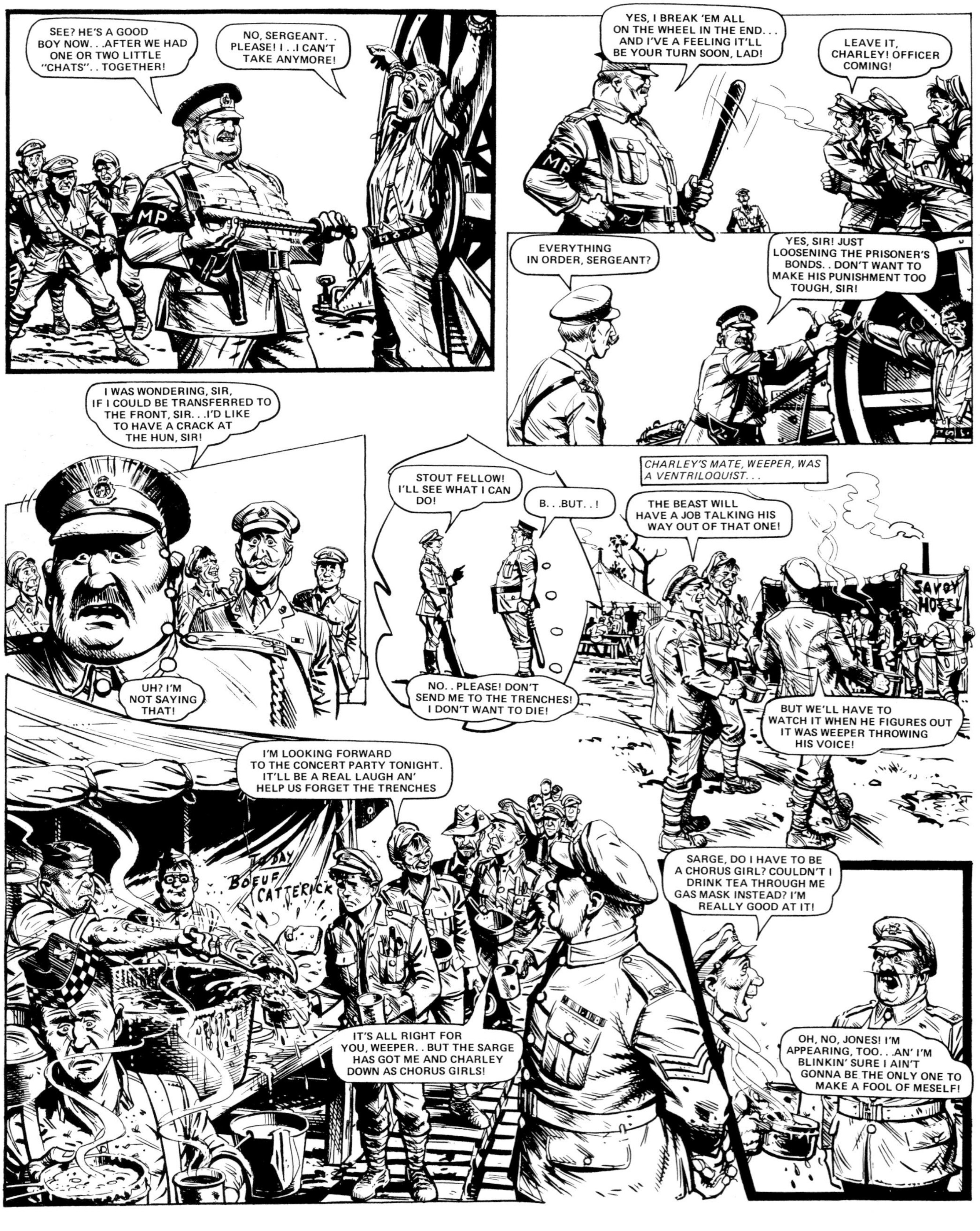

SEE? HE'S A GOOD BOY NOW. . .AFTER WE HAD ONE OR TWO LITTLE "CHATS". . TOGETHER!
NO, SERGEANT. . PLEASE! I . .I CAN'T TAKE ANYMORE!
MP
YES, I BREAK 'EM ALL ON THE WHEEL IN THE END. . . AND I'VE A FEELING IT'LL BE YOUR TURN SOON, LAD!
LEAVE IT, CHARLEY! OFFICER COMING!
MP
EVERYTHING IN ORDER, SERGEANT?
YES, SIR! JUST LOOSENING THE PRISONER'S BONDS. . DON'T WANT TO MAKE HIS PUNISHMENT TOO TOUGH, SIR!
I WAS WONDERING, SIR, IF I COULD BE TRANSFERRED TO THE FRONT, SIR. . .I'D LIKE TO HAVE A CRACK AT THE HUN, SIR!
UH? I'M NOT SAYING THAT!
STOUT FELLOW! I'LL SEE WHAT I CAN DO!
B. . .BUT. . !
NO. . PLEASE! DON'T SEND ME TO THE TRENCHES! I DON'T WANT TO DIE!
CHARLEY'S MATE, WEEPER, WAS A VENTRILOQUIST. . .
THE BEAST WILL HAVE A JOB TALKING HIS WAY OUT OF THAT ONE!
SAVOY HOTEL
BUT WE'LL HAVE TO WATCH IT WHEN HE FIGURES OUT IT WAS WEEPER THROWING HIS VOICE!
I'M LOOKING FORWARD TO THE CONCERT PARTY TONIGHT. IT'LL BE A REAL LAUGH AN' HELP US FORGET THE TRENCHES
TODAY BOEUF CATTERICK
IT'S ALL RIGHT FOR YOU, WEEPER. . BUT THE SARGE HAS GOT ME AND CHARLEY DOWN AS CHORUS GIRLS!
SARGE, DO I HAVE TO BE A CHORUS GIRL? COULDN'T I DRINK TEA THROUGH ME GAS MASK INSTEAD? I'M REALLY GOOD AT IT!
OH, NO, JONES! I'M APPEARING, TOO. . .AN' I'M BLINKIN' SURE I AIN'T GONNA BE THE ONLY ONE TO MAKE A FOOL OF MESELF!

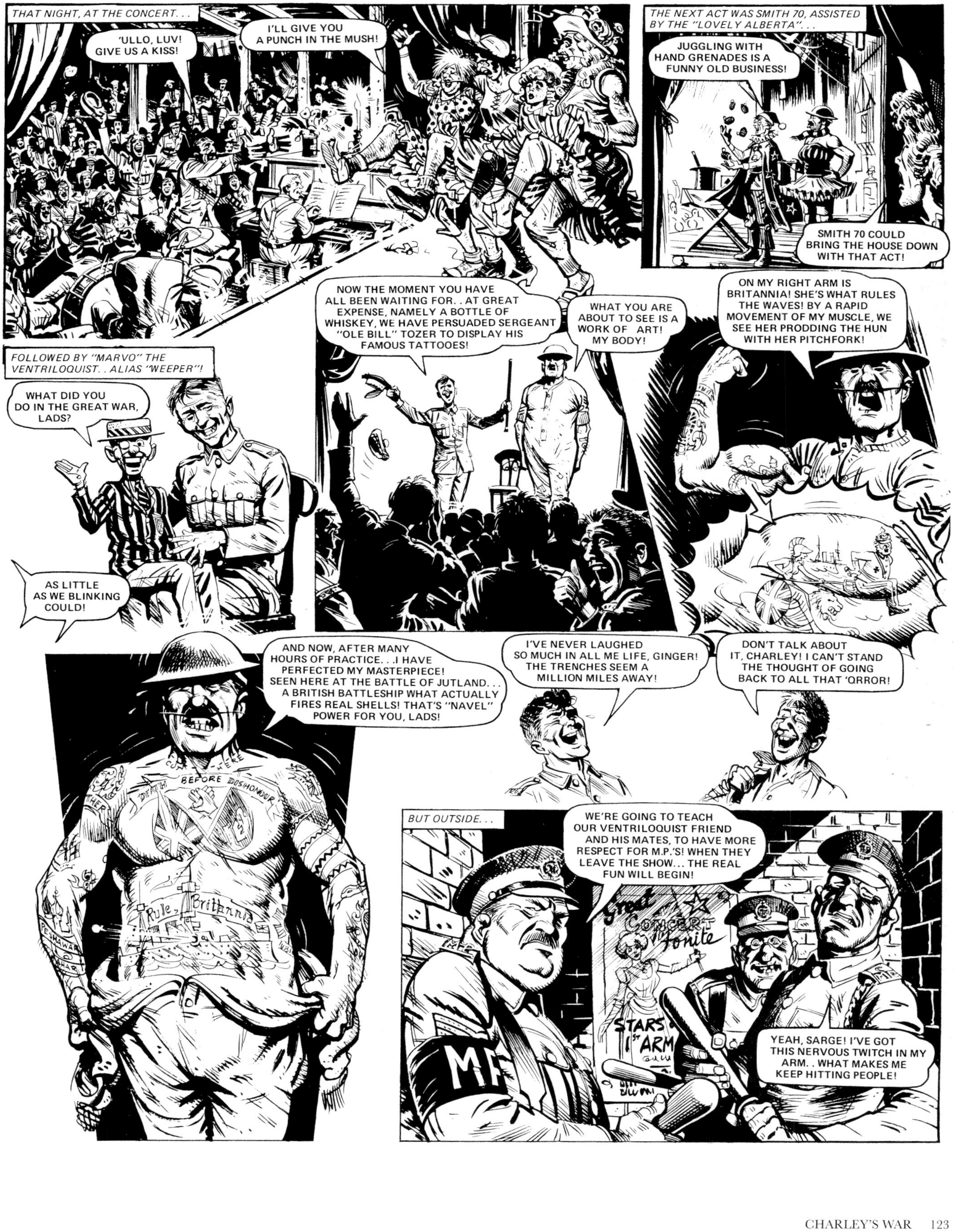

THAT NIGHT, AT THE CONCERT...
'ULLO, LUV! GIVE US A KISS!
I'LL GIVE YOU A PUNCH IN THE MUSH!
THE NEXT ACT WAS SMITH 70, ASSISTED BY THE "LOVELY ALBERTA"...
JUGGLING WITH HAND GRENADES IS A FUNNY OLD BUSINESS!
SMITH 70 COULD BRING THE HOUSE DOWN WITH THAT ACT!
FOLLOWED BY "MARVO" THE VENTRILOQUIST.. ALIAS "WEEPER"!
WHAT DID YOU DO IN THE GREAT WAR, LADS?
AS LITTLE AS WE BLINKING COULD!
NOW THE MOMENT YOU HAVE ALL BEEN WAITING FOR.. AT GREAT EXPENSE, NAMELY A BOTTLE OF WHISKEY, WE HAVE PERSUADED SERGEANT "OLE BILL" TOZER TO DISPLAY HIS FAMOUS TATTOOES!
WHAT YOU ARE ABOUT TO SEE IS A WORK OF ART! MY BODY!
ON MY RIGHT ARM IS BRITANNIA! SHE'S WHAT RULES THE WAVES! BY A RAPID MOVEMENT OF MY MUSCLE, WE SEE HER PRODDING THE HUN WITH HER PITCHFORK!
AND NOW, AFTER MANY HOURS OF PRACTICE.. I HAVE PERFECTED MY MASTERPIECE! SEEN HERE AT THE BATTLE OF JUTLAND... A BRITISH BATTLESHIP WHAT ACTUALLY FIRES REAL SHELLS! THAT'S "NAVEL" POWER FOR YOU, LADS!
DEATH BEFORE DISHONOUR
Rule, Britannia
I'VE NEVER LAUGHED SO MUCH IN ALL ME LIFE, GINGER! THE TRENCHES SEEM A MILLION MILES AWAY!
DON'T TALK ABOUT IT, CHARLEY! I CAN'T STAND THE THOUGHT OF GOING BACK TO ALL THAT 'ORROR!
BUT OUTSIDE...
WE'RE GOING TO TEACH OUR VENTRILOQUIST FRIEND AND HIS MATES, TO HAVE MORE RESPECT FOR M.P.'S! WHEN THEY LEAVE THE SHOW... THE REAL FUN WILL BEGIN!
Great Concert Tonite
YEAH, SARGE! I'VE GOT THIS NERVOUS TWITCH IN MY ARM.. WHAT MAKES ME KEEP HITTING PEOPLE!

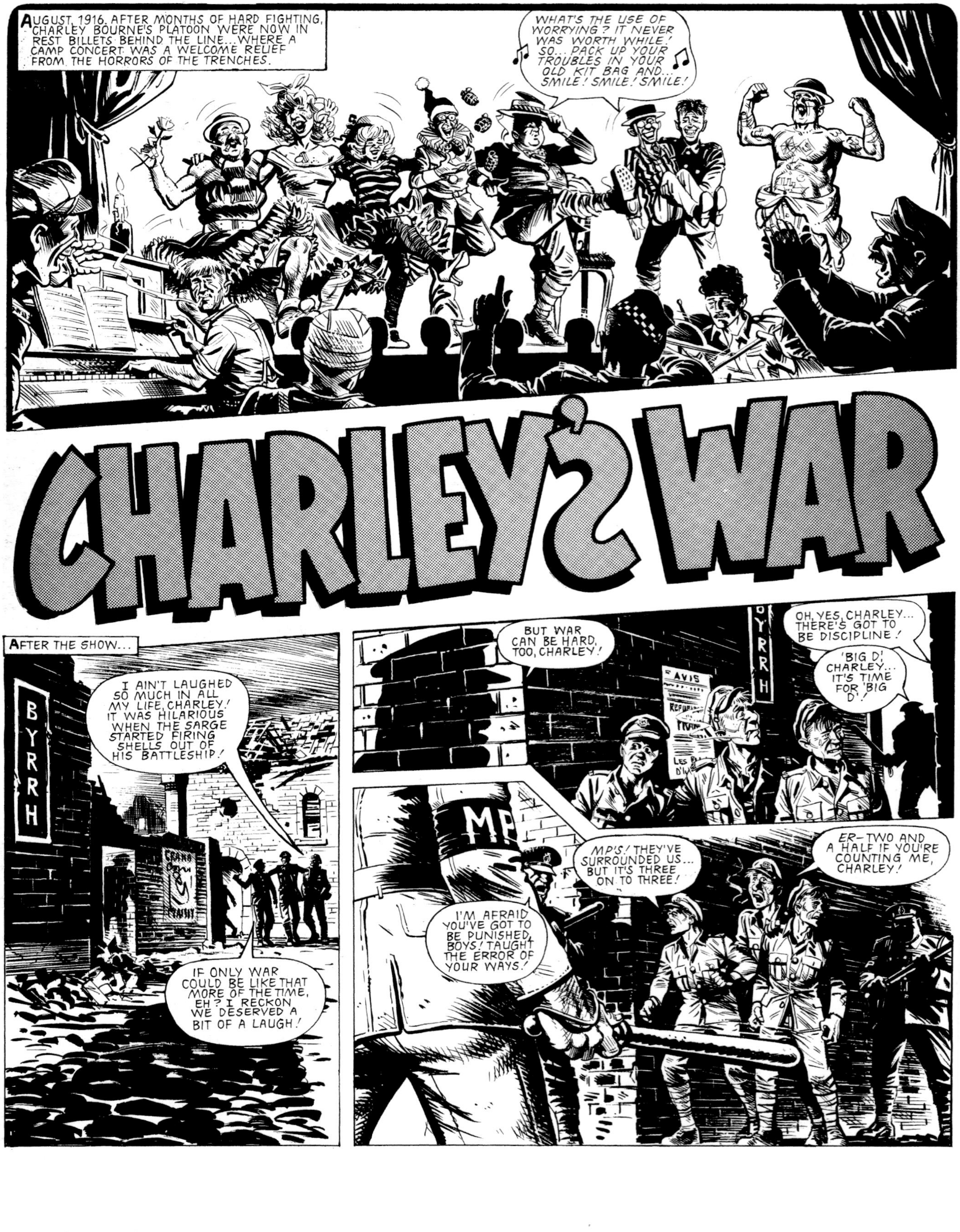
AUGUST 1916. AFTER MONTHS OF HARD FIGHTING, CHARLEY BOURNE'S PLATOON WERE NOW IN REST BILLETS BEHIND THE LINE... WHERE A CAMP CONCERT WAS A WELCOME RELIEF FROM THE HORRORS OF THE TRENCHES.
WHAT'S THE USE OF WORRYING? IT NEVER WAS WORTH WHILE! SO... PACK UP YOUR TROUBLES IN YOUR OLD KIT BAG AND... SMILE! SMILE! SMILE!
CHARLEY'S WAR
AFTER THE SHOW...
BYRRH
I AIN'T LAUGHED SO MUCH IN ALL MY LIFE, CHARLEY! IT WAS HILARIOUS WHEN THE SARGE STARTED FIRING SHELLS OUT OF HIS BATTLESHIP!
IF ONLY WAR COULD BE LIKE THAT MORE OF THE TIME, EH? I RECKON WE DESERVED A BIT OF A LAUGH!
BUT WAR CAN BE HARD, TOO, CHARLEY!
OH, YES, CHARLEY... THERE'S GOT TO BE DISCIPLINE!
'BIG D', CHARLEY... IT'S TIME FOR 'BIG D'!
AVIS
MP
MP'S! THEY'VE SURROUNDED US... BUT IT'S THREE ON TO THREE!
ER-TWO AND A HALF IF YOU'RE COUNTING ME, CHARLEY!
I'M AFRAID YOU'VE GOT TO BE PUNISHED, BOYS! TAUGHT THE ERROR OF YOUR WAYS!

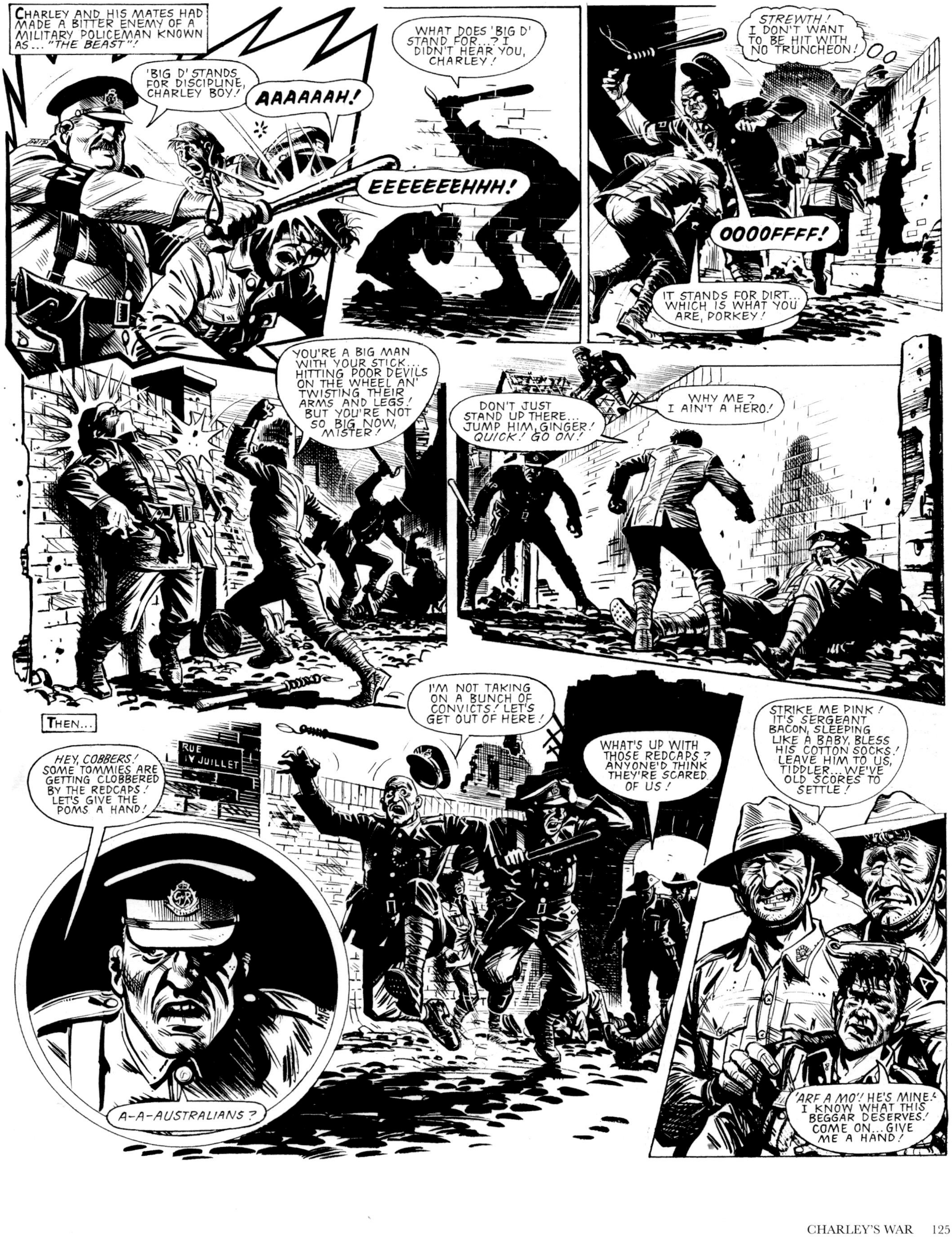
CHARLEY AND HIS MATES HAD MADE A BITTER ENEMY OF A MILITARY POLICEMAN KNOWN AS... "THE BEAST"!
'BIG D' STANDS FOR DISCIPLINE, CHARLEY BOY!
AAAAAAH!
EEEEEEEHHH!
WHAT DOES 'BIG D' STAND FOR...? I DIDN'T HEAR YOU, CHARLEY!
STREWTH! I DON'T WANT TO BE HIT WITH NO TRUNCHEON!
OOOOFFFF!
IT STANDS FOR DIRT... WHICH IS WHAT YOU ARE, PORKEY!
YOU'RE A BIG MAN WITH YOUR STICK... HITTING POOR DEVILS ON THE WHEEL AN' TWISTING THEIR ARMS AND LEGS! BUT YOU'RE NOT SO BIG NOW, MISTER!
DON'T JUST STAND UP THERE... JUMP HIM, GINGER! QUICK! GO ON!
WHY ME? I AIN'T A HERO!
THEN...
HEY, COBBERS! SOME TOMMIES ARE GETTING CLOBBERED BY THE REDCAPS! LET'S GIVE THE POMS A HAND!
RUE 14 JUILLET
A-A-AUSTRALIANS?
I'M NOT TAKING ON A BUNCH OF CONVICTS! LET'S GET OUT OF HERE!
WHAT'S UP WITH THOSE REDCAPS? ANYONE'D THINK THEY'RE SCARED OF US!
STRIKE ME PINK! IT'S SERGEANT BACON, SLEEPING LIKE A BABY, BLESS HIS COTTON SOCKS! LEAVE HIM TO US, TIDDLER... WE'VE OLD SCORES TO SETTLE!
'ARF A MO'! HE'S MINE! I KNOW WHAT THIS BEGGAR DESERVES! COME ON... GIVE ME A HAND!

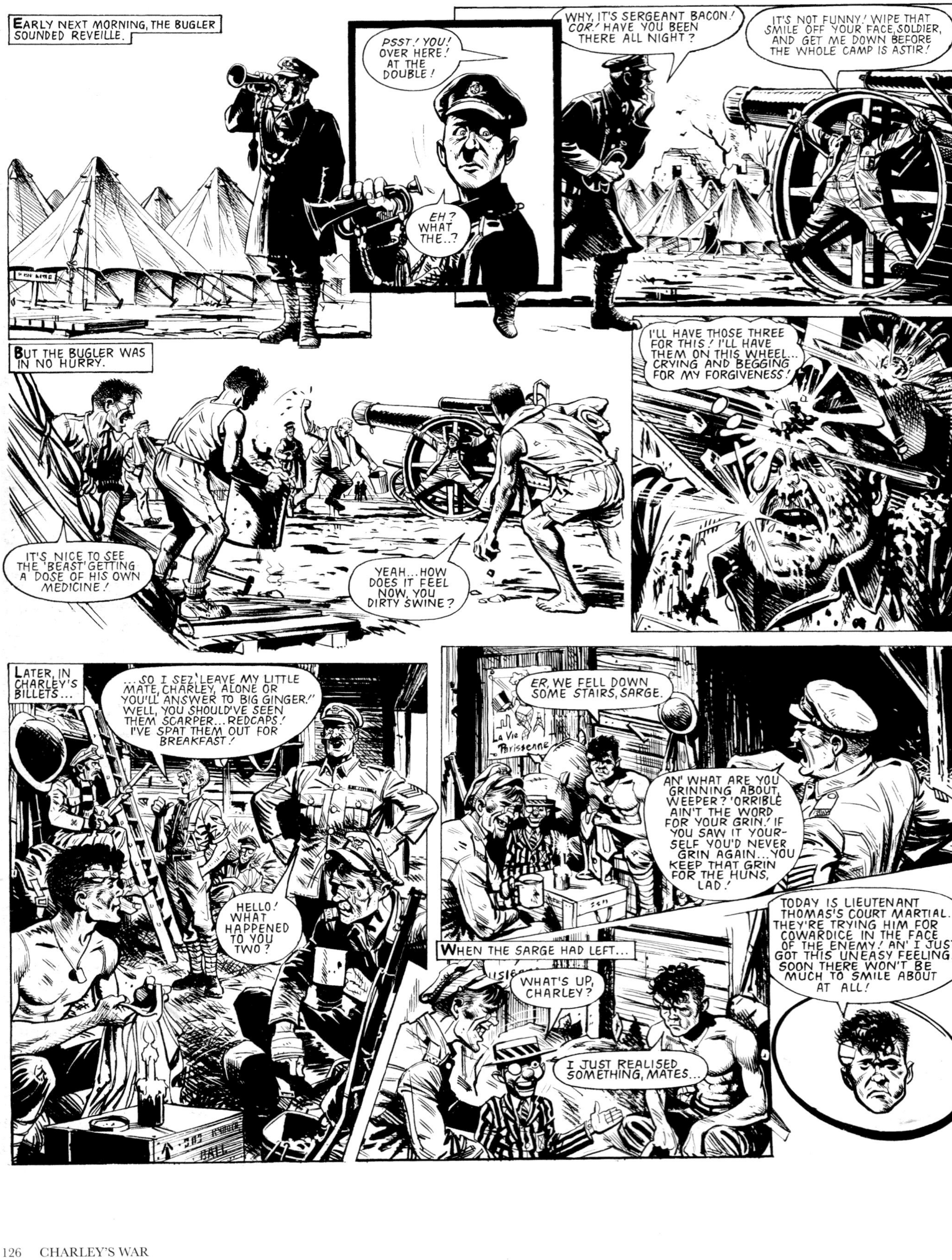
EARLY NEXT MORNING, THE BUGLER SOUNDED REVEILLE.
PSST! YOU! OVER HERE! AT THE DOUBLE!
EH? WHAT THE..?
WHY, IT'S SERGEANT BACON! COR! HAVE YOU BEEN THERE ALL NIGHT?
IT'S NOT FUNNY! WIPE THAT SMILE OFF YOUR FACE, SOLDIER, AND GET ME DOWN BEFORE THE WHOLE CAMP IS ASTIR!
BUT THE BUGLER WAS IN NO HURRY.
IT'S NICE TO SEE THE 'BEAST' GETTING A DOSE OF HIS OWN MEDICINE!
YEAH... HOW DOES IT FEEL NOW, YOU DIRTY SWINE?
I'LL HAVE THOSE THREE FOR THIS! I'LL HAVE THEM ON THIS WHEEL... CRYING AND BEGGING FOR MY FORGIVENESS!
LATER, IN CHARLEY'S BILLETS...
... SO I SEZ 'LEAVE MY LITTLE MATE, CHARLEY, ALONE OR YOU'LL ANSWER TO BIG GINGER!' WELL, YOU SHOULD'VE SEEN THEM SCARPER... REDCAPS! I'VE SPAT THEM OUT FOR BREAKFAST!
HELLO! WHAT HAPPENED TO YOU TWO?
ER, WE FELL DOWN SOME STAIRS, SARGE.
La Vie Parisienne
AN' WHAT ARE YOU GRINNING ABOUT, WEEPER? 'ORRIBLE AIN'T THE WORD FOR YOUR GRIN! IF YOU SAW IT YOURSELF YOU'D NEVER GRIN AGAIN... YOU KEEP THAT GRIN FOR THE HUNS, LAD!
WHEN THE SARGE HAD LEFT...
WHAT'S UP, CHARLEY?
I JUST REALISED SOMETHING, MATES...
TODAY IS LIEUTENANT THOMAS'S COURT MARTIAL... THEY'RE TRYING HIM FOR COWARDICE IN THE FACE OF THE ENEMY! AN' I JUST GOT THIS UNEASY FEELING... SOON THERE WON'T BE MUCH TO SMILE ABOUT AT ALL!

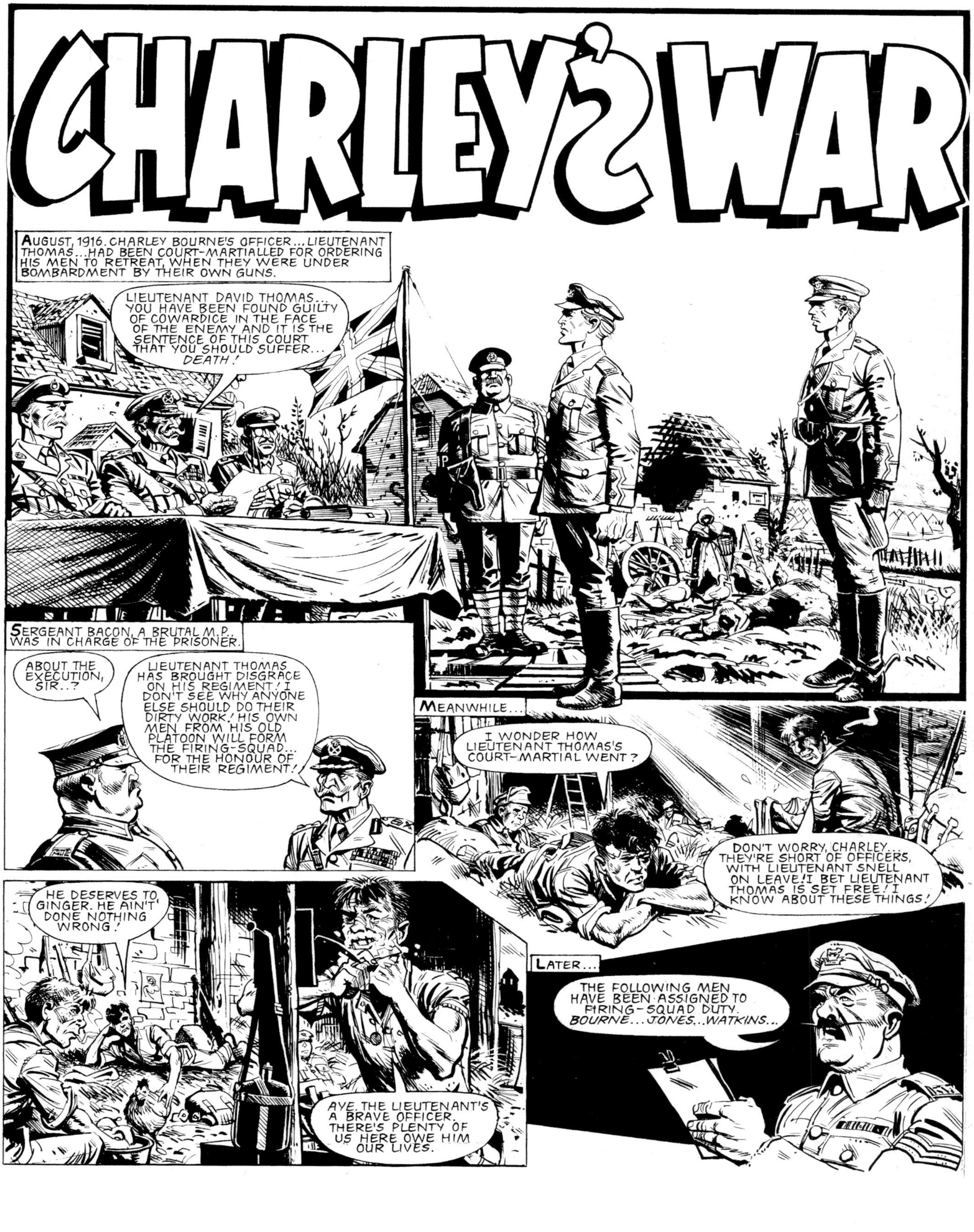
CHARLEY'S WAR
AUGUST, 1916. CHARLEY BOURNE'S OFFICER... LIEUTENANT THOMAS... HAD BEEN COURT-MARTIALLED FOR ORDERING HIS MEN TO RETREAT, WHEN THEY WERE UNDER BOMBARDMENT BY THEIR OWN GUNS.
LIEUTENANT DAVID THOMAS... YOU HAVE BEEN FOUND GUILTY OF COWARDICE IN THE FACE OF THE ENEMY AND IT IS THE SENTENCE OF THIS COURT THAT YOU SHOULD SUFFER... DEATH!
SERGEANT BACON, A BRUTAL M.P., WAS IN CHARGE OF THE PRISONER.
ABOUT THE EXECUTION, SIR..?
LIEUTENANT THOMAS HAS BROUGHT DISGRACE ON HIS REGIMENT! I DON'T SEE WHY ANYONE ELSE SHOULD DO THEIR DIRTY WORK! HIS OWN MEN FROM HIS OLD PLATOON WILL FORM THE FIRING-SQUAD... FOR THE HONOUR OF THEIR REGIMENT!
MEANWHILE...
I WONDER HOW LIEUTENANT THOMAS'S COURT-MARTIAL WENT?
DON'T WORRY, CHARLEY... THEY'RE SHORT OF OFFICERS, WITH LIEUTENANT SNELL ON LEAVE! I BET LIEUTENANT THOMAS IS SET FREE! I KNOW ABOUT THESE THINGS!
HE DESERVES TO, GINGER. HE AIN'T DONE NOTHING WRONG!
AYE, THE LIEUTENANT'S A BRAVE OFFICER. THERE'S PLENTY OF US HERE OWE HIM OUR LIVES.
LATER...
THE FOLLOWING MEN HAVE BEEN ASSIGNED TO FIRING-SQUAD DUTY. BOURNE... JONES... WATKINS...

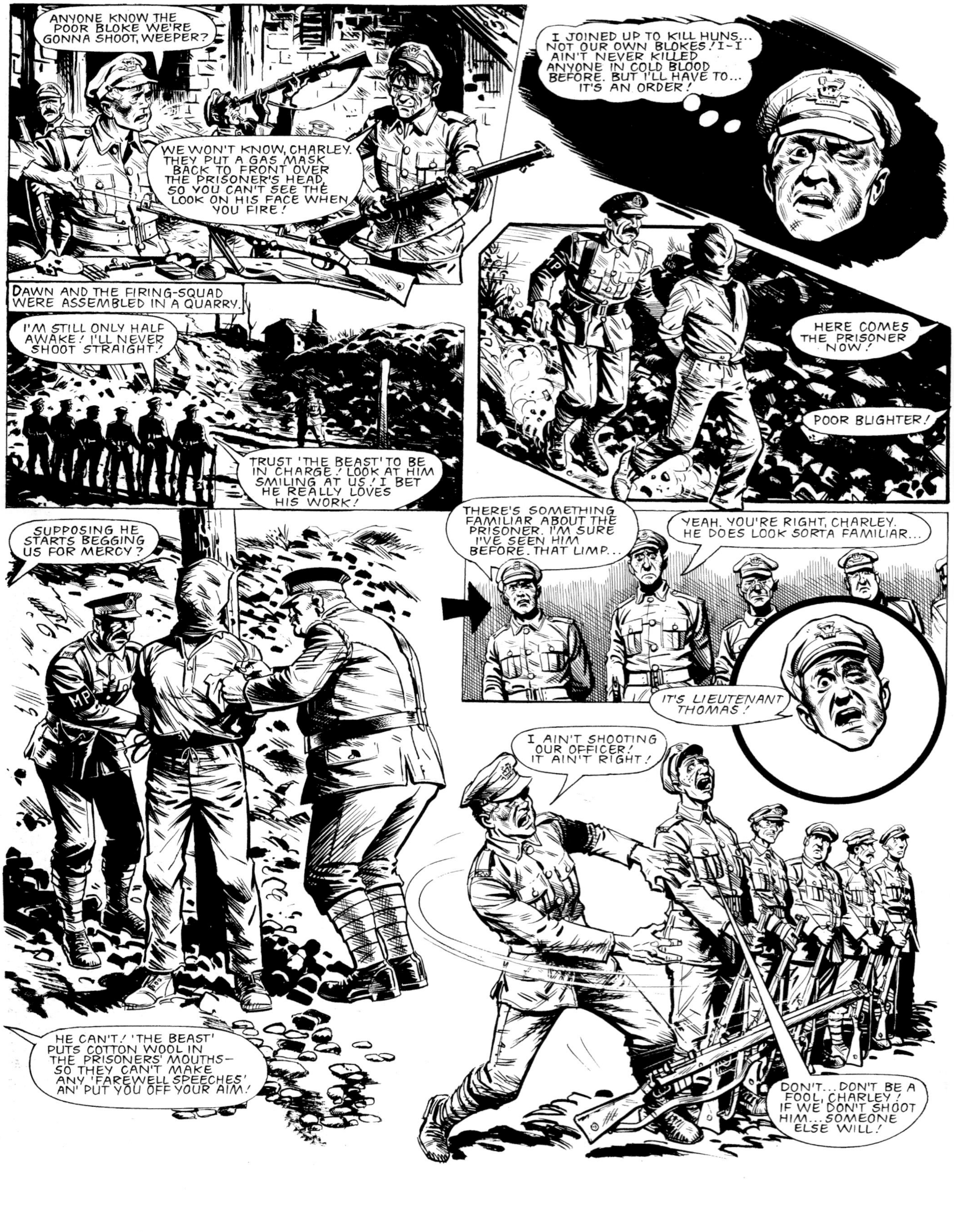

ANYONE KNOW THE POOR BLOKE WE'RE GONNA SHOOT, WEEPER?
WE WON'T KNOW, CHARLEY. THEY PUT A GAS MASK BACK TO FRONT OVER THE PRISONER'S HEAD SO YOU CAN'T SEE THE LOOK ON HIS FACE WHEN YOU FIRE!
I JOINED UP TO KILL HUNS... NOT OUR OWN BLOKES! I-I AIN'T NEVER KILLED ANYONE IN COLD BLOOD BEFORE. BUT I'LL HAVE TO... IT'S AN ORDER!
DAWN AND THE FIRING-SQUAD WERE ASSEMBLED IN A QUARRY.
I'M STILL ONLY HALF AWAKE! I'LL NEVER SHOOT STRAIGHT!
TRUST 'THE BEAST' TO BE IN CHARGE! LOOK AT HIM SMILING AT US! I BET HE REALLY LOVES HIS WORK!
HERE COMES THE PRISONER NOW!
POOR BLIGHTER!
SUPPOSING HE STARTS BEGGING US FOR MERCY?
HE CAN'T! 'THE BEAST' PUTS COTTON WOOL IN THE PRISONERS' MOUTHS— SO THEY CAN'T MAKE ANY 'FAREWELL SPEECHES' AN' PUT YOU OFF YOUR AIM!
THERE'S SOMETHING FAMILIAR ABOUT THE PRISONER. I'M SURE I'VE SEEN HIM BEFORE. THAT LIMP...
YEAH. YOU'RE RIGHT, CHARLEY. HE DOES LOOK SORTA FAMILIAR...
IT'S LIEUTENANT THOMAS!
I AIN'T SHOOTING OUR OFFICER! IT AIN'T RIGHT!
DON'T... DON'T BE A FOOL, CHARLEY! IF WE DON'T SHOOT HIM... SOMEONE ELSE WILL!

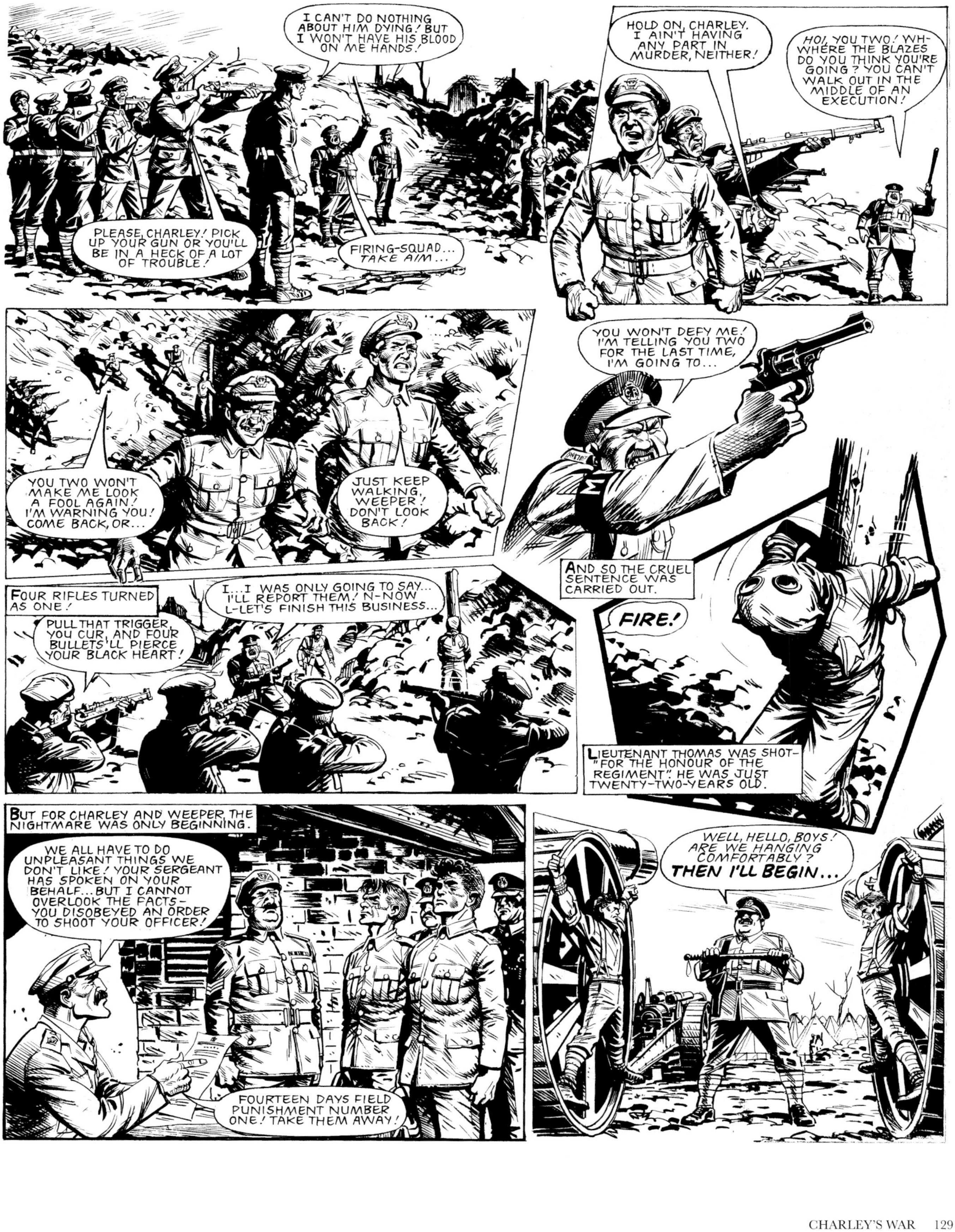
I CAN'T DO NOTHING ABOUT HIM DYING! BUT I WON'T HAVE HIS BLOOD ON ME HANDS!
PLEASE, CHARLEY! PICK UP YOUR GUN OR YOU'LL BE IN A HECK OF A LOT OF TROUBLE!
FIRING-SQUAD... TAKE AIM...
HOLD ON, CHARLEY. I AIN'T HAVING ANY PART IN MURDER, NEITHER!
HOI, YOU TWO! WH-WHERE THE BLAZES DO YOU THINK YOU'RE GOING? YOU CAN'T WALK OUT IN THE MIDDLE OF AN EXECUTION!
YOU TWO WON'T MAKE ME LOOK A FOOL AGAIN! I'M WARNING YOU! COME BACK, OR...
JUST KEEP WALKING, WEEPER! DON'T LOOK BACK!
YOU WON'T DEFY ME! I'M TELLING YOU TWO FOR THE LAST TIME, I'M GOING TO...
FOUR RIFLES TURNED AS ONE!
PULL THAT TRIGGER, YOU CUR, AND FOUR BULLETS'LL PIERCE YOUR BLACK HEART!
I...I WAS ONLY GOING TO SAY... I'LL REPORT THEM! N-NOW L-LET'S FINISH THIS BUSINESS...
AND SO THE CRUEL SENTENCE WAS CARRIED OUT.
FIRE!
LIEUTENANT THOMAS WAS SHOT- "FOR THE HONOUR OF THE REGIMENT". HE WAS JUST TWENTY-TWO-YEARS OLD.
BUT FOR CHARLEY AND WEEPER THE NIGHTMARE WAS ONLY BEGINNING.
WE ALL HAVE TO DO UNPLEASANT THINGS WE DON'T LIKE! YOUR SERGEANT HAS SPOKEN ON YOUR BEHALF... BUT I CANNOT OVERLOOK THE FACTS- YOU DISOBEYED AN ORDER TO SHOOT YOUR OFFICER!
FOURTEEN DAYS FIELD PUNISHMENT NUMBER ONE! TAKE THEM AWAY!
WELL, HELLO, BOYS! ARE WE HANGING COMFORTABLY? THEN I'LL BEGIN...

CHARLEY'S WAR

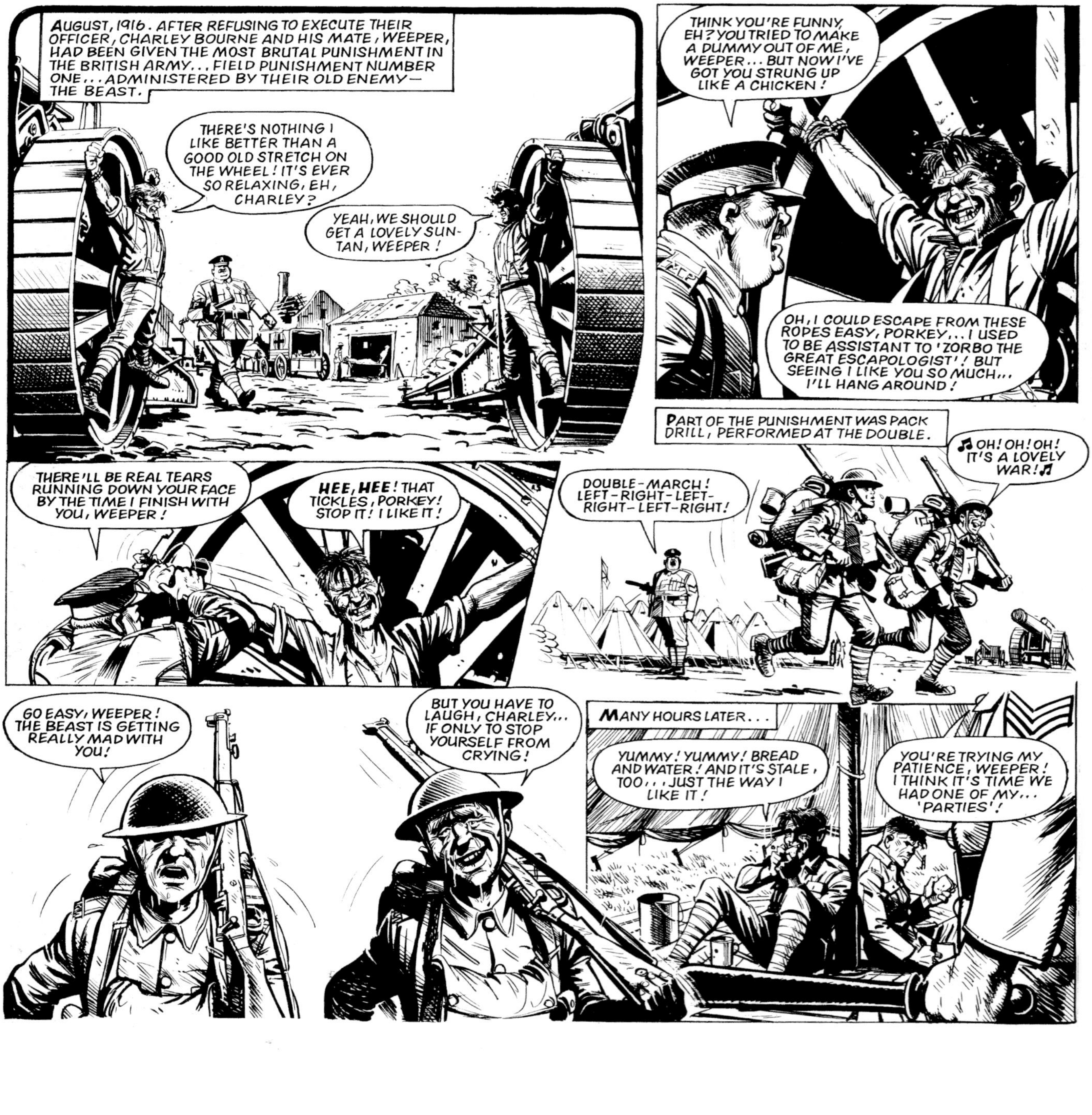

AUGUST, 1916. AFTER REFUSING TO EXECUTE THEIR OFFICER, CHARLEY BOURNE AND HIS MATE, WEEPER, HAD BEEN GIVEN THE MOST BRUTAL PUNISHMENT IN THE BRITISH ARMY... FIELD PUNISHMENT NUMBER ONE... ADMINISTERED BY THEIR OLD ENEMY— THE BEAST.
THERE'S NOTHING I LIKE BETTER THAN A GOOD OLD STRETCH ON THE WHEEL! IT'S EVER SO RELAXING, EH, CHARLEY?
YEAH, WE SHOULD GET A LOVELY SUN-TAN, WEEPER!
THINK YOU'RE FUNNY, EH? YOU TRIED TO MAKE A DUMMY OUT OF ME, WEEPER... BUT NOW I'VE GOT YOU STRUNG UP LIKE A CHICKEN!
OH, I COULD ESCAPE FROM THESE ROPES EASY, PORKEY... I USED TO BE ASSISTANT TO 'ZORBO THE GREAT ESCAPOLOGIST'! BUT SEEING I LIKE YOU SO MUCH... I'LL HANG AROUND!
THERE'LL BE REAL TEARS RUNNING DOWN YOUR FACE BY THE TIME I FINISH WITH YOU, WEEPER!
HEE, HEE! THAT TICKLES, PORKEY! STOP IT! I LIKE IT!
PART OF THE PUNISHMENT WAS PACK DRILL, PERFORMED AT THE DOUBLE.
DOUBLE-MARCH! LEFT-RIGHT-LEFT-RIGHT-LEFT-RIGHT!
♫ OH! OH! OH! IT'S A LOVELY WAR! ♫
GO EASY, WEEPER! THE BEAST IS GETTING REALLY MAD WITH YOU!
BUT YOU HAVE TO LAUGH, CHARLEY... IF ONLY TO STOP YOURSELF FROM CRYING!
MANY HOURS LATER...
YUMMY! YUMMY! BREAD AND WATER! AND IT'S STALE, TOO... JUST THE WAY I LIKE IT!
YOU'RE TRYING MY PATIENCE, WEEPER! I THINK IT'S TIME WE HAD ONE OF MY... 'PARTIES'!

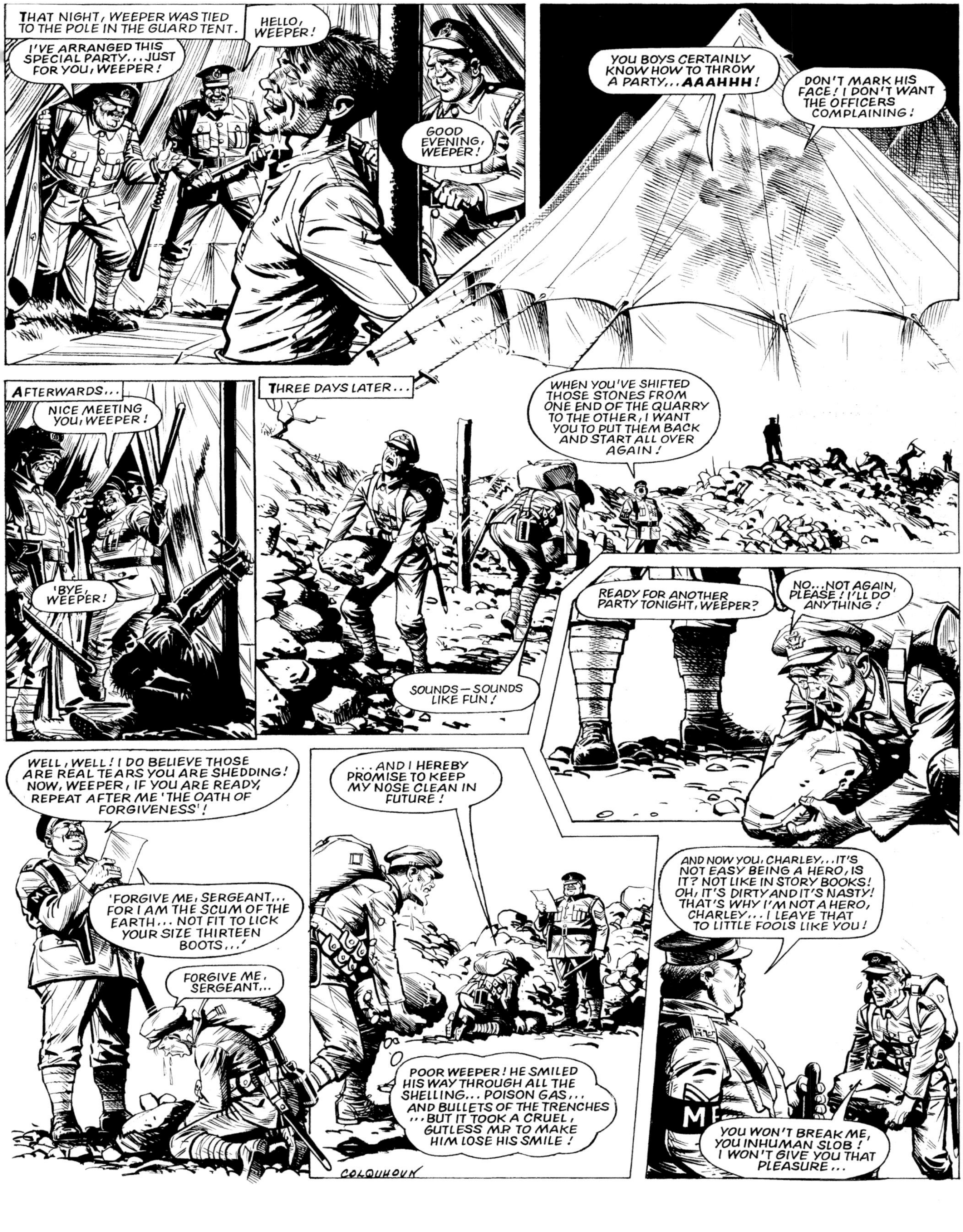
THAT NIGHT, WEEPER WAS TIED TO THE POLE IN THE GUARD TENT.
I'VE ARRANGED THIS SPECIAL PARTY... JUST FOR YOU, WEEPER!
HELLO, WEEPER!
GOOD EVENING, WEEPER!
YOU BOYS CERTAINLY KNOW HOW TO THROW A PARTY... AAAHHH!
DON'T MARK HIS FACE! I DON'T WANT THE OFFICERS COMPLAINING!
AFTERWARDS...
NICE MEETING YOU, WEEPER!
'BYE, WEEPER!
THREE DAYS LATER...
WHEN YOU'VE SHIFTED THOSE STONES FROM ONE END OF THE QUARRY TO THE OTHER, I WANT YOU TO PUT THEM BACK AND START ALL OVER AGAIN!
SOUNDS — SOUNDS LIKE FUN!
READY FOR ANOTHER PARTY TONIGHT, WEEPER?
NO... NOT AGAIN, PLEASE! I'LL DO ANYTHING!
WELL, WELL! I DO BELIEVE THOSE ARE REAL TEARS YOU ARE SHEDDING! NOW, WEEPER, IF YOU ARE READY, REPEAT AFTER ME 'THE OATH OF FORGIVENESS'!
'FORGIVE ME, SERGEANT... FOR I AM THE SCUM OF THE EARTH... NOT FIT TO LICK YOUR SIZE THIRTEEN BOOTS...'
FORGIVE ME, SERGEANT...
...AND I HEREBY PROMISE TO KEEP MY NOSE CLEAN IN FUTURE!
POOR WEEPER! HE SMILED HIS WAY THROUGH ALL THE SHELLING... POISON GAS... AND BULLETS OF THE TRENCHES ... BUT IT TOOK A CRUEL, GUTLESS M.P. TO MAKE HIM LOSE HIS SMILE!
COLQUHOUN
AND NOW YOU, CHARLEY... IT'S NOT EASY BEING A HERO, IS IT? NOT LIKE IN STORY BOOKS! OH, IT'S DIRTY AND IT'S NASTY! THAT'S WHY I'M NOT A HERO, CHARLEY... I LEAVE THAT TO LITTLE FOOLS LIKE YOU!
YOU WON'T BREAK ME, YOU INHUMAN SLOB! I WON'T GIVE YOU THAT PLEASURE...

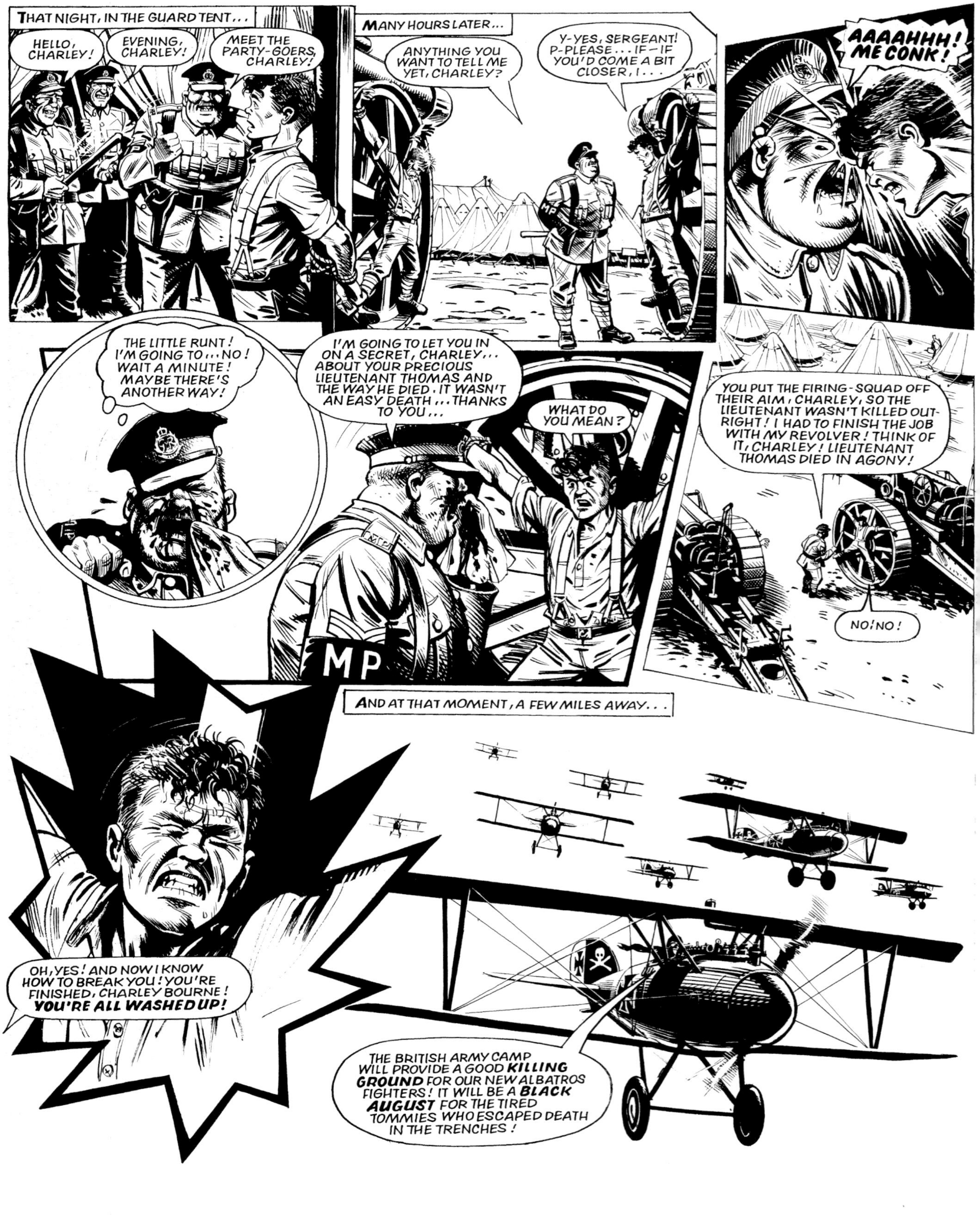

THAT NIGHT, IN THE GUARD TENT...
HELLO, CHARLEY!
EVENING, CHARLEY!
MEET THE PARTY-GOERS, CHARLEY!
MANY HOURS LATER...
ANYTHING YOU WANT TO TELL ME YET, CHARLEY?
Y-YES, SERGEANT! P-PLEASE... IF—IF YOU'D COME A BIT CLOSER, I...
AAAAHHH! ME CONK!
THE LITTLE RUNT! I'M GOING TO...NO! WAIT A MINUTE! MAYBE THERE'S ANOTHER WAY!
I'M GOING TO LET YOU IN ON A SECRET, CHARLEY... ABOUT YOUR PRECIOUS LIEUTENANT THOMAS AND THE WAY HE DIED. IT WASN'T AN EASY DEATH... THANKS TO YOU...
WHAT DO YOU MEAN?
YOU PUT THE FIRING-SQUAD OFF THEIR AIM, CHARLEY, SO THE LIEUTENANT WASN'T KILLED OUTRIGHT! I HAD TO FINISH THE JOB WITH MY REVOLVER! THINK OF IT, CHARLEY! LIEUTENANT THOMAS DIED IN AGONY!
NO! NO!
MP
OH, YES! AND NOW I KNOW HOW TO BREAK YOU! YOU'RE FINISHED, CHARLEY BOURNE! YOU'RE ALL WASHED UP!
AND AT THAT MOMENT, A FEW MILES AWAY...
THE BRITISH ARMY CAMP WILL PROVIDE A GOOD KILLING GROUND FOR OUR NEW ALBATROS FIGHTERS! IT WILL BE A BLACK AUGUST FOR THE TIRED TOMMIES WHO ESCAPED DEATH IN THE TRENCHES!

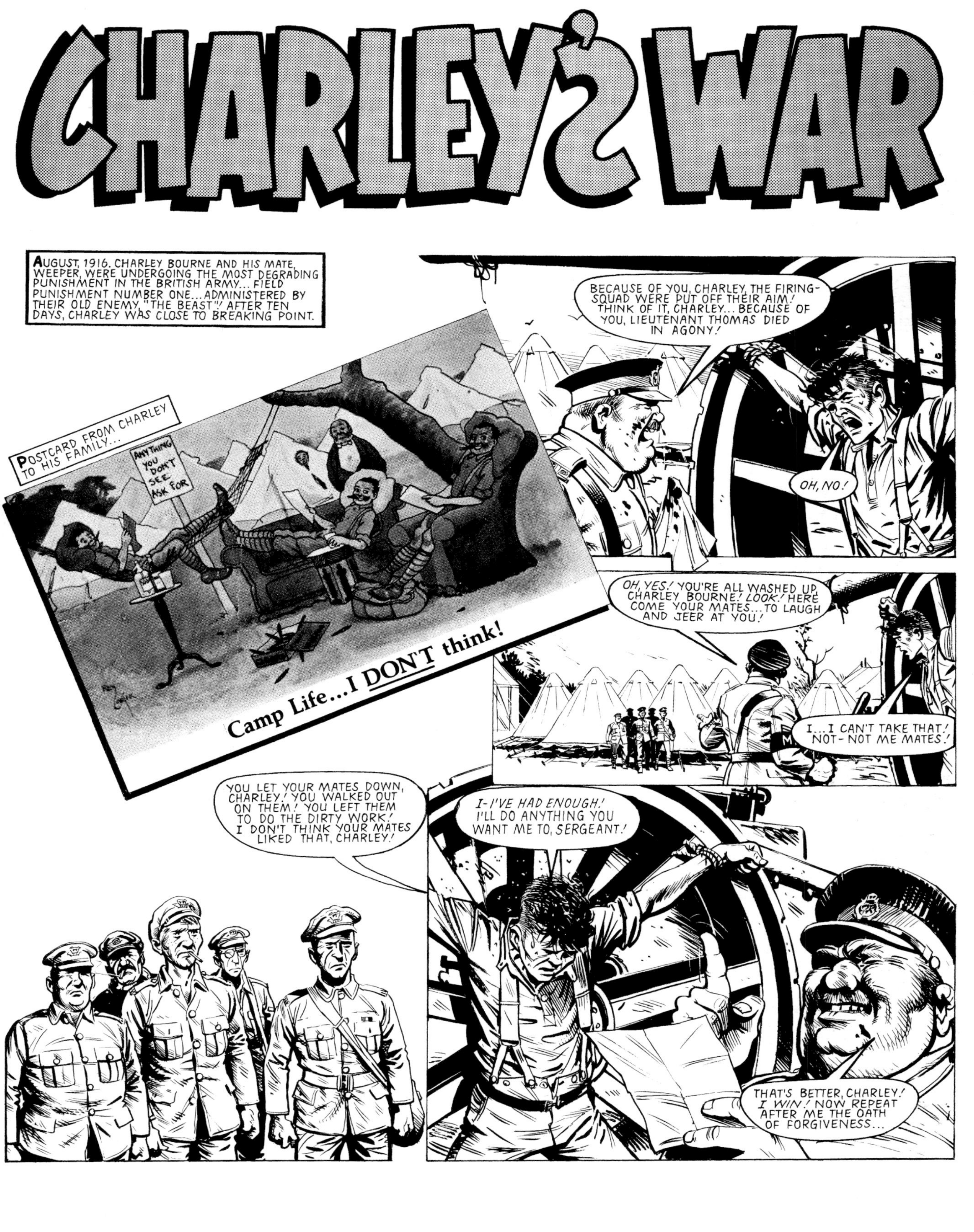
CHARLEY'S WAR
AUGUST, 1916. CHARLEY BOURNE AND HIS MATE, WEEPER, WERE UNDERGOING THE MOST DEGRADING PUNISHMENT IN THE BRITISH ARMY... FIELD PUNISHMENT NUMBER ONE... ADMINISTERED BY THEIR OLD ENEMY, "THE BEAST"! AFTER TEN DAYS, CHARLEY WAS CLOSE TO BREAKING POINT.
BECAUSE OF YOU, CHARLEY, THE FIRING-SQUAD WERE PUT OFF THEIR AIM! THINK OF IT, CHARLEY... BECAUSE OF YOU, LIEUTENANT THOMAS DIED IN AGONY!
OH, NO!
POSTCARD FROM CHARLEY TO HIS FAMILY...
ANYTHING YOU DON'T SEE ASK FOR
Camp Life...I DONT think!
OH, YES! YOU'RE ALL WASHED UP, CHARLEY BOURNE! LOOK! HERE COME YOUR MATES... TO LAUGH AND JEER AT YOU!
I... I CAN'T TAKE THAT! NOT- NOT ME MATES!
YOU LET YOUR MATES DOWN, CHARLEY! YOU WALKED OUT ON THEM! YOU LEFT THEM TO DO THE DIRTY WORK! I DON'T THINK YOUR MATES LIKED THAT, CHARLEY!
I-I'VE HAD ENOUGH! I'LL DO ANYTHING YOU WANT ME TO, SERGEANT!
THAT'S BETTER, CHARLEY! I WIN! NOW REPEAT AFTER ME THE OATH OF FORGIVENESS...

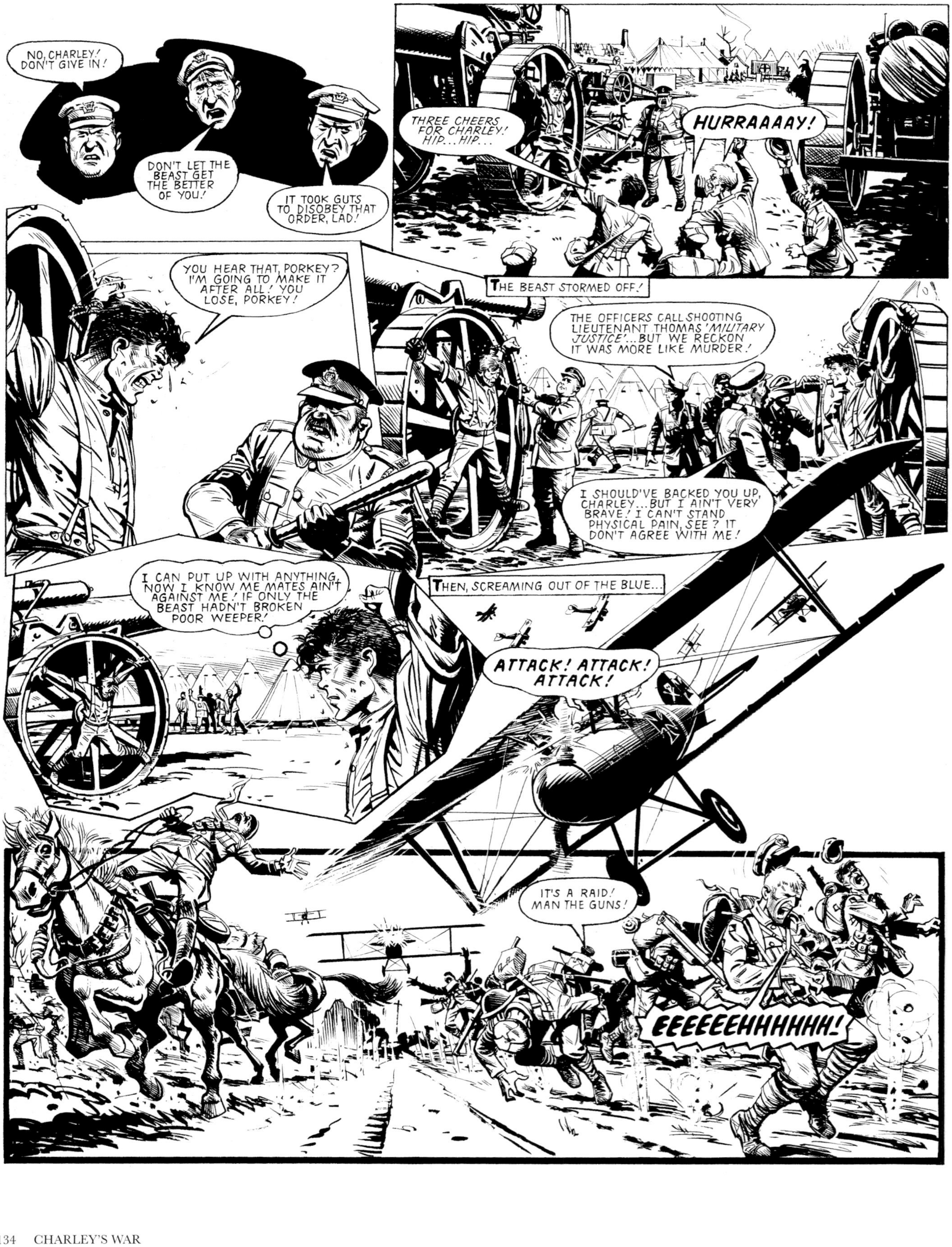
NO, CHARLEY! DON'T GIVE IN!
DON'T LET THE BEAST GET THE BETTER OF YOU!
IT TOOK GUTS TO DISOBEY THAT ORDER, LAD!
THREE CHEERS FOR CHARLEY! HIP...HIP...
HURRAAAAY!
YOU HEAR THAT, PORKEY? I'M GOING TO MAKE IT AFTER ALL! YOU LOSE, PORKEY!
THE BEAST STORMED OFF!
THE OFFICERS CALL SHOOTING LIEUTENANT THOMAS 'MILITARY JUSTICE'... BUT WE RECKON IT WAS MORE LIKE MURDER!
I SHOULD'VE BACKED YOU UP, CHARLEY... BUT I AIN'T VERY BRAVE! I CAN'T STAND PHYSICAL PAIN, SEE? IT DON'T AGREE WITH ME!
I CAN PUT UP WITH ANYTHING, NOW I KNOW ME MATES AIN'T AGAINST ME! IF ONLY THE BEAST HADN'T BROKEN POOR WEEPER!
THEN, SCREAMING OUT OF THE BLUE...
ATTACK! ATTACK! ATTACK!
IT'S A RAID! MAN THE GUNS!
EEEEEEHHHHHH!

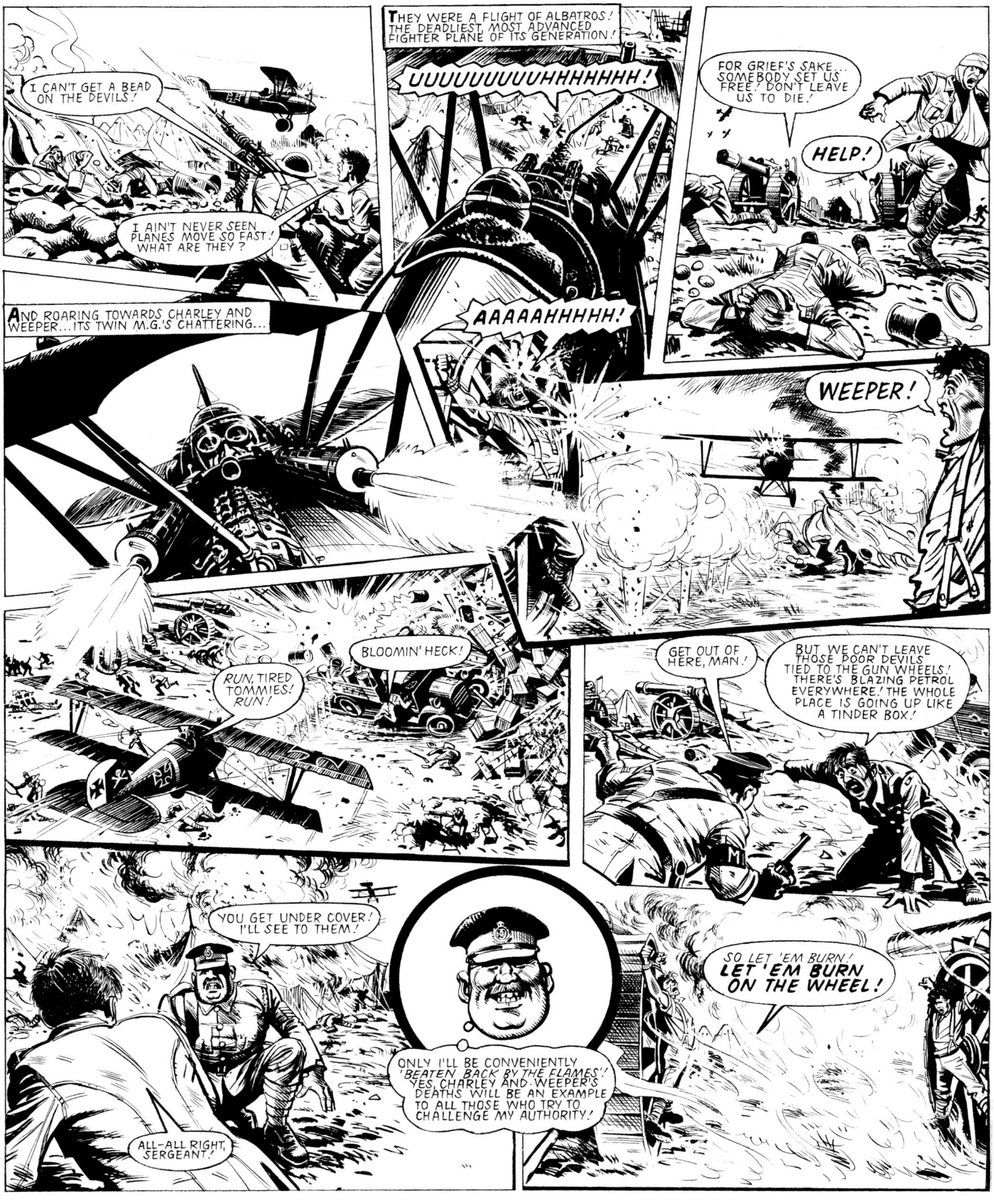
I CAN'T GET A BEAD ON THE DEVILS!
I AIN'T NEVER SEEN PLANES MOVE SO FAST! WHAT ARE THEY?
THEY WERE A FLIGHT OF ALBATROS! THE DEADLIEST, MOST ADVANCED FIGHTER PLANE OF ITS GENERATION!
UUUUUUUUUHHHHHHH!
FOR GRIEF'S SAKE... SOMEBODY SET US FREE! DON'T LEAVE US TO DIE!
HELP!
AND ROARING TOWARDS CHARLEY AND WEEPER... ITS TWIN M.G.'S CHATTERING...
AAAAAHHHHH!
WEEPER!
BLOOMIN' HECK!
RUN, TIRED TOMMIES! RUN!
GET OUT OF HERE, MAN!
BUT WE CAN'T LEAVE THOSE POOR DEVILS TIED TO THE GUN WHEELS! THERE'S BLAZING PETROL EVERYWHERE! THE WHOLE PLACE IS GOING UP LIKE A TINDER BOX!
YOU GET UNDER COVER! I'LL SEE TO THEM!
ALL-ALL RIGHT, SERGEANT!
SO LET 'EM BURN! LET 'EM BURN ON THE WHEEL!
ONLY I'LL BE CONVENIENTLY 'BEATEN BACK BY THE FLAMES'! YES, CHARLEY AND WEEPER'S DEATHS WILL BE AN EXAMPLE TO ALL THOSE WHO TRY TO CHALLENGE MY AUTHORITY!

CHARLEY'S WAR

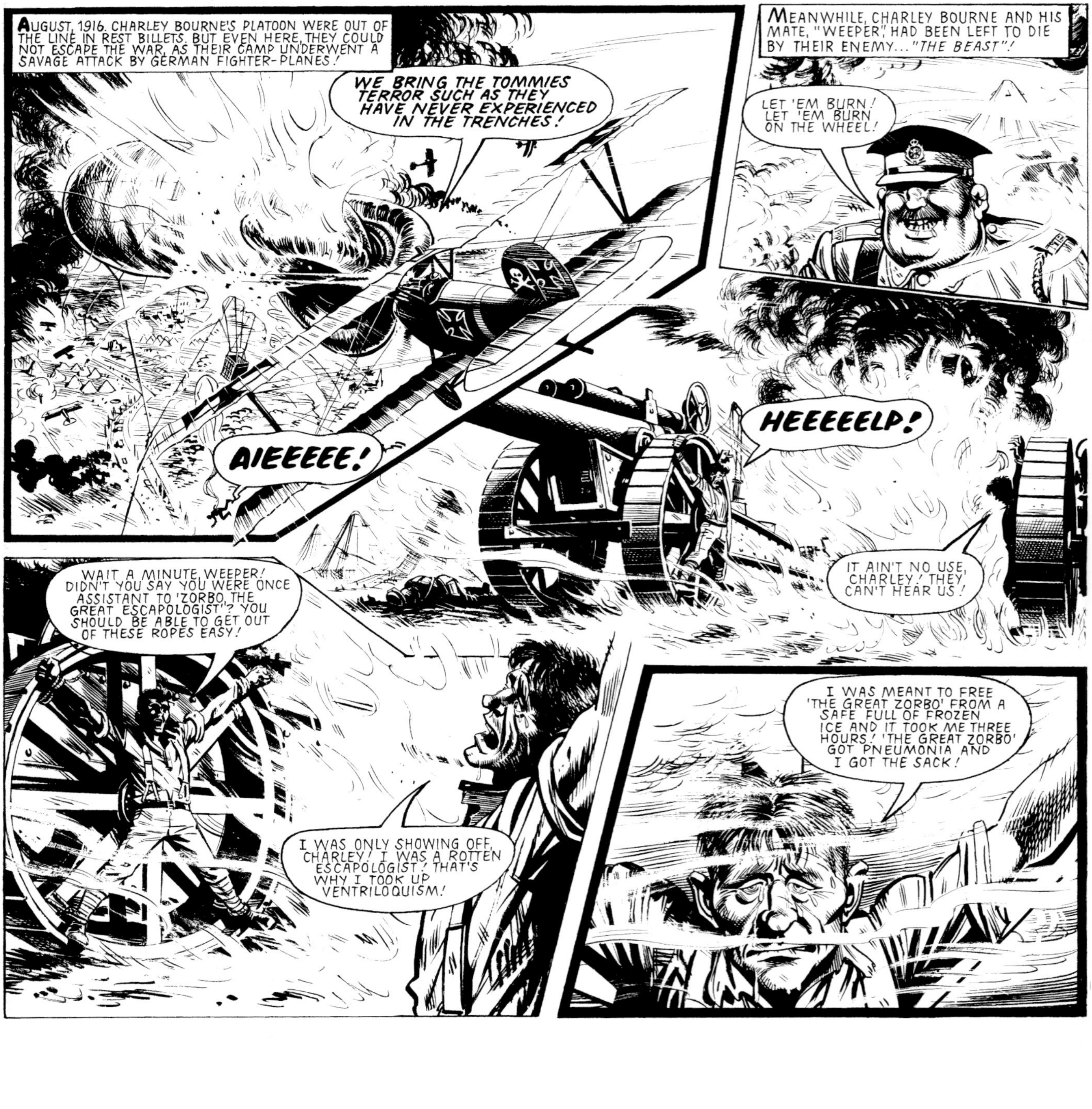

AUGUST, 1916. CHARLEY BOURNE'S PLATOON WERE OUT OF THE LINE IN REST BILLETS. BUT EVEN HERE, THEY COULD NOT ESCAPE THE WAR, AS THEIR CAMP UNDERWENT A SAVAGE ATTACK BY GERMAN FIGHTER-PLANES!
WE BRING THE TOMMIES TERROR SUCH AS THEY HAVE NEVER EXPERIENCED IN THE TRENCHES!
AIEEEEE!
MEANWHILE, CHARLEY BOURNE AND HIS MATE, "WEEPER", HAD BEEN LEFT TO DIE BY THEIR ENEMY... "THE BEAST"!
LET 'EM BURN! LET 'EM BURN ON THE WHEEL!
HEEEEELP!
IT AIN'T NO USE, CHARLEY! THEY CAN'T HEAR US!
WAIT A MINUTE, WEEPER! DIDN'T YOU SAY YOU WERE ONCE ASSISTANT TO 'ZORBO, THE GREAT ESCAPOLOGIST'? YOU SHOULD BE ABLE TO GET OUT OF THESE ROPES EASY!
I WAS ONLY SHOWING OFF, CHARLEY! I WAS A ROTTEN ESCAPOLOGIST! THAT'S WHY I TOOK UP VENTRILOQUISM!
I WAS MEANT TO FREE 'THE GREAT ZORBO' FROM A SAFE FULL OF FROZEN ICE AND IT TOOK ME THREE HOURS! 'THE GREAT ZORBO' GOT PNEUMONIA AND I GOT THE SACK!

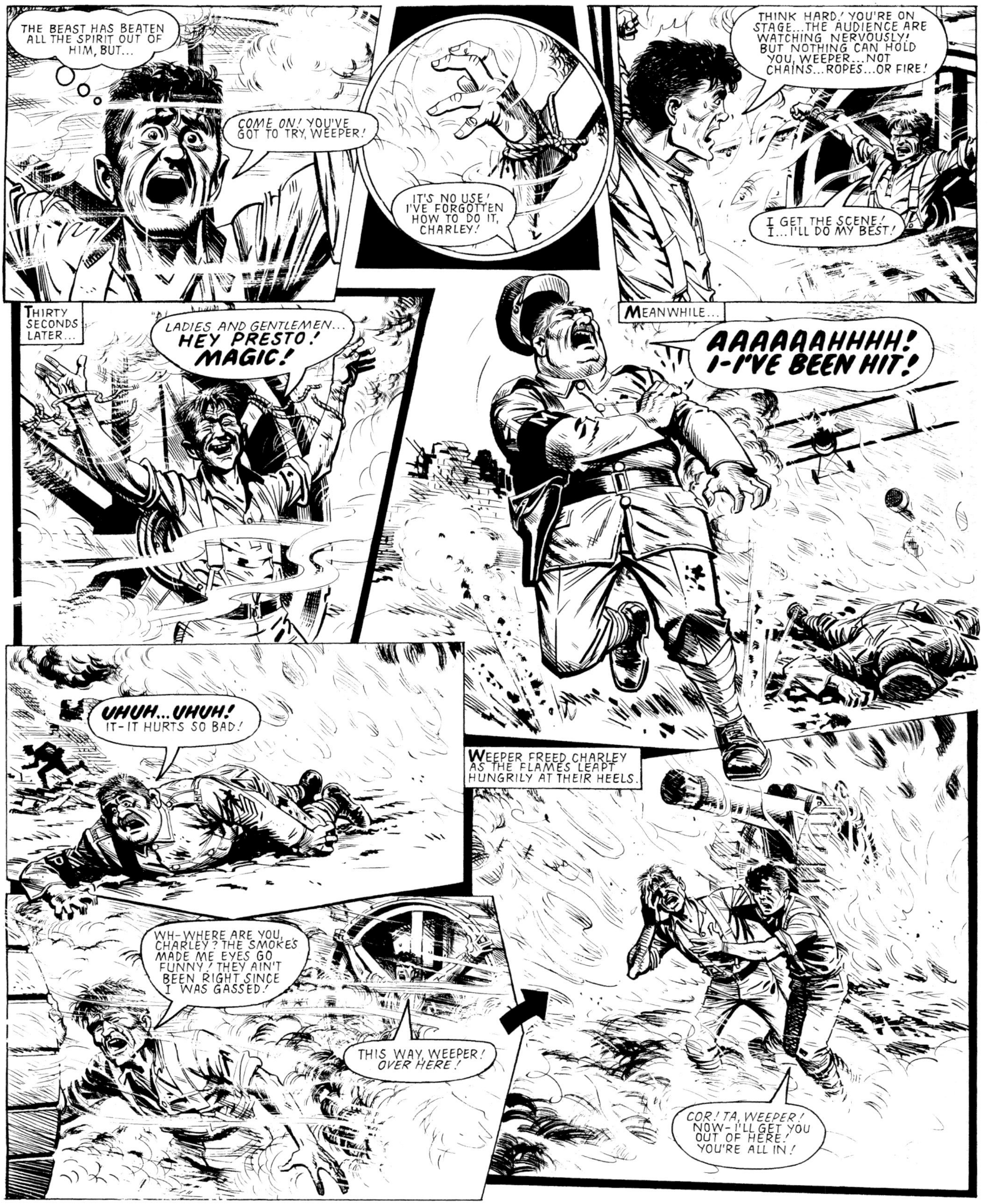
THE BEAST HAS BEATEN ALL THE SPIRIT OUT OF HIM, BUT...
COME ON! YOU'VE GOT TO TRY, WEEPER!
IT'S NO USE! I'VE FORGOTTEN HOW TO DO IT, CHARLEY!
THINK HARD! YOU'RE ON STAGE... THE AUDIENCE ARE WATCHING NERVOUSLY! BUT NOTHING CAN HOLD YOU, WEEPER... NOT CHAINS... ROPES... OR FIRE!
I GET THE SCENE! I... I'LL DO MY BEST!
THIRTY SECONDS LATER...
LADIES AND GENTLEMEN... HEY PRESTO! MAGIC!
MEANWHILE...
AAAAAAHHHH! I-I'VE BEEN HIT!
UHUH...UHUH! IT-IT HURTS SO BAD!
WH-WHERE ARE YOU, CHARLEY? THE SMOKE'S MADE ME EYES GO FUNNY! THEY AIN'T BEEN RIGHT SINCE I WAS GASSED!
THIS WAY, WEEPER! OVER HERE!
WEEPER FREED CHARLEY AS THE FLAMES LEAPT HUNGRILY AT THEIR HEELS.
COR! TA, WEEPER! NOW-I'LL GET YOU OUT OF HERE! YOU'RE ALL IN!

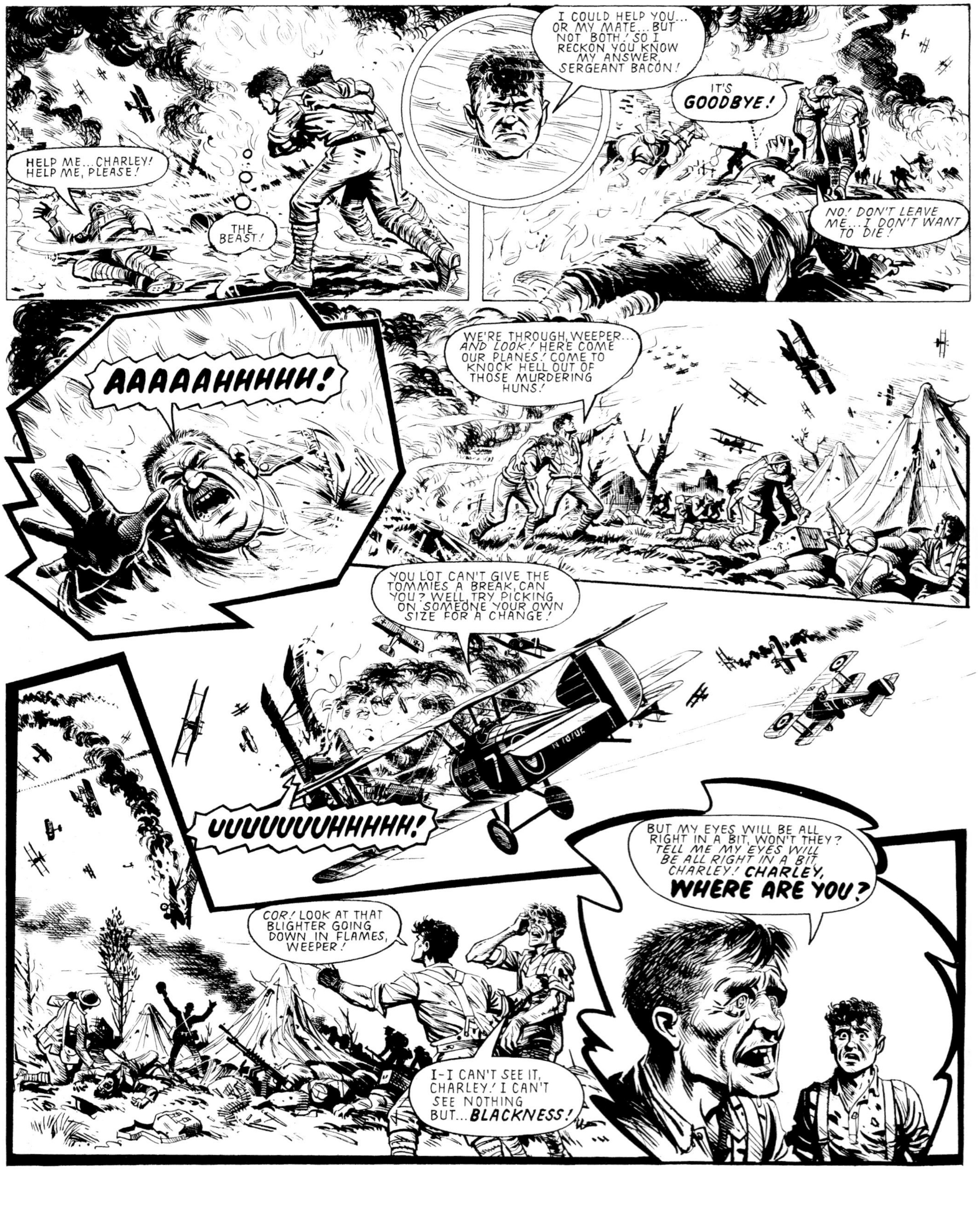

HELP ME... CHARLEY! HELP ME, PLEASE!
THE BEAST!
I COULD HELP YOU... OR MY MATE... BUT NOT BOTH! SO I RECKON YOU KNOW MY ANSWER, SERGEANT BACON!
IT'S GOODBYE!
NO! DON'T LEAVE ME... I DON'T WANT TO DIE!
AAAAAHHHHH!
WE'RE THROUGH, WEEPER... AND LOOK! HERE COME OUR PLANES! COME TO KNOCK HELL OUT OF THOSE MURDERING HUNS!
YOU LOT CAN'T GIVE THE TOMMIES A BREAK, CAN YOU? WELL, TRY PICKING ON SOMEONE YOUR OWN SIZE FOR A CHANGE!
UUUUUUUHHHHH!
COR! LOOK AT THAT BLIGHTER GOING DOWN IN FLAMES, WEEPER!
I-I CAN'T SEE IT, CHARLEY! I CAN'T SEE NOTHING BUT... BLACKNESS!
BUT MY EYES WILL BE ALL RIGHT IN A BIT, WON'T THEY? TELL ME MY EYES WILL BE ALL RIGHT IN A BIT, CHARLEY! CHARLEY, WHERE ARE YOU?

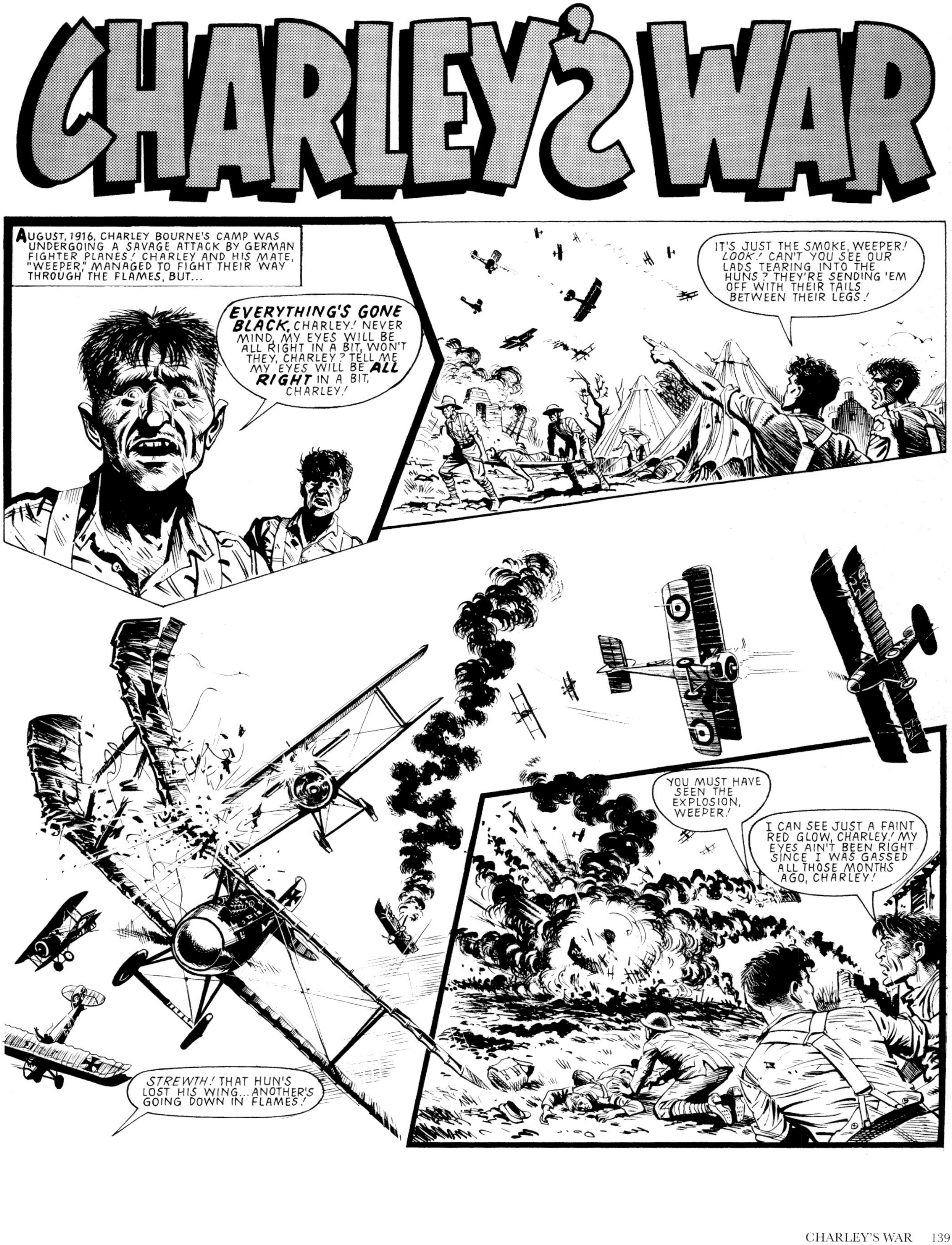
CHARLEY'S WAR
AUGUST, 1916, CHARLEY BOURNE'S CAMP WAS UNDERGOING A SAVAGE ATTACK BY GERMAN FIGHTER PLANES! CHARLEY AND HIS MATE, "WEEPER," MANAGED TO FIGHT THEIR WAY THROUGH THE FLAMES, BUT...
EVERYTHING'S GONE BLACK, CHARLEY! NEVER MIND, MY EYES WILL BE ALL RIGHT IN A BIT, WON'T THEY, CHARLEY? TELL ME MY EYES WILL BE ALL RIGHT IN A BIT, CHARLEY!
IT'S JUST THE SMOKE, WEEPER! LOOK! CAN'T YOU SEE OUR LADS TEARING INTO THE HUNS? THEY'RE SENDING 'EM OFF WITH THEIR TAILS BETWEEN THEIR LEGS!
STREWTH! THAT HUN'S LOST HIS WING... ANOTHER'S GOING DOWN IN FLAMES!
YOU MUST HAVE SEEN THE EXPLOSION, WEEPER!
I CAN SEE JUST A FAINT RED GLOW, CHARLEY! MY EYES AIN'T BEEN RIGHT SINCE I WAS GASSED ALL THOSE MONTHS AGO, CHARLEY!

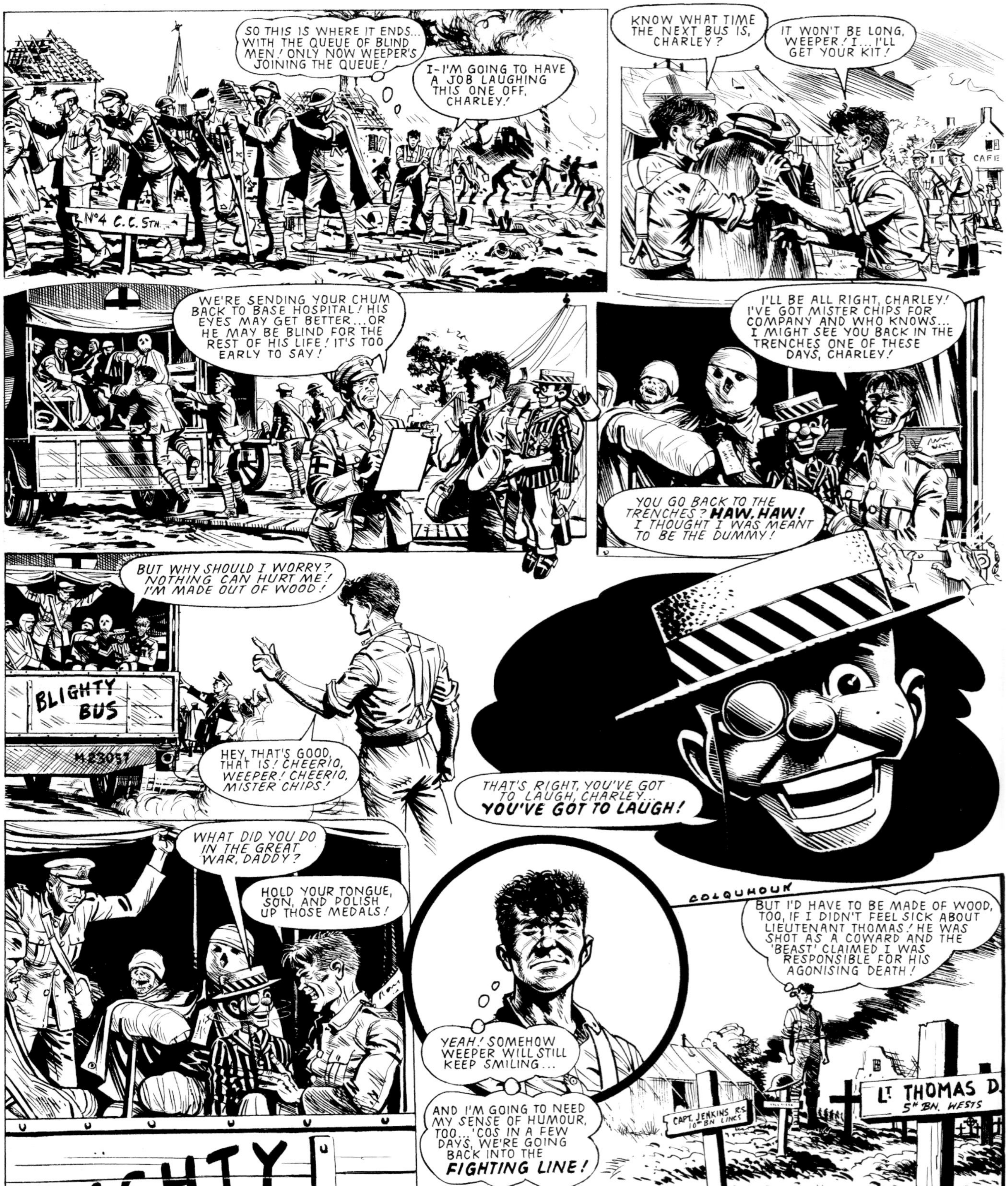
SO THIS IS WHERE IT ENDS... WITH THE QUEUE OF BLIND MEN! ONLY NOW WEEPER'S JOINING THE QUEUE!
I-I'M GOING TO HAVE A JOB LAUGHING THIS ONE OFF, CHARLEY!
Nº4 C.C. STN.
KNOW WHAT TIME THE NEXT BUS IS, CHARLEY?
IT WON'T BE LONG, WEEPER! I... I'LL GET YOUR KIT!
CAFE
WE'RE SENDING YOUR CHUM BACK TO BASE HOSPITAL! HIS EYES MAY GET BETTER... OR HE MAY BE BLIND FOR THE REST OF HIS LIFE! IT'S TOO EARLY TO SAY!
I'LL BE ALL RIGHT, CHARLEY! I'VE GOT MISTER CHIPS FOR COMPANY AND WHO KNOWS... I MIGHT SEE YOU BACK IN THE TRENCHES ONE OF THESE DAYS, CHARLEY!
YOU GO BACK TO THE TRENCHES? HAW, HAW! I THOUGHT I WAS MEANT TO BE THE DUMMY!
BUT WHY SHOULD I WORRY? NOTHING CAN HURT ME! I'M MADE OUT OF WOOD!
BLIGHTY BUS
M23051
HEY, THAT'S GOOD, THAT IS! CHEERIO, WEEPER! CHEERIO, MISTER CHIPS!
THAT'S RIGHT, YOU'VE GOT TO LAUGH, CHARLEY... YOU'VE GOT TO LAUGH!
WHAT DID YOU DO IN THE GREAT WAR, DADDY?
HOLD YOUR TONGUE, SON, AND POLISH UP THOSE MEDALS!
LIGHTY
COLQUHOUN
YEAH! SOMEHOW WEEPER WILL STILL KEEP SMILING...
AND I'M GOING TO NEED MY SENSE OF HUMOUR, TOO... 'COS IN A FEW DAYS, WE'RE GOING BACK INTO THE FIGHTING LINE!
BUT I'D HAVE TO BE MADE OF WOOD, TOO, IF I DIDN'T FEEL SICK ABOUT LIEUTENANT THOMAS! HE WAS SHOT AS A COWARD AND THE 'BEAST' CLAIMED I WAS RESPONSIBLE FOR HIS AGONISING DEATH!
CAPT. JENKINS RS. 10th BN LINCS
Lt THOMAS D. 5th BN. WESTS

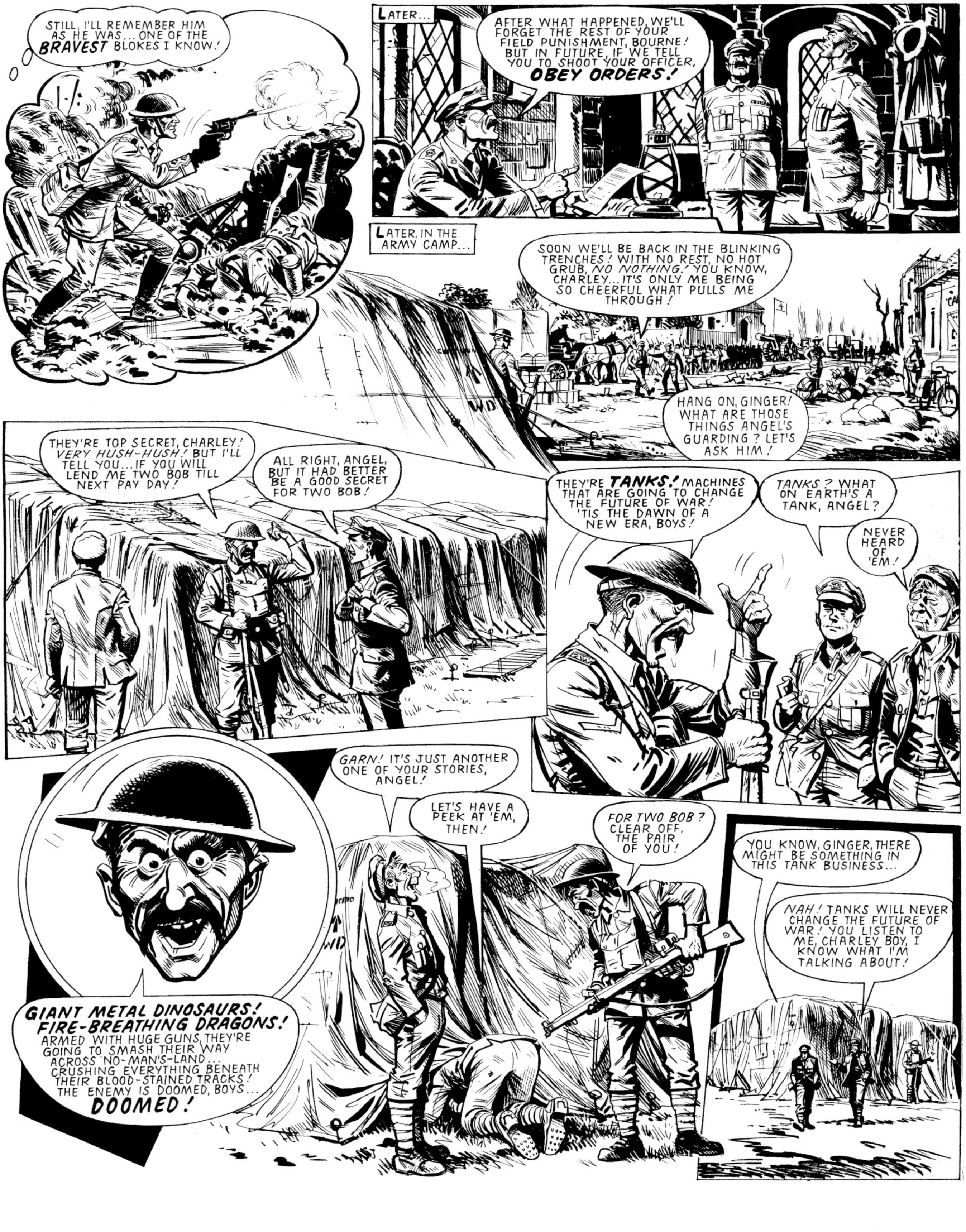
STILL, I'LL REMEMBER HIM AS HE WAS... ONE OF THE BRAVEST BLOKES I KNOW!
LATER...
AFTER WHAT HAPPENED, WE'LL FORGET THE REST OF YOUR FIELD PUNISHMENT, BOURNE! BUT IN FUTURE, IF WE TELL YOU TO SHOOT YOUR OFFICER, OBEY ORDERS!
LATER, IN THE ARMY CAMP...
SOON WE'LL BE BACK IN THE BLINKING TRENCHES! WITH NO REST, NO HOT GRUB, NO NOTHING! YOU KNOW, CHARLEY... IT'S ONLY ME BEING SO CHEERFUL WHAT PULLS ME THROUGH!
HANG ON, GINGER! WHAT ARE THOSE THINGS ANGEL'S GUARDING? LET'S ASK HIM!
THEY'RE TOP SECRET, CHARLEY! VERY HUSH-HUSH! BUT I'LL TELL YOU... IF YOU WILL LEND ME TWO BOB TILL NEXT PAY DAY!
ALL RIGHT, ANGEL, BUT IT HAD BETTER BE A GOOD SECRET FOR TWO BOB!
THEY'RE TANKS! MACHINES THAT ARE GOING TO CHANGE THE FUTURE OF WAR! 'TIS THE DAWN OF A NEW ERA, BOYS!
TANKS? WHAT ON EARTH'S A TANK, ANGEL?
NEVER HEARD OF 'EM!
GIANT METAL DINOSAURS! FIRE-BREATHING DRAGONS! ARMED WITH HUGE GUNS, THEY'RE GOING TO SMASH THEIR WAY ACROSS NO-MAN'S-LAND... CRUSHING EVERYTHING BENEATH THEIR BLOOD-STAINED TRACKS! THE ENEMY IS DOOMED, BOYS... DOOMED!
GARN! IT'S JUST ANOTHER ONE OF YOUR STORIES, ANGEL!
LET'S HAVE A PEEK AT 'EM, THEN!
FOR TWO BOB? CLEAR OFF, THE PAIR OF YOU!
YOU KNOW, GINGER, THERE MIGHT BE SOMETHING IN THIS TANK BUSINESS...
NAH! TANKS WILL NEVER CHANGE THE FUTURE OF WAR! YOU LISTEN TO ME, CHARLEY BOY, I KNOW WHAT I'M TALKING ABOUT!

CHARLEY'S WAR

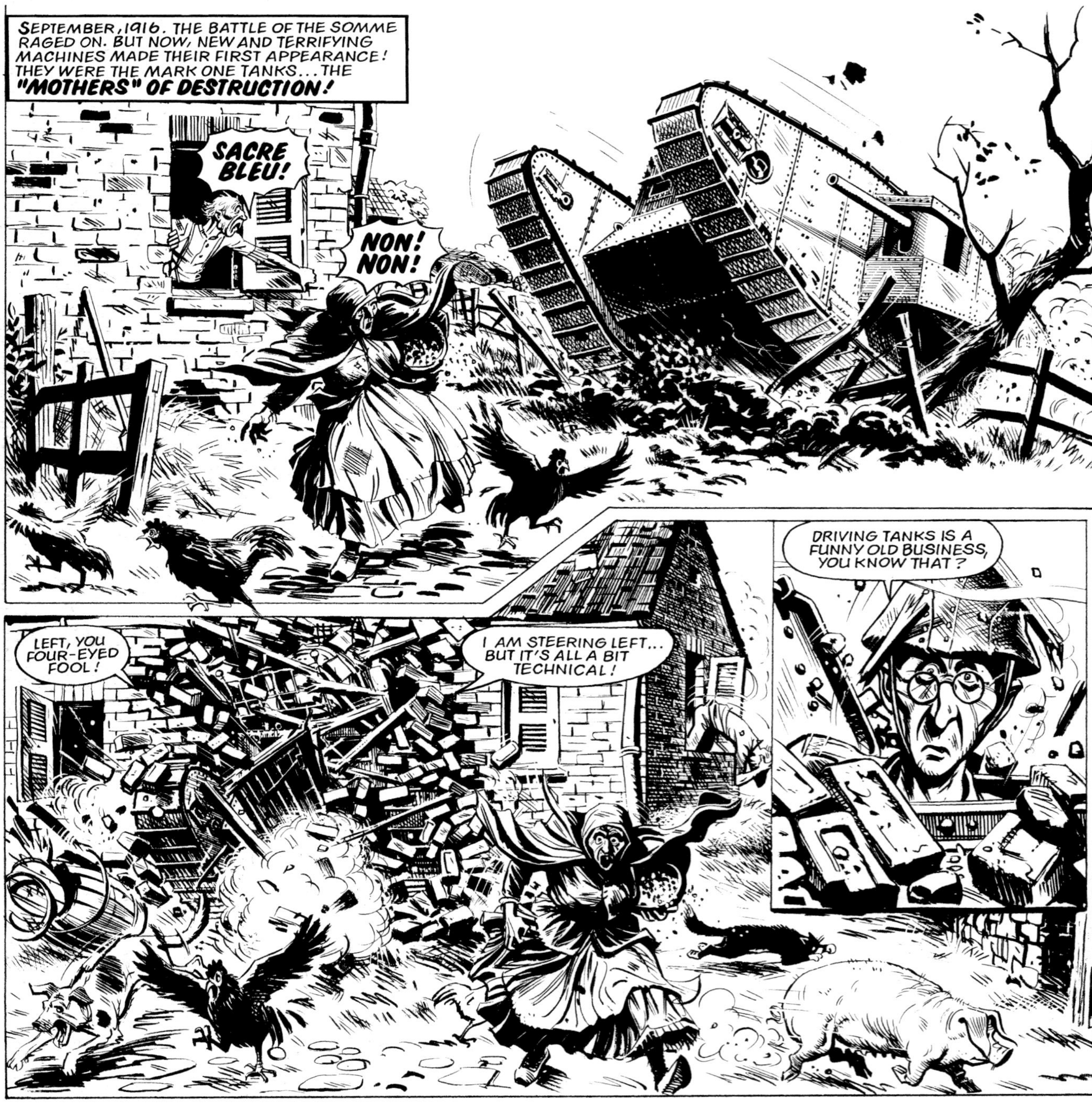
SEPTEMBER, 1916. THE BATTLE OF THE SOMME RAGED ON. BUT NOW, NEW AND TERRIFYING MACHINES MADE THEIR FIRST APPEARANCE! THEY WERE THE MARK ONE TANKS... THE "MOTHERS" OF DESTRUCTION!
SACRE BLEU!
NON! NON!
DRIVING TANKS IS A FUNNY OLD BUSINESS, YOU KNOW THAT?
LEFT, YOU FOUR-EYED FOOL!
I AM STEERING LEFT... BUT IT'S ALL A BIT TECHNICAL!

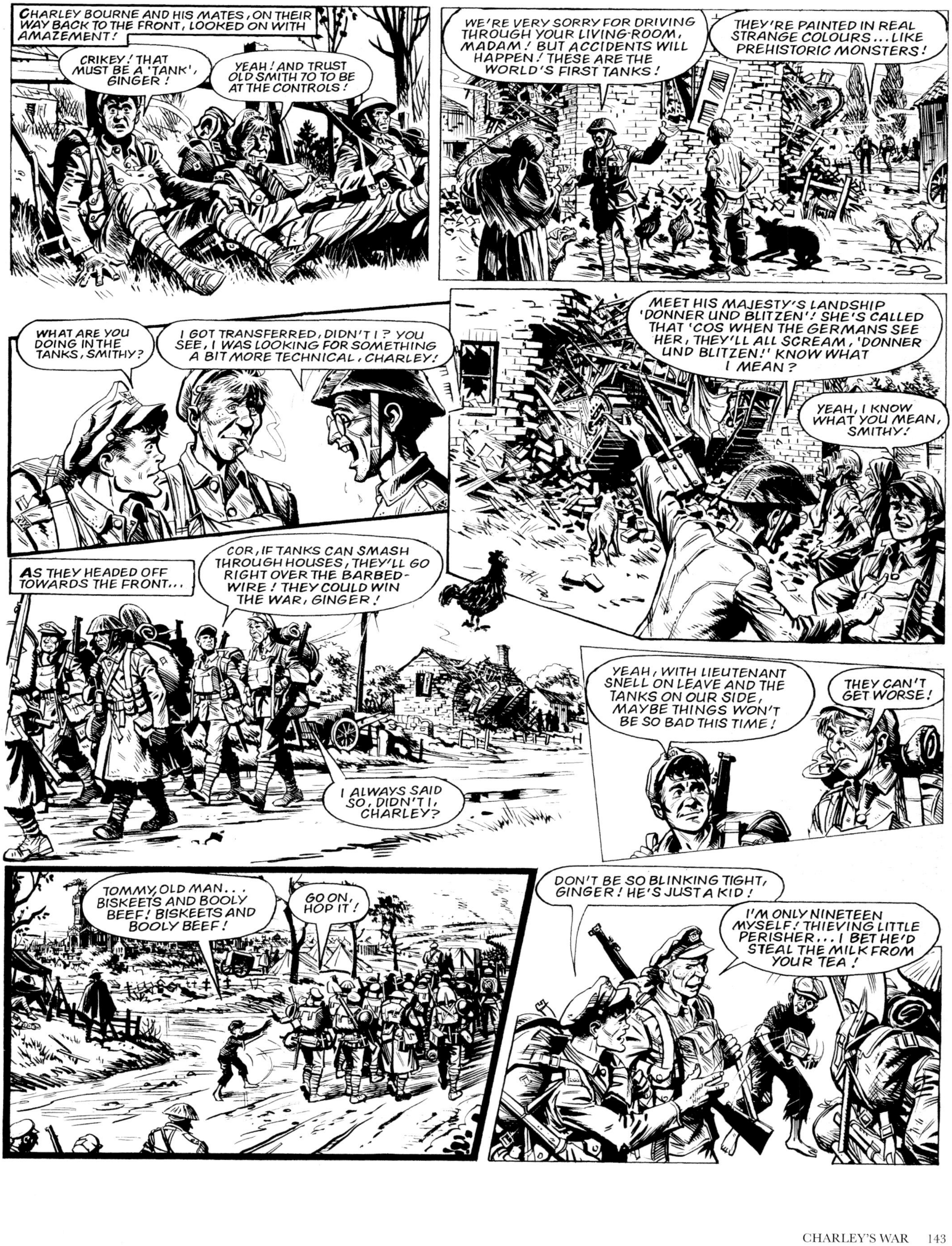
CHARLEY BOURNE AND HIS MATES, ON THEIR WAY BACK TO THE FRONT, LOOKED ON WITH AMAZEMENT!
CRIKEY! THAT MUST BE A 'TANK', GINGER!
YEAH! AND TRUST OLD SMITH 70 TO BE AT THE CONTROLS!
WE'RE VERY SORRY FOR DRIVING THROUGH YOUR LIVING-ROOM, MADAM! BUT ACCIDENTS WILL HAPPEN! THESE ARE THE WORLD'S FIRST TANKS!
THEY'RE PAINTED IN REAL STRANGE COLOURS... LIKE PREHISTORIC MONSTERS!
WHAT ARE YOU DOING IN THE TANKS, SMITHY?
I GOT TRANSFERRED, DIDN'T I? YOU SEE, I WAS LOOKING FOR SOMETHING A BIT MORE TECHNICAL, CHARLEY!
MEET HIS MAJESTY'S LANDSHIP 'DONNER UND BLITZEN'! SHE'S CALLED THAT 'COS WHEN THE GERMANS SEE HER, THEY'LL ALL SCREAM, 'DONNER UND BLITZEN!' KNOW WHAT I MEAN?
YEAH, I KNOW WHAT YOU MEAN, SMITHY!
AS THEY HEADED OFF TOWARDS THE FRONT...
COR, IF TANKS CAN SMASH THROUGH HOUSES, THEY'LL GO RIGHT OVER THE BARBED-WIRE! THEY COULD WIN THE WAR, GINGER!
I ALWAYS SAID SO, DIDN'T I, CHARLEY?
YEAH, WITH LIEUTENANT SNELL ON LEAVE AND THE TANKS ON OUR SIDE, MAYBE THINGS WON'T BE SO BAD THIS TIME!
THEY CAN'T GET WORSE!
TOMMY, OLD MAN... BISKEETS AND BOOLY BEEF! BISKEETS AND BOOLY BEEF!
GO ON, HOP IT!
DON'T BE SO BLINKING TIGHT, GINGER! HE'S JUST A KID!
I'M ONLY NINETEEN MYSELF! THIEVING LITTLE PERISHER... I BET HE'D STEAL THE MILK FROM YOUR TEA!

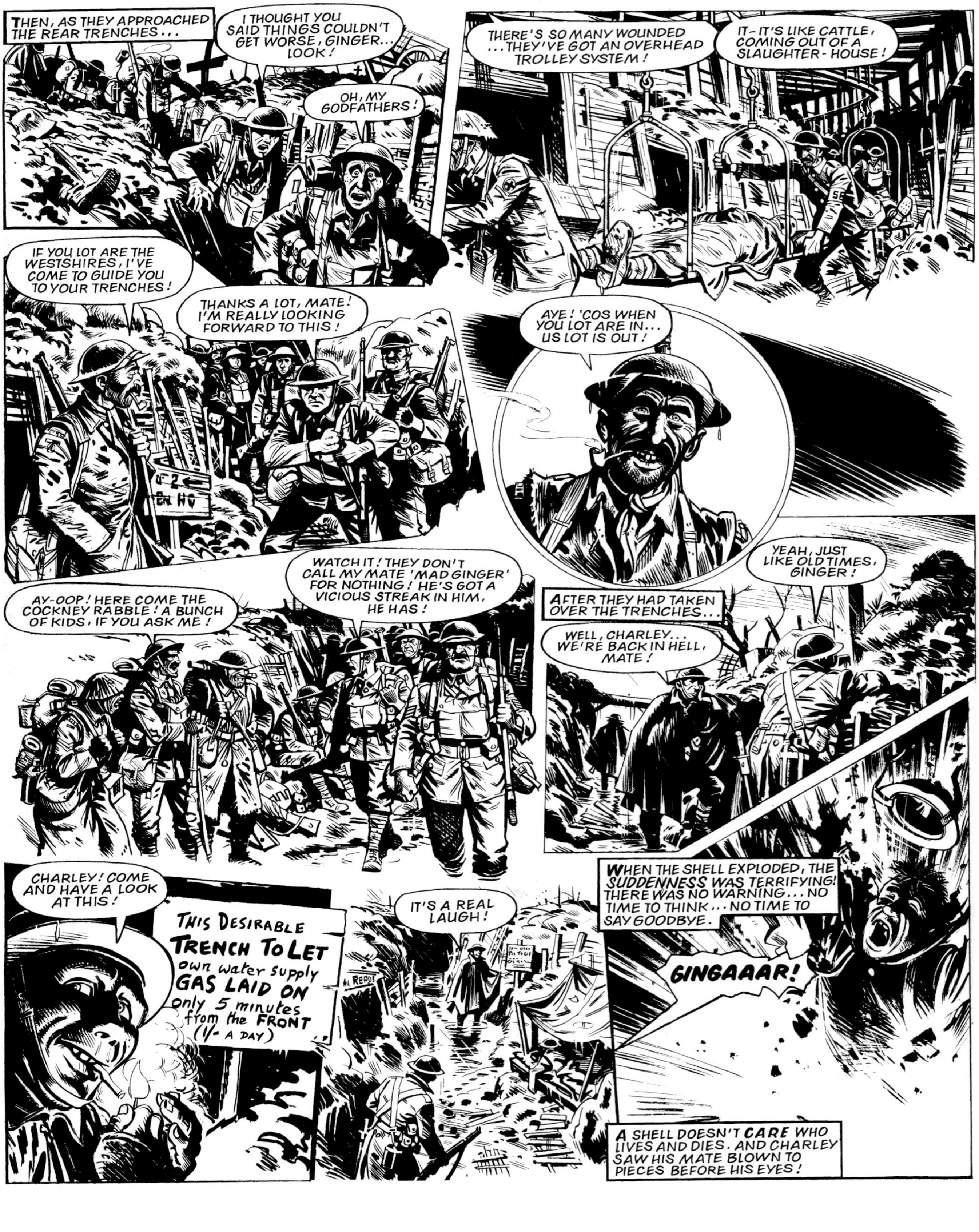
THEN, AS THEY APPROACHED THE REAR TRENCHES...
I THOUGHT YOU SAID THINGS COULDN'T GET WORSE, GINGER... LOOK!
OH, MY GODFATHERS!
THERE'S SO MANY WOUNDED ...THEY'VE GOT AN OVERHEAD TROLLEY SYSTEM!
IT- IT'S LIKE CATTLE, COMING OUT OF A SLAUGHTER-HOUSE!
IF YOU LOT ARE THE WESTSHIRES, I'VE COME TO GUIDE YOU TO YOUR TRENCHES!
THANKS A LOT, MATE! I'M REALLY LOOKING FORWARD TO THIS!
AYE! 'COS WHEN YOU LOT ARE IN... US LOT IS OUT!
AY-OOP! HERE COME THE COCKNEY RABBLE! A BUNCH OF KIDS, IF YOU ASK ME!
WATCH IT! THEY DON'T CALL MY MATE 'MAD GINGER' FOR NOTHING! HE'S GOT A VICIOUS STREAK IN HIM, HE HAS!
AFTER THEY HAD TAKEN OVER THE TRENCHES...
YEAH, JUST LIKE OLD TIMES, GINGER!
WELL, CHARLEY... WE'RE BACK IN HELL, MATE!
CHARLEY! COME AND HAVE A LOOK AT THIS!
THIS DESIRABLE TRENCH TO LET own water supply GAS LAID ON only 5 minutes from the FRONT (1/- A DAY)
IT'S A REAL LAUGH!
WHEN THE SHELL EXPLODED, THE SUDDENNESS WAS TERRIFYING! THERE WAS NO WARNING... NO TIME TO THINK... NO TIME TO SAY GOODBYE.
GINGAAAR!
A SHELL DOESN'T CARE WHO LIVES AND DIES. AND CHARLEY SAW HIS MATE BLOWN TO PIECES BEFORE HIS EYES!

CHARLEY'S WAR

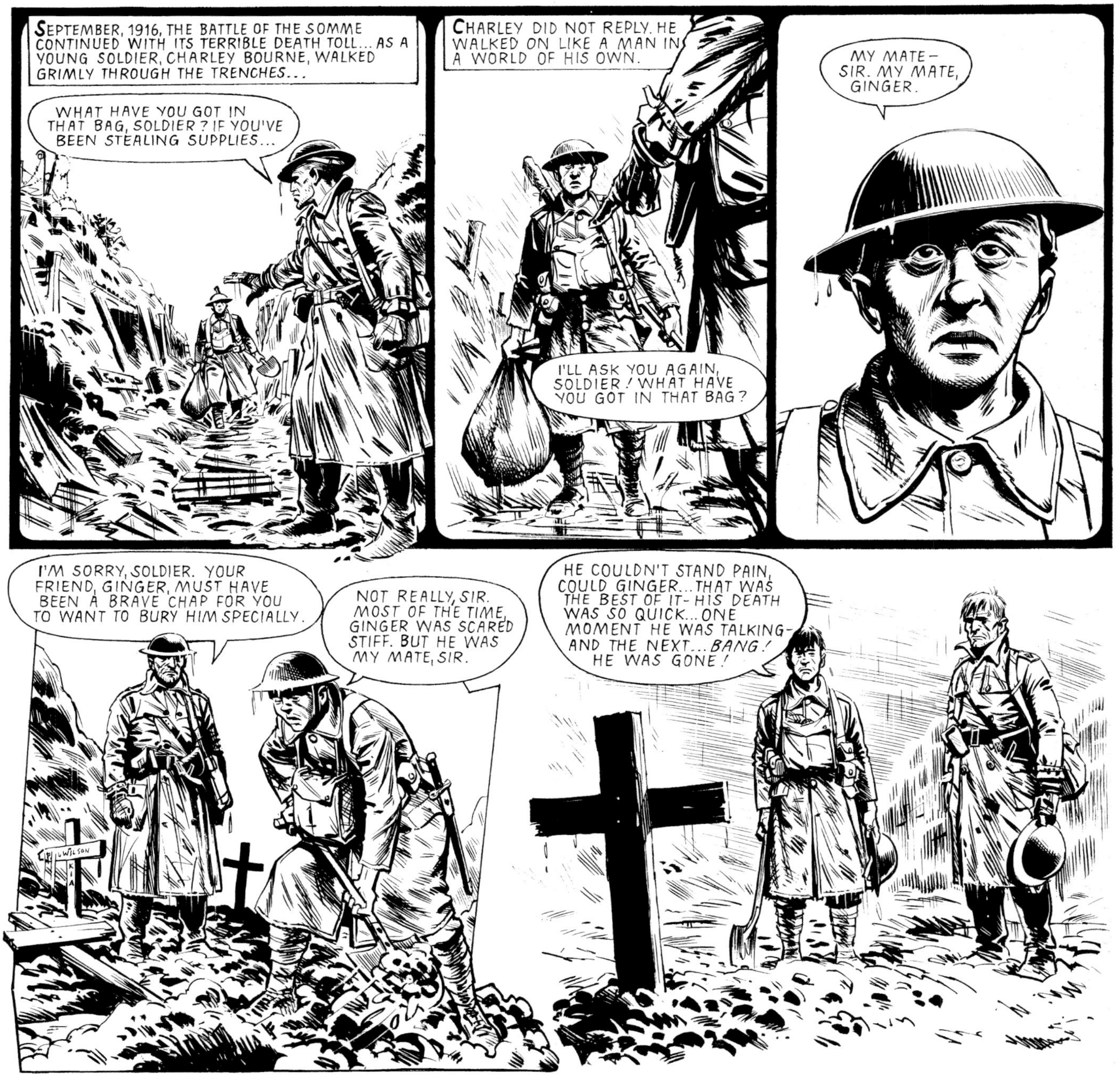
SEPTEMBER, 1916, THE BATTLE OF THE SOMME CONTINUED WITH ITS TERRIBLE DEATH TOLL... AS A YOUNG SOLDIER, CHARLEY BOURNE, WALKED GRIMLY THROUGH THE TRENCHES...
WHAT HAVE YOU GOT IN THAT BAG, SOLDIER? IF YOU'VE BEEN STEALING SUPPLIES...
CHARLEY DID NOT REPLY. HE WALKED ON LIKE A MAN IN A WORLD OF HIS OWN.
I'LL ASK YOU AGAIN, SOLDIER! WHAT HAVE YOU GOT IN THAT BAG?
MY MATE– SIR. MY MATE, GINGER.
I'M SORRY, SOLDIER. YOUR FRIEND, GINGER, MUST HAVE BEEN A BRAVE CHAP FOR YOU TO WANT TO BURY HIM SPECIALLY.
NOT REALLY, SIR. MOST OF THE TIME, GINGER WAS SCARED STIFF. BUT HE WAS MY MATE, SIR.
HE COULDN'T STAND PAIN, COULD GINGER... THAT WAS THE BEST OF IT- HIS DEATH WAS SO QUICK... ONE MOMENT HE WAS TALKING- AND THE NEXT... BANG! HE WAS GONE!

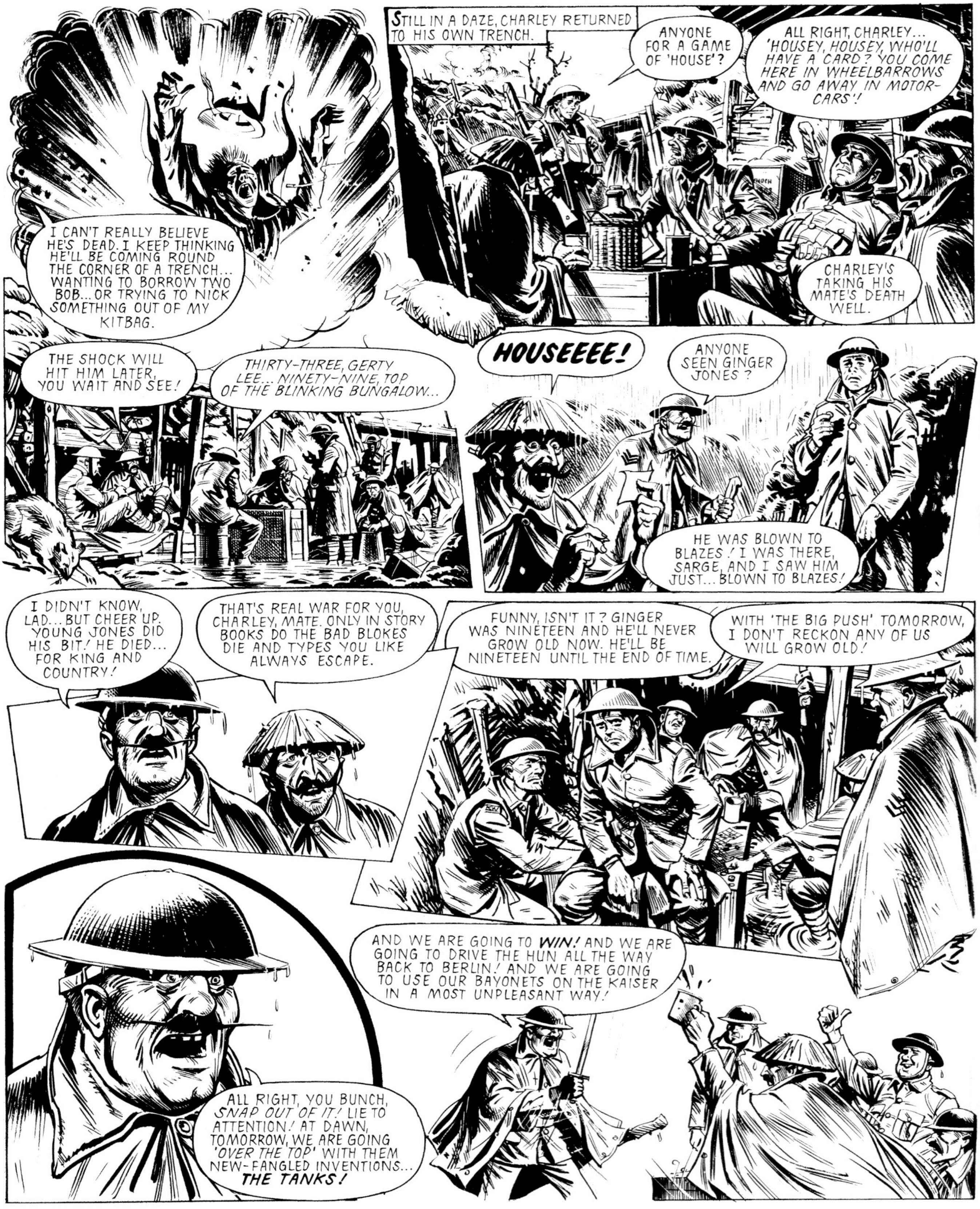
STILL IN A DAZE, CHARLEY RETURNED TO HIS OWN TRENCH.
I CAN'T REALLY BELIEVE HE'S DEAD. I KEEP THINKING HE'LL BE COMING ROUND THE CORNER OF A TRENCH... WANTING TO BORROW TWO BOB... OR TRYING TO NICK SOMETHING OUT OF MY KITBAG.
ANYONE FOR A GAME OF 'HOUSE'?
ALL RIGHT, CHARLEY... 'HOUSEY, HOUSEY, WHO'LL HAVE A CARD? YOU COME HERE IN WHEELBARROWS AND GO AWAY IN MOTOR-CARS'!
CHARLEY'S TAKING HIS MATE'S DEATH WELL.
THE SHOCK WILL HIT HIM LATER, YOU WAIT AND SEE!
THIRTY-THREE, GERTY LEE... NINETY-NINE, TOP OF THE BLINKING BUNGALOW...
HOUSEEEE!
ANYONE SEEN GINGER JONES?
HE WAS BLOWN TO BLAZES! I WAS THERE, SARGE, AND I SAW HIM JUST... BLOWN TO BLAZES!
I DIDN'T KNOW, LAD... BUT CHEER UP. YOUNG JONES DID HIS BIT! HE DIED... FOR KING AND COUNTRY!
THAT'S REAL WAR FOR YOU, CHARLEY, MATE. ONLY IN STORY BOOKS DO THE BAD BLOKES DIE AND TYPES YOU LIKE ALWAYS ESCAPE.
FUNNY, ISN'T IT? GINGER WAS NINETEEN AND HE'LL NEVER GROW OLD NOW. HE'LL BE NINETEEN UNTIL THE END OF TIME.
WITH 'THE BIG PUSH' TOMORROW, I DON'T RECKON ANY OF US WILL GROW OLD!
ALL RIGHT, YOU BUNCH, SNAP OUT OF IT! LIE TO ATTENTION! AT DAWN, TOMORROW, WE ARE GOING 'OVER THE TOP' WITH THEM NEW-FANGLED INVENTIONS... THE TANKS!
AND WE ARE GOING TO WIN! AND WE ARE GOING TO DRIVE THE HUN ALL THE WAY BACK TO BERLIN! AND WE ARE GOING TO USE OUR BAYONETS ON THE KAISER IN A MOST UNPLEASANT WAY!

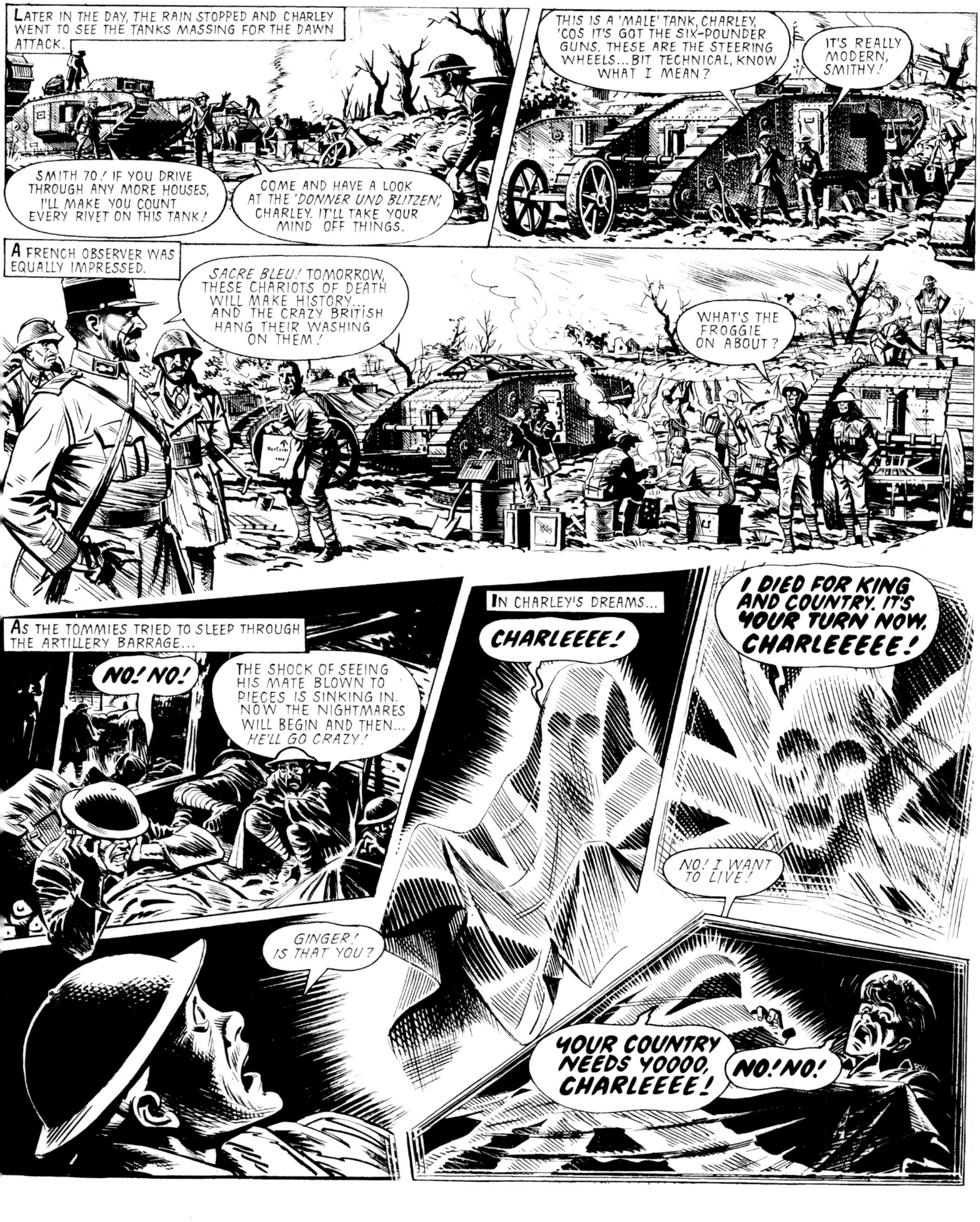
LATER IN THE DAY, THE RAIN STOPPED AND CHARLEY WENT TO SEE THE TANKS MASSING FOR THE DAWN ATTACK.
SMITH 70! IF YOU DRIVE THROUGH ANY MORE HOUSES, I'LL MAKE YOU COUNT EVERY RIVET ON THIS TANK!
COME AND HAVE A LOOK AT THE 'DONNER UND BLITZEN', CHARLEY. IT'LL TAKE YOUR MIND OFF THINGS.
THIS IS A 'MALE' TANK, CHARLEY, 'COS IT'S GOT THE SIX-POUNDER GUNS. THESE ARE THE STEERING WHEELS... BIT TECHNICAL, KNOW WHAT I MEAN?
IT'S REALLY MODERN, SMITHY!
A FRENCH OBSERVER WAS EQUALLY IMPRESSED.
SACRE BLEU! TOMORROW, THESE CHARIOTS OF DEATH WILL MAKE HISTORY... AND THE CRAZY BRITISH HANG THEIR WASHING ON THEM!
WHAT'S THE FROGGIE ON ABOUT?
AS THE TOMMIES TRIED TO SLEEP THROUGH THE ARTILLERY BARRAGE...
NO! NO!
THE SHOCK OF SEEING HIS MATE BLOWN TO PIECES IS SINKING IN. NOW THE NIGHTMARES WILL BEGIN AND THEN... HE'LL GO CRAZY!
GINGER! IS THAT YOU?
IN CHARLEY'S DREAMS...
CHARLEEEE!
I DIED FOR KING AND COUNTRY. IT'S YOUR TURN NOW, CHARLEEEEE!
NO! I WANT TO LIVE!
YOUR COUNTRY NEEDS YOOOO, CHARLEEEE!
NO! NO!

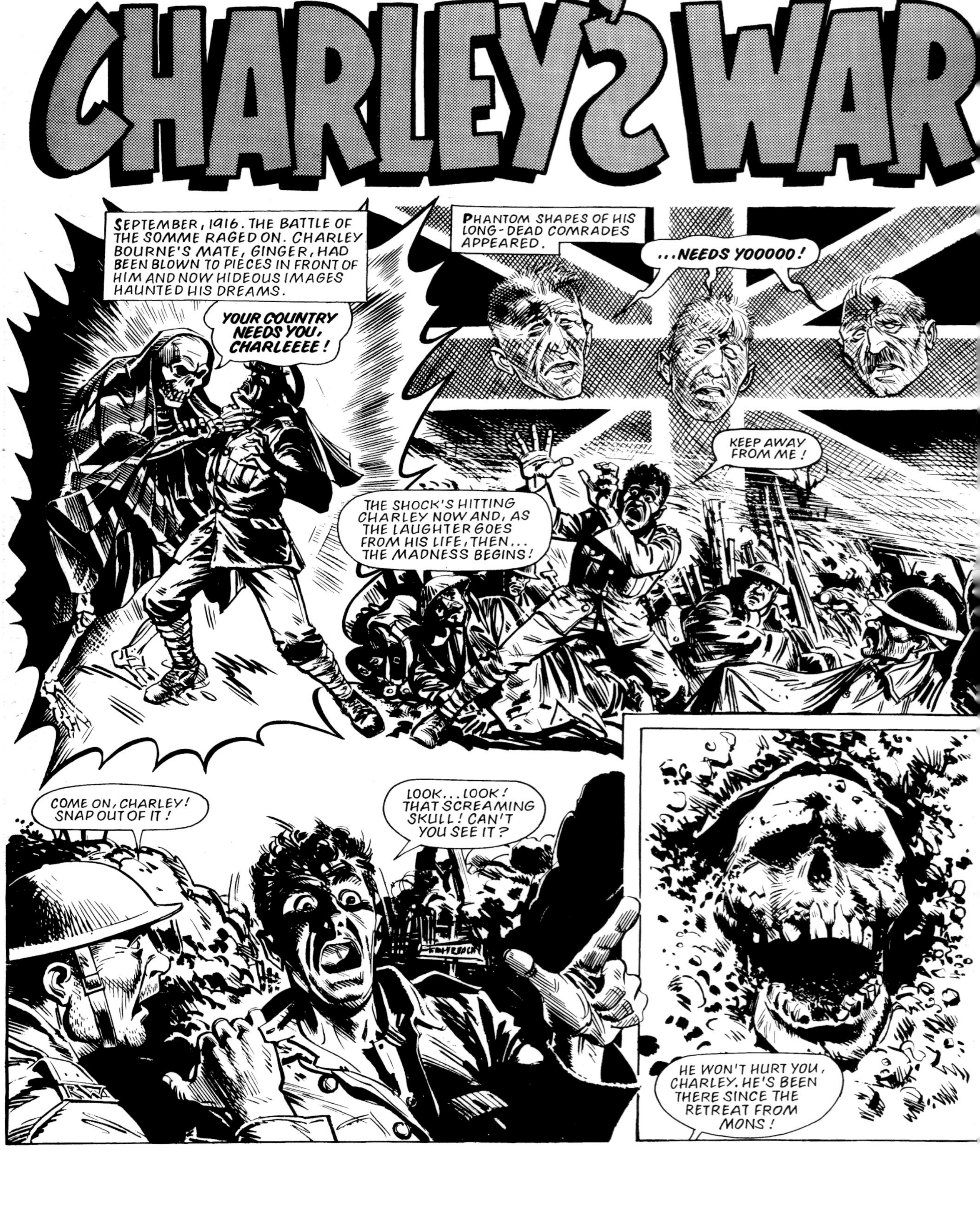
CHARLEY'S WAR
SEPTEMBER, 1916. THE BATTLE OF THE SOMME RAGED ON. CHARLEY BOURNE'S MATE, GINGER, HAD BEEN BLOWN TO PIECES IN FRONT OF HIM AND NOW HIDEOUS IMAGES HAUNTED HIS DREAMS.
YOUR COUNTRY NEEDS YOU, CHARLEEEE!
PHANTOM SHAPES OF HIS LONG-DEAD COMRADES APPEARED.
...NEEDS YOOOOO!
KEEP AWAY FROM ME!
THE SHOCK'S HITTING CHARLEY NOW AND, AS THE LAUGHTER GOES FROM HIS LIFE, THEN... THE MADNESS BEGINS!
COME ON, CHARLEY! SNAP OUT OF IT!
LOOK... LOOK! THAT SCREAMING SKULL! CAN'T YOU SEE IT?
HE WON'T HURT YOU, CHARLEY. HE'S BEEN THERE SINCE THE RETREAT FROM MONS!

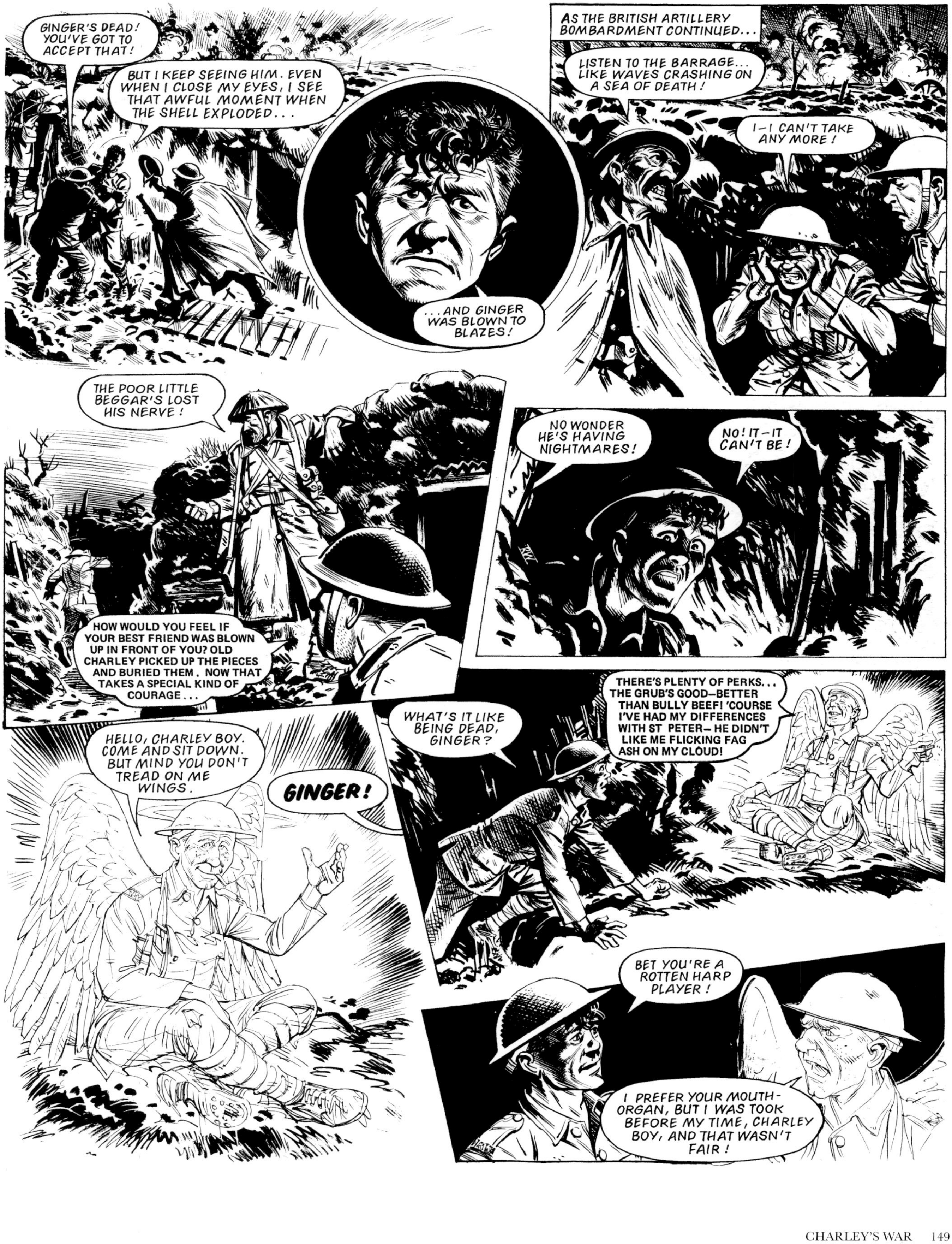

GINGER'S DEAD! YOU'VE GOT TO ACCEPT THAT!
BUT I KEEP SEEING HIM. EVEN WHEN I CLOSE MY EYES, I SEE THAT AWFUL MOMENT WHEN THE SHELL EXPLODED...
...AND GINGER WAS BLOWN TO BLAZES!
AS THE BRITISH ARTILLERY BOMBARDMENT CONTINUED...
LISTEN TO THE BARRAGE... LIKE WAVES CRASHING ON A SEA OF DEATH!
I-I CAN'T TAKE ANY MORE!
THE POOR LITTLE BEGGAR'S LOST HIS NERVE!
HOW WOULD YOU FEEL IF YOUR BEST FRIEND WAS BLOWN UP IN FRONT OF YOU? OLD CHARLEY PICKED UP THE PIECES AND BURIED THEM. NOW THAT TAKES A SPECIAL KIND OF COURAGE...
NO WONDER HE'S HAVING NIGHTMARES!
NO! IT-IT CAN'T BE!
WHAT'S IT LIKE BEING DEAD, GINGER?
THERE'S PLENTY OF PERKS... THE GRUB'S GOOD-BETTER THAN BULLY BEEF! 'COURSE I'VE HAD MY DIFFERENCES WITH ST PETER- HE DIDN'T LIKE ME FLICKING FAG ASH ON MY CLOUD!
GINGER!
HELLO, CHARLEY BOY. COME AND SIT DOWN. BUT MIND YOU DON'T TREAD ON ME WINGS.
BET YOU'RE A ROTTEN HARP PLAYER!
I PREFER YOUR MOUTH-ORGAN, BUT I WAS TOOK BEFORE MY TIME, CHARLEY BOY, AND THAT WASN'T FAIR!

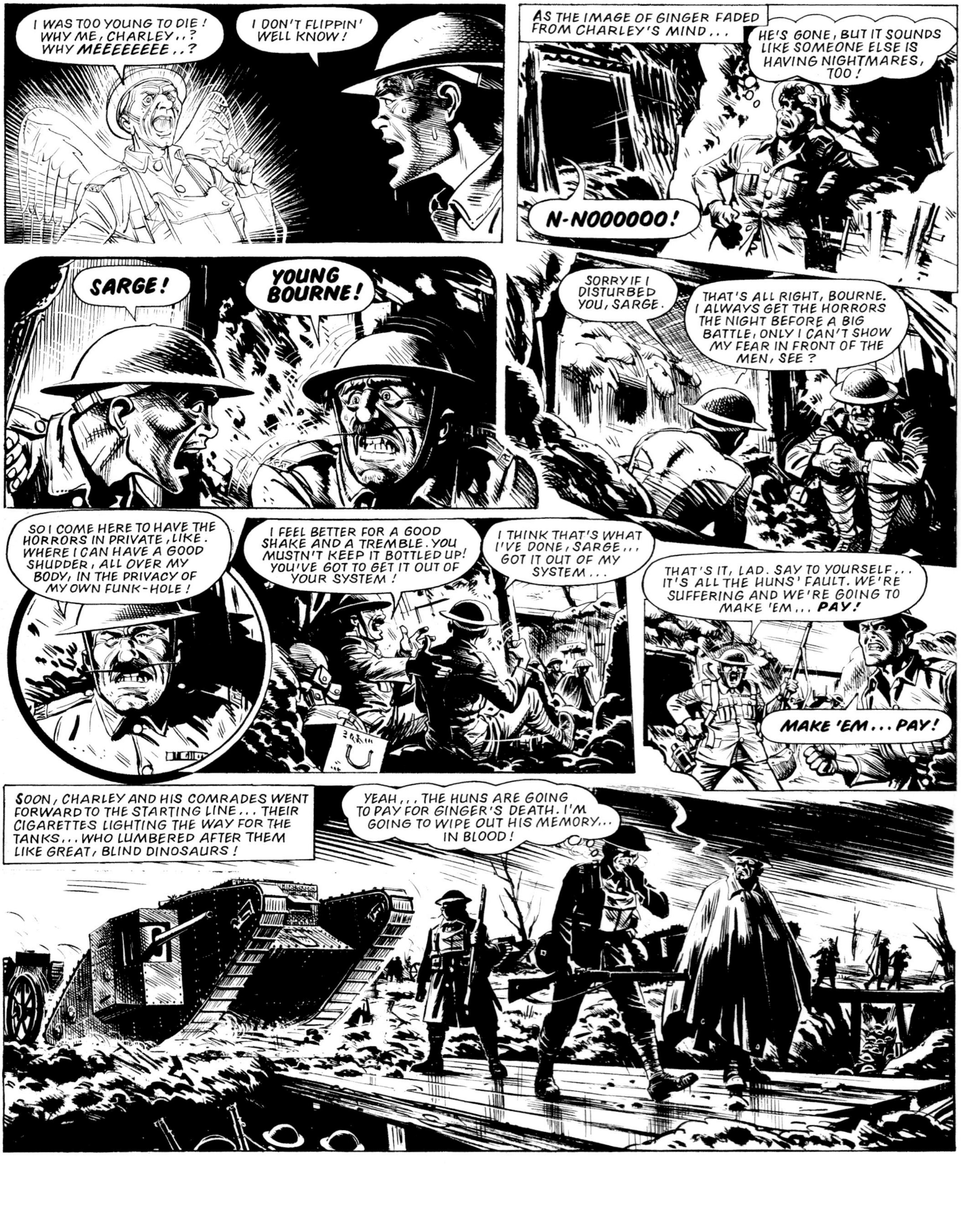
I WAS TOO YOUNG TO DIE! WHY ME, CHARLEY..? WHY MEEEEEEE..?
I DON'T FLIPPIN' WELL KNOW!
AS THE IMAGE OF GINGER FADED FROM CHARLEY'S MIND...
HE'S GONE, BUT IT SOUNDS LIKE SOMEONE ELSE IS HAVING NIGHTMARES, TOO!
N-NOOOOOO!
SARGE!
YOUNG BOURNE!
SORRY IF I DISTURBED YOU, SARGE.
THAT'S ALL RIGHT, BOURNE. I ALWAYS GET THE HORRORS THE NIGHT BEFORE A BIG BATTLE, ONLY I CAN'T SHOW MY FEAR IN FRONT OF THE MEN, SEE?
SO I COME HERE TO HAVE THE HORRORS IN PRIVATE, LIKE. WHERE I CAN HAVE A GOOD SHUDDER, ALL OVER MY BODY, IN THE PRIVACY OF MY OWN FUNK-HOLE!
I FEEL BETTER FOR A GOOD SHAKE AND A TREMBLE. YOU MUSTN'T KEEP IT BOTTLED UP! YOU'VE GOT TO GET IT OUT OF YOUR SYSTEM!
I THINK THAT'S WHAT I'VE DONE, SARGE... GOT IT OUT OF MY SYSTEM...
THAT'S IT, LAD. SAY TO YOURSELF... IT'S ALL THE HUNS' FAULT. WE'RE SUFFERING AND WE'RE GOING TO MAKE 'EM... PAY!
MAKE 'EM... PAY!
SOON, CHARLEY AND HIS COMRADES WENT FORWARD TO THE STARTING LINE... THEIR CIGARETTES LIGHTING THE WAY FOR THE TANKS... WHO LUMBERED AFTER THEM LIKE GREAT, BLIND DINOSAURS!
YEAH... THE HUNS ARE GOING TO PAY FOR GINGER'S DEATH. I'M GOING TO WIPE OUT HIS MEMORY... IN BLOOD!

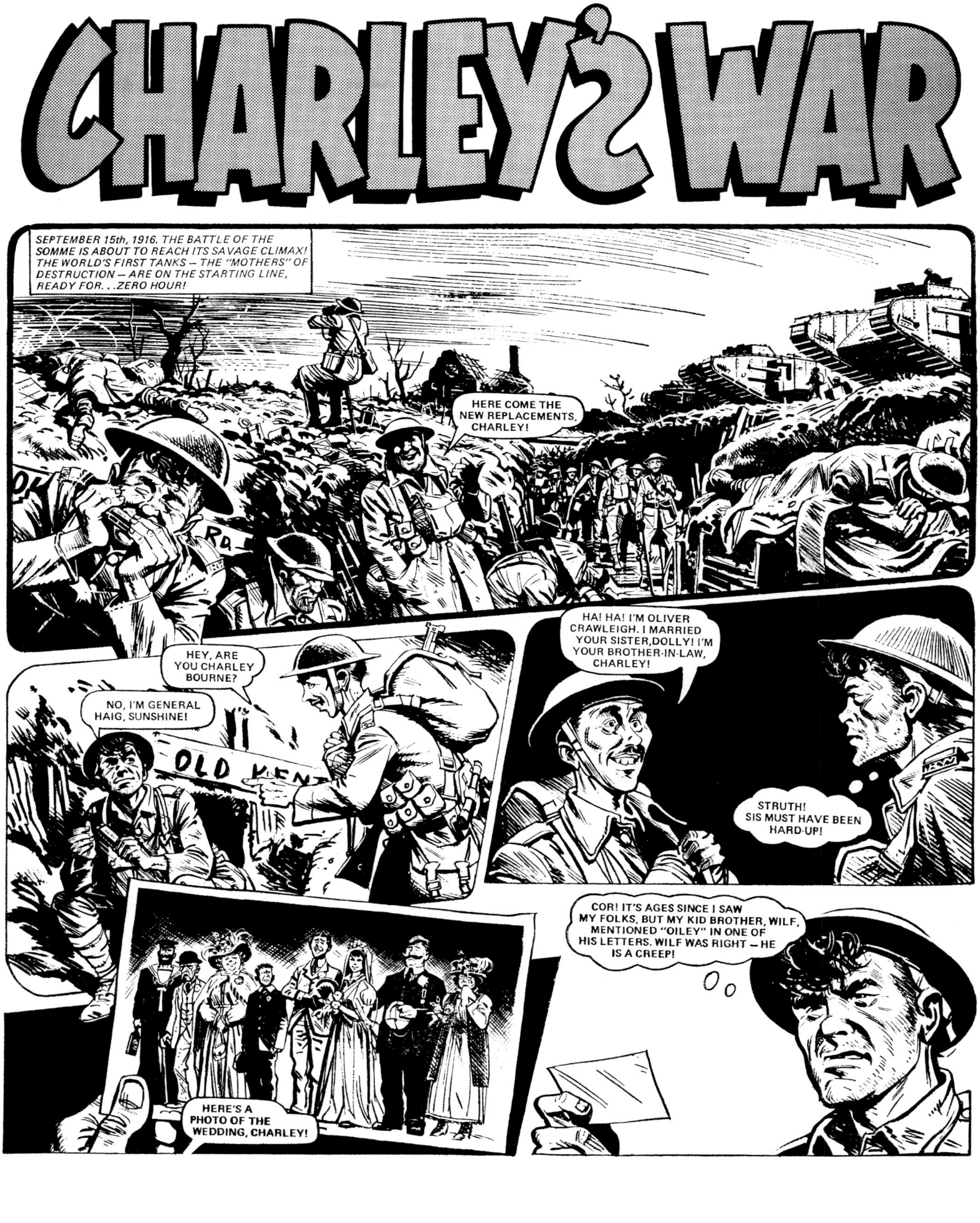
CHARLEY'S WAR
SEPTEMBER 15th, 1916. THE BATTLE OF THE SOMME IS ABOUT TO REACH ITS SAVAGE CLIMAX! THE WORLD'S FIRST TANKS – THE "MOTHERS" OF DESTRUCTION – ARE ON THE STARTING LINE, READY FOR. . .ZERO HOUR!
HERE COME THE NEW REPLACEMENTS, CHARLEY!
HEY, ARE YOU CHARLEY BOURNE?
NO, I'M GENERAL HAIG, SUNSHINE!
OLD KENT
HA! HA! I'M OLIVER CRAWLEIGH. I MARRIED YOUR SISTER, DOLLY! I'M YOUR BROTHER-IN-LAW, CHARLEY!
STRUTH! SIS MUST HAVE BEEN HARD-UP!
HERE'S A PHOTO OF THE WEDDING, CHARLEY!
COR! IT'S AGES SINCE I SAW MY FOLKS, BUT MY KID BROTHER, WILF, MENTIONED "OILEY" IN ONE OF HIS LETTERS. WILF WAS RIGHT – HE IS A CREEP!

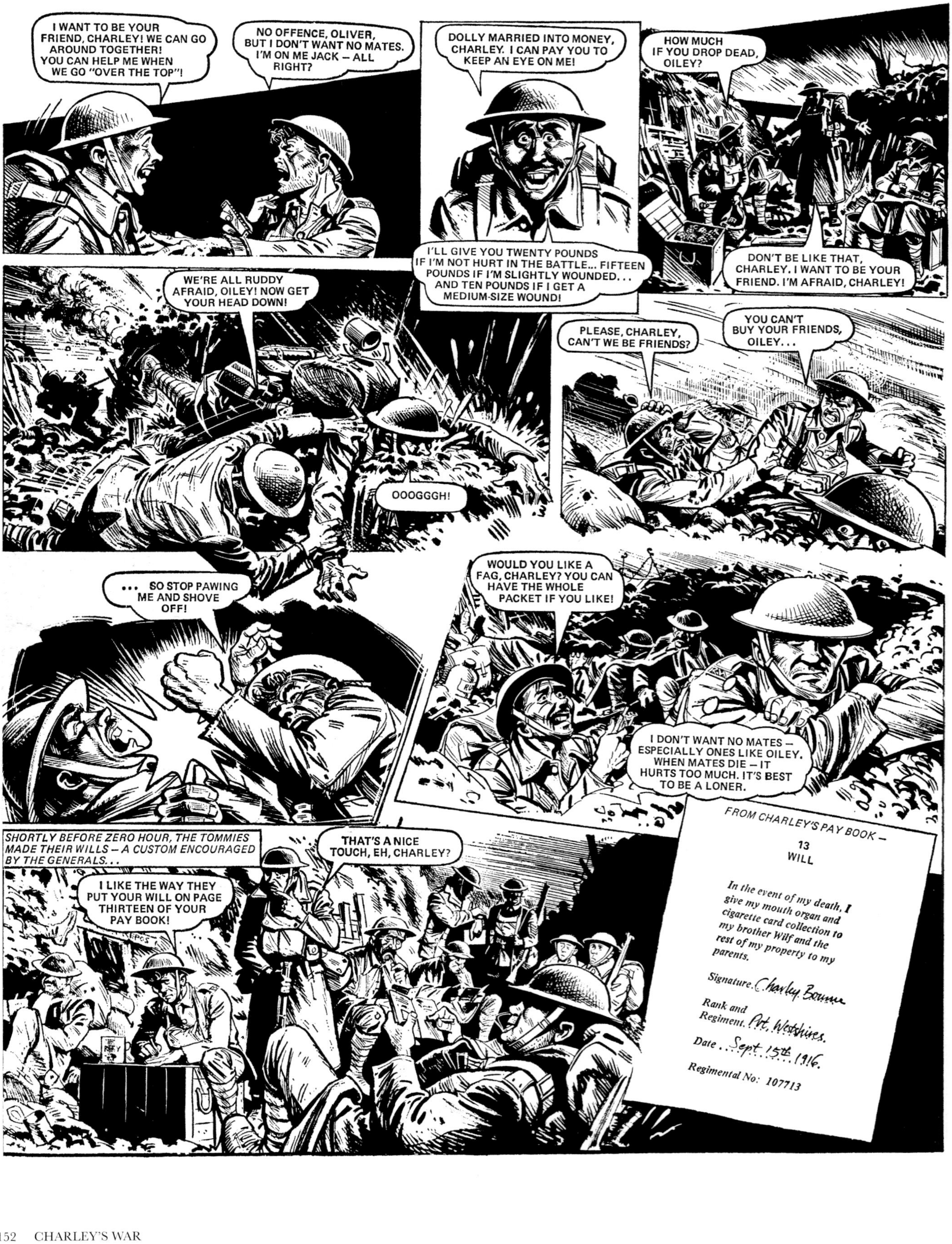
I WANT TO BE YOUR FRIEND, CHARLEY! WE CAN GO AROUND TOGETHER! YOU CAN HELP ME WHEN WE GO "OVER THE TOP"!
NO OFFENCE, OLIVER, BUT I DON'T WANT NO MATES. I'M ON ME JACK – ALL RIGHT?
DOLLY MARRIED INTO MONEY, CHARLEY. I CAN PAY YOU TO KEEP AN EYE ON ME!
I'LL GIVE YOU TWENTY POUNDS IF I'M NOT HURT IN THE BATTLE... FIFTEEN POUNDS IF I'M SLIGHTLY WOUNDED... AND TEN POUNDS IF I GET A MEDIUM-SIZE WOUND!
HOW MUCH IF YOU DROP DEAD, OILEY?
DON'T BE LIKE THAT, CHARLEY. I WANT TO BE YOUR FRIEND. I'M AFRAID, CHARLEY!
WE'RE ALL RUDDY AFRAID, OILEY! NOW GET YOUR HEAD DOWN!
OOOGGGH!
PLEASE, CHARLEY, CAN'T WE BE FRIENDS?
YOU CAN'T BUY YOUR FRIENDS, OILEY...
... SO STOP PAWING ME AND SHOVE OFF!
WOULD YOU LIKE A FAG, CHARLEY? YOU CAN HAVE THE WHOLE PACKET IF YOU LIKE!
I DON'T WANT NO MATES – ESPECIALLY ONES LIKE OILEY. WHEN MATES DIE – IT HURTS TOO MUCH. IT'S BEST TO BE A LONER.
SHORTLY BEFORE ZERO HOUR, THE TOMMIES MADE THEIR WILLS – A CUSTOM ENCOURAGED BY THE GENERALS...
THAT'S A NICE TOUCH, EH, CHARLEY?
I LIKE THE WAY THEY PUT YOUR WILL ON PAGE THIRTEEN OF YOUR PAY BOOK!
FROM CHARLEY'S PAY BOOK –
13
WILL
In the event of my death, I give my mouth organ and cigarette card collection to my brother Wilf and the rest of my property to my parents.
Signature. Charley Bourne
Rank and Regiment. Pvt. Westshires.
Date ..Sept. 15th. 1916.
Regimental No: 107713

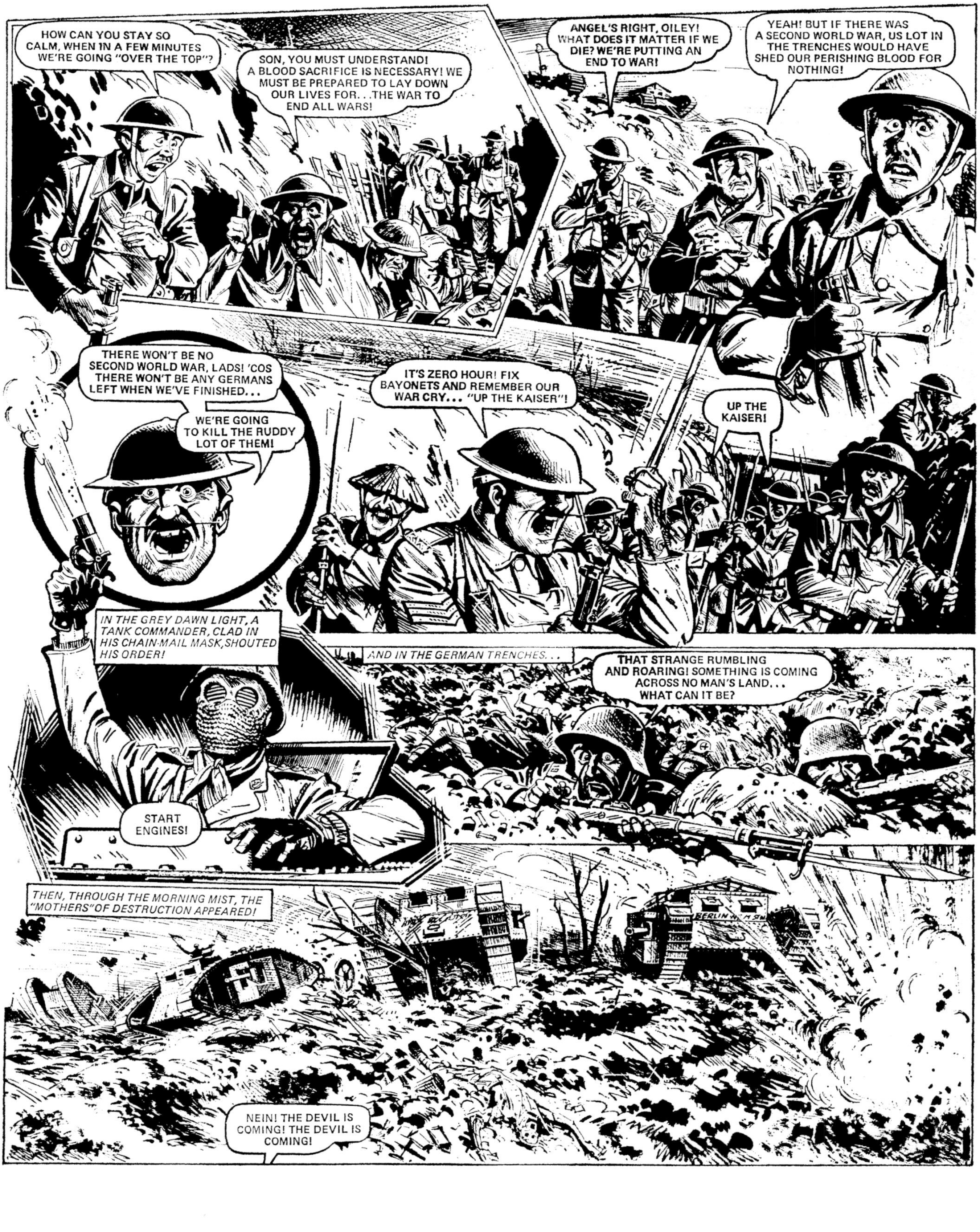
HOW CAN YOU STAY SO CALM, WHEN IN A FEW MINUTES WE'RE GOING "OVER THE TOP"?
SON, YOU MUST UNDERSTAND! A BLOOD SACRIFICE IS NECESSARY! WE MUST BE PREPARED TO LAY DOWN OUR LIVES FOR. . .THE WAR TO END ALL WARS!
ANGEL'S RIGHT, OILEY! WHAT DOES IT MATTER IF WE DIE? WE'RE PUTTING AN END TO WAR!
YEAH! BUT IF THERE WAS A SECOND WORLD WAR, US LOT IN THE TRENCHES WOULD HAVE SHED OUR PERISHING BLOOD FOR NOTHING!
THERE WON'T BE NO SECOND WORLD WAR, LADS! 'COS THERE WON'T BE ANY GERMANS LEFT WHEN WE'VE FINISHED...
WE'RE GOING TO KILL THE RUDDY LOT OF THEM!
IT'S ZERO HOUR! FIX BAYONETS AND REMEMBER OUR WAR CRY... "UP THE KAISER"!
UP THE KAISER!
IN THE GREY DAWN LIGHT, A TANK COMMANDER, CLAD IN HIS CHAIN-MAIL MASK, SHOUTED HIS ORDER!
START ENGINES!
AND IN THE GERMAN TRENCHES...
THAT STRANGE RUMBLING AND ROARING! SOMETHING IS COMING ACROSS NO MAN'S LAND... WHAT CAN IT BE?
THEN, THROUGH THE MORNING MIST, THE "MOTHERS" OF DESTRUCTION APPEARED!
NEIN! THE DEVIL IS COMING! THE DEVIL IS COMING!

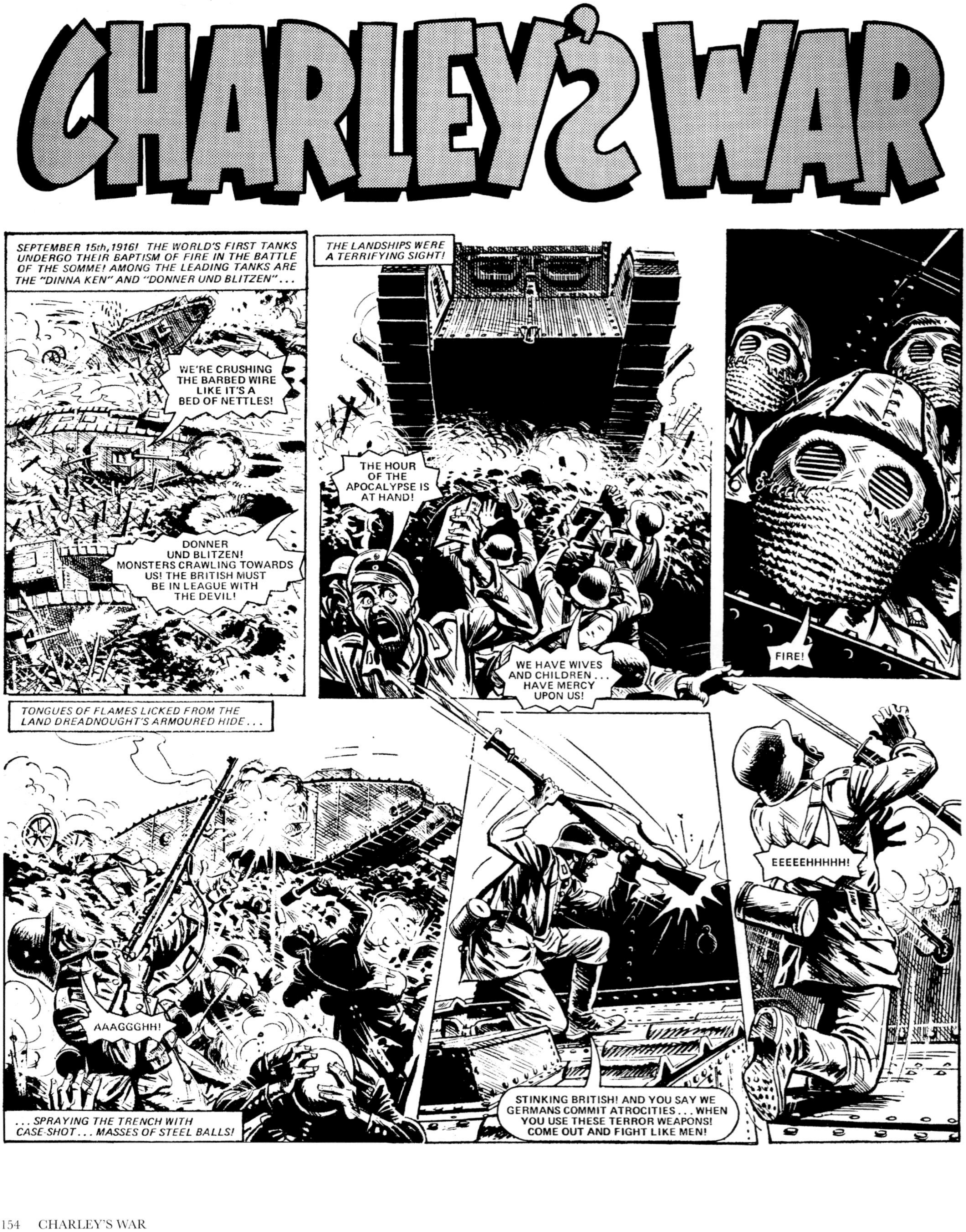
CHARLEY'S WAR
SEPTEMBER 15th,1916! THE WORLD'S FIRST TANKS UNDERGO THEIR BAPTISM OF FIRE IN THE BATTLE OF THE SOMME! AMONG THE LEADING TANKS ARE THE "DINNA KEN" AND "DONNER UND BLITZEN"...
WE'RE CRUSHING THE BARBED WIRE LIKE IT'S A BED OF NETTLES!
DONNER UND BLITZEN! MONSTERS CRAWLING TOWARDS US! THE BRITISH MUST BE IN LEAGUE WITH THE DEVIL!
THE LANDSHIPS WERE A TERRIFYING SIGHT!
THE HOUR OF THE APOCALYPSE IS AT HAND!
WE HAVE WIVES AND CHILDREN... HAVE MERCY UPON US!
FIRE!
TONGUES OF FLAMES LICKED FROM THE LAND DREADNOUGHT'S ARMOURED HIDE...
AAAGGGHH!
... SPRAYING THE TRENCH WITH CASE-SHOT... MASSES OF STEEL BALLS!
STINKING BRITISH! AND YOU SAY WE GERMANS COMMIT ATROCITIES... WHEN YOU USE THESE TERROR WEAPONS! COME OUT AND FIGHT LIKE MEN!
EEEEEHHHHH!

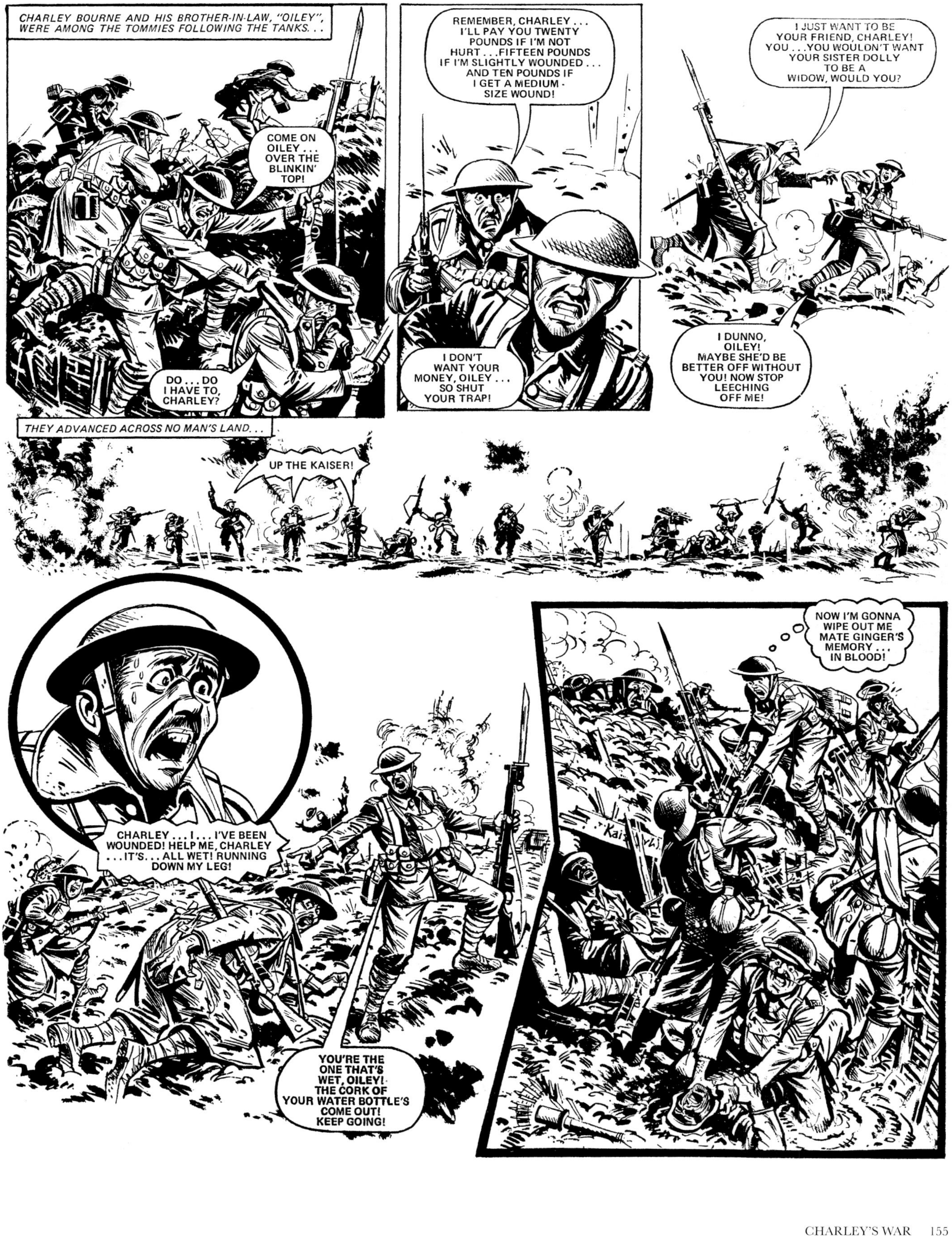

CHARLEY BOURNE AND HIS BROTHER-IN-LAW, "OILEY", WERE AMONG THE TOMMIES FOLLOWING THE TANKS...
COME ON OILEY... OVER THE BLINKIN' TOP!
DO... DO I HAVE TO, CHARLEY?
REMEMBER, CHARLEY... I'LL PAY YOU TWENTY POUNDS IF I'M NOT HURT... FIFTEEN POUNDS IF I'M SLIGHTLY WOUNDED... AND TEN POUNDS IF I GET A MEDIUM - SIZE WOUND!
I DON'T WANT YOUR MONEY, OILEY... SO SHUT YOUR TRAP!
I JUST WANT TO BE YOUR FRIEND, CHARLEY! YOU... YOU WOULDN'T WANT YOUR SISTER DOLLY TO BE A WIDOW, WOULD YOU?
I DUNNO, OILEY! MAYBE SHE'D BE BETTER OFF WITHOUT YOU! NOW STOP LEECHING OFF ME!
THEY ADVANCED ACROSS NO MAN'S LAND...
UP THE KAISER!
CHARLEY... I... I'VE BEEN WOUNDED! HELP ME, CHARLEY... IT'S... ALL WET! RUNNING DOWN MY LEG!
YOU'RE THE ONE THAT'S WET, OILEY! THE CORK OF YOUR WATER BOTTLE'S COME OUT! KEEP GOING!
NOW I'M GONNA WIPE OUT ME MATE GINGER'S MEMORY... IN BLOOD!

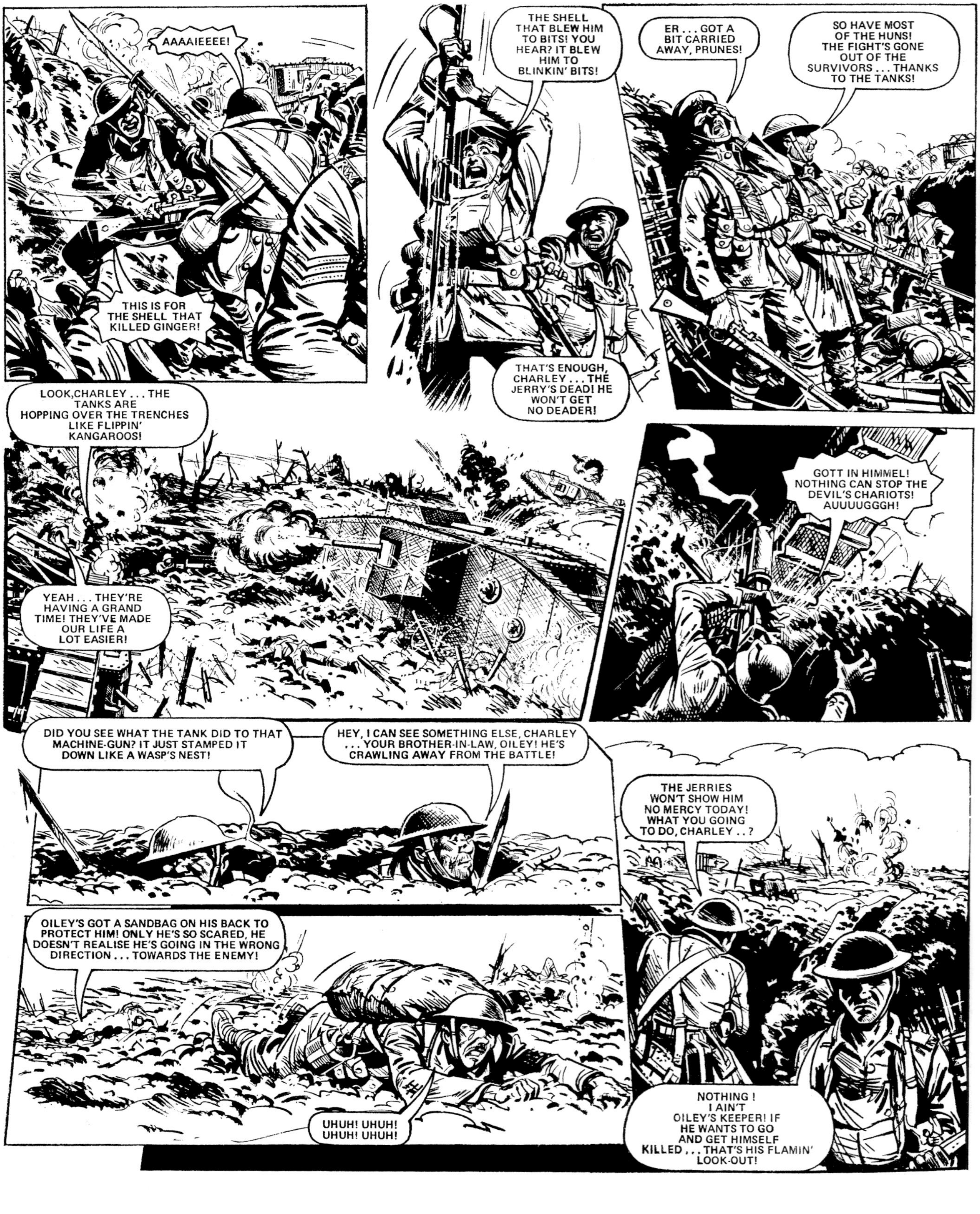
AAAAIEEEE!
THIS IS FOR THE SHELL THAT KILLED GINGER!
THE SHELL THAT BLEW HIM TO BITS! YOU HEAR? IT BLEW HIM TO BLINKIN' BITS!
THAT'S ENOUGH, CHARLEY . . . THE JERRY'S DEAD! HE WON'T GET NO DEADER!
ER . . . GOT A BIT CARRIED AWAY, PRUNES!
SO HAVE MOST OF THE HUNS! THE FIGHT'S GONE OUT OF THE SURVIVORS . . . THANKS TO THE TANKS!
LOOK,CHARLEY . . . THE TANKS ARE HOPPING OVER THE TRENCHES LIKE FLIPPIN' KANGAROOS!
YEAH . . . THEY'RE HAVING A GRAND TIME! THEY'VE MADE OUR LIFE A LOT EASIER!
GOTT IN HIMMEL! NOTHING CAN STOP THE DEVIL'S CHARIOTS! AUUUUGGGH!
DID YOU SEE WHAT THE TANK DID TO THAT MACHINE-GUN? IT JUST STAMPED IT DOWN LIKE A WASP'S NEST!
HEY, I CAN SEE SOMETHING ELSE, CHARLEY . . . YOUR BROTHER-IN-LAW, OILEY! HE'S CRAWLING AWAY FROM THE BATTLE!
OILEY'S GOT A SANDBAG ON HIS BACK TO PROTECT HIM! ONLY HE'S SO SCARED, HE DOESN'T REALISE HE'S GOING IN THE WRONG DIRECTION . . . TOWARDS THE ENEMY!
UHUH! UHUH! UHUH! UHUH!
THE JERRIES WON'T SHOW HIM NO MERCY TODAY! WHAT YOU GOING TO DO, CHARLEY . . ?
NOTHING ! I AIN'T OILEY'S KEEPER! IF HE WANTS TO GO AND GET HIMSELF KILLED , , , THAT'S HIS FLAMIN' LOOK-OUT!

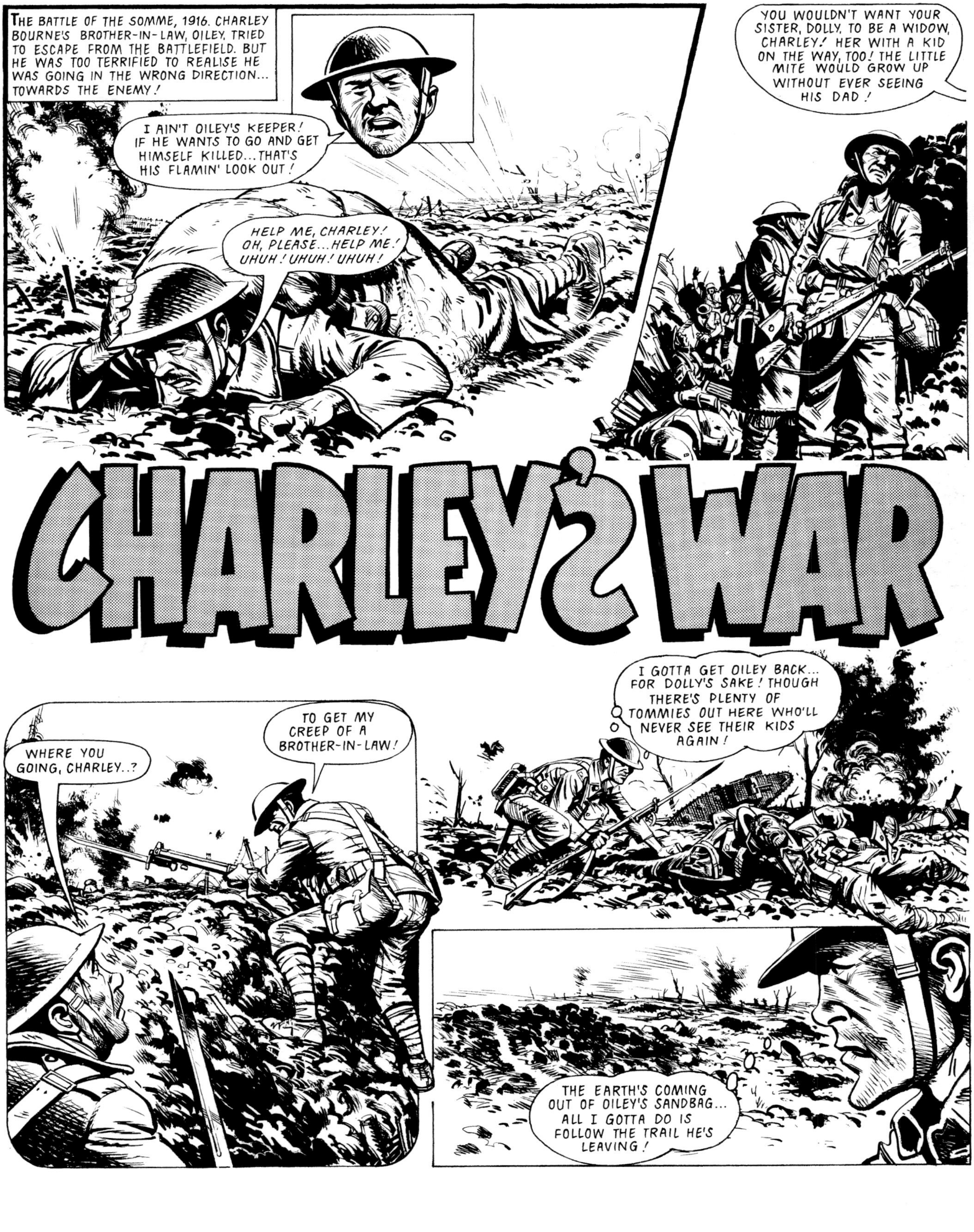
THE BATTLE OF THE SOMME, 1916. CHARLEY BOURNE'S BROTHER-IN-LAW, OILEY, TRIED TO ESCAPE FROM THE BATTLEFIELD. BUT HE WAS TOO TERRIFIED TO REALISE HE WAS GOING IN THE WRONG DIRECTION... TOWARDS THE ENEMY!
I AIN'T OILEY'S KEEPER! IF HE WANTS TO GO AND GET HIMSELF KILLED... THAT'S HIS FLAMIN' LOOK OUT!
HELP ME, CHARLEY! OH, PLEASE... HELP ME! UHUH! UHUH! UHUH!
YOU WOULDN'T WANT YOUR SISTER, DOLLY, TO BE A WIDOW, CHARLEY! HER WITH A KID ON THE WAY, TOO! THE LITTLE MITE WOULD GROW UP WITHOUT EVER SEEING HIS DAD!
CHARLEY'S WAR
WHERE YOU GOING, CHARLEY..?
TO GET MY CREEP OF A BROTHER-IN-LAW!
I GOTTA GET OILEY BACK... FOR DOLLY'S SAKE! THOUGH THERE'S PLENTY OF TOMMIES OUT HERE WHO'LL NEVER SEE THEIR KIDS AGAIN!
THE EARTH'S COMING OUT OF OILEY'S SANDBAG... ALL I GOTTA DO IS FOLLOW THE TRAIL HE'S LEAVING!

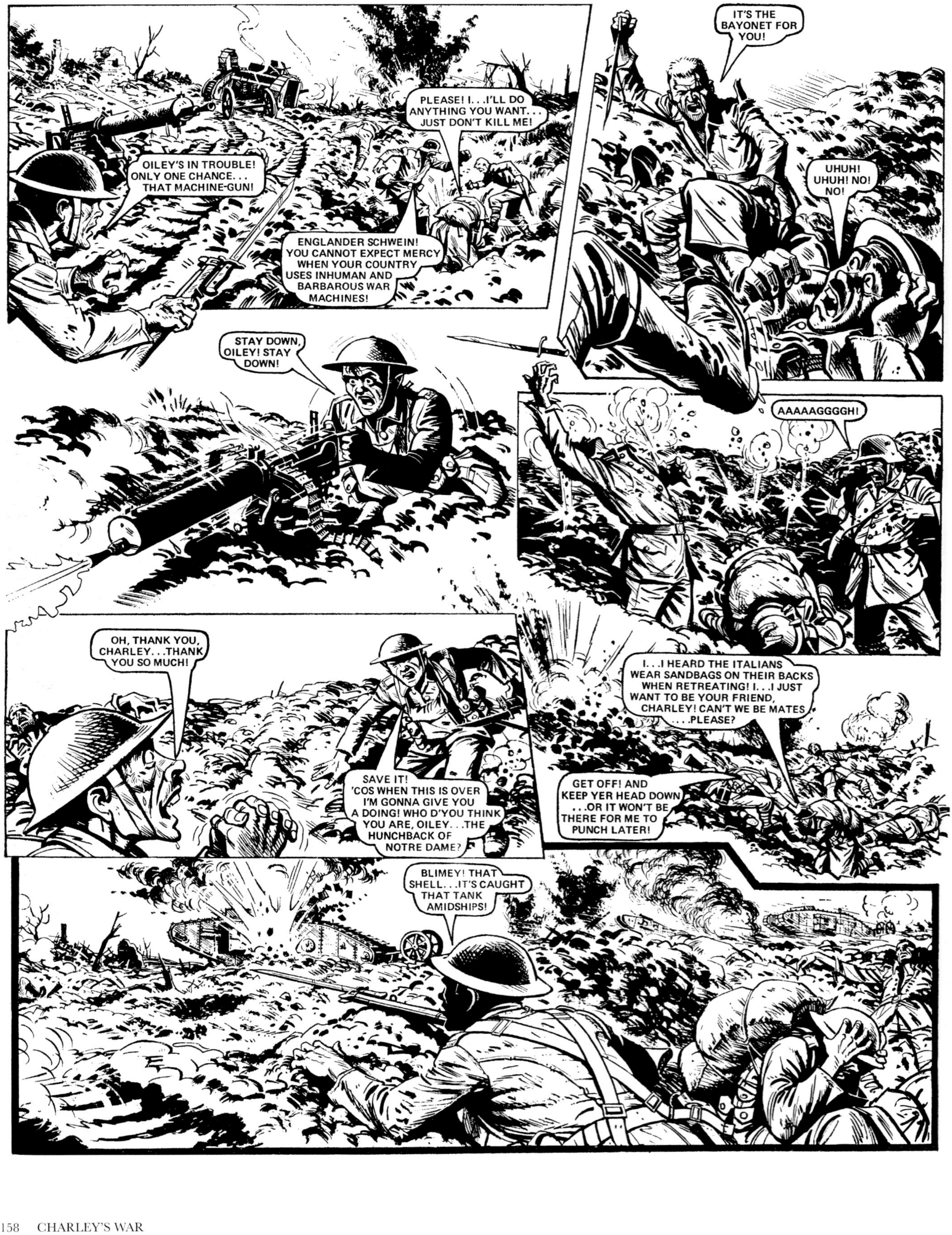
OILEY'S IN TROUBLE! ONLY ONE CHANCE... THAT MACHINE-GUN!
PLEASE! I...I'LL DO ANYTHING YOU WANT... JUST DON'T KILL ME!
ENGLANDER SCHWEIN! YOU CANNOT EXPECT MERCY WHEN YOUR COUNTRY USES INHUMAN AND BARBAROUS WAR MACHINES!
IT'S THE BAYONET FOR YOU!
UHUH! UHUH! NO! NO!
STAY DOWN, OILEY! STAY DOWN!
AAAAAGGGGH!
OH, THANK YOU, CHARLEY...THANK YOU SO MUCH!
SAVE IT! 'COS WHEN THIS IS OVER I'M GONNA GIVE YOU A DOING! WHO D'YOU THINK YOU ARE, OILEY...THE HUNCHBACK OF NOTRE DAME?
I...I HEARD THE ITALIANS WEAR SANDBAGS ON THEIR BACKS WHEN RETREATING! I...I JUST WANT TO BE YOUR FRIEND, CHARLEY! CAN'T WE BE MATES ...PLEASE?
GET OFF! AND KEEP YER HEAD DOWN ...OR IT WON'T BE THERE FOR ME TO PUNCH LATER!
BLIMEY! THAT SHELL...IT'S CAUGHT THAT TANK AMIDSHIPS!

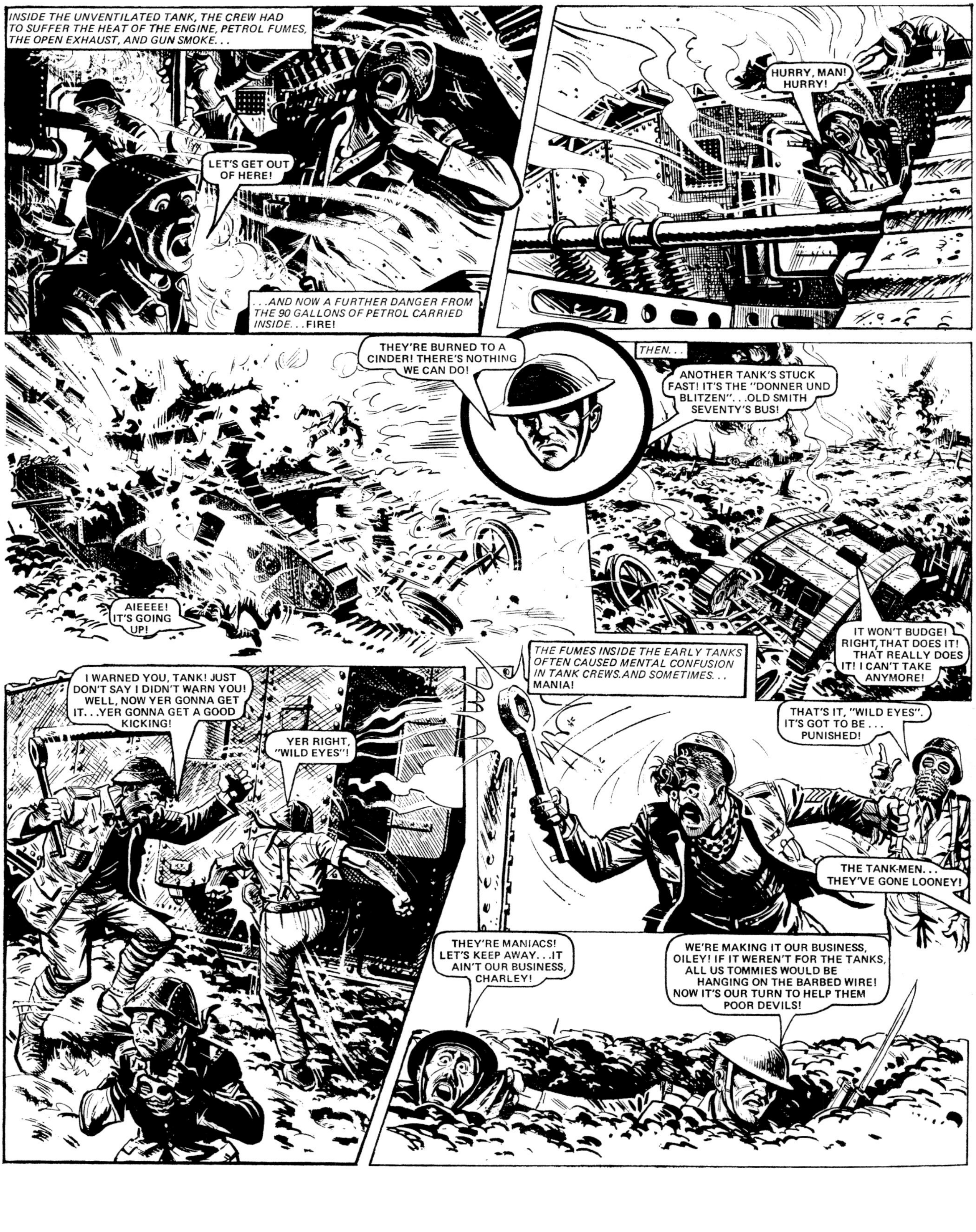
INSIDE THE UNVENTILATED TANK, THE CREW HAD TO SUFFER THE HEAT OF THE ENGINE, PETROL FUMES, THE OPEN EXHAUST, AND GUN SMOKE...
LET'S GET OUT OF HERE!
...AND NOW A FURTHER DANGER FROM THE 90 GALLONS OF PETROL CARRIED INSIDE...FIRE!
HURRY, MAN! HURRY!
AIEEEE! IT'S GOING UP!
THEY'RE BURNED TO A CINDER! THERE'S NOTHING WE CAN DO!
THEN...
ANOTHER TANK'S STUCK FAST! IT'S THE "DONNER UND BLITZEN"...OLD SMITH SEVENTY'S BUS!
IT WON'T BUDGE! RIGHT, THAT DOES IT! THAT REALLY DOES IT! I CAN'T TAKE ANYMORE!
THE FUMES INSIDE THE EARLY TANKS OFTEN CAUSED MENTAL CONFUSION IN TANK CREWS. AND SOMETIMES... MANIA!
I WARNED YOU, TANK! JUST DON'T SAY I DIDN'T WARN YOU! WELL, NOW YER GONNA GET IT...YER GONNA GET A GOOD KICKING!
YER RIGHT, "WILD EYES"!
THAT'S IT, "WILD EYES". IT'S GOT TO BE... PUNISHED!
THE TANK-MEN... THEY'VE GONE LOONEY!
THEY'RE MANIACS! LET'S KEEP AWAY...IT AIN'T OUR BUSINESS, CHARLEY!
WE'RE MAKING IT OUR BUSINESS, OILEY! IF IT WEREN'T FOR THE TANKS, ALL US TOMMIES WOULD BE HANGING ON THE BARBED WIRE! NOW IT'S OUR TURN TO HELP THEM POOR DEVILS!

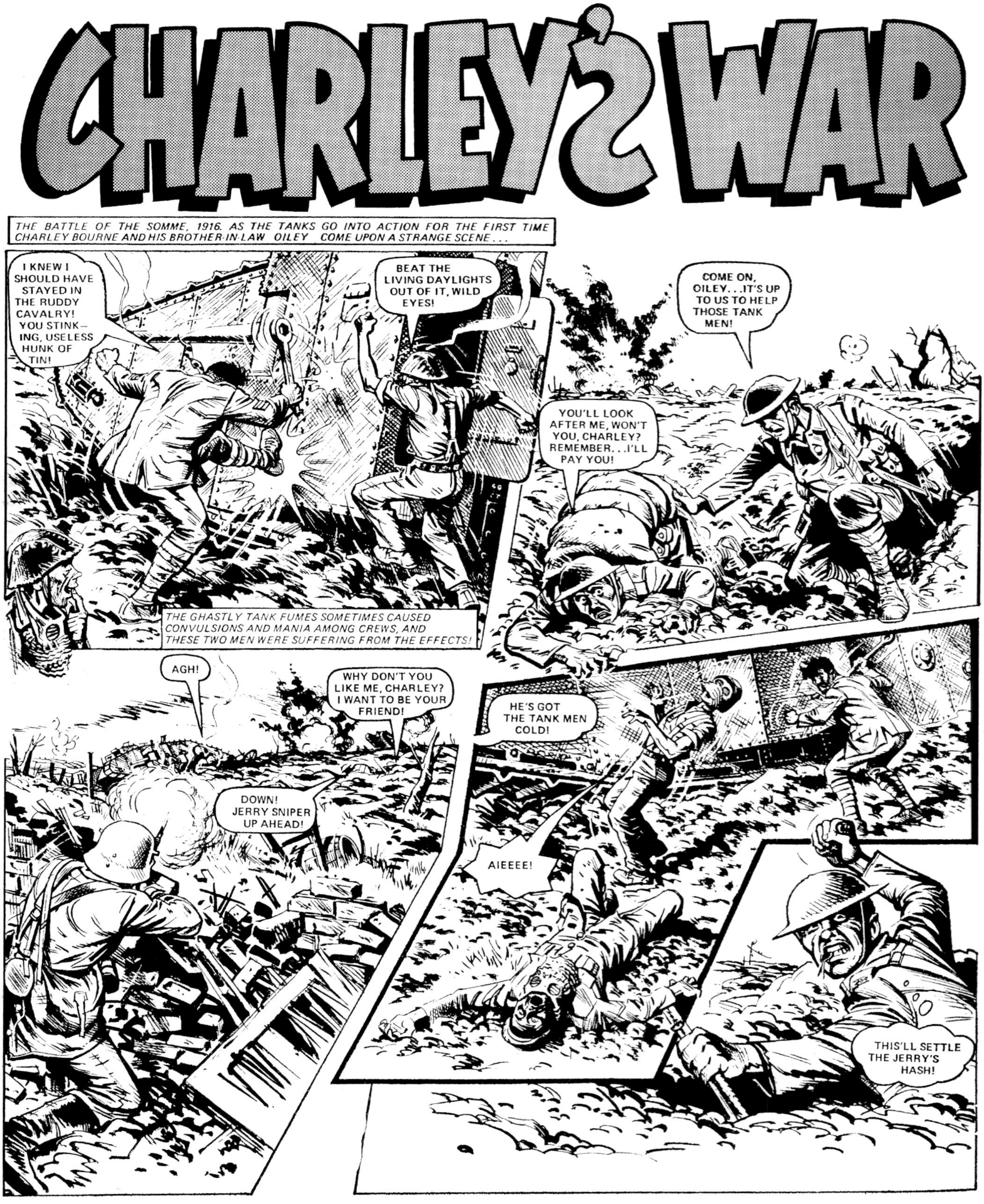
CHARLEY'S WAR
THE BATTLE OF THE SOMME, 1916. AS THE TANKS GO INTO ACTION FOR THE FIRST TIME CHARLEY BOURNE AND HIS BROTHER-IN-LAW OILEY COME UPON A STRANGE SCENE...
I KNEW I SHOULD HAVE STAYED IN THE RUDDY CAVALRY! YOU STINK-ING, USELESS HUNK OF TIN!
BEAT THE LIVING DAYLIGHTS OUT OF IT, WILD EYES!
THE GHASTLY TANK FUMES SOMETIMES CAUSED CONVULSIONS AND MANIA AMONG CREWS, AND THESE TWO MEN WERE SUFFERING FROM THE EFFECTS!
COME ON, OILEY...IT'S UP TO US TO HELP THOSE TANK MEN!
YOU'LL LOOK AFTER ME, WON'T YOU, CHARLEY? REMEMBER...I'LL PAY YOU!
AGH!
WHY DON'T YOU LIKE ME, CHARLEY? I WANT TO BE YOUR FRIEND!
DOWN! JERRY SNIPER UP AHEAD!
HE'S GOT THE TANK MEN COLD!
AIEEEE!
THIS'LL SETTLE THE JERRY'S HASH!

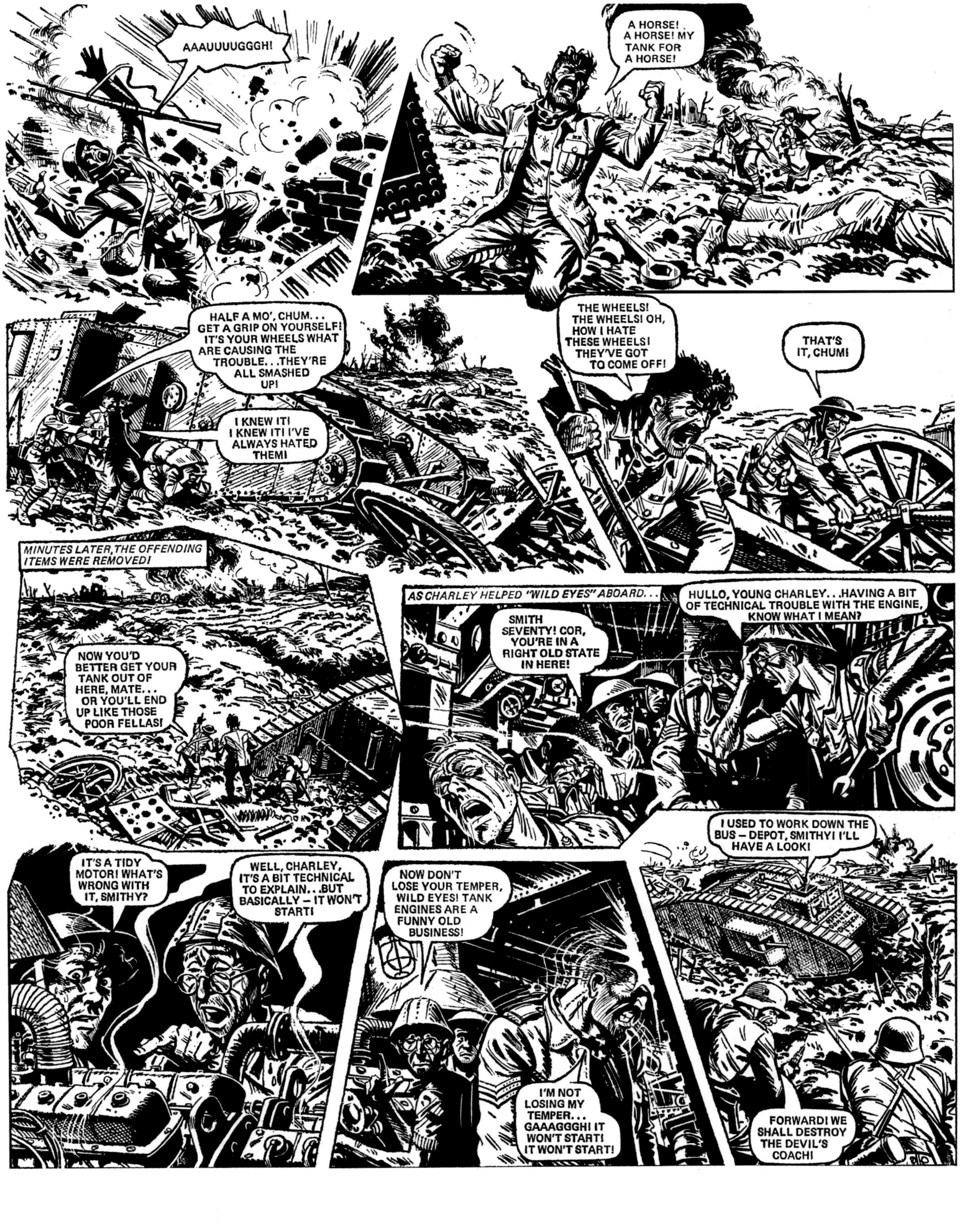
AAAUUUUGGGH!
A HORSE! A HORSE! MY TANK FOR A HORSE!
HALF A MO', CHUM... GET A GRIP ON YOURSELF! IT'S YOUR WHEELS WHAT ARE CAUSING THE TROUBLE... THEY'RE ALL SMASHED UP!
I KNEW IT! I KNEW IT! I'VE ALWAYS HATED THEM!
THE WHEELS! THE WHEELS! OH, HOW I HATE THESE WHEELS! THEY'VE GOT TO COME OFF!
THAT'S IT, CHUM!
MINUTES LATER, THE OFFENDING ITEMS WERE REMOVED!
NOW YOU'D BETTER GET YOUR TANK OUT OF HERE, MATE... OR YOU'LL END UP LIKE THOSE POOR FELLAS!
AS CHARLEY HELPED "WILD EYES" ABOARD...
SMITH SEVENTY! COR, YOU'RE IN A RIGHT OLD STATE IN HERE!
HULLO, YOUNG CHARLEY... HAVING A BIT OF TECHNICAL TROUBLE WITH THE ENGINE, KNOW WHAT I MEAN?
IT'S A TIDY MOTOR! WHAT'S WRONG WITH IT, SMITHY?
WELL, CHARLEY, IT'S A BIT TECHNICAL TO EXPLAIN... BUT BASICALLY — IT WON'T START!
NOW DON'T LOSE YOUR TEMPER, WILD EYES! TANK ENGINES ARE A FUNNY OLD BUSINESS!
I'M NOT LOSING MY TEMPER... GAAAGGGH! IT WON'T START! IT WON'T START!
I USED TO WORK DOWN THE BUS – DEPOT, SMITHY! I'LL HAVE A LOOK!
FORWARD! WE SHALL DESTROY THE DEVIL'S COACH!

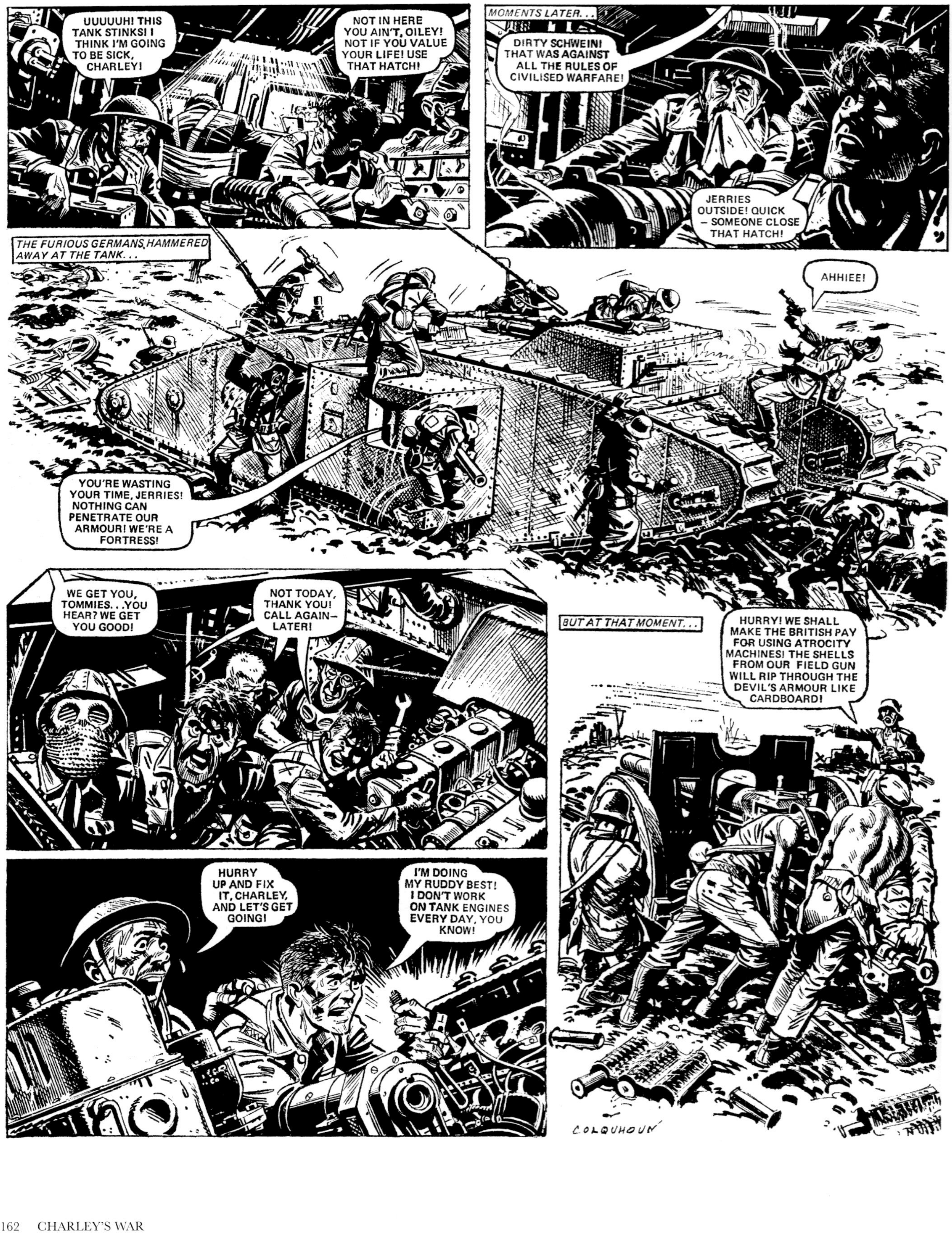
UUUUUH! THIS TANK STINKS! I THINK I'M GOING TO BE SICK, CHARLEY!
NOT IN HERE YOU AIN'T, OILEY! NOT IF YOU VALUE YOUR LIFE! USE THAT HATCH!
MOMENTS LATER...
DIRTY SCHWEIN! THAT WAS AGAINST ALL THE RULES OF CIVILISED WARFARE!
JERRIES OUTSIDE! QUICK – SOMEONE CLOSE THAT HATCH!
THE FURIOUS GERMANS HAMMERED AWAY AT THE TANK...
AHHIEE!
YOU'RE WASTING YOUR TIME, JERRIES! NOTHING CAN PENETRATE OUR ARMOUR! WE'RE A FORTRESS!
WE GET YOU, TOMMIES...YOU HEAR? WE GET YOU GOOD!
NOT TODAY, THANK YOU! CALL AGAIN– LATER!
HURRY UP AND FIX IT, CHARLEY, AND LET'S GET GOING!
I'M DOING MY RUDDY BEST! I DON'T WORK ON TANK ENGINES EVERY DAY, YOU KNOW!
BUT AT THAT MOMENT...
HURRY! WE SHALL MAKE THE BRITISH PAY FOR USING ATROCITY MACHINES! THE SHELLS FROM OUR FIELD GUN WILL RIP THROUGH THE DEVIL'S ARMOUR LIKE CARDBOARD!
COLQUHOUN

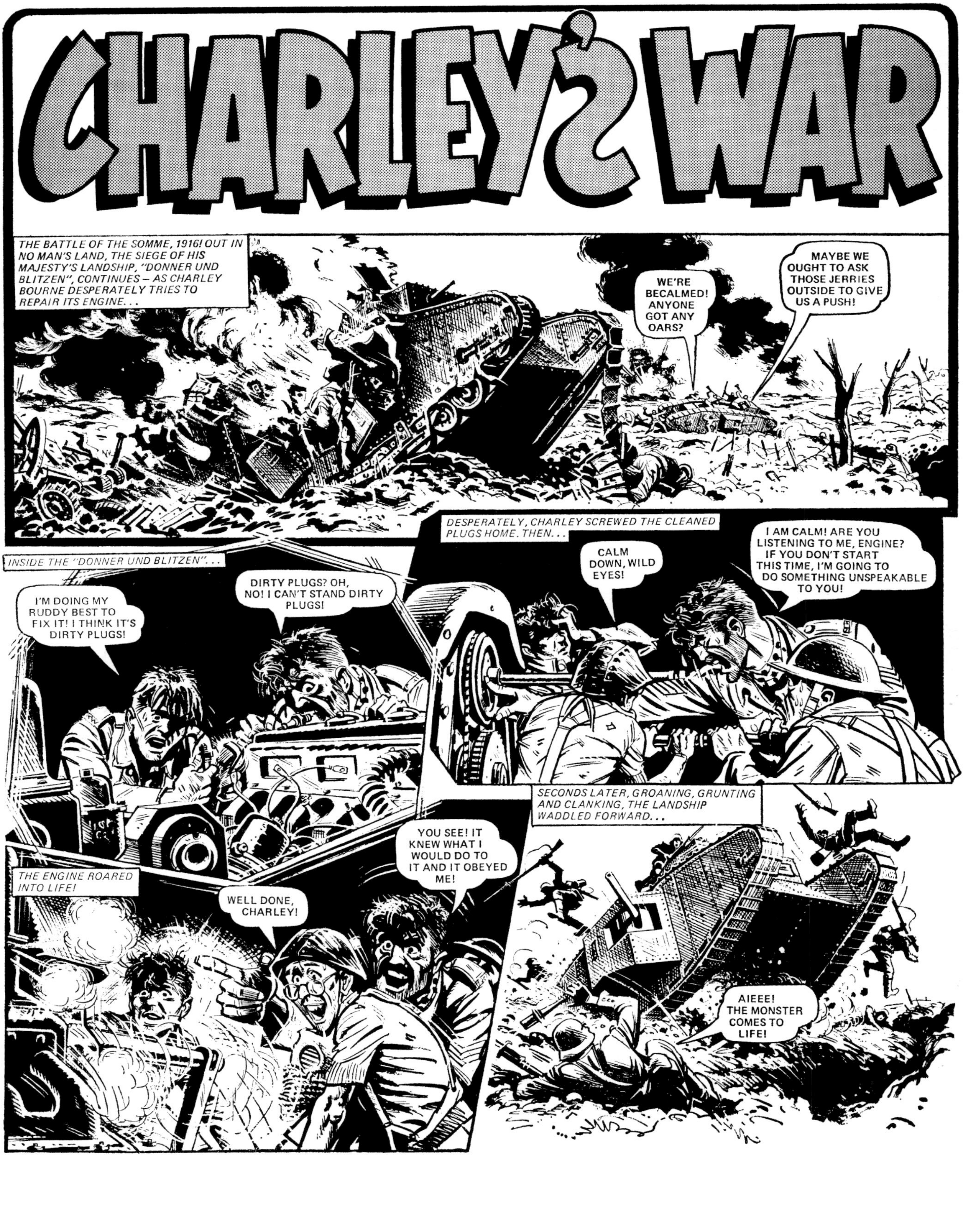
CHARLEY'S WAR
THE BATTLE OF THE SOMME, 1916! OUT IN NO MAN'S LAND, THE SIEGE OF HIS MAJESTY'S LANDSHIP, "DONNER UND BLITZEN", CONTINUES – AS CHARLEY BOURNE DESPERATELY TRIES TO REPAIR ITS ENGINE...
WE'RE BECALMED! ANYONE GOT ANY OARS?
MAYBE WE OUGHT TO ASK THOSE JERRIES OUTSIDE TO GIVE US A PUSH!
INSIDE THE "DONNER UND BLITZEN"...
I'M DOING MY RUDDY BEST TO FIX IT! I THINK IT'S DIRTY PLUGS!
DIRTY PLUGS? OH, NO! I CAN'T STAND DIRTY PLUGS!
DESPERATELY, CHARLEY SCREWED THE CLEANED PLUGS HOME. THEN...
CALM DOWN, WILD EYES!
I AM CALM! ARE YOU LISTENING TO ME, ENGINE? IF YOU DON'T START THIS TIME, I'M GOING TO DO SOMETHING UNSPEAKABLE TO YOU!
THE ENGINE ROARED INTO LIFE!
WELL DONE, CHARLEY!
YOU SEE! IT KNEW WHAT I WOULD DO TO IT AND IT OBEYED ME!
SECONDS LATER, GROANING, GRUNTING AND CLANKING, THE LANDSHIP WADDLED FORWARD...
AIEEE! THE MONSTER COMES TO LIFE!

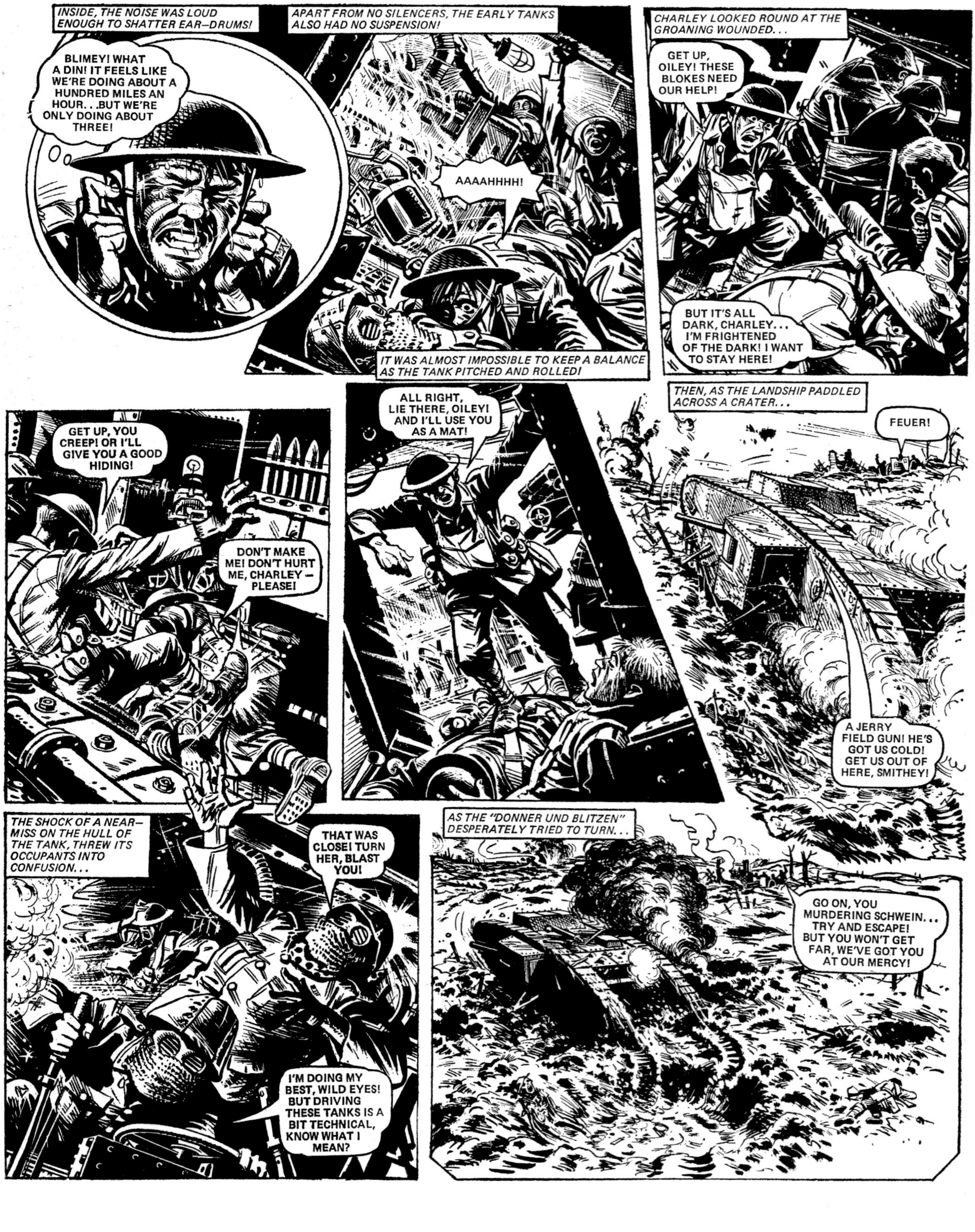
INSIDE, THE NOISE WAS LOUD ENOUGH TO SHATTER EAR-DRUMS!
BLIMEY! WHAT A DIN! IT FEELS LIKE WE'RE DOING ABOUT A HUNDRED MILES AN HOUR. . .BUT WE'RE ONLY DOING ABOUT THREE!
APART FROM NO SILENCERS, THE EARLY TANKS ALSO HAD NO SUSPENSION!
AAAAHHHH!
IT WAS ALMOST IMPOSSIBLE TO KEEP A BALANCE AS THE TANK PITCHED AND ROLLED!
CHARLEY LOOKED ROUND AT THE GROANING WOUNDED. . .
GET UP, OILEY! THESE BLOKES NEED OUR HELP!
BUT IT'S ALL DARK, CHARLEY. . . I'M FRIGHTENED OF THE DARK! I WANT TO STAY HERE!
GET UP, YOU CREEP! OR I'LL GIVE YOU A GOOD HIDING!
DON'T MAKE ME! DON'T HURT ME, CHARLEY — PLEASE!
ALL RIGHT, LIE THERE, OILEY! AND I'LL USE YOU AS A MAT!
THEN, AS THE LANDSHIP PADDLED ACROSS A CRATER. . .
FEUER!
A JERRY FIELD GUN! HE'S GOT US COLD! GET US OUT OF HERE, SMITHEY!
THE SHOCK OF A NEAR-MISS ON THE HULL OF THE TANK, THREW ITS OCCUPANTS INTO CONFUSION. . .
THAT WAS CLOSE! TURN HER, BLAST YOU!
I'M DOING MY BEST, WILD EYES! BUT DRIVING THESE TANKS IS A BIT TECHNICAL, KNOW WHAT I MEAN?
AS THE "DONNER UND BLITZEN" DESPERATELY TRIED TO TURN. . .
GO ON, YOU MURDERING SCHWEIN. . . TRY AND ESCAPE! BUT YOU WON'T GET FAR, WE'VE GOT YOU AT OUR MERCY!

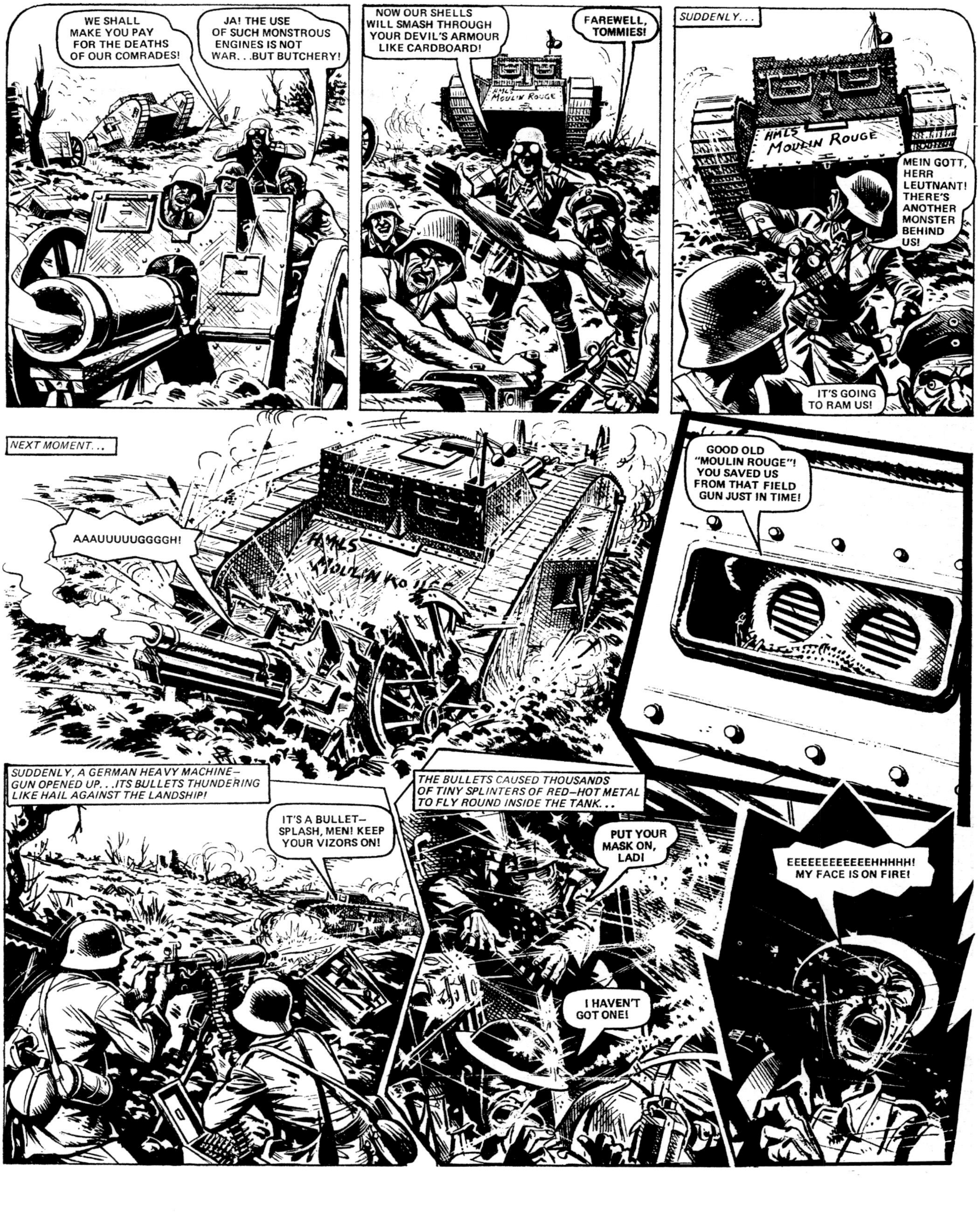
WE SHALL MAKE YOU PAY FOR THE DEATHS OF OUR COMRADES!
JA! THE USE OF SUCH MONSTROUS ENGINES IS NOT WAR. . .BUT BUTCHERY!
NOW OUR SHELLS WILL SMASH THROUGH YOUR DEVIL'S ARMOUR LIKE CARDBOARD!
FAREWELL, TOMMIES!
HMLS MOULIN ROUGE
SUDDENLY. . .
HMLS MOULIN ROUGE
MEIN GOTT, HERR LEUTNANT! THERE'S ANOTHER MONSTER BEHIND US!
IT'S GOING TO RAM US!
NEXT MOMENT. . .
AAAUUUUUGGGGH!
GOOD OLD "MOULIN ROUGE"! YOU SAVED US FROM THAT FIELD GUN JUST IN TIME!
SUDDENLY, A GERMAN HEAVY MACHINE-GUN OPENED UP. . .ITS BULLETS THUNDERING LIKE HAIL AGAINST THE LANDSHIP!
IT'S A BULLET-SPLASH, MEN! KEEP YOUR VIZORS ON!
THE BULLETS CAUSED THOUSANDS OF TINY SPLINTERS OF RED-HOT METAL TO FLY ROUND INSIDE THE TANK. . .
PUT YOUR MASK ON, LAD!
I HAVEN'T GOT ONE!
EEEEEEEEEEEEHHHHH! MY FACE IS ON FIRE!

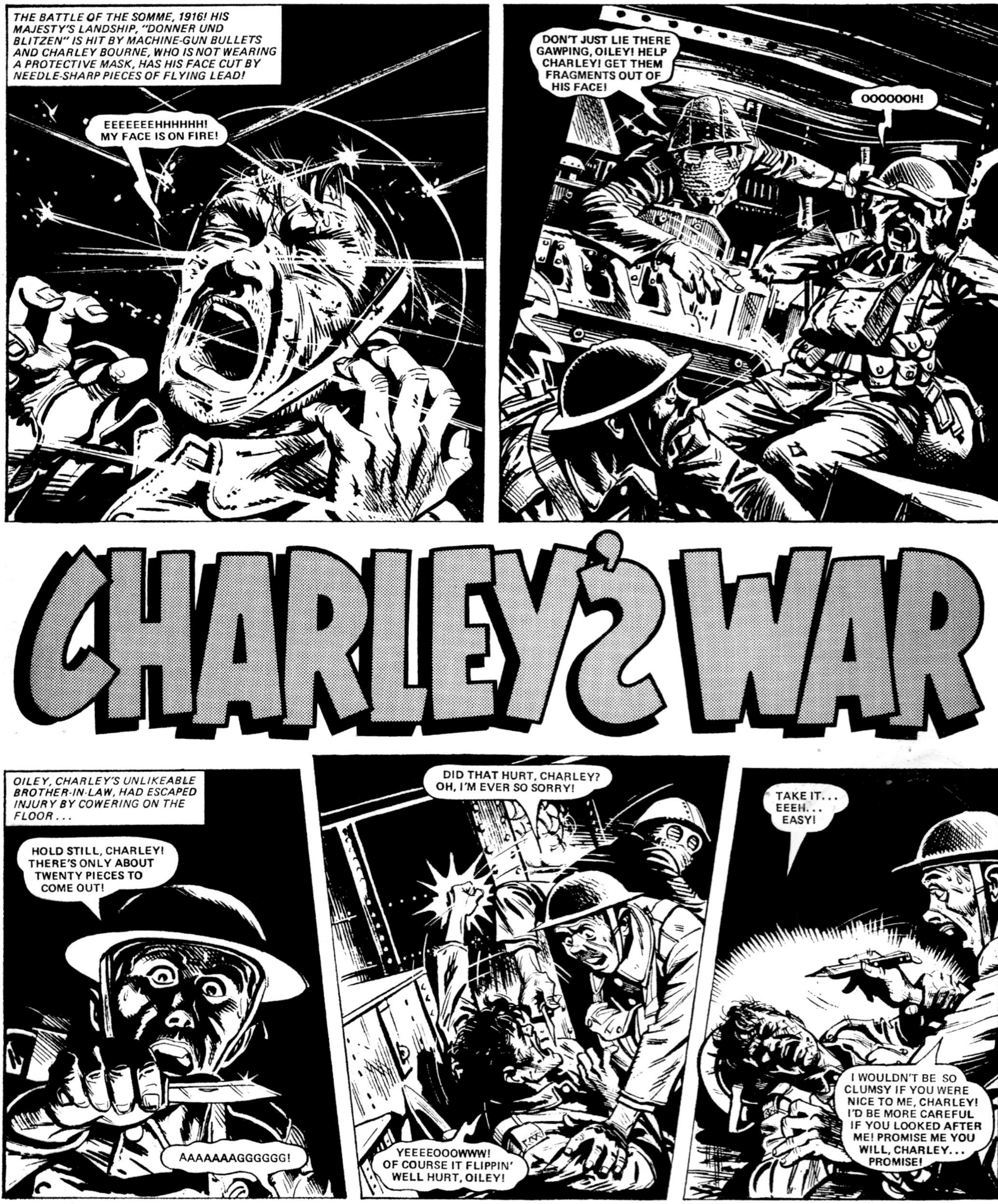
THE BATTLE OF THE SOMME, 1916! HIS MAJESTY'S LANDSHIP, "DONNER UND BLITZEN" IS HIT BY MACHINE-GUN BULLETS AND CHARLEY BOURNE, WHO IS NOT WEARING A PROTECTIVE MASK, HAS HIS FACE CUT BY NEEDLE-SHARP PIECES OF FLYING LEAD!
EEEEEEEHHHHHH! MY FACE IS ON FIRE!
DON'T JUST LIE THERE GAWPING, OILEY! HELP CHARLEY! GET THEM FRAGMENTS OUT OF HIS FACE!
OOOOOOH!
CHARLEY'S WAR
OILEY, CHARLEY'S UNLIKEABLE BROTHER-IN-LAW, HAD ESCAPED INJURY BY COWERING ON THE FLOOR . . .
HOLD STILL, CHARLEY! THERE'S ONLY ABOUT TWENTY PIECES TO COME OUT!
AAAAAAAGGGGGG!
DID THAT HURT, CHARLEY? OH, I'M EVER SO SORRY!
YEEEEOOOWWW! OF COURSE IT FLIPPIN' WELL HURT, OILEY!
TAKE IT . . . EEEH . . . EASY!
I WOULDN'T BE SO CLUMSY IF YOU WERE NICE TO ME, CHARLEY! I'D BE MORE CAREFUL IF YOU LOOKED AFTER ME! PROMISE ME YOU WILL, CHARLEY . . . PROMISE!

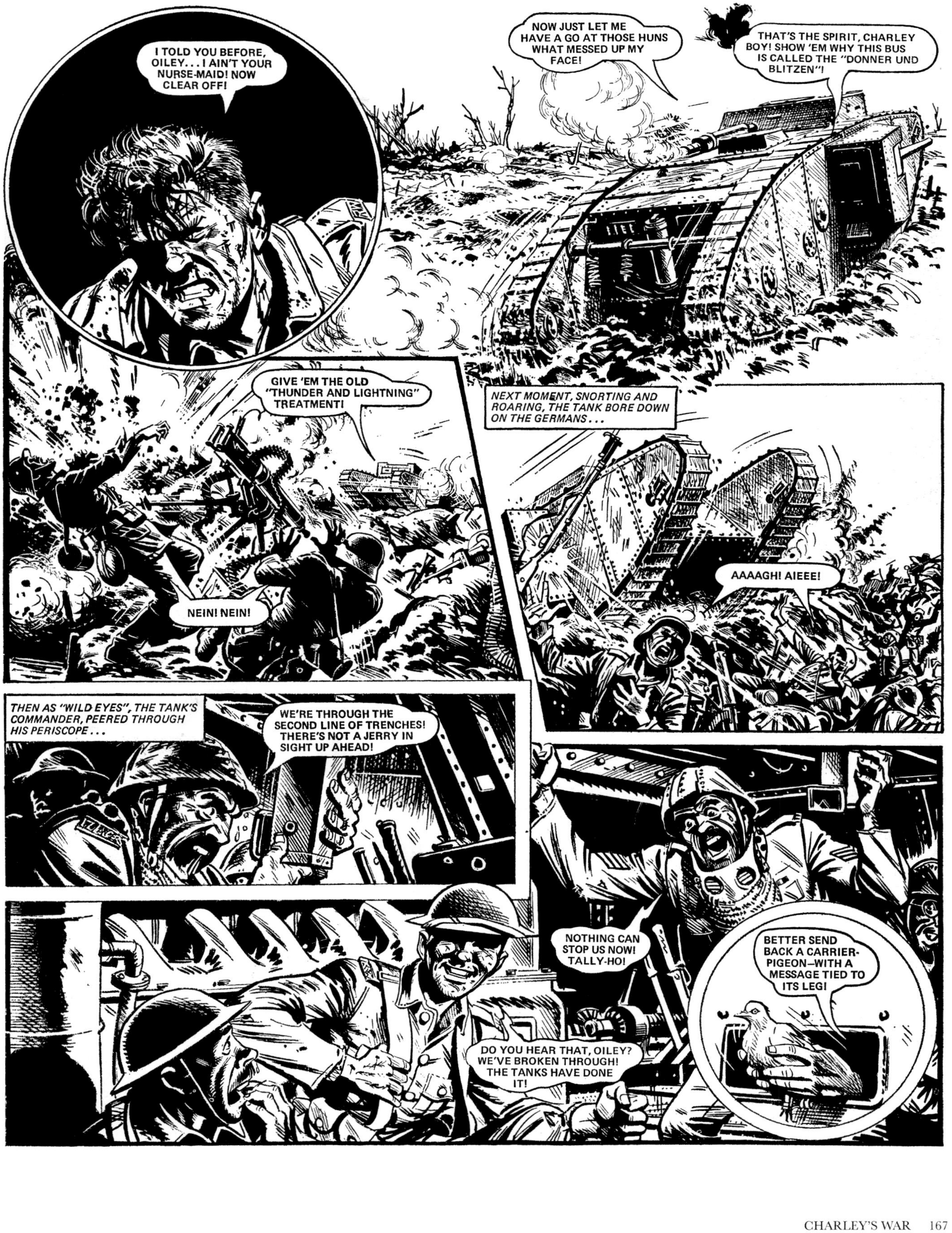
I TOLD YOU BEFORE, OILEY... I AIN'T YOUR NURSE-MAID! NOW CLEAR OFF!
NOW JUST LET ME HAVE A GO AT THOSE HUNS WHAT MESSED UP MY FACE!
THAT'S THE SPIRIT, CHARLEY BOY! SHOW 'EM WHY THIS BUS IS CALLED THE "DONNER UND BLITZEN"!
GIVE 'EM THE OLD "THUNDER AND LIGHTNING" TREATMENT!
NEIN! NEIN!
NEXT MOMENT, SNORTING AND ROARING, THE TANK BORE DOWN ON THE GERMANS...
AAAAGH! AIEEE!
THEN AS "WILD EYES", THE TANK'S COMMANDER, PEERED THROUGH HIS PERISCOPE...
WE'RE THROUGH THE SECOND LINE OF TRENCHES! THERE'S NOT A JERRY IN SIGHT UP AHEAD!
NOTHING CAN STOP US NOW! TALLY-HO!
DO YOU HEAR THAT, OILEY? WE'VE BROKEN THROUGH! THE TANKS HAVE DONE IT!
BETTER SEND BACK A CARRIER-PIGEON—WITH A MESSAGE TIED TO ITS LEG!

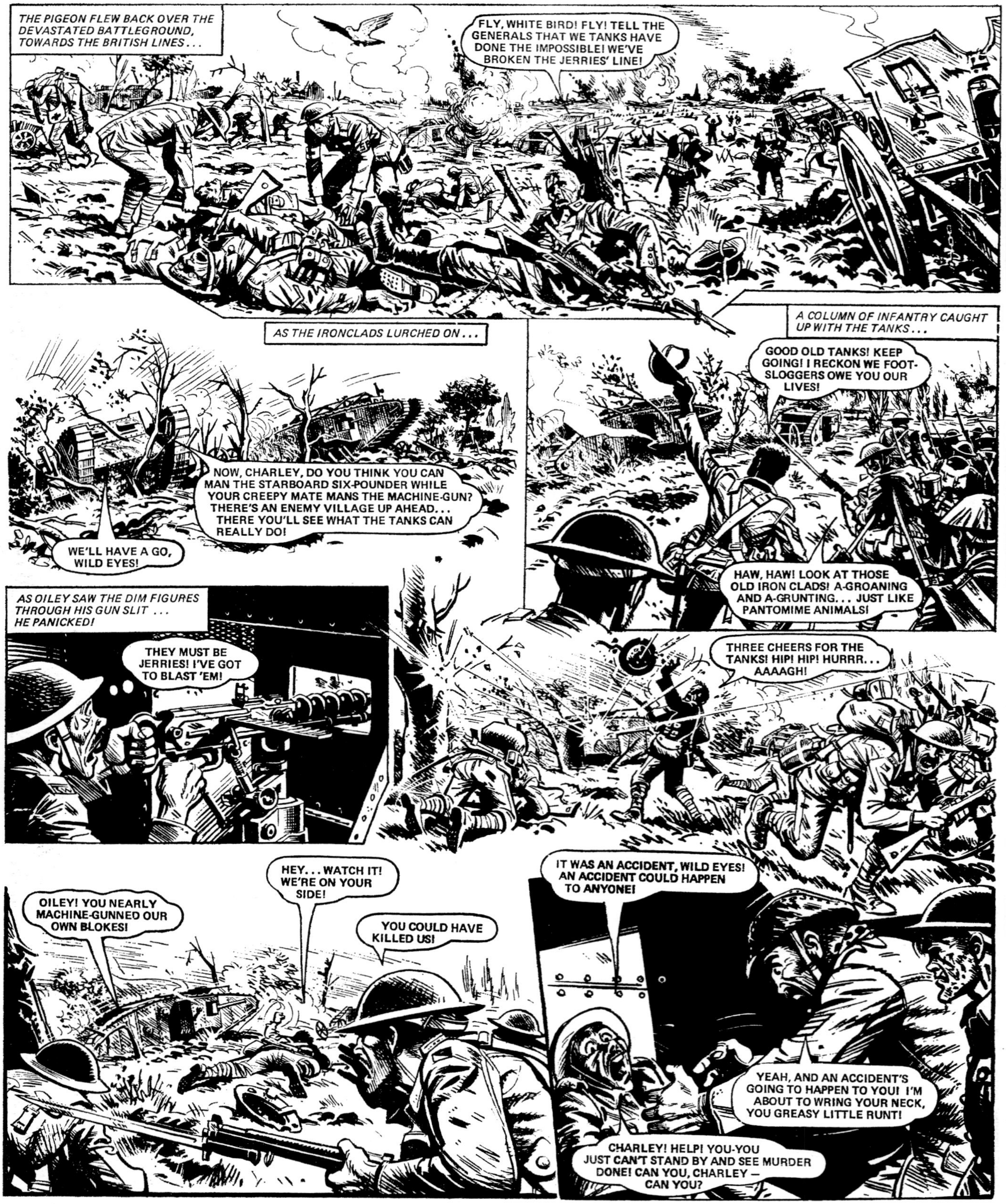
THE PIGEON FLEW BACK OVER THE DEVASTATED BATTLEGROUND, TOWARDS THE BRITISH LINES . . .
FLY, WHITE BIRD! FLY! TELL THE GENERALS THAT WE TANKS HAVE DONE THE IMPOSSIBLE! WE'VE BROKEN THE JERRIES' LINE!
AS THE IRONCLADS LURCHED ON . . .
NOW, CHARLEY, DO YOU THINK YOU CAN MAN THE STARBOARD SIX-POUNDER WHILE YOUR CREEPY MATE MANS THE MACHINE-GUN? THERE'S AN ENEMY VILLAGE UP AHEAD . . . THERE YOU'LL SEE WHAT THE TANKS CAN REALLY DO!
WE'LL HAVE A GO, WILD EYES!
A COLUMN OF INFANTRY CAUGHT UP WITH THE TANKS . . .
GOOD OLD TANKS! KEEP GOING! I RECKON WE FOOT-SLOGGERS OWE YOU OUR LIVES!
HAW, HAW! LOOK AT THOSE OLD IRON CLADS! A-GROANING AND A-GRUNTING . . . JUST LIKE PANTOMIME ANIMALS!
AS OILEY SAW THE DIM FIGURES THROUGH HIS GUN SLIT . . . HE PANICKED!
THEY MUST BE JERRIES! I'VE GOT TO BLAST 'EM!
THREE CHEERS FOR THE TANKS! HIP! HIP! HURRR . . . AAAAGH!
OILEY! YOU NEARLY MACHINE-GUNNED OUR OWN BLOKES!
HEY . . . WATCH IT! WE'RE ON YOUR SIDE!
YOU COULD HAVE KILLED US!
IT WAS AN ACCIDENT, WILD EYES! AN ACCIDENT COULD HAPPEN TO ANYONE!
YEAH, AND AN ACCIDENT'S GOING TO HAPPEN TO YOU! I'M ABOUT TO WRING YOUR NECK, YOU GREASY LITTLE RUNT!
CHARLEY! HELP! YOU-YOU JUST CAN'T STAND BY AND SEE MURDER DONE! CAN YOU, CHARLEY — CAN YOU?

CHARLEY'S WAR

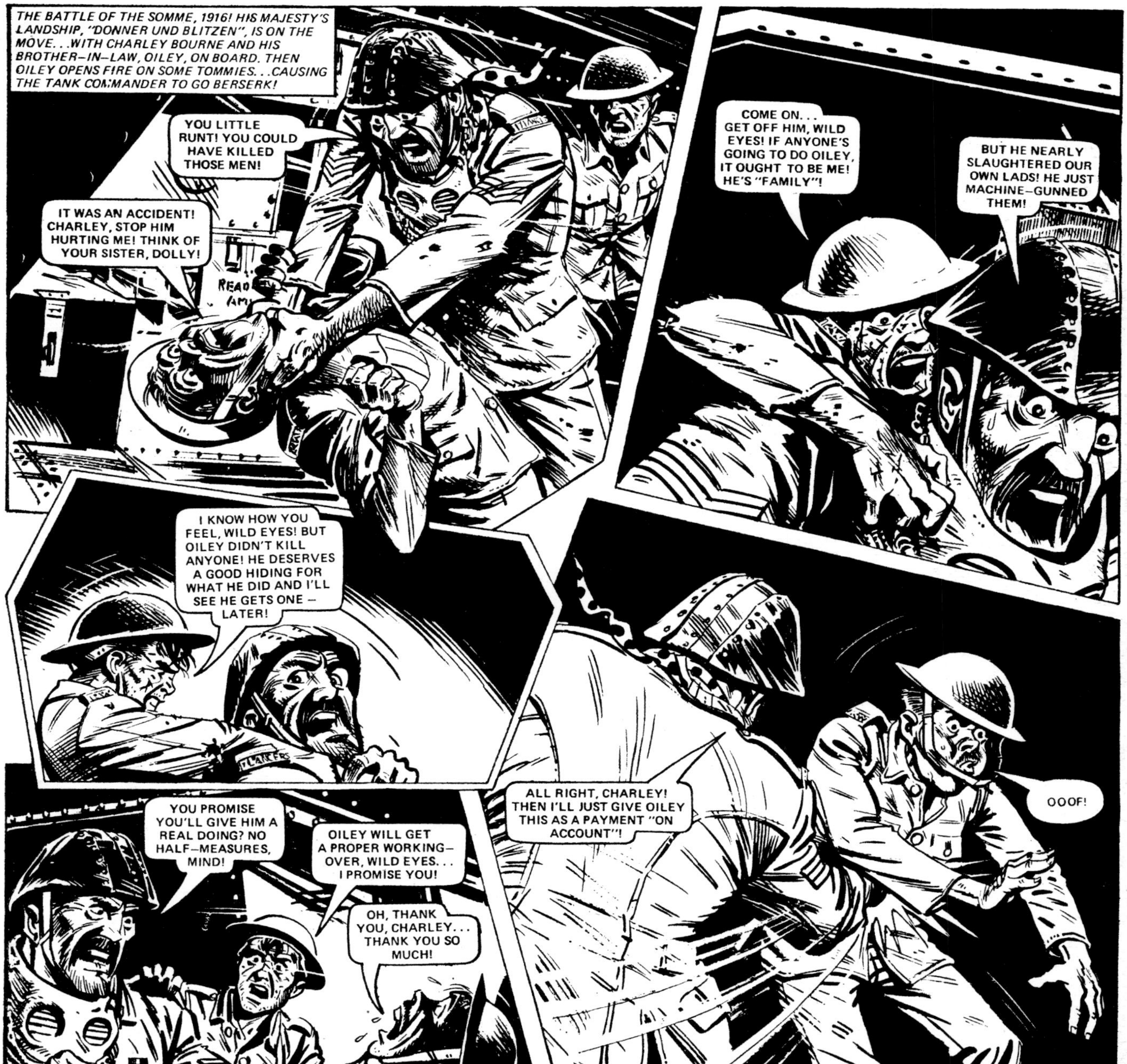
THE BATTLE OF THE SOMME, 1916! HIS MAJESTY'S LANDSHIP, "DONNER UND BLITZEN", IS ON THE MOVE. . .WITH CHARLEY BOURNE AND HIS BROTHER–IN–LAW, OILEY, ON BOARD. THEN OILEY OPENS FIRE ON SOME TOMMIES. . .CAUSING THE TANK COMMANDER TO GO BERSERK!
YOU LITTLE RUNT! YOU COULD HAVE KILLED THOSE MEN!
IT WAS AN ACCIDENT! CHARLEY, STOP HIM HURTING ME! THINK OF YOUR SISTER, DOLLY!
COME ON. . . GET OFF HIM, WILD EYES! IF ANYONE'S GOING TO DO OILEY, IT OUGHT TO BE ME! HE'S "FAMILY"!
BUT HE NEARLY SLAUGHTERED OUR OWN LADS! HE JUST MACHINE–GUNNED THEM!
I KNOW HOW YOU FEEL, WILD EYES! BUT OILEY DIDN'T KILL ANYONE! HE DESERVES A GOOD HIDING FOR WHAT HE DID AND I'LL SEE HE GETS ONE – LATER!
YOU PROMISE YOU'LL GIVE HIM A REAL DOING? NO HALF–MEASURES, MIND!
OILEY WILL GET A PROPER WORKING–OVER, WILD EYES. . . I PROMISE YOU!
OH, THANK YOU, CHARLEY. . . THANK YOU SO MUCH!
ALL RIGHT, CHARLEY! THEN I'LL JUST GIVE OILEY THIS AS A PAYMENT "ON ACCOUNT"!
OOOF!

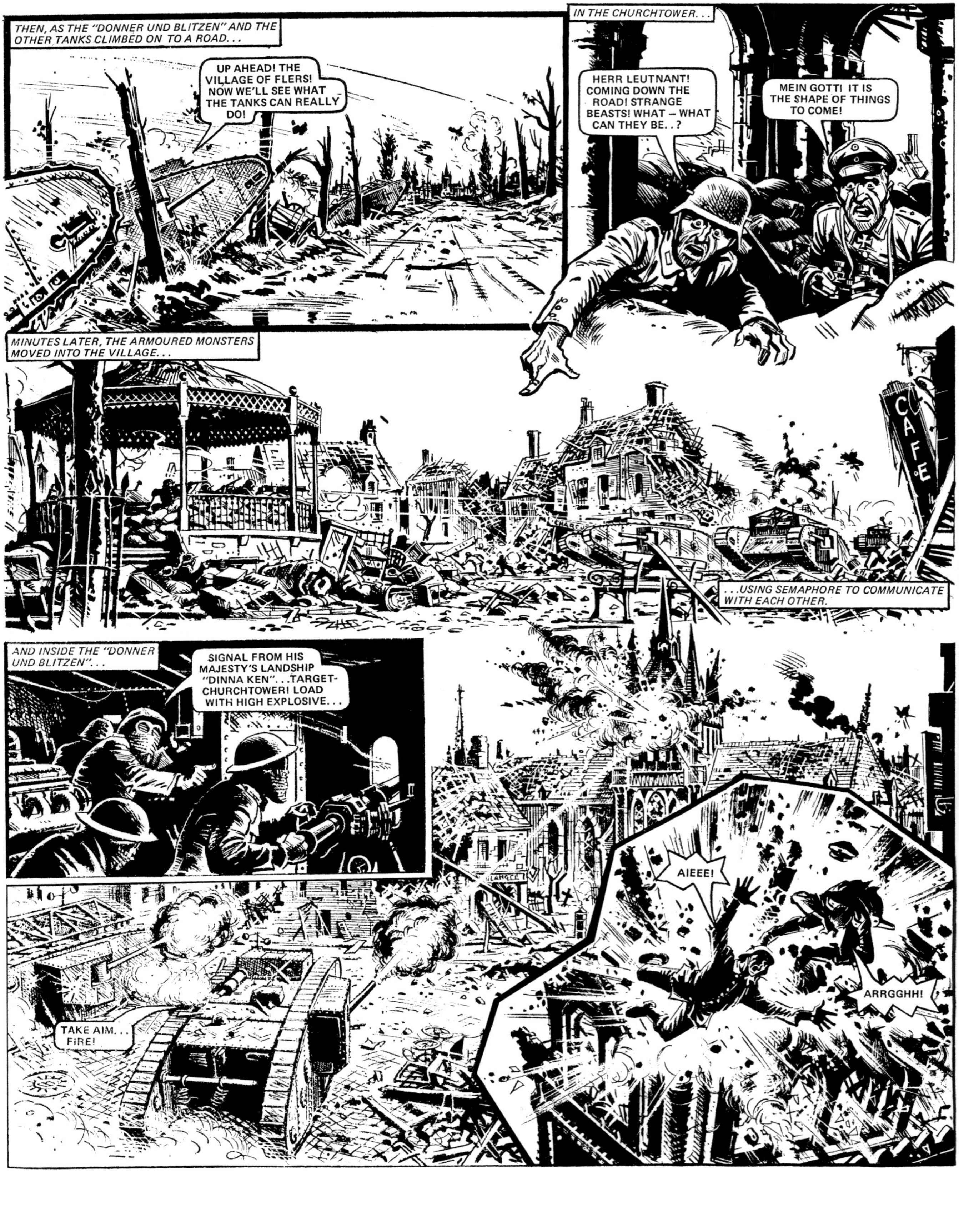
THEN, AS THE "DONNER UND BLITZEN" AND THE OTHER TANKS CLIMBED ON TO A ROAD...
UP AHEAD! THE VILLAGE OF FLERS! NOW WE'LL SEE WHAT THE TANKS CAN REALLY DO!
IN THE CHURCHTOWER...
HERR LEUTNANT! COMING DOWN THE ROAD! STRANGE BEASTS! WHAT – WHAT CAN THEY BE..?
MEIN GOTT! IT IS THE SHAPE OF THINGS TO COME!
MINUTES LATER, THE ARMOURED MONSTERS MOVED INTO THE VILLAGE...
CAFE
...USING SEMAPHORE TO COMMUNICATE WITH EACH OTHER.
AND INSIDE THE "DONNER UND BLITZEN"...
SIGNAL FROM HIS MAJESTY'S LANDSHIP "DINNA KEN"...TARGET-CHURCHTOWER! LOAD WITH HIGH EXPLOSIVE...
TAKE AIM... FIRE!
AIEEE!
ARRGGHH!

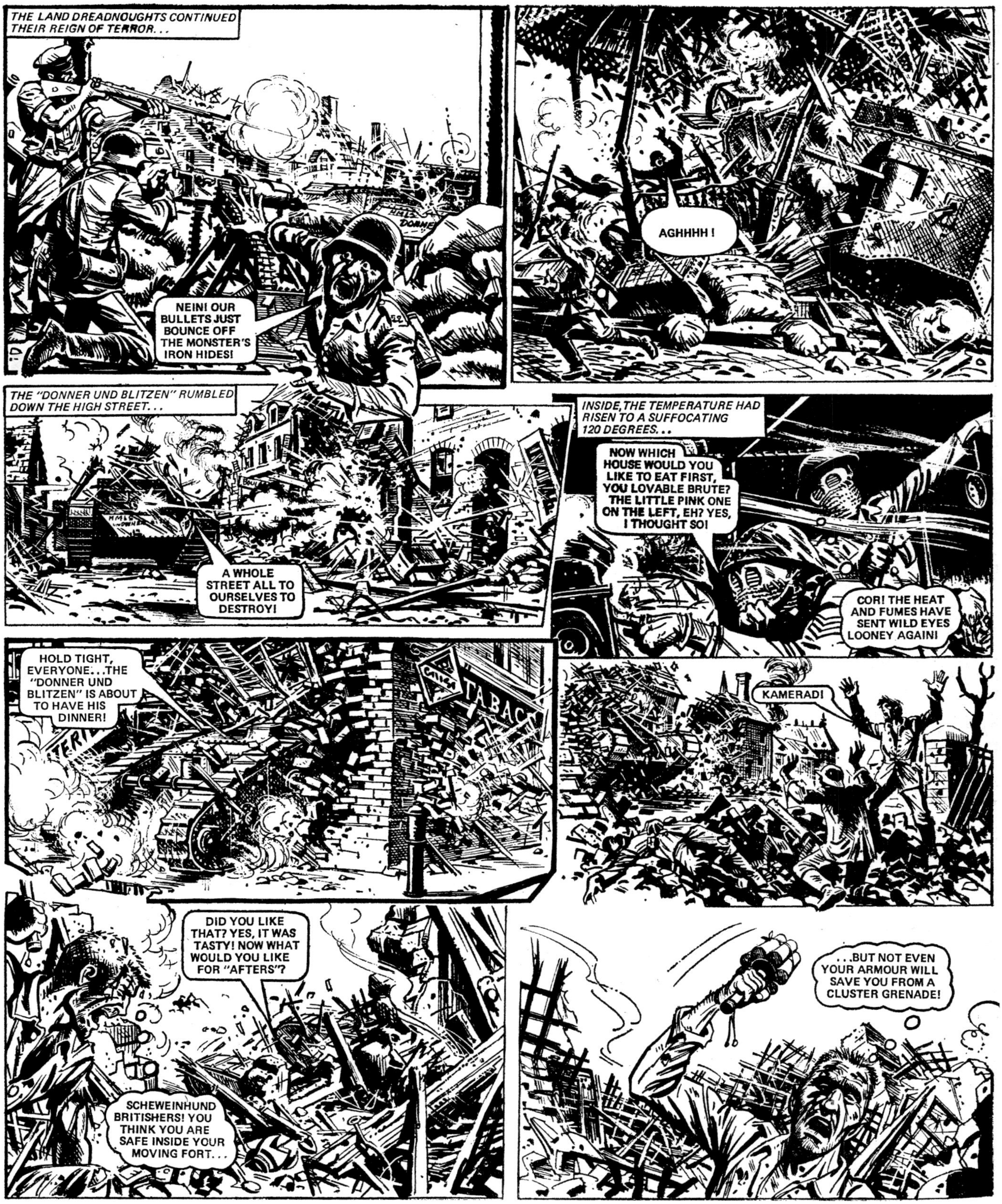
THE LAND DREADNOUGHTS CONTINUED THEIR REIGN OF TERROR...
NEIN! OUR BULLETS JUST BOUNCE OFF THE MONSTER'S IRON HIDES!
AGHHHH!
THE "DONNER UND BLITZEN" RUMBLED DOWN THE HIGH STREET...
A WHOLE STREET ALL TO OURSELVES TO DESTROY!
INSIDE, THE TEMPERATURE HAD RISEN TO A SUFFOCATING 120 DEGREES...
NOW WHICH HOUSE WOULD YOU LIKE TO EAT FIRST, YOU LOVABLE BRUTE? THE LITTLE PINK ONE ON THE LEFT, EH? YES, I THOUGHT SO!
COR! THE HEAT AND FUMES HAVE SENT WILD EYES LOONEY AGAIN!
HOLD TIGHT, EVERYONE...THE "DONNER UND BLITZEN" IS ABOUT TO HAVE HIS DINNER!
TABAC
KAMERAD!
DID YOU LIKE THAT? YES, IT WAS TASTY! NOW WHAT WOULD YOU LIKE FOR "AFTERS"?
SCHEWEINHUND BRITISHERS! YOU THINK YOU ARE SAFE INSIDE YOUR MOVING FORT...
...BUT NOT EVEN YOUR ARMOUR WILL SAVE YOU FROM A CLUSTER GRENADE!

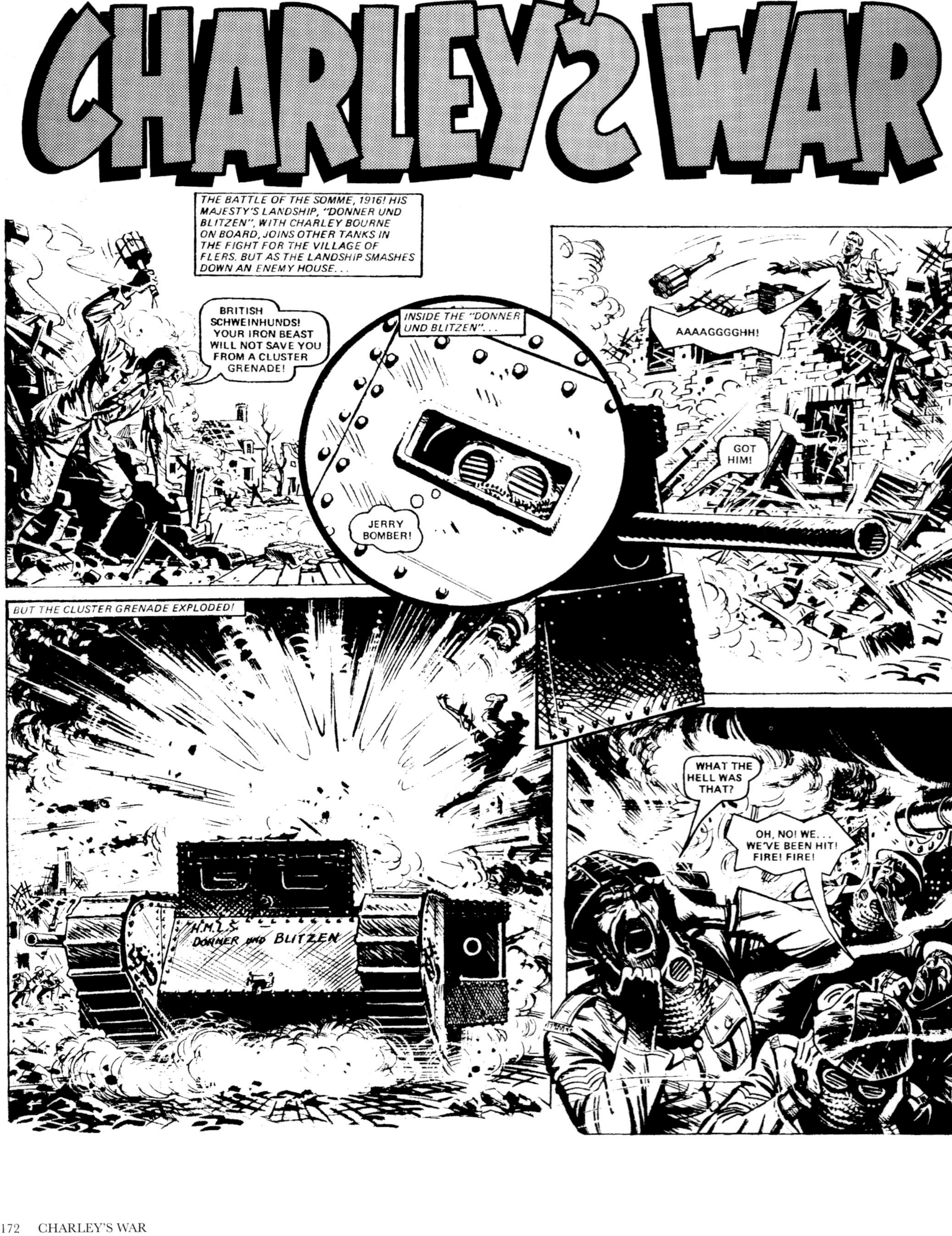
CHARLEY'S WAR
THE BATTLE OF THE SOMME, 1916! HIS MAJESTY'S LANDSHIP, "DONNER UND BLITZEN", WITH CHARLEY BOURNE ON BOARD, JOINS OTHER TANKS IN THE FIGHT FOR THE VILLAGE OF FLERS. BUT AS THE LANDSHIP SMASHES DOWN AN ENEMY HOUSE...
BRITISH SCHWEINHUNDS! YOUR IRON BEAST WILL NOT SAVE YOU FROM A CLUSTER GRENADE!
INSIDE THE "DONNER UND BLITZEN"...
JERRY BOMBER!
AAAAGGGGHH!
GOT HIM!
BUT THE CLUSTER GRENADE EXPLODED!
H.M.L.S. DONNER UND BLITZEN
WHAT THE HELL WAS THAT?
OH, NO! WE... WE'VE BEEN HIT! FIRE! FIRE!

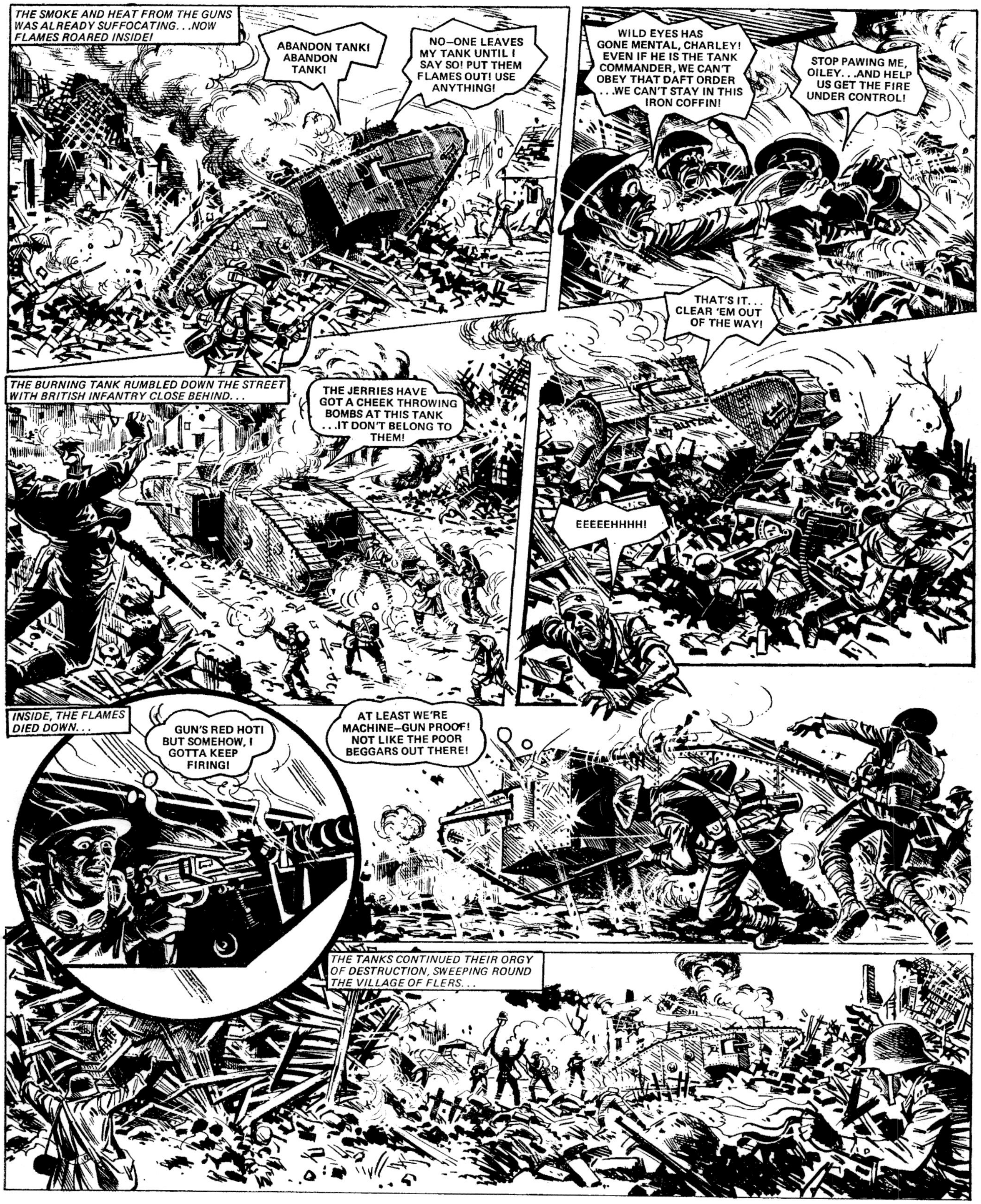

THE SMOKE AND HEAT FROM THE GUNS WAS ALREADY SUFFOCATING. . .NOW FLAMES ROARED INSIDE!
ABANDON TANK! ABANDON TANK!
NO—ONE LEAVES MY TANK UNTIL I SAY SO! PUT THEM FLAMES OUT! USE ANYTHING!
WILD EYES HAS GONE MENTAL, CHARLEY! EVEN IF HE IS THE TANK COMMANDER, WE CAN'T OBEY THAT DAFT ORDER . . .WE CAN'T STAY IN THIS IRON COFFIN!
STOP PAWING ME, OILEY. . .AND HELP US GET THE FIRE UNDER CONTROL!
THE BURNING TANK RUMBLED DOWN THE STREET WITH BRITISH INFANTRY CLOSE BEHIND. . .
THE JERRIES HAVE GOT A CHEEK THROWING BOMBS AT THIS TANK . . .IT DON'T BELONG TO THEM!
THAT'S IT. . . CLEAR 'EM OUT OF THE WAY!
EEEEEHHHH!
INSIDE, THE FLAMES DIED DOWN. . .
GUN'S RED HOT! BUT SOMEHOW, I GOTTA KEEP FIRING!
AT LEAST WE'RE MACHINE—GUN PROOF! NOT LIKE THE POOR BEGGARS OUT THERE!
THE TANKS CONTINUED THEIR ORGY OF DESTRUCTION, SWEEPING ROUND THE VILLAGE OF FLERS. . .

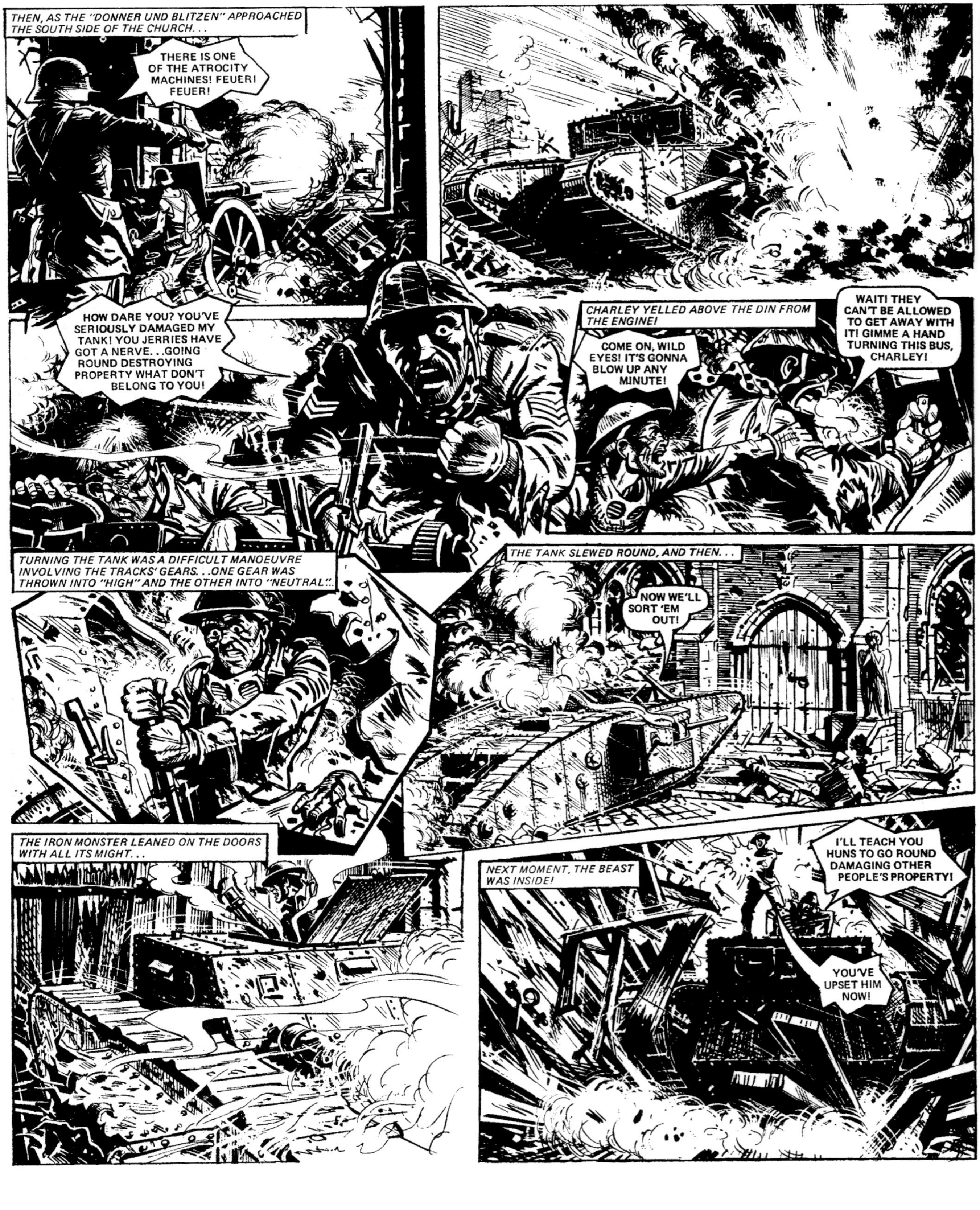
THEN, AS THE "DONNER UND BLITZEN" APPROACHED THE SOUTH SIDE OF THE CHURCH...
THERE IS ONE OF THE ATROCITY MACHINES! FEUER! FEUER!
HOW DARE YOU? YOU'VE SERIOUSLY DAMAGED MY TANK! YOU JERRIES HAVE GOT A NERVE... GOING ROUND DESTROYING PROPERTY WHAT DON'T BELONG TO YOU!
CHARLEY YELLED ABOVE THE DIN FROM THE ENGINE!
COME ON, WILD EYES! IT'S GONNA BLOW UP ANY MINUTE!
WAIT! THEY CAN'T BE ALLOWED TO GET AWAY WITH IT! GIMME A HAND TURNING THIS BUS, CHARLEY!
TURNING THE TANK WAS A DIFFICULT MANOEUVRE INVOLVING THE TRACKS' GEARS... ONE GEAR WAS THROWN INTO "HIGH" AND THE OTHER INTO "NEUTRAL"...
THE TANK SLEWED ROUND, AND THEN...
NOW WE'LL SORT 'EM OUT!
THE IRON MONSTER LEANED ON THE DOORS WITH ALL ITS MIGHT...
NEXT MOMENT, THE BEAST WAS INSIDE!
I'LL TEACH YOU HUNS TO GO ROUND DAMAGING OTHER PEOPLE'S PROPERTY!
YOU'VE UPSET HIM NOW!

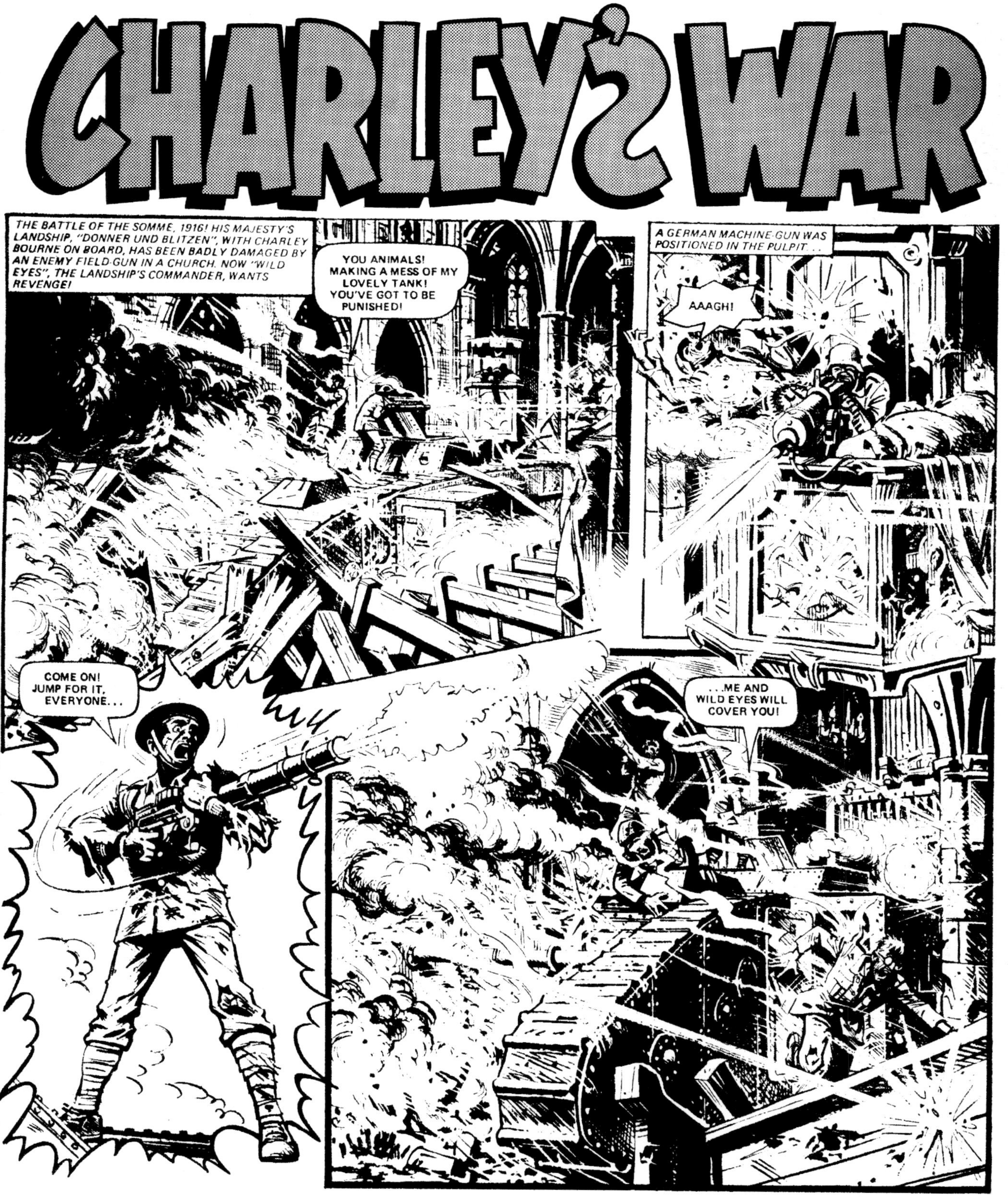
CHARLEY'S WAR
THE BATTLE OF THE SOMME, 1916! HIS MAJESTY'S LANDSHIP, "DONNER UND BLITZEN", WITH CHARLEY BOURNE ON BOARD, HAS BEEN BADLY DAMAGED BY AN ENEMY FIELD-GUN IN A CHURCH. NOW "WILD EYES", THE LANDSHIP'S COMMANDER, WANTS REVENGE!
YOU ANIMALS! MAKING A MESS OF MY LOVELY TANK! YOU'VE GOT TO BE PUNISHED!
A GERMAN MACHINE-GUN WAS POSITIONED IN THE PULPIT . . .
AAAGH!
COME ON! JUMP FOR IT, EVERYONE . . .
. . .ME AND WILD EYES WILL COVER YOU!

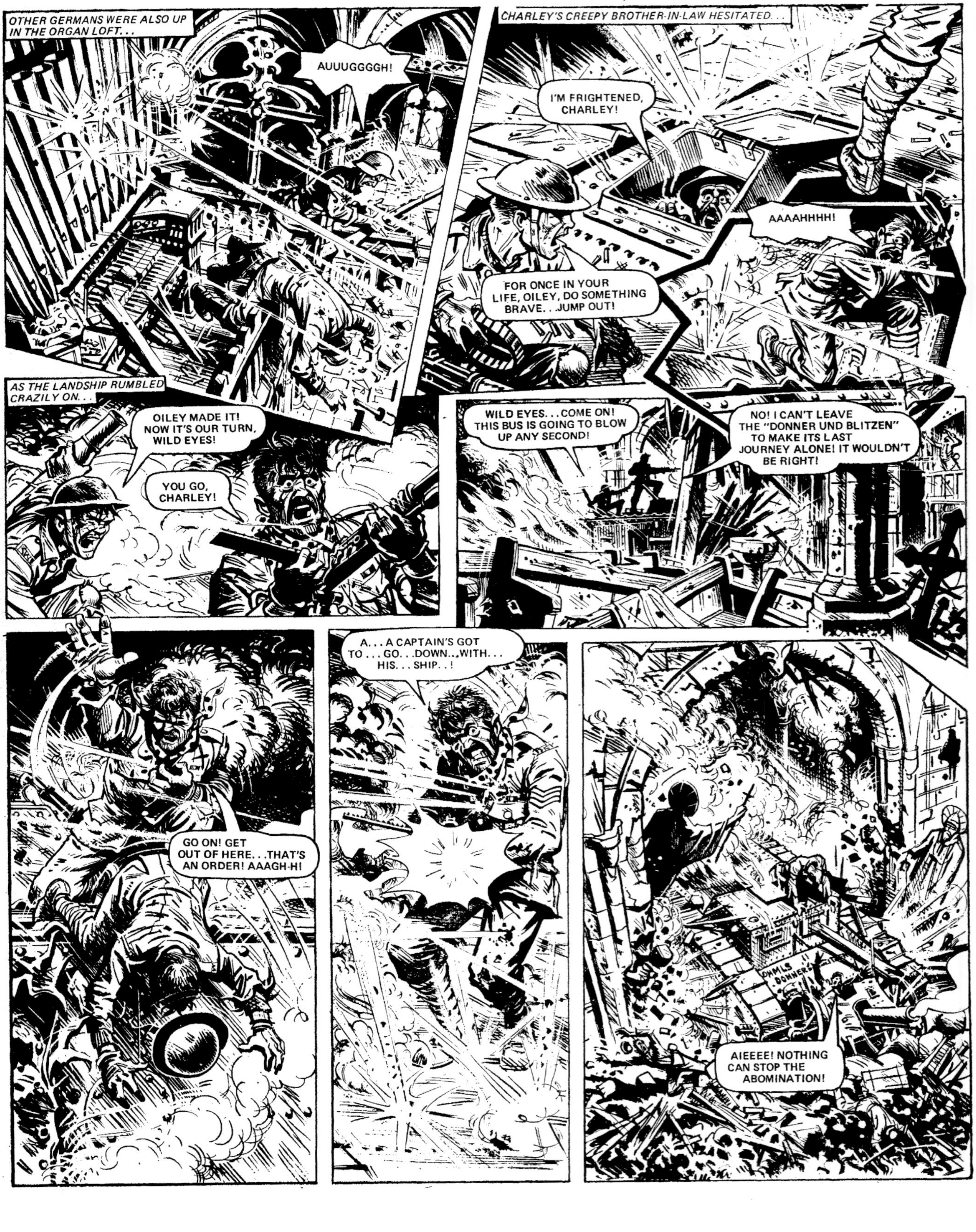

OTHER GERMANS WERE ALSO UP IN THE ORGAN LOFT...
AUUUGGGGH!
CHARLEY'S CREEPY BROTHER-IN-LAW HESITATED...
I'M FRIGHTENED, CHARLEY!
FOR ONCE IN YOUR LIFE, OILEY, DO SOMETHING BRAVE...JUMP OUT!
AAAAHHHH!
AS THE LANDSHIP RUMBLED CRAZILY ON...
OILEY MADE IT! NOW IT'S OUR TURN, WILD EYES!
YOU GO, CHARLEY!
WILD EYES...COME ON! THIS BUS IS GOING TO BLOW UP ANY SECOND!
NO! I CAN'T LEAVE THE "DONNER UND BLITZEN" TO MAKE ITS LAST JOURNEY ALONE! IT WOULDN'T BE RIGHT!
GO ON! GET OUT OF HERE...THAT'S AN ORDER! AAAGH-H!
A...A CAPTAIN'S GOT TO...GO...DOWN...WITH...HIS...SHIP..!
AIEEEE! NOTHING CAN STOP THE ABOMINATION!

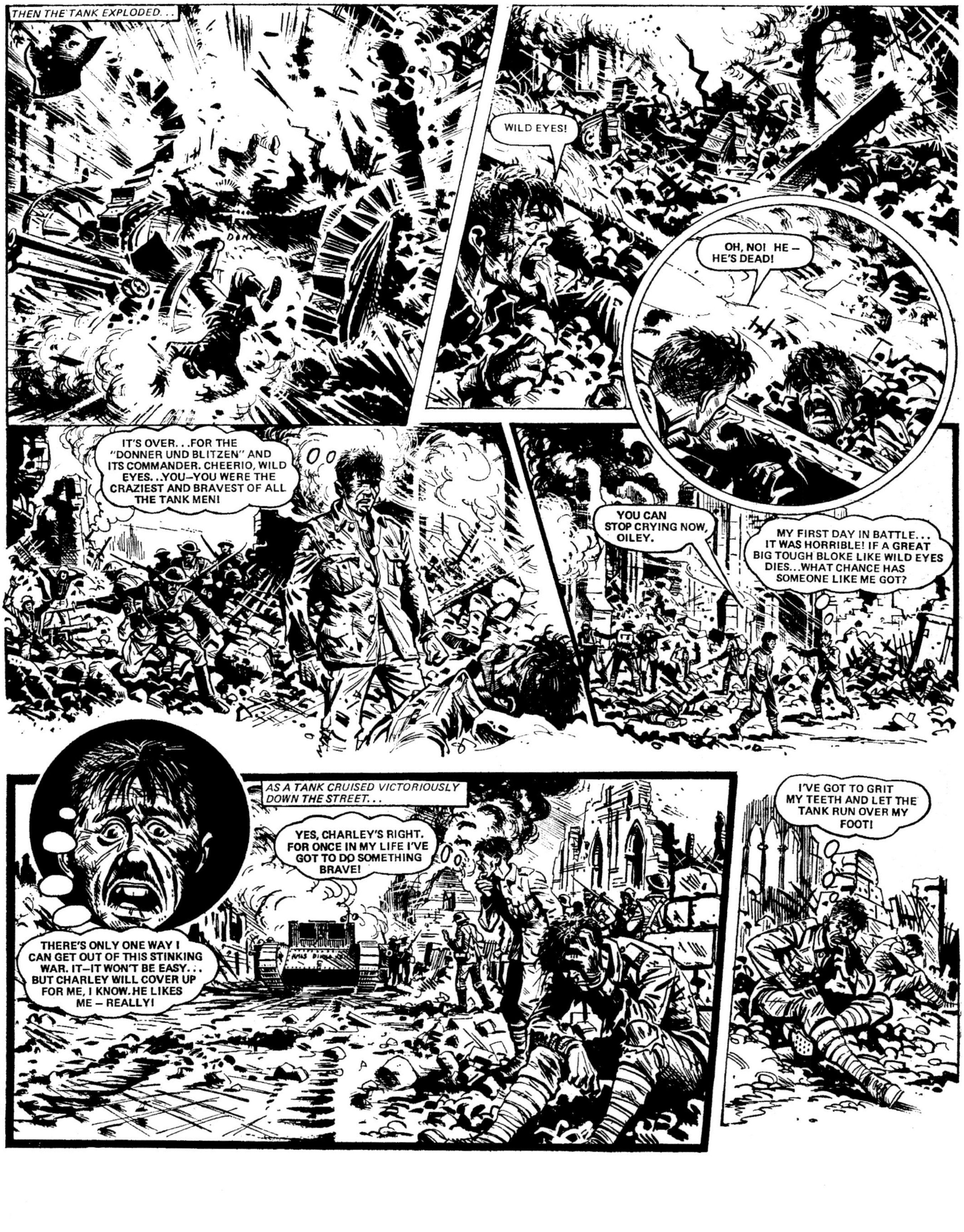
THEN THE TANK EXPLODED...
WILD EYES!
OH, NO! HE – HE'S DEAD!
IT'S OVER...FOR THE "DONNER UND BLITZEN" AND ITS COMMANDER. CHEERIO, WILD EYES...YOU–YOU WERE THE CRAZIEST AND BRAVEST OF ALL THE TANK MEN!
YOU CAN STOP CRYING NOW, OILEY.
MY FIRST DAY IN BATTLE... IT WAS HORRIBLE! IF A GREAT BIG TOUGH BLOKE LIKE WILD EYES DIES...WHAT CHANCE HAS SOMEONE LIKE ME GOT?
THERE'S ONLY ONE WAY I CAN GET OUT OF THIS STINKING WAR. IT–IT WON'T BE EASY... BUT CHARLEY WILL COVER UP FOR ME, I KNOW. HE LIKES ME – REALLY!
AS A TANK CRUISED VICTORIOUSLY DOWN THE STREET...
YES, CHARLEY'S RIGHT. FOR ONCE IN MY LIFE I'VE GOT TO DO SOMETHING BRAVE!
I'VE GOT TO GRIT MY TEETH AND LET THE TANK RUN OVER MY FOOT!

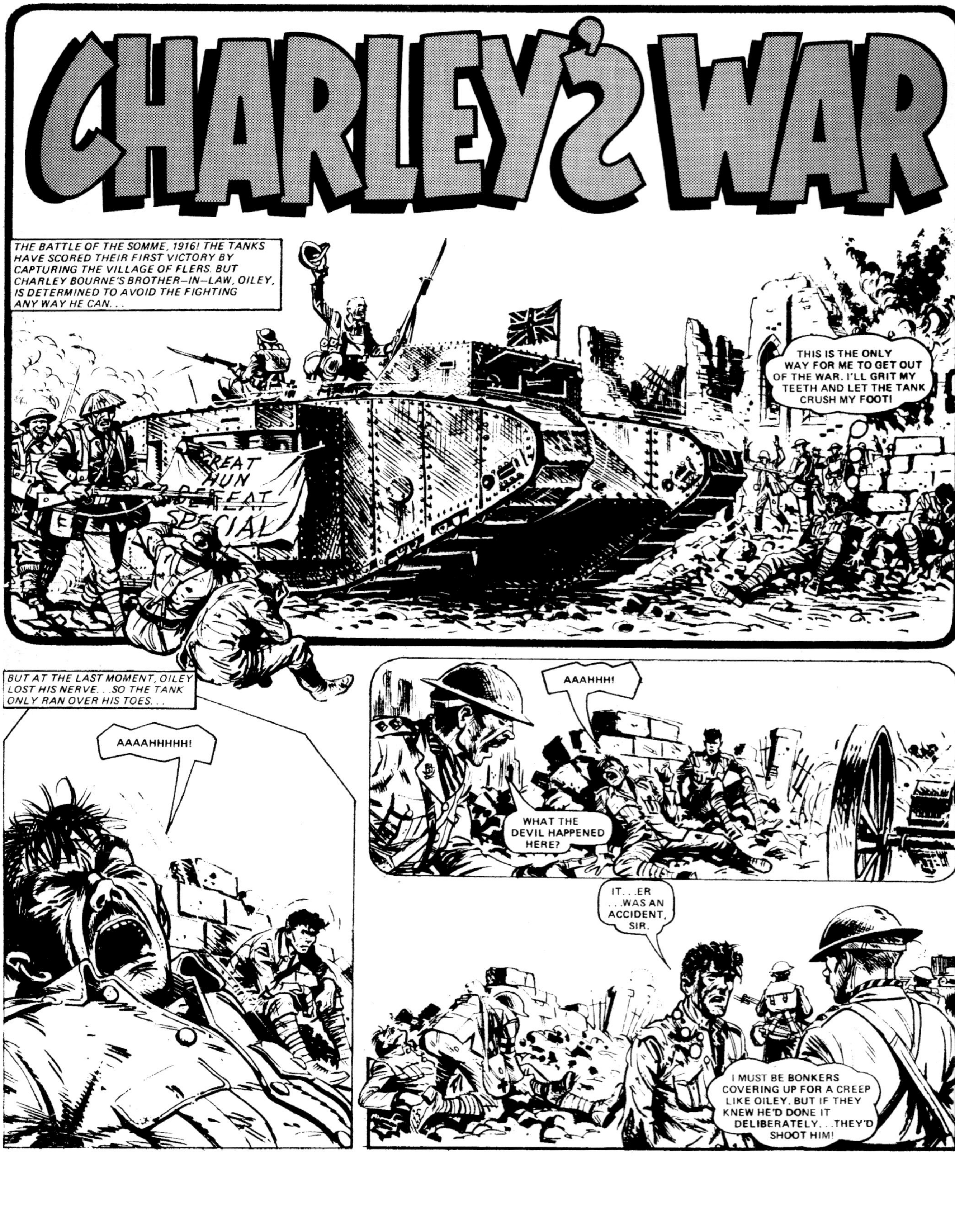
CHARLEY'S WAR
THE BATTLE OF THE SOMME, 1916! THE TANKS HAVE SCORED THEIR FIRST VICTORY BY CAPTURING THE VILLAGE OF FLERS. BUT CHARLEY BOURNE'S BROTHER-IN-LAW, OILEY, IS DETERMINED TO AVOID THE FIGHTING ANY WAY HE CAN...
GREAT HUN DEFEAT SPECIAL
THIS IS THE ONLY WAY FOR ME TO GET OUT OF THE WAR. I'LL GRIT MY TEETH AND LET THE TANK CRUSH MY FOOT!
BUT AT THE LAST MOMENT, OILEY LOST HIS NERVE...SO THE TANK ONLY RAN OVER HIS TOES...
AAAAHHHHH!
AAAHHH!
WHAT THE DEVIL HAPPENED HERE?
IT...ER ...WAS AN ACCIDENT, SIR.
I MUST BE BONKERS COVERING UP FOR A CREEP LIKE OILEY. BUT IF THEY KNEW HE'D DONE IT DELIBERATELY...THEY'D SHOOT HIM!

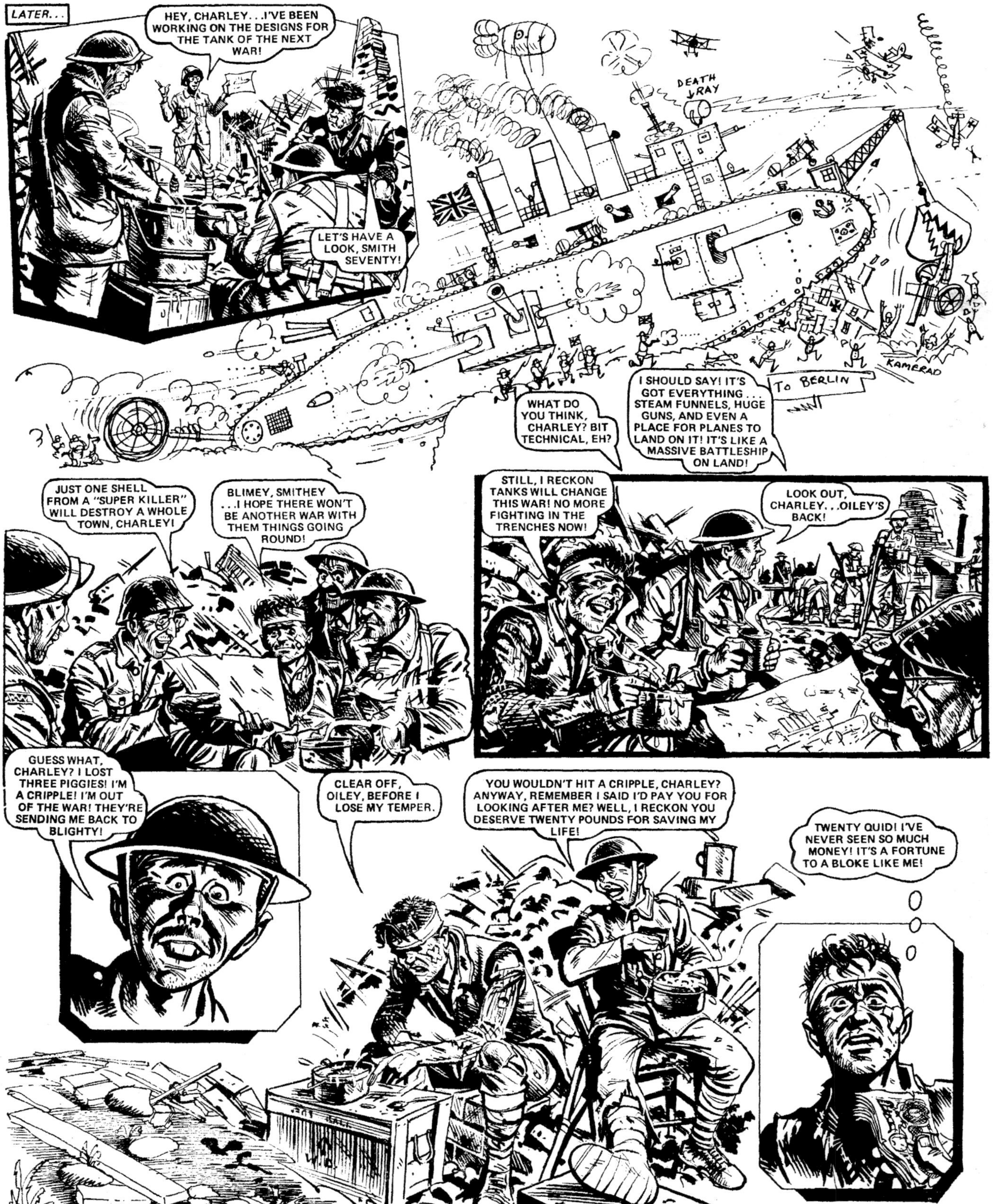
LATER...
HEY, CHARLEY...I'VE BEEN WORKING ON THE DESIGNS FOR THE TANK OF THE NEXT WAR!
LET'S HAVE A LOOK, SMITH SEVENTY!
DEATH RAY
KAMERAD
To BERLIN
WHAT DO YOU THINK, CHARLEY? BIT TECHNICAL, EH?
I SHOULD SAY! IT'S GOT EVERYTHING... STEAM FUNNELS, HUGE GUNS, AND EVEN A PLACE FOR PLANES TO LAND ON IT! IT'S LIKE A MASSIVE BATTLESHIP ON LAND!
JUST ONE SHELL FROM A "SUPER KILLER" WILL DESTROY A WHOLE TOWN, CHARLEY!
BLIMEY, SMITHEY ...I HOPE THERE WON'T BE ANOTHER WAR WITH THEM THINGS GOING ROUND!
STILL, I RECKON TANKS WILL CHANGE THIS WAR! NO MORE FIGHTING IN THE TRENCHES NOW!
LOOK OUT, CHARLEY...OILEY'S BACK!
GUESS WHAT, CHARLEY? I LOST THREE PIGGIES! I'M A CRIPPLE! I'M OUT OF THE WAR! THEY'RE SENDING ME BACK TO BLIGHTY!
CLEAR OFF, OILEY, BEFORE I LOSE MY TEMPER.
YOU WOULDN'T HIT A CRIPPLE, CHARLEY? ANYWAY, REMEMBER I SAID I'D PAY YOU FOR LOOKING AFTER ME? WELL, I RECKON YOU DESERVE TWENTY POUNDS FOR SAVING MY LIFE!
TWENTY QUID! I'VE NEVER SEEN SO MUCH MONEY! IT'S A FORTUNE TO A BLOKE LIKE ME!
COLQUHOUN

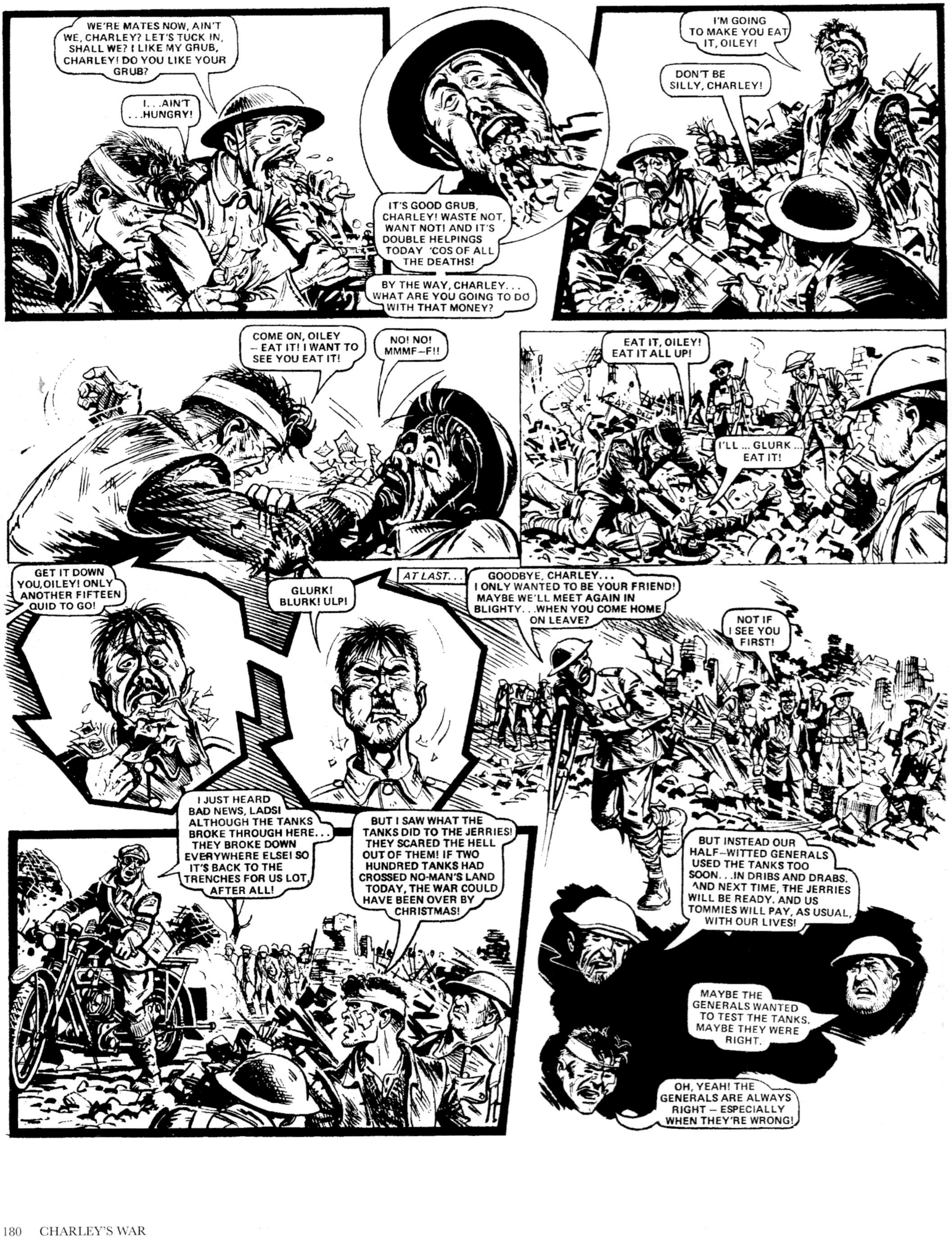
WE'RE MATES NOW, AIN'T WE, CHARLEY? LET'S TUCK IN, SHALL WE? I LIKE MY GRUB, CHARLEY! DO YOU LIKE YOUR GRUB?
I...AIN'T ...HUNGRY!
IT'S GOOD GRUB, CHARLEY! WASTE NOT, WANT NOT! AND IT'S DOUBLE HELPINGS TODAY 'COS OF ALL THE DEATHS!
BY THE WAY, CHARLEY... WHAT ARE YOU GOING TO DO WITH THAT MONEY?
I'M GOING TO MAKE YOU EAT IT, OILEY!
DON'T BE SILLY, CHARLEY!
COME ON, OILEY – EAT IT! I WANT TO SEE YOU EAT IT!
NO! NO! MMMF–F!!
EAT IT, OILEY! EAT IT ALL UP!
I'LL ... GLURK ... EAT IT!
GET IT DOWN YOU,OILEY! ONLY ANOTHER FIFTEEN QUID TO GO!
GLURK! BLURK! ULP!
AT LAST...
GOODBYE, CHARLEY... I ONLY WANTED TO BE YOUR FRIEND! MAYBE WE'LL MEET AGAIN IN BLIGHTY...WHEN YOU COME HOME ON LEAVE?
NOT IF I SEE YOU FIRST!
I JUST HEARD BAD NEWS, LADS! ALTHOUGH THE TANKS BROKE THROUGH HERE... THEY BROKE DOWN EVERYWHERE ELSE! SO IT'S BACK TO THE TRENCHES FOR US LOT, AFTER ALL!
BUT I SAW WHAT THE TANKS DID TO THE JERRIES! THEY SCARED THE HELL OUT OF THEM! IF TWO HUNDRED TANKS HAD CROSSED NO-MAN'S LAND TODAY, THE WAR COULD HAVE BEEN OVER BY CHRISTMAS!
BUT INSTEAD OUR HALF-WITTED GENERALS USED THE TANKS TOO SOON...IN DRIBS AND DRABS. AND NEXT TIME, THE JERRIES WILL BE READY. AND US TOMMIES WILL PAY, AS USUAL, WITH OUR LIVES!
MAYBE THE GENERALS WANTED TO TEST THE TANKS. MAYBE THEY WERE RIGHT.
OH, YEAH! THE GENERALS ARE ALWAYS RIGHT – ESPECIALLY WHEN THEY'RE WRONG!

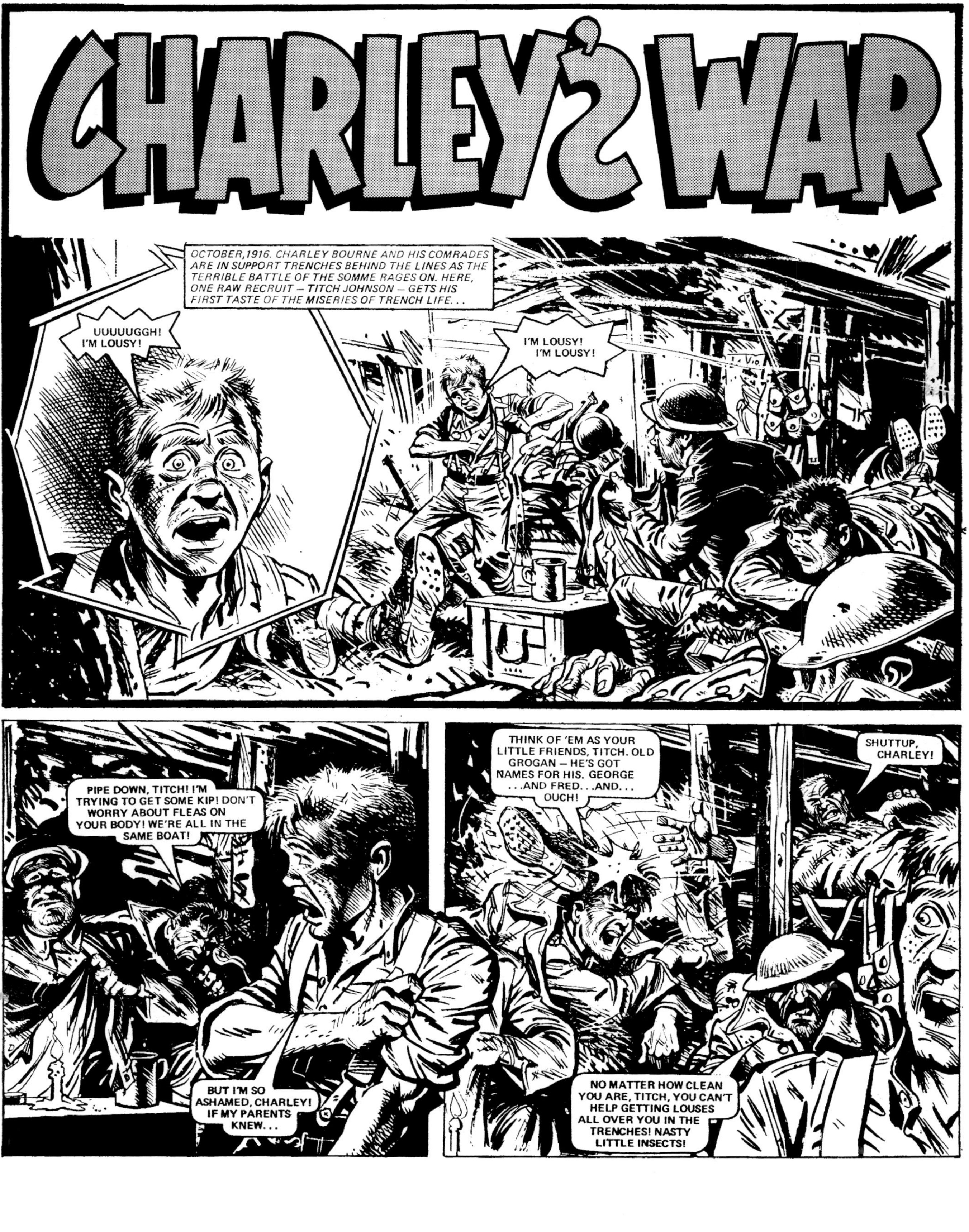
CHARLEY'S WAR
OCTOBER, 1916. CHARLEY BOURNE AND HIS COMRADES ARE IN SUPPORT TRENCHES BEHIND THE LINES AS THE TERRIBLE BATTLE OF THE SOMME RAGES ON. HERE, ONE RAW RECRUIT — TITCH JOHNSON — GETS HIS FIRST TASTE OF THE MISERIES OF TRENCH LIFE. . .
UUUUUGGH! I'M LOUSY!
I'M LOUSY! I'M LOUSY!
PIPE DOWN, TITCH! I'M TRYING TO GET SOME KIP! DON'T WORRY ABOUT FLEAS ON YOUR BODY! WE'RE ALL IN THE SAME BOAT!
BUT I'M SO ASHAMED, CHARLEY! IF MY PARENTS KNEW. . .
THINK OF 'EM AS YOUR LITTLE FRIENDS, TITCH. OLD GROGAN — HE'S GOT NAMES FOR HIS. GEORGE . . .AND FRED. . .AND. . . OUCH!
SHUTTUP, CHARLEY!
NO MATTER HOW CLEAN YOU ARE, TITCH, YOU CAN'T HELP GETTING LOUSES ALL OVER YOU IN THE TRENCHES! NASTY LITTLE INSECTS!

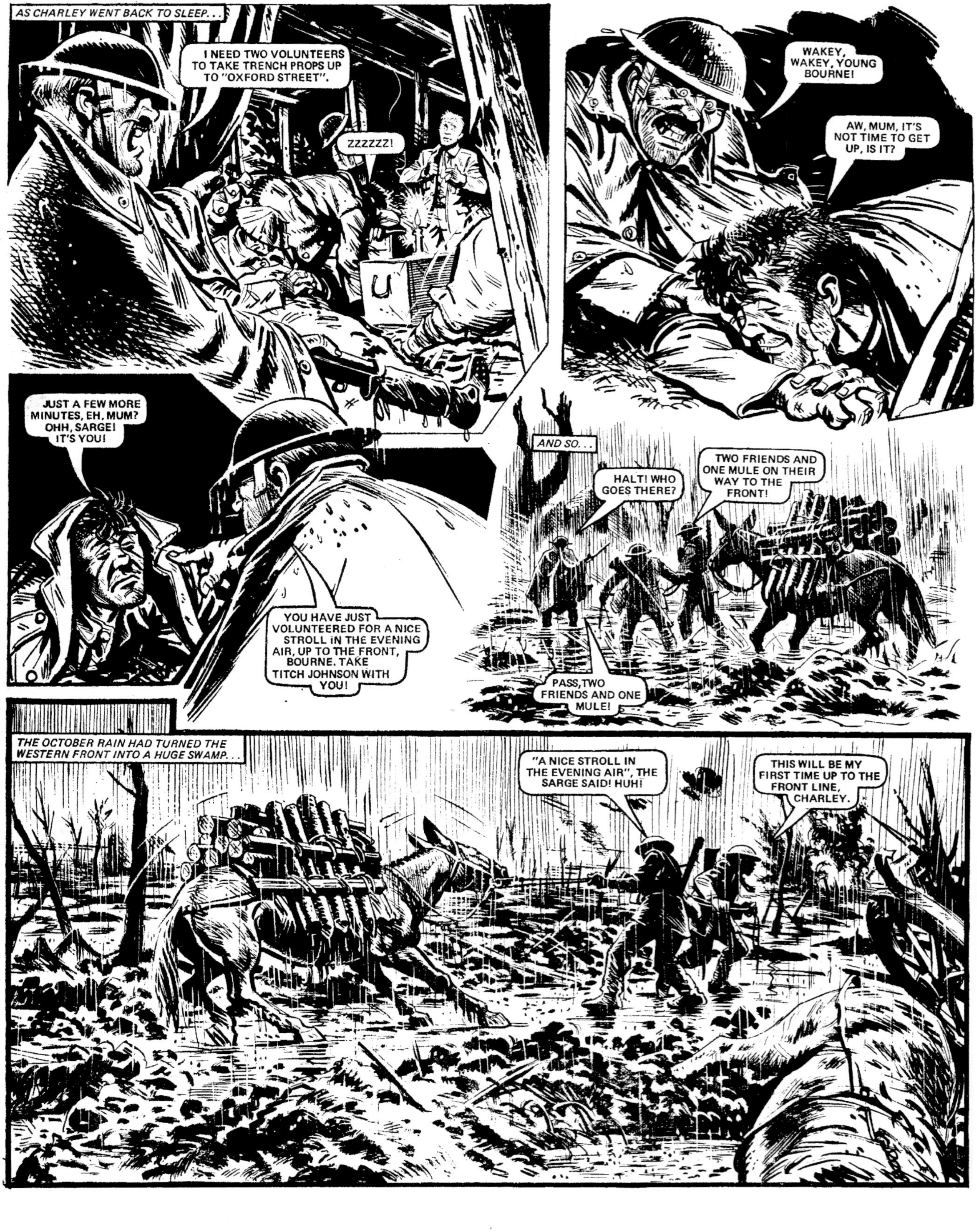
AS CHARLEY WENT BACK TO SLEEP. . .
I NEED TWO VOLUNTEERS TO TAKE TRENCH PROPS UP TO "OXFORD STREET".
ZZZZZZ!
WAKEY, WAKEY, YOUNG BOURNE!
AW, MUM, IT'S NOT TIME TO GET UP, IS IT?
JUST A FEW MORE MINUTES, EH, MUM? OHH, SARGE! IT'S YOU!
YOU HAVE JUST VOLUNTEERED FOR A NICE STROLL IN THE EVENING AIR, UP TO THE FRONT, BOURNE. TAKE TITCH JOHNSON WITH YOU!
AND SO. . .
HALT! WHO GOES THERE?
TWO FRIENDS AND ONE MULE ON THEIR WAY TO THE FRONT!
PASS, TWO FRIENDS AND ONE MULE!
THE OCTOBER RAIN HAD TURNED THE WESTERN FRONT INTO A HUGE SWAMP. . .
"A NICE STROLL IN THE EVENING AIR", THE SARGE SAID! HUH!
THIS WILL BE MY FIRST TIME UP TO THE FRONT LINE, CHARLEY.

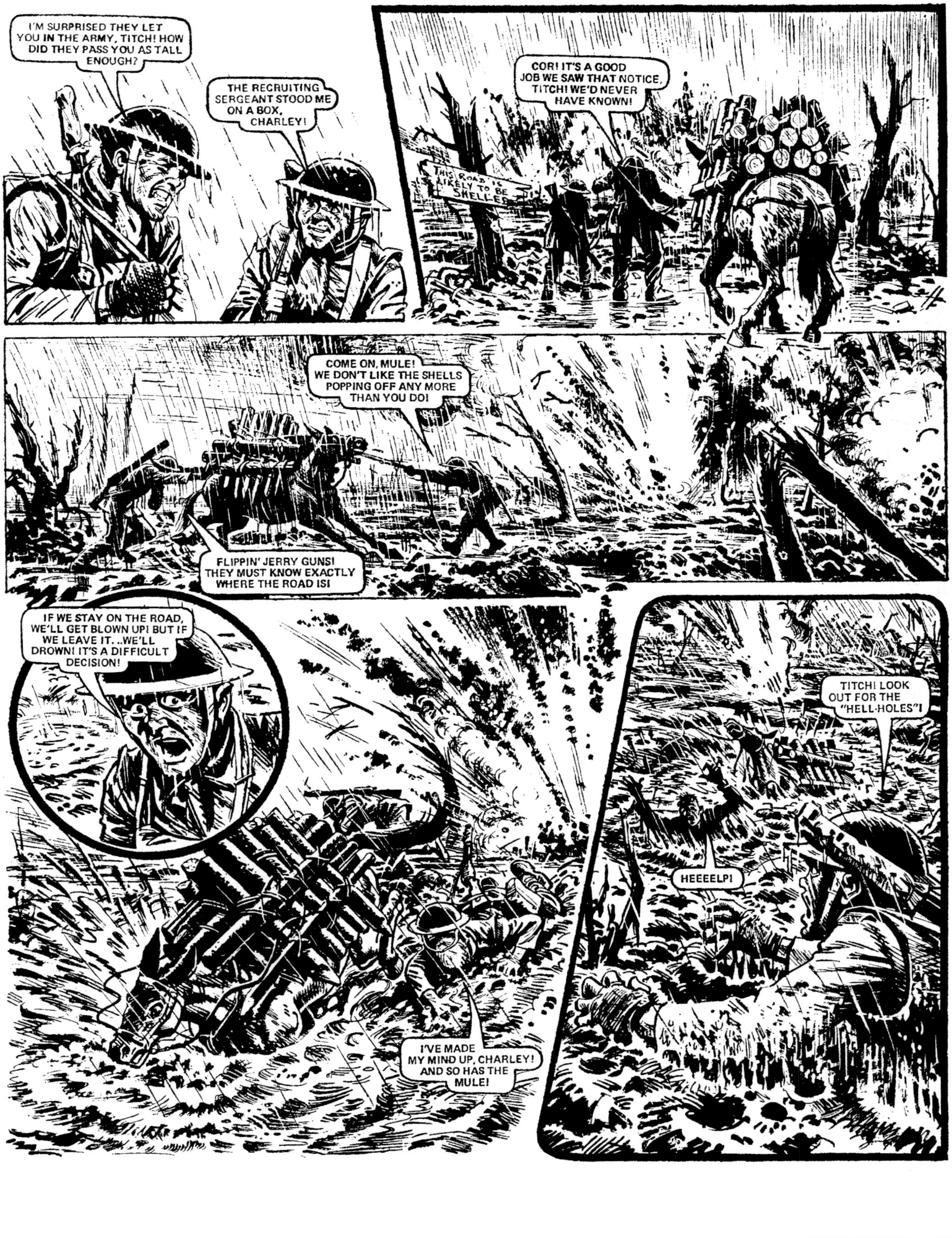
I'M SURPRISED THEY LET YOU IN THE ARMY, TITCH! HOW DID THEY PASS YOU AS TALL ENOUGH?
THE RECRUITING SERGEANT STOOD ME ON A BOX, CHARLEY!
CORI IT'S A GOOD JOB WE SAW THAT NOTICE, TITCH! WE'D NEVER HAVE KNOWN!
THIS ROAD IS LIKELY TO BE SHELLED
COME ON, MULE! WE DON'T LIKE THE SHELLS POPPING OFF ANY MORE THAN YOU DO!
FLIPPIN' JERRY GUNS! THEY MUST KNOW EXACTLY WHERE THE ROAD IS!
IF WE STAY ON THE ROAD, WE'LL GET BLOWN UP! BUT IF WE LEAVE IT. ..WE'LL DROWN! IT'S A DIFFICULT DECISION!
I'VE MADE MY MIND UP, CHARLEY! AND SO HAS THE MULE!
TITCH! LOOK OUT FOR THE "HELL-HOLES"!
HEEEELP!

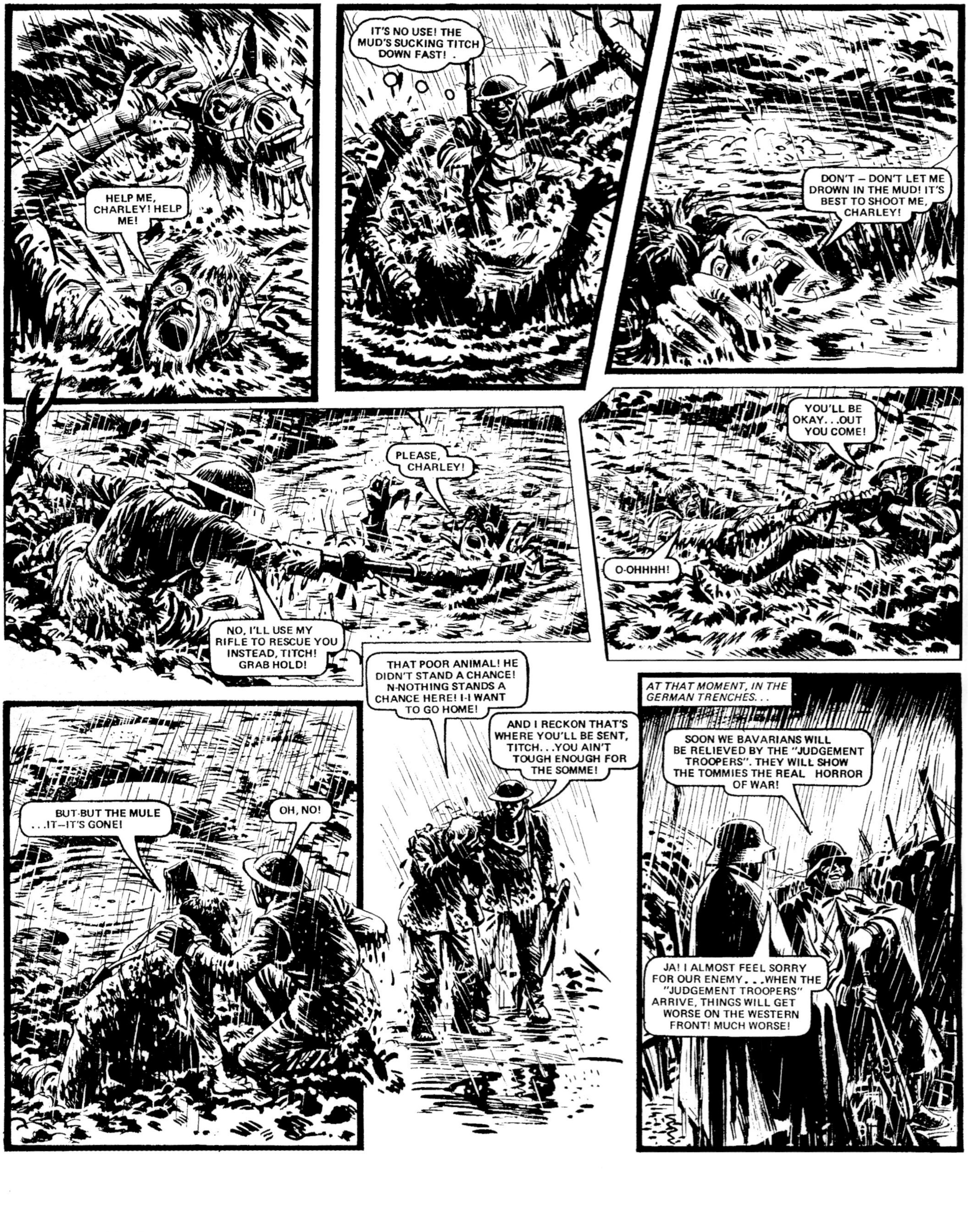
HELP ME, CHARLEY! HELP ME!
IT'S NO USE! THE MUD'S SUCKING TITCH DOWN FAST!
DON'T – DON'T LET ME DROWN IN THE MUD! IT'S BEST TO SHOOT ME, CHARLEY!
PLEASE, CHARLEY!
NO, I'LL USE MY RIFLE TO RESCUE YOU INSTEAD, TITCH! GRAB HOLD!
YOU'LL BE OKAY. . .OUT YOU COME!
O-OHHHH!
BUT-BUT THE MULE . . .IT–IT'S GONE!
OH, NO!
THAT POOR ANIMAL! HE DIDN'T STAND A CHANCE! N-NOTHING STANDS A CHANCE HERE! I-I WANT TO GO HOME!
AND I RECKON THAT'S WHERE YOU'LL BE SENT, TITCH. . .YOU AIN'T TOUGH ENOUGH FOR THE SOMME!
AT THAT MOMENT, IN THE GERMAN TRENCHES. . .
SOON WE BAVARIANS WILL BE RELIEVED BY THE "JUDGEMENT TROOPERS". THEY WILL SHOW THE TOMMIES THE REAL HORROR OF WAR!
JA! I ALMOST FEEL SORRY FOR OUR ENEMY. . .WHEN THE "JUDGEMENT TROOPERS" ARRIVE, THINGS WILL GET WORSE ON THE WESTERN FRONT! MUCH WORSE!

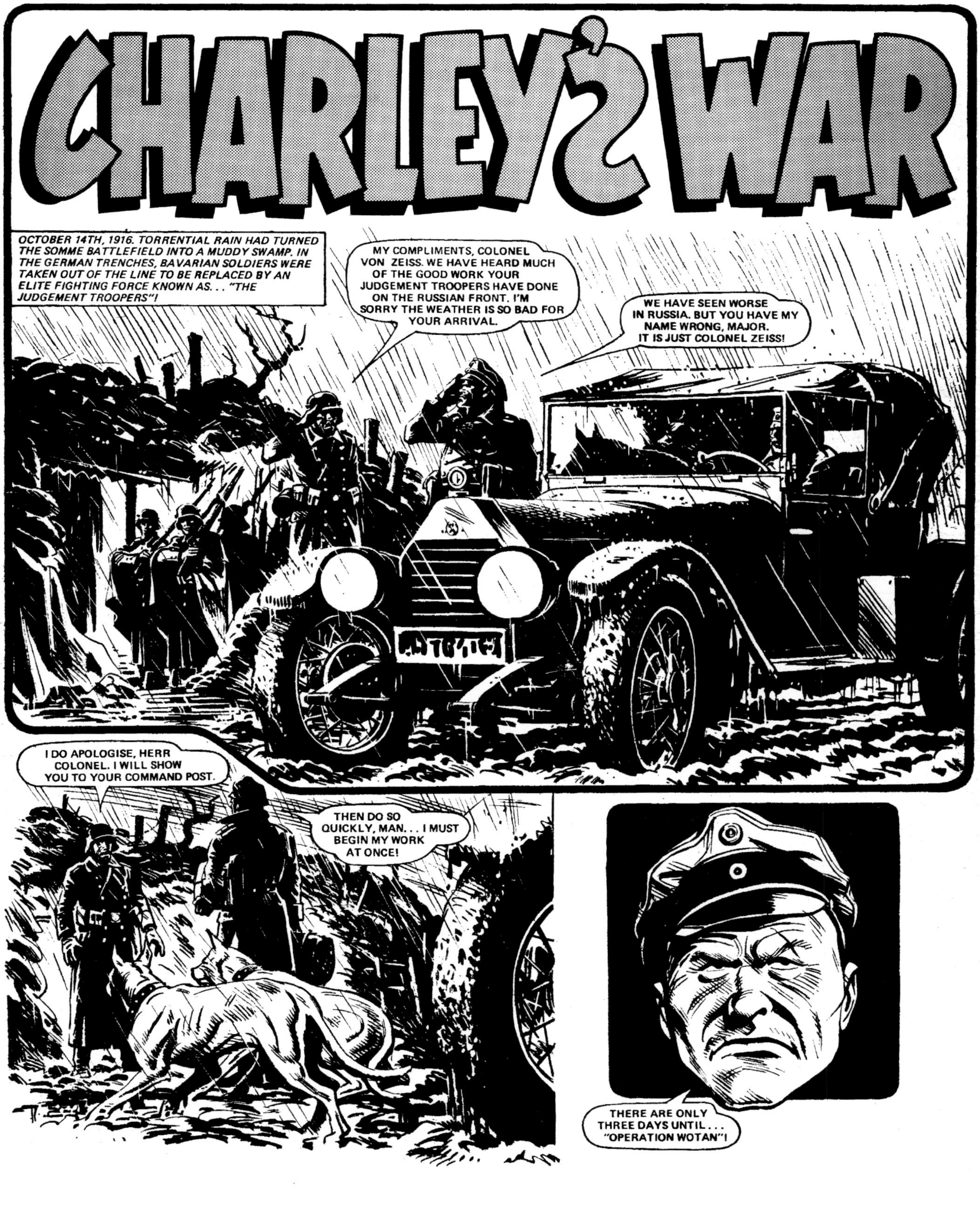
CHARLEY'S WAR
OCTOBER 14TH, 1916. TORRENTIAL RAIN HAD TURNED THE SOMME BATTLEFIELD INTO A MUDDY SWAMP. IN THE GERMAN TRENCHES, BAVARIAN SOLDIERS WERE TAKEN OUT OF THE LINE TO BE REPLACED BY AN ELITE FIGHTING FORCE KNOWN AS... "THE JUDGEMENT TROOPERS"!
MY COMPLIMENTS, COLONEL VON ZEISS. WE HAVE HEARD MUCH OF THE GOOD WORK YOUR JUDGEMENT TROOPERS HAVE DONE ON THE RUSSIAN FRONT. I'M SORRY THE WEATHER IS SO BAD FOR YOUR ARRIVAL.
WE HAVE SEEN WORSE IN RUSSIA. BUT YOU HAVE MY NAME WRONG, MAJOR. IT IS JUST COLONEL ZEISS!
I DO APOLOGISE, HERR COLONEL. I WILL SHOW YOU TO YOUR COMMAND POST.
THEN DO SO QUICKLY, MAN... I MUST BEGIN MY WORK AT ONCE!
THERE ARE ONLY THREE DAYS UNTIL... "OPERATION WOTAN"!

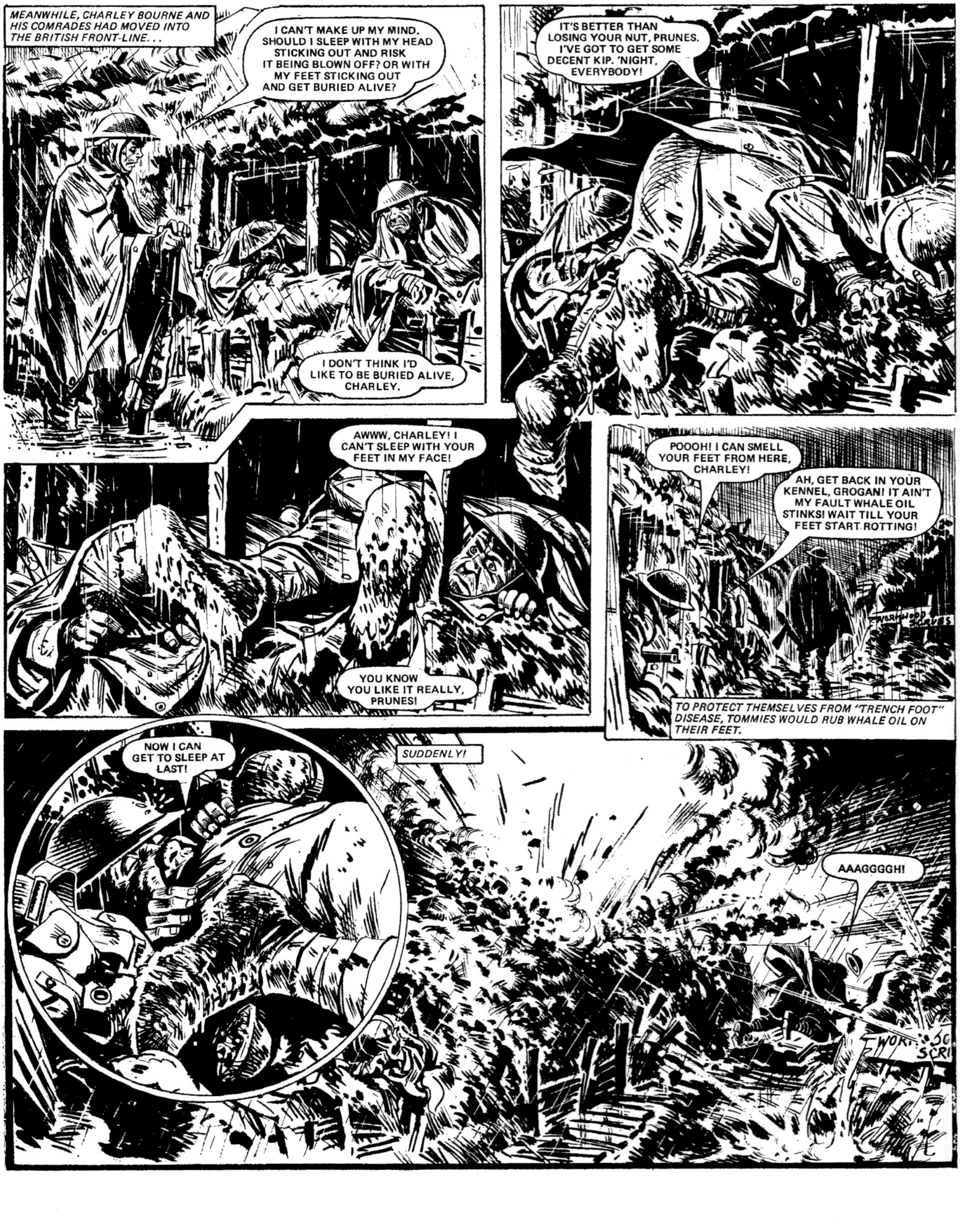

MEANWHILE, CHARLEY BOURNE AND HIS COMRADES HAD MOVED INTO THE BRITISH FRONT-LINE. . .
I CAN'T MAKE UP MY MIND. SHOULD I SLEEP WITH MY HEAD STICKING OUT AND RISK IT BEING BLOWN OFF? OR WITH MY FEET STICKING OUT AND GET BURIED ALIVE?
I DON'T THINK I'D LIKE TO BE BURIED ALIVE, CHARLEY.
IT'S BETTER THAN LOSING YOUR NUT, PRUNES. I'VE GOT TO GET SOME DECENT KIP. 'NIGHT, EVERYBODY!
AWWW, CHARLEY! I CAN'T SLEEP WITH YOUR FEET IN MY FACE!
YOU KNOW YOU LIKE IT REALLY, PRUNES!
POOOH! I CAN SMELL YOUR FEET FROM HERE, CHARLEY!
AH, GET BACK IN YOUR KENNEL, GROGAN! IT AIN'T MY FAULT WHALE OIL STINKS! WAIT TILL YOUR FEET START ROTTING!
TO PROTECT THEMSELVES FROM "TRENCH FOOT" DISEASE, TOMMIES WOULD RUB WHALE OIL ON THEIR FEET.
NOW I CAN GET TO SLEEP AT LAST!
SUDDENLY!
AAAGGGGH!

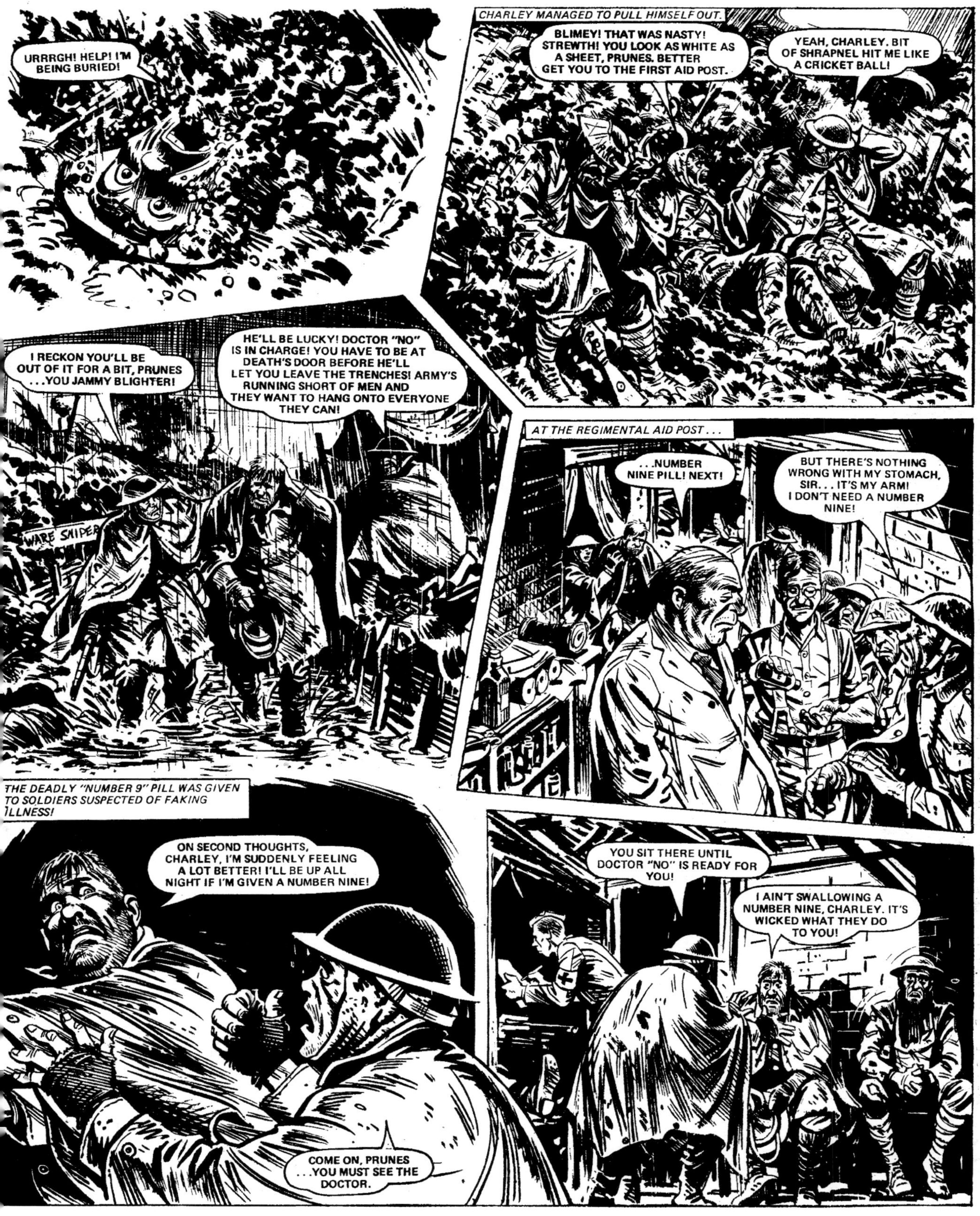
URRRGH! HELP! I'M BEING BURIED!
CHARLEY MANAGED TO PULL HIMSELF OUT.
BLIMEY! THAT WAS NASTY! STREWTH! YOU LOOK AS WHITE AS A SHEET, PRUNES. BETTER GET YOU TO THE FIRST AID POST.
YEAH, CHARLEY. BIT OF SHRAPNEL HIT ME LIKE A CRICKET BALL!
I RECKON YOU'LL BE OUT OF IT FOR A BIT, PRUNES . . . YOU JAMMY BLIGHTER!
HE'LL BE LUCKY! DOCTOR "NO" IS IN CHARGE! YOU HAVE TO BE AT DEATH'S DOOR BEFORE HE'LL LET YOU LEAVE THE TRENCHES! ARMY'S RUNNING SHORT OF MEN AND THEY WANT TO HANG ONTO EVERYONE THEY CAN!
WARE SNIPER
AT THE REGIMENTAL AID POST . . .
. . . NUMBER NINE PILL! NEXT!
BUT THERE'S NOTHING WRONG WITH MY STOMACH, SIR . . . IT'S MY ARM! I DON'T NEED A NUMBER NINE!
THE DEADLY "NUMBER 9" PILL WAS GIVEN TO SOLDIERS SUSPECTED OF FAKING ILLNESS!
ON SECOND THOUGHTS, CHARLEY, I'M SUDDENLY FEELING A LOT BETTER! I'LL BE UP ALL NIGHT IF I'M GIVEN A NUMBER NINE!
COME ON, PRUNES . . . YOU MUST SEE THE DOCTOR.
YOU SIT THERE UNTIL DOCTOR "NO" IS READY FOR YOU!
I AIN'T SWALLOWING A NUMBER NINE, CHARLEY. IT'S WICKED WHAT THEY DO TO YOU!

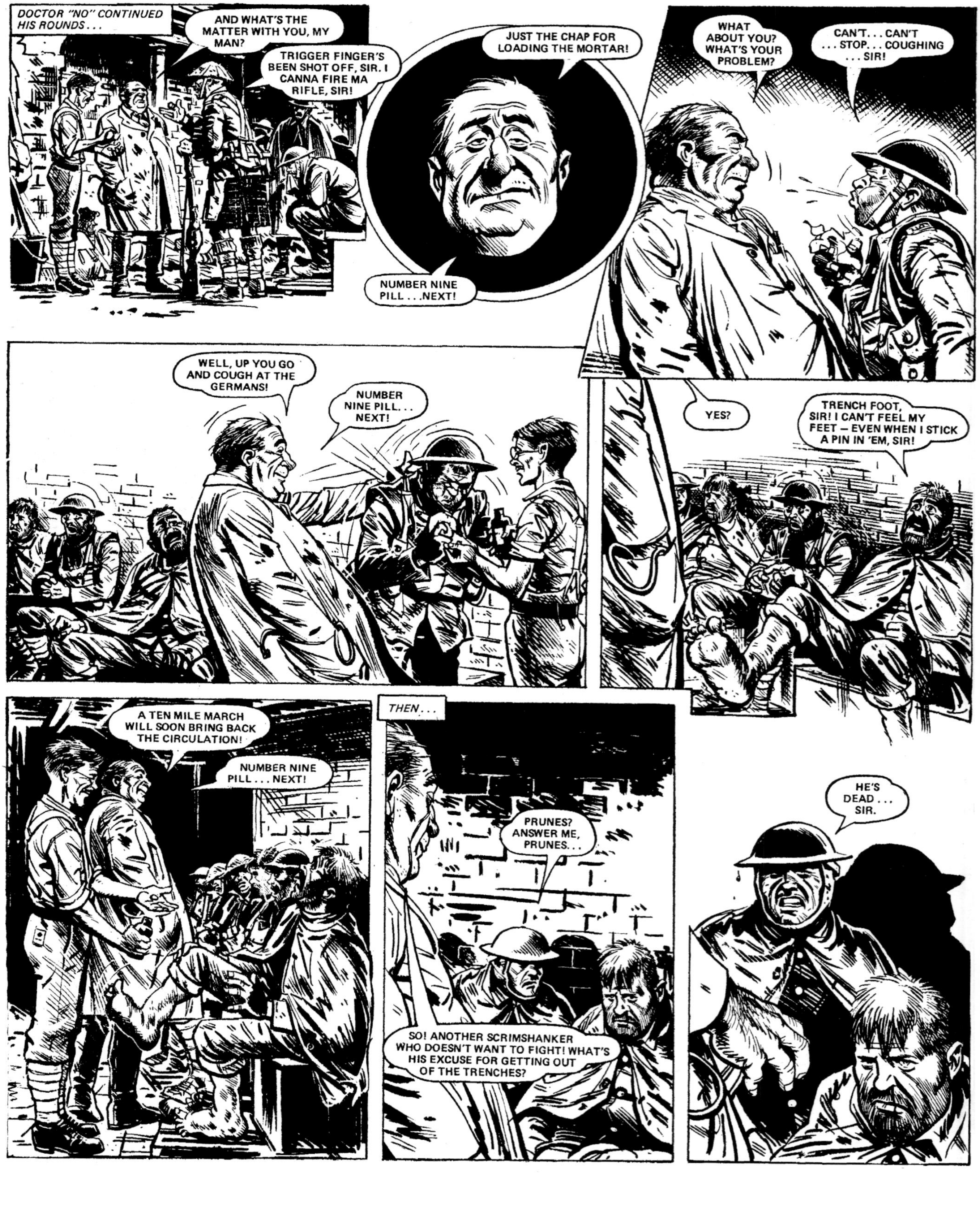
DOCTOR "NO" CONTINUED HIS ROUNDS . . .
AND WHAT'S THE MATTER WITH YOU, MY MAN?
TRIGGER FINGER'S BEEN SHOT OFF, SIR. I CANNA FIRE MA RIFLE, SIR!
JUST THE CHAP FOR LOADING THE MORTAR!
NUMBER NINE PILL . . . NEXT!
WHAT ABOUT YOU? WHAT'S YOUR PROBLEM?
CAN'T . . . CAN'T . . . STOP . . . COUGHING . . . SIR!
WELL, UP YOU GO AND COUGH AT THE GERMANS!
NUMBER NINE PILL . . . NEXT!
YES?
TRENCH FOOT, SIR! I CAN'T FEEL MY FEET – EVEN WHEN I STICK A PIN IN 'EM, SIR!
A TEN MILE MARCH WILL SOON BRING BACK THE CIRCULATION!
NUMBER NINE PILL . . . NEXT!
THEN . . .
SO! ANOTHER SCRIMSHANKER WHO DOESN'T WANT TO FIGHT! WHAT'S HIS EXCUSE FOR GETTING OUT OF THE TRENCHES?
PRUNES? ANSWER ME, PRUNES. . .
HE'S DEAD . . . SIR.

CHARLEY'S WAR

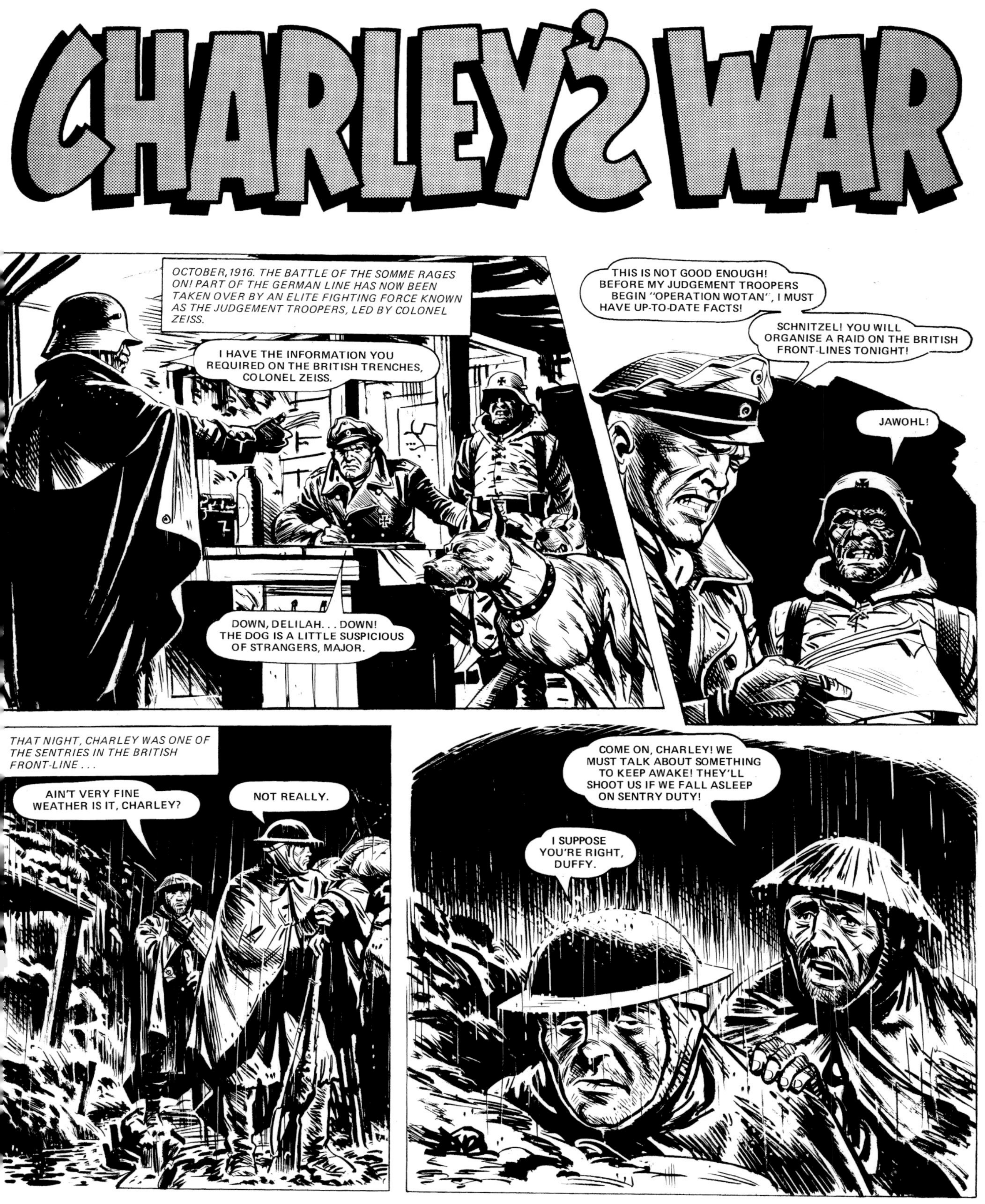

OCTOBER, 1916. THE BATTLE OF THE SOMME RAGES ON! PART OF THE GERMAN LINE HAS NOW BEEN TAKEN OVER BY AN ELITE FIGHTING FORCE KNOWN AS THE JUDGEMENT TROOPERS, LED BY COLONEL ZEISS.
I HAVE THE INFORMATION YOU REQUIRED ON THE BRITISH TRENCHES, COLONEL ZEISS.
DOWN, DELILAH. . . DOWN! THE DOG IS A LITTLE SUSPICIOUS OF STRANGERS, MAJOR.
THIS IS NOT GOOD ENOUGH! BEFORE MY JUDGEMENT TROOPERS BEGIN "OPERATION WOTAN", I MUST HAVE UP-TO-DATE FACTS!
SCHNITZEL! YOU WILL ORGANISE A RAID ON THE BRITISH FRONT-LINES TONIGHT!
JAWOHL!
THAT NIGHT, CHARLEY WAS ONE OF THE SENTRIES IN THE BRITISH FRONT-LINE . . .
AIN'T VERY FINE WEATHER IS IT, CHARLEY?
NOT REALLY.
COME ON, CHARLEY! WE MUST TALK ABOUT SOMETHING TO KEEP AWAKE! THEY'LL SHOOT US IF WE FALL ASLEEP ON SENTRY DUTY!
I SUPPOSE YOU'RE RIGHT, DUFFY.

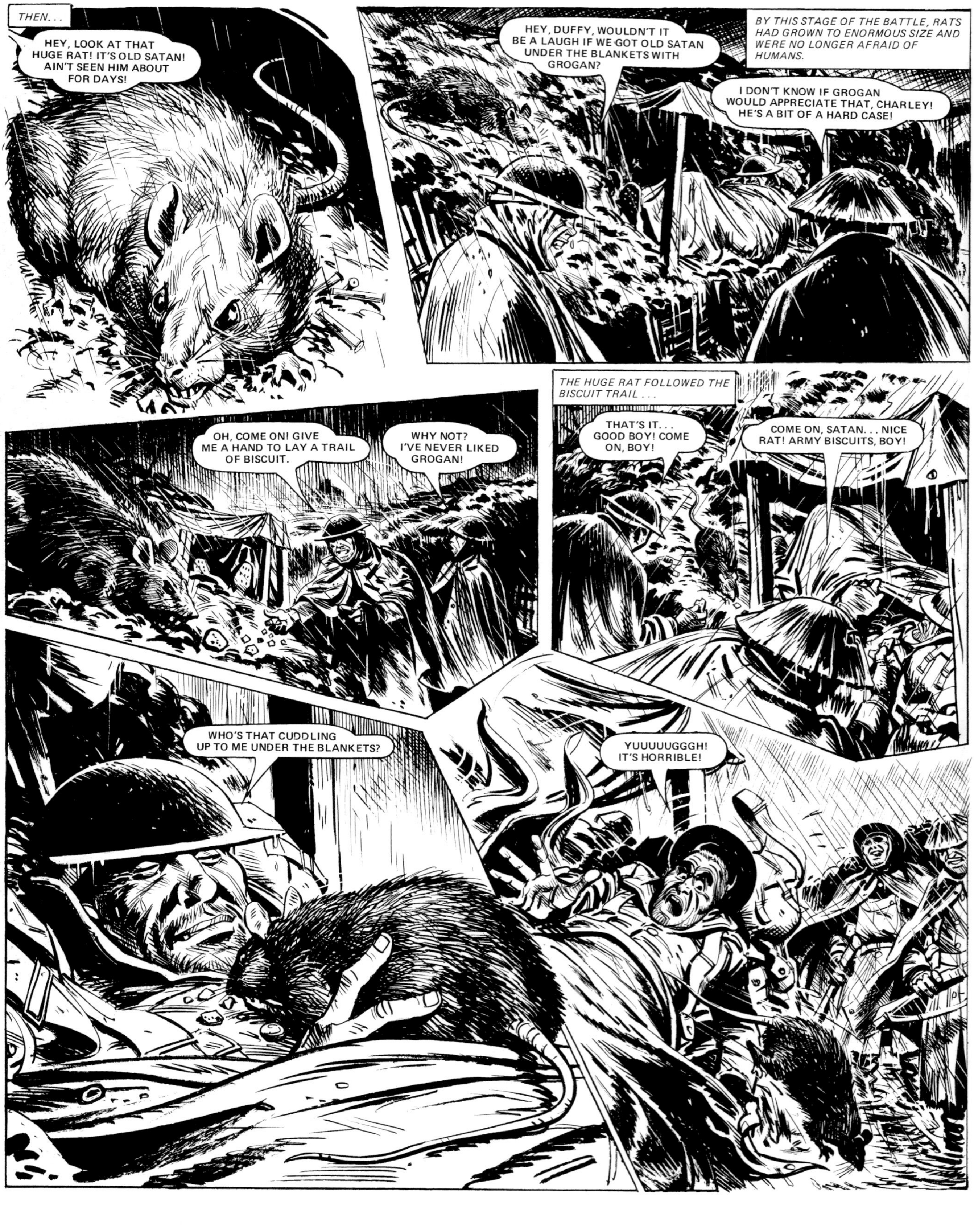
THEN...
HEY, LOOK AT THAT HUGE RAT! IT'S OLD SATAN! AIN'T SEEN HIM ABOUT FOR DAYS!
HEY, DUFFY, WOULDN'T IT BE A LAUGH IF WE GOT OLD SATAN UNDER THE BLANKETS WITH GROGAN?
BY THIS STAGE OF THE BATTLE, RATS HAD GROWN TO ENORMOUS SIZE AND WERE NO LONGER AFRAID OF HUMANS.
I DON'T KNOW IF GROGAN WOULD APPRECIATE THAT, CHARLEY! HE'S A BIT OF A HARD CASE!
OH, COME ON! GIVE ME A HAND TO LAY A TRAIL OF BISCUIT.
WHY NOT? I'VE NEVER LIKED GROGAN!
THE HUGE RAT FOLLOWED THE BISCUIT TRAIL...
THAT'S IT... GOOD BOY! COME ON, BOY!
COME ON, SATAN... NICE RAT! ARMY BISCUITS, BOY!
WHO'S THAT CUDDLING UP TO ME UNDER THE BLANKETS?
YUUUUUGGGH! IT'S HORRIBLE!

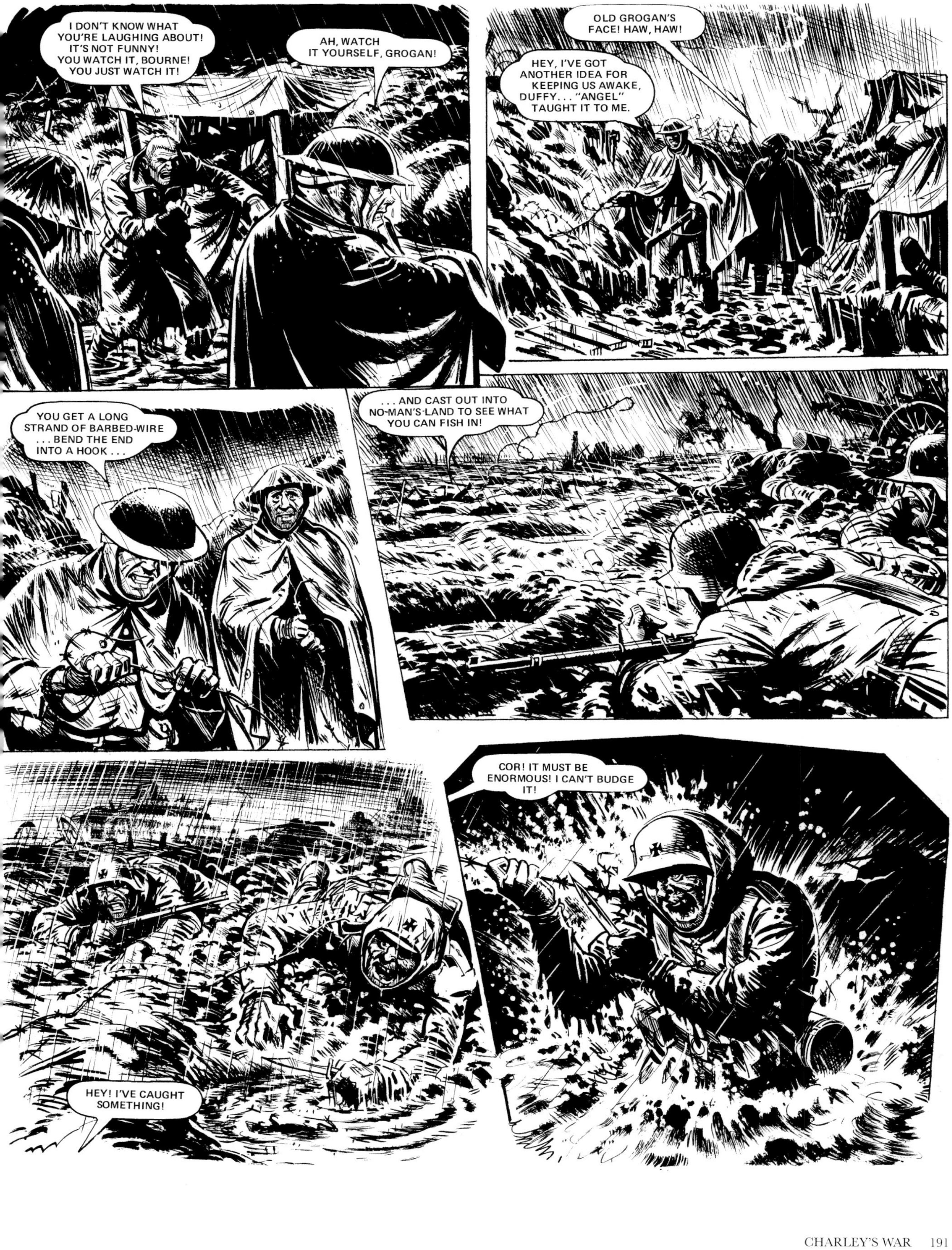
I DON'T KNOW WHAT YOU'RE LAUGHING ABOUT! IT'S NOT FUNNY! YOU WATCH IT, BOURNE! YOU JUST WATCH IT!
AH, WATCH IT YOURSELF, GROGAN!
OLD GROGAN'S FACE! HAW, HAW!
HEY, I'VE GOT ANOTHER IDEA FOR KEEPING US AWAKE, DUFFY... "ANGEL" TAUGHT IT TO ME.
YOU GET A LONG STRAND OF BARBED-WIRE ... BEND THE END INTO A HOOK ...
... AND CAST OUT INTO NO-MAN'S-LAND TO SEE WHAT YOU CAN FISH IN!
HEY! I'VE CAUGHT SOMETHING!
COR! IT MUST BE ENORMOUS! I CAN'T BUDGE IT!

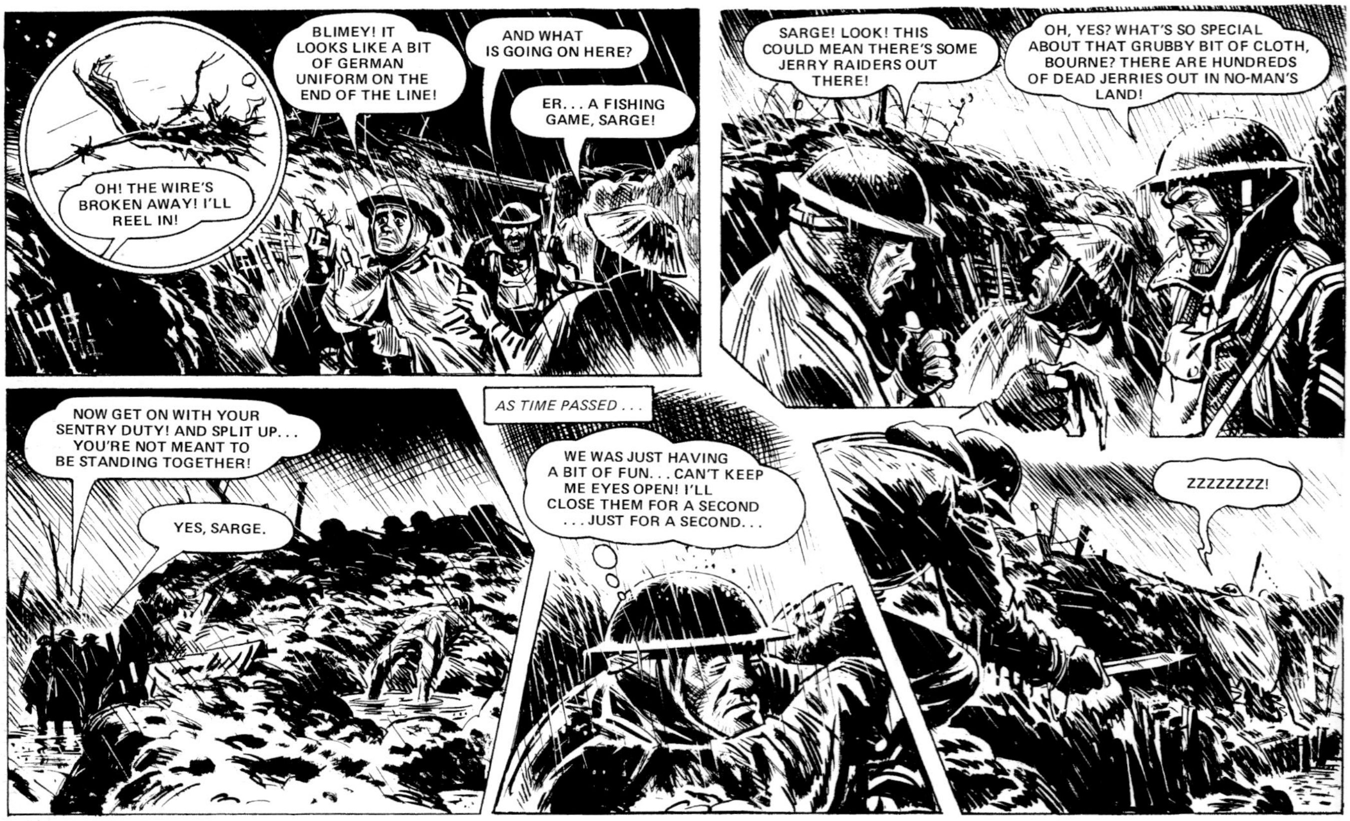
OH! THE WIRE'S BROKEN AWAY! I'LL REEL IN!
BLIMEY! IT LOOKS LIKE A BIT OF GERMAN UNIFORM ON THE END OF THE LINE!
AND WHAT IS GOING ON HERE?
ER... A FISHING GAME, SARGE!
SARGE! LOOK! THIS COULD MEAN THERE'S SOME JERRY RAIDERS OUT THERE!
OH, YES? WHAT'S SO SPECIAL ABOUT THAT GRUBBY BIT OF CLOTH, BOURNE? THERE ARE HUNDREDS OF DEAD JERRIES OUT IN NO-MAN'S LAND!
NOW GET ON WITH YOUR SENTRY DUTY! AND SPLIT UP... YOU'RE NOT MEANT TO BE STANDING TOGETHER!
YES, SARGE.
AS TIME PASSED...
WE WAS JUST HAVING A BIT OF FUN... CAN'T KEEP ME EYES OPEN! I'LL CLOSE THEM FOR A SECOND ... JUST FOR A SECOND...
ZZZZZZZZ!

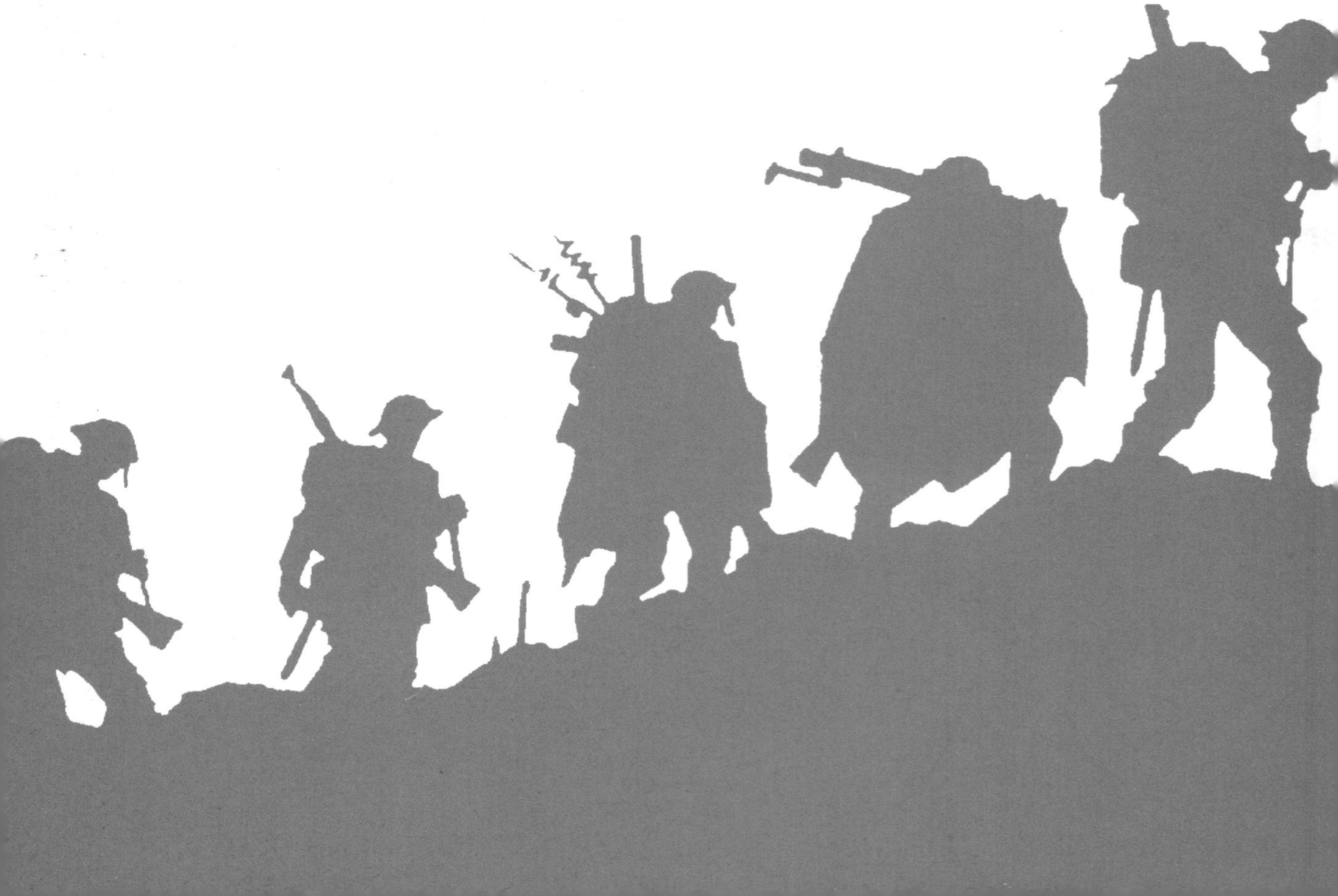

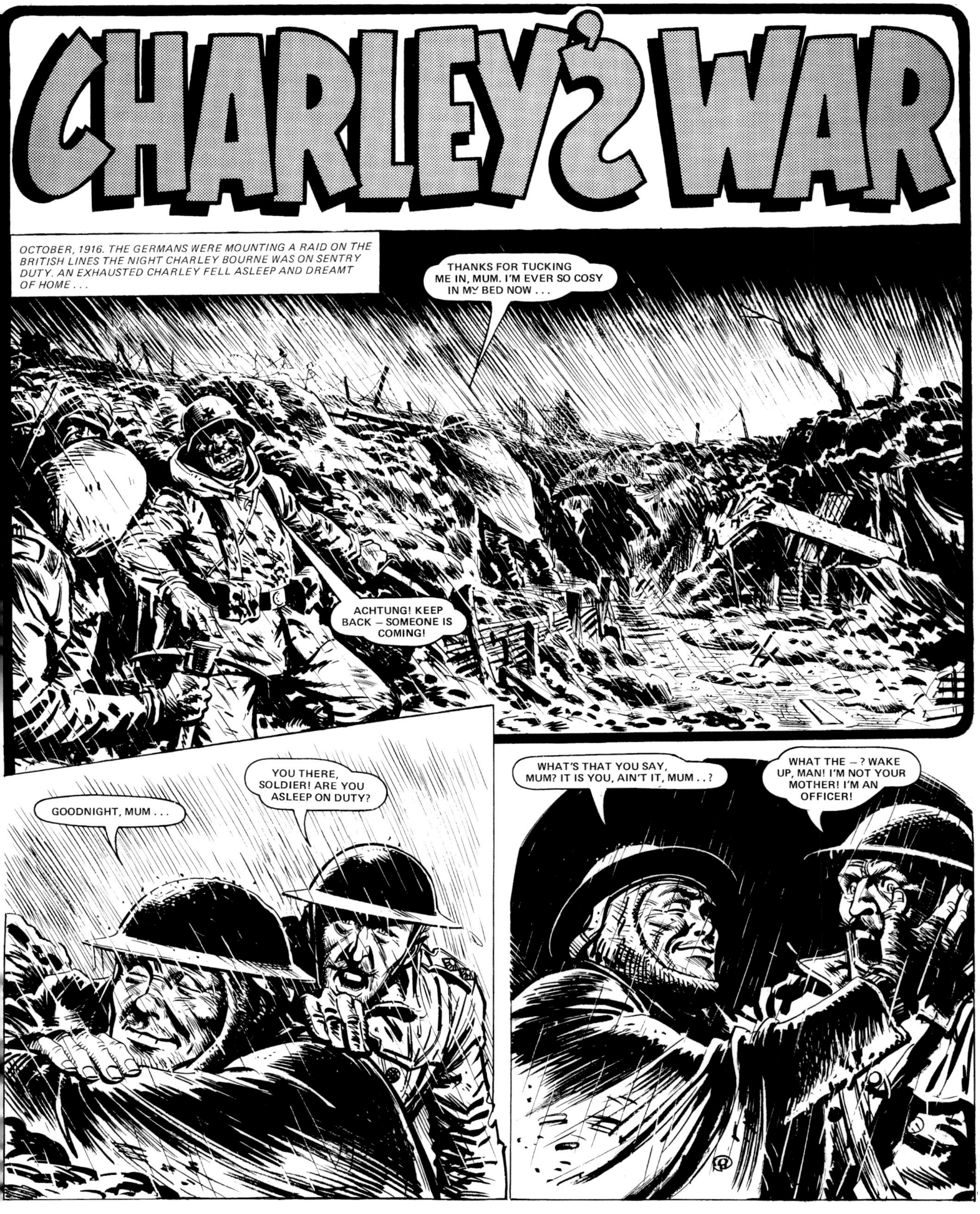
CHARLEY'S WAR
OCTOBER, 1916. THE GERMANS WERE MOUNTING A RAID ON THE BRITISH LINES THE NIGHT CHARLEY BOURNE WAS ON SENTRY DUTY. AN EXHAUSTED CHARLEY FELL ASLEEP AND DREAMT OF HOME . . .
THANKS FOR TUCKING ME IN, MUM. I'M EVER SO COSY IN MY BED NOW . . .
ACHTUNG! KEEP BACK – SOMEONE IS COMING!
GOODNIGHT, MUM . . .
YOU THERE, SOLDIER! ARE YOU ASLEEP ON DUTY?
WHAT'S THAT YOU SAY, MUM? IT IS YOU, AIN'T IT, MUM . . ?
WHAT THE – ? WAKE UP, MAN! I'M NOT YOUR MOTHER! I'M AN OFFICER!

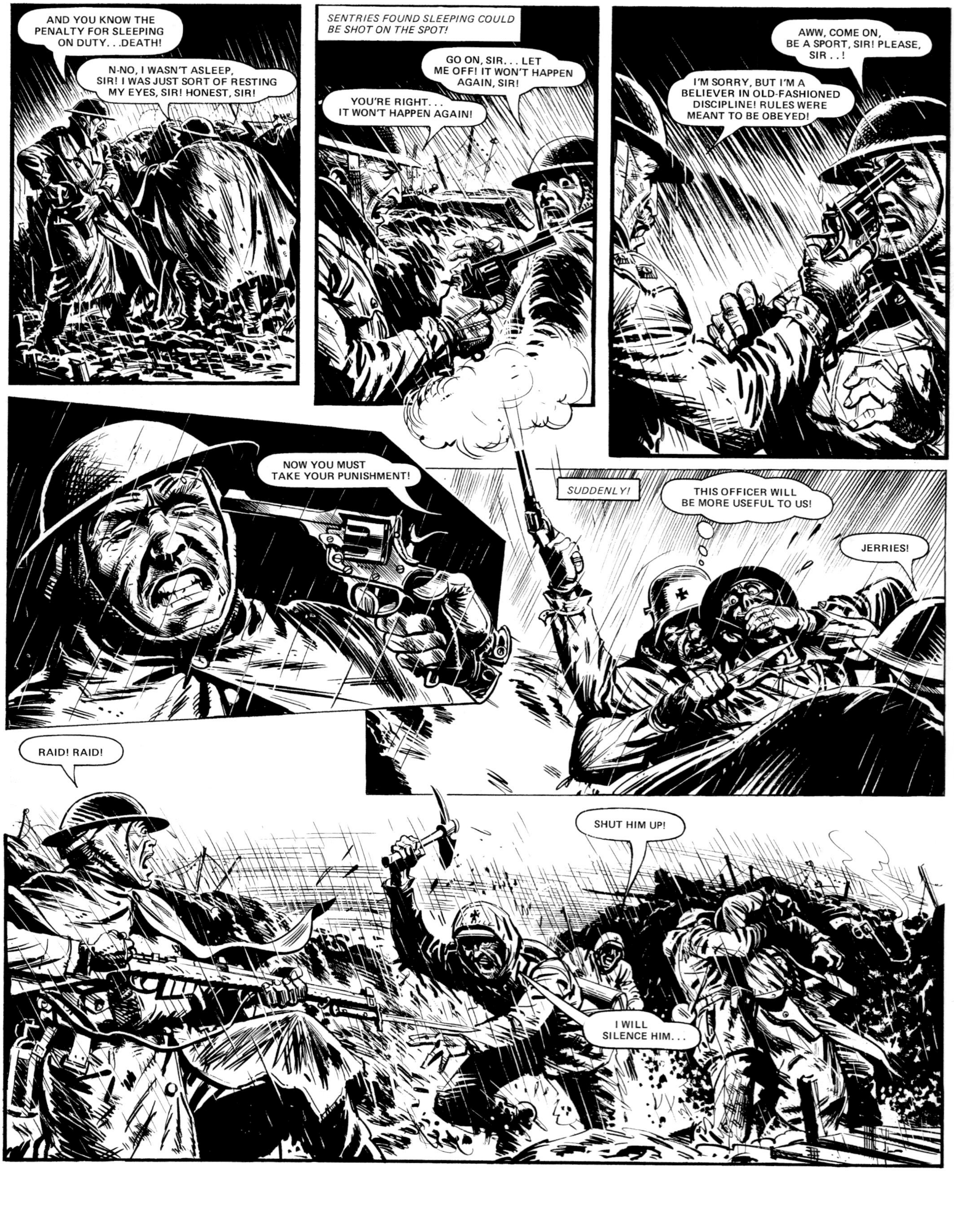
AND YOU KNOW THE PENALTY FOR SLEEPING ON DUTY. . .DEATH!
N-NO, I WASN'T ASLEEP, SIR! I WAS JUST SORT OF RESTING MY EYES, SIR! HONEST, SIR!
SENTRIES FOUND SLEEPING COULD BE SHOT ON THE SPOT!
GO ON, SIR. . . LET ME OFF! IT WON'T HAPPEN AGAIN, SIR!
YOU'RE RIGHT. . . IT WON'T HAPPEN AGAIN!
AWW, COME ON, BE A SPORT, SIR! PLEASE, SIR . . !
I'M SORRY, BUT I'M A BELIEVER IN OLD-FASHIONED DISCIPLINE! RULES WERE MEANT TO BE OBEYED!
NOW YOU MUST TAKE YOUR PUNISHMENT!
SUDDENLY!
THIS OFFICER WILL BE MORE USEFUL TO US!
JERRIES!
RAID! RAID!
SHUT HIM UP!
I WILL SILENCE HIM. . .

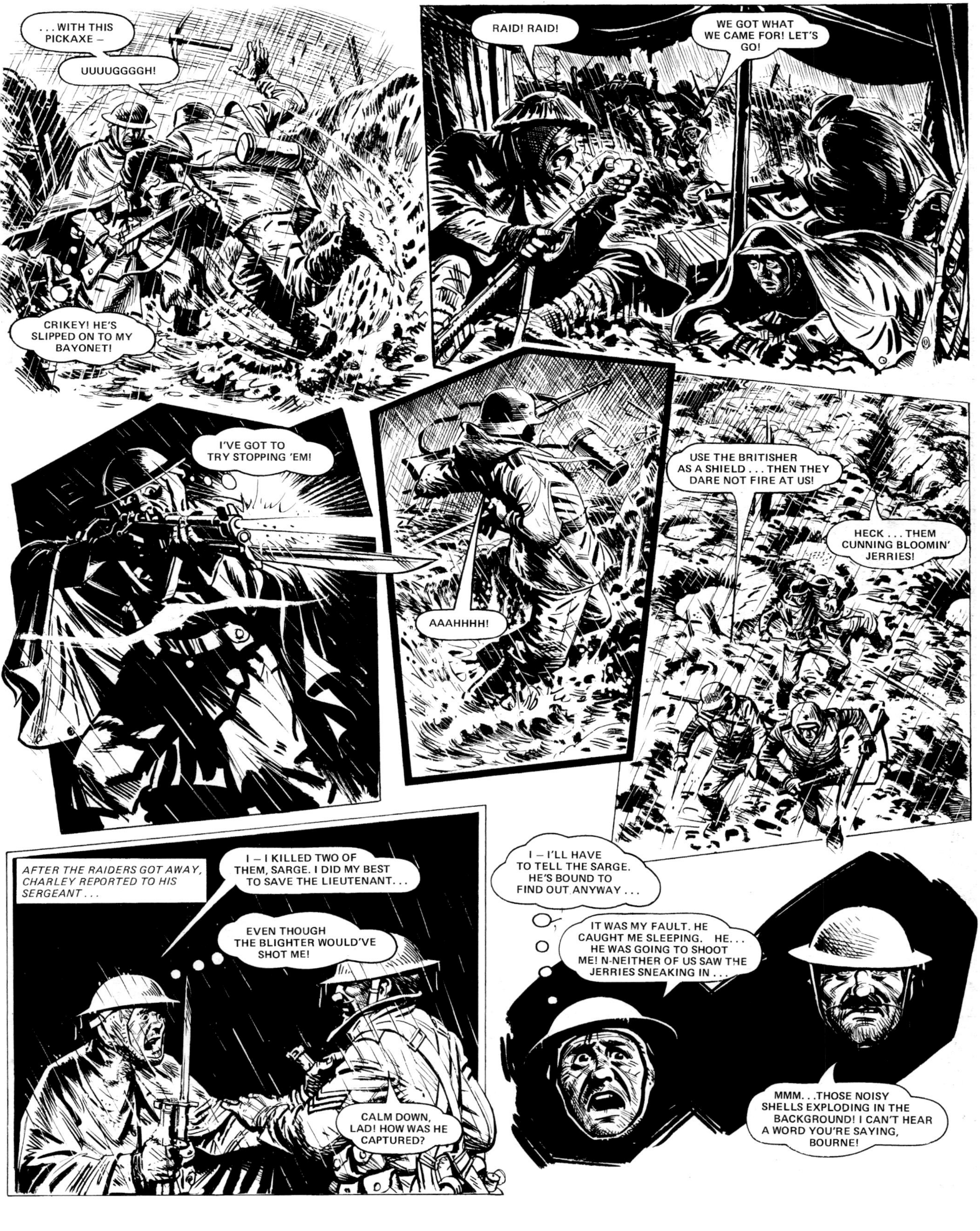

. . . WITH THIS PICKAXE –
UUUUGGGGH!
CRIKEY! HE'S SLIPPED ON TO MY BAYONET!
RAID! RAID!
WE GOT WHAT WE CAME FOR! LET'S GO!
I'VE GOT TO TRY STOPPING 'EM!
AAAHHHH!
USE THE BRITISHER AS A SHIELD . . . THEN THEY DARE NOT FIRE AT US!
HECK . . . THEM CUNNING BLOOMIN' JERRIES!
AFTER THE RAIDERS GOT AWAY, CHARLEY REPORTED TO HIS SERGEANT . . .
I – I KILLED TWO OF THEM, SARGE. I DID MY BEST TO SAVE THE LIEUTENANT . . .
EVEN THOUGH THE BLIGHTER WOULD'VE SHOT ME!
CALM DOWN, LAD! HOW WAS HE CAPTURED?
I – I'LL HAVE TO TELL THE SARGE. HE'S BOUND TO FIND OUT ANYWAY . . .
IT WAS MY FAULT. HE CAUGHT ME SLEEPING. HE. . . HE WAS GOING TO SHOOT ME! N-NEITHER OF US SAW THE JERRIES SNEAKING IN . . .
MMM. . .THOSE NOISY SHELLS EXPLODING IN THE BACKGROUND! I CAN'T HEAR A WORD YOU'RE SAYING, BOURNE!

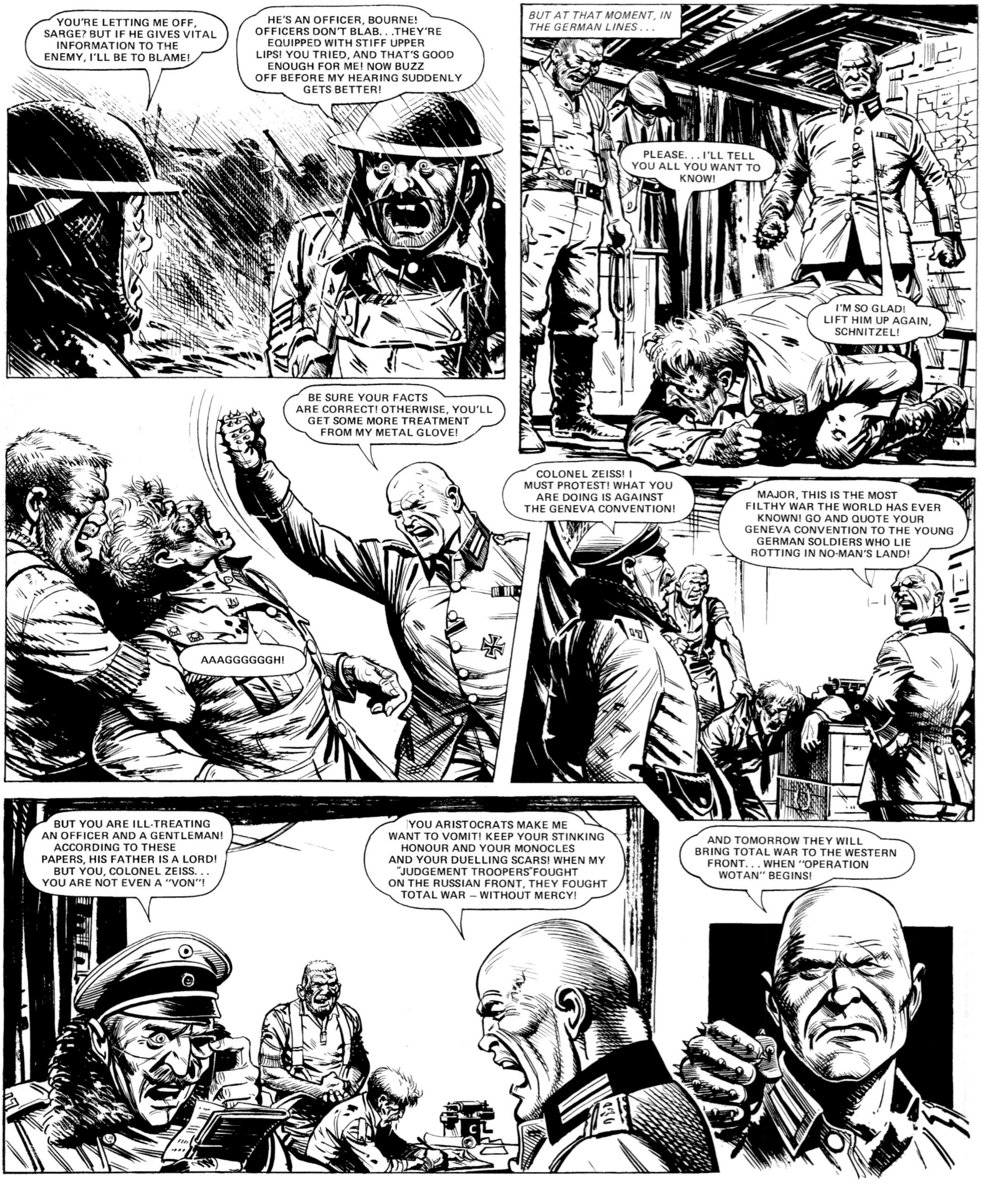
YOU'RE LETTING ME OFF, SARGE? BUT IF HE GIVES VITAL INFORMATION TO THE ENEMY, I'LL BE TO BLAME!
HE'S AN OFFICER, BOURNE! OFFICERS DON'T BLAB. . .THEY'RE EQUIPPED WITH STIFF UPPER LIPS! YOU TRIED, AND THAT'S GOOD ENOUGH FOR ME! NOW BUZZ OFF BEFORE MY HEARING SUDDENLY GETS BETTER!
BUT AT THAT MOMENT, IN THE GERMAN LINES . . .
PLEASE. . . I'LL TELL YOU ALL YOU WANT TO KNOW!
I'M SO GLAD! LIFT HIM UP AGAIN, SCHNITZEL!
BE SURE YOUR FACTS ARE CORRECT! OTHERWISE, YOU'LL GET SOME MORE TREATMENT FROM MY METAL GLOVE!
AAAGGGGGGH!
COLONEL ZEISS! I MUST PROTEST! WHAT YOU ARE DOING IS AGAINST THE GENEVA CONVENTION!
MAJOR, THIS IS THE MOST FILTHY WAR THE WORLD HAS EVER KNOWN! GO AND QUOTE YOUR GENEVA CONVENTION TO THE YOUNG GERMAN SOLDIERS WHO LIE ROTTING IN NO-MAN'S LAND!
BUT YOU ARE ILL-TREATING AN OFFICER AND A GENTLEMAN! ACCORDING TO THESE PAPERS, HIS FATHER IS A LORD! BUT YOU, COLONEL ZEISS. . . YOU ARE NOT EVEN A "VON"!
YOU ARISTOCRATS MAKE ME WANT TO VOMIT! KEEP YOUR STINKING HONOUR AND YOUR MONOCLES AND YOUR DUELLING SCARS! WHEN MY "JUDGEMENT TROOPERS" FOUGHT ON THE RUSSIAN FRONT, THEY FOUGHT TOTAL WAR – WITHOUT MERCY!
AND TOMORROW THEY WILL BRING TOTAL WAR TO THE WESTERN FRONT. . . WHEN "OPERATION WOTAN" BEGINS!

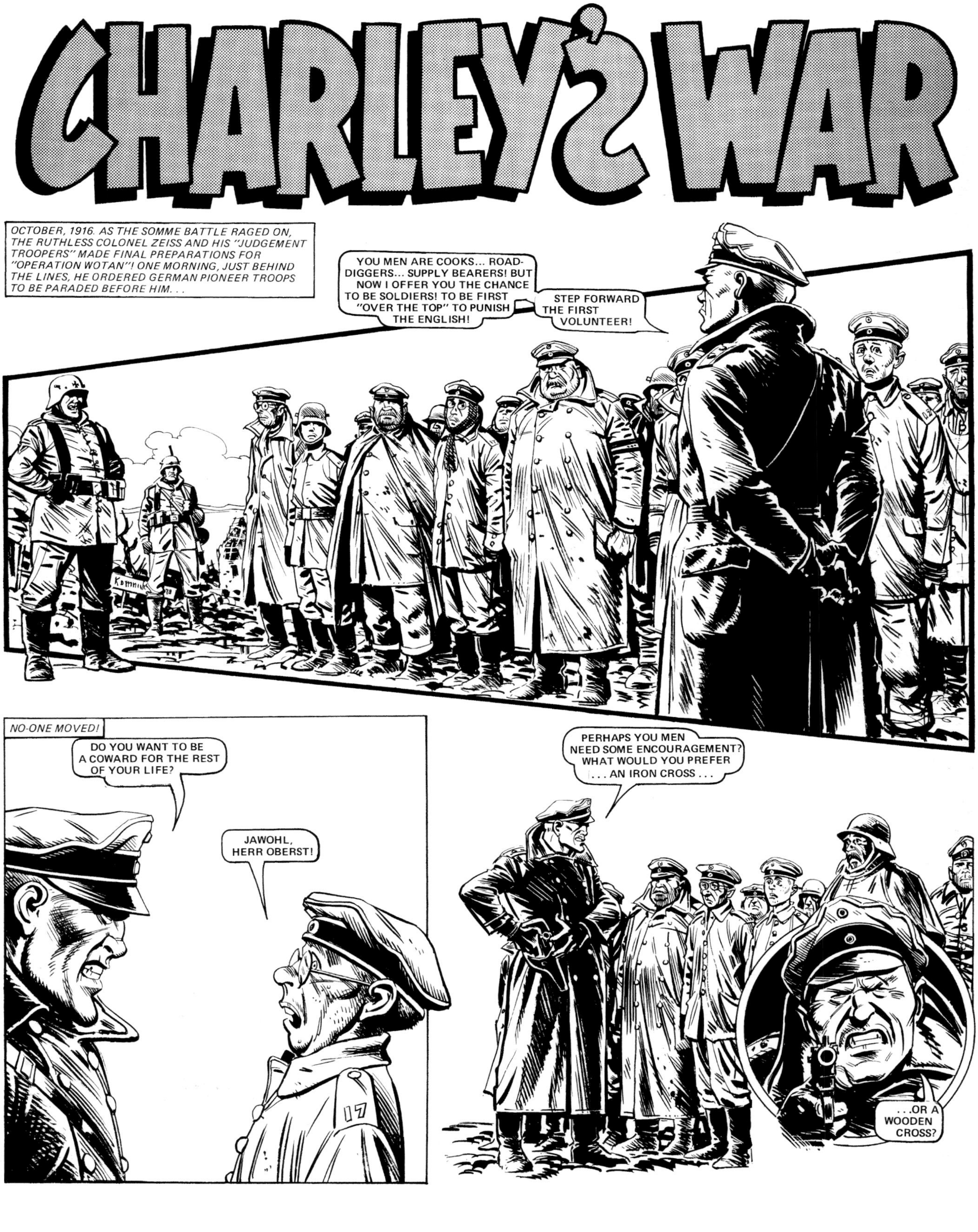
CHARLEY'S WAR
OCTOBER, 1916. AS THE SOMME BATTLE RAGED ON, THE RUTHLESS COLONEL ZEISS AND HIS "JUDGEMENT TROOPERS" MADE FINAL PREPARATIONS FOR "OPERATION WOTAN"! ONE MORNING, JUST BEHIND THE LINES, HE ORDERED GERMAN PIONEER TROOPS TO BE PARADED BEFORE HIM...
YOU MEN ARE COOKS... ROAD-DIGGERS... SUPPLY BEARERS! BUT NOW I OFFER YOU THE CHANCE TO BE SOLDIERS! TO BE FIRST "OVER THE TOP" TO PUNISH THE ENGLISH!
STEP FORWARD THE FIRST VOLUNTEER!
NO-ONE MOVED!
DO YOU WANT TO BE A COWARD FOR THE REST OF YOUR LIFE?
JAWOHL, HERR OBERST!
17
PERHAPS YOU MEN NEED SOME ENCOURAGEMENT? WHAT WOULD YOU PREFER . . . AN IRON CROSS . . .
. . .OR A WOODEN CROSS?

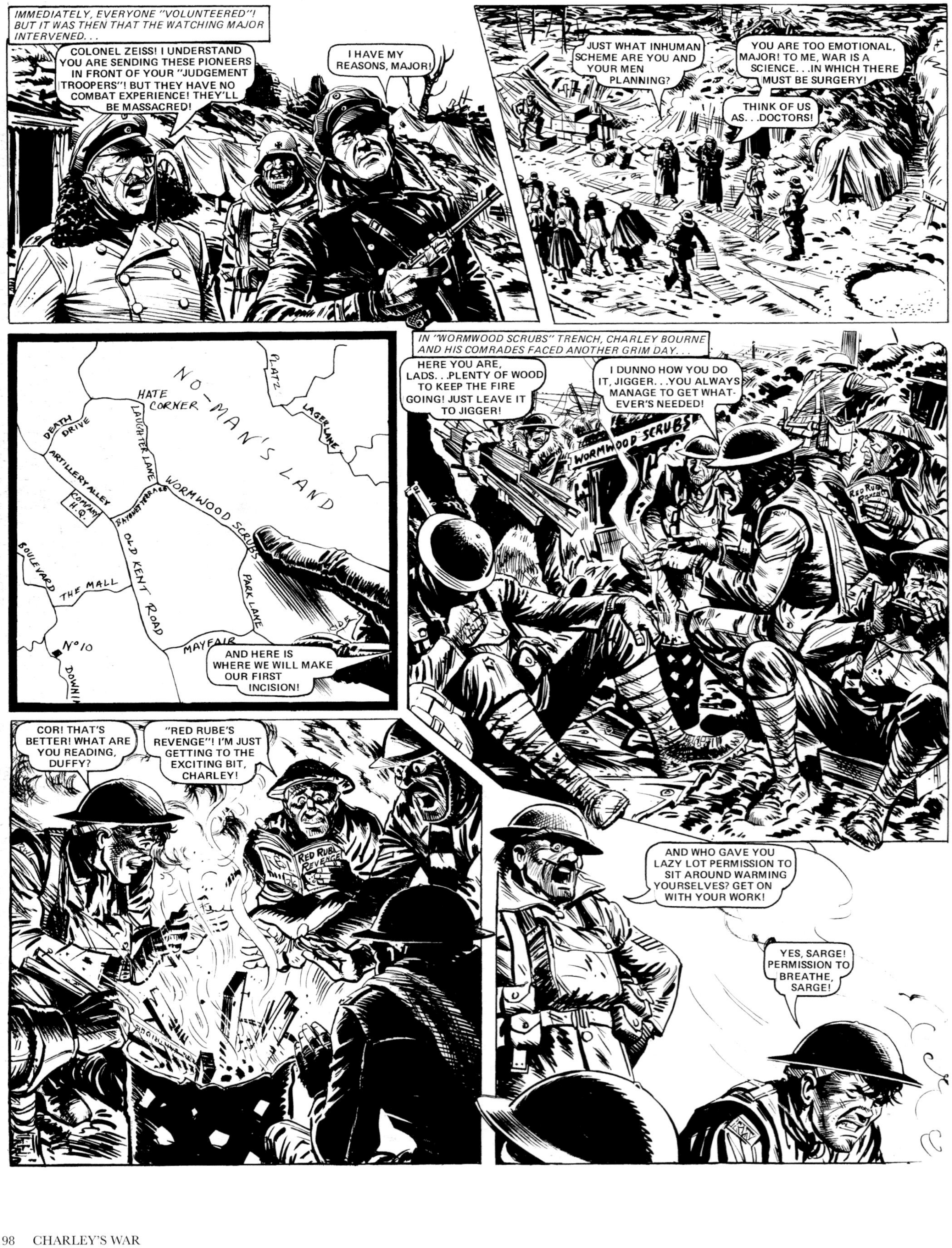
IMMEDIATELY, EVERYONE "VOLUNTEERED"! BUT IT WAS THEN THAT THE WATCHING MAJOR INTERVENED...
COLONEL ZEISS! I UNDERSTAND YOU ARE SENDING THESE PIONEERS IN FRONT OF YOUR "JUDGEMENT TROOPERS"! BUT THEY HAVE NO COMBAT EXPERIENCE! THEY'LL BE MASSACRED!
I HAVE MY REASONS, MAJOR!
JUST WHAT INHUMAN SCHEME ARE YOU AND YOUR MEN PLANNING?
YOU ARE TOO EMOTIONAL, MAJOR! TO ME, WAR IS A SCIENCE...IN WHICH THERE MUST BE SURGERY!
THINK OF US AS...DOCTORS!
NO-MAN'S LAND
PLATZ
HATE CORNER
LAGER LANE
DEATH DRIVE
LAUGHTER LANE
ARTILLERY ALLEY
WORMWOOD SCRUBS
COMPANY H.Q.
BAYONET TERRACE
OLD KENT ROAD
BOULEVARD
THE MALL
PARK LANE
No 10
MAYFAIR
DOWNIN
AND HERE IS WHERE WE WILL MAKE OUR FIRST INCISION!
IN "WORMWOOD SCRUBS" TRENCH, CHARLEY BOURNE AND HIS COMRADES FACED ANOTHER GRIM DAY...
HERE YOU ARE, LADS...PLENTY OF WOOD TO KEEP THE FIRE GOING! JUST LEAVE IT TO JIGGER!
I DUNNO HOW YOU DO IT, JIGGER...YOU ALWAYS MANAGE TO GET WHAT-EVER'S NEEDED!
WORMWOOD SCRUBS
COR! THAT'S BETTER! WHAT ARE YOU READING, DUFFY?
"RED RUBE'S REVENGE"! I'M JUST GETTING TO THE EXCITING BIT, CHARLEY!
RED RUBE REVENGE
AND WHO GAVE YOU LAZY LOT PERMISSION TO SIT AROUND WARMING YOURSELVES? GET ON WITH YOUR WORK!
YES, SARGE! PERMISSION TO BREATHE, SARGE!

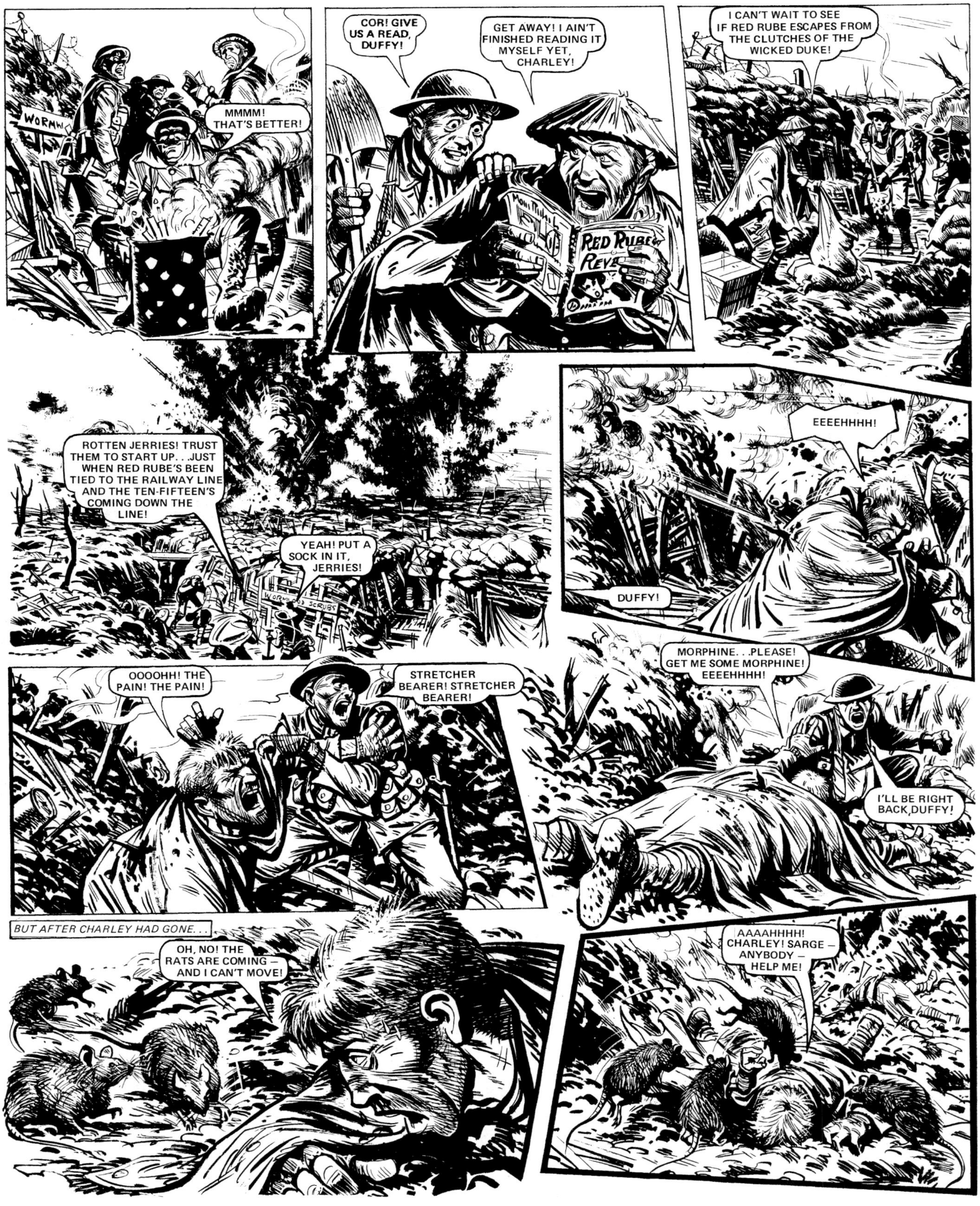
MMMM! THAT'S BETTER!
COR! GIVE US A READ, DUFFY!
GET AWAY! I AIN'T FINISHED READING IT MYSELF YET, CHARLEY!
I CAN'T WAIT TO SEE IF RED RUBE ESCAPES FROM THE CLUTCHES OF THE WICKED DUKE!
ROTTEN JERRIES! TRUST THEM TO START UP. . .JUST WHEN RED RUBE'S BEEN TIED TO THE RAILWAY LINE AND THE TEN-FIFTEEN'S COMING DOWN THE LINE!
YEAH! PUT A SOCK IN IT, JERRIES!
EEEEHHHH!
DUFFY!
OOOOHH! THE PAIN! THE PAIN!
STRETCHER BEARER! STRETCHER BEARER!
MORPHINE. . .PLEASE! GET ME SOME MORPHINE! EEEEHHHH!
I'LL BE RIGHT BACK, DUFFY!
BUT AFTER CHARLEY HAD GONE. . .
OH, NO! THE RATS ARE COMING — AND I CAN'T MOVE!
AAAAHHHH! CHARLEY! SARGE — ANYBODY — HELP ME!

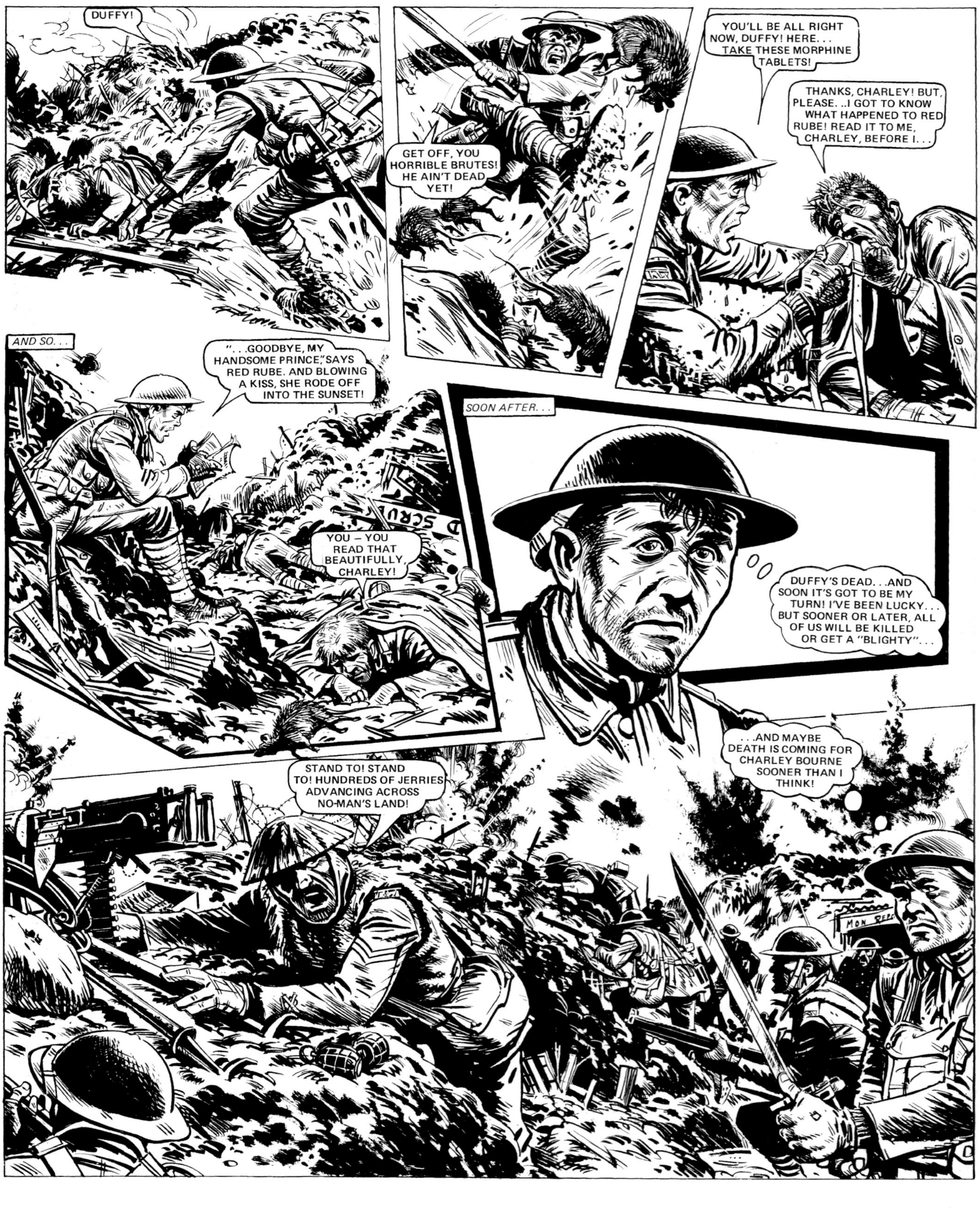
DUFFY!
GET OFF, YOU HORRIBLE BRUTES! HE AIN'T DEAD YET!
YOU'LL BE ALL RIGHT NOW, DUFFY! HERE... TAKE THESE MORPHINE TABLETS!
THANKS, CHARLEY! BUT, PLEASE. ..I GOT TO KNOW WHAT HAPPENED TO RED RUBE! READ IT TO ME, CHARLEY, BEFORE I...
AND SO...
"...GOODBYE, MY HANDSOME PRINCE," SAYS RED RUBE. AND BLOWING A KISS, SHE RODE OFF INTO THE SUNSET!
YOU – YOU READ THAT BEAUTIFULLY, CHARLEY!
SOON AFTER...
DUFFY'S DEAD...AND SOON IT'S GOT TO BE MY TURN! I'VE BEEN LUCKY... BUT SOONER OR LATER, ALL OF US WILL BE KILLED OR GET A "BLIGHTY"...
STAND TO! STAND TO! HUNDREDS OF JERRIES ADVANCING ACROSS NO-MAN'S LAND!
...AND MAYBE DEATH IS COMING FOR CHARLEY BOURNE SOONER THAN I THINK!

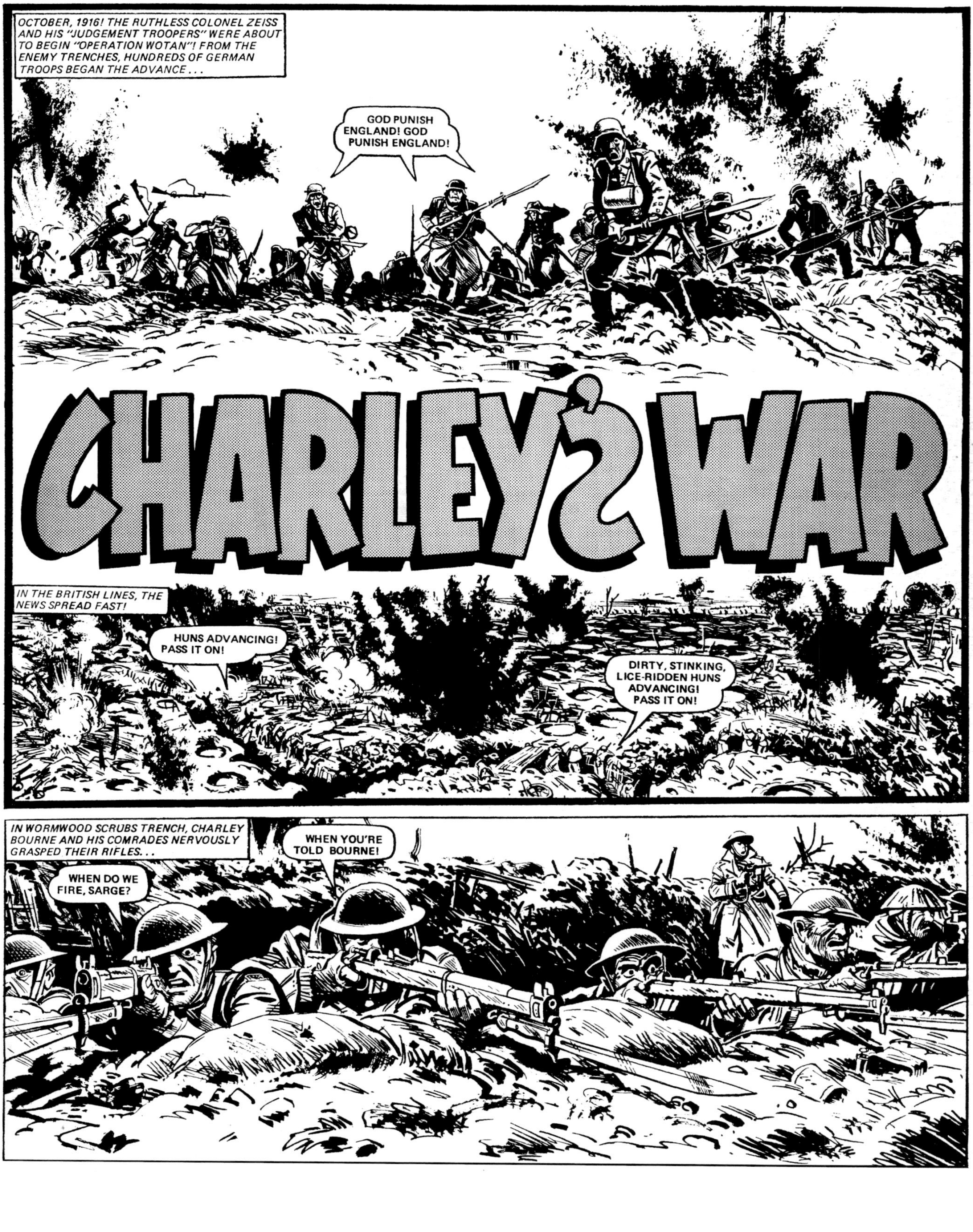
OCTOBER, 1916! THE RUTHLESS COLONEL ZEISS AND HIS "JUDGEMENT TROOPERS" WERE ABOUT TO BEGIN "OPERATION WOTAN"! FROM THE ENEMY TRENCHES, HUNDREDS OF GERMAN TROOPS BEGAN THE ADVANCE . . .
GOD PUNISH ENGLAND! GOD PUNISH ENGLAND!
CHARLEY'S WAR
IN THE BRITISH LINES, THE NEWS SPREAD FAST!
HUNS ADVANCING! PASS IT ON!
DIRTY, STINKING, LICE-RIDDEN HUNS ADVANCING! PASS IT ON!
IN WORMWOOD SCRUBS TRENCH, CHARLEY BOURNE AND HIS COMRADES NERVOUSLY GRASPED THEIR RIFLES. . .
WHEN DO WE FIRE, SARGE?
WHEN YOU'RE TOLD BOURNE!

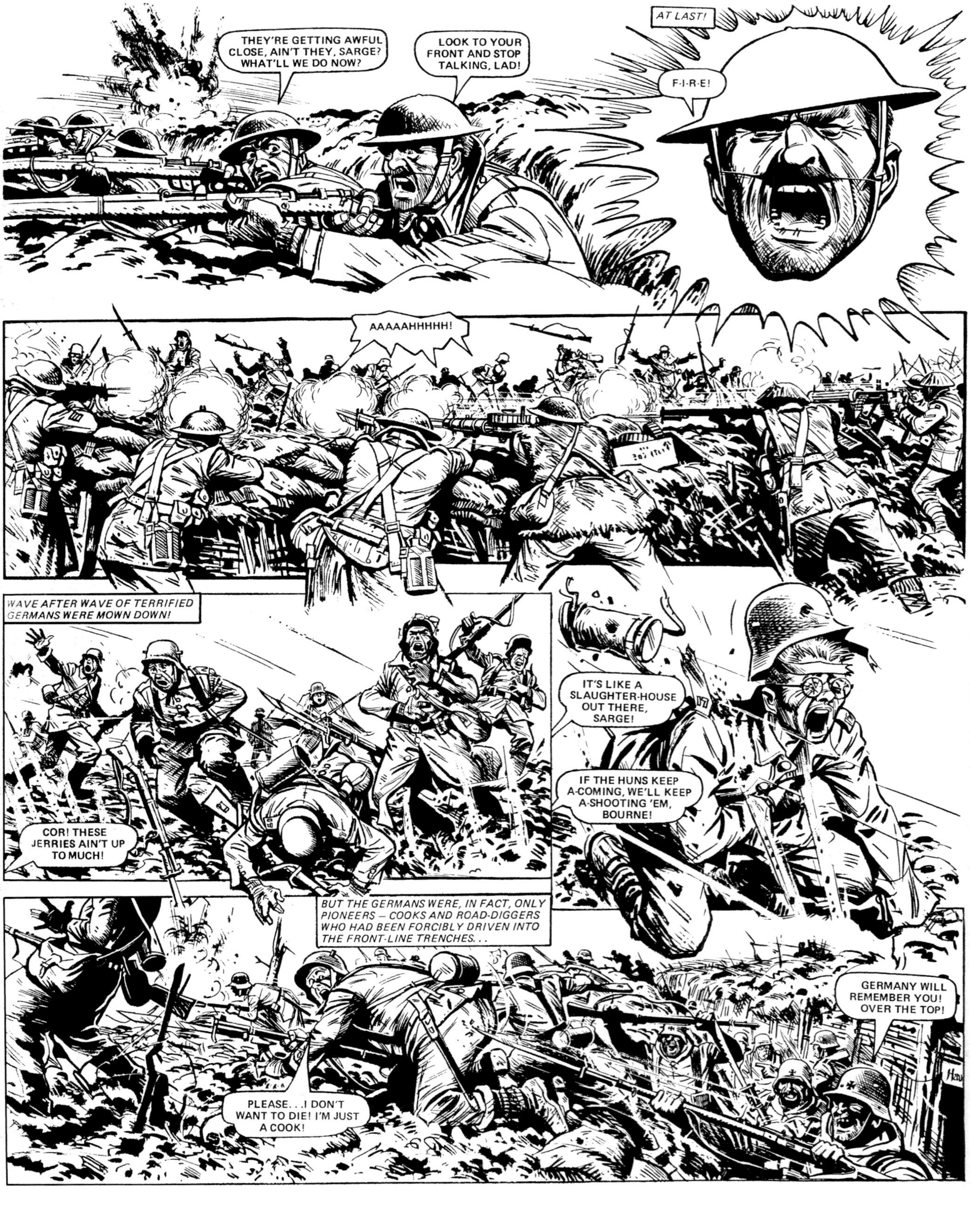
THEY'RE GETTING AWFUL CLOSE, AIN'T THEY, SARGE? WHAT'LL WE DO NOW?
LOOK TO YOUR FRONT AND STOP TALKING, LAD!
AT LAST!
F-I-R-E!
AAAAAHHHHH!
WAVE AFTER WAVE OF TERRIFIED GERMANS WERE MOWN DOWN!
COR! THESE JERRIES AIN'T UP TO MUCH!
IT'S LIKE A SLAUGHTER-HOUSE OUT THERE, SARGE!
IF THE HUNS KEEP A-COMING, WE'LL KEEP A-SHOOTING 'EM, BOURNE!
BUT THE GERMANS WERE, IN FACT, ONLY PIONEERS – COOKS AND ROAD-DIGGERS WHO HAD BEEN FORCIBLY DRIVEN INTO THE FRONT-LINE TRENCHES...
PLEASE... I DON'T WANT TO DIE! I'M JUST A COOK!
GERMANY WILL REMEMBER YOU! OVER THE TOP!

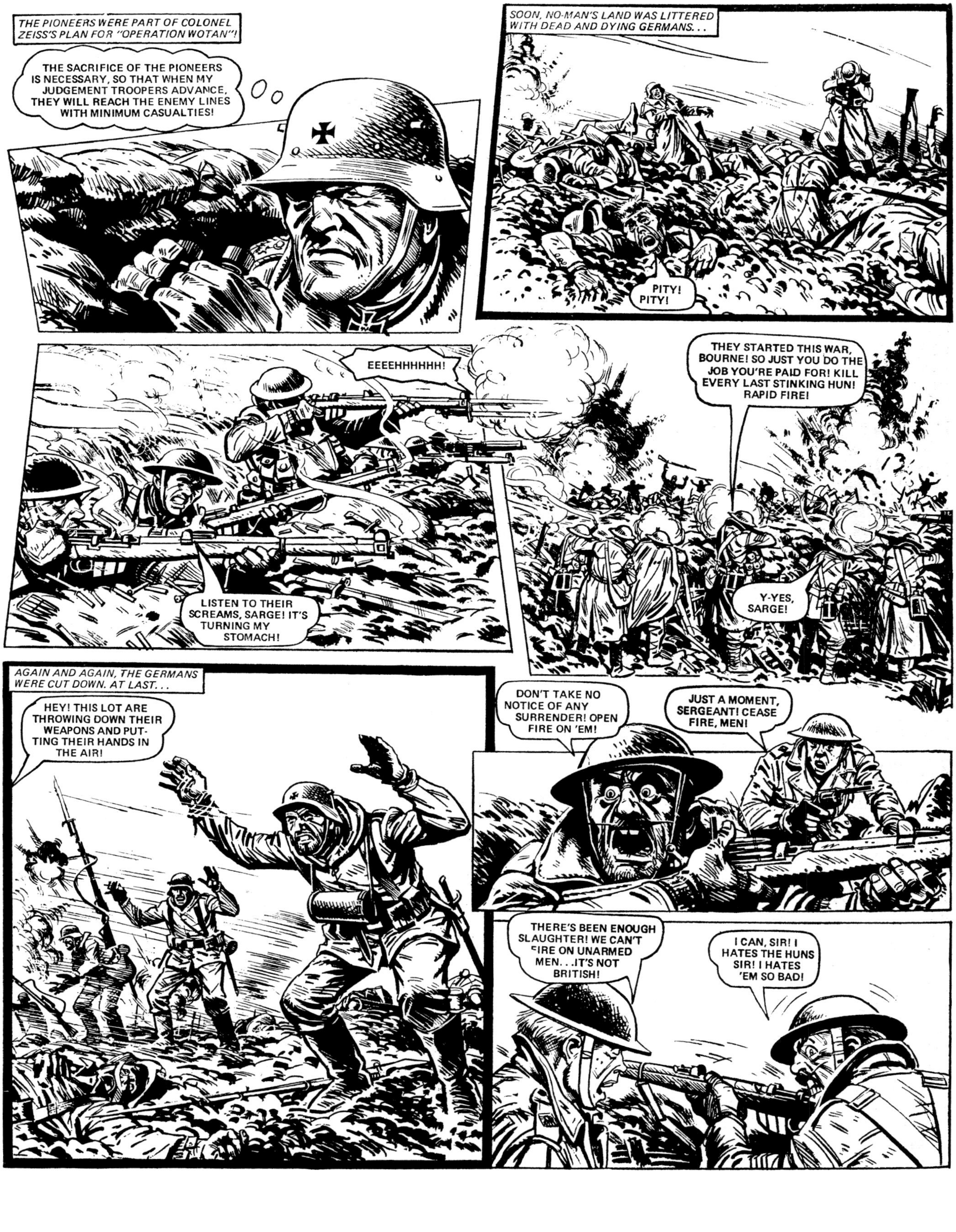
THE PIONEERS WERE PART OF COLONEL ZEISS'S PLAN FOR "OPERATION WOTAN"!
THE SACRIFICE OF THE PIONEERS IS NECESSARY, SO THAT WHEN MY JUDGEMENT TROOPERS ADVANCE, THEY WILL REACH THE ENEMY LINES WITH MINIMUM CASUALTIES!
SOON, NO-MAN'S LAND WAS LITTERED WITH DEAD AND DYING GERMANS. . .
PITY! PITY!
EEEEHHHHHHH!
LISTEN TO THEIR SCREAMS, SARGE! IT'S TURNING MY STOMACH!
THEY STARTED THIS WAR, BOURNE! SO JUST YOU DO THE JOB YOU'RE PAID FOR! KILL EVERY LAST STINKING HUN! RAPID FIRE!
Y-YES, SARGE!
AGAIN AND AGAIN, THE GERMANS WERE CUT DOWN. AT LAST. . .
HEY! THIS LOT ARE THROWING DOWN THEIR WEAPONS AND PUTTING THEIR HANDS IN THE AIR!
DON'T TAKE NO NOTICE OF ANY SURRENDER! OPEN FIRE ON 'EM!
JUST A MOMENT, SERGEANT! CEASE FIRE, MEN!
THERE'S BEEN ENOUGH SLAUGHTER! WE CAN'T FIRE ON UNARMED MEN. . . IT'S NOT BRITISH!
I CAN, SIR! I HATES THE HUNS SIR! I HATES 'EM SO BAD!

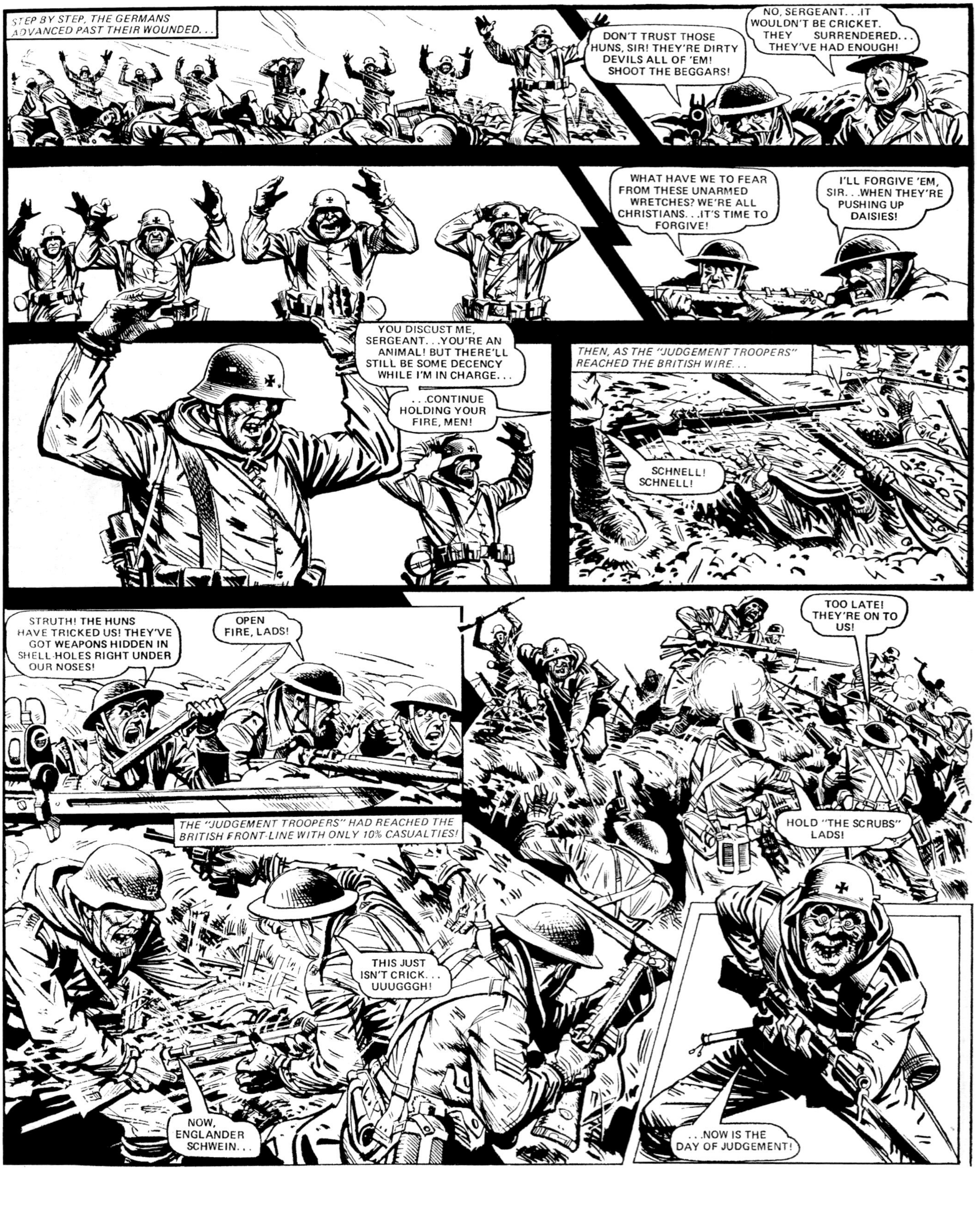

STEP BY STEP, THE GERMANS ADVANCED PAST THEIR WOUNDED...
DON'T TRUST THOSE HUNS, SIR! THEY'RE DIRTY DEVILS ALL OF 'EM! SHOOT THE BEGGARS!
NO, SERGEANT...IT WOULDN'T BE CRICKET. THEY SURRENDERED... THEY'VE HAD ENOUGH!
WHAT HAVE WE TO FEAR FROM THESE UNARMED WRETCHES? WE'RE ALL CHRISTIANS...IT'S TIME TO FORGIVE!
I'LL FORGIVE 'EM, SIR...WHEN THEY'RE PUSHING UP DAISIES!
YOU DISGUST ME, SERGEANT...YOU'RE AN ANIMAL! BUT THERE'LL STILL BE SOME DECENCY WHILE I'M IN CHARGE...
...CONTINUE HOLDING YOUR FIRE, MEN!
THEN, AS THE "JUDGEMENT TROOPERS" REACHED THE BRITISH WIRE...
SCHNELL! SCHNELL!
STRUTH! THE HUNS HAVE TRICKED US! THEY'VE GOT WEAPONS HIDDEN IN SHELL-HOLES RIGHT UNDER OUR NOSES!
OPEN FIRE, LADS!
TOO LATE! THEY'RE ON TO US!
HOLD "THE SCRUBS" LADS!
THE "JUDGEMENT TROOPERS" HAD REACHED THE BRITISH FRONT-LINE WITH ONLY 10% CASUALTIES!
THIS JUST ISN'T CRICK... UUUGGGH!
NOW, ENGLANDER SCHWEIN...
...NOW IS THE DAY OF JUDGEMENT!

CHARLEY'S WAR

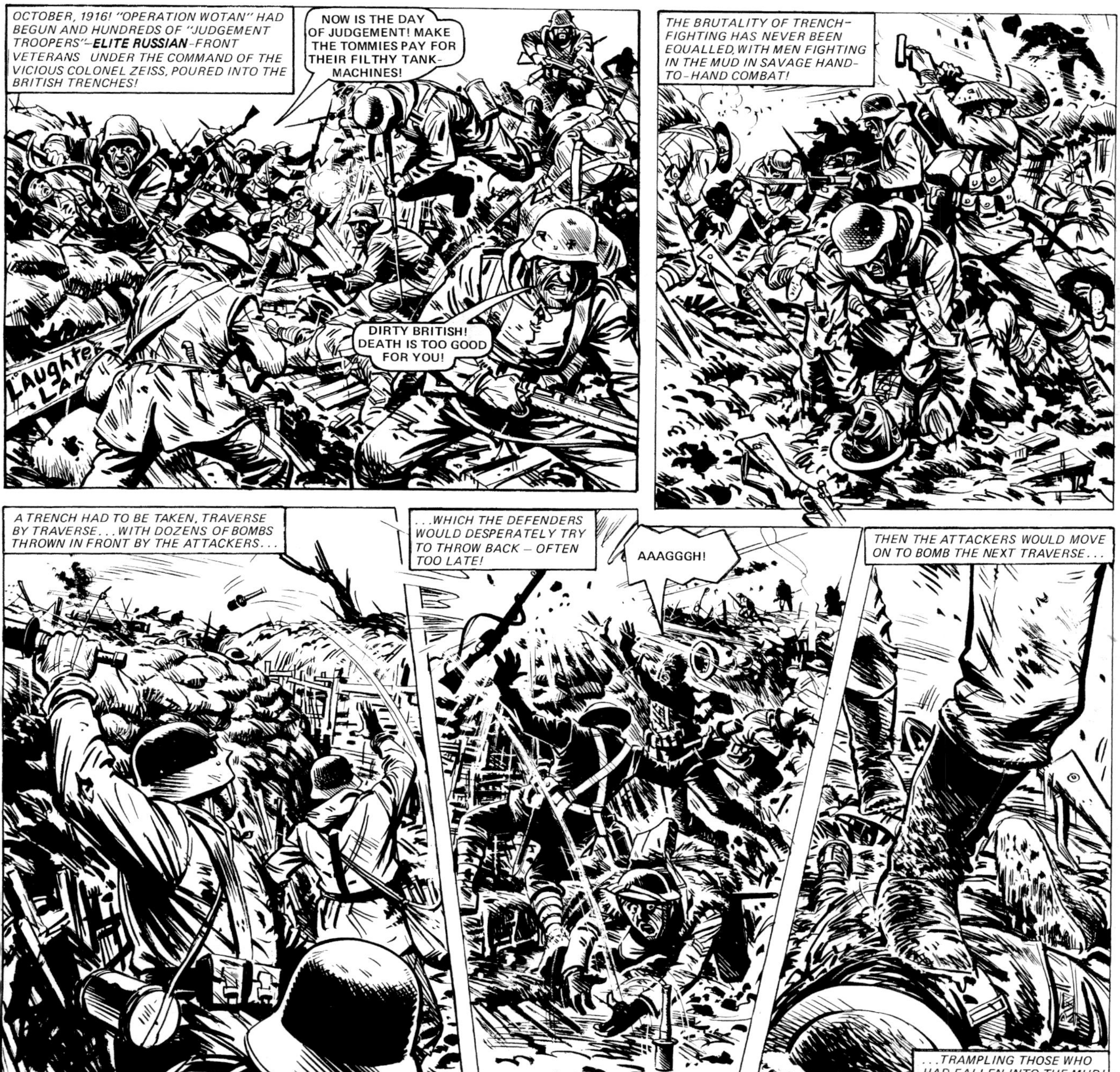
OCTOBER, 1916! "OPERATION WOTAN" HAD BEGUN AND HUNDREDS OF "JUDGEMENT TROOPERS"—ELITE RUSSIAN-FRONT VETERANS UNDER THE COMMAND OF THE VICIOUS COLONEL ZEISS, POURED INTO THE BRITISH TRENCHES!
NOW IS THE DAY OF JUDGEMENT! MAKE THE TOMMIES PAY FOR THEIR FILTHY TANK-MACHINES!
DIRTY BRITISH! DEATH IS TOO GOOD FOR YOU!
THE BRUTALITY OF TRENCH-FIGHTING HAS NEVER BEEN EQUALLED, WITH MEN FIGHTING IN THE MUD IN SAVAGE HAND-TO-HAND COMBAT!
A TRENCH HAD TO BE TAKEN, TRAVERSE BY TRAVERSE... WITH DOZENS OF BOMBS THROWN IN FRONT BY THE ATTACKERS...
...WHICH THE DEFENDERS WOULD DESPERATELY TRY TO THROW BACK – OFTEN TOO LATE!
AAAGGGH!
THEN THE ATTACKERS WOULD MOVE ON TO BOMB THE NEXT TRAVERSE...
...TRAMPLING THOSE WHO HAD FALLEN, INTO THE MUD!

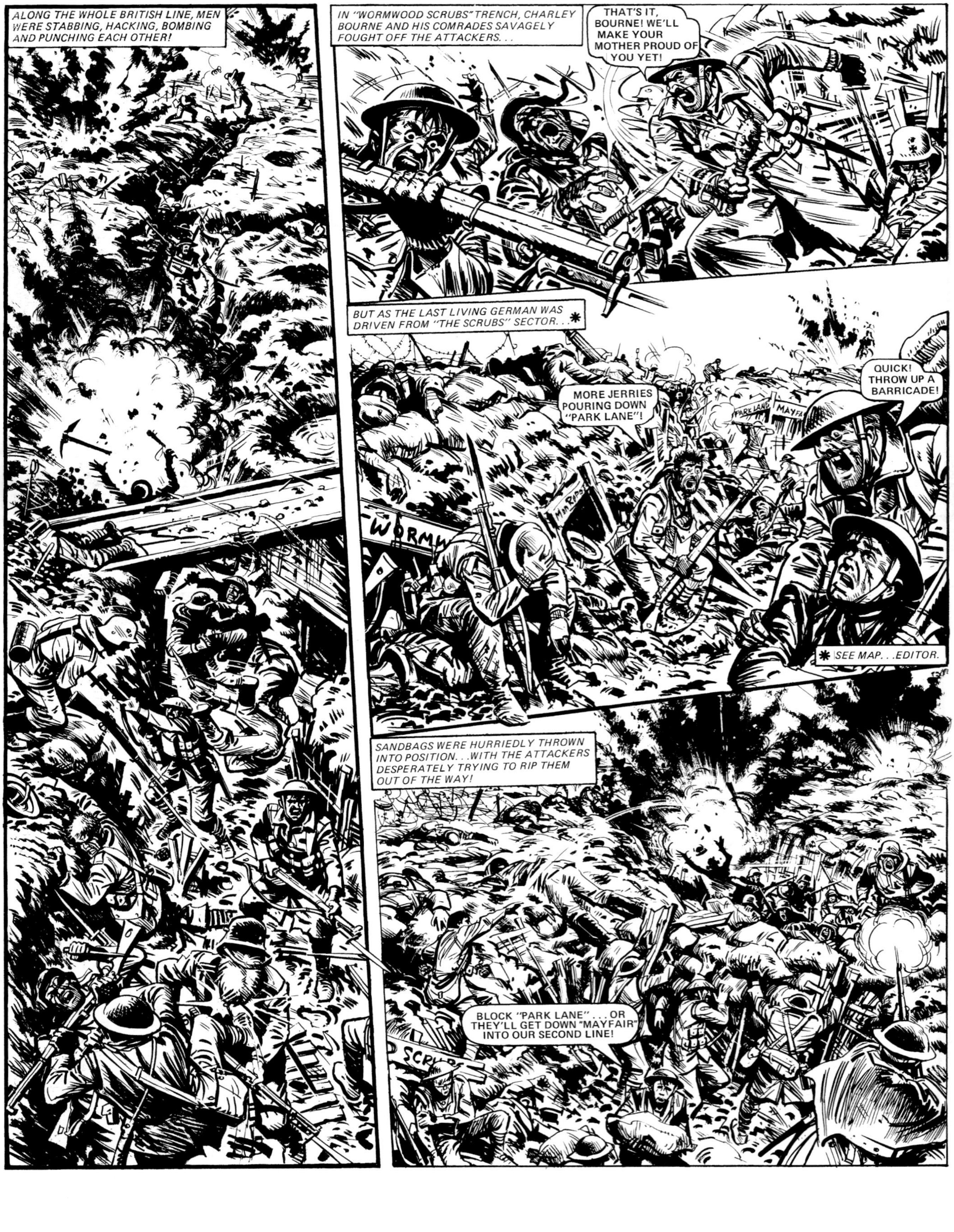
ALONG THE WHOLE BRITISH LINE, MEN WERE STABBING, HACKING, BOMBING AND PUNCHING EACH OTHER!
IN "WORMWOOD SCRUBS" TRENCH, CHARLEY BOURNE AND HIS COMRADES SAVAGELY FOUGHT OFF THE ATTACKERS...
THAT'S IT, BOURNE! WE'LL MAKE YOUR MOTHER PROUD OF YOU YET!
BUT AS THE LAST LIVING GERMAN WAS DRIVEN FROM "THE SCRUBS" SECTOR...*
MORE JERRIES POURING DOWN "PARK LANE"!
QUICK! THROW UP A BARRICADE!
* SEE MAP... EDITOR.
SANDBAGS WERE HURRIEDLY THROWN INTO POSITION... WITH THE ATTACKERS DESPERATELY TRYING TO RIP THEM OUT OF THE WAY!
BLOCK "PARK LANE"... OR THEY'LL GET DOWN "MAYFAIR" INTO OUR SECOND LINE!

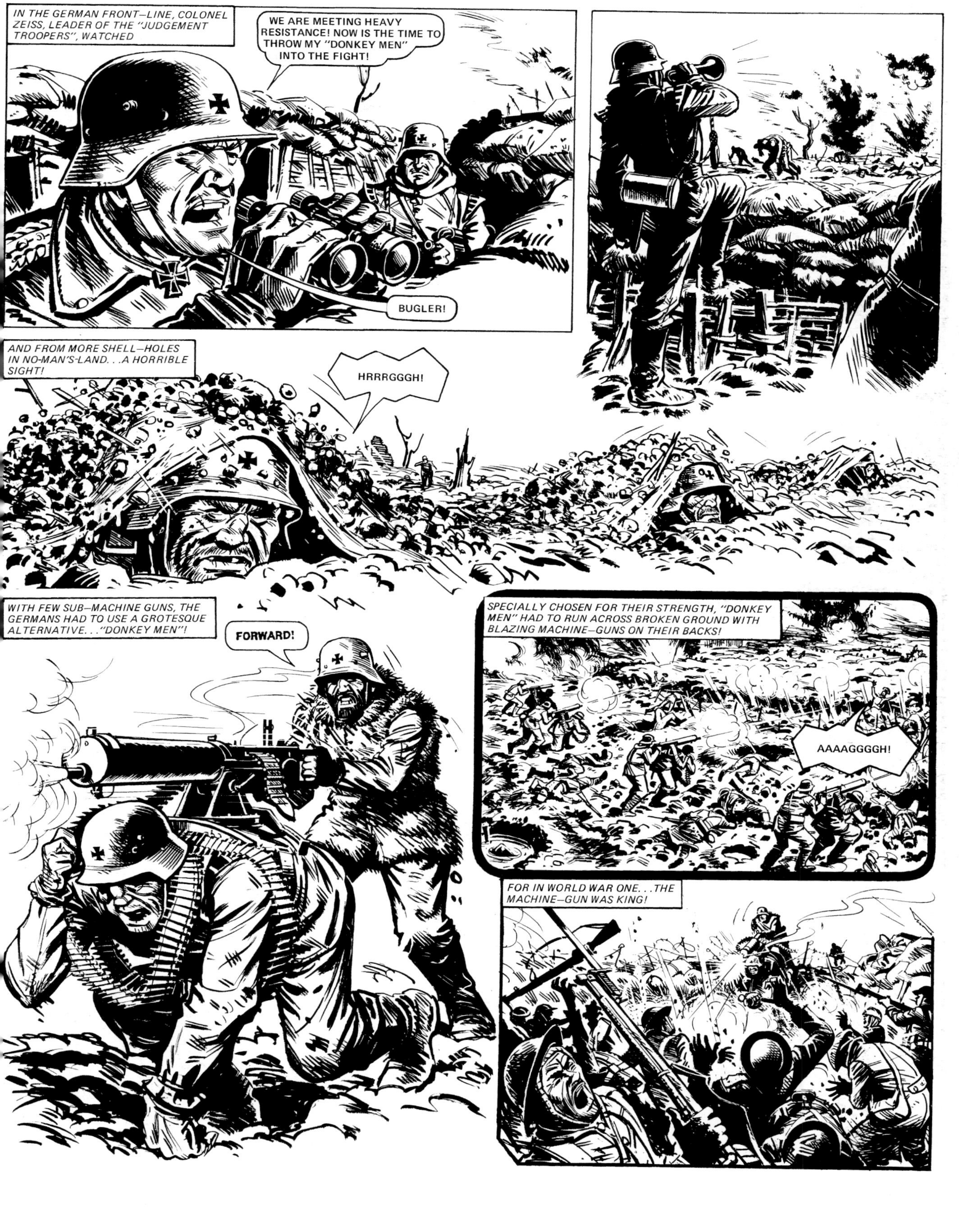
IN THE GERMAN FRONT—LINE, COLONEL ZEISS, LEADER OF THE "JUDGEMENT TROOPERS", WATCHED
WE ARE MEETING HEAVY RESISTANCE! NOW IS THE TIME TO THROW MY "DONKEY MEN" INTO THE FIGHT!
BUGLER!
AND FROM MORE SHELL—HOLES IN NO-MAN'S-LAND. . .A HORRIBLE SIGHT!
HRRRGGGH!
WITH FEW SUB—MACHINE GUNS, THE GERMANS HAD TO USE A GROTESQUE ALTERNATIVE. . ."DONKEY MEN"!
FORWARD!
SPECIALLY CHOSEN FOR THEIR STRENGTH, "DONKEY MEN" HAD TO RUN ACROSS BROKEN GROUND WITH BLAZING MACHINE—GUNS ON THEIR BACKS!
AAAAGGGGH!
FOR IN WORLD WAR ONE. . .THE MACHINE—GUN WAS KING!

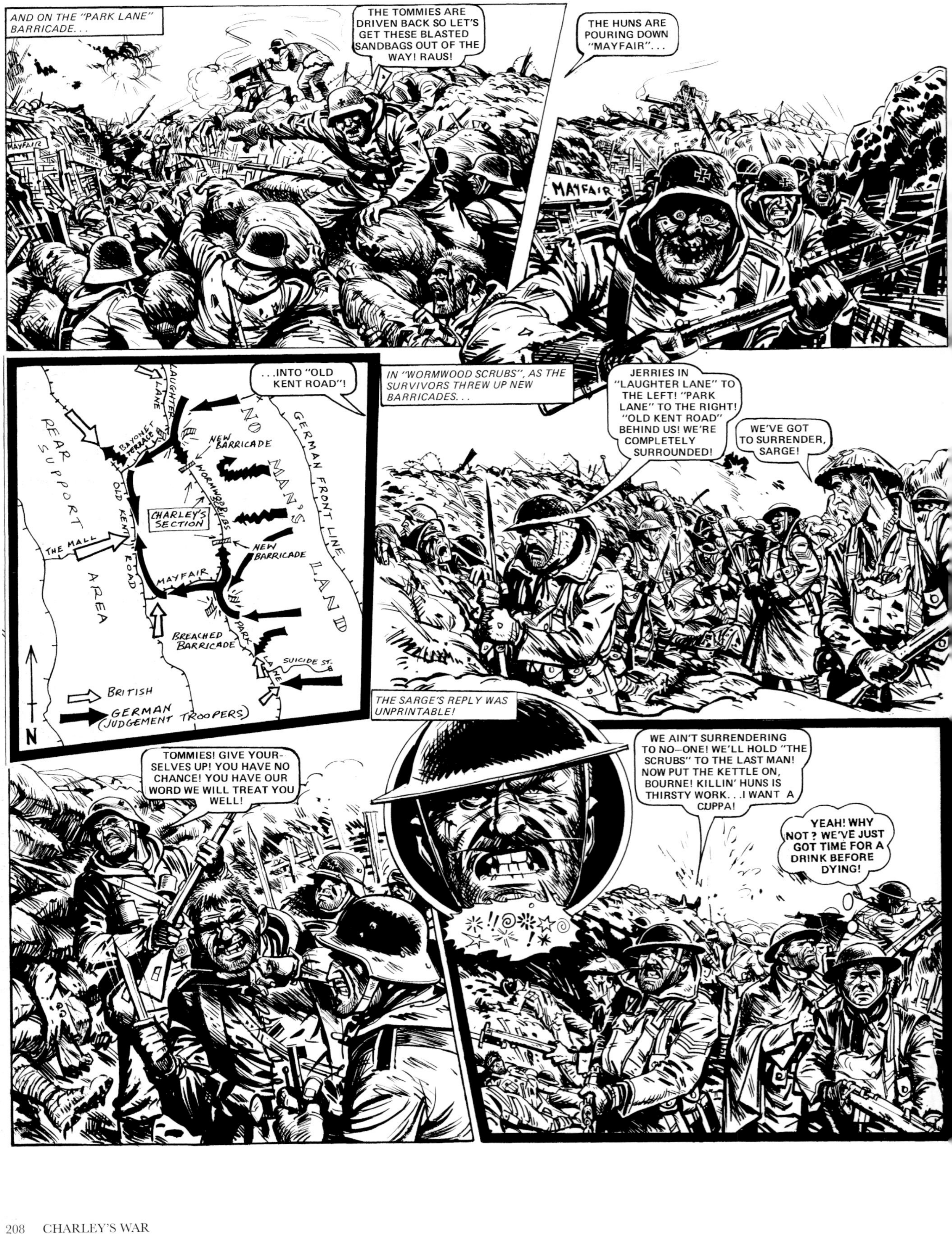
AND ON THE "PARK LANE" BARRICADE...
THE TOMMIES ARE DRIVEN BACK SO LET'S GET THESE BLASTED SANDBAGS OUT OF THE WAY! RAUS!
MAYFAIR
THE HUNS ARE POURING DOWN "MAYFAIR"...
MAYFAIR
...INTO "OLD KENT ROAD"!
LAUGHTER LANE
NO MAN'S LAND
GERMAN FRONT LINE
REAR SUPPORT AREA
BAYONET TERRACE
NEW BARRICADE
WORMWOOD SCRUBS
CHARLEY'S SECTION
OLD KENT ROAD
THE MALL
NEW BARRICADE
MAYFAIR
BREACHED BARRICADE
PARK LANE
SUICIDE ST.
BRITISH
GERMAN (JUDGEMENT TROOPERS)
N
IN "WORMWOOD SCRUBS", AS THE SURVIVORS THREW UP NEW BARRICADES...
JERRIES IN "LAUGHTER LANE" TO THE LEFT! "PARK LANE" TO THE RIGHT! "OLD KENT ROAD" BEHIND US! WE'RE COMPLETELY SURROUNDED!
WE'VE GOT TO SURRENDER, SARGE!
THE SARGE'S REPLY WAS UNPRINTABLE!
TOMMIES! GIVE YOURSELVES UP! YOU HAVE NO CHANCE! YOU HAVE OUR WORD WE WILL TREAT YOU WELL!
WE AIN'T SURRENDERING TO NO-ONE! WE'LL HOLD "THE SCRUBS" TO THE LAST MAN! NOW PUT THE KETTLE ON, BOURNE! KILLIN' HUNS IS THIRSTY WORK...I WANT A CUPPA!
YEAH! WHY NOT? WE'VE JUST GOT TIME FOR A DRINK BEFORE DYING!

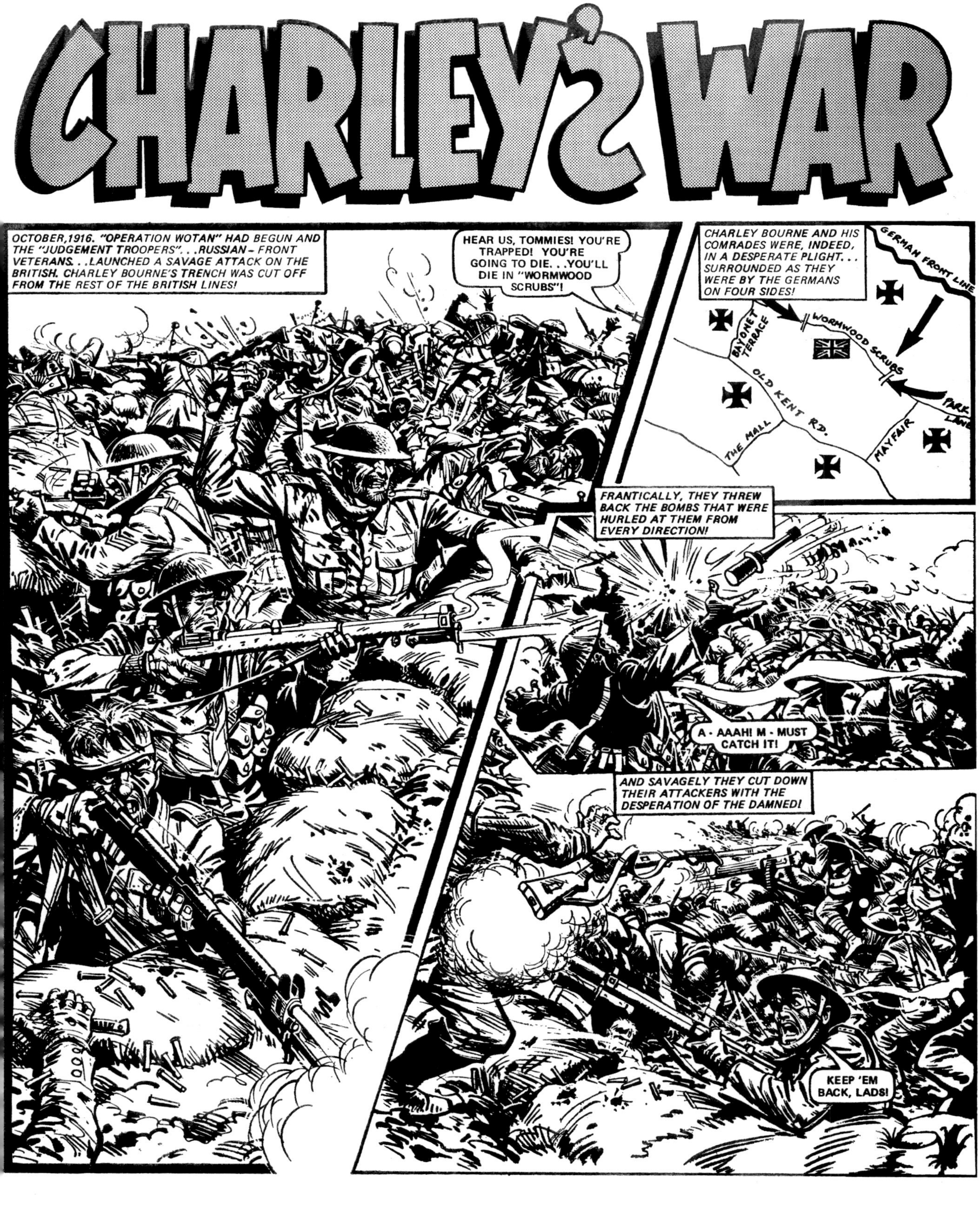
CHARLEY'S WAR
OCTOBER, 1916. "OPERATION WOTAN" HAD BEGUN AND THE "JUDGEMENT TROOPERS". . .RUSSIAN - FRONT VETERANS. . .LAUNCHED A SAVAGE ATTACK ON THE BRITISH. CHARLEY BOURNE'S TRENCH WAS CUT OFF FROM THE REST OF THE BRITISH LINES!
HEAR US, TOMMIES! YOU'RE TRAPPED! YOU'RE GOING TO DIE. . .YOU'LL DIE IN "WORMWOOD SCRUBS"!
CHARLEY BOURNE AND HIS COMRADES WERE, INDEED, IN A DESPERATE PLIGHT. . . SURROUNDED AS THEY WERE BY THE GERMANS ON FOUR SIDES!
GERMAN FRONT LINE
WORMWOOD SCRUBS
BAYONET TERRACE
OLD KENT RD.
PARK LANE
THE MALL
MAYFAIR
FRANTICALLY, THEY THREW BACK THE BOMBS THAT WERE HURLED AT THEM FROM EVERY DIRECTION!
A - AAAH! M - MUST CATCH IT!
AND SAVAGELY THEY CUT DOWN THEIR ATTACKERS WITH THE DESPERATION OF THE DAMNED!
KEEP 'EM BACK, LADS!

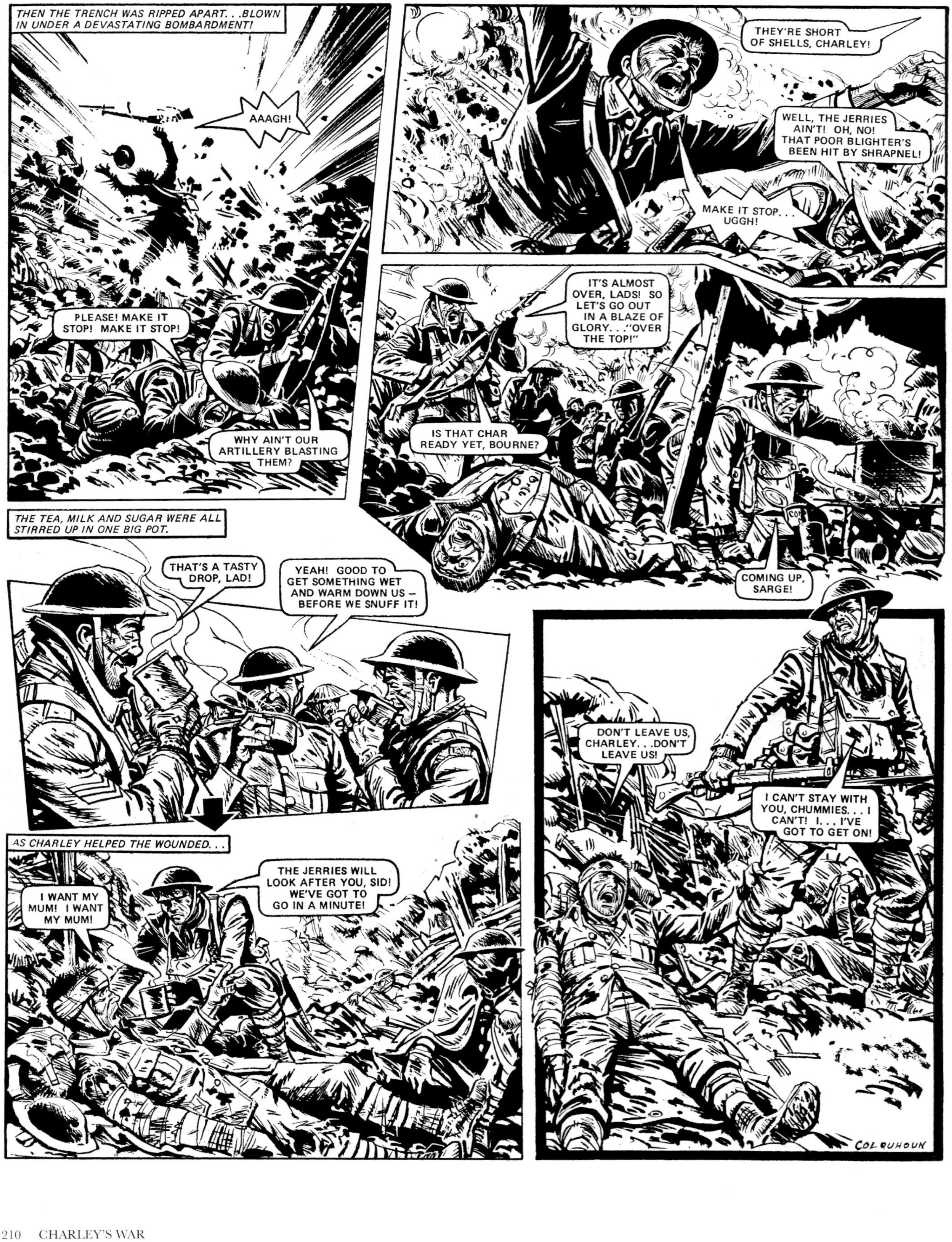

THEN THE TRENCH WAS RIPPED APART. . .BLOWN IN UNDER A DEVASTATING BOMBARDMENT!
AAAGH!
PLEASE! MAKE IT STOP! MAKE IT STOP!
WHY AIN'T OUR ARTILLERY BLASTING THEM?
THEY'RE SHORT OF SHELLS, CHARLEY!
WELL, THE JERRIES AIN'T! OH, NO! THAT POOR BLIGHTER'S BEEN HIT BY SHRAPNEL!
MAKE IT STOP. . . UGGH!
IT'S ALMOST OVER, LADS! SO LET'S GO OUT IN A BLAZE OF GLORY. . ."OVER THE TOP!"
IS THAT CHAR READY YET, BOURNE?
COMING UP, SARGE!
THE TEA, MILK AND SUGAR WERE ALL STIRRED UP IN ONE BIG POT.
THAT'S A TASTY DROP, LAD!
YEAH! GOOD TO GET SOMETHING WET AND WARM DOWN US – BEFORE WE SNUFF IT!
AS CHARLEY HELPED THE WOUNDED. . .
I WANT MY MUM! I WANT MY MUM!
THE JERRIES WILL LOOK AFTER YOU, SID! WE'VE GOT TO GO IN A MINUTE!
DON'T LEAVE US, CHARLEY. . .DON'T LEAVE US!
I CAN'T STAY WITH YOU, CHUMMIES. . . I CAN'T! I. . . I'VE GOT TO GET ON!
COLQUHOUN

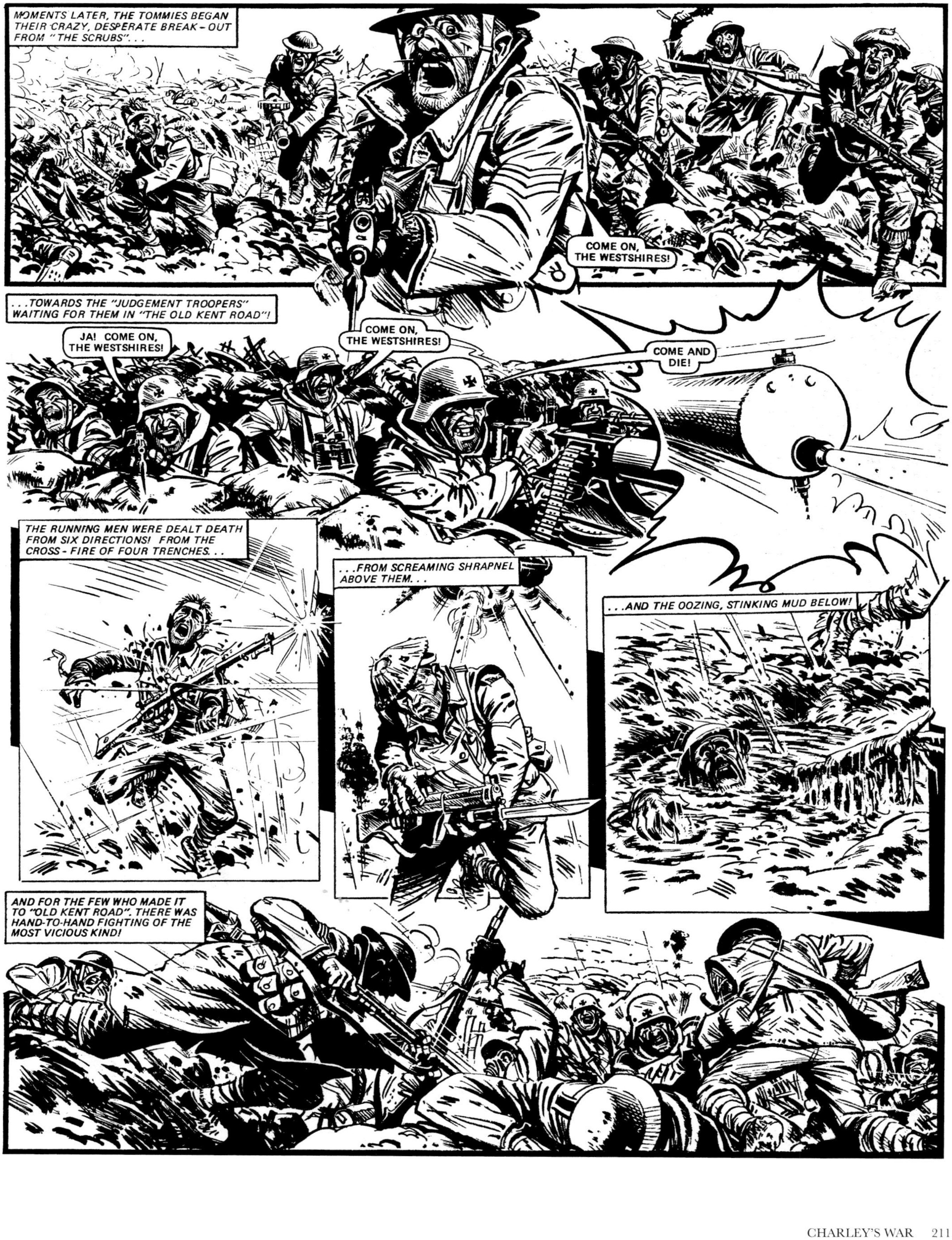
MOMENTS LATER, THE TOMMIES BEGAN THEIR CRAZY, DESPERATE BREAK - OUT FROM "THE SCRUBS"...
COME ON, THE WESTSHIRES!
...TOWARDS THE "JUDGEMENT TROOPERS" WAITING FOR THEM IN "THE OLD KENT ROAD"!
JA! COME ON, THE WESTSHIRES!
COME ON, THE WESTSHIRES!
COME AND DIE!
THE RUNNING MEN WERE DEALT DEATH FROM SIX DIRECTIONS! FROM THE CROSS - FIRE OF FOUR TRENCHES...
...FROM SCREAMING SHRAPNEL ABOVE THEM...
...AND THE OOZING, STINKING MUD BELOW!
AND FOR THE FEW WHO MADE IT TO "OLD KENT ROAD", THERE WAS HAND-TO-HAND FIGHTING OF THE MOST VICIOUS KIND!

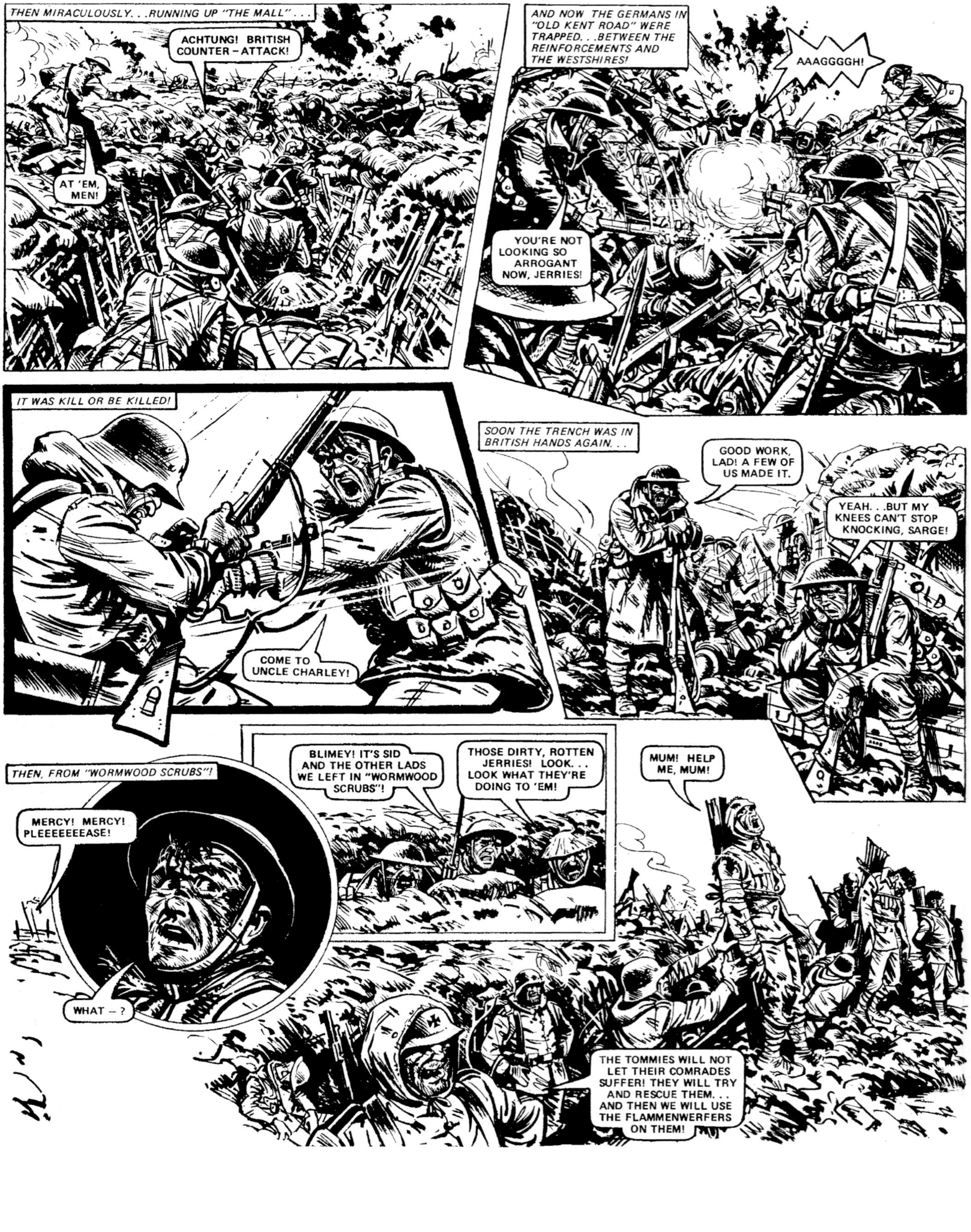
THEN MIRACULOUSLY. . .RUNNING UP "THE MALL". . .
ACHTUNG! BRITISH COUNTER – ATTACK!
AT 'EM, MEN!
AND NOW THE GERMANS IN "OLD KENT ROAD" WERE TRAPPED. . .BETWEEN THE REINFORCEMENTS AND THE WESTSHIRES!
AAAGGGGH!
YOU'RE NOT LOOKING SO ARROGANT NOW, JERRIES!
IT WAS KILL OR BE KILLED!
COME TO UNCLE CHARLEY!
SOON THE TRENCH WAS IN BRITISH HANDS AGAIN. . .
GOOD WORK, LAD! A FEW OF US MADE IT.
YEAH. . .BUT MY KNEES CAN'T STOP KNOCKING, SARGE!
OLD K
THEN, FROM "WORMWOOD SCRUBS"!
MERCY! MERCY! PLEEEEEEEASE!
WHAT – ?
BLIMEY! IT'S SID AND THE OTHER LADS WE LEFT IN "WORMWOOD SCRUBS"!
THOSE DIRTY, ROTTEN JERRIES! LOOK. . . LOOK WHAT THEY'RE DOING TO 'EM!
MUM! HELP ME, MUM!
THE TOMMIES WILL NOT LET THEIR COMRADES SUFFER! THEY WILL TRY AND RESCUE THEM. . . AND THEN WE WILL USE THE FLAMMENWERFERS ON THEM!

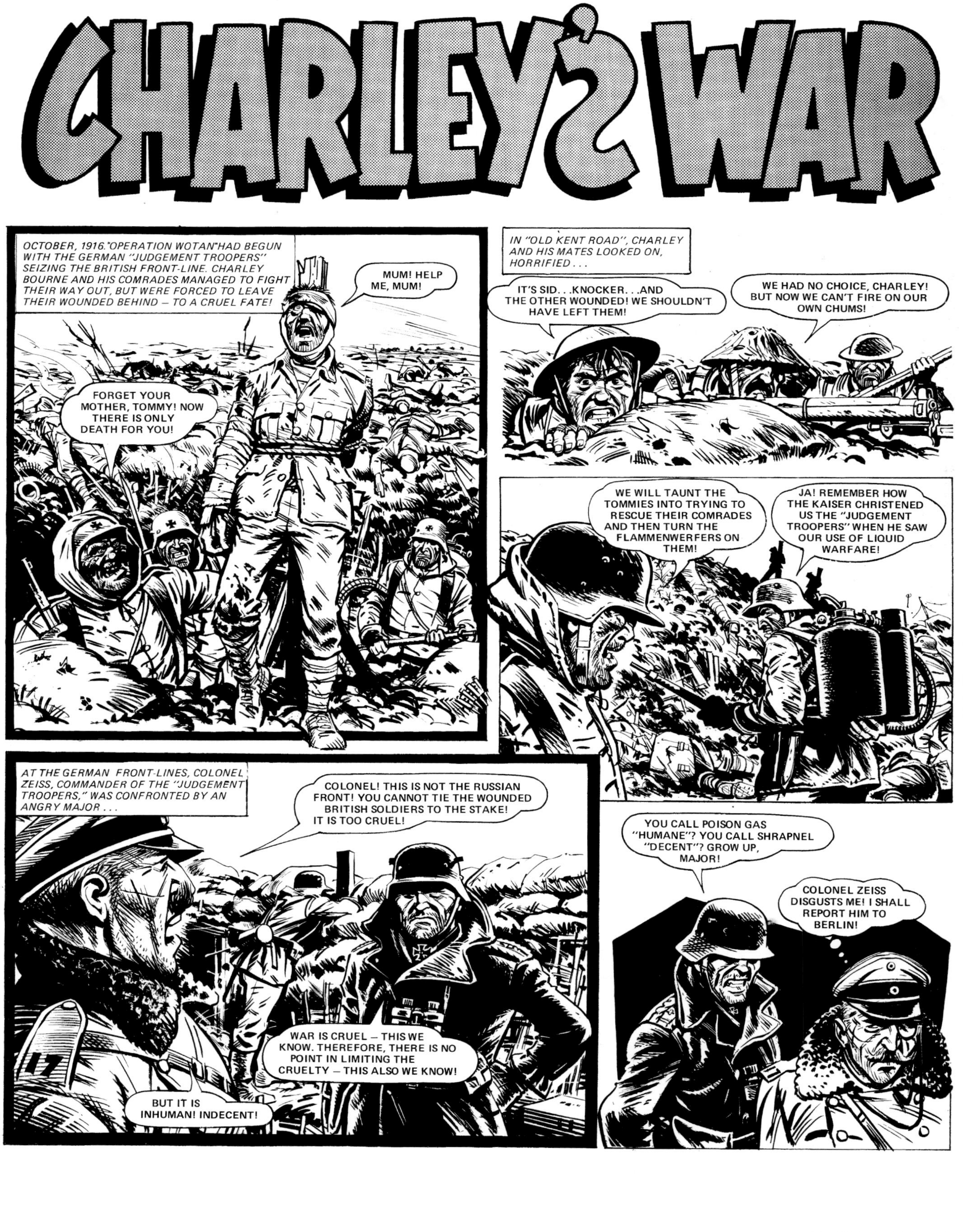
CHARLEY'S WAR
OCTOBER, 1916. "OPERATION WOTAN" HAD BEGUN WITH THE GERMAN "JUDGEMENT TROOPERS" SEIZING THE BRITISH FRONT-LINE. CHARLEY BOURNE AND HIS COMRADES MANAGED TO FIGHT THEIR WAY OUT, BUT WERE FORCED TO LEAVE THEIR WOUNDED BEHIND – TO A CRUEL FATE!
MUM! HELP ME, MUM!
FORGET YOUR MOTHER, TOMMY! NOW THERE IS ONLY DEATH FOR YOU!
IN "OLD KENT ROAD", CHARLEY AND HIS MATES LOOKED ON, HORRIFIED . . .
IT'S SID. . .KNOCKER. . .AND THE OTHER WOUNDED! WE SHOULDN'T HAVE LEFT THEM!
WE HAD NO CHOICE, CHARLEY! BUT NOW WE CAN'T FIRE ON OUR OWN CHUMS!
WE WILL TAUNT THE TOMMIES INTO TRYING TO RESCUE THEIR COMRADES AND THEN TURN THE FLAMMENWERFERS ON THEM!
JA! REMEMBER HOW THE KAISER CHRISTENED US THE "JUDGEMENT TROOPERS" WHEN HE SAW OUR USE OF LIQUID WARFARE!
AT THE GERMAN FRONT-LINES, COLONEL ZEISS, COMMANDER OF THE "JUDGEMENT TROOPERS," WAS CONFRONTED BY AN ANGRY MAJOR . . .
COLONEL! THIS IS NOT THE RUSSIAN FRONT! YOU CANNOT TIE THE WOUNDED BRITISH SOLDIERS TO THE STAKE! IT IS TOO CRUEL!
WAR IS CRUEL – THIS WE KNOW. THEREFORE, THERE IS NO POINT IN LIMITING THE CRUELTY – THIS ALSO WE KNOW!
BUT IT IS INHUMAN! INDECENT!
YOU CALL POISON GAS "HUMANE"? YOU CALL SHRAPNEL "DECENT"? GROW UP, MAJOR!
COLONEL ZEISS DISGUSTS ME! I SHALL REPORT HIM TO BERLIN!

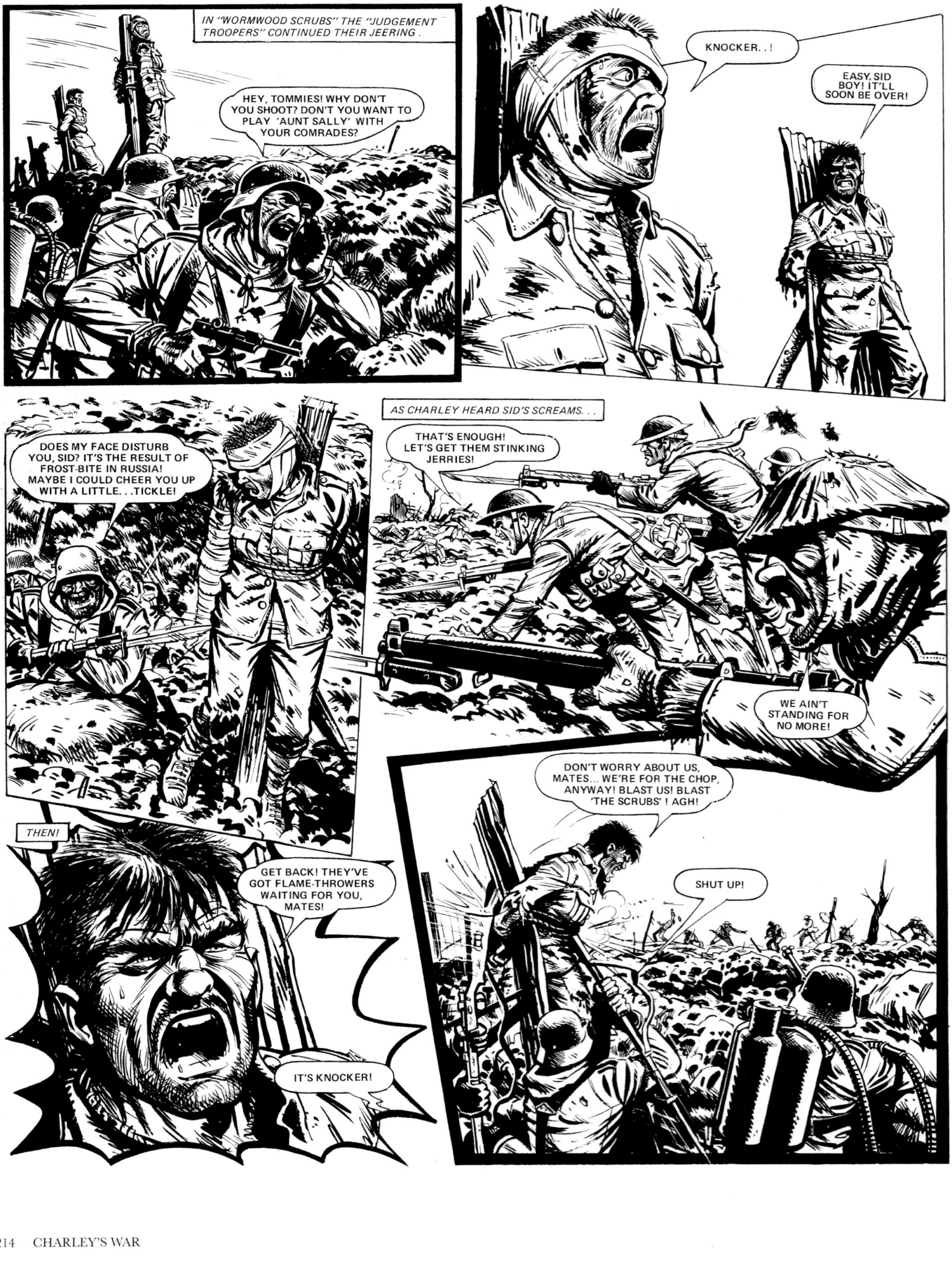
IN "WORMWOOD SCRUBS" THE "JUDGEMENT TROOPERS" CONTINUED THEIR JEERING.
HEY, TOMMIES! WHY DON'T YOU SHOOT? DON'T YOU WANT TO PLAY 'AUNT SALLY' WITH YOUR COMRADES?
KNOCKER..!
EASY, SID BOY! IT'LL SOON BE OVER!
DOES MY FACE DISTURB YOU, SID? IT'S THE RESULT OF FROST-BITE IN RUSSIA! MAYBE I COULD CHEER YOU UP WITH A LITTLE...TICKLE!
AS CHARLEY HEARD SID'S SCREAMS...
THAT'S ENOUGH! LET'S GET THEM STINKING JERRIES!
WE AIN'T STANDING FOR NO MORE!
THEN!
GET BACK! THEY'VE GOT FLAME-THROWERS WAITING FOR YOU, MATES!
IT'S KNOCKER!
DON'T WORRY ABOUT US, MATES... WE'RE FOR THE CHOP, ANYWAY! BLAST US! BLAST 'THE SCRUBS'! AGH!
SHUT UP!

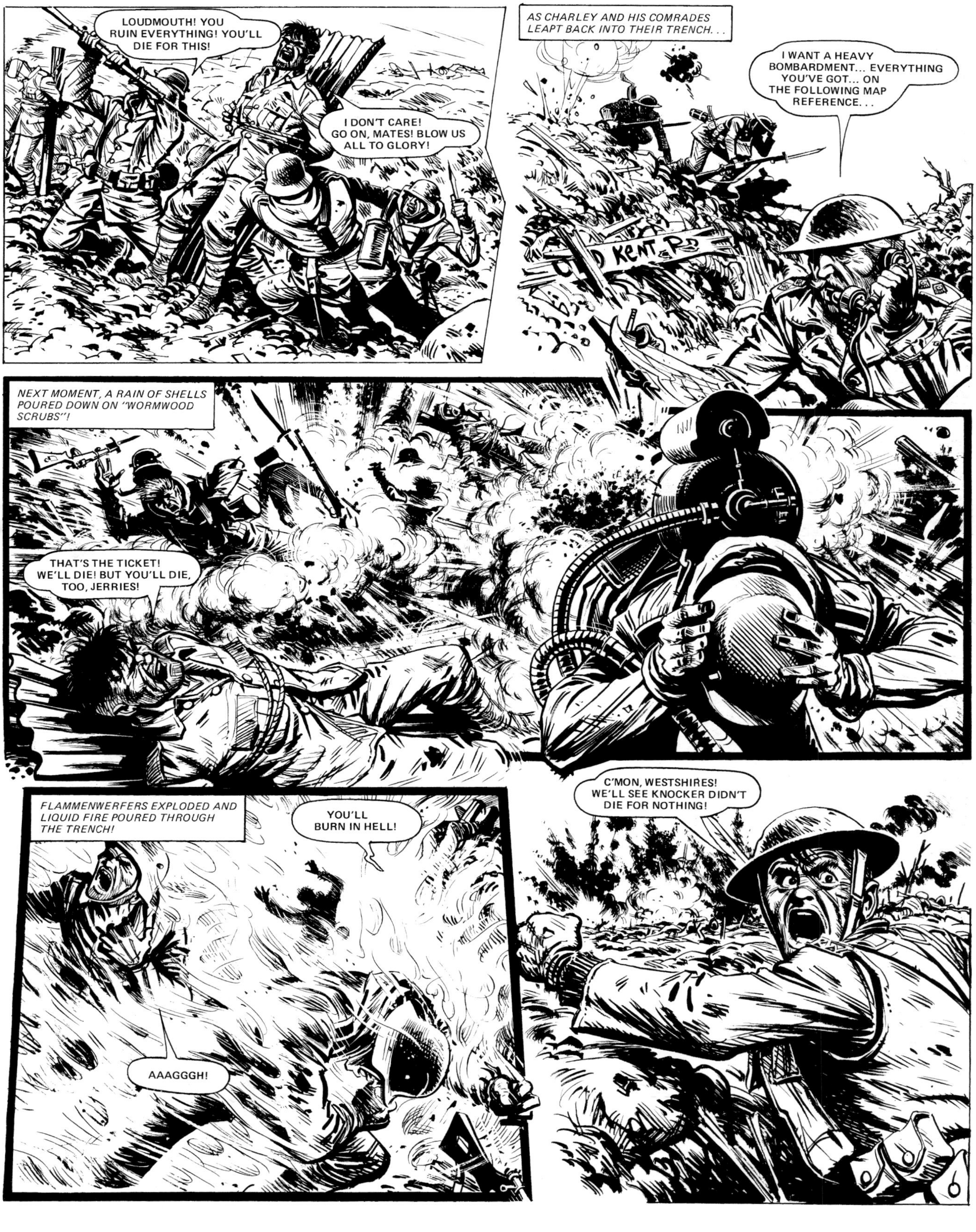

LOUDMOUTH! YOU RUIN EVERYTHING! YOU'LL DIE FOR THIS!
I DON'T CARE! GO ON, MATES! BLOW US ALL TO GLORY!
AS CHARLEY AND HIS COMRADES LEAPT BACK INTO THEIR TRENCH...
I WANT A HEAVY BOMBARDMENT... EVERYTHING YOU'VE GOT... ON THE FOLLOWING MAP REFERENCE...
OLD KENT RD
NEXT MOMENT, A RAIN OF SHELLS POURED DOWN ON "WORMWOOD SCRUBS"!
THAT'S THE TICKET! WE'LL DIE! BUT YOU'LL DIE, TOO, JERRIES!
FLAMMENWERFERS EXPLODED AND LIQUID FIRE POURED THROUGH THE TRENCH!
YOU'LL BURN IN HELL!
AAAGGGH!
C'MON, WESTSHIRES! WE'LL SEE KNOCKER DIDN'T DIE FOR NOTHING!

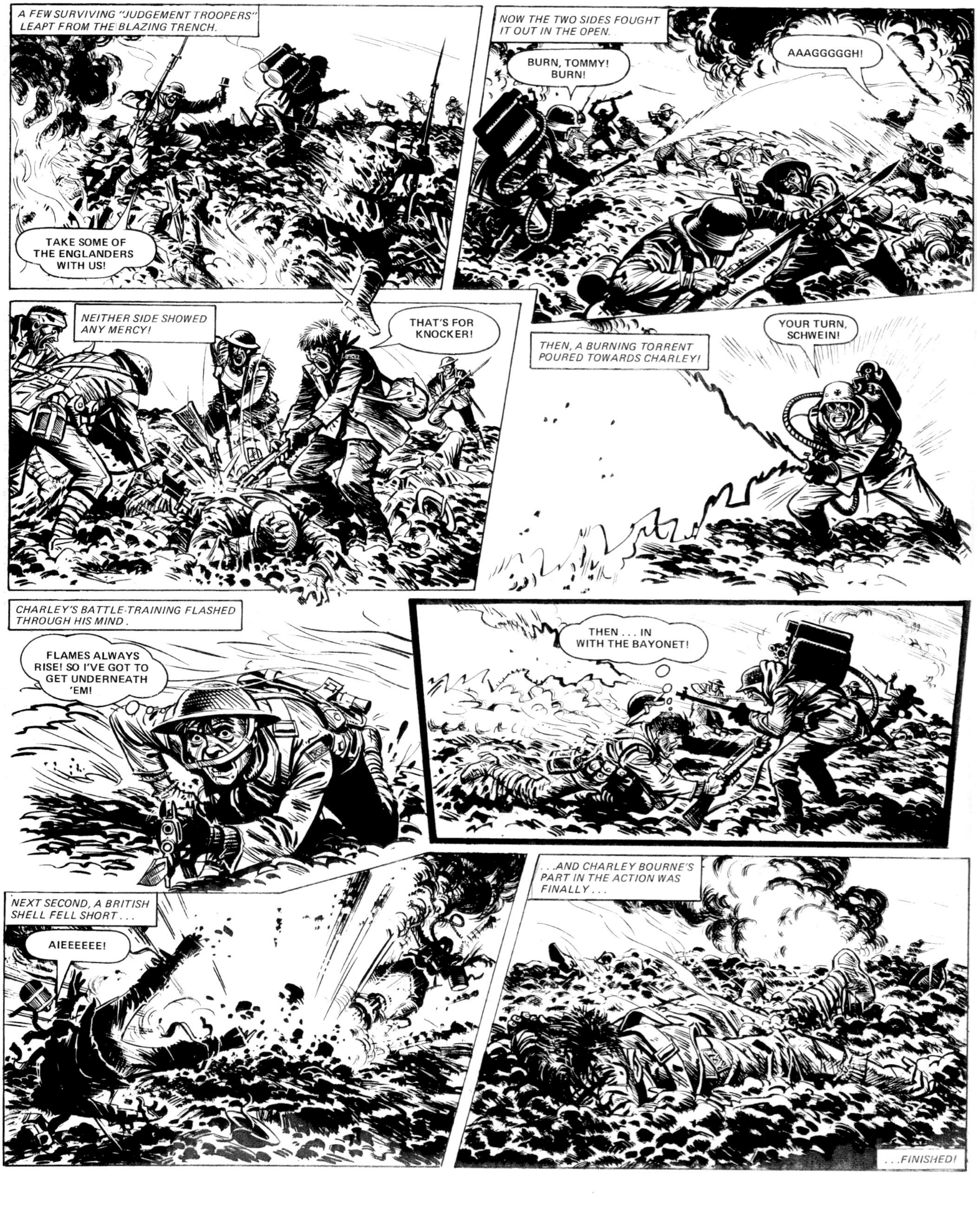
A FEW SURVIVING "JUDGEMENT TROOPERS" LEAPT FROM THE BLAZING TRENCH.
TAKE SOME OF THE ENGLANDERS WITH US!
NOW THE TWO SIDES FOUGHT IT OUT IN THE OPEN.
BURN, TOMMY! BURN!
AAAGGGGGH!
NEITHER SIDE SHOWED ANY MERCY!
THAT'S FOR KNOCKER!
THEN, A BURNING TORRENT POURED TOWARDS CHARLEY!
YOUR TURN, SCHWEIN!
CHARLEY'S BATTLE-TRAINING FLASHED THROUGH HIS MIND.
FLAMES ALWAYS RISE! SO I'VE GOT TO GET UNDERNEATH 'EM!
THEN . . . IN WITH THE BAYONET!
NEXT SECOND, A BRITISH SHELL FELL SHORT . . .
AIEEEEEE!
. . .AND CHARLEY BOURNE'S PART IN THE ACTION WAS FINALLY . . .
. . .FINISHED!

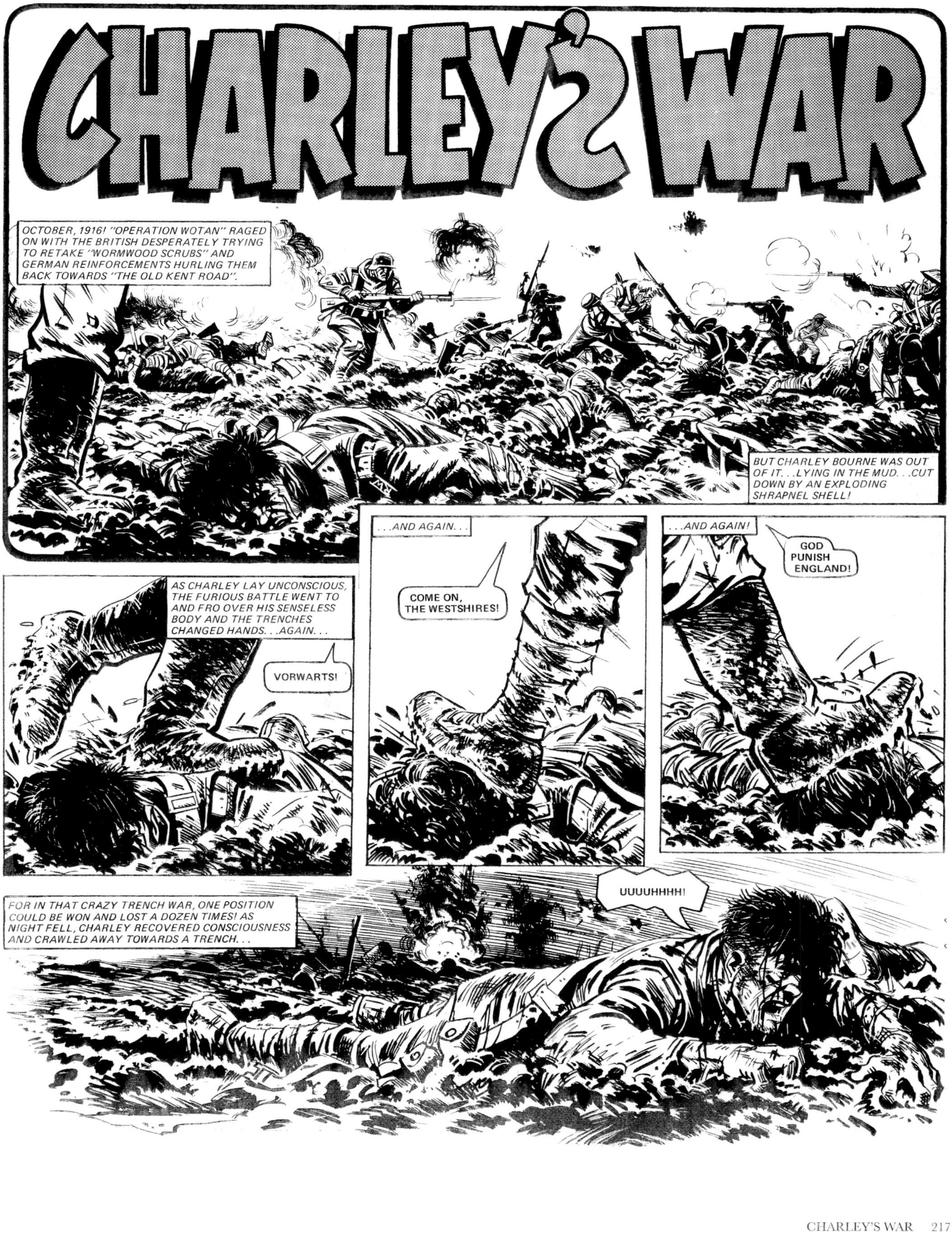
CHARLEY'S WAR
OCTOBER, 1916! "OPERATION WOTAN" RAGED ON WITH THE BRITISH DESPERATELY TRYING TO RETAKE "WORMWOOD SCRUBS" AND GERMAN REINFORCEMENTS HURLING THEM BACK TOWARDS "THE OLD KENT ROAD".
BUT CHARLEY BOURNE WAS OUT OF IT. . .LYING IN THE MUD. . .CUT DOWN BY AN EXPLODING SHRAPNEL SHELL!
AS CHARLEY LAY UNCONSCIOUS, THE FURIOUS BATTLE WENT TO AND FRO OVER HIS SENSELESS BODY AND THE TRENCHES CHANGED HANDS. . .AGAIN. . .
VORWARTS!
. . .AND AGAIN. . .
COME ON, THE WESTSHIRES!
. . .AND AGAIN!
GOD PUNISH ENGLAND!
FOR IN THAT CRAZY TRENCH WAR, ONE POSITION COULD BE WON AND LOST A DOZEN TIMES! AS NIGHT FELL, CHARLEY RECOVERED CONSCIOUSNESS AND CRAWLED AWAY TOWARDS A TRENCH. . .
UUUUHHHH!

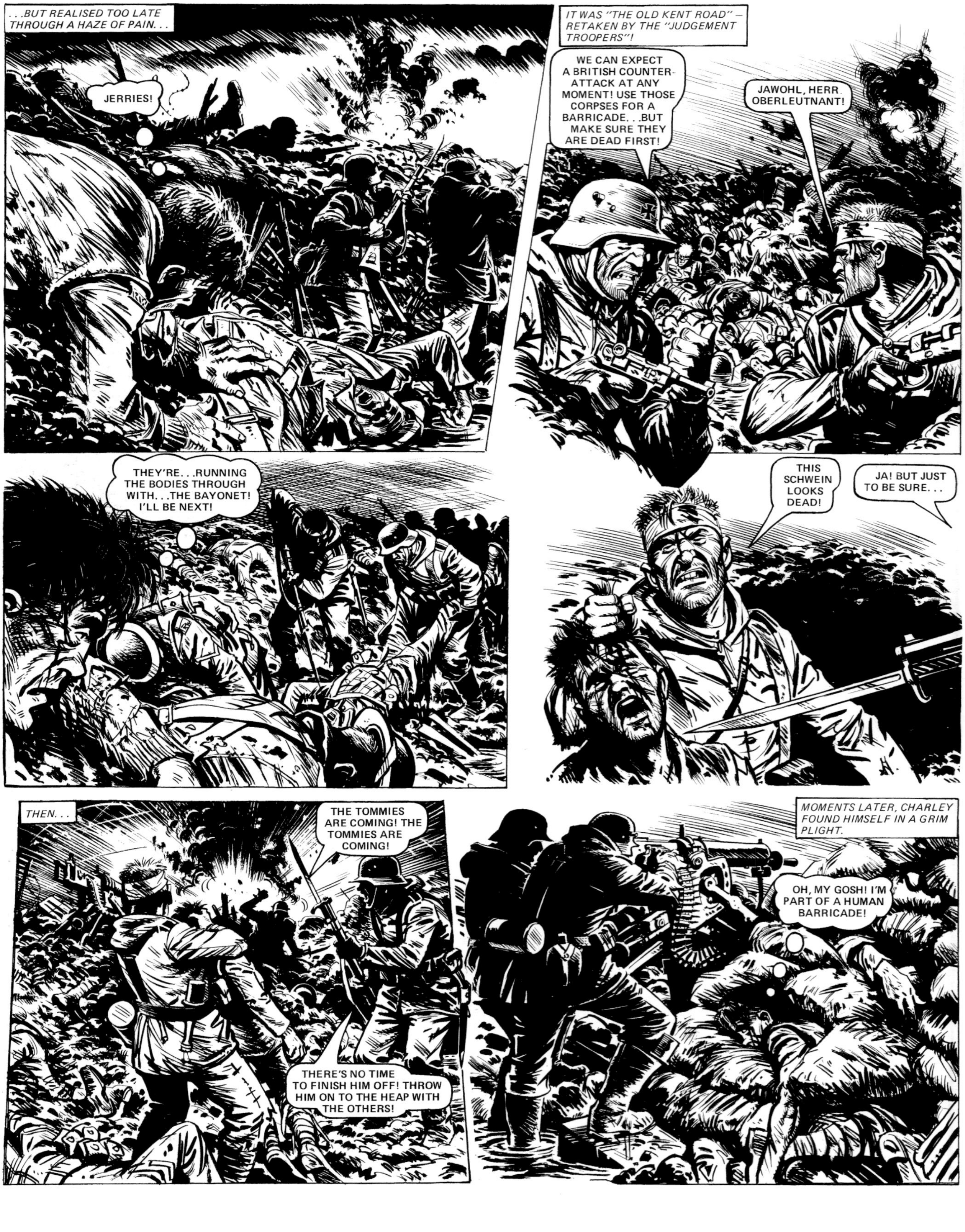
...BUT REALISED TOO LATE THROUGH A HAZE OF PAIN...
JERRIES!
IT WAS "THE OLD KENT ROAD" – RETAKEN BY THE "JUDGEMENT TROOPERS"!
WE CAN EXPECT A BRITISH COUNTER-ATTACK AT ANY MOMENT! USE THOSE CORPSES FOR A BARRICADE...BUT MAKE SURE THEY ARE DEAD FIRST!
JAWOHL, HERR OBERLEUTNANT!
THEY'RE...RUNNING THE BODIES THROUGH WITH...THE BAYONET! I'LL BE NEXT!
THIS SCHWEIN LOOKS DEAD!
JA! BUT JUST TO BE SURE...
THEN...
THE TOMMIES ARE COMING! THE TOMMIES ARE COMING!
THERE'S NO TIME TO FINISH HIM OFF! THROW HIM ON TO THE HEAP WITH THE OTHERS!
MOMENTS LATER, CHARLEY FOUND HIMSELF IN A GRIM PLIGHT.
OH, MY GOSH! I'M PART OF A HUMAN BARRICADE!

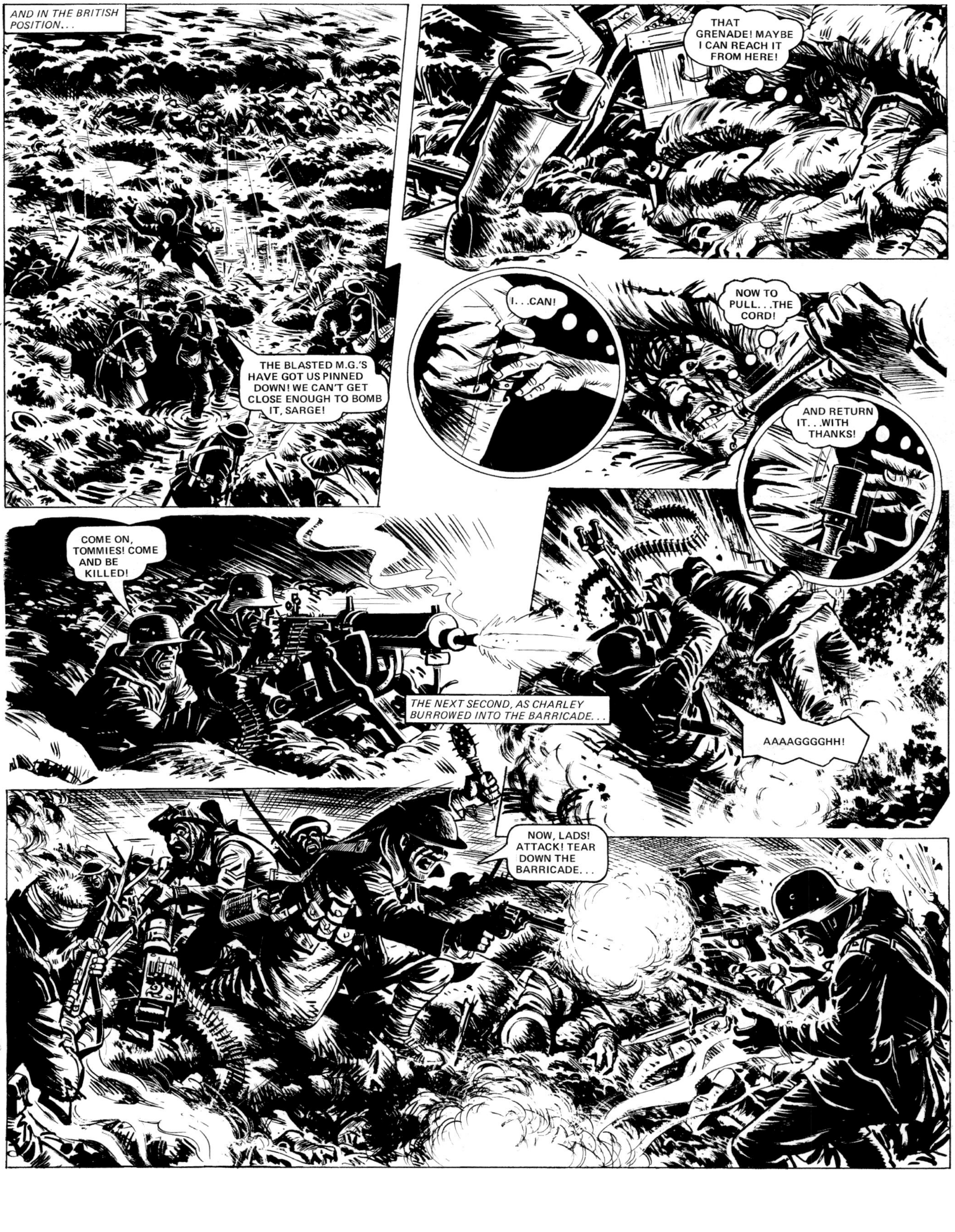
AND IN THE BRITISH POSITION...
THE BLASTED M.G.'S HAVE GOT US PINNED DOWN! WE CAN'T GET CLOSE ENOUGH TO BOMB IT, SARGE!
THAT GRENADE! MAYBE I CAN REACH IT FROM HERE!
I...CAN!
NOW TO PULL...THE CORD!
AND RETURN IT...WITH THANKS!
COME ON, TOMMIES! COME AND BE KILLED!
THE NEXT SECOND, AS CHARLEY BURROWED INTO THE BARRICADE...
AAAAGGGGHH!
NOW, LADS! ATTACK! TEAR DOWN THE BARRICADE...

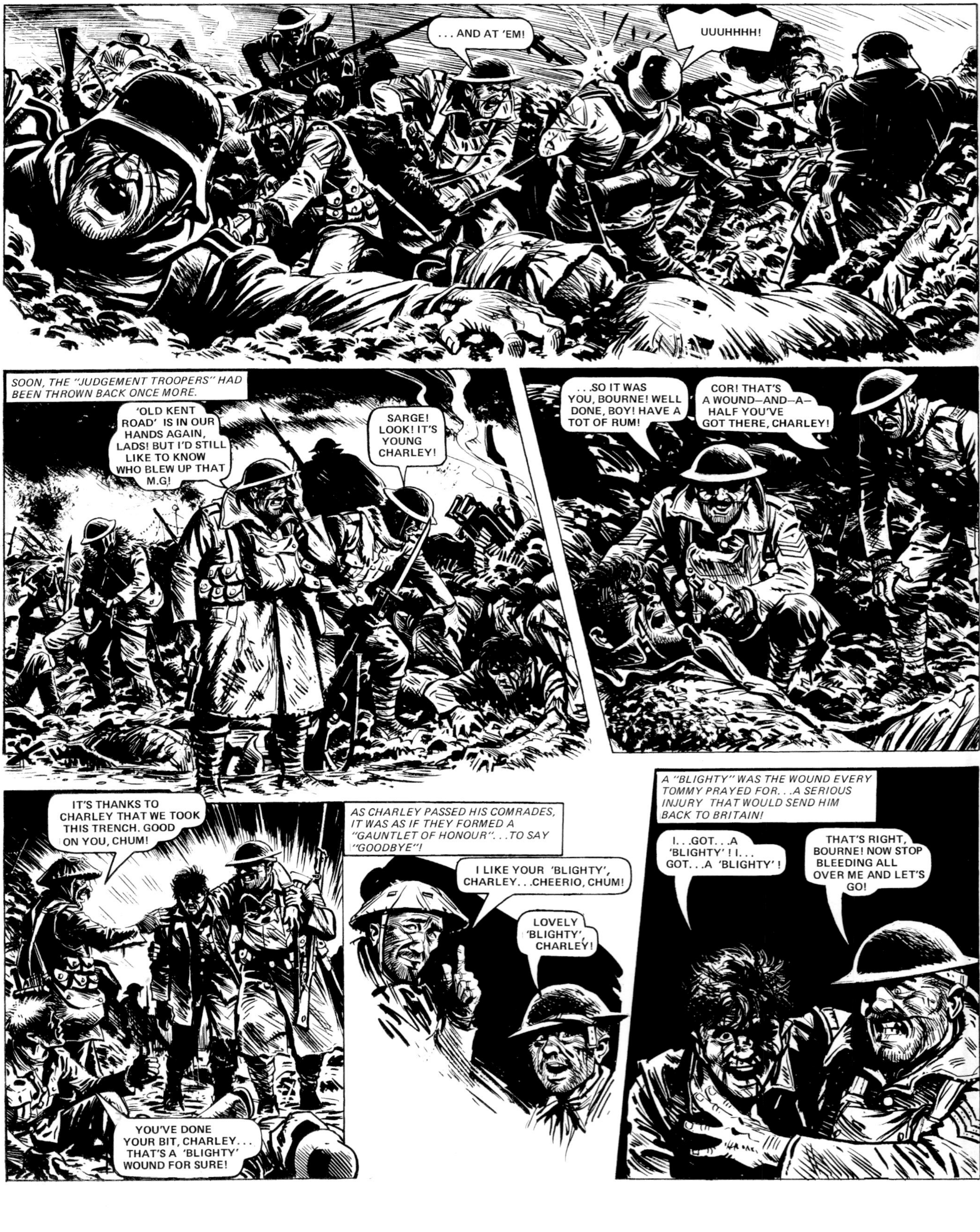
. . . AND AT 'EM!
UUUHHHH!
SOON, THE "JUDGEMENT TROOPERS" HAD BEEN THROWN BACK ONCE MORE.
'OLD KENT ROAD' IS IN OUR HANDS AGAIN, LADS! BUT I'D STILL LIKE TO KNOW WHO BLEW UP THAT M.G!
SARGE! LOOK! IT'S YOUNG CHARLEY!
. . .SO IT WAS YOU, BOURNE! WELL DONE, BOY! HAVE A TOT OF RUM!
COR! THAT'S A WOUND—AND—A—HALF YOU'VE GOT THERE, CHARLEY!
IT'S THANKS TO CHARLEY THAT WE TOOK THIS TRENCH. GOOD ON YOU, CHUM!
YOU'VE DONE YOUR BIT, CHARLEY. . . THAT'S A 'BLIGHTY' WOUND FOR SURE!
AS CHARLEY PASSED HIS COMRADES, IT WAS AS IF THEY FORMED A "GAUNTLET OF HONOUR". . . TO SAY "GOODBYE"!
I LIKE YOUR 'BLIGHTY', CHARLEY. . .CHEERIO, CHUM!
LOVELY 'BLIGHTY', CHARLEY!
A "BLIGHTY" WAS THE WOUND EVERY TOMMY PRAYED FOR. . .A SERIOUS INJURY THAT WOULD SEND HIM BACK TO BRITAIN!
I. . .GOT. . .A 'BLIGHTY' ! I. . . GOT. . .A 'BLIGHTY' !
THAT'S RIGHT, BOURNE! NOW STOP BLEEDING ALL OVER ME AND LET'S GO!

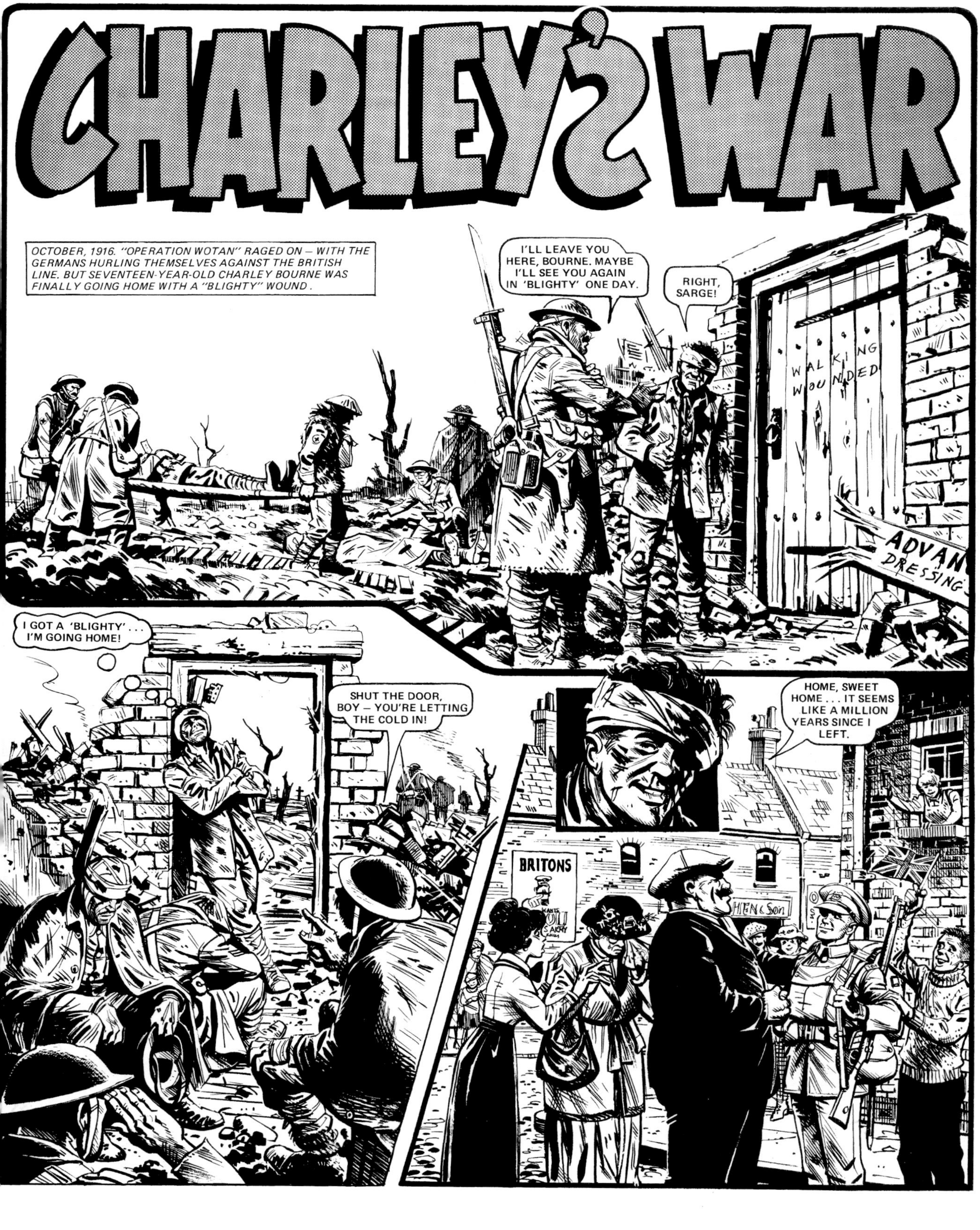
CHARLEY'S WAR
OCTOBER, 1916. "OPERATION WOTAN" RAGED ON – WITH THE GERMANS HURLING THEMSELVES AGAINST THE BRITISH LINE. BUT SEVENTEEN-YEAR-OLD CHARLEY BOURNE WAS FINALLY GOING HOME WITH A "BLIGHTY" WOUND.
I'LL LEAVE YOU HERE, BOURNE. MAYBE I'LL SEE YOU AGAIN IN 'BLIGHTY' ONE DAY.
RIGHT, SARGE!
WALKING WOUNDED
ADVAN DRESSING
I GOT A 'BLIGHTY' . . . I'M GOING HOME!
SHUT THE DOOR, BOY – YOU'RE LETTING THE COLD IN!
HOME, SWEET HOME . . . IT SEEMS LIKE A MILLION YEARS SINCE I LEFT.
BRITONS

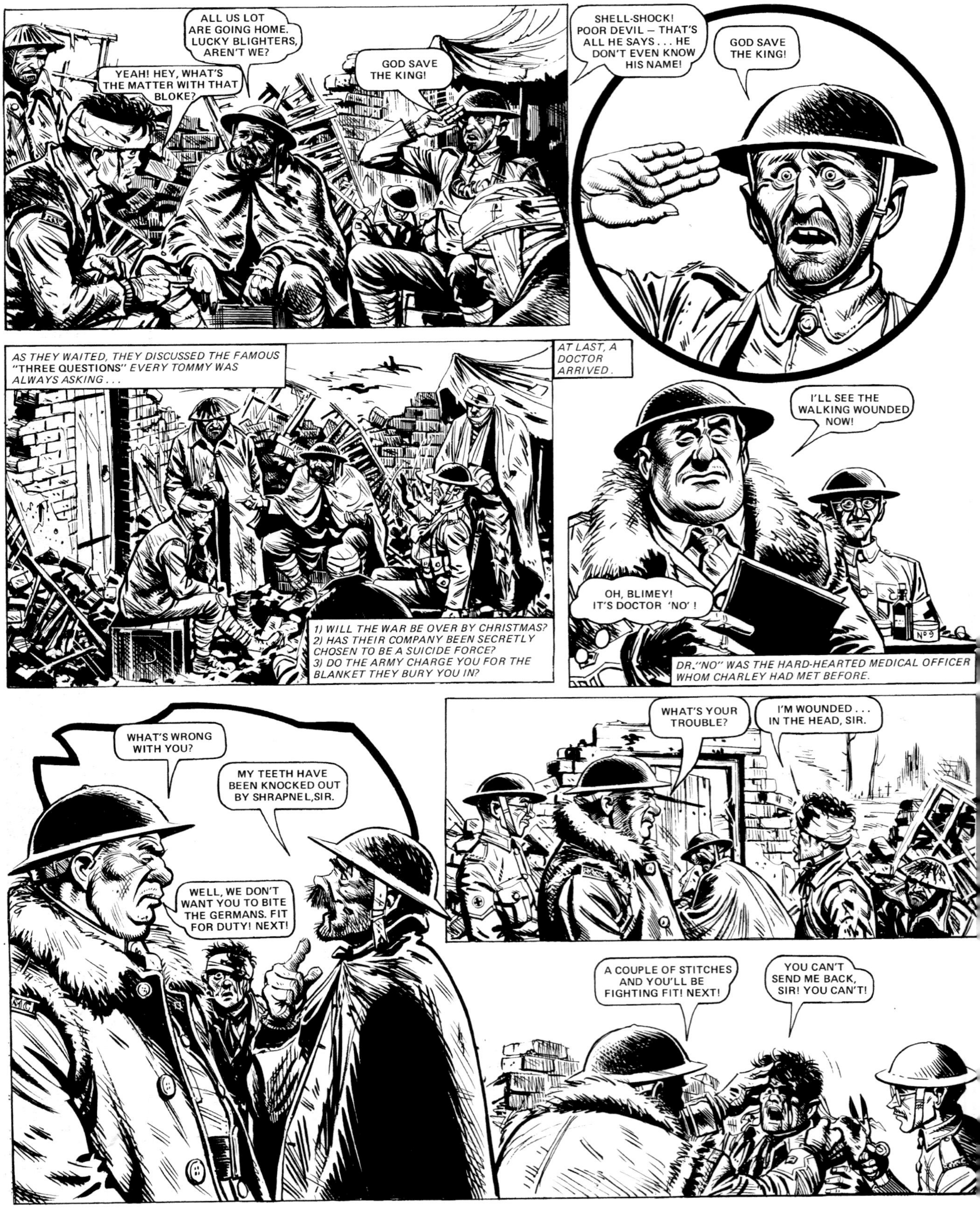
ALL US LOT ARE GOING HOME. LUCKY BLIGHTERS, AREN'T WE?
YEAH! HEY, WHAT'S THE MATTER WITH THAT BLOKE?
GOD SAVE THE KING!
SHELL-SHOCK! POOR DEVIL — THAT'S ALL HE SAYS . . . HE DON'T EVEN KNOW HIS NAME!
GOD SAVE THE KING!
AS THEY WAITED, THEY DISCUSSED THE FAMOUS "THREE QUESTIONS" EVERY TOMMY WAS ALWAYS ASKING . . .
1) WILL THE WAR BE OVER BY CHRISTMAS? 2) HAS THEIR COMPANY BEEN SECRETLY CHOSEN TO BE A SUICIDE FORCE? 3) DO THE ARMY CHARGE YOU FOR THE BLANKET THEY BURY YOU IN?
AT LAST, A DOCTOR ARRIVED.
I'LL SEE THE WALKING WOUNDED NOW!
OH, BLIMEY! IT'S DOCTOR 'NO'!
DR. "NO" WAS THE HARD-HEARTED MEDICAL OFFICER WHOM CHARLEY HAD MET BEFORE.
WHAT'S WRONG WITH YOU?
MY TEETH HAVE BEEN KNOCKED OUT BY SHRAPNEL, SIR.
WELL, WE DON'T WANT YOU TO BITE THE GERMANS. FIT FOR DUTY! NEXT!
WHAT'S YOUR TROUBLE?
I'M WOUNDED . . . IN THE HEAD, SIR.
A COUPLE OF STITCHES AND YOU'LL BE FIGHTING FIT! NEXT!
YOU CAN'T SEND ME BACK, SIR! YOU CAN'T!

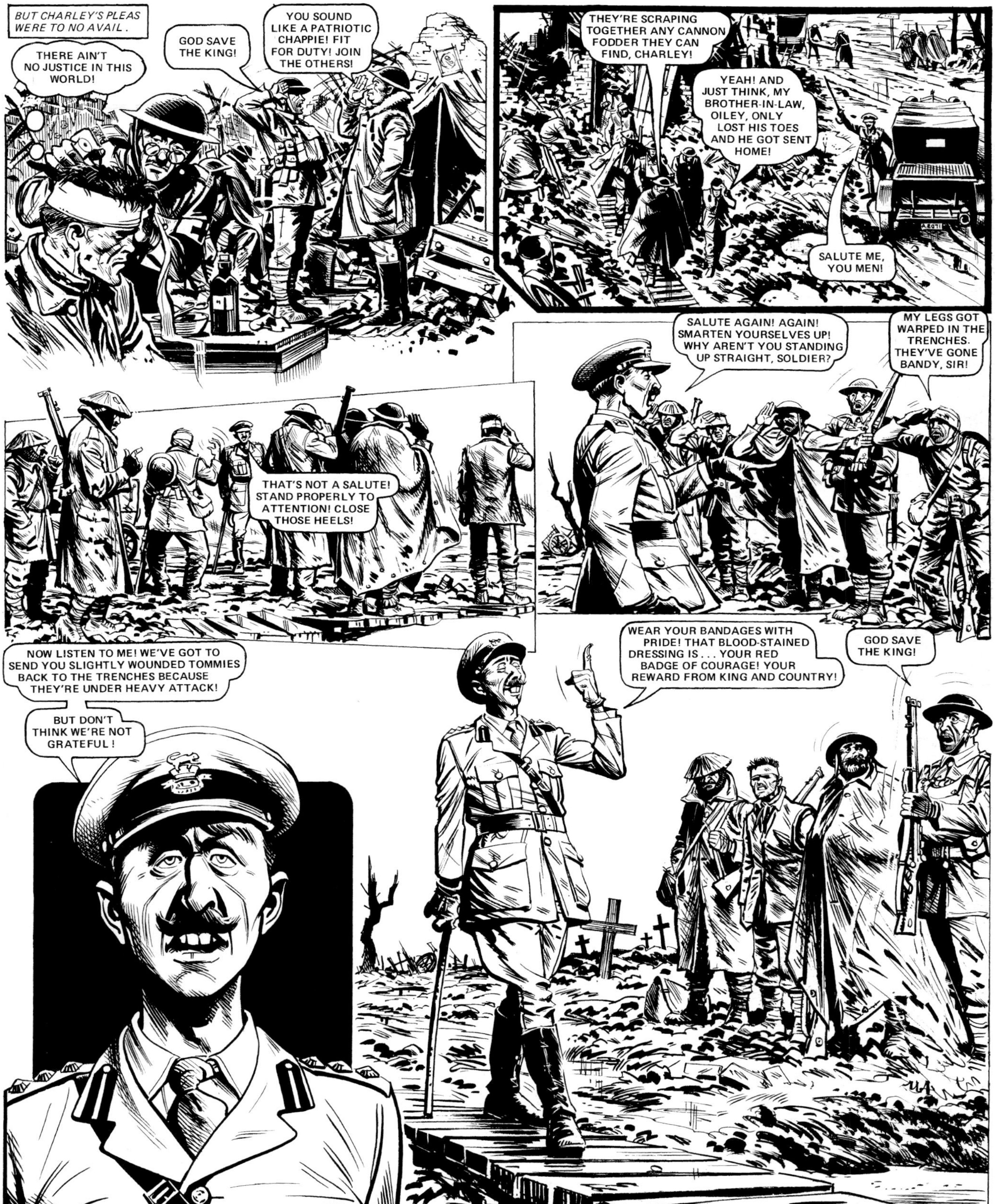

BUT CHARLEY'S PLEAS WERE TO NO AVAIL.
THERE AIN'T NO JUSTICE IN THIS WORLD!
GOD SAVE THE KING!
YOU SOUND LIKE A PATRIOTIC CHAPPIE! FIT FOR DUTY! JOIN THE OTHERS!
THEY'RE SCRAPING TOGETHER ANY CANNON FODDER THEY CAN FIND, CHARLEY!
YEAH! AND JUST THINK, MY BROTHER-IN-LAW, OILEY, ONLY LOST HIS TOES AND HE GOT SENT HOME!
SALUTE ME, YOU MEN!
THAT'S NOT A SALUTE! STAND PROPERLY TO ATTENTION! CLOSE THOSE HEELS!
SALUTE AGAIN! AGAIN! SMARTEN YOURSELVES UP! WHY AREN'T YOU STANDING UP STRAIGHT, SOLDIER?
MY LEGS GOT WARPED IN THE TRENCHES. THEY'VE GONE BANDY, SIR!
NOW LISTEN TO ME! WE'VE GOT TO SEND YOU SLIGHTLY WOUNDED TOMMIES BACK TO THE TRENCHES BECAUSE THEY'RE UNDER HEAVY ATTACK!
BUT DON'T THINK WE'RE NOT GRATEFUL!
WEAR YOUR BANDAGES WITH PRIDE! THAT BLOOD-STAINED DRESSING IS . . . YOUR RED BADGE OF COURAGE! YOUR REWARD FROM KING AND COUNTRY!
GOD SAVE THE KING!

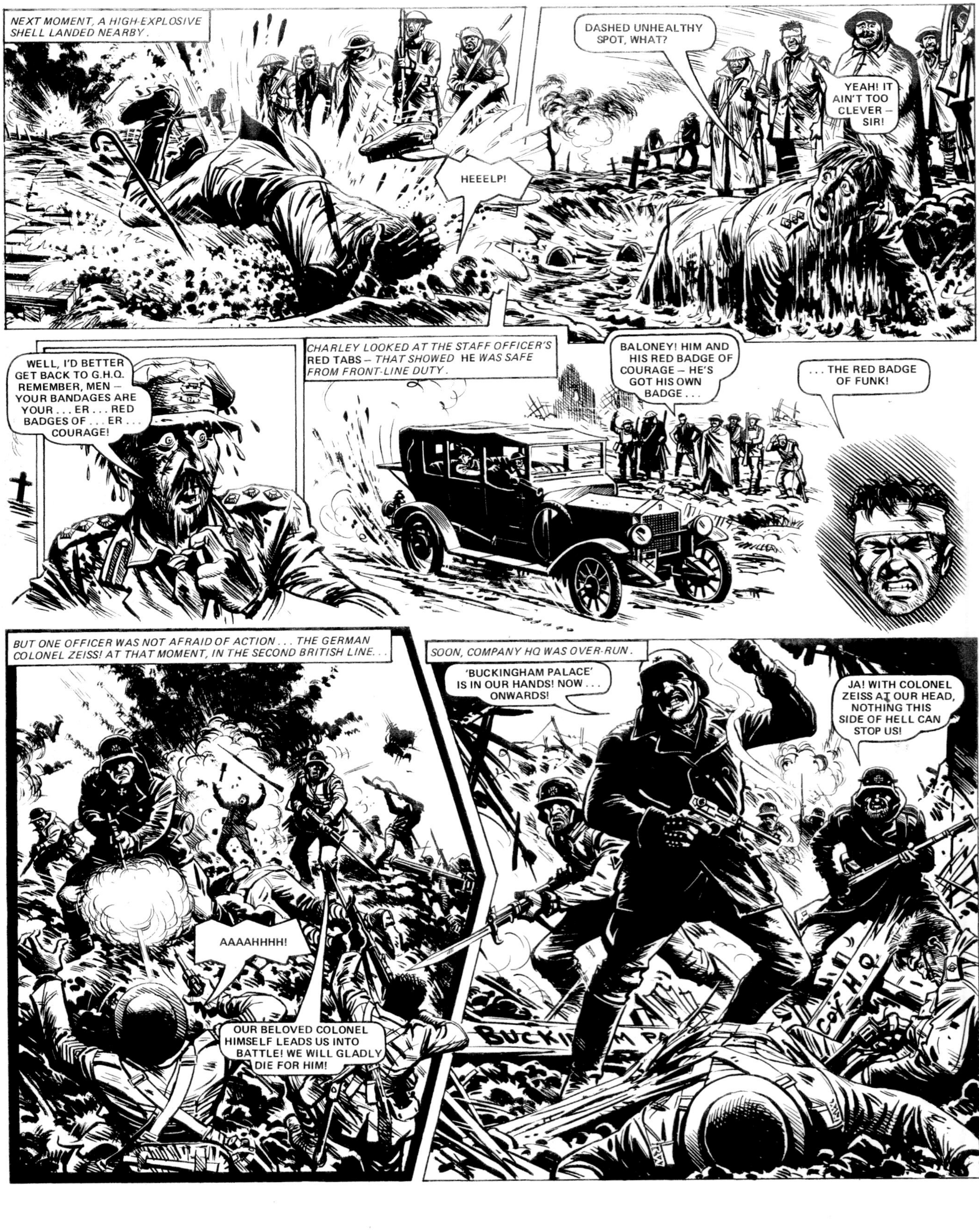
NEXT MOMENT, A HIGH-EXPLOSIVE SHELL LANDED NEARBY.
HEEELP!
DASHED UNHEALTHY SPOT, WHAT?
YEAH! IT AIN'T TOO CLEVER – SIR!
WELL, I'D BETTER GET BACK TO G.H.Q. REMEMBER, MEN – YOUR BANDAGES ARE YOUR . . . ER . . . RED BADGES OF . . . ER . . . COURAGE!
CHARLEY LOOKED AT THE STAFF OFFICER'S RED TABS – THAT SHOWED HE WAS SAFE FROM FRONT-LINE DUTY.
BALONEY! HIM AND HIS RED BADGE OF COURAGE – HE'S GOT HIS OWN BADGE . . .
. . . THE RED BADGE OF FUNK!
BUT ONE OFFICER WAS NOT AFRAID OF ACTION . . . THE GERMAN COLONEL ZEISS! AT THAT MOMENT, IN THE SECOND BRITISH LINE . . .
AAAAHHHH!
OUR BELOVED COLONEL HIMSELF LEADS US INTO BATTLE! WE WILL GLADLY DIE FOR HIM!
SOON, COMPANY HQ WAS OVER-RUN.
'BUCKINGHAM PALACE' IS IN OUR HANDS! NOW . . . ONWARDS!
JA! WITH COLONEL ZEISS AT OUR HEAD, NOTHING THIS SIDE OF HELL CAN STOP US!
COY H.Q.

CHARLEY'S WAR

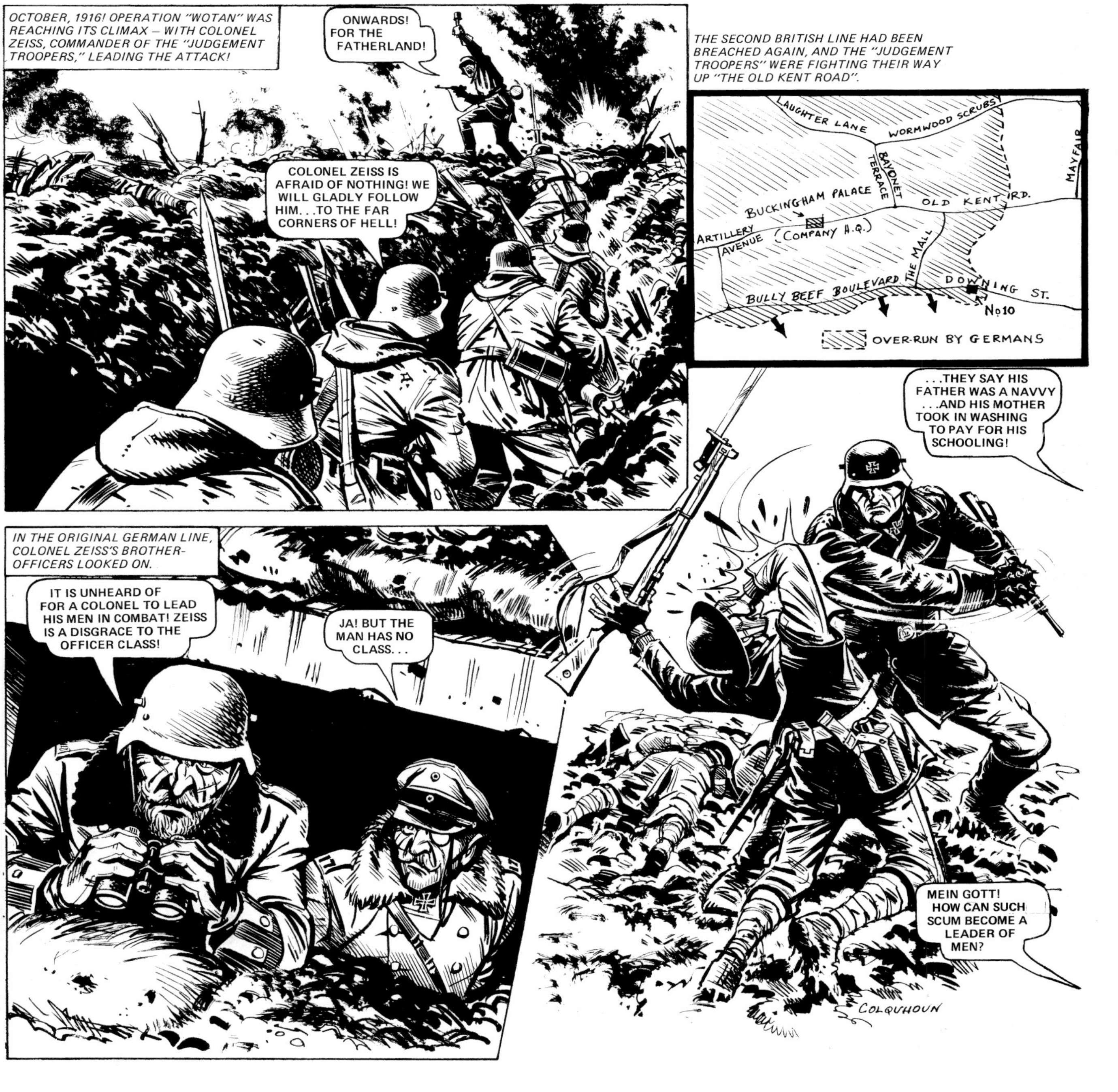

OCTOBER, 1916! OPERATION "WOTAN" WAS REACHING ITS CLIMAX – WITH COLONEL ZEISS, COMMANDER OF THE "JUDGEMENT TROOPERS," LEADING THE ATTACK!
ONWARDS! FOR THE FATHERLAND!
COLONEL ZEISS IS AFRAID OF NOTHING! WE WILL GLADLY FOLLOW HIM. . .TO THE FAR CORNERS OF HELL!
THE SECOND BRITISH LINE HAD BEEN BREACHED AGAIN, AND THE "JUDGEMENT TROOPERS" WERE FIGHTING THEIR WAY UP "THE OLD KENT ROAD".
LAUGHTER LANE
WORMWOOD SCRUBS
BAYONET TERRACE
MAYFAIR
OLD KENT RD.
BUCKINGHAM PALACE
ARTILLERY AVENUE
(COMPANY H.Q.)
THE MALL
BULLY BEEF BOULEVARD
DOWNING ST.
No10
OVER-RUN BY GERMANS
IN THE ORIGINAL GERMAN LINE, COLONEL ZEISS'S BROTHER-OFFICERS LOOKED ON.
IT IS UNHEARD OF FOR A COLONEL TO LEAD HIS MEN IN COMBAT! ZEISS IS A DISGRACE TO THE OFFICER CLASS!
JA! BUT THE MAN HAS NO CLASS. . .
. . .THEY SAY HIS FATHER WAS A NAVVY . . .AND HIS MOTHER TOOK IN WASHING TO PAY FOR HIS SCHOOLING!
MEIN GOTT! HOW CAN SUCH SCUM BECOME A LEADER OF MEN?
COLQUHOUN

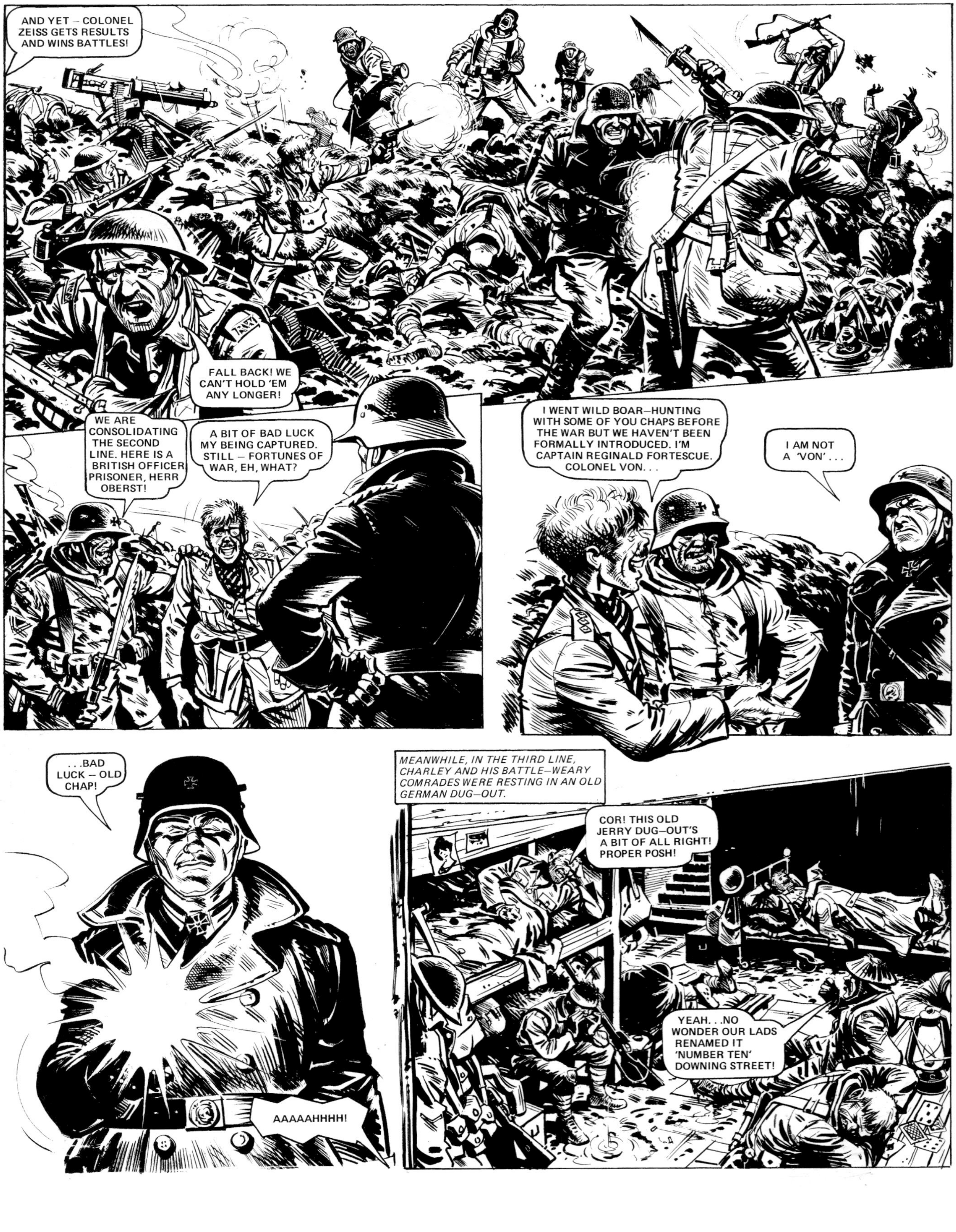
AND YET – COLONEL ZEISS GETS RESULTS AND WINS BATTLES!
FALL BACK! WE CAN'T HOLD 'EM ANY LONGER!
WE ARE CONSOLIDATING THE SECOND LINE. HERE IS A BRITISH OFFICER PRISONER, HERR OBERST!
A BIT OF BAD LUCK MY BEING CAPTURED. STILL – FORTUNES OF WAR, EH, WHAT?
I WENT WILD BOAR–HUNTING WITH SOME OF YOU CHAPS BEFORE THE WAR BUT WE HAVEN'T BEEN FORMALLY INTRODUCED. I'M CAPTAIN REGINALD FORTESCUE. COLONEL VON. . .
I AM NOT A 'VON'. . .
. . .BAD LUCK – OLD CHAP!
AAAAAHHHH!
MEANWHILE, IN THE THIRD LINE, CHARLEY AND HIS BATTLE–WEARY COMRADES WERE RESTING IN AN OLD GERMAN DUG–OUT.
COR! THIS OLD JERRY DUG–OUT'S A BIT OF ALL RIGHT! PROPER POSH!
YEAH. . .NO WONDER OUR LADS RENAMED IT 'NUMBER TEN' DOWNING STREET!

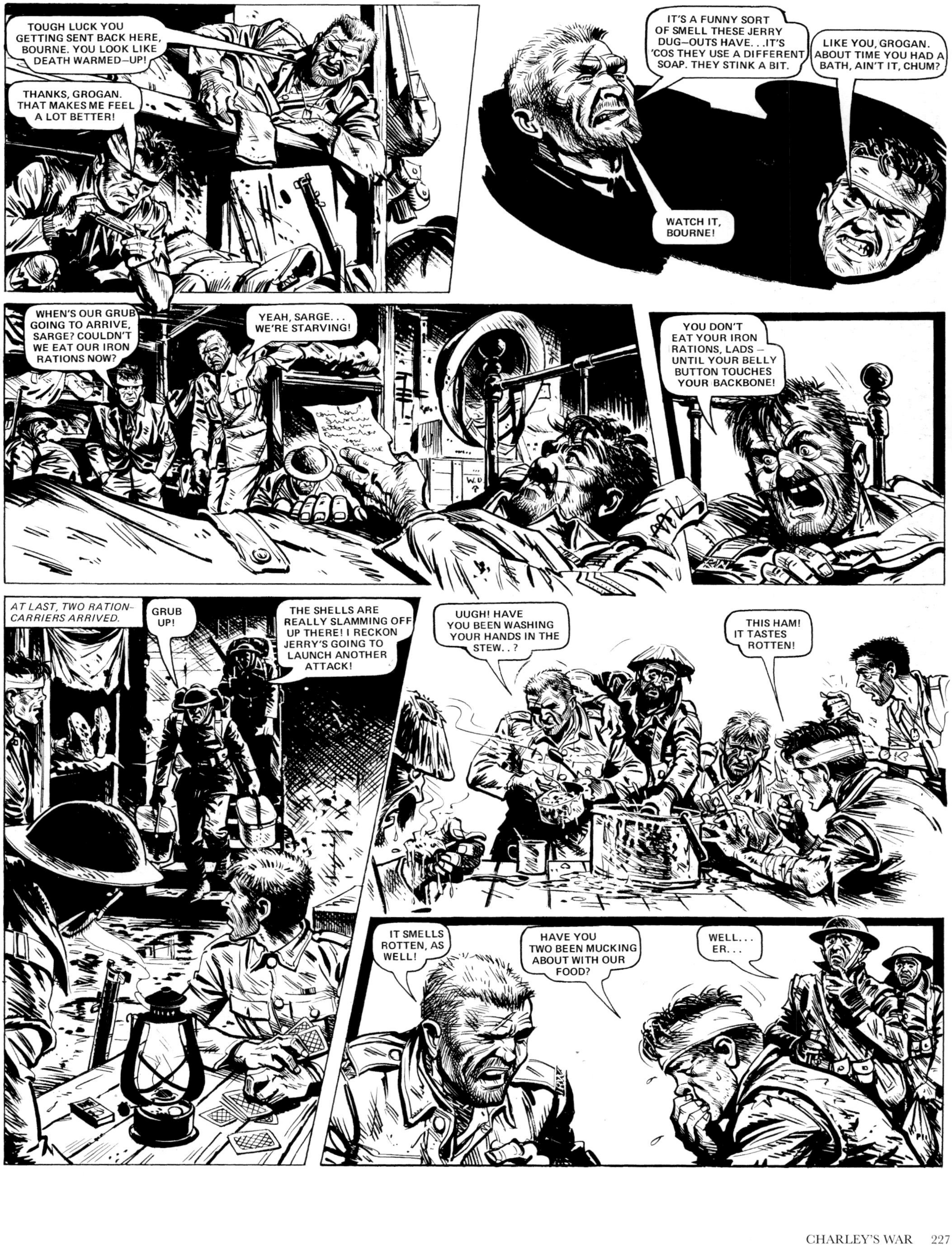
TOUGH LUCK YOU GETTING SENT BACK HERE, BOURNE. YOU LOOK LIKE DEATH WARMED-UP!
THANKS, GROGAN. THAT MAKES ME FEEL A LOT BETTER!
IT'S A FUNNY SORT OF SMELL THESE JERRY DUG-OUTS HAVE. . .IT'S 'COS THEY USE A DIFFERENT SOAP. THEY STINK A BIT.
LIKE YOU, GROGAN. ABOUT TIME YOU HAD A BATH, AIN'T IT, CHUM?
WATCH IT, BOURNE!
WHEN'S OUR GRUB GOING TO ARRIVE, SARGE? COULDN'T WE EAT OUR IRON RATIONS NOW?
YEAH, SARGE. . . WE'RE STARVING!
YOU DON'T EAT YOUR IRON RATIONS, LADS – UNTIL YOUR BELLY BUTTON TOUCHES YOUR BACKBONE!
AT LAST, TWO RATION-CARRIERS ARRIVED.
GRUB UP!
THE SHELLS ARE REALLY SLAMMING OFF UP THERE! I RECKON JERRY'S GOING TO LAUNCH ANOTHER ATTACK!
UUGH! HAVE YOU BEEN WASHING YOUR HANDS IN THE STEW. . ?
THIS HAM! IT TASTES ROTTEN!
IT SMELLS ROTTEN, AS WELL!
HAVE YOU TWO BEEN MUCKING ABOUT WITH OUR FOOD?
WELL. . . ER. . .

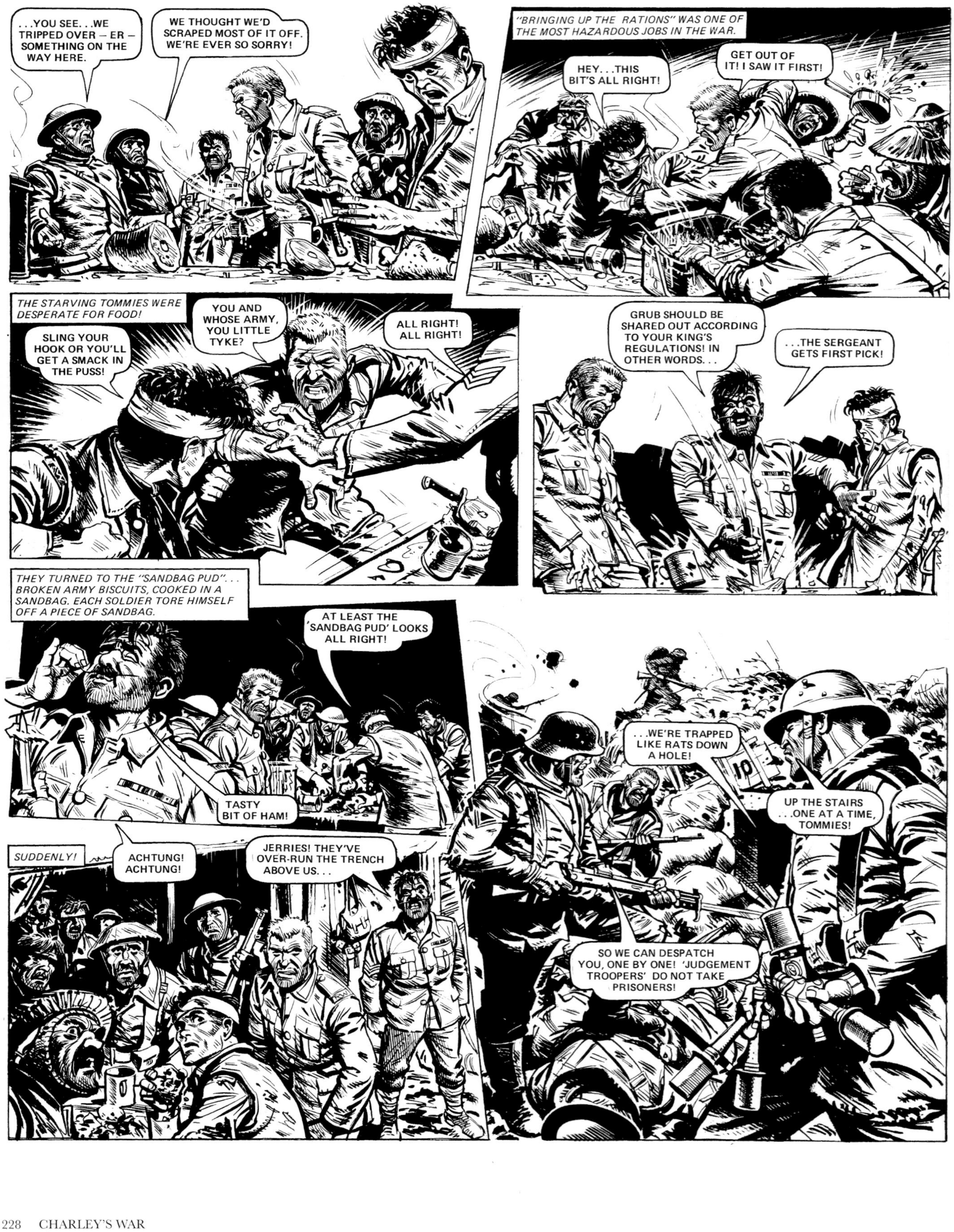

. . .YOU SEE. . .WE TRIPPED OVER — ER — SOMETHING ON THE WAY HERE.
WE THOUGHT WE'D SCRAPED MOST OF IT OFF. WE'RE EVER SO SORRY!
"BRINGING UP THE RATIONS" WAS ONE OF THE MOST HAZARDOUS JOBS IN THE WAR.
HEY. . .THIS BIT'S ALL RIGHT!
GET OUT OF IT! I SAW IT FIRST!
THE STARVING TOMMIES WERE DESPERATE FOR FOOD!
SLING YOUR HOOK OR YOU'LL GET A SMACK IN THE PUSS!
YOU AND WHOSE ARMY, YOU LITTLE TYKE?
ALL RIGHT! ALL RIGHT!
GRUB SHOULD BE SHARED OUT ACCORDING TO YOUR KING'S REGULATIONS! IN OTHER WORDS. . .
. . .THE SERGEANT GETS FIRST PICK!
THEY TURNED TO THE "SANDBAG PUD". . . BROKEN ARMY BISCUITS, COOKED IN A SANDBAG. EACH SOLDIER TORE HIMSELF OFF A PIECE OF SANDBAG.
AT LEAST THE 'SANDBAG PUD' LOOKS ALL RIGHT!
TASTY BIT OF HAM!
SUDDENLY!
ACHTUNG! ACHTUNG!
JERRIES! THEY'VE OVER-RUN THE TRENCH ABOVE US. . .
. . .WE'RE TRAPPED LIKE RATS DOWN A HOLE!
UP THE STAIRS . . .ONE AT A TIME, TOMMIES!
SO WE CAN DESPATCH YOU, ONE BY ONE! 'JUDGEMENT TROOPERS' DO NOT TAKE PRISONERS!

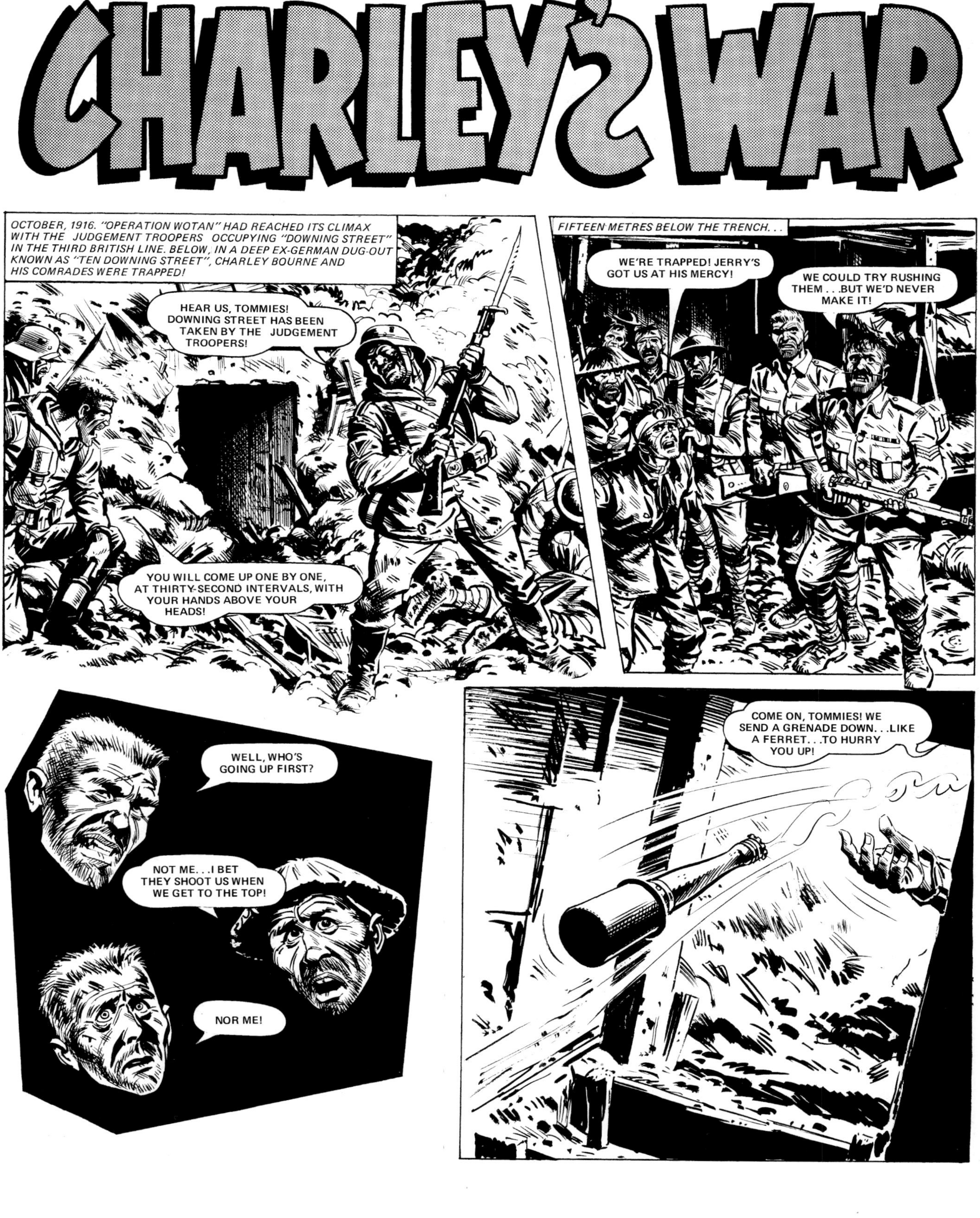
CHARLEY'S WAR
OCTOBER, 1916. "OPERATION WOTAN" HAD REACHED ITS CLIMAX WITH THE JUDGEMENT TROOPERS OCCUPYING "DOWNING STREET" IN THE THIRD BRITISH LINE. BELOW, IN A DEEP EX-GERMAN DUG-OUT KNOWN AS "TEN DOWNING STREET", CHARLEY BOURNE AND HIS COMRADES WERE TRAPPED!
HEAR US, TOMMIES! DOWNING STREET HAS BEEN TAKEN BY THE JUDGEMENT TROOPERS!
YOU WILL COME UP ONE BY ONE, AT THIRTY-SECOND INTERVALS, WITH YOUR HANDS ABOVE YOUR HEADS!
FIFTEEN METRES BELOW THE TRENCH. . .
WE'RE TRAPPED! JERRY'S GOT US AT HIS MERCY!
WE COULD TRY RUSHING THEM . . .BUT WE'D NEVER MAKE IT!
WELL, WHO'S GOING UP FIRST?
NOT ME. . .I BET THEY SHOOT US WHEN WE GET TO THE TOP!
NOR ME!
COME ON, TOMMIES! WE SEND A GRENADE DOWN. . .LIKE A FERRET. . .TO HURRY YOU UP!

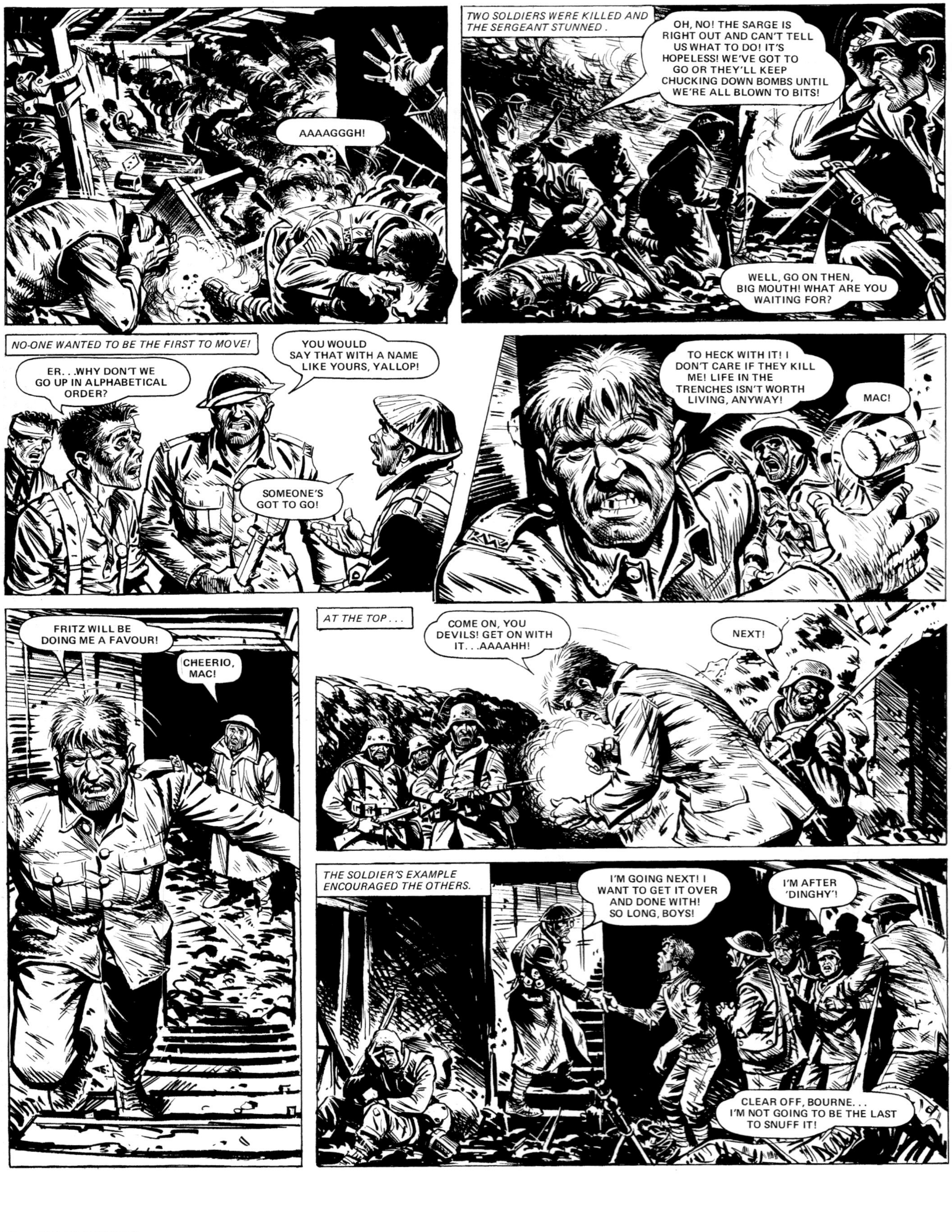
AAAAGGGH!
TWO SOLDIERS WERE KILLED AND THE SERGEANT STUNNED.
OH, NO! THE SARGE IS RIGHT OUT AND CAN'T TELL US WHAT TO DO! IT'S HOPELESS! WE'VE GOT TO GO OR THEY'LL KEEP CHUCKING DOWN BOMBS UNTIL WE'RE ALL BLOWN TO BITS!
WELL, GO ON THEN, BIG MOUTH! WHAT ARE YOU WAITING FOR?
NO-ONE WANTED TO BE THE FIRST TO MOVE!
ER. . .WHY DON'T WE GO UP IN ALPHABETICAL ORDER?
YOU WOULD SAY THAT WITH A NAME LIKE YOURS, YALLOP!
SOMEONE'S GOT TO GO!
TO HECK WITH IT! I DON'T CARE IF THEY KILL ME! LIFE IN THE TRENCHES ISN'T WORTH LIVING, ANYWAY!
MAC!
FRITZ WILL BE DOING ME A FAVOUR!
CHEERIO, MAC!
AT THE TOP . . .
COME ON, YOU DEVILS! GET ON WITH IT. . .AAAAHH!
NEXT!
THE SOLDIER'S EXAMPLE ENCOURAGED THE OTHERS.
I'M GOING NEXT! I WANT TO GET IT OVER AND DONE WITH! SO LONG, BOYS!
I'M AFTER 'DINGHY'!
CLEAR OFF, BOURNE. . . I'M NOT GOING TO BE THE LAST TO SNUFF IT!

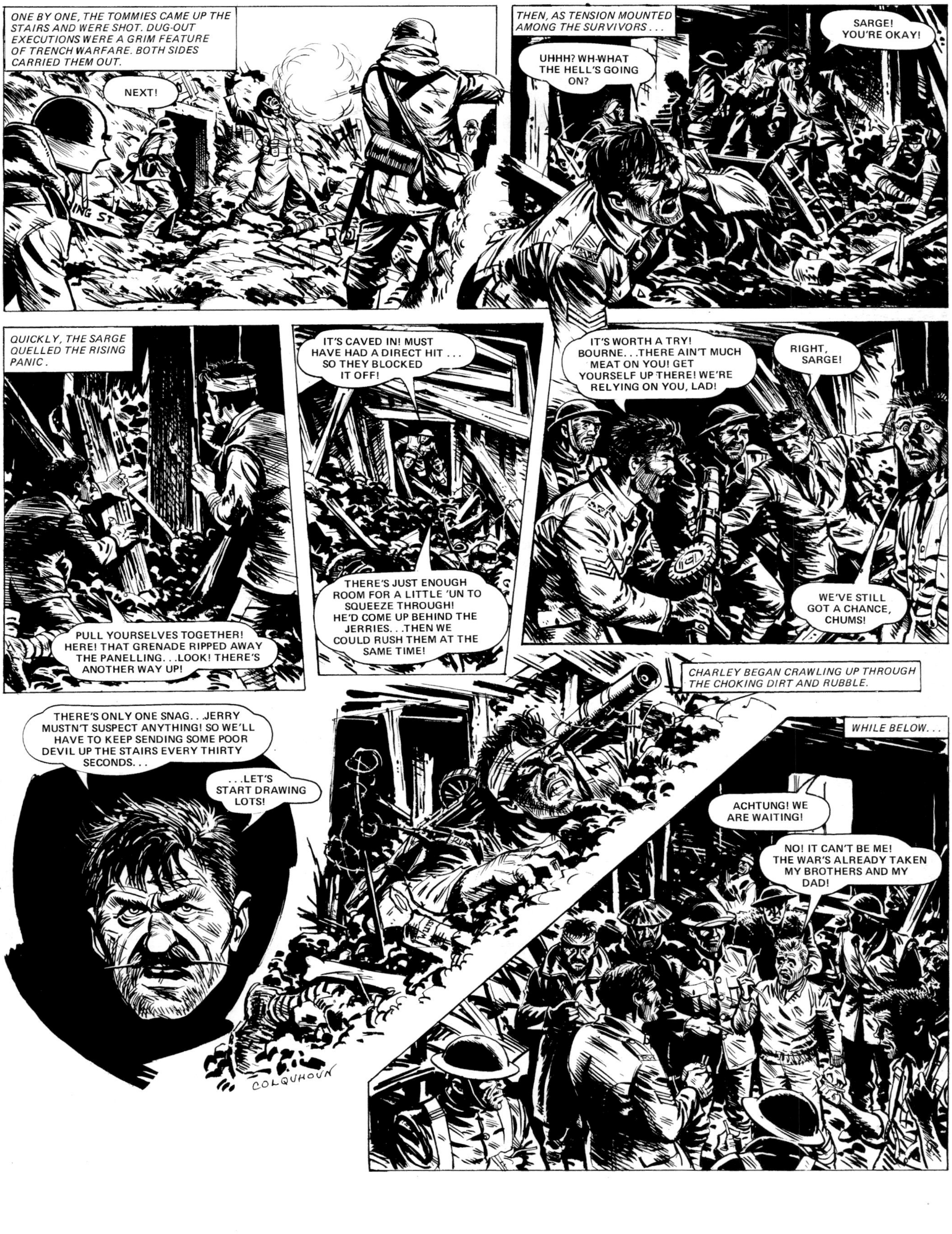

ONE BY ONE, THE TOMMIES CAME UP THE STAIRS AND WERE SHOT. DUG-OUT EXECUTIONS WERE A GRIM FEATURE OF TRENCH WARFARE. BOTH SIDES CARRIED THEM OUT.
NEXT!
THEN, AS TENSION MOUNTED AMONG THE SURVIVORS . . .
UHHH? WH-WHAT THE HELL'S GOING ON?
SARGE! YOU'RE OKAY!
QUICKLY, THE SARGE QUELLED THE RISING PANIC.
PULL YOURSELVES TOGETHER! HERE! THAT GRENADE RIPPED AWAY THE PANELLING. . .LOOK! THERE'S ANOTHER WAY UP!
IT'S CAVED IN! MUST HAVE HAD A DIRECT HIT . . . SO THEY BLOCKED IT OFF!
THERE'S JUST ENOUGH ROOM FOR A LITTLE 'UN TO SQUEEZE THROUGH! HE'D COME UP BEHIND THE JERRIES. . .THEN WE COULD RUSH THEM AT THE SAME TIME!
IT'S WORTH A TRY! BOURNE. . .THERE AIN'T MUCH MEAT ON YOU! GET YOURSELF UP THERE! WE'RE RELYING ON YOU, LAD!
RIGHT, SARGE!
WE'VE STILL GOT A CHANCE, CHUMS!
THERE'S ONLY ONE SNAG. . .JERRY MUSTN'T SUSPECT ANYTHING! SO WE'LL HAVE TO KEEP SENDING SOME POOR DEVIL UP THE STAIRS EVERY THIRTY SECONDS. . .
. . .LET'S START DRAWING LOTS!
CHARLEY BEGAN CRAWLING UP THROUGH THE CHOKING DIRT AND RUBBLE.
COLQUHOUN
WHILE BELOW. . .
ACHTUNG! WE ARE WAITING!
NO! IT CAN'T BE ME! THE WAR'S ALREADY TAKEN MY BROTHERS AND MY DAD!

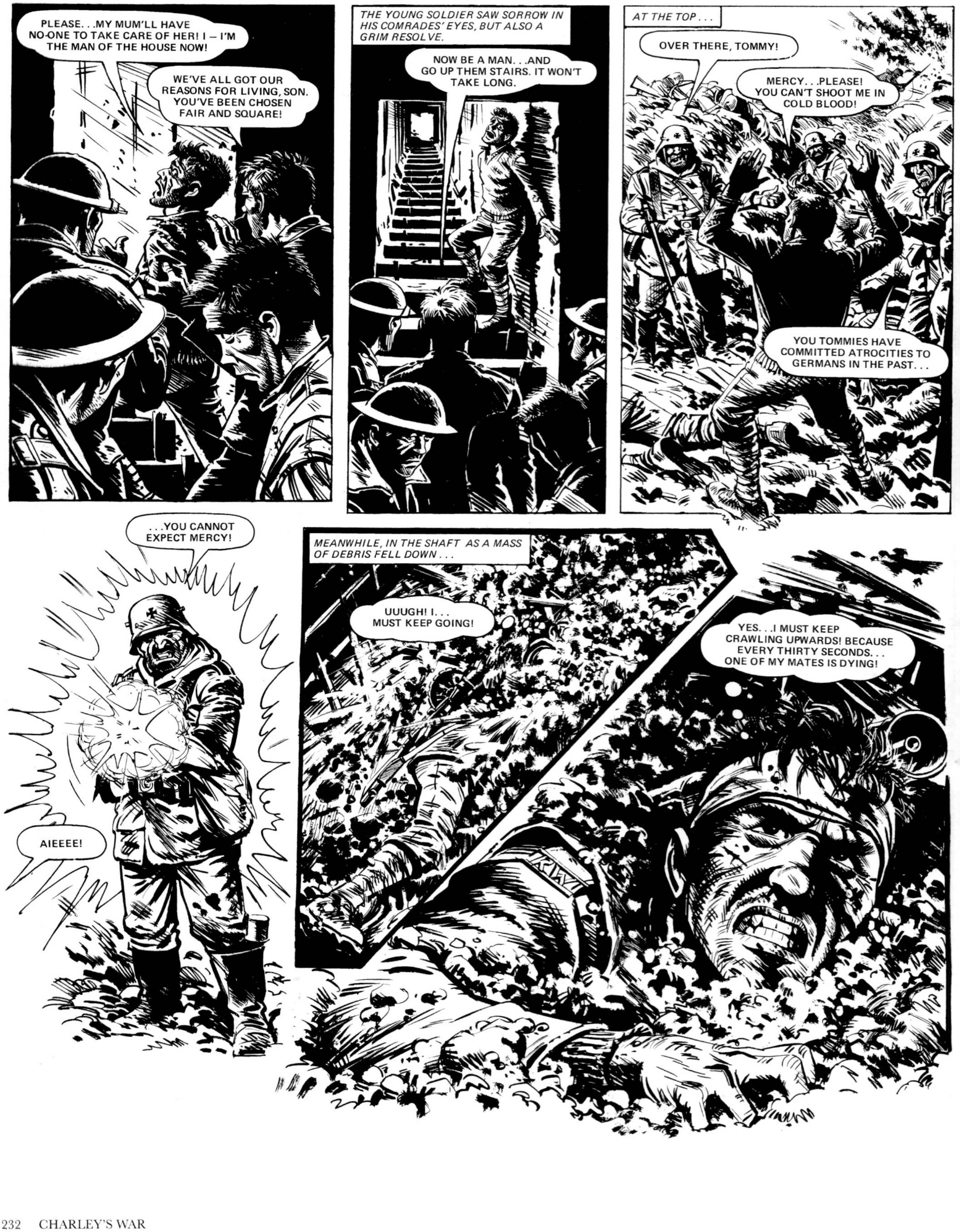
PLEASE. . .MY MUM'LL HAVE NO-ONE TO TAKE CARE OF HER! I – I'M THE MAN OF THE HOUSE NOW!
WE'VE ALL GOT OUR REASONS FOR LIVING, SON. YOU'VE BEEN CHOSEN FAIR AND SQUARE!
THE YOUNG SOLDIER SAW SORROW IN HIS COMRADES' EYES, BUT ALSO A GRIM RESOLVE.
NOW BE A MAN. . .AND GO UP THEM STAIRS. IT WON'T TAKE LONG.
AT THE TOP . . .
OVER THERE, TOMMY!
MERCY. . .PLEASE! YOU CAN'T SHOOT ME IN COLD BLOOD!
YOU TOMMIES HAVE COMMITTED ATROCITIES TO GERMANS IN THE PAST. . .
. . .YOU CANNOT EXPECT MERCY!
AIEEEE!
MEANWHILE, IN THE SHAFT AS A MASS OF DEBRIS FELL DOWN . . .
UUUGH! I. . . MUST KEEP GOING!
YES. . .I MUST KEEP CRAWLING UPWARDS! BECAUSE EVERY THIRTY SECONDS. . . ONE OF MY MATES IS DYING!

CHARLEY'S WAR

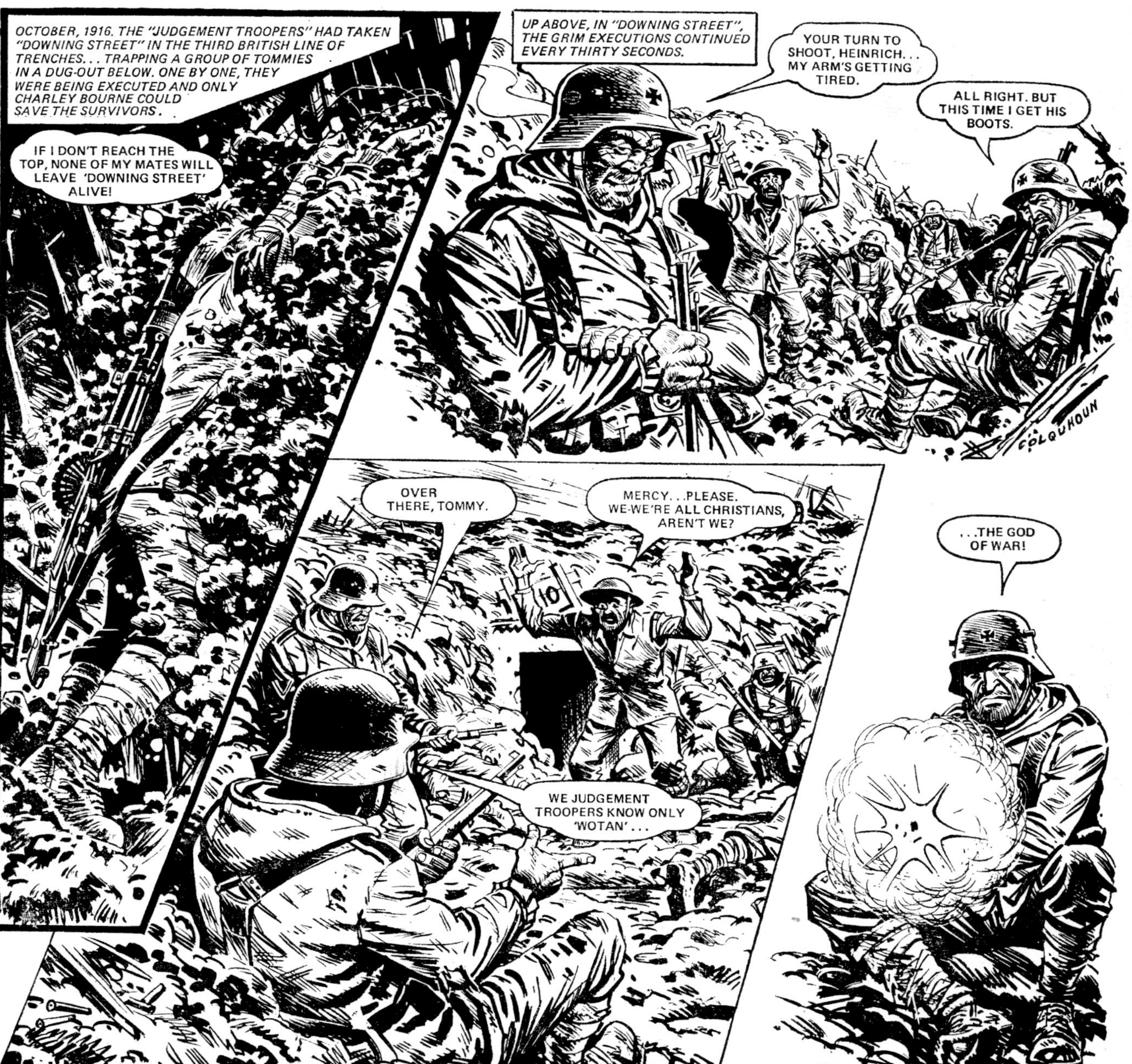

OCTOBER, 1916. THE "JUDGEMENT TROOPERS" HAD TAKEN "DOWNING STREET" IN THE THIRD BRITISH LINE OF TRENCHES... TRAPPING A GROUP OF TOMMIES IN A DUG-OUT BELOW. ONE BY ONE, THEY WERE BEING EXECUTED AND ONLY CHARLEY BOURNE COULD SAVE THE SURVIVORS.
IF I DON'T REACH THE TOP, NONE OF MY MATES WILL LEAVE 'DOWNING STREET' ALIVE!
UP ABOVE, IN "DOWNING STREET", THE GRIM EXECUTIONS CONTINUED EVERY THIRTY SECONDS.
YOUR TURN TO SHOOT, HEINRICH... MY ARM'S GETTING TIRED.
ALL RIGHT. BUT THIS TIME I GET HIS BOOTS.
COLQUHOUN
OVER THERE, TOMMY.
MERCY... PLEASE. WE-WE'RE ALL CHRISTIANS, AREN'T WE?
WE JUDGEMENT TROOPERS KNOW ONLY 'WOTAN'...
...THE GOD OF WAR!

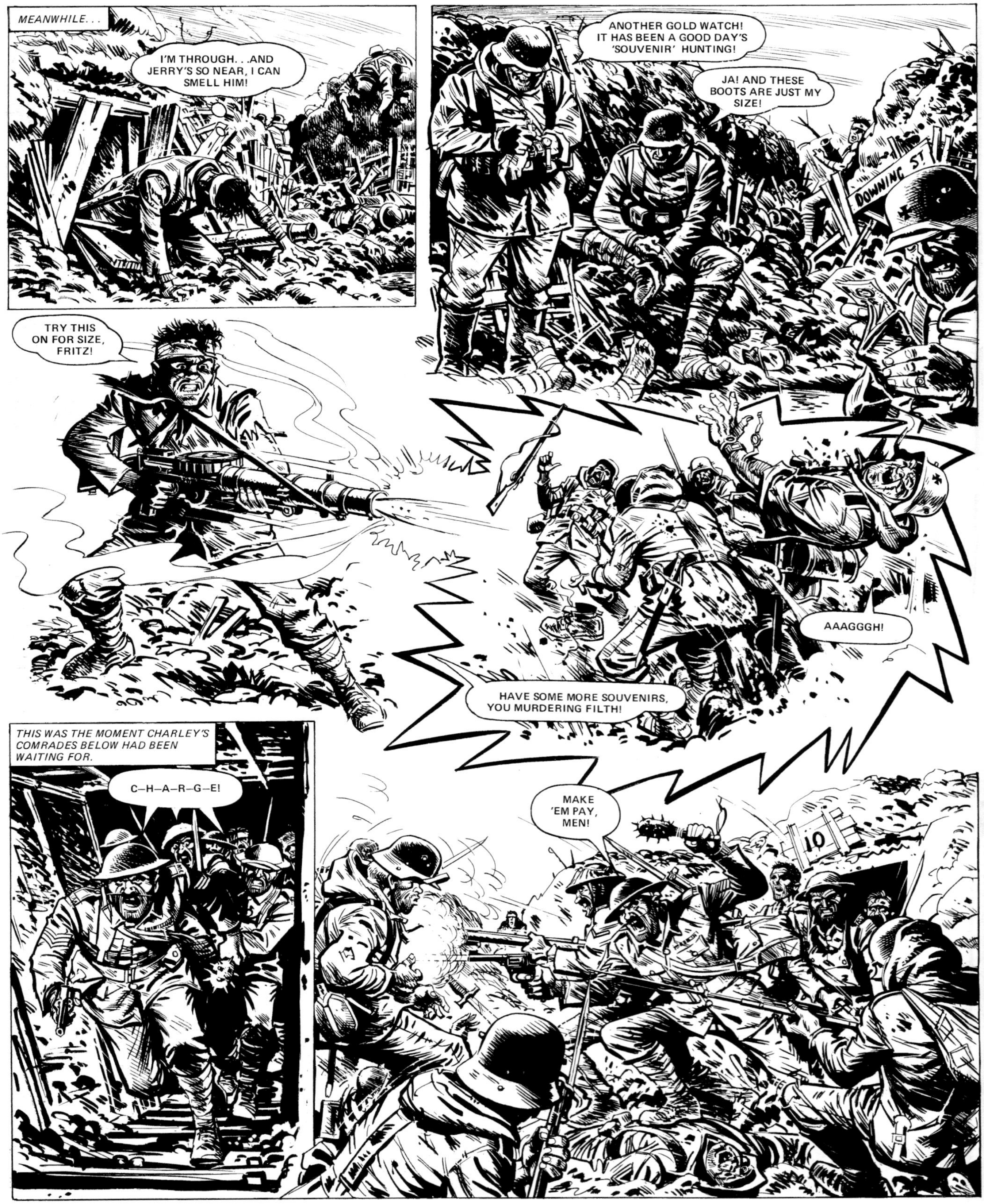
MEANWHILE...
I'M THROUGH...AND JERRY'S SO NEAR, I CAN SMELL HIM!
ANOTHER GOLD WATCH! IT HAS BEEN A GOOD DAY'S 'SOUVENIR' HUNTING!
JA! AND THESE BOOTS ARE JUST MY SIZE!
DOWNING ST
TRY THIS ON FOR SIZE, FRITZ!
AAAGGGH!
HAVE SOME MORE SOUVENIRS, YOU MURDERING FILTH!
THIS WAS THE MOMENT CHARLEY'S COMRADES BELOW HAD BEEN WAITING FOR.
C–H–A–R–G–E!
MAKE 'EM PAY, MEN!
10

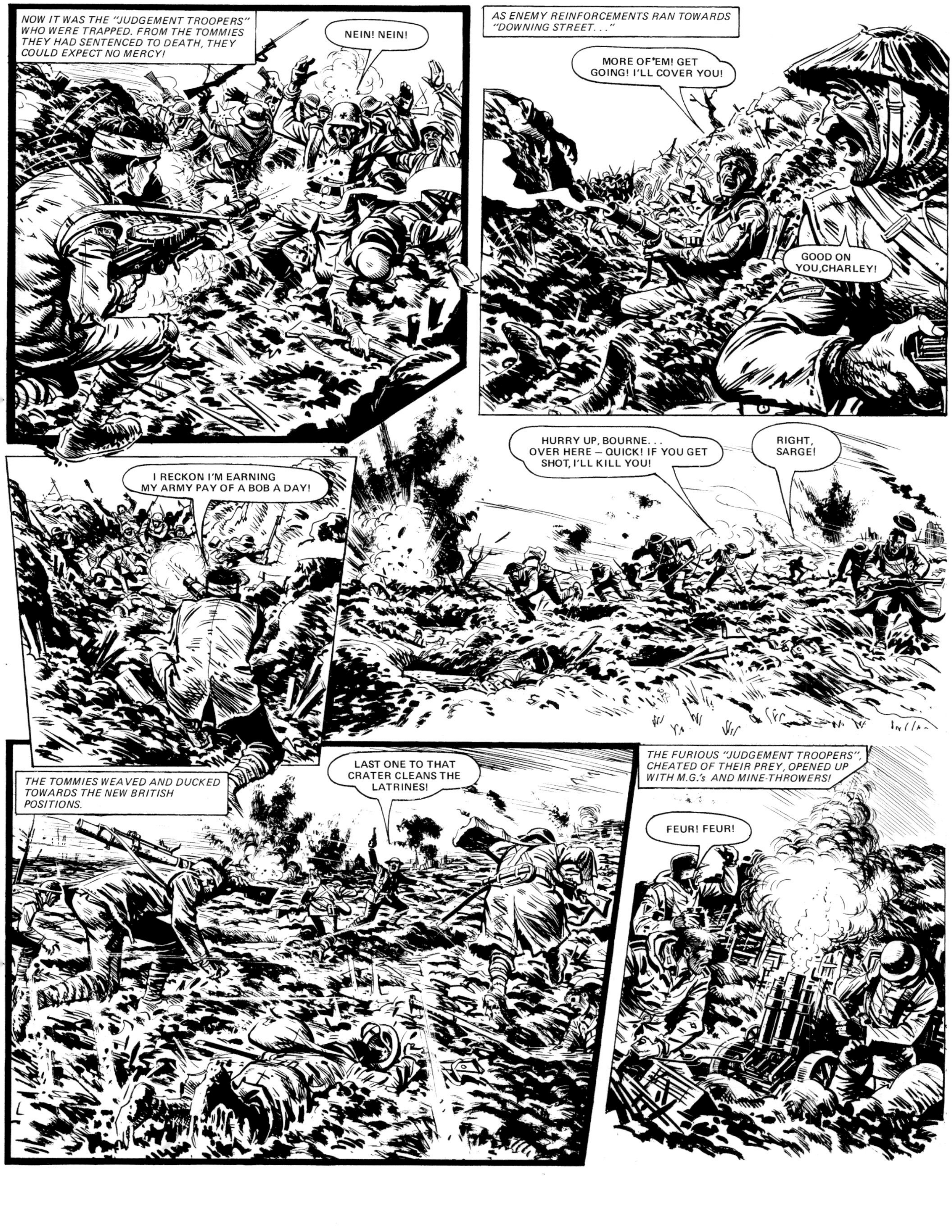
NOW IT WAS THE "JUDGEMENT TROOPERS" WHO WERE TRAPPED. FROM THE TOMMIES THEY HAD SENTENCED TO DEATH, THEY COULD EXPECT NO MERCY!
NEIN! NEIN!
AS ENEMY REINFORCEMENTS RAN TOWARDS "DOWNING STREET..."
MORE OF 'EM! GET GOING! I'LL COVER YOU!
GOOD ON YOU,CHARLEY!
I RECKON I'M EARNING MY ARMY PAY OF A BOB A DAY!
HURRY UP, BOURNE... OVER HERE – QUICK! IF YOU GET SHOT, I'LL KILL YOU!
RIGHT, SARGE!
THE TOMMIES WEAVED AND DUCKED TOWARDS THE NEW BRITISH POSITIONS.
LAST ONE TO THAT CRATER CLEANS THE LATRINES!
THE FURIOUS "JUDGEMENT TROOPERS", CHEATED OF THEIR PREY, OPENED UP WITH M.G.'s AND MINE-THROWERS!
FEUR! FEUR!

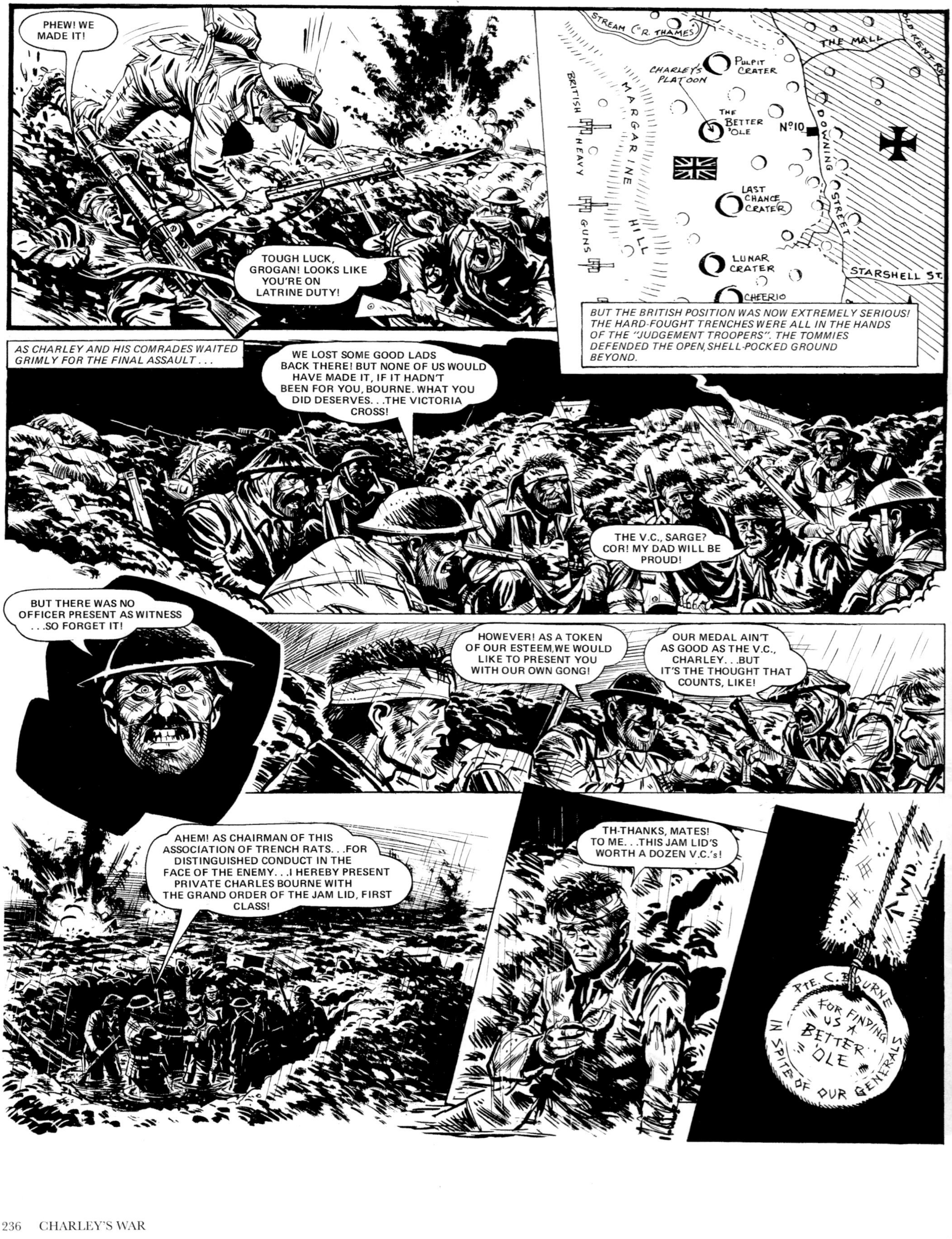
PHEW! WE MADE IT!
TOUGH LUCK, GROGAN! LOOKS LIKE YOU'RE ON LATRINE DUTY!
STREAM ("R. THAMES")
THE MALL
OLD KENT RD
PULPIT CRATER
CHARLEY'S PLATOON
BRITISH HEAVY GUNS
MARGARINE HILL
THE BETTER 'OLE
Nº10
DOWNING STREET
LAST CHANCE CRATER
LUNAR CRATER
STARSHELL ST.
CHEERIO
BUT THE BRITISH POSITION WAS NOW EXTREMELY SERIOUS! THE HARD-FOUGHT TRENCHES WERE ALL IN THE HANDS OF THE "JUDGEMENT TROOPERS". THE TOMMIES DEFENDED THE OPEN, SHELL-POCKED GROUND BEYOND.
AS CHARLEY AND HIS COMRADES WAITED GRIMLY FOR THE FINAL ASSAULT . . .
WE LOST SOME GOOD LADS BACK THERE! BUT NONE OF US WOULD HAVE MADE IT, IF IT HADN'T BEEN FOR YOU, BOURNE. WHAT YOU DID DESERVES. . .THE VICTORIA CROSS!
THE V.C., SARGE? COR! MY DAD WILL BE PROUD!
BUT THERE WAS NO OFFICER PRESENT AS WITNESS . . .SO FORGET IT!
HOWEVER! AS A TOKEN OF OUR ESTEEM, WE WOULD LIKE TO PRESENT YOU WITH OUR OWN GONG!
OUR MEDAL AIN'T AS GOOD AS THE V.C., CHARLEY. . .BUT IT'S THE THOUGHT THAT COUNTS, LIKE!
AHEM! AS CHAIRMAN OF THIS ASSOCIATION OF TRENCH RATS. . .FOR DISTINGUISHED CONDUCT IN THE FACE OF THE ENEMY. . .I HEREBY PRESENT PRIVATE CHARLES BOURNE WITH THE GRAND ORDER OF THE JAM LID, FIRST CLASS!
TH-THANKS, MATES! TO ME. . .THIS JAM LID'S WORTH A DOZEN V.C.'s!
PTE. C. BOURNE
FOR FINDING US A BETTER 'OLE
IN SPITE OF OUR GENERALS

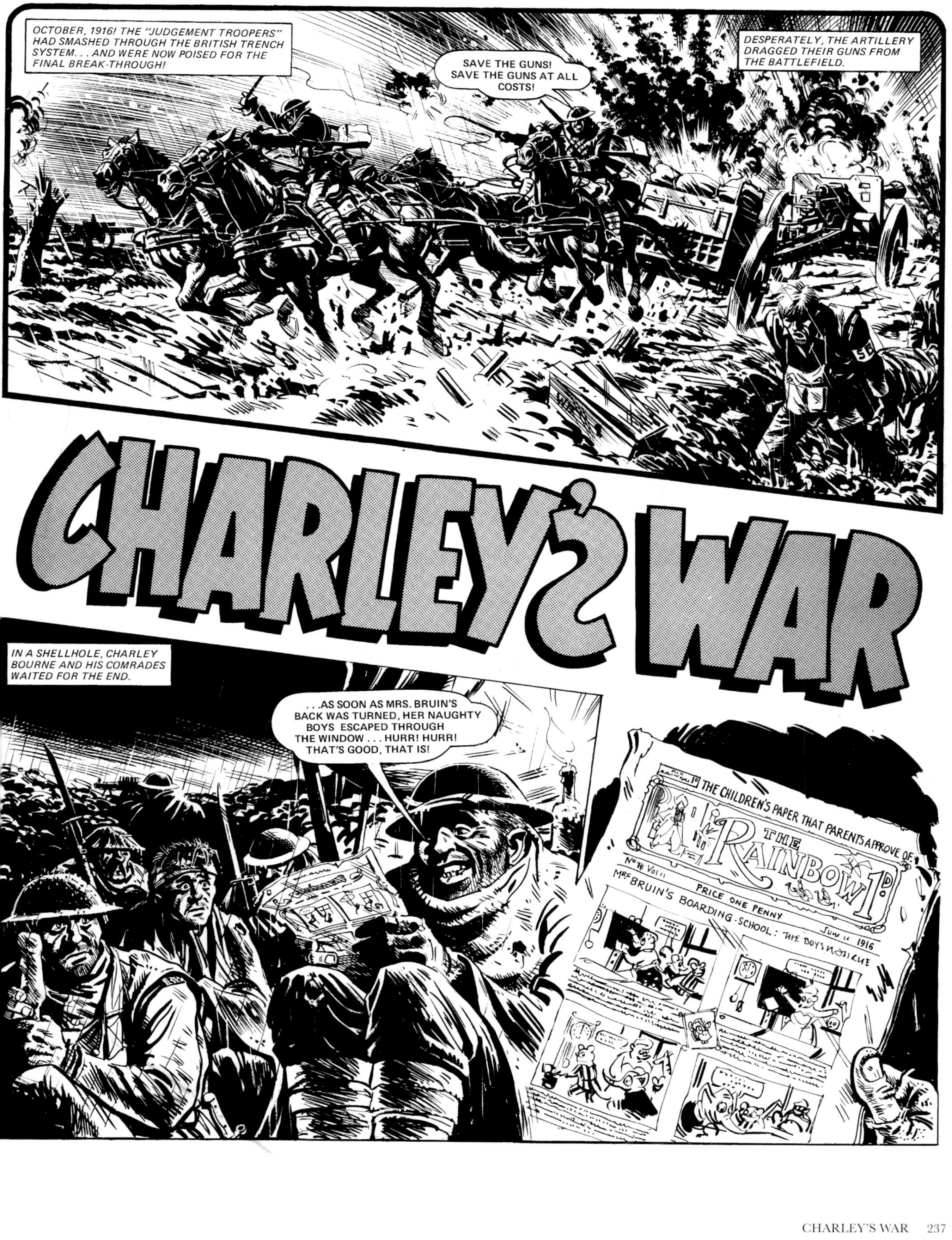
OCTOBER, 1916! THE "JUDGEMENT TROOPERS" HAD SMASHED THROUGH THE BRITISH TRENCH SYSTEM. . . AND WERE NOW POISED FOR THE FINAL BREAK-THROUGH!
SAVE THE GUNS! SAVE THE GUNS AT ALL COSTS!
DESPERATELY, THE ARTILLERY DRAGGED THEIR GUNS FROM THE BATTLEFIELD.
CHARLEY'S WAR
IN A SHELLHOLE, CHARLEY BOURNE AND HIS COMRADES WAITED FOR THE END.
. . .AS SOON AS MRS. BRUIN'S BACK WAS TURNED, HER NAUGHTY BOYS ESCAPED THROUGH THE WINDOW . . . HURR! HURR! THAT'S GOOD, THAT IS!
THE CHILDREN'S PAPER THAT PARENTS APPROVE OF.
THE RAINBOW 1d.
PRICE ONE PENNY
MRS BRUIN'S BOARDING-SCHOOL:
1916

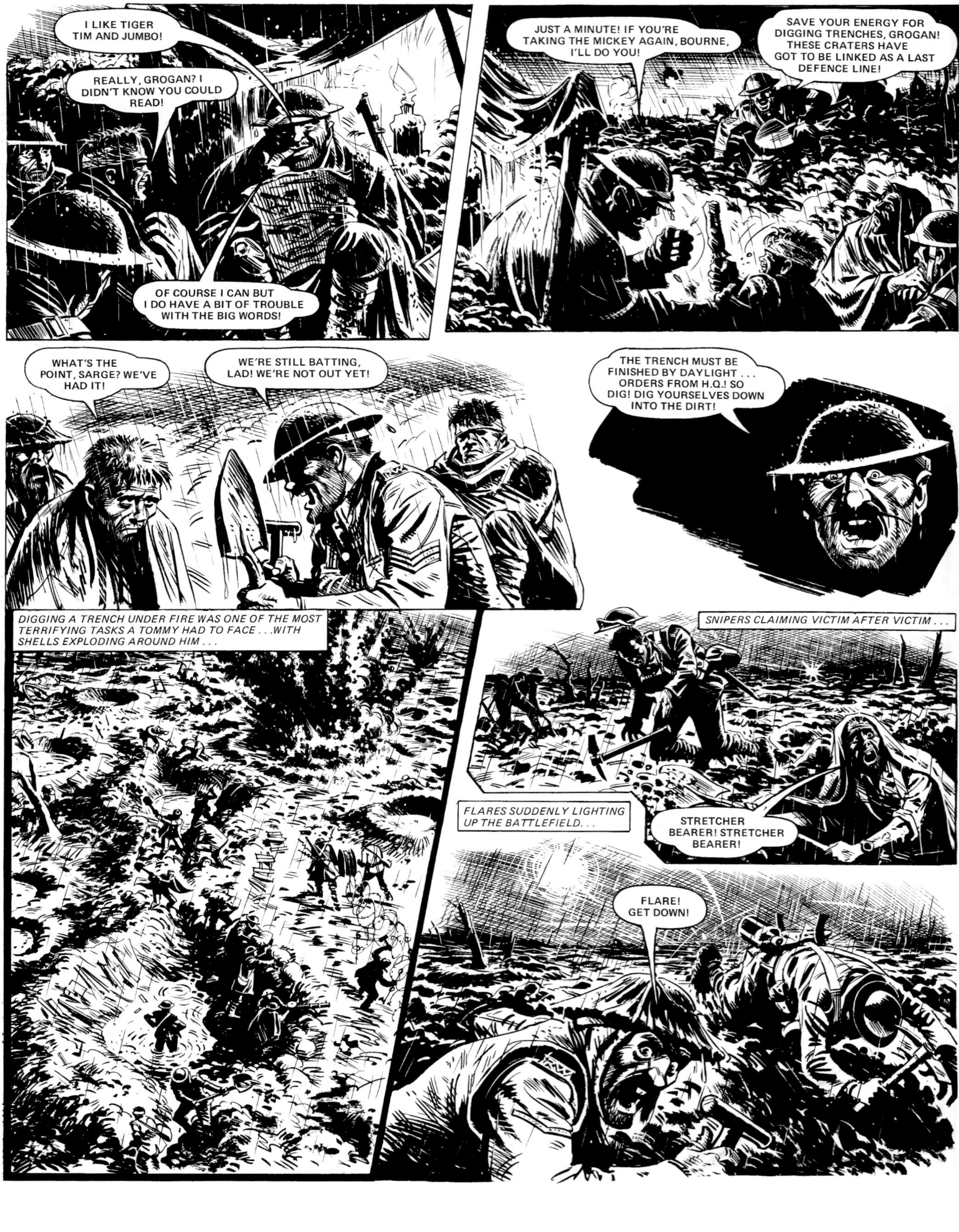
I LIKE TIGER TIM AND JUMBO!
REALLY, GROGAN? I DIDN'T KNOW YOU COULD READ!
OF COURSE I CAN BUT I DO HAVE A BIT OF TROUBLE WITH THE BIG WORDS!
JUST A MINUTE! IF YOU'RE TAKING THE MICKEY AGAIN, BOURNE, I'LL DO YOU!
SAVE YOUR ENERGY FOR DIGGING TRENCHES, GROGAN! THESE CRATERS HAVE GOT TO BE LINKED AS A LAST DEFENCE LINE!
WHAT'S THE POINT, SARGE? WE'VE HAD IT!
WE'RE STILL BATTING, LAD! WE'RE NOT OUT YET!
THE TRENCH MUST BE FINISHED BY DAYLIGHT . . . ORDERS FROM H.Q.! SO DIG! DIG YOURSELVES DOWN INTO THE DIRT!
DIGGING A TRENCH UNDER FIRE WAS ONE OF THE MOST TERRIFYING TASKS A TOMMY HAD TO FACE . . . WITH SHELLS EXPLODING AROUND HIM . . .
SNIPERS CLAIMING VICTIM AFTER VICTIM . . .
STRETCHER BEARER! STRETCHER BEARER!
FLARES SUDDENLY LIGHTING UP THE BATTLEFIELD. . .
FLARE! GET DOWN!

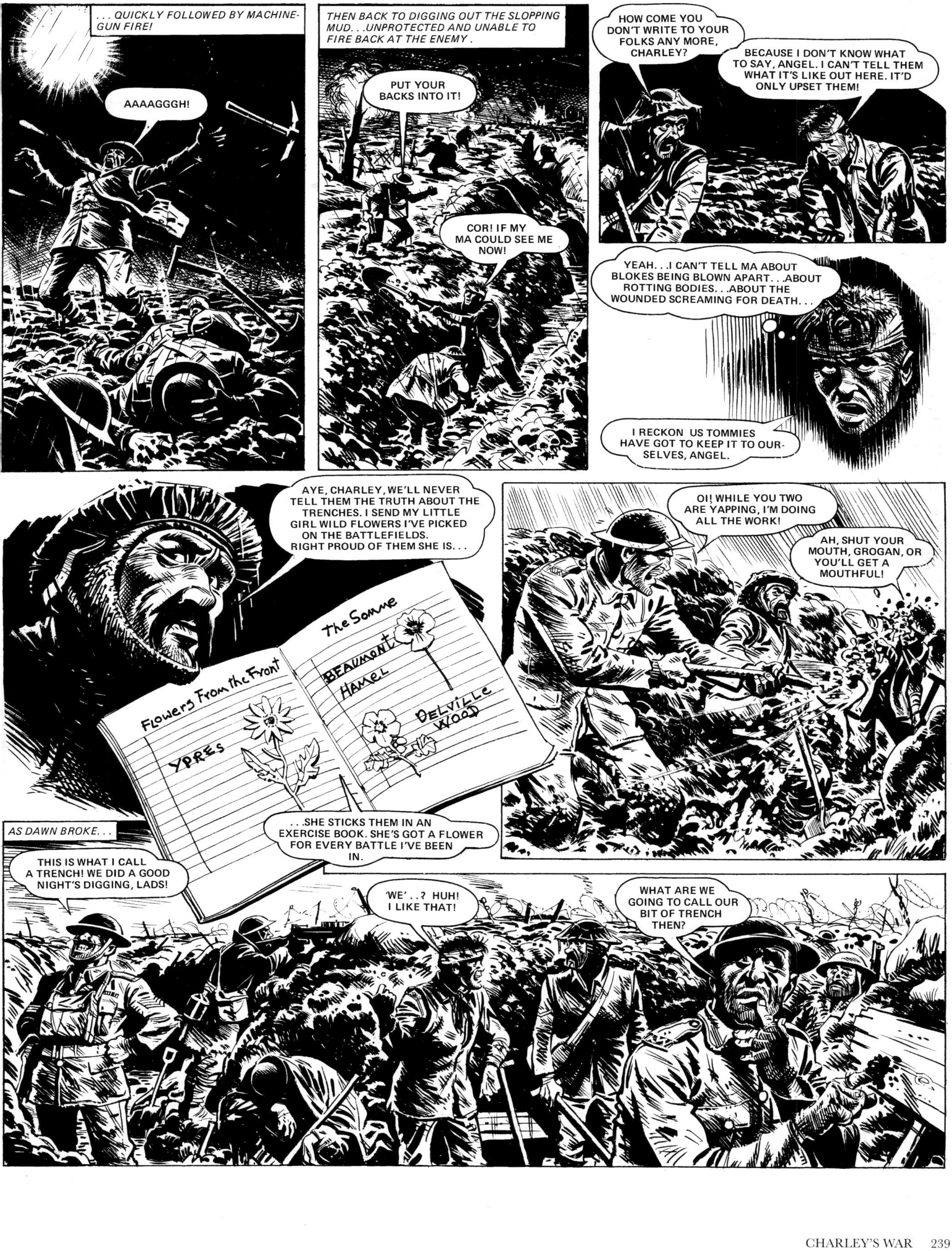

. . . QUICKLY FOLLOWED BY MACHINE-GUN FIRE!
AAAAGGGH!
THEN BACK TO DIGGING OUT THE SLOPPING MUD. . .UNPROTECTED AND UNABLE TO FIRE BACK AT THE ENEMY .
PUT YOUR BACKS INTO IT!
COR! IF MY MA COULD SEE ME NOW!
HOW COME YOU DON'T WRITE TO YOUR FOLKS ANY MORE, CHARLEY?
BECAUSE I DON'T KNOW WHAT TO SAY, ANGEL. I CAN'T TELL THEM WHAT IT'S LIKE OUT HERE. IT'D ONLY UPSET THEM!
YEAH. . .I CAN'T TELL MA ABOUT BLOKES BEING BLOWN APART. . .ABOUT ROTTING BODIES. . .ABOUT THE WOUNDED SCREAMING FOR DEATH. . .
I RECKON US TOMMIES HAVE GOT TO KEEP IT TO OUR-SELVES, ANGEL.
AYE, CHARLEY, WE'LL NEVER TELL THEM THE TRUTH ABOUT THE TRENCHES. I SEND MY LITTLE GIRL WILD FLOWERS I'VE PICKED ON THE BATTLEFIELDS. RIGHT PROUD OF THEM SHE IS. . .
Flowers From the Front
YPRES
The Somme
BEAUMONT HAMEL
DELVILLE WOOD
. . .SHE STICKS THEM IN AN EXERCISE BOOK. SHE'S GOT A FLOWER FOR EVERY BATTLE I'VE BEEN IN.
OI! WHILE YOU TWO ARE YAPPING, I'M DOING ALL THE WORK!
AH, SHUT YOUR MOUTH, GROGAN, OR YOU'LL GET A MOUTHFUL!
AS DAWN BROKE. . .
THIS IS WHAT I CALL A TRENCH! WE DID A GOOD NIGHT'S DIGGING, LADS!
'WE' . .? HUH! I LIKE THAT!
WHAT ARE WE GOING TO CALL OUR BIT OF TRENCH THEN?

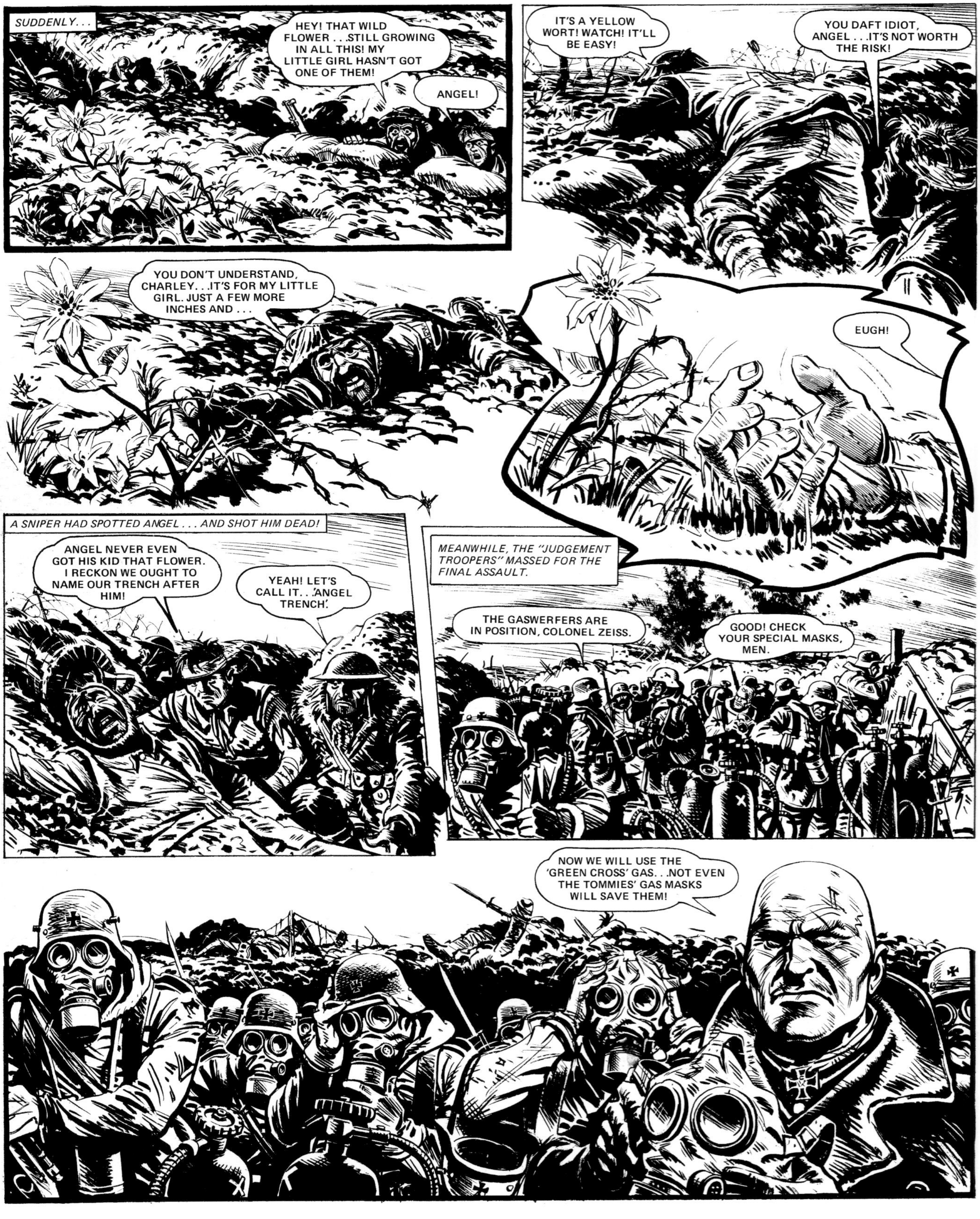
SUDDENLY. . .
HEY! THAT WILD FLOWER . . .STILL GROWING IN ALL THIS! MY LITTLE GIRL HASN'T GOT ONE OF THEM!
ANGEL!
IT'S A YELLOW WORT! WATCH! IT'LL BE EASY!
YOU DAFT IDIOT, ANGEL . . .IT'S NOT WORTH THE RISK!
YOU DON'T UNDERSTAND, CHARLEY. . .IT'S FOR MY LITTLE GIRL. JUST A FEW MORE INCHES AND . . .
EUGH!
A SNIPER HAD SPOTTED ANGEL . . . AND SHOT HIM DEAD!
ANGEL NEVER EVEN GOT HIS KID THAT FLOWER. I RECKON WE OUGHT TO NAME OUR TRENCH AFTER HIM!
YEAH! LET'S CALL IT. . .'ANGEL TRENCH'.
MEANWHILE, THE "JUDGEMENT TROOPERS" MASSED FOR THE FINAL ASSAULT.
THE GASWERFERS ARE IN POSITION, COLONEL ZEISS.
GOOD! CHECK YOUR SPECIAL MASKS, MEN.
NOW WE WILL USE THE 'GREEN CROSS' GAS. . .NOT EVEN THE TOMMIES' GAS MASKS WILL SAVE THEM!

CHARLEY'S WAR

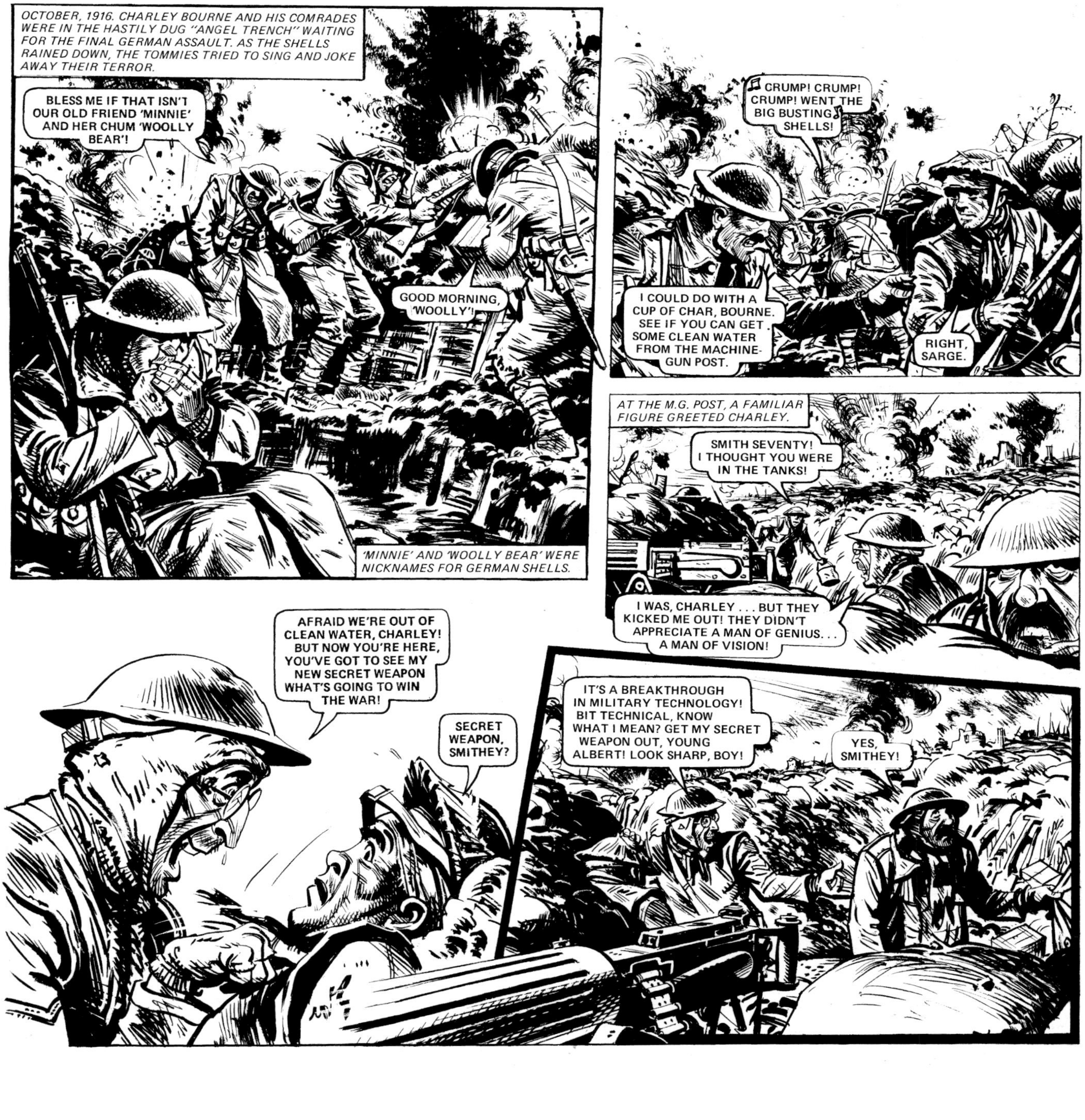

OCTOBER, 1916. CHARLEY BOURNE AND HIS COMRADES WERE IN THE HASTILY DUG "ANGEL TRENCH" WAITING FOR THE FINAL GERMAN ASSAULT. AS THE SHELLS RAINED DOWN, THE TOMMIES TRIED TO SING AND JOKE AWAY THEIR TERROR.
BLESS ME IF THAT ISN'T OUR OLD FRIEND 'MINNIE' AND HER CHUM 'WOOLLY BEAR'!
GOOD MORNING, 'WOOLLY'!
'MINNIE' AND 'WOOLLY BEAR' WERE NICKNAMES FOR GERMAN SHELLS.
♫ CRUMP! CRUMP! CRUMP! WENT THE BIG BUSTING ♫ SHELLS!
I COULD DO WITH A CUP OF CHAR, BOURNE. SEE IF YOU CAN GET SOME CLEAN WATER FROM THE MACHINE-GUN POST.
RIGHT, SARGE.
AT THE M.G. POST, A FAMILIAR FIGURE GREETED CHARLEY.
SMITH SEVENTY! I THOUGHT YOU WERE IN THE TANKS!
I WAS, CHARLEY . . . BUT THEY KICKED ME OUT! THEY DIDN'T APPRECIATE A MAN OF GENIUS. . . A MAN OF VISION!
AFRAID WE'RE OUT OF CLEAN WATER, CHARLEY! BUT NOW YOU'RE HERE, YOU'VE GOT TO SEE MY NEW SECRET WEAPON WHAT'S GOING TO WIN THE WAR!
SECRET WEAPON, SMITHEY?
IT'S A BREAKTHROUGH IN MILITARY TECHNOLOGY! BIT TECHNICAL, KNOW WHAT I MEAN? GET MY SECRET WEAPON OUT, YOUNG ALBERT! LOOK SHARP, BOY!
YES, SMITHEY!

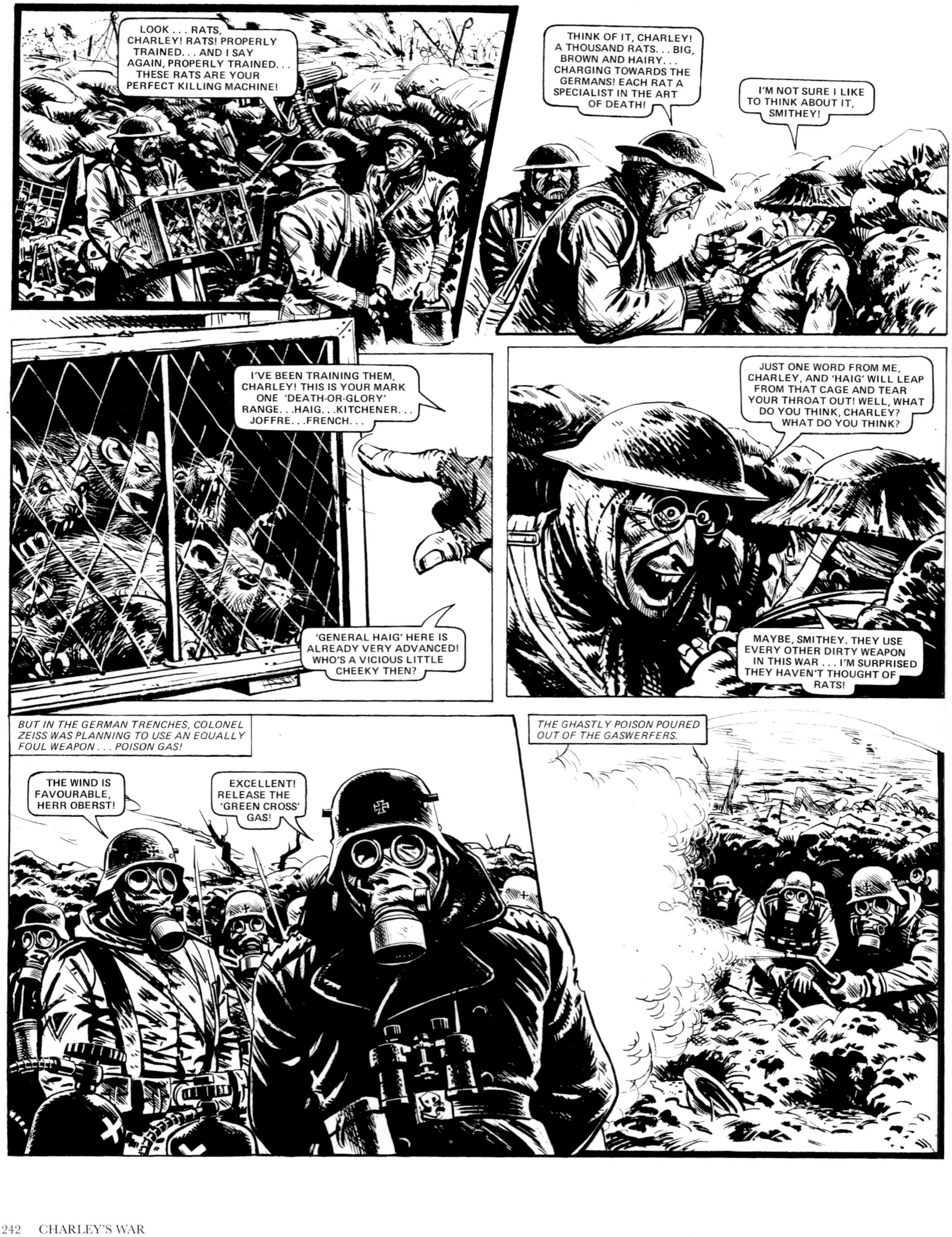
LOOK . . . RATS, CHARLEY! RATS! PROPERLY TRAINED. . . AND I SAY AGAIN, PROPERLY TRAINED. . . THESE RATS ARE YOUR PERFECT KILLING MACHINE!
THINK OF IT, CHARLEY! A THOUSAND RATS. . . BIG, BROWN AND HAIRY. . . CHARGING TOWARDS THE GERMANS! EACH RAT A SPECIALIST IN THE ART OF DEATH!
I'M NOT SURE I LIKE TO THINK ABOUT IT, SMITHEY!
I'VE BEEN TRAINING THEM, CHARLEY! THIS IS YOUR MARK ONE 'DEATH-OR-GLORY' RANGE. . . HAIG. . . KITCHENER. . . JOFFRE. . . FRENCH. . .
'GENERAL HAIG' HERE IS ALREADY VERY ADVANCED! WHO'S A VICIOUS LITTLE CHEEKY THEN?
JUST ONE WORD FROM ME, CHARLEY, AND 'HAIG' WILL LEAP FROM THAT CAGE AND TEAR YOUR THROAT OUT! WELL, WHAT DO YOU THINK, CHARLEY? WHAT DO YOU THINK?
MAYBE, SMITHEY. THEY USE EVERY OTHER DIRTY WEAPON IN THIS WAR . . . I'M SURPRISED THEY HAVEN'T THOUGHT OF RATS!
BUT IN THE GERMAN TRENCHES, COLONEL ZEISS WAS PLANNING TO USE AN EQUALLY FOUL WEAPON . . . POISON GAS!
THE WIND IS FAVOURABLE, HERR OBERST!
EXCELLENT! RELEASE THE 'GREEN CROSS' GAS!
THE GHASTLY POISON POURED OUT OF THE GASWERFERS.

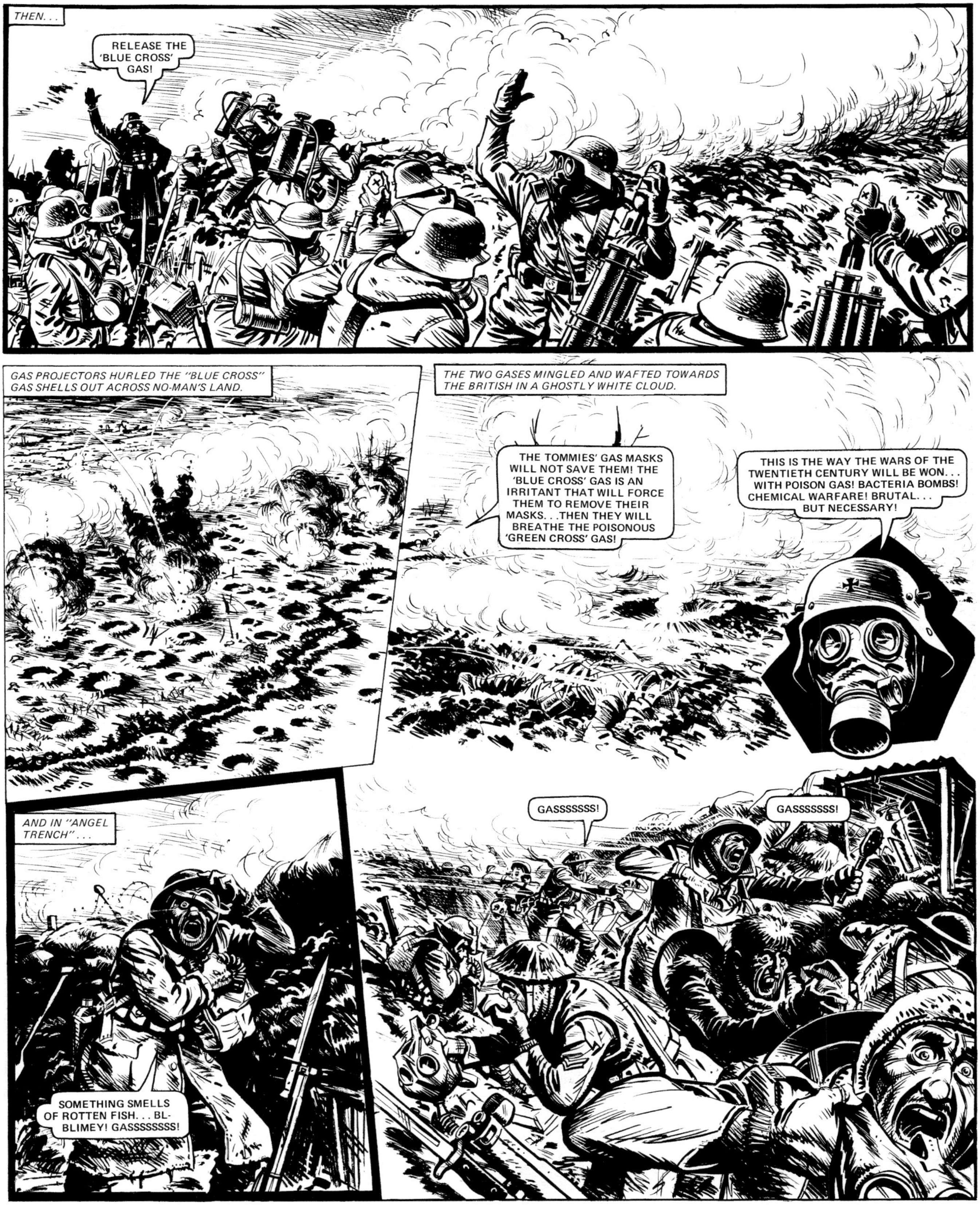

THEN...
RELEASE THE 'BLUE CROSS' GAS!
GAS PROJECTORS HURLED THE "BLUE CROSS" GAS SHELLS OUT ACROSS NO-MAN'S LAND.
THE TWO GASES MINGLED AND WAFTED TOWARDS THE BRITISH IN A GHOSTLY WHITE CLOUD.
THE TOMMIES' GAS MASKS WILL NOT SAVE THEM! THE 'BLUE CROSS' GAS IS AN IRRITANT THAT WILL FORCE THEM TO REMOVE THEIR MASKS...THEN THEY WILL BREATHE THE POISONOUS 'GREEN CROSS' GAS!
THIS IS THE WAY THE WARS OF THE TWENTIETH CENTURY WILL BE WON... WITH POISON GAS! BACTERIA BOMBS! CHEMICAL WARFARE! BRUTAL... BUT NECESSARY!
AND IN "ANGEL TRENCH"...
SOMETHING SMELLS OF ROTTEN FISH... BL-BLIMEY! GASSSSSSSS!
GASSSSSSS!
GASSSSSSS!

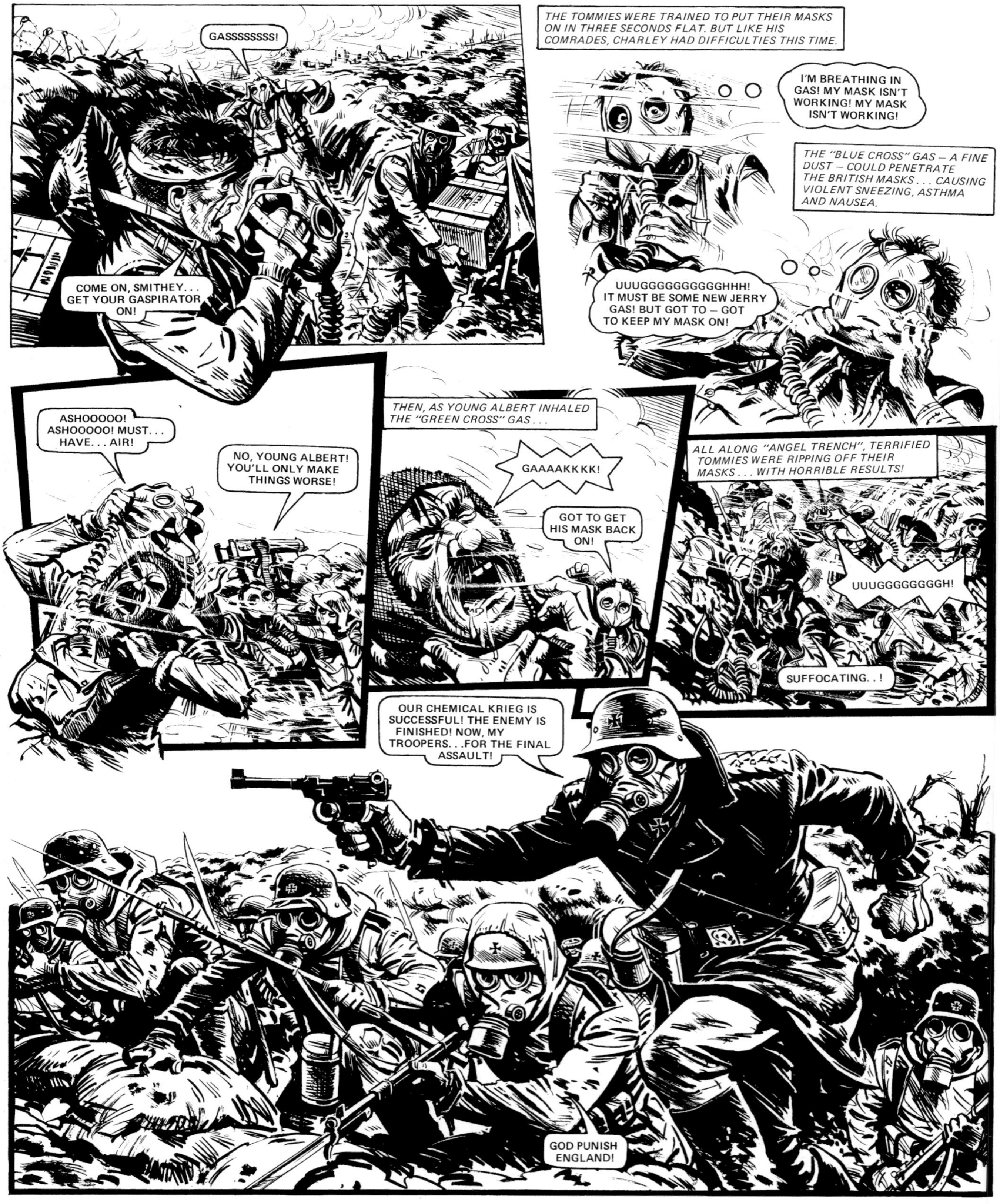

GASSSSSSSS!
COME ON, SMITHEY... GET YOUR GASPIRATOR ON!
THE TOMMIES WERE TRAINED TO PUT THEIR MASKS ON IN THREE SECONDS FLAT. BUT LIKE HIS COMRADES, CHARLEY HAD DIFFICULTIES THIS TIME.
I'M BREATHING IN GAS! MY MASK ISN'T WORKING! MY MASK ISN'T WORKING!
THE "BLUE CROSS" GAS – A FINE DUST – COULD PENETRATE THE BRITISH MASKS... CAUSING VIOLENT SNEEZING, ASTHMA AND NAUSEA.
UUUGGGGGGGGGGHHH! IT MUST BE SOME NEW JERRY GAS! BUT GOT TO – GOT TO KEEP MY MASK ON!
ASHOOOOO! ASHOOOOO! MUST... HAVE... AIR!
NO, YOUNG ALBERT! YOU'LL ONLY MAKE THINGS WORSE!
THEN, AS YOUNG ALBERT INHALED THE "GREEN CROSS" GAS...
GAAAAKKKK!
GOT TO GET HIS MASK BACK ON!
ALL ALONG "ANGEL TRENCH", TERRIFIED TOMMIES WERE RIPPING OFF THEIR MASKS... WITH HORRIBLE RESULTS!
UUUGGGGGGGGH!
SUFFOCATING..!
OUR CHEMICAL KRIEG IS SUCCESSFUL! THE ENEMY IS FINISHED! NOW, MY TROOPERS...FOR THE FINAL ASSAULT!
GOD PUNISH ENGLAND!

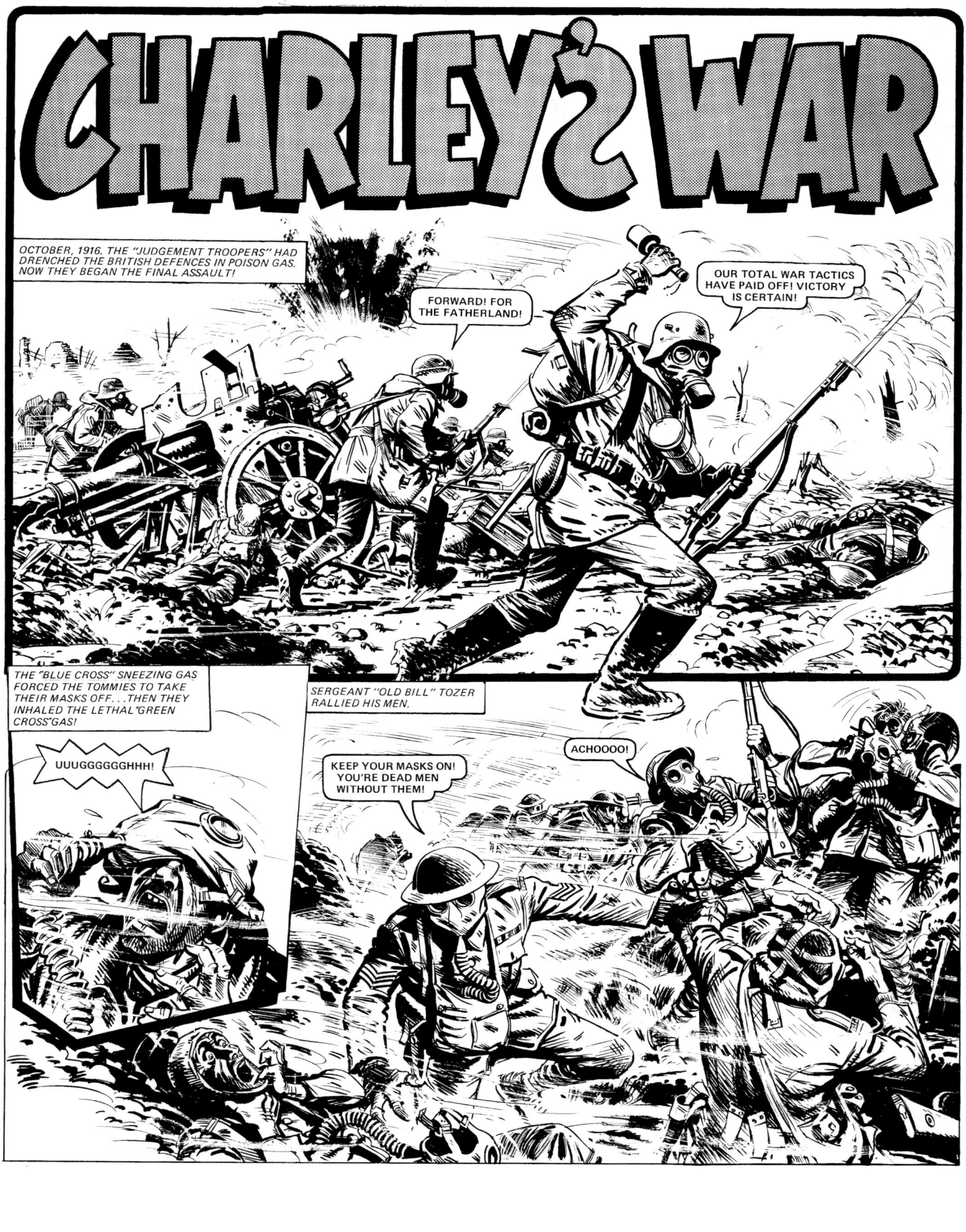
CHARLEY'S WAR
OCTOBER, 1916. THE "JUDGEMENT TROOPERS" HAD DRENCHED THE BRITISH DEFENCES IN POISON GAS. NOW THEY BEGAN THE FINAL ASSAULT!
FORWARD! FOR THE FATHERLAND!
OUR TOTAL WAR TACTICS HAVE PAID OFF! VICTORY IS CERTAIN!
THE "BLUE CROSS" SNEEZING GAS FORCED THE TOMMIES TO TAKE THEIR MASKS OFF. . .THEN THEY INHALED THE LETHAL "GREEN CROSS" GAS!
UUUGGGGGGHHH!
SERGEANT "OLD BILL" TOZER RALLIED HIS MEN.
KEEP YOUR MASKS ON! YOU'RE DEAD MEN WITHOUT THEM!
ACHOOOO!

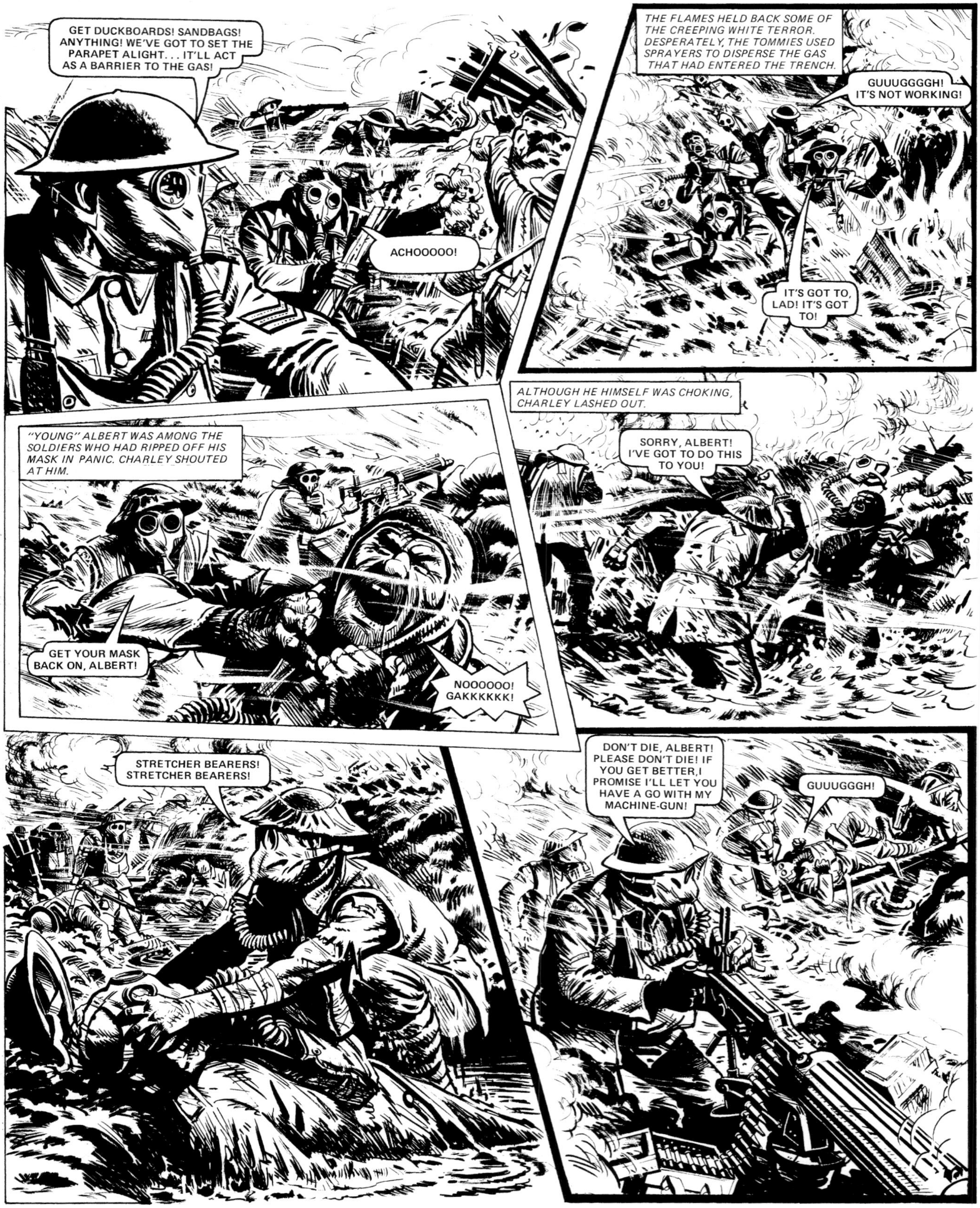
GET DUCKBOARDS! SANDBAGS! ANYTHING! WE'VE GOT TO SET THE PARAPET ALIGHT... IT'LL ACT AS A BARRIER TO THE GAS!
ACHOOOOO!
THE FLAMES HELD BACK SOME OF THE CREEPING WHITE TERROR. DESPERATELY, THE TOMMIES USED SPRAYERS TO DISPERSE THE GAS THAT HAD ENTERED THE TRENCH.
GUUUGGGGH! IT'S NOT WORKING!
IT'S GOT TO, LAD! IT'S GOT TO!
"YOUNG" ALBERT WAS AMONG THE SOLDIERS WHO HAD RIPPED OFF HIS MASK IN PANIC. CHARLEY SHOUTED AT HIM.
GET YOUR MASK BACK ON, ALBERT!
NOOOOOO! GAKKKKKK!
ALTHOUGH HE HIMSELF WAS CHOKING, CHARLEY LASHED OUT.
SORRY, ALBERT! I'VE GOT TO DO THIS TO YOU!
STRETCHER BEARERS! STRETCHER BEARERS!
DON'T DIE, ALBERT! PLEASE DON'T DIE! IF YOU GET BETTER, I PROMISE I'LL LET YOU HAVE A GO WITH MY MACHINE-GUN!
GUUUGGGH!

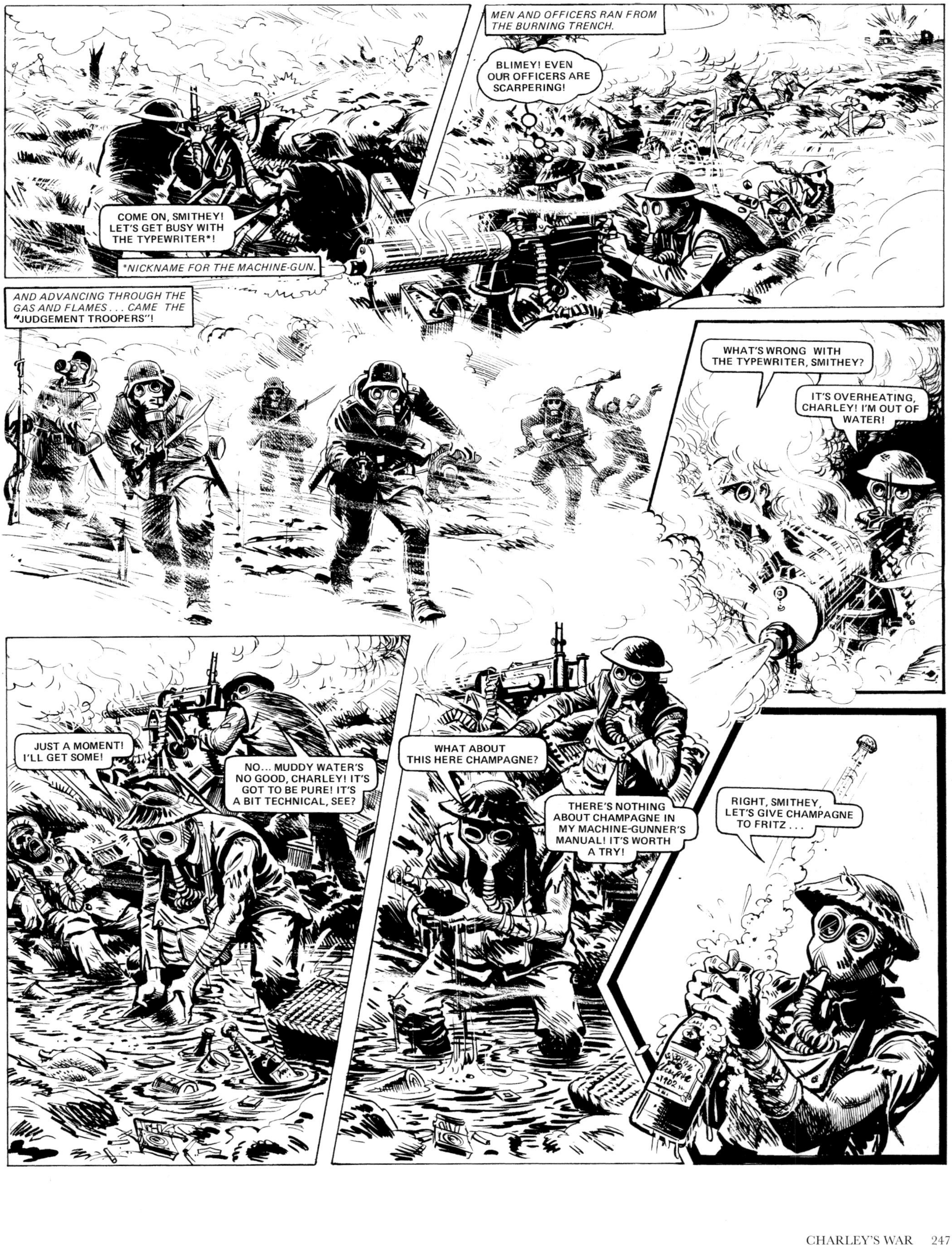
COME ON, SMITHEY! LET'S GET BUSY WITH THE TYPEWRITER*!
*NICKNAME FOR THE MACHINE-GUN.
MEN AND OFFICERS RAN FROM THE BURNING TRENCH.
BLIMEY! EVEN OUR OFFICERS ARE SCARPERING!
AND ADVANCING THROUGH THE GAS AND FLAMES . . . CAME THE "JUDGEMENT TROOPERS"!
WHAT'S WRONG WITH THE TYPEWRITER, SMITHEY?
IT'S OVERHEATING, CHARLEY! I'M OUT OF WATER!
JUST A MOMENT! I'LL GET SOME!
NO... MUDDY WATER'S NO GOOD, CHARLEY! IT'S GOT TO BE PURE! IT'S A BIT TECHNICAL, SEE?
WHAT ABOUT THIS HERE CHAMPAGNE?
THERE'S NOTHING ABOUT CHAMPAGNE IN MY MACHINE-GUNNER'S MANUAL! IT'S WORTH A TRY!
RIGHT, SMITHEY, LET'S GIVE CHAMPAGNE TO FRITZ . . .

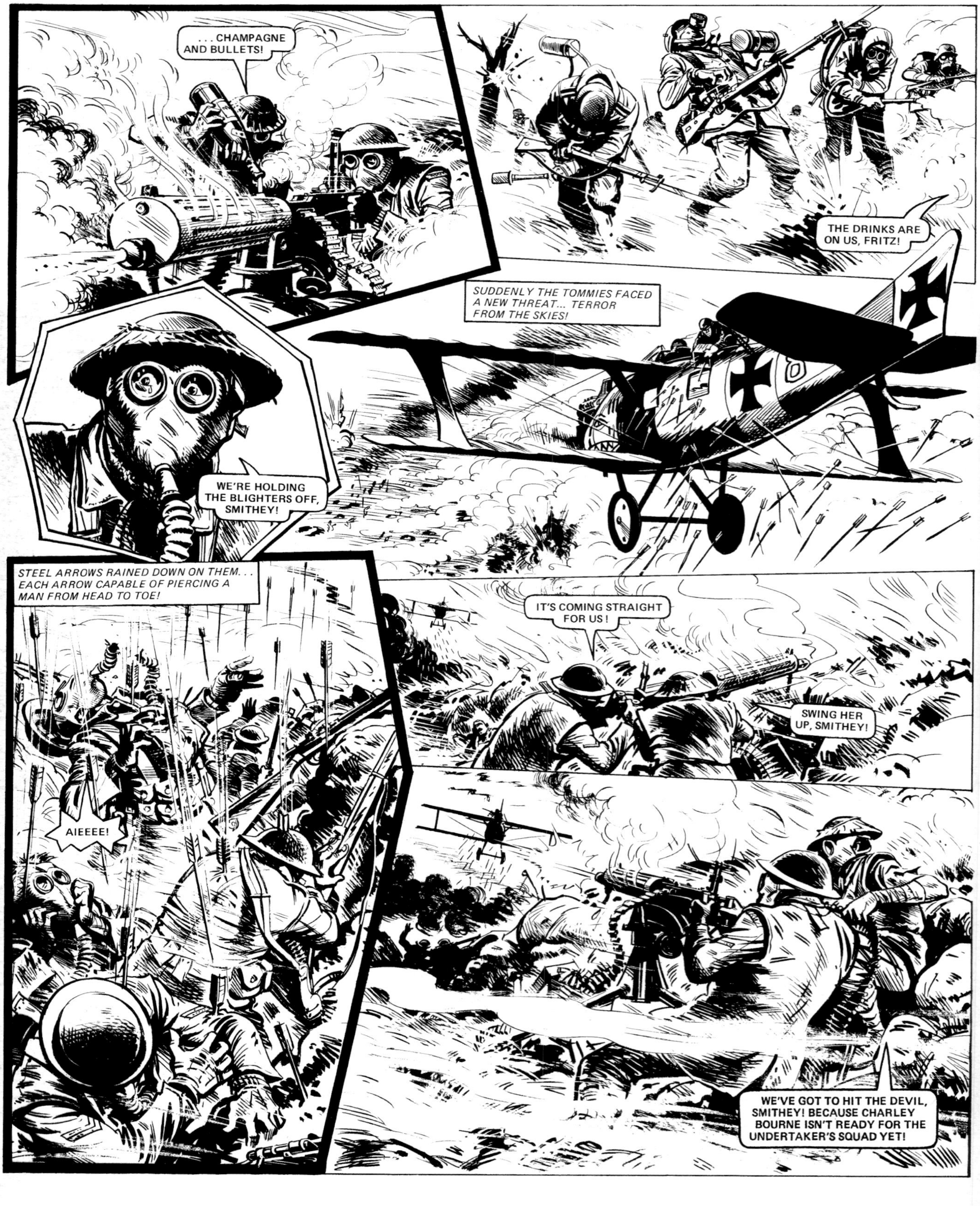
. . . CHAMPAGNE AND BULLETS!
THE DRINKS ARE ON US, FRITZ!
SUDDENLY THE TOMMIES FACED A NEW THREAT... TERROR FROM THE SKIES!
WE'RE HOLDING THE BLIGHTERS OFF, SMITHEY!
STEEL ARROWS RAINED DOWN ON THEM... EACH ARROW CAPABLE OF PIERCING A MAN FROM HEAD TO TOE!
AIEEEE!
IT'S COMING STRAIGHT FOR US!
SWING HER UP, SMITHEY!
WE'VE GOT TO HIT THE DEVIL, SMITHEY! BECAUSE CHARLEY BOURNE ISN'T READY FOR THE UNDERTAKER'S SQUAD YET!

CHARLEY'S WAR

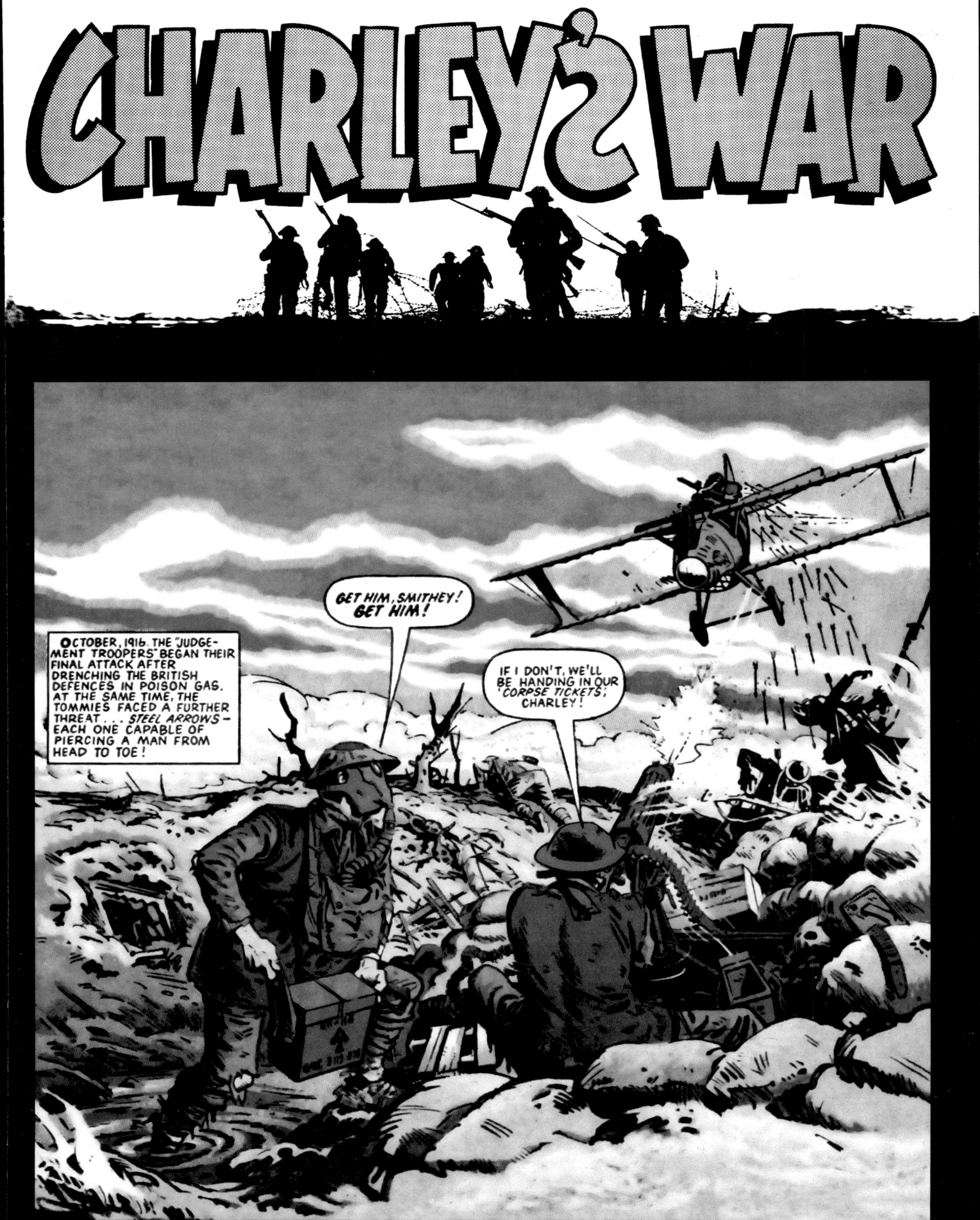
OCTOBER, 1916. THE "JUDGEMENT TROOPERS" BEGAN THEIR FINAL ATTACK AFTER DRENCHING THE BRITISH DEFENCES IN POISON GAS. AT THE SAME TIME, THE TOMMIES FACED A FURTHER THREAT . . . STEEL ARROWS – EACH ONE CAPABLE OF PIERCING A MAN FROM HEAD TO TOE!
GET HIM, SMITHEY! GET HIM!
IF I DON'T, WE'LL BE HANDING IN OUR 'CORPSE TICKETS', CHARLEY!

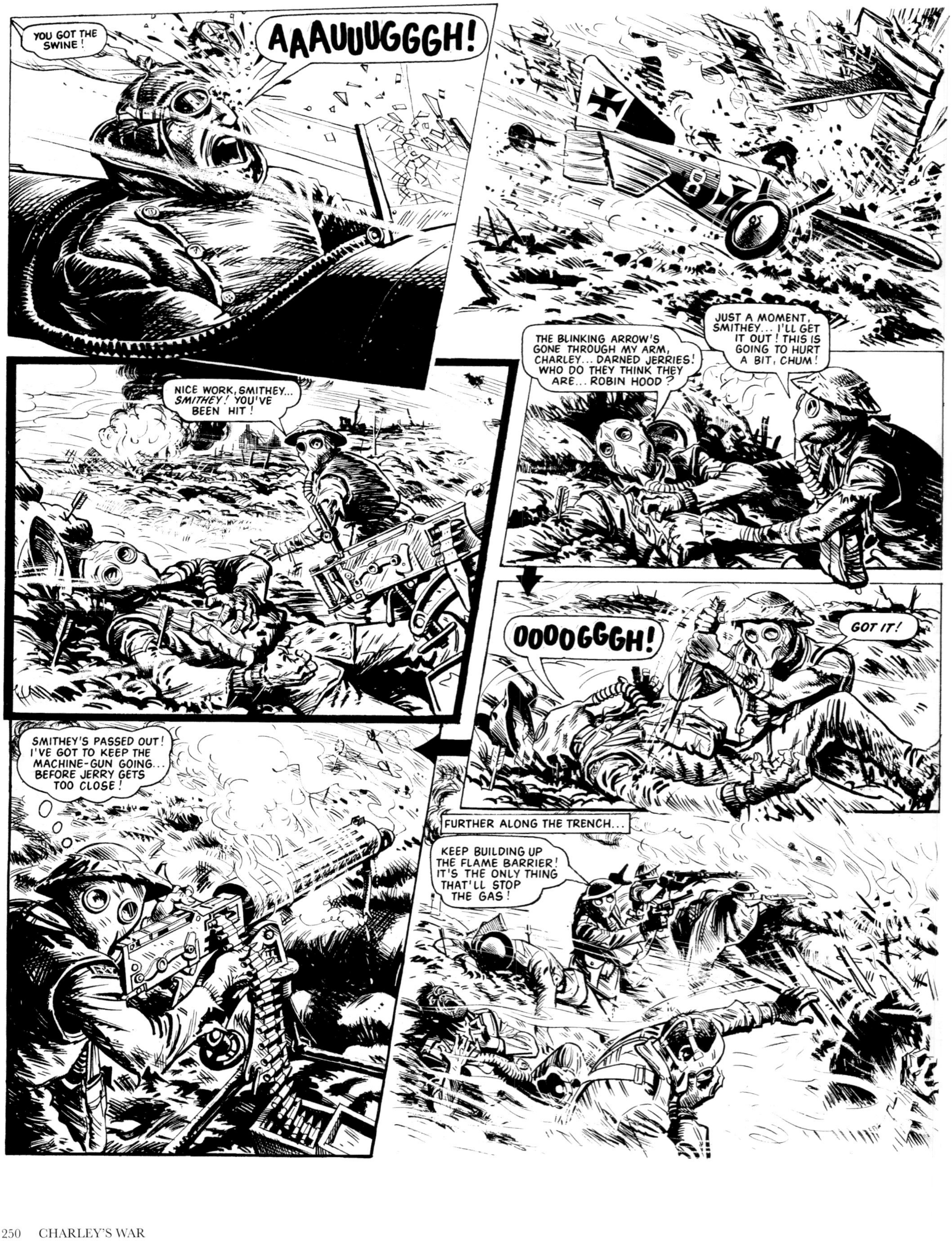
YOU GOT THE SWINE!
AAAUUUGGGH!
NICE WORK, SMITHEY... SMITHEY! YOU'VE BEEN HIT!
THE BLINKING ARROW'S GONE THROUGH MY ARM, CHARLEY... DARNED JERRIES! WHO DO THEY THINK THEY ARE... ROBIN HOOD?
JUST A MOMENT, SMITHEY... I'LL GET IT OUT! THIS IS GOING TO HURT A BIT, CHUM!
SMITHEY'S PASSED OUT! I'VE GOT TO KEEP THE MACHINE-GUN GOING... BEFORE JERRY GETS TOO CLOSE!
OOOOGGGH!
GOT IT!
FURTHER ALONG THE TRENCH...
KEEP BUILDING UP THE FLAME BARRIER! IT'S THE ONLY THING THAT'LL STOP THE GAS!

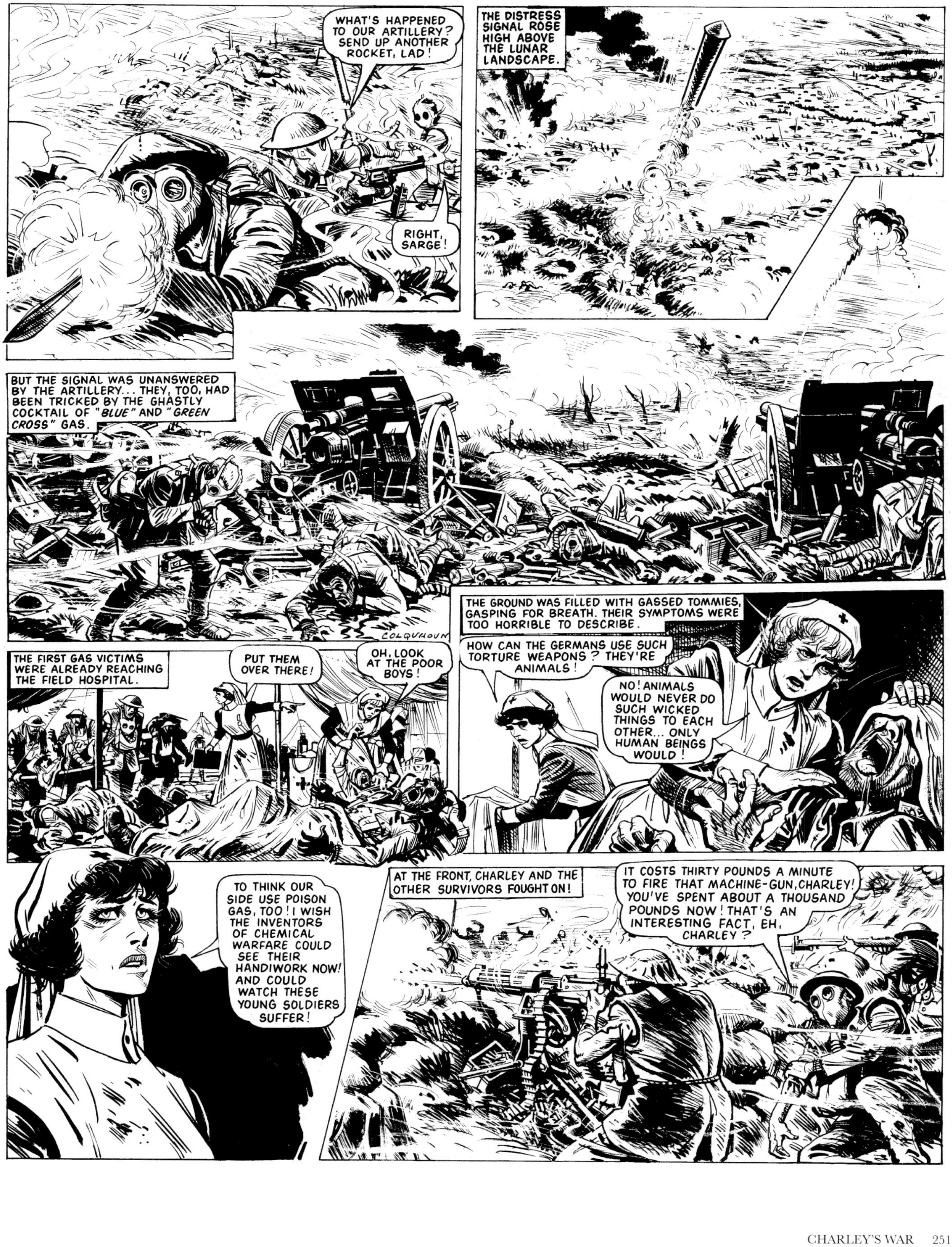
WHAT'S HAPPENED TO OUR ARTILLERY? SEND UP ANOTHER ROCKET, LAD!
RIGHT, SARGE!
THE DISTRESS SIGNAL ROSE HIGH ABOVE THE LUNAR LANDSCAPE.
BUT THE SIGNAL WAS UNANSWERED BY THE ARTILLERY... THEY, TOO, HAD BEEN TRICKED BY THE GHASTLY COCKTAIL OF "BLUE" AND "GREEN CROSS" GAS.
COLQUHOUN
THE FIRST GAS VICTIMS WERE ALREADY REACHING THE FIELD HOSPITAL.
PUT THEM OVER THERE!
OH, LOOK AT THE POOR BOYS!
THE GROUND WAS FILLED WITH GASSED TOMMIES, GASPING FOR BREATH. THEIR SYMPTOMS WERE TOO HORRIBLE TO DESCRIBE.
HOW CAN THE GERMANS USE SUCH TORTURE WEAPONS? THEY'RE ANIMALS!
NO! ANIMALS WOULD NEVER DO SUCH WICKED THINGS TO EACH OTHER... ONLY HUMAN BEINGS WOULD!
TO THINK OUR SIDE USE POISON GAS, TOO! I WISH THE INVENTORS OF CHEMICAL WARFARE COULD SEE THEIR HANDIWORK NOW! AND COULD WATCH THESE YOUNG SOLDIERS SUFFER!
AT THE FRONT, CHARLEY AND THE OTHER SURVIVORS FOUGHT ON!
IT COSTS THIRTY POUNDS A MINUTE TO FIRE THAT MACHINE-GUN, CHARLEY! YOU'VE SPENT ABOUT A THOUSAND POUNDS NOW! THAT'S AN INTERESTING FACT, EH, CHARLEY?

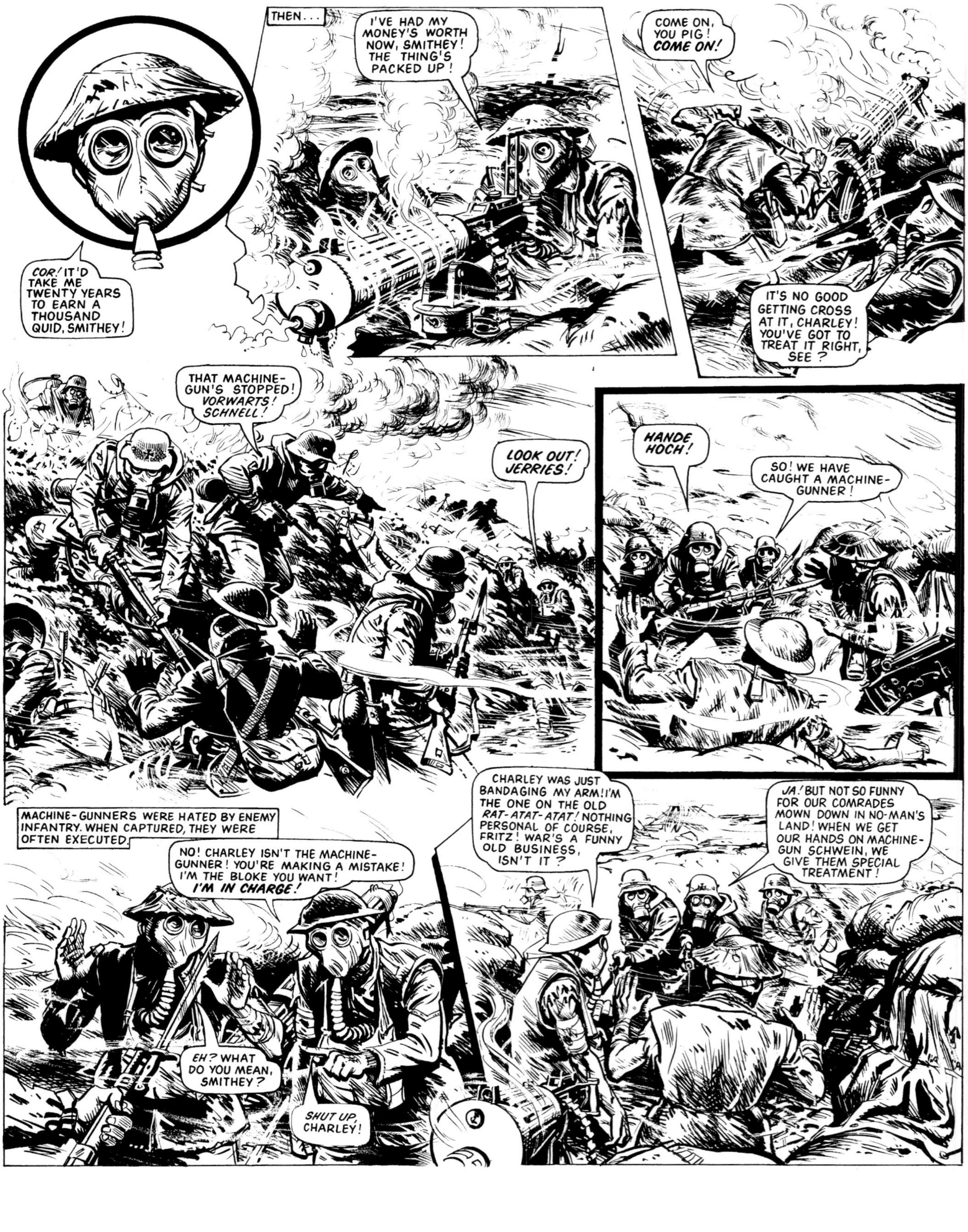
COR! IT'D TAKE ME TWENTY YEARS TO EARN A THOUSAND QUID, SMITHEY!
THEN...
I'VE HAD MY MONEY'S WORTH NOW, SMITHEY! THE THING'S PACKED UP!
COME ON, YOU PIG! COME ON!
IT'S NO GOOD GETTING CROSS AT IT, CHARLEY! YOU'VE GOT TO TREAT IT RIGHT, SEE?
THAT MACHINE-GUN'S STOPPED! VORWARTS! SCHNELL!
LOOK OUT! JERRIES!
HANDE HOCH!
SO! WE HAVE CAUGHT A MACHINE-GUNNER!
MACHINE-GUNNERS WERE HATED BY ENEMY INFANTRY. WHEN CAPTURED, THEY WERE OFTEN EXECUTED.
NO! CHARLEY ISN'T THE MACHINE-GUNNER! YOU'RE MAKING A MISTAKE! I'M THE BLOKE YOU WANT! I'M IN CHARGE!
EH? WHAT DO YOU MEAN, SMITHEY?
SHUT UP, CHARLEY!
CHARLEY WAS JUST BANDAGING MY ARM! I'M THE ONE ON THE OLD RAT-ATAT-ATAT! NOTHING PERSONAL OF COURSE, FRITZ! WAR'S A FUNNY OLD BUSINESS, ISN'T IT?
JA! BUT NOT SO FUNNY FOR OUR COMRADES MOWN DOWN IN NO-MAN'S LAND! WHEN WE GET OUR HANDS ON MACHINE-GUN SCHWEIN, WE GIVE THEM SPECIAL TREATMENT!

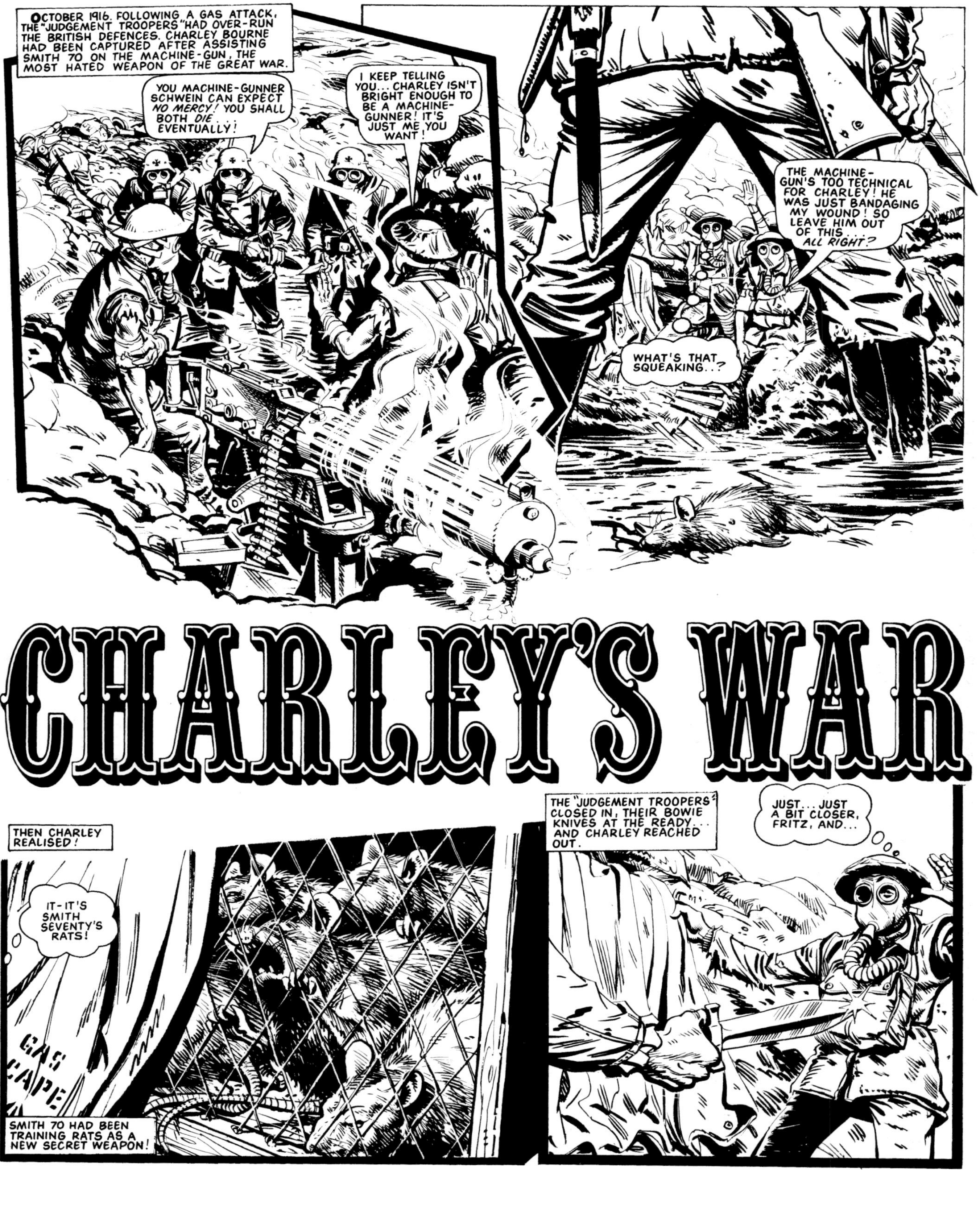

OCTOBER 1916. FOLLOWING A GAS ATTACK, THE "JUDGEMENT TROOPERS" HAD OVER-RUN THE BRITISH DEFENCES. CHARLEY BOURNE HAD BEEN CAPTURED AFTER ASSISTING SMITH 70 ON THE MACHINE-GUN, THE MOST HATED WEAPON OF THE GREAT WAR.
YOU MACHINE-GUNNER SCHWEIN CAN EXPECT NO MERCY! YOU SHALL BOTH DIE . . . EVENTUALLY!
I KEEP TELLING YOU... CHARLEY ISN'T BRIGHT ENOUGH TO BE A MACHINE-GUNNER! IT'S JUST ME YOU WANT!
THE MACHINE-GUN'S TOO TECHNICAL FOR CHARLEY! HE WAS JUST BANDAGING MY WOUND! SO LEAVE HIM OUT OF THIS . . . ALL RIGHT?
WHAT'S THAT SQUEAKING..?
CHARLEY'S WAR
THEN CHARLEY REALISED!
IT-IT'S SMITH SEVENTY'S RATS!
GAS CAPE
SMITH 70 HAD BEEN TRAINING RATS AS A NEW SECRET WEAPON!
THE "JUDGEMENT TROOPERS" CLOSED IN, THEIR BOWIE KNIVES AT THE READY . . . AND CHARLEY REACHED OUT.
JUST... JUST A BIT CLOSER, FRITZ, AND...

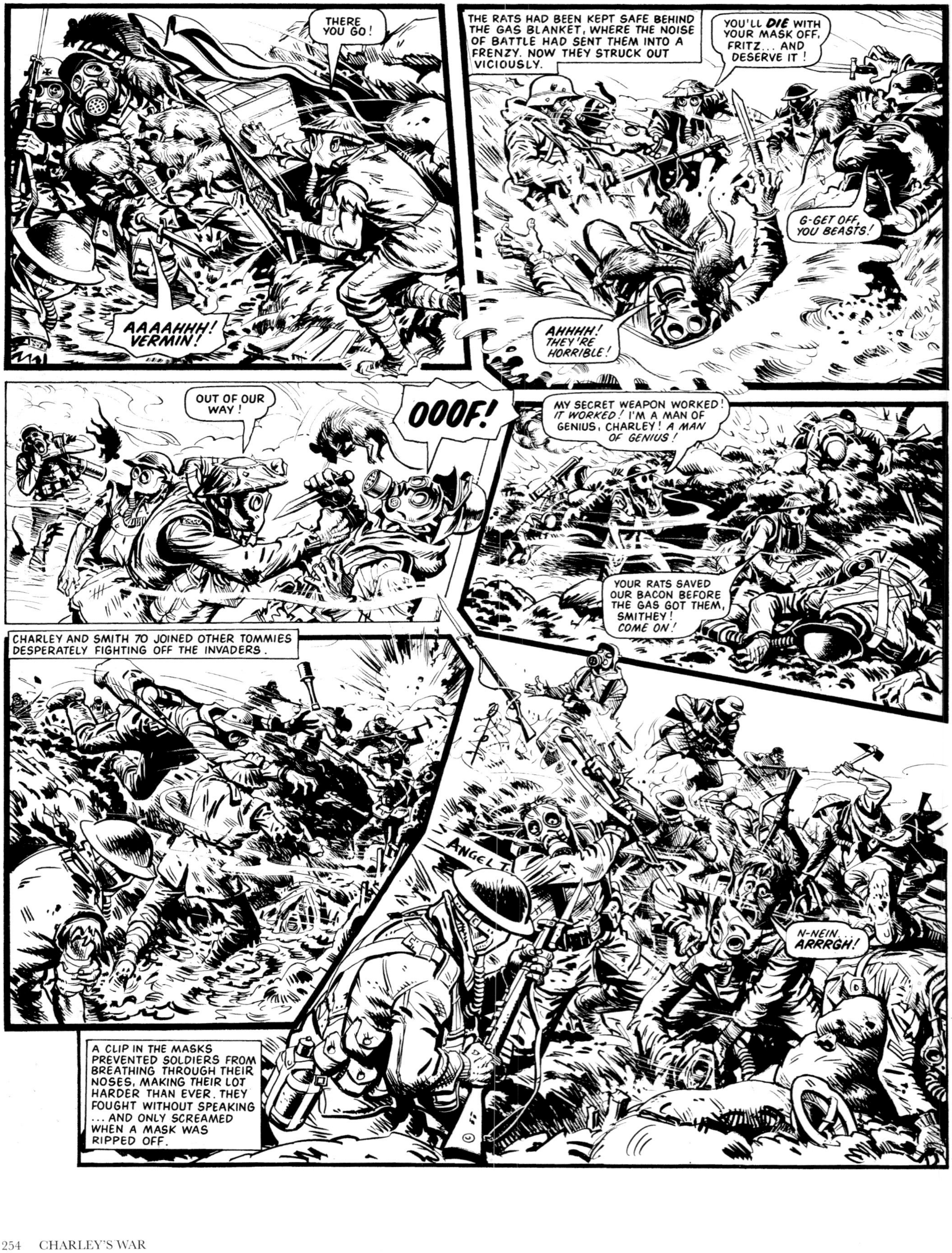
THERE YOU GO!
AAAAHHH! VERMIN!
THE RATS HAD BEEN KEPT SAFE BEHIND THE GAS BLANKET, WHERE THE NOISE OF BATTLE HAD SENT THEM INTO A FRENZY. NOW THEY STRUCK OUT VICIOUSLY.
YOU'LL DIE WITH YOUR MASK OFF, FRITZ... AND DESERVE IT!
G-GET OFF, YOU BEASTS!
AHHHH! THEY'RE HORRIBLE!
OUT OF OUR WAY!
OOOF!
MY SECRET WEAPON WORKED! IT WORKED! I'M A MAN OF GENIUS, CHARLEY! A MAN OF GENIUS!
YOUR RATS SAVED OUR BACON BEFORE THE GAS GOT THEM, SMITHEY! COME ON!
CHARLEY AND SMITH 70 JOINED OTHER TOMMIES DESPERATELY FIGHTING OFF THE INVADERS.
ANGEL T
N-NEIN... ARRRGH!
A CLIP IN THE MASKS PREVENTED SOLDIERS FROM BREATHING THROUGH THEIR NOSES, MAKING THEIR LOT HARDER THAN EVER. THEY FOUGHT WITHOUT SPEAKING ... AND ONLY SCREAMED WHEN A MASK WAS RIPPED OFF.

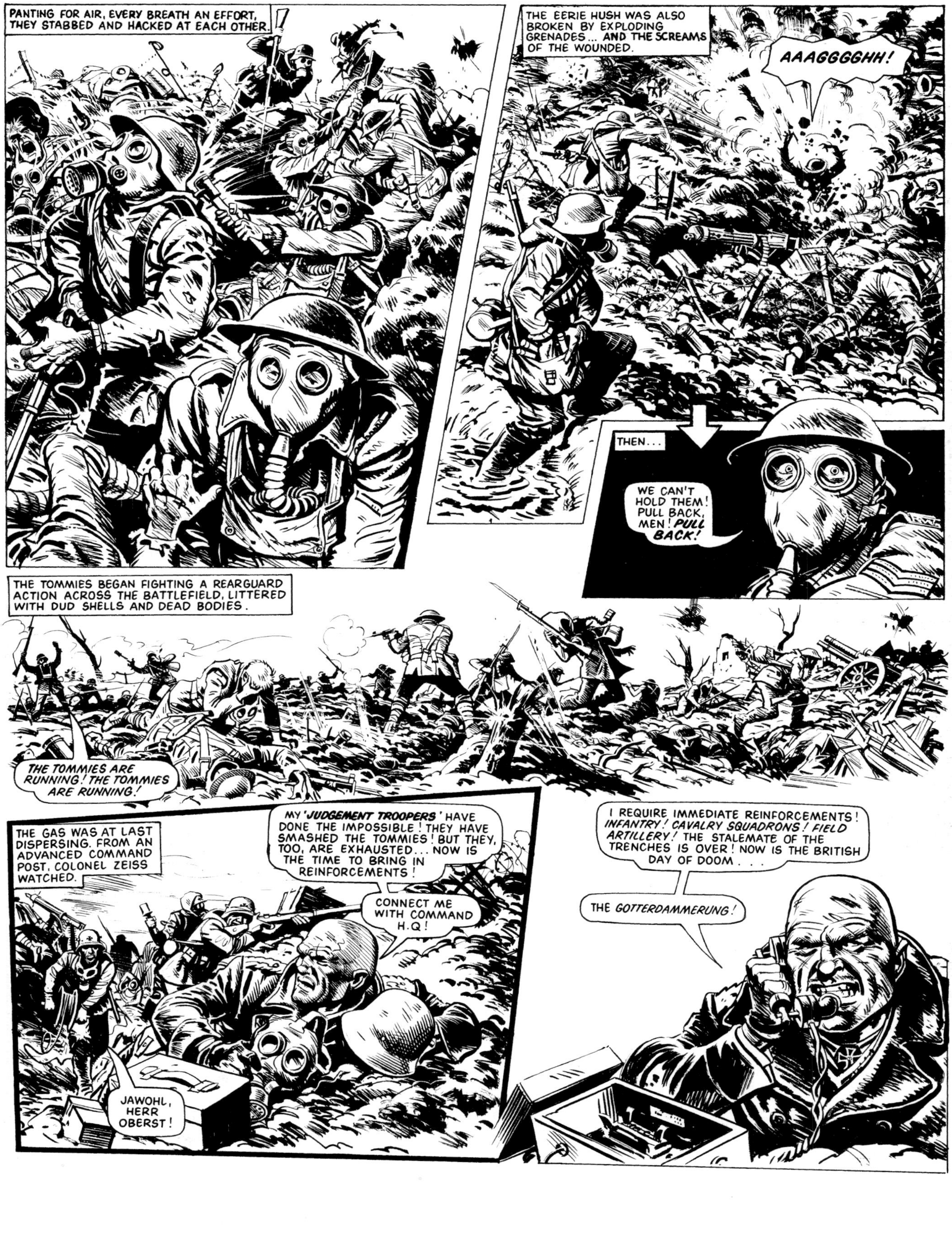
PANTING FOR AIR, EVERY BREATH AN EFFORT, THEY STABBED AND HACKED AT EACH OTHER.
THE EERIE HUSH WAS ALSO BROKEN BY EXPLODING GRENADES... AND THE SCREAMS OF THE WOUNDED.
AAAGGGGHH!
THEN...
WE CAN'T HOLD THEM! PULL BACK, MEN! PULL BACK!
THE TOMMIES BEGAN FIGHTING A REARGUARD ACTION ACROSS THE BATTLEFIELD, LITTERED WITH DUD SHELLS AND DEAD BODIES.
THE TOMMIES ARE RUNNING! THE TOMMIES ARE RUNNING!
THE GAS WAS AT LAST DISPERSING. FROM AN ADVANCED COMMAND POST, COLONEL ZEISS WATCHED.
MY 'JUDGEMENT TROOPERS' HAVE DONE THE IMPOSSIBLE! THEY HAVE SMASHED THE TOMMIES! BUT THEY, TOO, ARE EXHAUSTED... NOW IS THE TIME TO BRING IN REINFORCEMENTS!
CONNECT ME WITH COMMAND H.Q!
JAWOHL, HERR OBERST!
I REQUIRE IMMEDIATE REINFORCEMENTS! INFANTRY! CAVALRY SQUADRONS! FIELD ARTILLERY! THE STALEMATE OF THE TRENCHES IS OVER! NOW IS THE BRITISH DAY OF DOOM . . .
THE GOTTERDAMMERUNG!

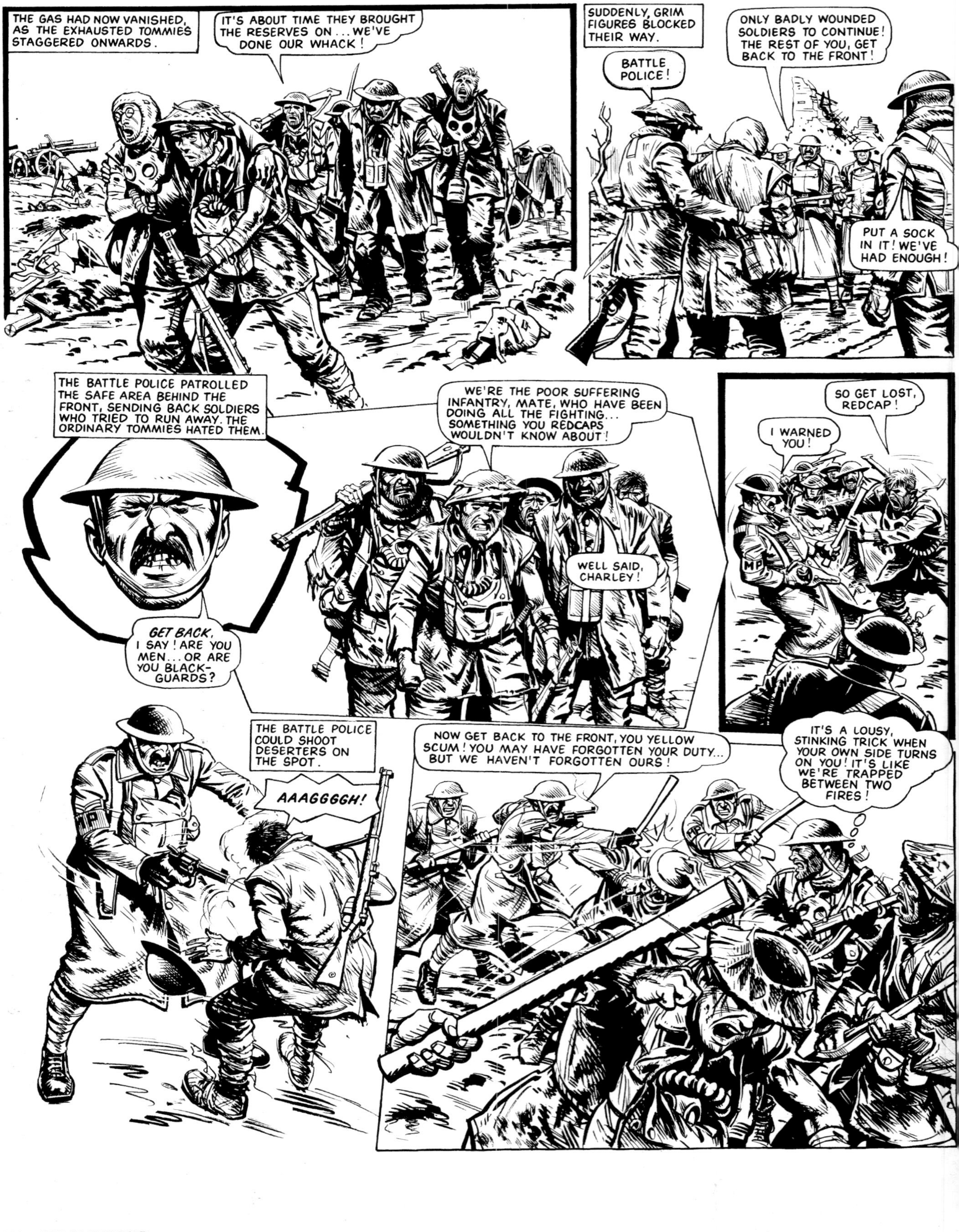

THE GAS HAD NOW VANISHED, AS THE EXHAUSTED TOMMIES STAGGERED ONWARDS.
IT'S ABOUT TIME THEY BROUGHT THE RESERVES ON... WE'VE DONE OUR WHACK!
SUDDENLY, GRIM FIGURES BLOCKED THEIR WAY.
BATTLE POLICE!
ONLY BADLY WOUNDED SOLDIERS TO CONTINUE! THE REST OF YOU, GET BACK TO THE FRONT!
PUT A SOCK IN IT! WE'VE HAD ENOUGH!
THE BATTLE POLICE PATROLLED THE SAFE AREA BEHIND THE FRONT, SENDING BACK SOLDIERS WHO TRIED TO RUN AWAY. THE ORDINARY TOMMIES HATED THEM.
GET BACK, I SAY! ARE YOU MEN... OR ARE YOU BLACK-GUARDS?
WE'RE THE POOR SUFFERING INFANTRY, MATE, WHO HAVE BEEN DOING ALL THE FIGHTING... SOMETHING YOU REDCAPS WOULDN'T KNOW ABOUT!
WELL SAID, CHARLEY!
SO GET LOST, REDCAP!
I WARNED YOU!
MP
THE BATTLE POLICE COULD SHOOT DESERTERS ON THE SPOT.
AAAGGGGH!
NOW GET BACK TO THE FRONT, YOU YELLOW SCUM! YOU MAY HAVE FORGOTTEN YOUR DUTY... BUT WE HAVEN'T FORGOTTEN OURS!
IT'S A LOUSY, STINKING TRICK WHEN YOUR OWN SIDE TURNS ON YOU! IT'S LIKE WE'RE TRAPPED BETWEEN TWO FIRES!

CHARLEY'S WAR

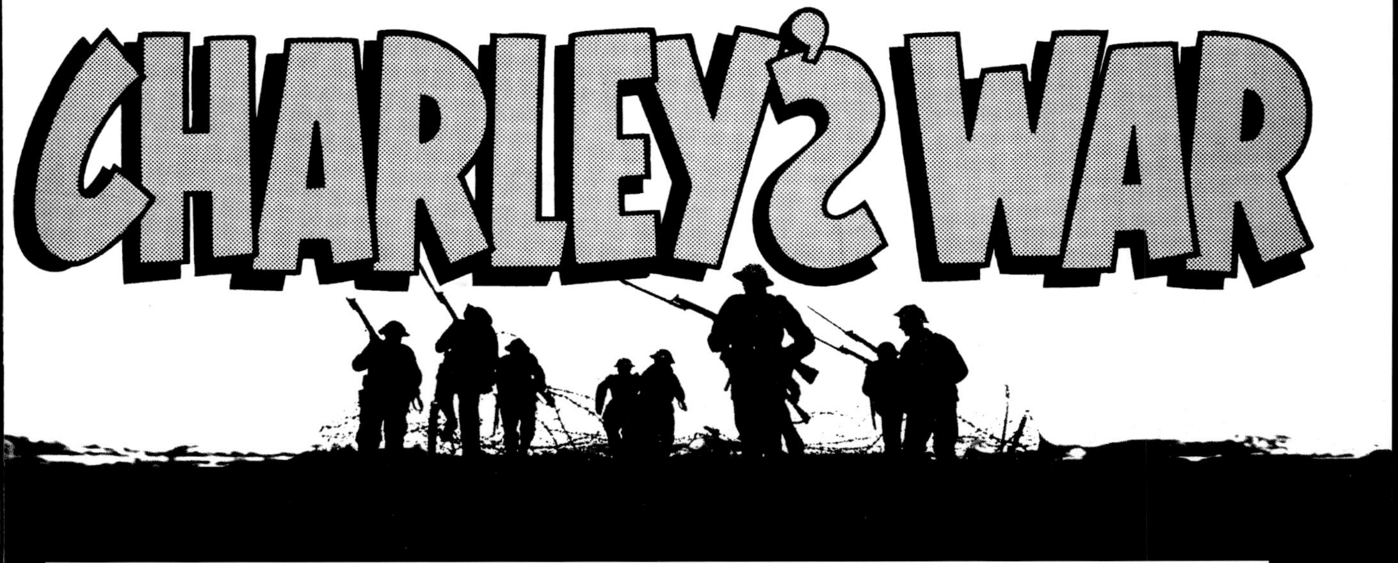

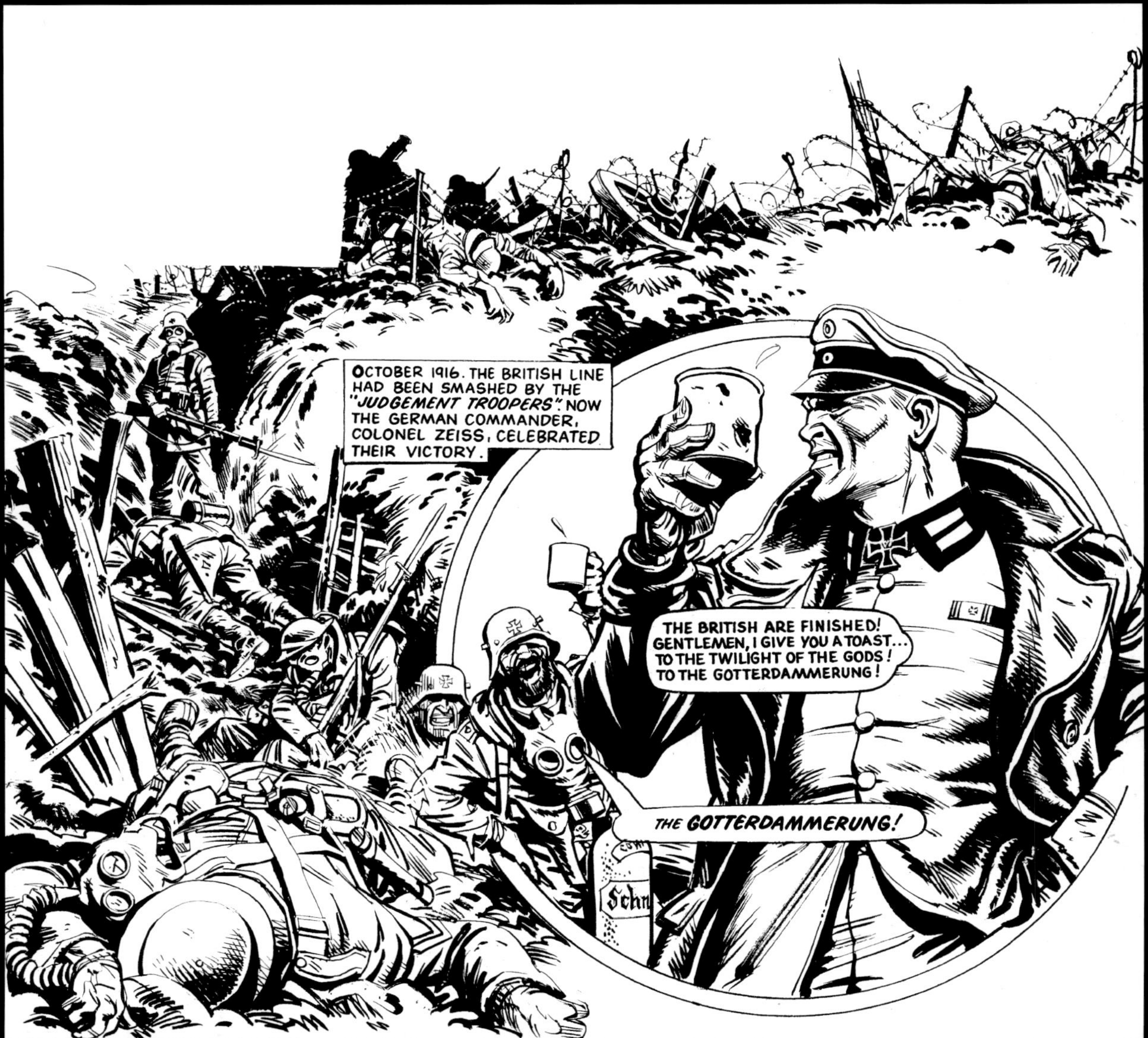

OCTOBER 1916. THE BRITISH LINE HAD BEEN SMASHED BY THE "JUDGEMENT TROOPERS". NOW THE GERMAN COMMANDER, COLONEL ZEISS, CELEBRATED THEIR VICTORY.
THE BRITISH ARE FINISHED! GENTLEMEN, I GIVE YOU A TOAST... TO THE TWILIGHT OF THE GODS! TO THE GOTTERDAMMERUNG!
THE GOTTERDAMMERUNG!

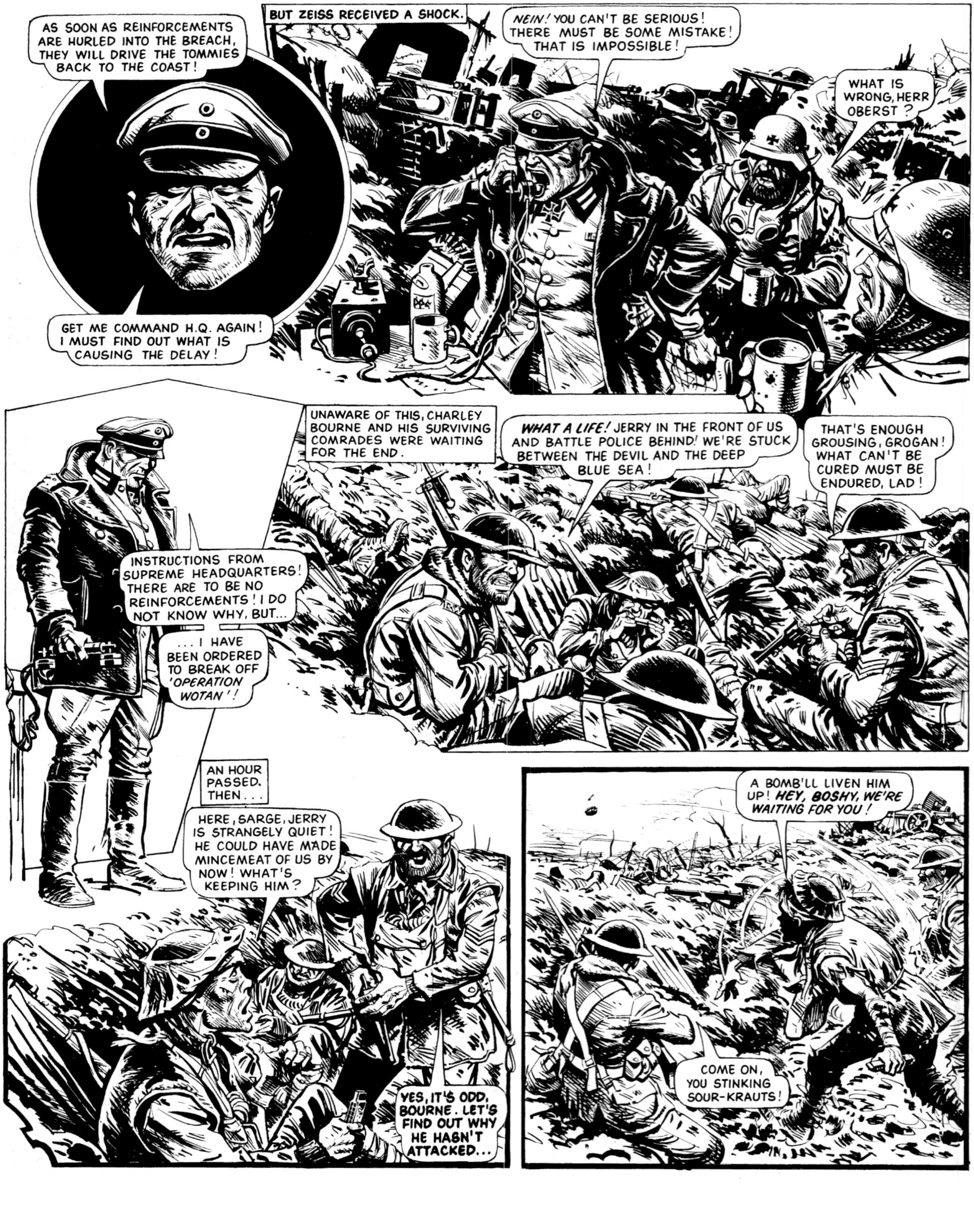
AS SOON AS REINFORCEMENTS ARE HURLED INTO THE BREACH, THEY WILL DRIVE THE TOMMIES BACK TO THE COAST!
GET ME COMMAND H.Q. AGAIN! I MUST FIND OUT WHAT IS CAUSING THE DELAY!
BUT ZEISS RECEIVED A SHOCK.
NEIN! YOU CAN'T BE SERIOUS! THERE MUST BE SOME MISTAKE! THAT IS IMPOSSIBLE!
WHAT IS WRONG, HERR OBERST?
INSTRUCTIONS FROM SUPREME HEADQUARTERS! THERE ARE TO BE NO REINFORCEMENTS! I DO NOT KNOW WHY, BUT...
... I HAVE BEEN ORDERED TO BREAK OFF 'OPERATION WOTAN'!
UNAWARE OF THIS, CHARLEY BOURNE AND HIS SURVIVING COMRADES WERE WAITING FOR THE END.
WHAT A LIFE! JERRY IN THE FRONT OF US AND BATTLE POLICE BEHIND! WE'RE STUCK BETWEEN THE DEVIL AND THE DEEP BLUE SEA!
THAT'S ENOUGH GROUSING, GROGAN! WHAT CAN'T BE CURED MUST BE ENDURED, LAD!
AN HOUR PASSED. THEN...
HERE, SARGE, JERRY IS STRANGELY QUIET! HE COULD HAVE MADE MINCEMEAT OF US BY NOW! WHAT'S KEEPING HIM?
YES, IT'S ODD, BOURNE. LET'S FIND OUT WHY HE HASN'T ATTACKED...
A BOMB'LL LIVEN HIM UP! HEY, BOSHY, WE'RE WAITING FOR YOU!
COME ON, YOU STINKING SOUR-KRAUTS!

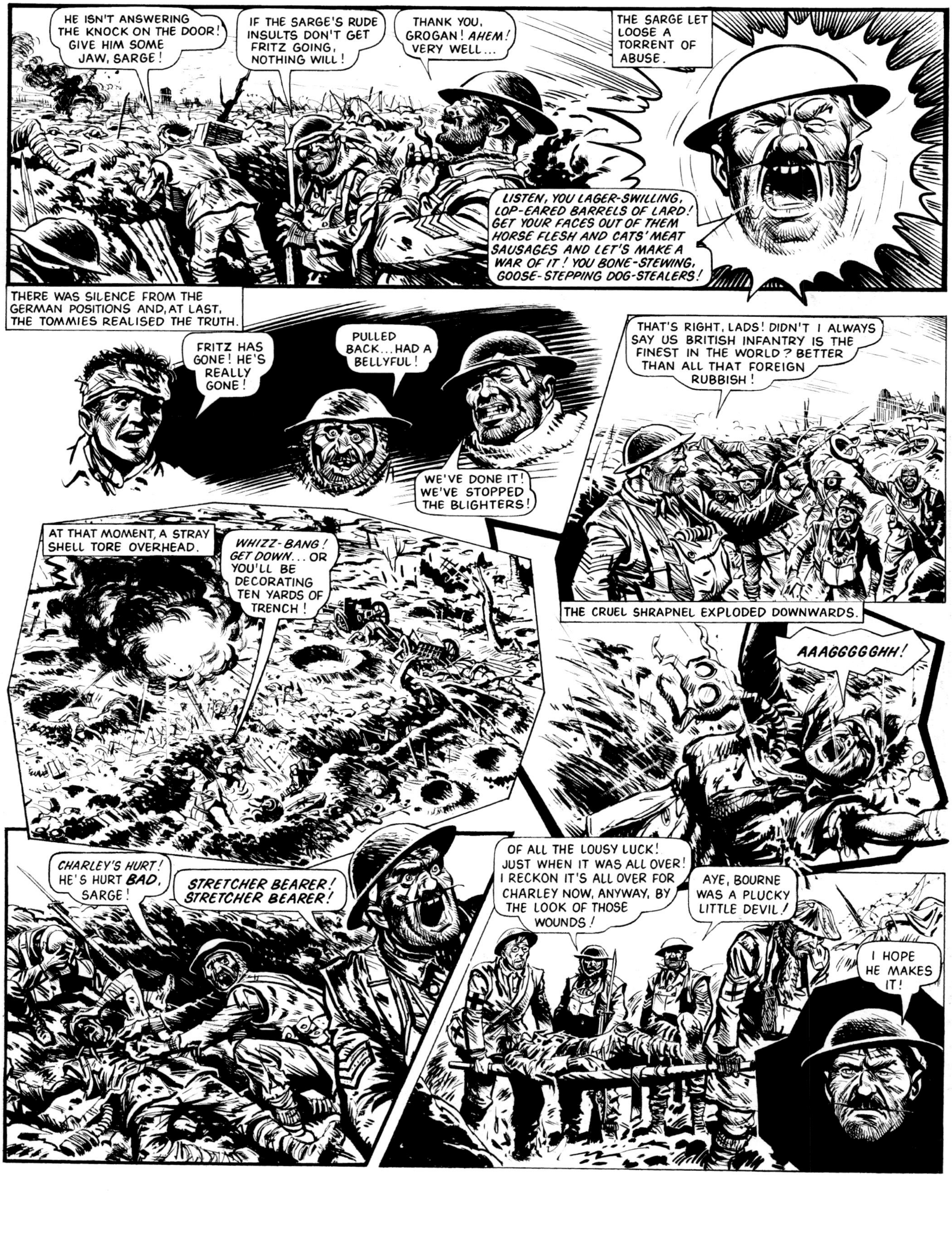
HE ISN'T ANSWERING THE KNOCK ON THE DOOR! GIVE HIM SOME JAW, SARGE!
IF THE SARGE'S RUDE INSULTS DON'T GET FRITZ GOING, NOTHING WILL!
THANK YOU, GROGAN! AHEM! VERY WELL...
THE SARGE LET LOOSE A TORRENT OF ABUSE.
LISTEN, YOU LAGER-SWILLING, LOP-EARED BARRELS OF LARD! GET YOUR FACES OUT OF THEM HORSE FLESH AND CATS' MEAT SAUSAGES AND LET'S MAKE A WAR OF IT! YOU BONE-STEWING, GOOSE-STEPPING DOG-STEALERS!
THERE WAS SILENCE FROM THE GERMAN POSITIONS AND, AT LAST, THE TOMMIES REALISED THE TRUTH.
FRITZ HAS GONE! HE'S REALLY GONE!
PULLED BACK... HAD A BELLYFUL!
WE'VE DONE IT! WE'VE STOPPED THE BLIGHTERS!
THAT'S RIGHT, LADS! DIDN'T I ALWAYS SAY US BRITISH INFANTRY IS THE FINEST IN THE WORLD? BETTER THAN ALL THAT FOREIGN RUBBISH!
AT THAT MOMENT, A STRAY SHELL TORE OVERHEAD.
WHIZZ-BANG! GET DOWN... OR YOU'LL BE DECORATING TEN YARDS OF TRENCH!
THE CRUEL SHRAPNEL EXPLODED DOWNWARDS.
AAAGGGGGHH!
CHARLEY'S HURT! HE'S HURT BAD, SARGE!
STRETCHER BEARER! STRETCHER BEARER!
OF ALL THE LOUSY LUCK! JUST WHEN IT WAS ALL OVER! I RECKON IT'S ALL OVER FOR CHARLEY NOW, ANYWAY, BY THE LOOK OF THOSE WOUNDS!
AYE, BOURNE WAS A PLUCKY LITTLE DEVIL!
I HOPE HE MAKES IT!

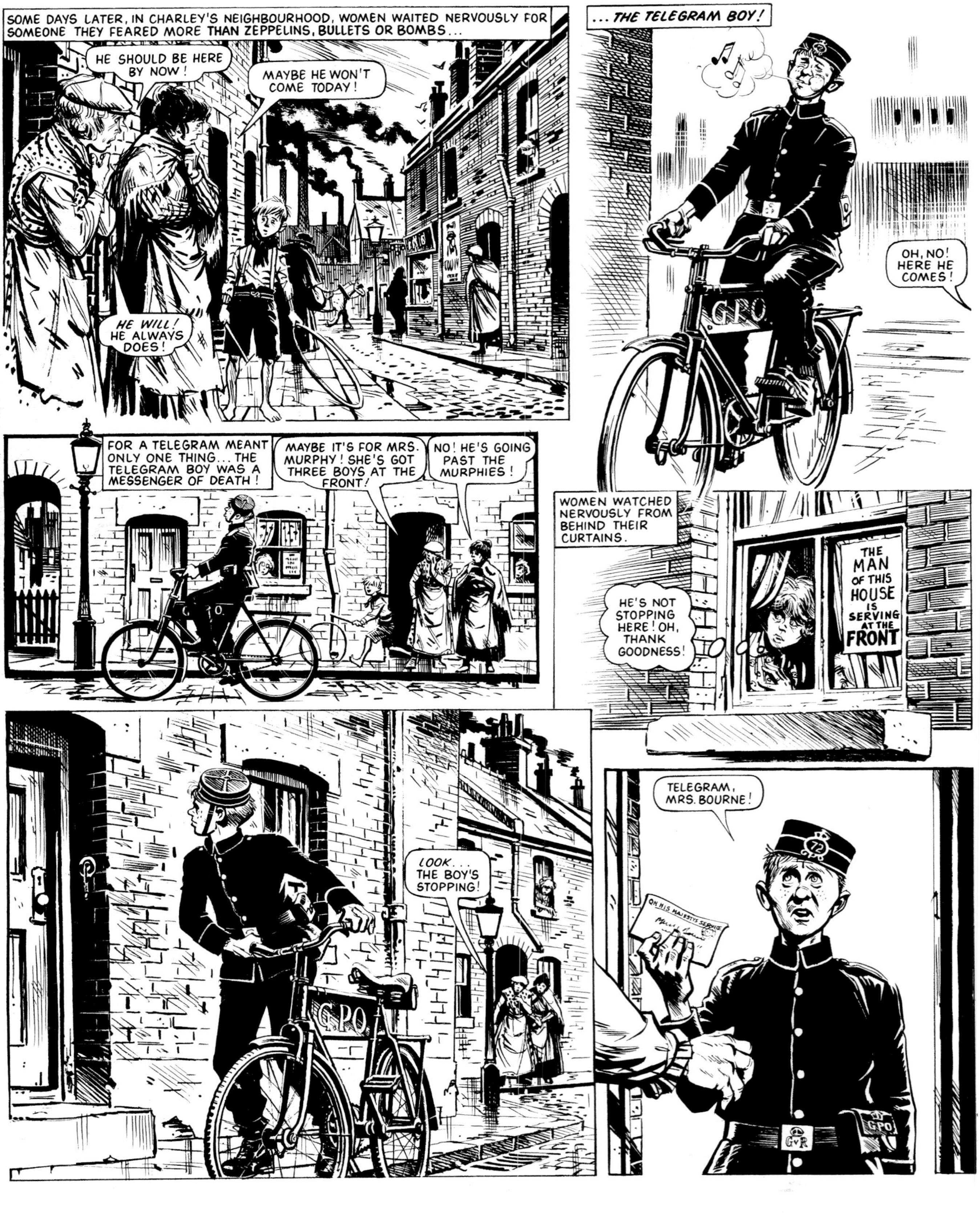
SOME DAYS LATER, IN CHARLEY'S NEIGHBOURHOOD, WOMEN WAITED NERVOUSLY FOR SOMEONE THEY FEARED MORE THAN ZEPPELINS, BULLETS OR BOMBS...
HE SHOULD BE HERE BY NOW!
MAYBE HE WON'T COME TODAY!
HE WILL! HE ALWAYS DOES!
...THE TELEGRAM BOY!
OH, NO! HERE HE COMES!
FOR A TELEGRAM MEANT ONLY ONE THING... THE TELEGRAM BOY WAS A MESSENGER OF DEATH!
MAYBE IT'S FOR MRS. MURPHY! SHE'S GOT THREE BOYS AT THE FRONT!
NO! HE'S GOING PAST THE MURPHIES!
WOMEN WATCHED NERVOUSLY FROM BEHIND THEIR CURTAINS.
THE MAN OF THIS HOUSE IS SERVING AT THE FRONT
HE'S NOT STOPPING HERE! OH, THANK GOODNESS!
LOOK... THE BOY'S STOPPING!
TELEGRAM, MRS. BOURNE!
ON HIS MAJESTY'S SERVICE

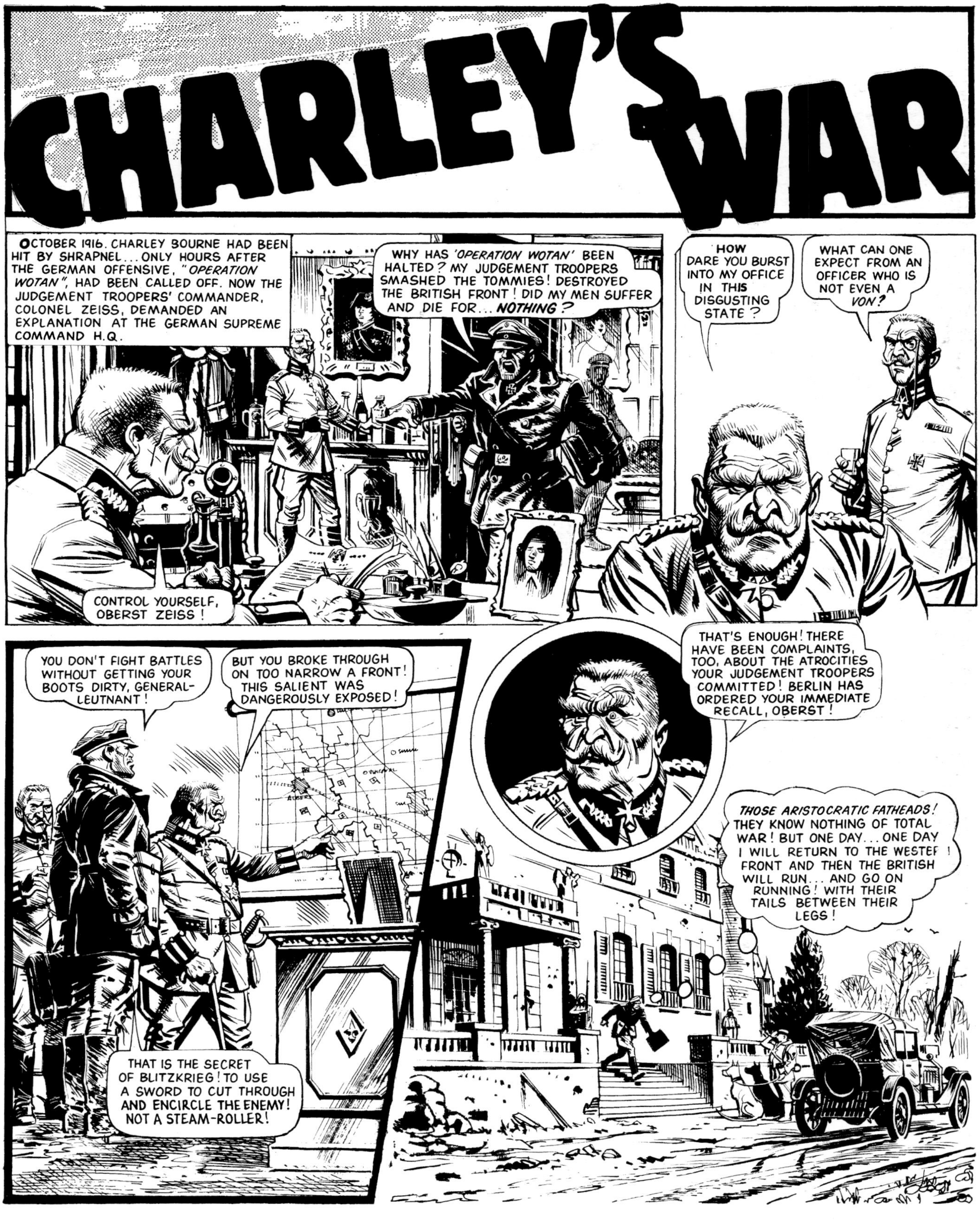
CHARLEY'S WAR
OCTOBER 1916. CHARLEY BOURNE HAD BEEN HIT BY SHRAPNEL... ONLY HOURS AFTER THE GERMAN OFFENSIVE, "OPERATION WOTAN", HAD BEEN CALLED OFF. NOW THE JUDGEMENT TROOPERS' COMMANDER, COLONEL ZEISS, DEMANDED AN EXPLANATION AT THE GERMAN SUPREME COMMAND H.Q.
WHY HAS 'OPERATION WOTAN' BEEN HALTED? MY JUDGEMENT TROOPERS SMASHED THE TOMMIES! DESTROYED THE BRITISH FRONT! DID MY MEN SUFFER AND DIE FOR... NOTHING?
CONTROL YOURSELF, OBERST ZEISS!
HOW DARE YOU BURST INTO MY OFFICE IN THIS DISGUSTING STATE?
WHAT CAN ONE EXPECT FROM AN OFFICER WHO IS NOT EVEN A VON?
YOU DON'T FIGHT BATTLES WITHOUT GETTING YOUR BOOTS DIRTY, GENERAL-LEUTNANT!
BUT YOU BROKE THROUGH ON TOO NARROW A FRONT! THIS SALIENT WAS DANGEROUSLY EXPOSED!
THAT IS THE SECRET OF BLITZKRIEG! TO USE A SWORD TO CUT THROUGH AND ENCIRCLE THE ENEMY! NOT A STEAM-ROLLER!
THAT'S ENOUGH! THERE HAVE BEEN COMPLAINTS, TOO, ABOUT THE ATROCITIES YOUR JUDGEMENT TROOPERS COMMITTED! BERLIN HAS ORDERED YOUR IMMEDIATE RECALL, OBERST!
THOSE ARISTOCRATIC FATHEADS! THEY KNOW NOTHING OF TOTAL WAR! BUT ONE DAY... ONE DAY I WILL RETURN TO THE WESTER FRONT AND THEN THE BRITISH WILL RUN... AND GO ON RUNNING! WITH THEIR TAILS BETWEEN THEIR LEGS!

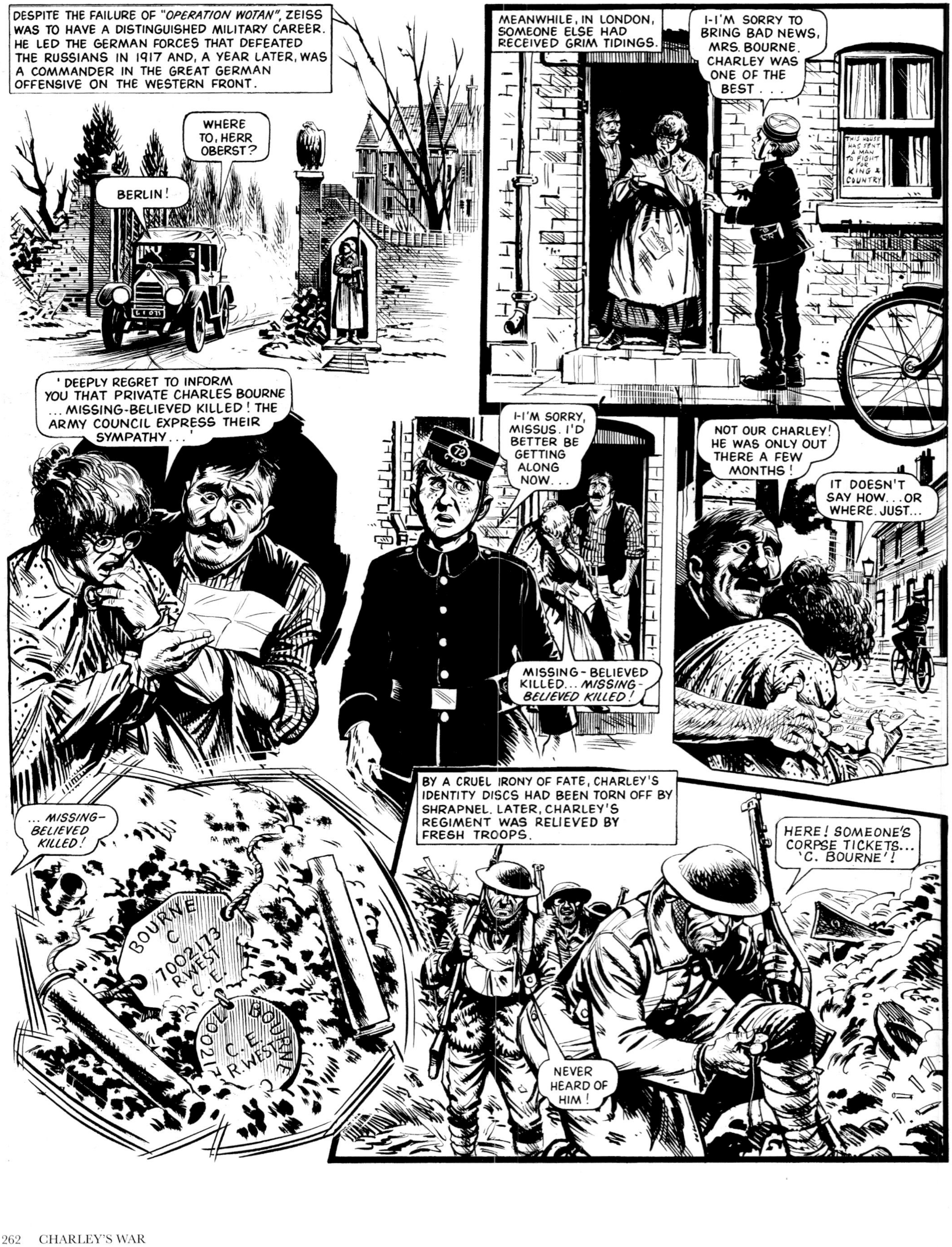

DESPITE THE FAILURE OF "OPERATION WOTAN", ZEISS WAS TO HAVE A DISTINGUISHED MILITARY CAREER. HE LED THE GERMAN FORCES THAT DEFEATED THE RUSSIANS IN 1917 AND, A YEAR LATER, WAS A COMMANDER IN THE GREAT GERMAN OFFENSIVE ON THE WESTERN FRONT.
WHERE TO, HERR OBERST?
BERLIN!
MEANWHILE, IN LONDON, SOMEONE ELSE HAD RECEIVED GRIM TIDINGS.
I-I'M SORRY TO BRING BAD NEWS, MRS. BOURNE. CHARLEY WAS ONE OF THE BEST . . .
THIS HOUSE HAS SENT A MAN TO FIGHT FOR KING & COUNTRY
'DEEPLY REGRET TO INFORM YOU THAT PRIVATE CHARLES BOURNE ... MISSING-BELIEVED KILLED! THE ARMY COUNCIL EXPRESS THEIR SYMPATHY...'
I-I'M SORRY, MISSUS. I'D BETTER BE GETTING ALONG NOW...
MISSING-BELIEVED KILLED... MISSING-BELIEVED KILLED!
NOT OUR CHARLEY! HE WAS ONLY OUT THERE A FEW MONTHS!
IT DOESN'T SAY HOW...OR WHERE. JUST...
... MISSING-BELIEVED KILLED!
BOURNE C 7002173 R.WEST C.E.
BOURNE C.E. 7002173 R.WEST
BY A CRUEL IRONY OF FATE, CHARLEY'S IDENTITY DISCS HAD BEEN TORN OFF BY SHRAPNEL. LATER, CHARLEY'S REGIMENT WAS RELIEVED BY FRESH TROOPS.
HERE! SOMEONE'S CORPSE TICKETS... 'C. BOURNE'!
NEVER HEARD OF HIM!

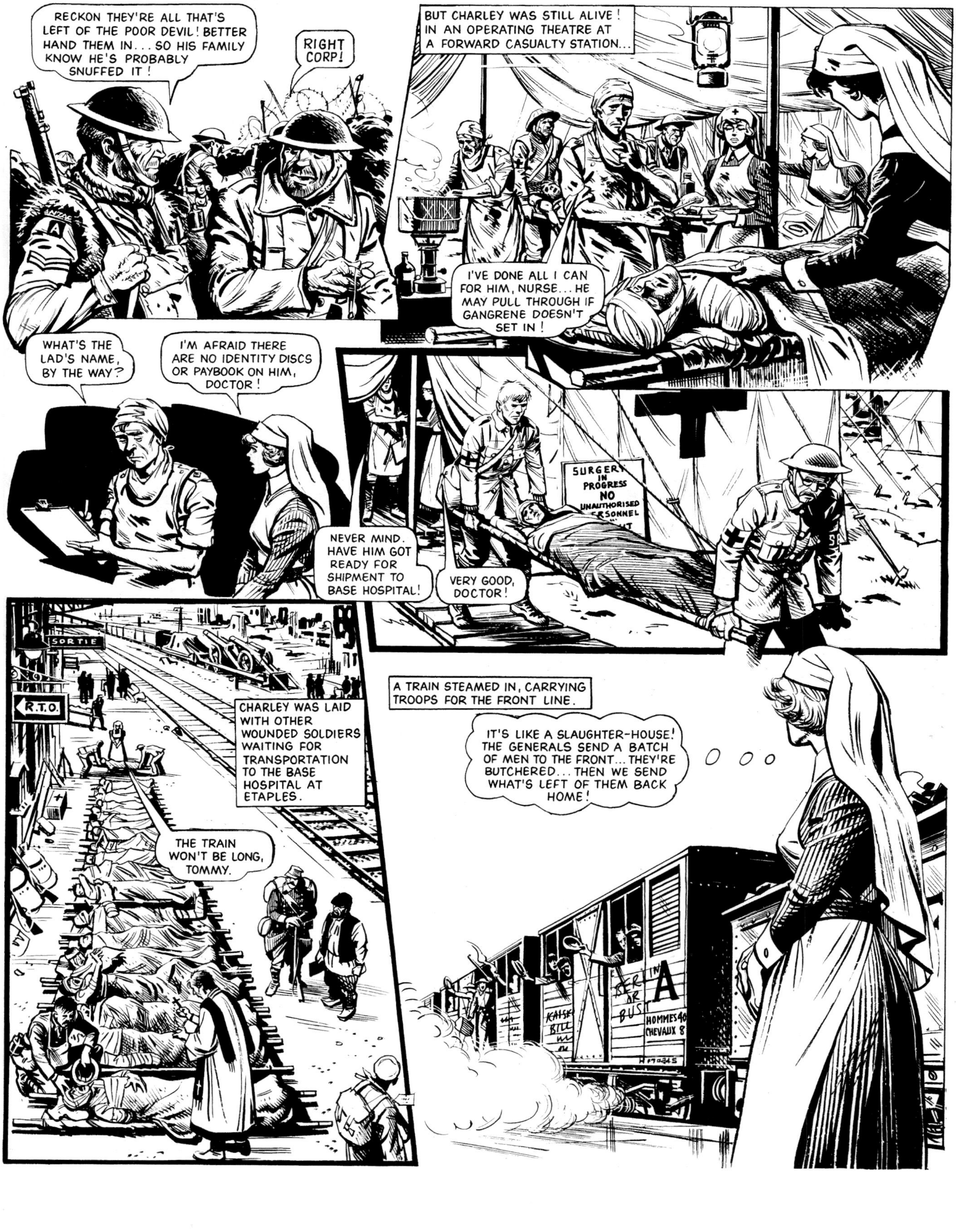

RECKON THEY'RE ALL THAT'S LEFT OF THE POOR DEVIL! BETTER HAND THEM IN... SO HIS FAMILY KNOW HE'S PROBABLY SNUFFED IT!
RIGHT CORP!
BUT CHARLEY WAS STILL ALIVE! IN AN OPERATING THEATRE AT A FORWARD CASUALTY STATION...
I'VE DONE ALL I CAN FOR HIM, NURSE... HE MAY PULL THROUGH IF GANGRENE DOESN'T SET IN!
WHAT'S THE LAD'S NAME, BY THE WAY?
I'M AFRAID THERE ARE NO IDENTITY DISCS OR PAYBOOK ON HIM, DOCTOR!
NEVER MIND. HAVE HIM GOT READY FOR SHIPMENT TO BASE HOSPITAL!
VERY GOOD, DOCTOR!
IN PROGRESS
NO
UNAUTHORISED
SORTIE
R.T.O.
CHARLEY WAS LAID WITH OTHER WOUNDED SOLDIERS WAITING FOR TRANSPORTATION TO THE BASE HOSPITAL AT ETAPLES.
THE TRAIN WON'T BE LONG, TOMMY.
A TRAIN STEAMED IN, CARRYING TROOPS FOR THE FRONT LINE.
IT'S LIKE A SLAUGHTER-HOUSE! THE GENERALS SEND A BATCH OF MEN TO THE FRONT... THEY'RE BUTCHERED... THEN WE SEND WHAT'S LEFT OF THEM BACK HOME!
HOMMES 40
CHEVAUX 8

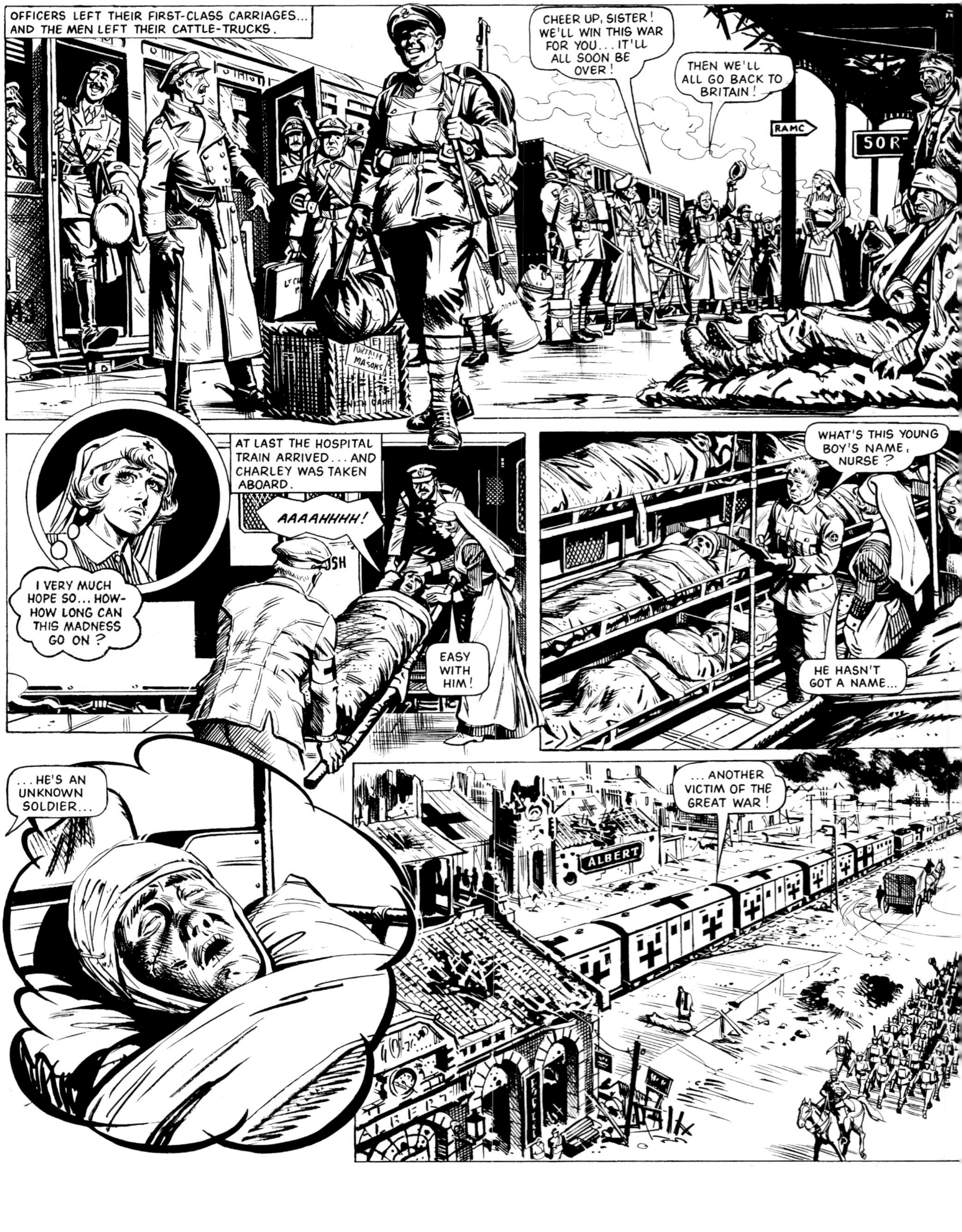

OFFICERS LEFT THEIR FIRST-CLASS CARRIAGES... AND THE MEN LEFT THEIR CATTLE-TRUCKS.
CHEER UP, SISTER! WE'LL WIN THIS WAR FOR YOU... IT'LL ALL SOON BE OVER!
THEN WE'LL ALL GO BACK TO BRITAIN!
RAMC
I VERY MUCH HOPE SO... HOW-HOW LONG CAN THIS MADNESS GO ON?
AT LAST THE HOSPITAL TRAIN ARRIVED... AND CHARLEY WAS TAKEN ABOARD.
AAAAHHHH!
EASY WITH HIM!
WHAT'S THIS YOUNG BOY'S NAME, NURSE?
HE HASN'T GOT A NAME...
...HE'S AN UNKNOWN SOLDIER...
...ANOTHER VICTIM OF THE GREAT WAR!
ALBERT

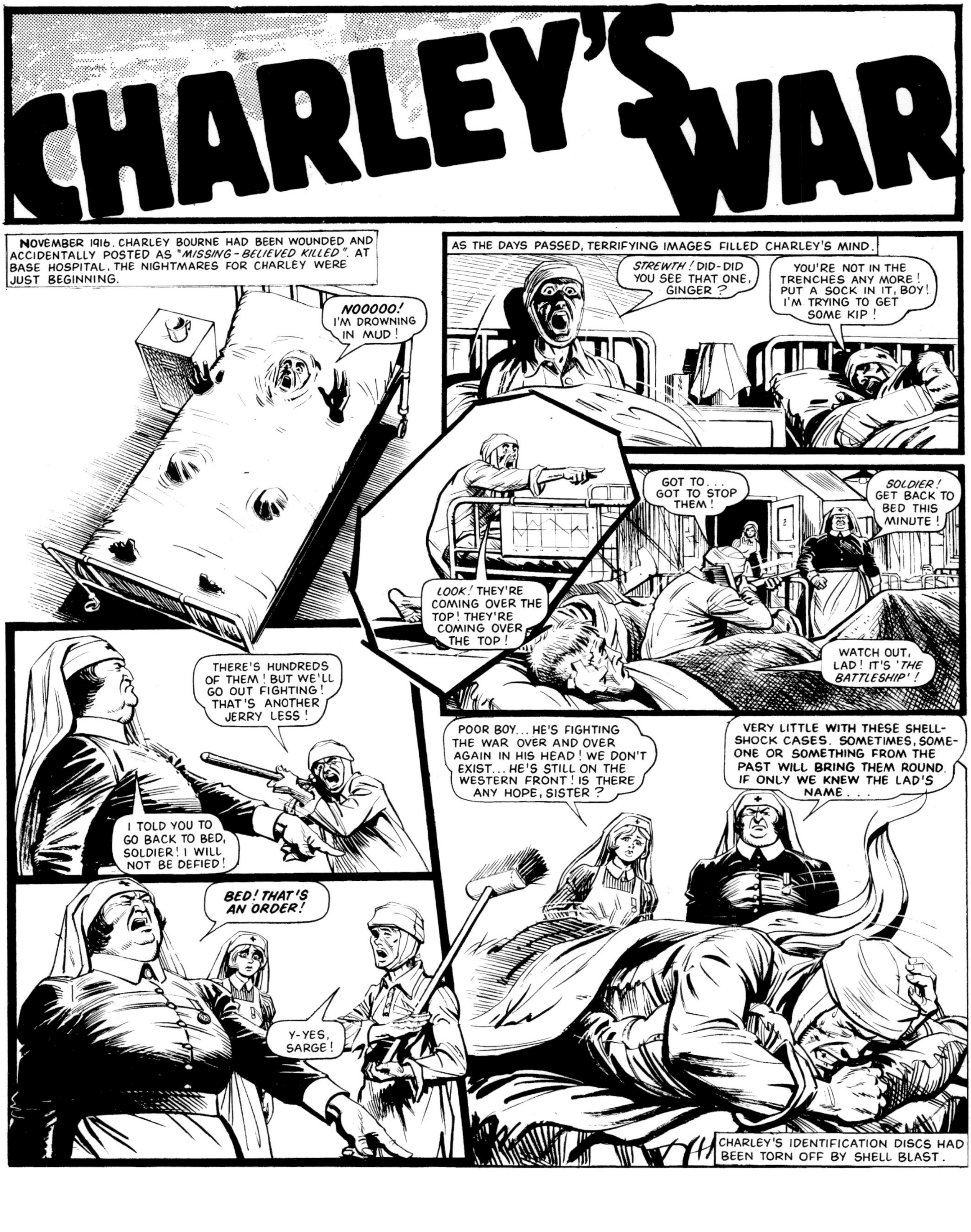
CHARLEY'S WAR
NOVEMBER 1916. CHARLEY BOURNE HAD BEEN WOUNDED AND ACCIDENTALLY POSTED AS "MISSING-BELIEVED KILLED". AT BASE HOSPITAL, THE NIGHTMARES FOR CHARLEY WERE JUST BEGINNING.
NOOOOO! I'M DROWNING IN MUD!
AS THE DAYS PASSED, TERRIFYING IMAGES FILLED CHARLEY'S MIND.
STREWTH! DID-DID YOU SEE THAT ONE, GINGER?
YOU'RE NOT IN THE TRENCHES ANY MORE! PUT A SOCK IN IT, BOY! I'M TRYING TO GET SOME KIP!
LOOK! THEY'RE COMING OVER THE TOP! THEY'RE COMING OVER THE TOP!
GOT TO... GOT TO STOP THEM!
SOLDIER! GET BACK TO BED THIS MINUTE!
WATCH OUT, LAD! IT'S 'THE BATTLESHIP'!
THERE'S HUNDREDS OF THEM! BUT WE'LL GO OUT FIGHTING! THAT'S ANOTHER JERRY LESS!
I TOLD YOU TO GO BACK TO BED, SOLDIER! I WILL NOT BE DEFIED!
BED! THAT'S AN ORDER!
Y-YES, SARGE!
POOR BOY... HE'S FIGHTING THE WAR OVER AND OVER AGAIN IN HIS HEAD! WE DON'T EXIST... HE'S STILL ON THE WESTERN FRONT! IS THERE ANY HOPE, SISTER?
VERY LITTLE WITH THESE SHELL-SHOCK CASES. SOMETIMES, SOME-ONE OR SOMETHING FROM THE PAST WILL BRING THEM ROUND. IF ONLY WE KNEW THE LAD'S NAME...
CHARLEY'S IDENTIFICATION DISCS HAD BEEN TORN OFF BY SHELL BLAST.

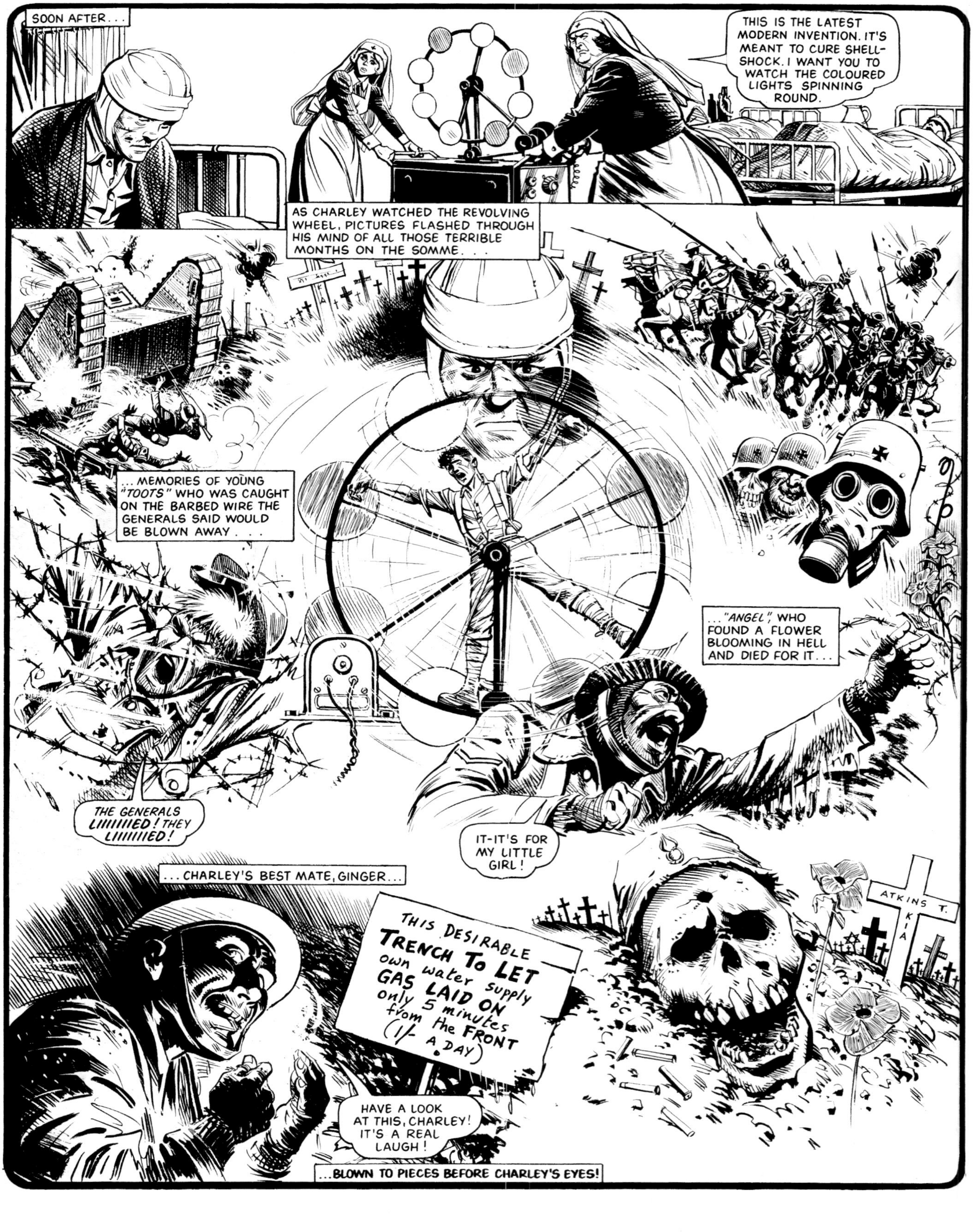

SOON AFTER...
THIS IS THE LATEST MODERN INVENTION. IT'S MEANT TO CURE SHELL-SHOCK. I WANT YOU TO WATCH THE COLOURED LIGHTS SPINNING ROUND.
AS CHARLEY WATCHED THE REVOLVING WHEEL, PICTURES FLASHED THROUGH HIS MIND OF ALL THOSE TERRIBLE MONTHS ON THE SOMME...
...MEMORIES OF YOUNG "TOOTS" WHO WAS CAUGHT ON THE BARBED WIRE THE GENERALS SAID WOULD BE BLOWN AWAY...
THE GENERALS LIIIIIIED! THEY LIIIIIIED!
..."ANGEL", WHO FOUND A FLOWER BLOOMING IN HELL AND DIED FOR IT...
IT-IT'S FOR MY LITTLE GIRL!
...CHARLEY'S BEST MATE, GINGER...
THIS DESIRABLE TRENCH TO LET own water supply GAS LAID ON only 5 minutes from the FRONT (1/- A DAY)
HAVE A LOOK AT THIS, CHARLEY! IT'S A REAL LAUGH!
ATKINS T. KIA
...BLOWN TO PIECES BEFORE CHARLEY'S EYES!

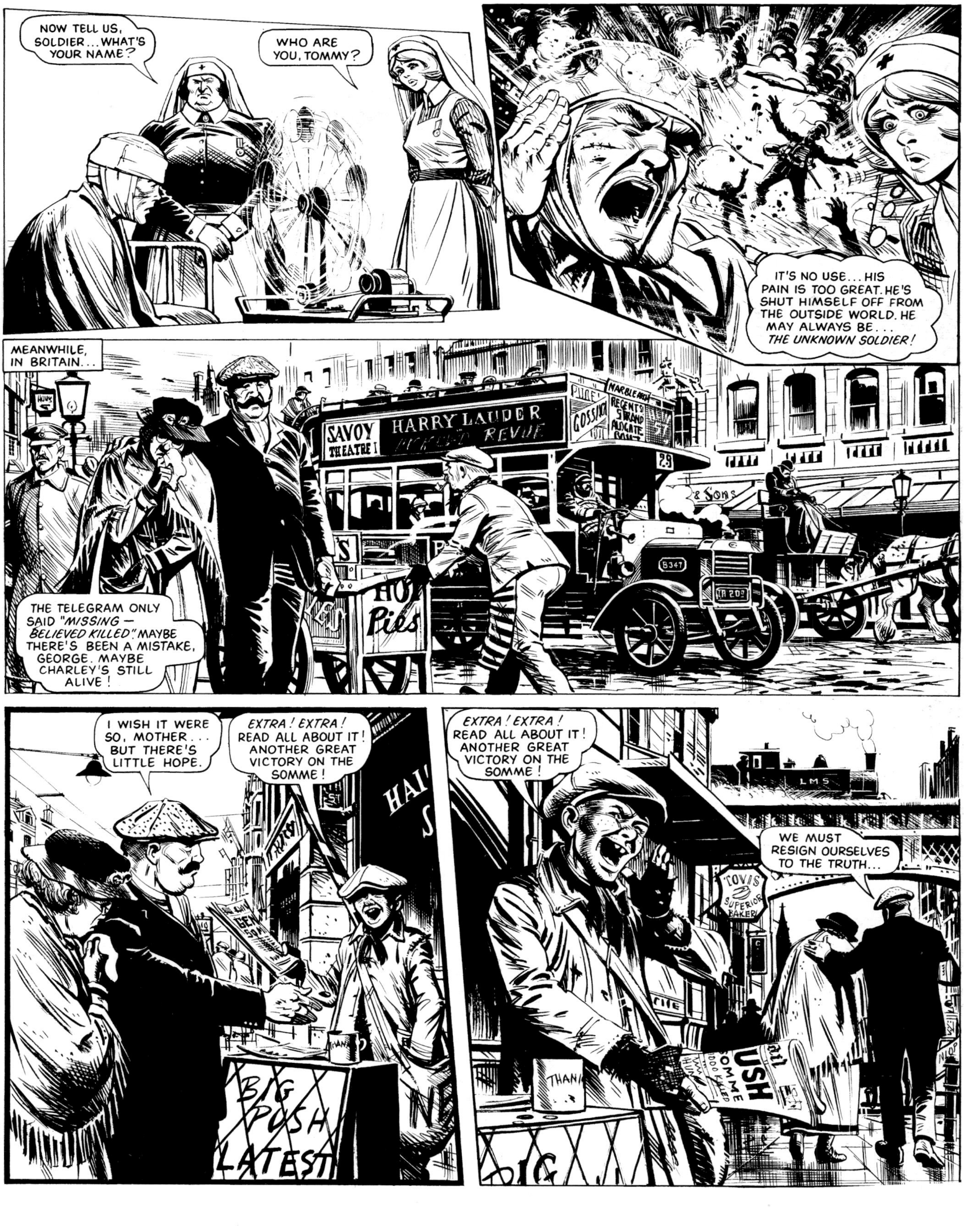
NOW TELL US, SOLDIER... WHAT'S YOUR NAME?
WHO ARE YOU, TOMMY?
IT'S NO USE... HIS PAIN IS TOO GREAT. HE'S SHUT HIMSELF OFF FROM THE OUTSIDE WORLD. HE MAY ALWAYS BE... *THE UNKNOWN SOLDIER!*
MEANWHILE, IN BRITAIN...
SAVOY THEATRE
HARRY LAUDER
REVUE
THE TELEGRAM ONLY SAID *"MISSING — BELIEVED KILLED"*. MAYBE THERE'S BEEN A MISTAKE, GEORGE. MAYBE CHARLEY'S STILL ALIVE!
I WISH IT WERE SO, MOTHER... BUT THERE'S LITTLE HOPE.
EXTRA! EXTRA! READ ALL ABOUT IT! ANOTHER GREAT VICTORY ON THE SOMME!
BIG PUSH LATEST
EXTRA! EXTRA! READ ALL ABOUT IT! ANOTHER GREAT VICTORY ON THE SOMME!
LMS
WE MUST RESIGN OURSELVES TO THE TRUTH...
TOVIS SUPERIOR BAKERY

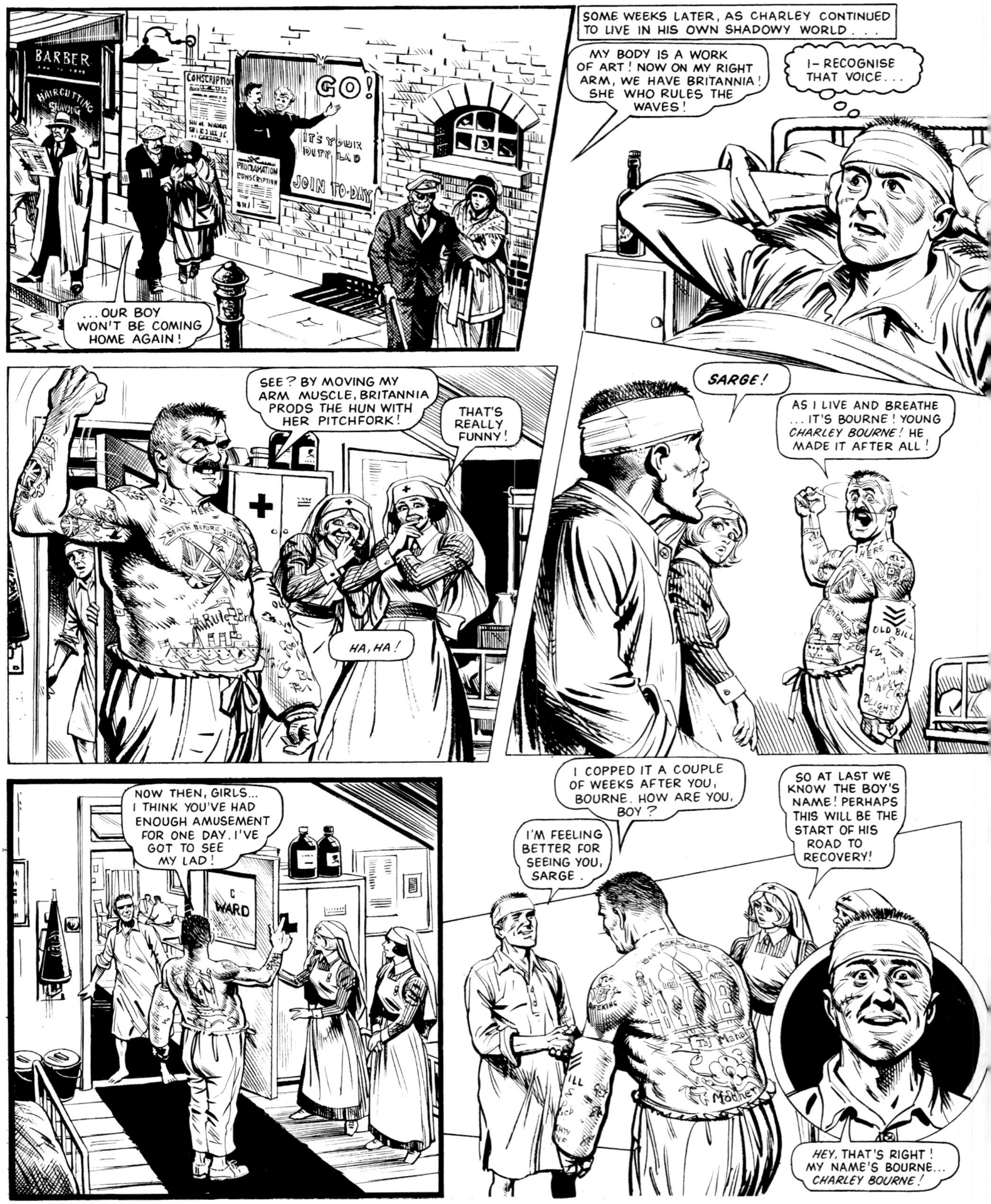
BARBER
HAIRCUTTING SHAVING
CONSCRIPTION
PROCLAMATION CONSCRIPTION
GO!
IT'S YOUR DUTY LAD
JOIN TO-DAY
... OUR BOY WON'T BE COMING HOME AGAIN!
SOME WEEKS LATER, AS CHARLEY CONTINUED TO LIVE IN HIS OWN SHADOWY WORLD . . .
MY BODY IS A WORK OF ART! NOW ON MY RIGHT ARM, WE HAVE BRITANNIA! SHE WHO RULES THE WAVES!
I- RECOGNISE THAT VOICE . . .
SEE? BY MOVING MY ARM MUSCLE, BRITANNIA PRODS THE HUN WITH HER PITCHFORK!
THAT'S REALLY FUNNY!
HA, HA!
SARGE!
AS I LIVE AND BREATHE ... IT'S BOURNE! YOUNG CHARLEY BOURNE! HE MADE IT AFTER ALL!
NOW THEN, GIRLS... I THINK YOU'VE HAD ENOUGH AMUSEMENT FOR ONE DAY. I'VE GOT TO SEE MY LAD!
C WARD
I COPPED IT A COUPLE OF WEEKS AFTER YOU, BOURNE. HOW ARE YOU, BOY?
I'M FEELING BETTER FOR SEEING YOU, SARGE.
SO AT LAST WE KNOW THE BOY'S NAME! PERHAPS THIS WILL BE THE START OF HIS ROAD TO RECOVERY!
HEY, THAT'S RIGHT! MY NAME'S BOURNE... CHARLEY BOURNE!

WINTER, 1916. IN THE EAST END OF LONDON, THE BOURNE FAMILY MOURNED THE LOSS OF THEIR SON... UNAWARE THAT CHARLEY WAS STILL ALIVE AND RECOVERING FROM HIS WOUNDS IN FRANCE.

I WONDER HOW CHARLEY DIED? HE... HE NEVER DID SAY WHAT IT WAS LIKE IN FRANCE.

COME AWAY, MOTHER. I'M SURE OUR SON DIED QUICKLY... WITH LITTLE PAIN.

CHARLEY'S WAR

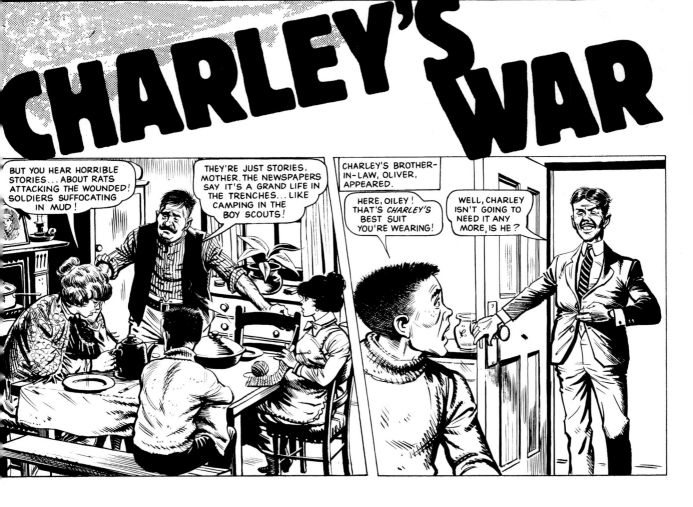

BUT YOU HEAR HORRIBLE STORIES... ABOUT RATS ATTACKING THE WOUNDED! SOLDIERS SUFFOCATING IN MUD!

THEY'RE JUST STORIES, MOTHER. THE NEWSPAPERS SAY IT'S A GRAND LIFE IN THE TRENCHES... LIKE CAMPING IN THE BOY SCOUTS!

CHARLEY'S BROTHER-IN-LAW, OLIVER, APPEARED.

HERE, OILEY! THAT'S *CHARLEY'S* BEST SUIT YOU'RE WEARING!

WELL, CHARLEY ISN'T GOING TO NEED IT ANY MORE, IS HE?

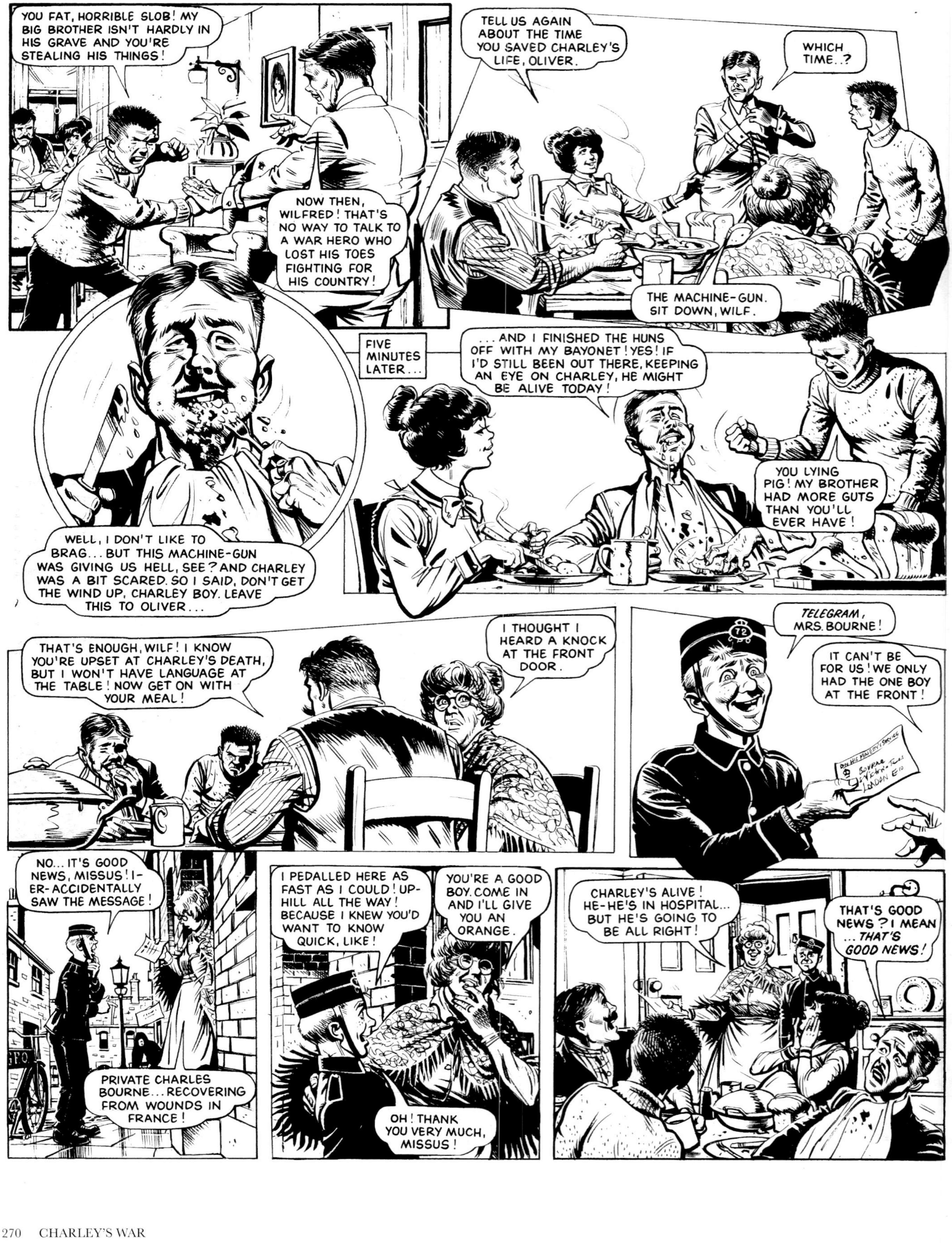

YOU FAT, HORRIBLE SLOB! MY BIG BROTHER ISN'T HARDLY IN HIS GRAVE AND YOU'RE STEALING HIS THINGS!
NOW THEN, WILFRED! THAT'S NO WAY TO TALK TO A WAR HERO WHO LOST HIS TOES FIGHTING FOR HIS COUNTRY!
TELL US AGAIN ABOUT THE TIME YOU SAVED CHARLEY'S LIFE, OLIVER.
WHICH TIME..?
THE MACHINE-GUN. SIT DOWN, WILF.
WELL, I DON'T LIKE TO BRAG... BUT THIS MACHINE-GUN WAS GIVING US HELL, SEE? AND CHARLEY WAS A BIT SCARED. SO I SAID, DON'T GET THE WIND UP, CHARLEY BOY. LEAVE THIS TO OLIVER...
FIVE MINUTES LATER...
...AND I FINISHED THE HUNS OFF WITH MY BAYONET! YES! IF I'D STILL BEEN OUT THERE, KEEPING AN EYE ON CHARLEY, HE MIGHT BE ALIVE TODAY!
YOU LYING PIG! MY BROTHER HAD MORE GUTS THAN YOU'LL EVER HAVE!
THAT'S ENOUGH, WILF! I KNOW YOU'RE UPSET AT CHARLEY'S DEATH, BUT I WON'T HAVE LANGUAGE AT THE TABLE! NOW GET ON WITH YOUR MEAL!
I THOUGHT I HEARD A KNOCK AT THE FRONT DOOR.
TELEGRAM, MRS. BOURNE!
IT CAN'T BE FOR US! WE ONLY HAD THE ONE BOY AT THE FRONT!
NO... IT'S GOOD NEWS, MISSUS! I-ER-ACCIDENTALLY SAW THE MESSAGE!
PRIVATE CHARLES BOURNE... RECOVERING FROM WOUNDS IN FRANCE!
I PEDALLED HERE AS FAST AS I COULD! UP-HILL ALL THE WAY! BECAUSE I KNEW YOU'D WANT TO KNOW QUICK, LIKE!
YOU'RE A GOOD BOY. COME IN AND I'LL GIVE YOU AN ORANGE.
OH! THANK YOU VERY MUCH, MISSUS!
CHARLEY'S ALIVE! HE-HE'S IN HOSPITAL... BUT HE'S GOING TO BE ALL RIGHT!
THAT'S GOOD NEWS? I MEAN ...THAT'S GOOD NEWS!

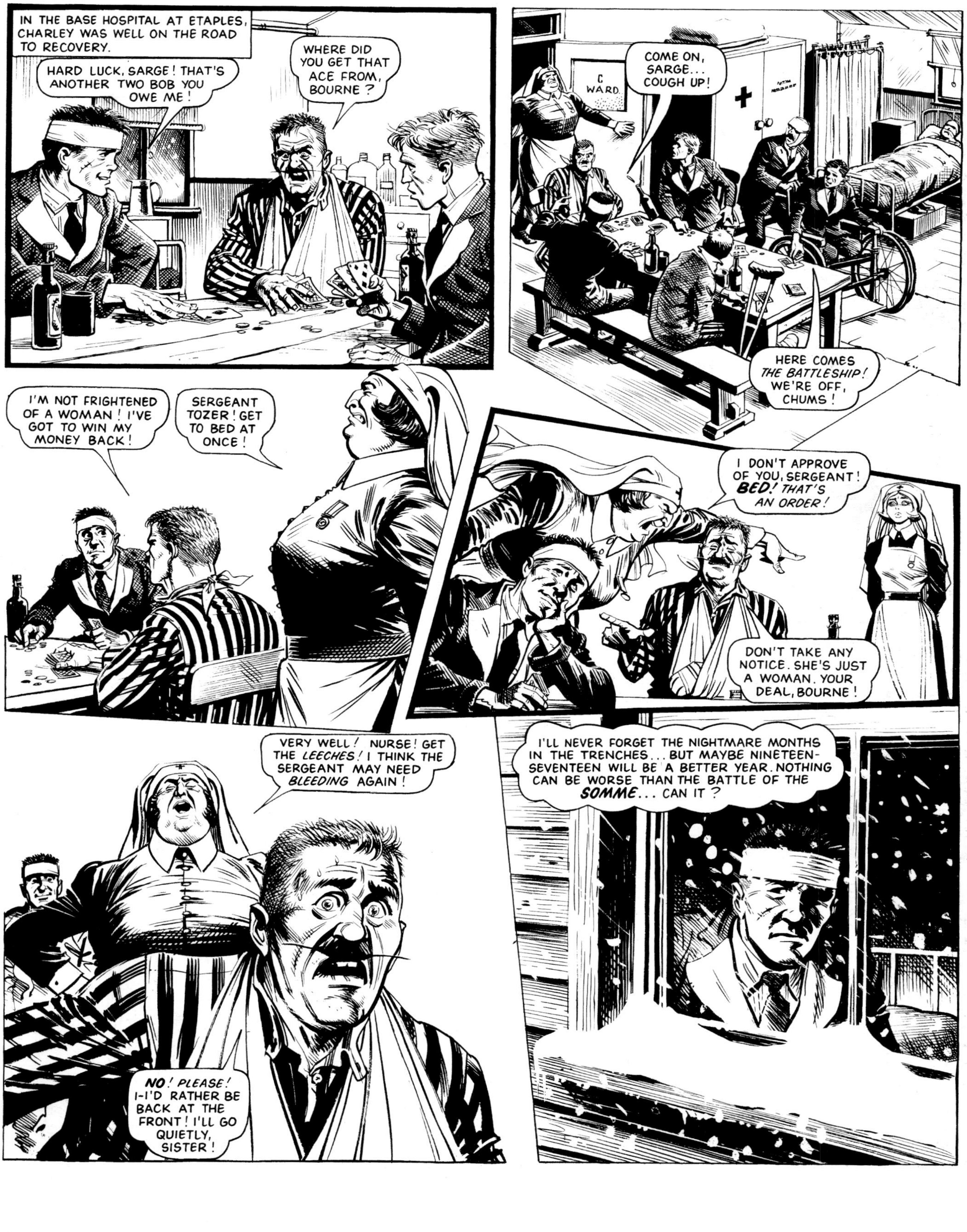

IN THE BASE HOSPITAL AT ETAPLES, CHARLEY WAS WELL ON THE ROAD TO RECOVERY.
HARD LUCK, SARGE! THAT'S ANOTHER TWO BOB YOU OWE ME!
WHERE DID YOU GET THAT ACE FROM, BOURNE?
C WARD
COME ON, SARGE... COUGH UP!
HERE COMES THE BATTLESHIP! WE'RE OFF, CHUMS!
I'M NOT FRIGHTENED OF A WOMAN! I'VE GOT TO WIN MY MONEY BACK!
SERGEANT TOZER! GET TO BED AT ONCE!
I DON'T APPROVE OF YOU, SERGEANT! BED! THAT'S AN ORDER!
DON'T TAKE ANY NOTICE. SHE'S JUST A WOMAN. YOUR DEAL, BOURNE!
VERY WELL! NURSE! GET THE LEECHES! I THINK THE SERGEANT MAY NEED BLEEDING AGAIN!
NO! PLEASE! I-I'D RATHER BE BACK AT THE FRONT! I'LL GO QUIETLY, SISTER!
I'LL NEVER FORGET THE NIGHTMARE MONTHS IN THE TRENCHES... BUT MAYBE NINETEEN-SEVENTEEN WILL BE A BETTER YEAR. NOTHING CAN BE WORSE THAN THE BATTLE OF THE SOMME... CAN IT?

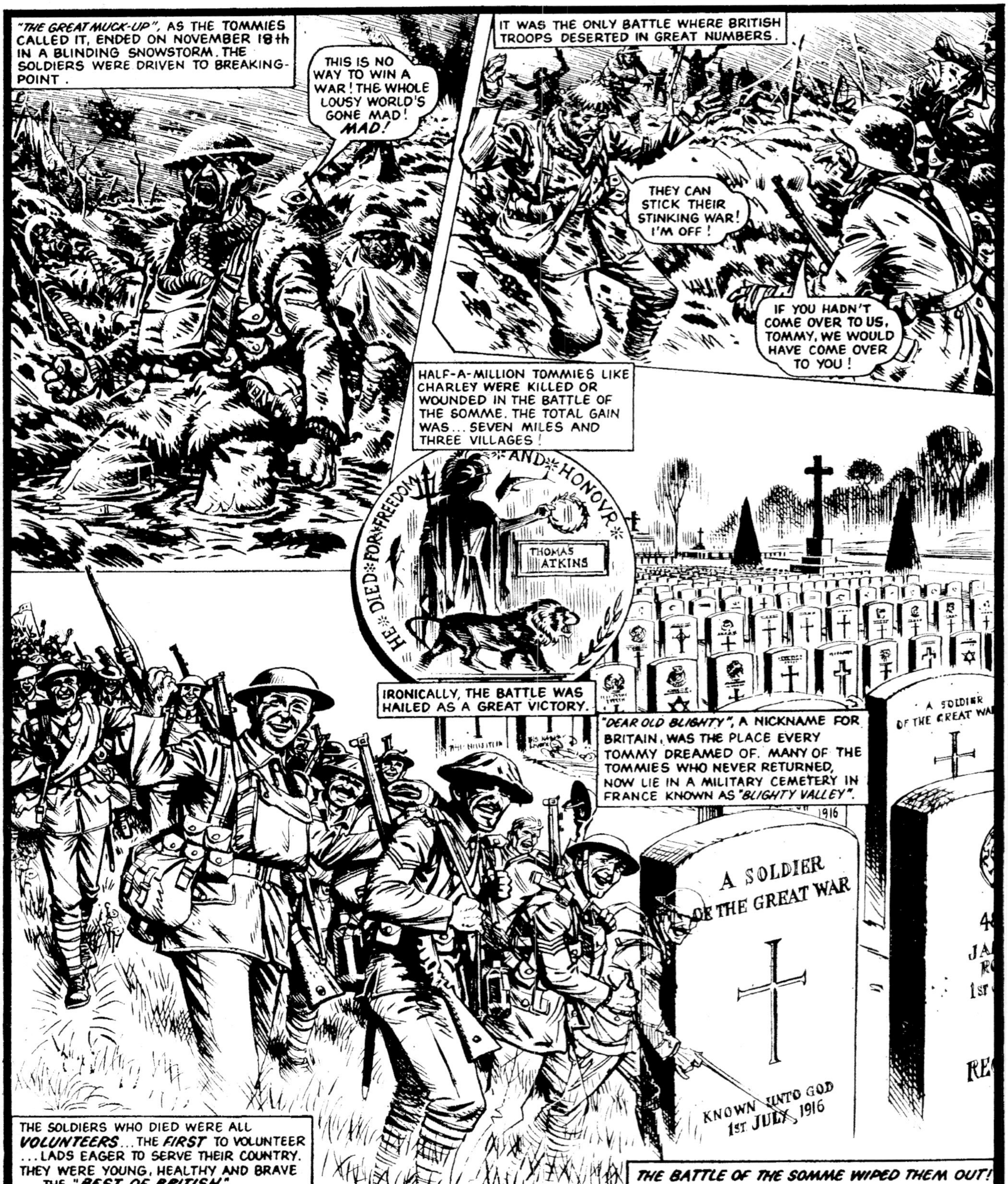
"THE GREAT MUCK-UP", AS THE TOMMIES CALLED IT, ENDED ON NOVEMBER 18th IN A BLINDING SNOWSTORM. THE SOLDIERS WERE DRIVEN TO BREAKING-POINT.
THIS IS NO WAY TO WIN A WAR! THE WHOLE LOUSY WORLD'S GONE MAD! MAD!
IT WAS THE ONLY BATTLE WHERE BRITISH TROOPS DESERTED IN GREAT NUMBERS.
THEY CAN STICK THEIR STINKING WAR! I'M OFF!
IF YOU HADN'T COME OVER TO US, TOMMY, WE WOULD HAVE COME OVER TO YOU!
HALF-A-MILLION TOMMIES LIKE CHARLEY WERE KILLED OR WOUNDED IN THE BATTLE OF THE SOMME. THE TOTAL GAIN WAS... SEVEN MILES AND THREE VILLAGES!
HE DIED FOR FREEDOM AND HONOVR
THOMAS ATKINS
IRONICALLY, THE BATTLE WAS HAILED AS A GREAT VICTORY.
"DEAR OLD BLIGHTY", A NICKNAME FOR BRITAIN, WAS THE PLACE EVERY TOMMY DREAMED OF. MANY OF THE TOMMIES WHO NEVER RETURNED, NOW LIE IN A MILITARY CEMETERY IN FRANCE KNOWN AS "BLIGHTY VALLEY".
A SOLDIER OF THE GREAT WAR
A SOLDIER OF THE GREAT WAR
KNOWN UNTO GOD
1ST JULY, 1916
THE SOLDIERS WHO DIED WERE ALL VOLUNTEERS... THE FIRST TO VOLUNTEER ...LADS EAGER TO SERVE THEIR COUNTRY. THEY WERE YOUNG, HEALTHY AND BRAVE ... THE "BEST OF BRITISH".
THE BATTLE OF THE SOMME WIPED THEM OUT!

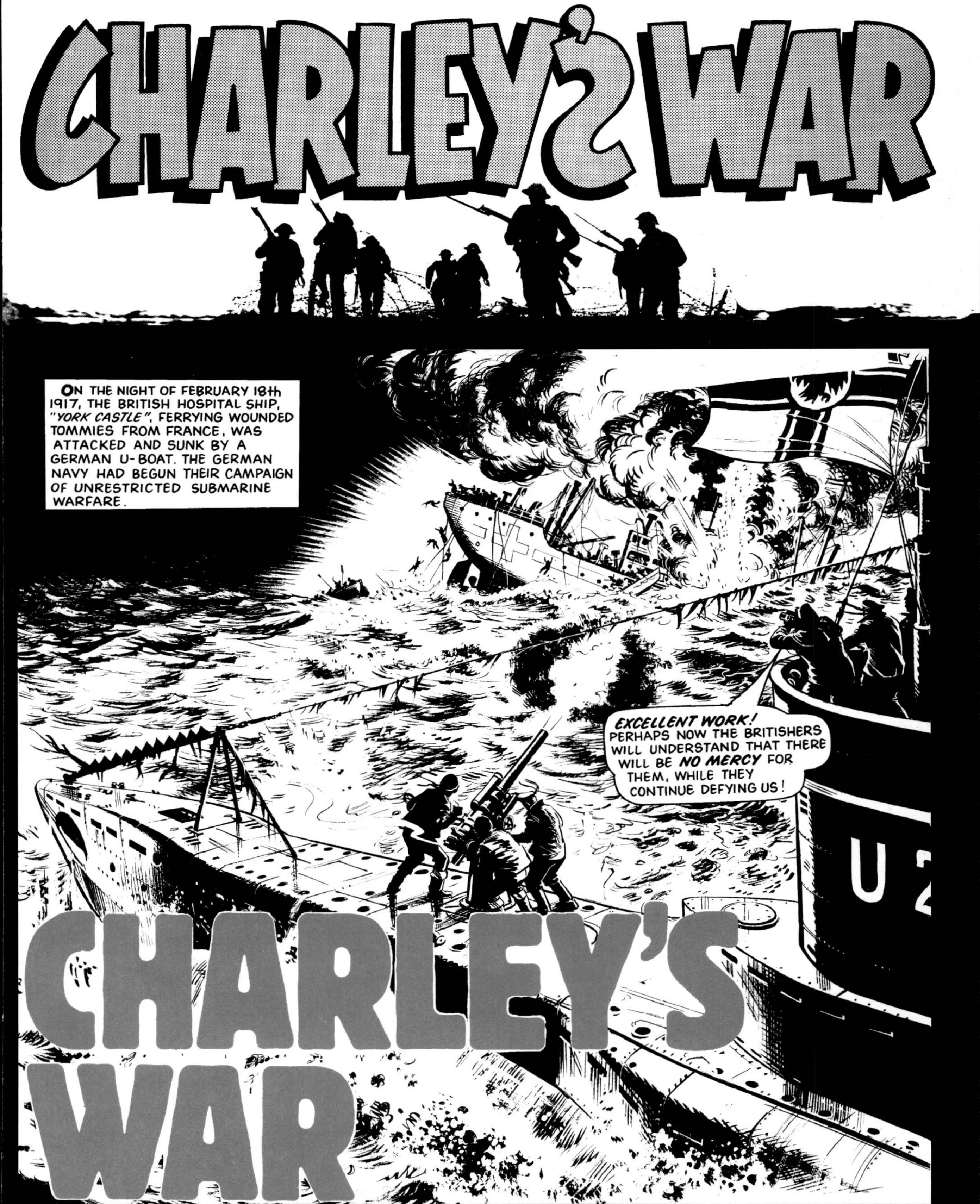
CHARLEY'S WAR
ON THE NIGHT OF FEBRUARY 18th 1917, THE BRITISH HOSPITAL SHIP, "YORK CASTLE", FERRYING WOUNDED TOMMIES FROM FRANCE, WAS ATTACKED AND SUNK BY A GERMAN U-BOAT. THE GERMAN NAVY HAD BEGUN THEIR CAMPAIGN OF UNRESTRICTED SUBMARINE WARFARE.
EXCELLENT WORK! PERHAPS NOW THE BRITISHERS WILL UNDERSTAND THAT THERE WILL BE NO MERCY FOR THEM, WHILE THEY CONTINUE DEFYING US!
U 2
CHARLEY'S WAR

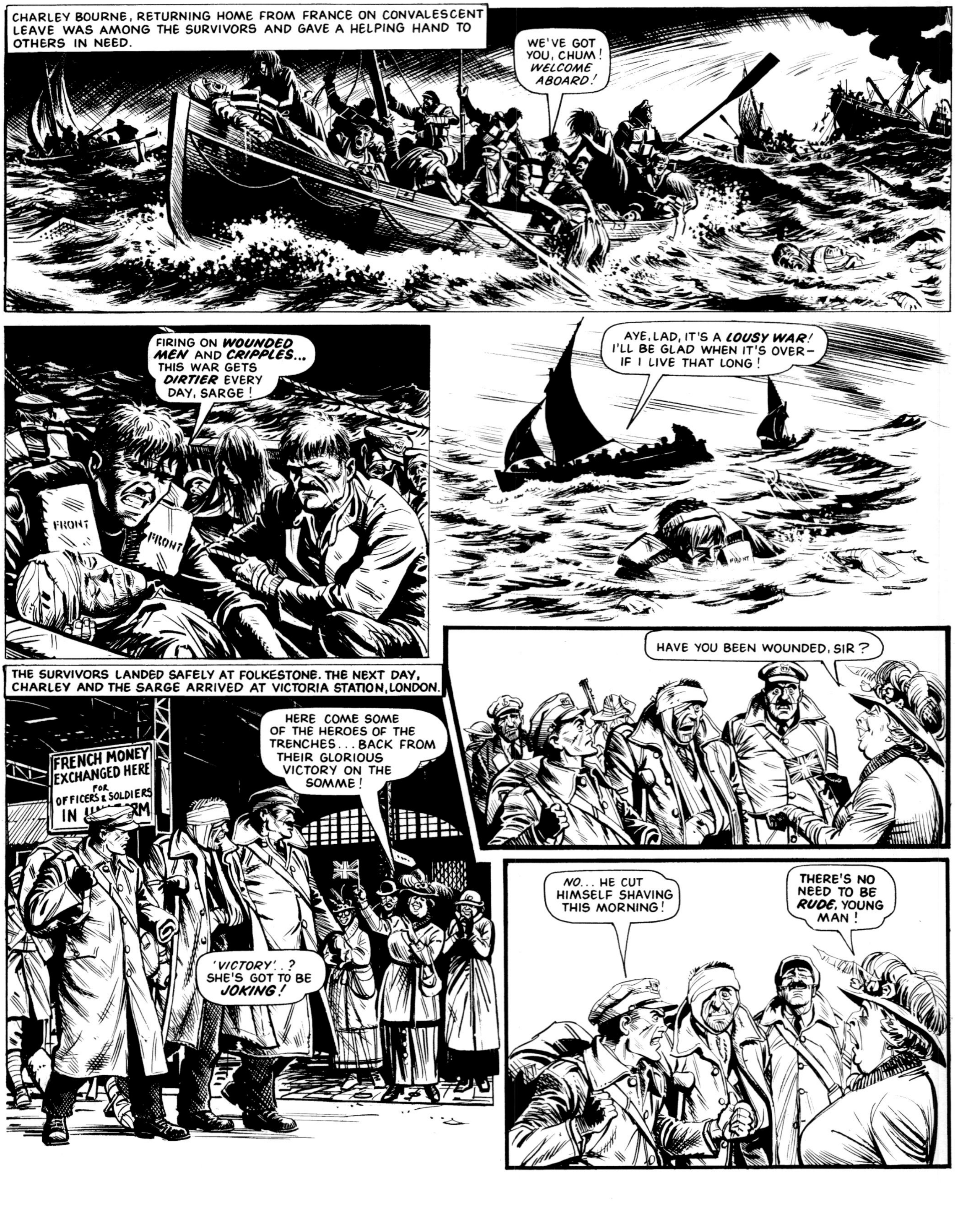
CHARLEY BOURNE, RETURNING HOME FROM FRANCE ON CONVALESCENT LEAVE WAS AMONG THE SURVIVORS AND GAVE A HELPING HAND TO OTHERS IN NEED.
WE'VE GOT YOU, CHUM! WELCOME ABOARD!
FIRING ON WOUNDED MEN AND CRIPPLES... THIS WAR GETS DIRTIER EVERY DAY, SARGE!
FRONT
FRONT
AYE, LAD, IT'S A LOUSY WAR! I'LL BE GLAD WHEN IT'S OVER– IF I LIVE THAT LONG!
THE SURVIVORS LANDED SAFELY AT FOLKESTONE. THE NEXT DAY, CHARLEY AND THE SARGE ARRIVED AT VICTORIA STATION, LONDON.
FRENCH MONEY EXCHANGED HERE FOR OFFICERS & SOLDIERS
HERE COME SOME OF THE HEROES OF THE TRENCHES... BACK FROM THEIR GLORIOUS VICTORY ON THE SOMME!
'VICTORY'..? SHE'S GOT TO BE JOKING!
HAVE YOU BEEN WOUNDED, SIR?
NO... HE CUT HIMSELF SHAVING THIS MORNING!
THERE'S NO NEED TO BE RUDE, YOUNG MAN!

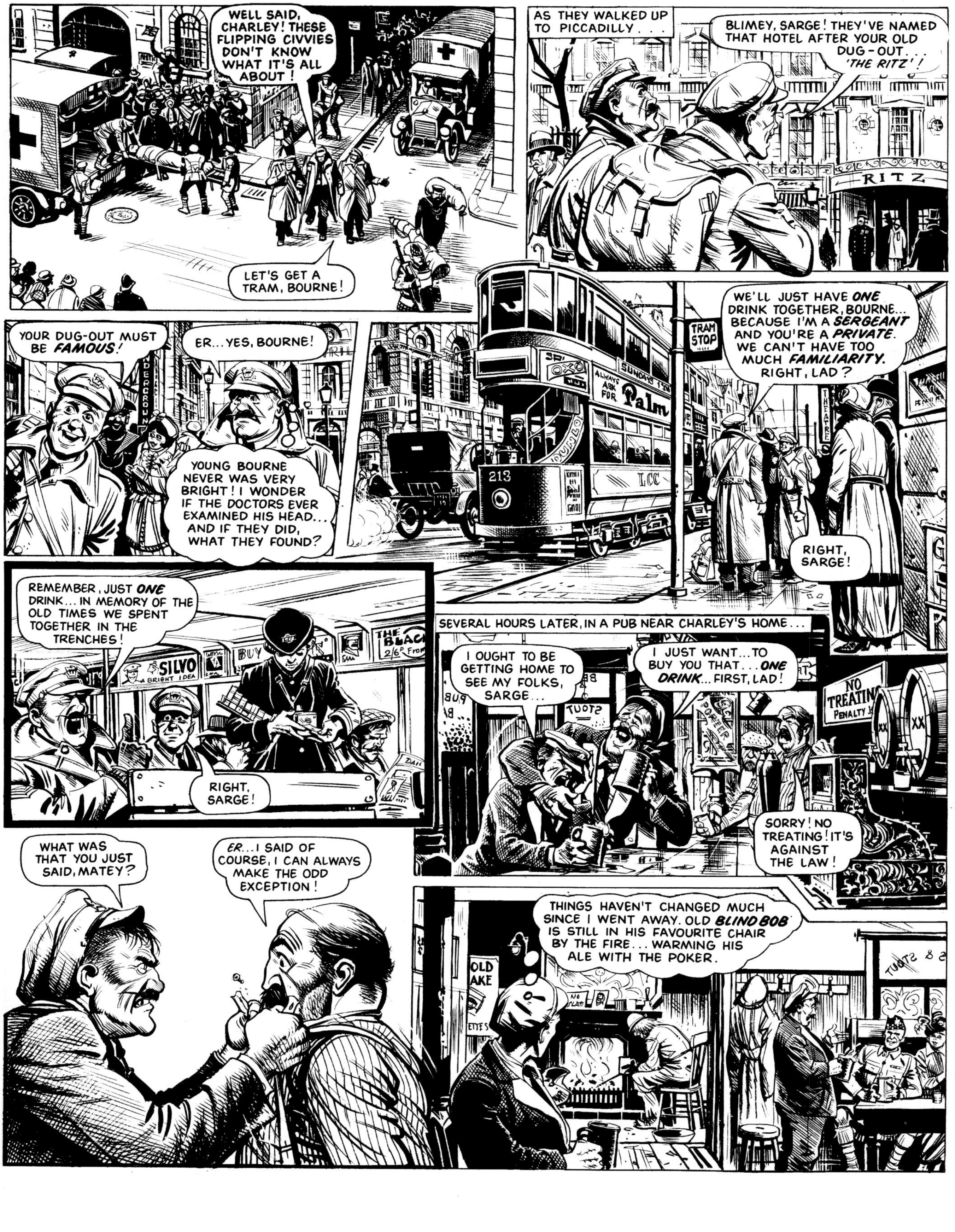
WELL SAID, CHARLEY! THESE FLIPPING CIVVIES DON'T KNOW WHAT IT'S ALL ABOUT!
LET'S GET A TRAM, BOURNE!
AS THEY WALKED UP TO PICCADILLY . . .
BLIMEY, SARGE! THEY'VE NAMED THAT HOTEL AFTER YOUR OLD DUG-OUT . . . 'THE RITZ'!
RITZ
YOUR DUG-OUT MUST BE FAMOUS!
ER... YES, BOURNE!
YOUNG BOURNE NEVER WAS VERY BRIGHT! I WONDER IF THE DOCTORS EVER EXAMINED HIS HEAD... AND IF THEY DID, WHAT THEY FOUND?
WE'LL JUST HAVE ONE DRINK TOGETHER, BOURNE... BECAUSE I'M A SERGEANT AND YOU'RE A PRIVATE. WE CAN'T HAVE TOO MUCH FAMILIARITY. RIGHT, LAD?
TRAM STOP
OXO
ALWAYS ASK FOR Palm
213
LCC
RIGHT, SARGE!
REMEMBER, JUST ONE DRINK... IN MEMORY OF THE OLD TIMES WE SPENT TOGETHER IN THE TRENCHES!
SILVO BRIGHT IDEA
RIGHT, SARGE!
SEVERAL HOURS LATER, IN A PUB NEAR CHARLEY'S HOME . . .
I OUGHT TO BE GETTING HOME TO SEE MY FOLKS, SARGE . . .
I JUST WANT... TO BUY YOU THAT... ONE DRINK... FIRST, LAD!
NO TREATING PENALTY
SORRY! NO TREATING! IT'S AGAINST THE LAW!
WHAT WAS THAT YOU JUST SAID, MATEY?
ER... I SAID OF COURSE, I CAN ALWAYS MAKE THE ODD EXCEPTION!
THINGS HAVEN'T CHANGED MUCH SINCE I WENT AWAY. OLD BLIND BOB IS STILL IN HIS FAVOURITE CHAIR BY THE FIRE... WARMING HIS ALE WITH THE POKER.

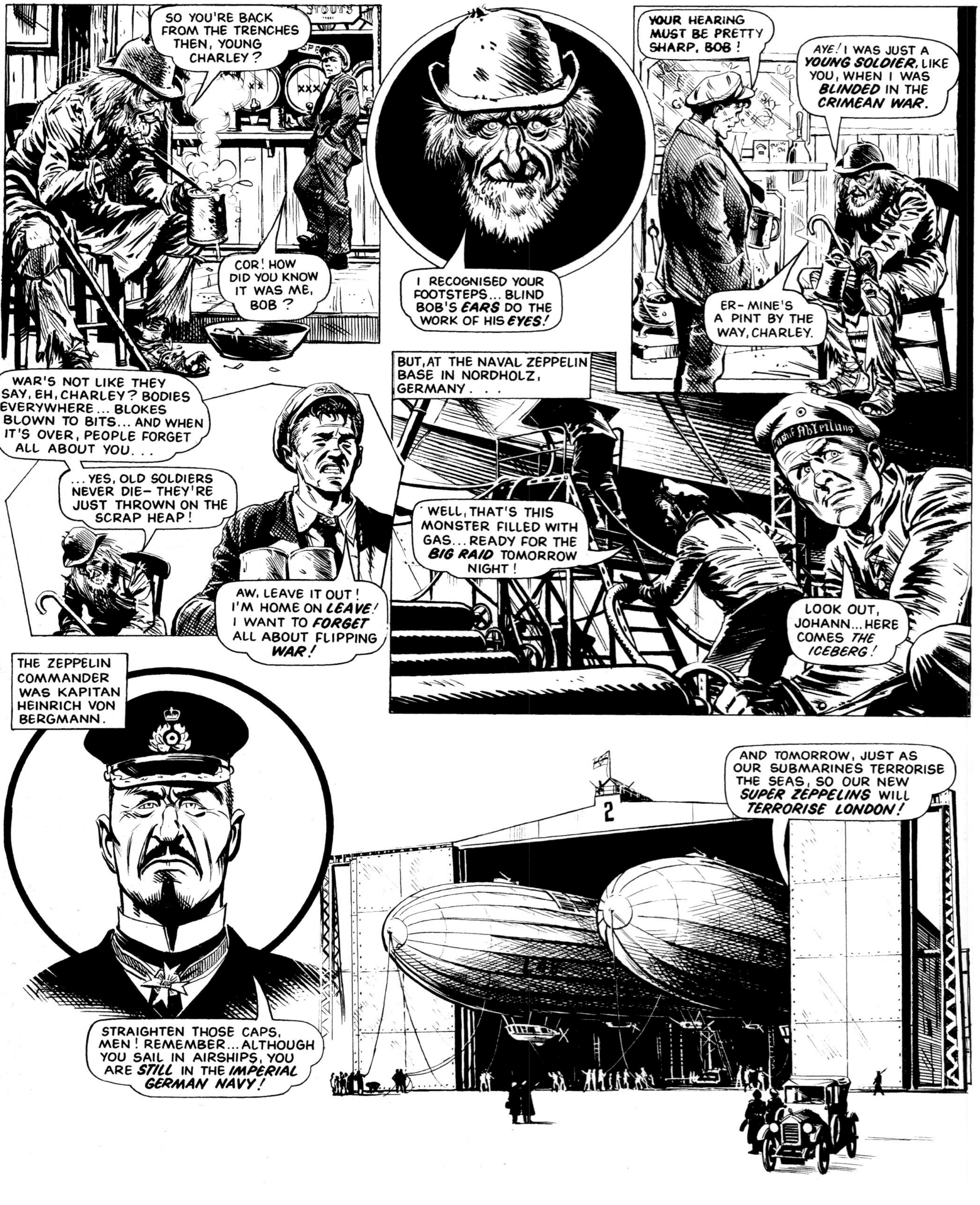
SO YOU'RE BACK FROM THE TRENCHES THEN, YOUNG CHARLEY?
COR! HOW DID YOU KNOW IT WAS ME, BOB?
I RECOGNISED YOUR FOOTSTEPS... BLIND BOB'S EARS DO THE WORK OF HIS EYES!
YOUR HEARING MUST BE PRETTY SHARP, BOB!
AYE! I WAS JUST A YOUNG SOLDIER, LIKE YOU, WHEN I WAS BLINDED IN THE CRIMEAN WAR.
ER-MINE'S A PINT BY THE WAY, CHARLEY.
WAR'S NOT LIKE THEY SAY, EH, CHARLEY? BODIES EVERYWHERE... BLOKES BLOWN TO BITS... AND WHEN IT'S OVER, PEOPLE FORGET ALL ABOUT YOU...
...YES, OLD SOLDIERS NEVER DIE- THEY'RE JUST THROWN ON THE SCRAP HEAP!
AW, LEAVE IT OUT! I'M HOME ON LEAVE! I WANT TO FORGET ALL ABOUT FLIPPING WAR!
BUT, AT THE NAVAL ZEPPELIN BASE IN NORDHOLZ, GERMANY . . .
WELL, THAT'S THIS MONSTER FILLED WITH GAS... READY FOR THE BIG RAID TOMORROW NIGHT!
LOOK OUT, JOHANN... HERE COMES THE ICEBERG!
THE ZEPPELIN COMMANDER WAS KAPITAN HEINRICH VON BERGMANN.
STRAIGHTEN THOSE CAPS, MEN! REMEMBER... ALTHOUGH YOU SAIL IN AIRSHIPS, YOU ARE STILL IN THE IMPERIAL GERMAN NAVY!
AND TOMORROW, JUST AS OUR SUBMARINES TERRORISE THE SEAS, SO OUR NEW SUPER ZEPPELINS WILL TERRORISE LONDON!
2

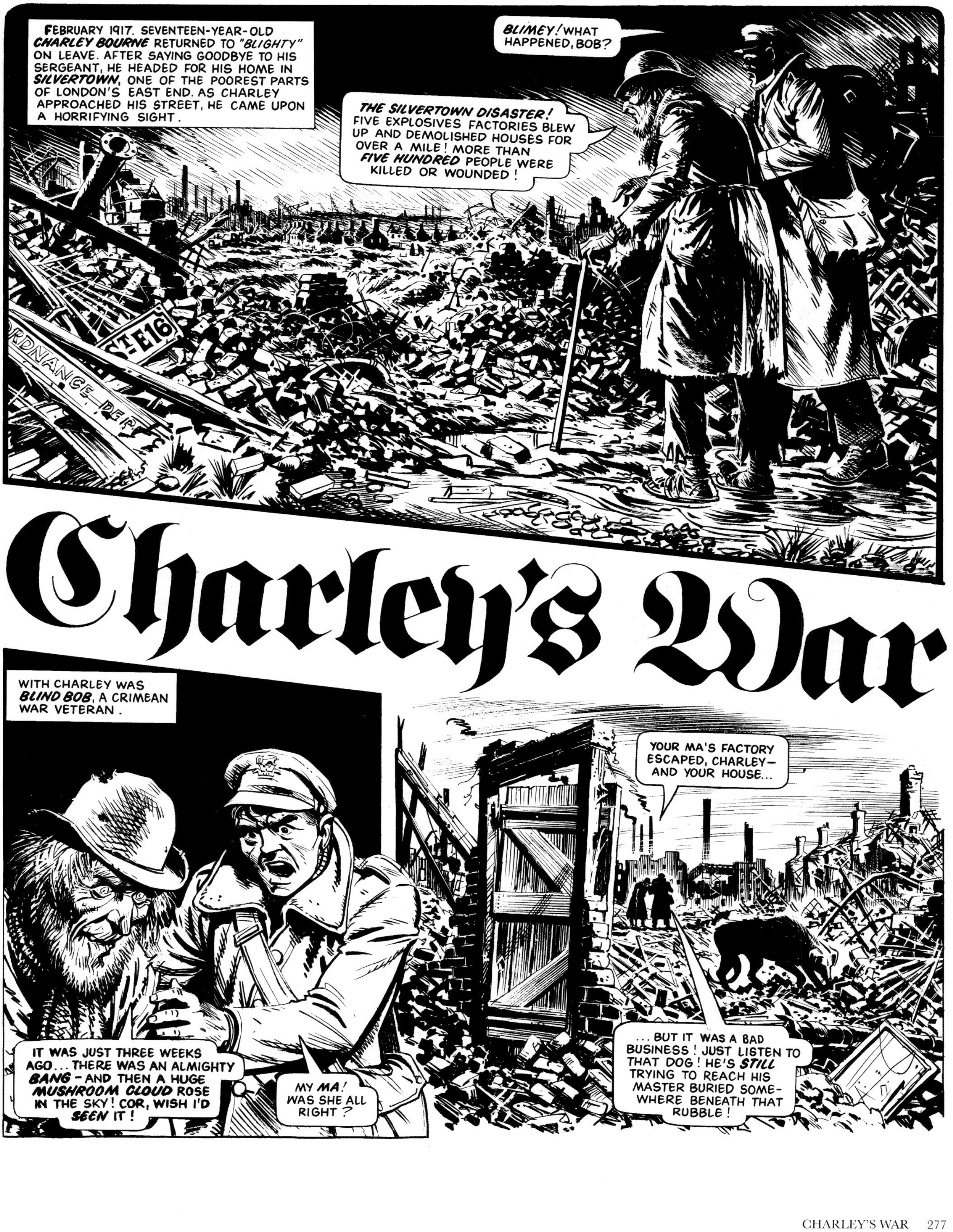
FEBRUARY 1917. SEVENTEEN-YEAR-OLD CHARLEY BOURNE RETURNED TO "BLIGHTY" ON LEAVE. AFTER SAYING GOODBYE TO HIS SERGEANT, HE HEADED FOR HIS HOME IN SILVERTOWN, ONE OF THE POOREST PARTS OF LONDON'S EAST END. AS CHARLEY APPROACHED HIS STREET, HE CAME UPON A HORRIFYING SIGHT.
BLIMEY! WHAT HAPPENED, BOB?
THE SILVERTOWN DISASTER! FIVE EXPLOSIVE FACTORIES BLEW UP AND DEMOLISHED HOUSES FOR OVER A MILE! MORE THAN FIVE HUNDRED PEOPLE WERE KILLED OR WOUNDED!
St. E16
ORDNANCE DEP
Charley's War
WITH CHARLEY WAS BLIND BOB, A CRIMEAN WAR VETERAN.
IT WAS JUST THREE WEEKS AGO... THERE WAS AN ALMIGHTY BANG – AND THEN A HUGE MUSHROOM CLOUD ROSE IN THE SKY! COR, WISH I'D SEEN IT!
MY MA! WAS SHE ALL RIGHT?
YOUR MA'S FACTORY ESCAPED, CHARLEY– AND YOUR HOUSE...
... BUT IT WAS A BAD BUSINESS! JUST LISTEN TO THAT DOG! HE'S STILL TRYING TO REACH HIS MASTER BURIED SOMEWHERE BENEATH THAT RUBBLE!

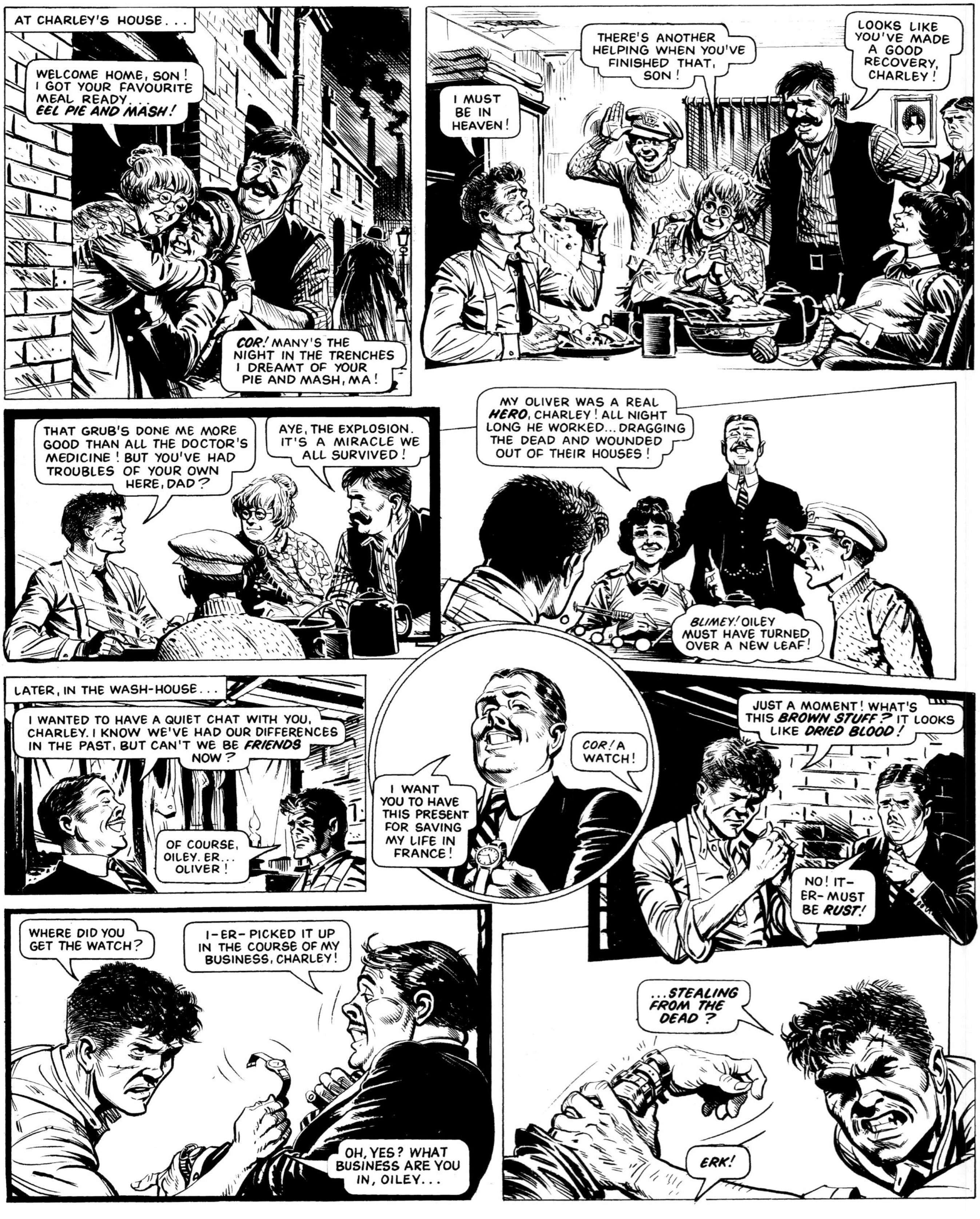
AT CHARLEY'S HOUSE...
WELCOME HOME, SON! I GOT YOUR FAVOURITE MEAL READY... EEL PIE AND MASH!
COR! MANY'S THE NIGHT IN THE TRENCHES I DREAMT OF YOUR PIE AND MASH, MA!
I MUST BE IN HEAVEN!
THERE'S ANOTHER HELPING WHEN YOU'VE FINISHED THAT, SON!
LOOKS LIKE YOU'VE MADE A GOOD RECOVERY, CHARLEY!
THAT GRUB'S DONE ME MORE GOOD THAN ALL THE DOCTOR'S MEDICINE! BUT YOU'VE HAD TROUBLES OF YOUR OWN HERE, DAD?
AYE, THE EXPLOSION. IT'S A MIRACLE WE ALL SURVIVED!
MY OLIVER WAS A REAL HERO, CHARLEY! ALL NIGHT LONG HE WORKED... DRAGGING THE DEAD AND WOUNDED OUT OF THEIR HOUSES!
BLIMEY! OILEY MUST HAVE TURNED OVER A NEW LEAF!
LATER, IN THE WASH-HOUSE...
I WANTED TO HAVE A QUIET CHAT WITH YOU, CHARLEY. I KNOW WE'VE HAD OUR DIFFERENCES IN THE PAST, BUT CAN'T WE BE FRIENDS NOW?
OF COURSE, OILEY. ER... OLIVER!
I WANT YOU TO HAVE THIS PRESENT FOR SAVING MY LIFE IN FRANCE!
COR! A WATCH!
JUST A MOMENT! WHAT'S THIS BROWN STUFF? IT LOOKS LIKE DRIED BLOOD!
NO! IT-ER-MUST BE RUST!
WHERE DID YOU GET THE WATCH?
I-ER-PICKED IT UP IN THE COURSE OF MY BUSINESS, CHARLEY!
OH, YES? WHAT BUSINESS ARE YOU IN, OILEY...
...STEALING FROM THE DEAD?
ERK!

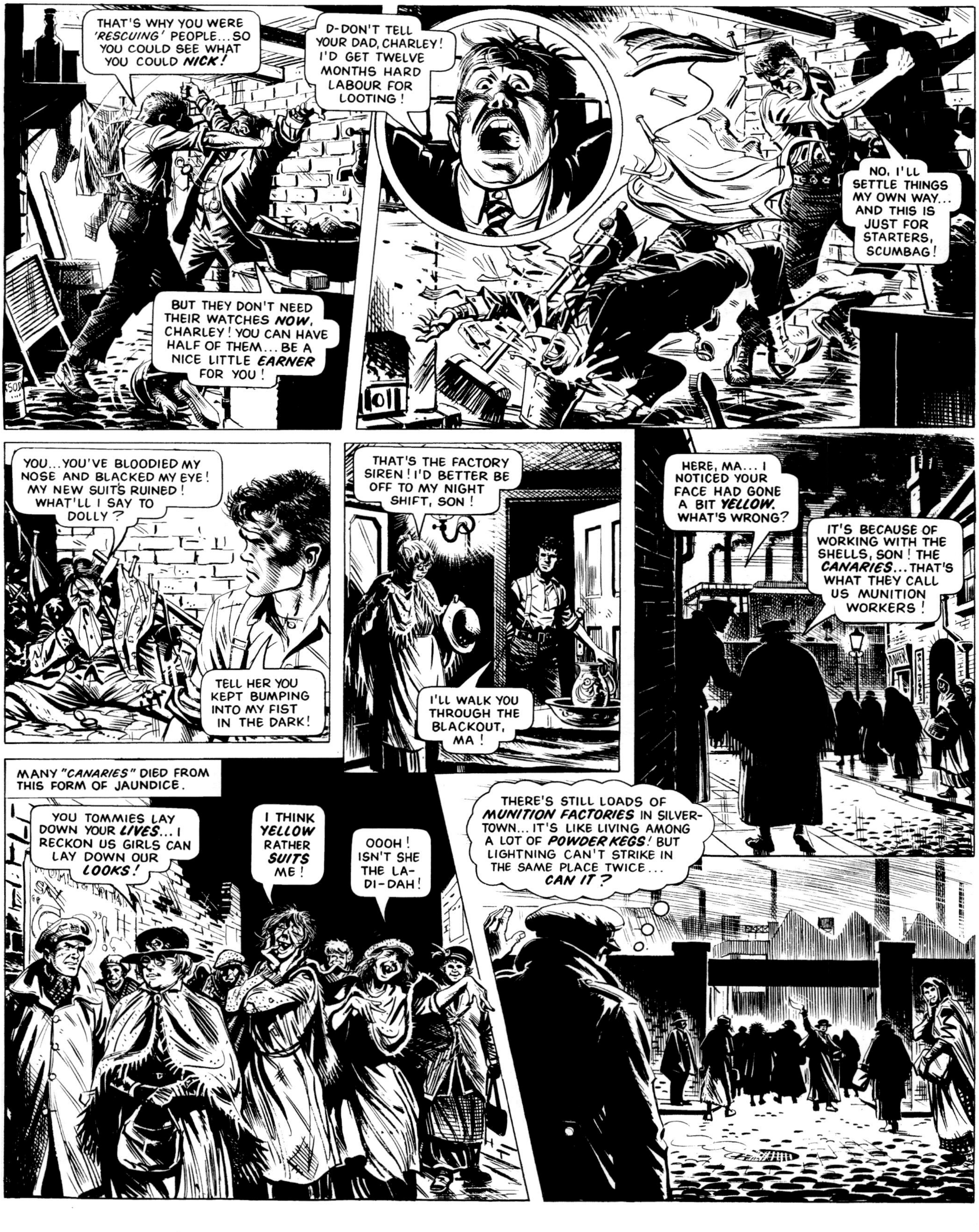

THAT'S WHY YOU WERE 'RESCUING' PEOPLE... SO YOU COULD SEE WHAT YOU COULD NICK!
D-DON'T TELL YOUR DAD, CHARLEY! I'D GET TWELVE MONTHS HARD LABOUR FOR LOOTING!
BUT THEY DON'T NEED THEIR WATCHES NOW, CHARLEY! YOU CAN HAVE HALF OF THEM... BE A NICE LITTLE EARNER FOR YOU!
NO, I'LL SETTLE THINGS MY OWN WAY... AND THIS IS JUST FOR STARTERS, SCUMBAG!
YOU... YOU'VE BLOODIED MY NOSE AND BLACKED MY EYE! MY NEW SUIT'S RUINED! WHAT'LL I SAY TO DOLLY?
TELL HER YOU KEPT BUMPING INTO MY FIST IN THE DARK!
THAT'S THE FACTORY SIREN! I'D BETTER BE OFF TO MY NIGHT SHIFT, SON!
I'LL WALK YOU THROUGH THE BLACKOUT, MA!
HERE, MA... I NOTICED YOUR FACE HAD GONE A BIT YELLOW. WHAT'S WRONG?
IT'S BECAUSE OF WORKING WITH THE SHELLS, SON! THE CANARIES... THAT'S WHAT THEY CALL US MUNITION WORKERS!
MANY "CANARIES" DIED FROM THIS FORM OF JAUNDICE.
YOU TOMMIES LAY DOWN YOUR LIVES... I RECKON US GIRLS CAN LAY DOWN OUR LOOKS!
I THINK YELLOW RATHER SUITS ME!
OOOH! ISN'T SHE THE LA-DI-DAH!
THERE'S STILL LOADS OF MUNITION FACTORIES IN SILVERTOWN... IT'S LIKE LIVING AMONG A LOT OF POWDER KEGS! BUT LIGHTNING CAN'T STRIKE IN THE SAME PLACE TWICE... CAN IT?

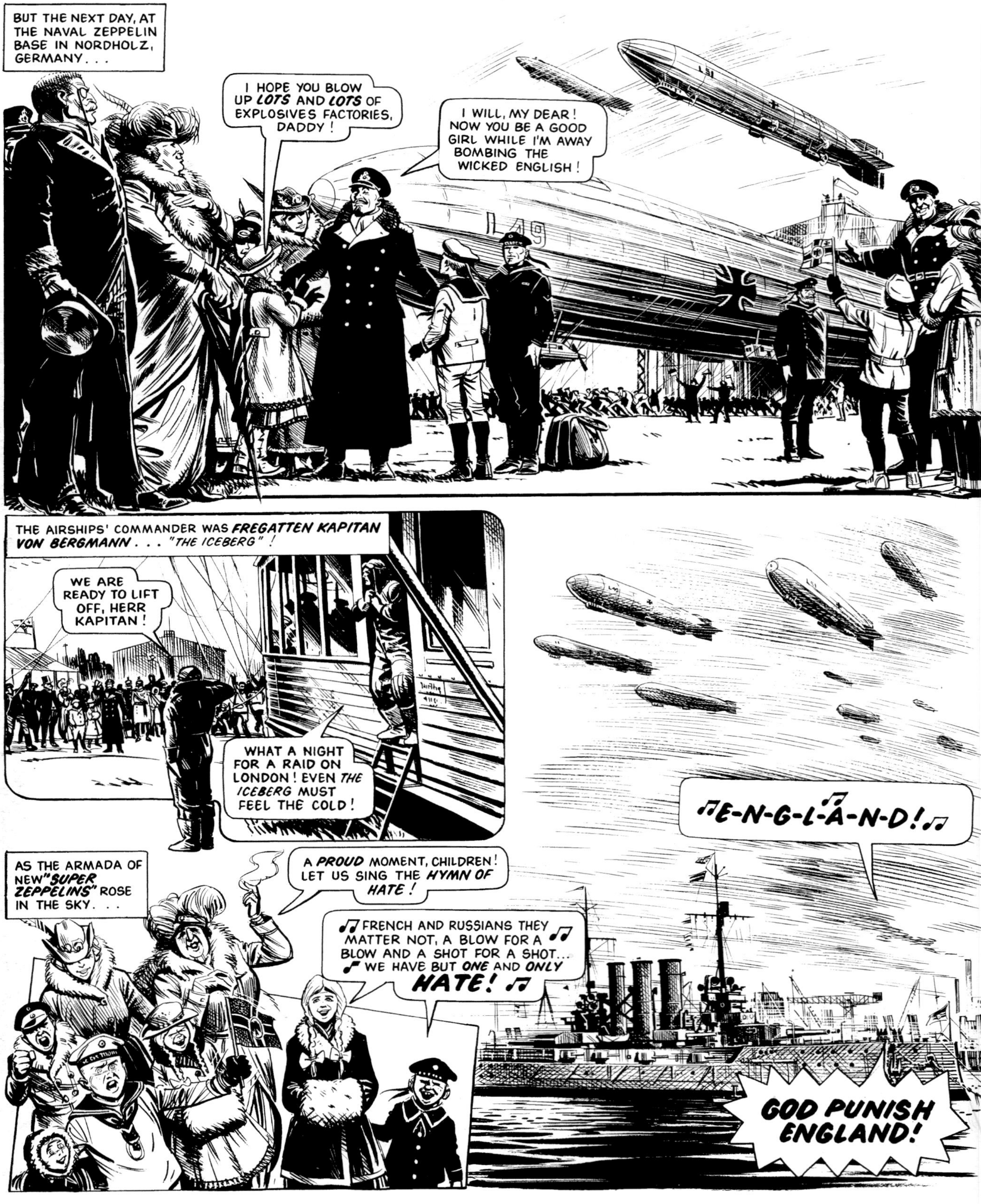

BUT THE NEXT DAY, AT THE NAVAL ZEPPELIN BASE IN NORDHOLZ, GERMANY . . .
I HOPE YOU BLOW UP LOTS AND LOTS OF EXPLOSIVES FACTORIES, DADDY!
I WILL, MY DEAR! NOW YOU BE A GOOD GIRL WHILE I'M AWAY BOMBING THE WICKED ENGLISH!
L 49
THE AIRSHIPS' COMMANDER WAS FREGATTEN KAPITAN VON BERGMANN . . . "THE ICEBERG"!
WE ARE READY TO LIFT OFF, HERR KAPITAN!
WHAT A NIGHT FOR A RAID ON LONDON! EVEN THE ICEBERG MUST FEEL THE COLD!
♫E-N-G-L-A-N-D!♫
AS THE ARMADA OF NEW "SUPER ZEPPELINS" ROSE IN THE SKY. . .
A PROUD MOMENT, CHILDREN! LET US SING THE HYMN OF HATE!
♫FRENCH AND RUSSIANS THEY MATTER NOT, A BLOW FOR A BLOW AND A SHOT FOR A SHOT... WE HAVE BUT ONE AND ONLY HATE! ♫
GOD PUNISH ENGLAND!

CHARLEY'S WAR

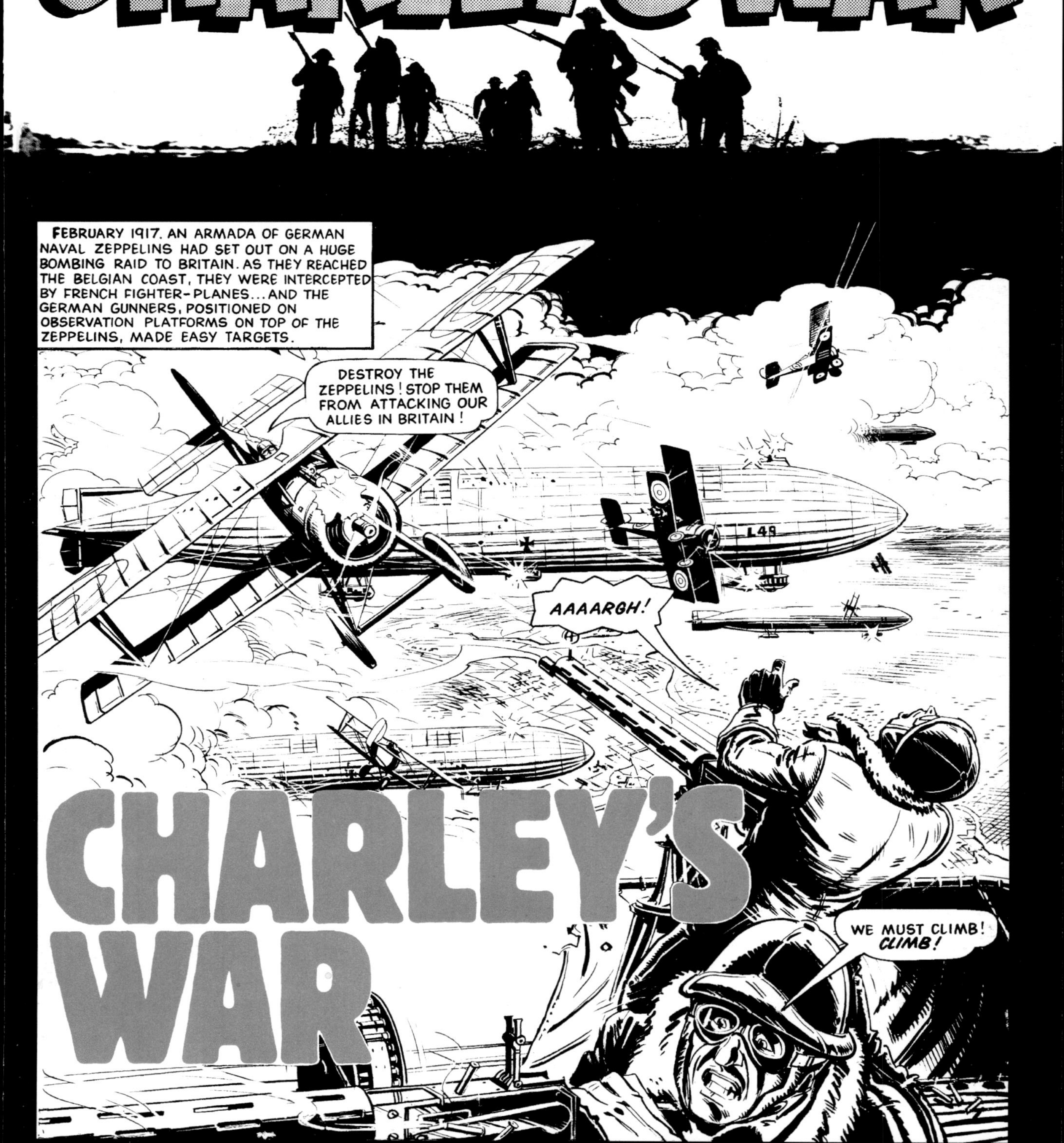

FEBRUARY 1917. AN ARMADA OF GERMAN NAVAL ZEPPELINS HAD SET OUT ON A HUGE BOMBING RAID TO BRITAIN. AS THEY REACHED THE BELGIAN COAST, THEY WERE INTERCEPTED BY FRENCH FIGHTER-PLANES... AND THE GERMAN GUNNERS, POSITIONED ON OBSERVATION PLATFORMS ON TOP OF THE ZEPPELINS, MADE EASY TARGETS.
DESTROY THE ZEPPELINS! STOP THEM FROM ATTACKING OUR ALLIES IN BRITAIN!
L49
AAAARGH!
CHARLEY'S WAR
WE MUST CLIMB! CLIMB!

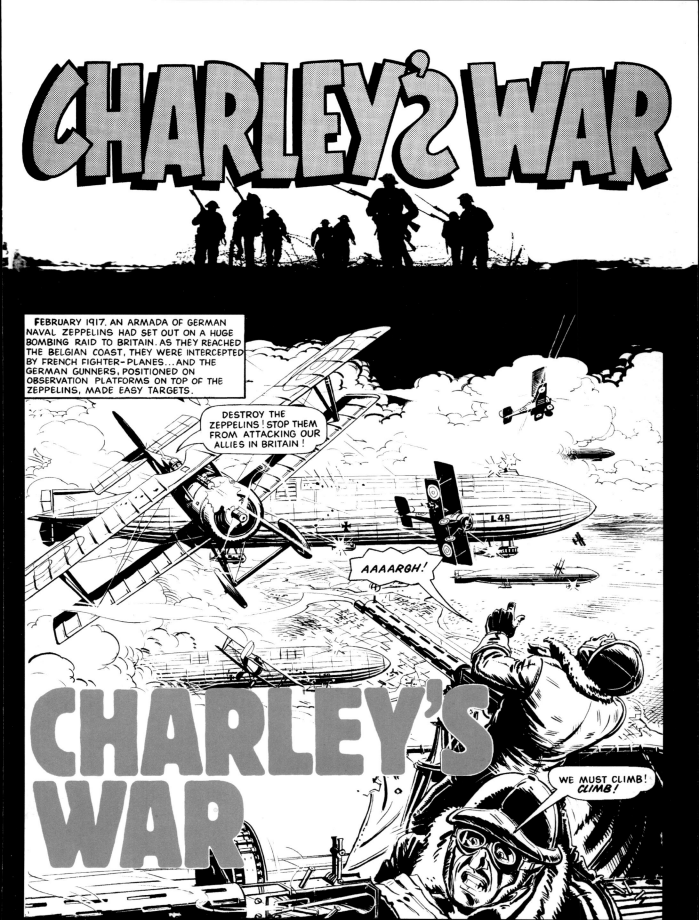

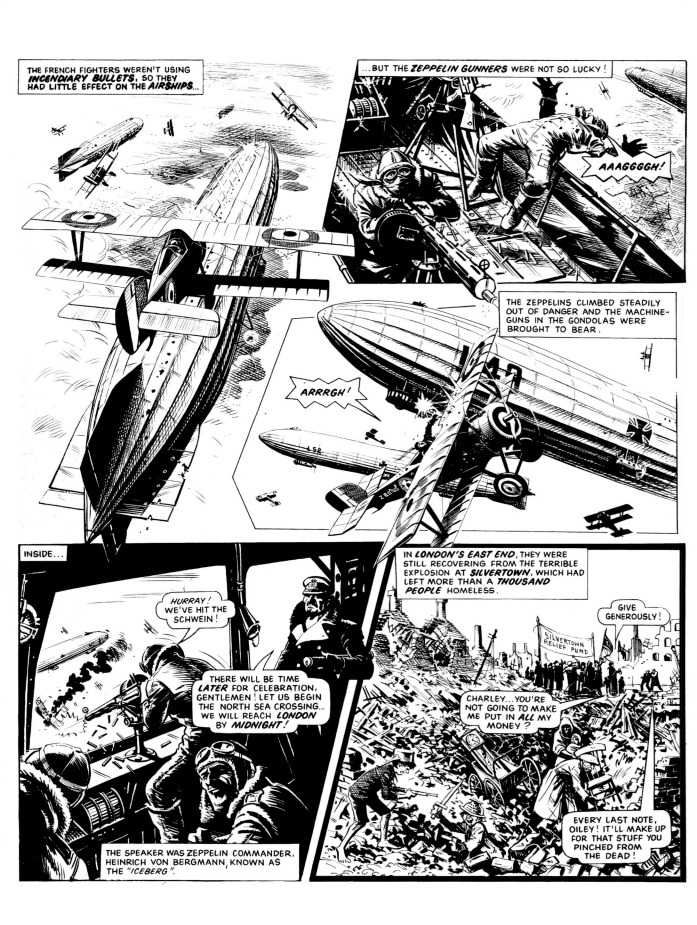

THE FRENCH FIGHTERS WEREN'T USING *INCENDIARY BULLETS*, SO THEY HAD LITTLE EFFECT ON THE *AIRSHIPS*...

...BUT THE *ZEPPELIN GUNNERS* WERE NOT SO LUCKY!

AAAGGGGH!

THE ZEPPELINS CLIMBED STEADILY OUT OF DANGER AND THE MACHINE-GUNS IN THE GONDOLAS WERE BROUGHT TO BEAR.

ARRRGH!

INSIDE...

HURRAY! WE'VE HIT THE SCHWEIN!

THERE WILL BE TIME *LATER* FOR CELEBRATION, GENTLEMEN! LET US BEGIN THE NORTH SEA CROSSING... WE WILL REACH *LONDON* BY *MIDNIGHT!*

THE SPEAKER WAS ZEPPELIN COMMANDER, HEINRICH VON BERGMANN, KNOWN AS THE "ICEBERG".

IN *LONDON'S EAST END*, THEY WERE STILL RECOVERING FROM THE TERRIBLE EXPLOSION AT *SILVERTOWN*, WHICH HAD LEFT MORE THAN A *THOUSAND PEOPLE* HOMELESS.

GIVE GENEROUSLY!

SILVERTOWN RELIEF FUND

CHARLEY...YOU'RE NOT GOING TO MAKE ME PUT IN *ALL* MY MONEY?

EVERY LAST NOTE, OILEY! IT'LL MAKE UP FOR THAT STUFF YOU PINCHED FROM THE DEAD!

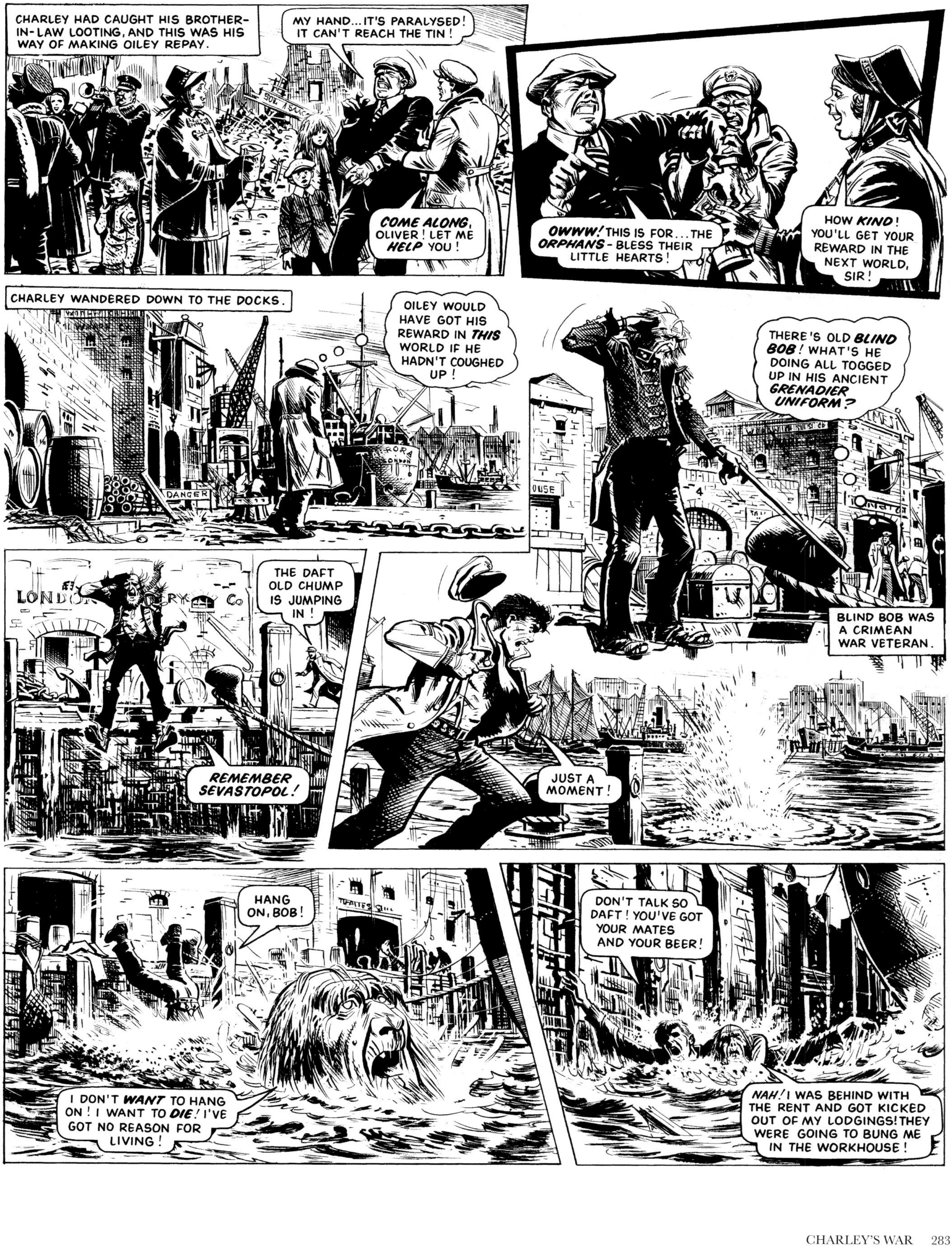
CHARLEY HAD CAUGHT HIS BROTHER-IN-LAW LOOTING, AND THIS WAS HIS WAY OF MAKING OILEY REPAY.
MY HAND... IT'S PARALYSED! IT CAN'T REACH THE TIN!
COME ALONG, OLIVER! LET ME HELP YOU!
OWWW! THIS IS FOR... THE ORPHANS - BLESS THEIR LITTLE HEARTS!
HOW KIND! YOU'LL GET YOUR REWARD IN THE NEXT WORLD, SIR!
CHARLEY WANDERED DOWN TO THE DOCKS.
OILEY WOULD HAVE GOT HIS REWARD IN THIS WORLD IF HE HADN'T COUGHED UP!
DANGER
THERE'S OLD BLIND BOB! WHAT'S HE DOING ALL TOGGED UP IN HIS ANCIENT GRENADIER UNIFORM?
BLIND BOB WAS A CRIMEAN WAR VETERAN.
THE DAFT OLD CHUMP IS JUMPING IN!
REMEMBER SEVASTOPOL!
JUST A MOMENT!
HANG ON, BOB!
I DON'T WANT TO HANG ON! I WANT TO DIE! I'VE GOT NO REASON FOR LIVING!
DON'T TALK SO DAFT! YOU'VE GOT YOUR MATES AND YOUR BEER!
NAH! I WAS BEHIND WITH THE RENT AND GOT KICKED OUT OF MY LODGINGS! THEY WERE GOING TO BUNG ME IN THE WORKHOUSE!

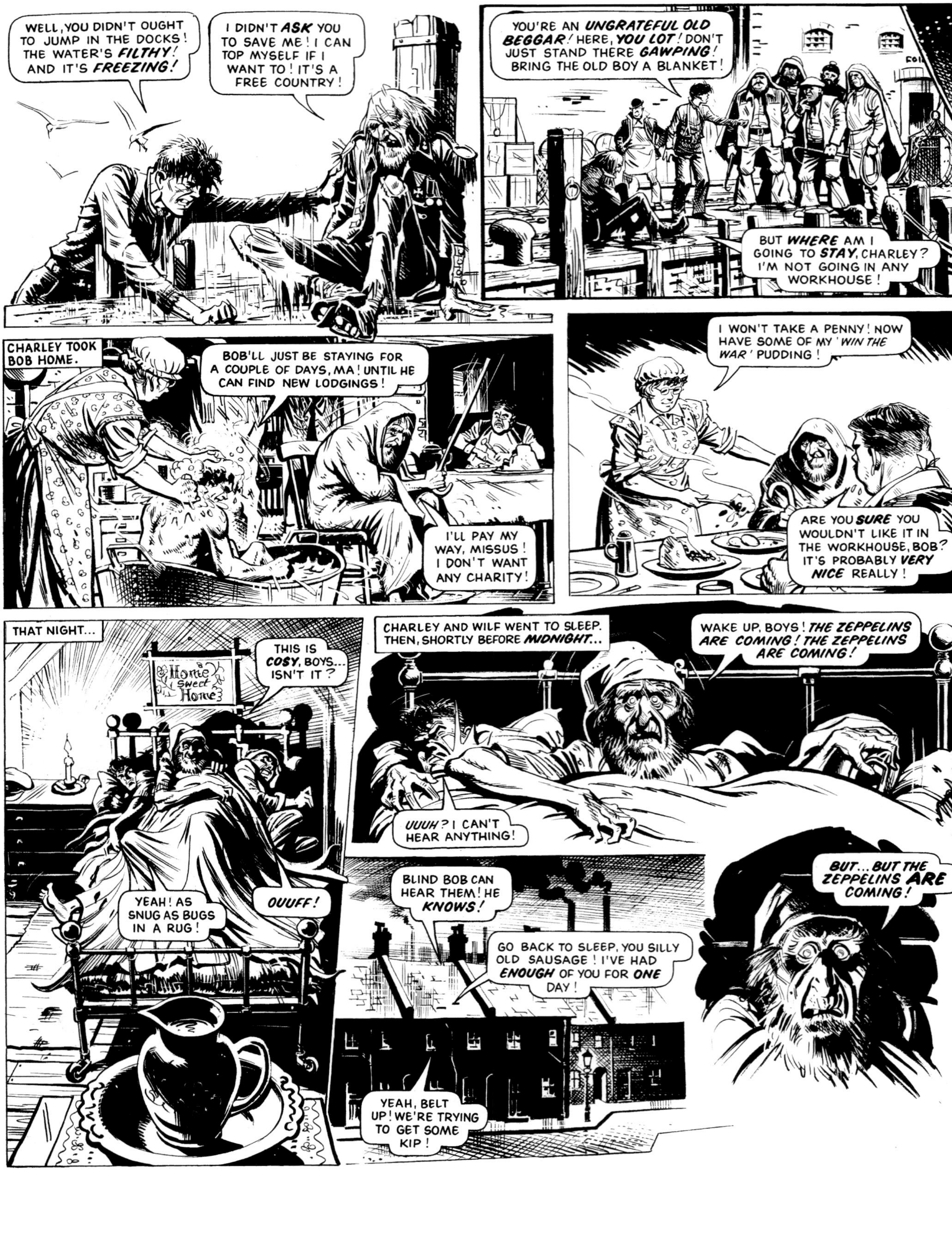
WELL, YOU DIDN'T OUGHT TO JUMP IN THE DOCKS! THE WATER'S FILTHY! AND IT'S FREEZING!
I DIDN'T ASK YOU TO SAVE ME! I CAN TOP MYSELF IF I WANT TO! IT'S A FREE COUNTRY!
YOU'RE AN UNGRATEFUL OLD BEGGAR! HERE, YOU LOT! DON'T JUST STAND THERE GAWPING! BRING THE OLD BOY A BLANKET!
BUT WHERE AM I GOING TO STAY, CHARLEY? I'M NOT GOING IN ANY WORKHOUSE!
CHARLEY TOOK BOB HOME.
BOB'LL JUST BE STAYING FOR A COUPLE OF DAYS, MA! UNTIL HE CAN FIND NEW LODGINGS!
I'LL PAY MY WAY, MISSUS! I DON'T WANT ANY CHARITY!
I WON'T TAKE A PENNY! NOW HAVE SOME OF MY 'WIN THE WAR' PUDDING!
ARE YOU SURE YOU WOULDN'T LIKE IT IN THE WORKHOUSE, BOB? IT'S PROBABLY VERY NICE REALLY!
THAT NIGHT...
Home Sweet Home
THIS IS COSY, BOYS... ISN'T IT?
YEAH! AS SNUG AS BUGS IN A RUG!
OUUFF!
CHARLEY AND WILF WENT TO SLEEP. THEN, SHORTLY BEFORE MIDNIGHT...
WAKE UP, BOYS! THE ZEPPELINS ARE COMING! THE ZEPPELINS ARE COMING!
UUUH? I CAN'T HEAR ANYTHING!
BLIND BOB CAN HEAR THEM! HE KNOWS!
GO BACK TO SLEEP, YOU SILLY OLD SAUSAGE! I'VE HAD ENOUGH OF YOU FOR ONE DAY!
YEAH, BELT UP! WE'RE TRYING TO GET SOME KIP!
BUT... BUT THE ZEPPELINS ARE COMING!

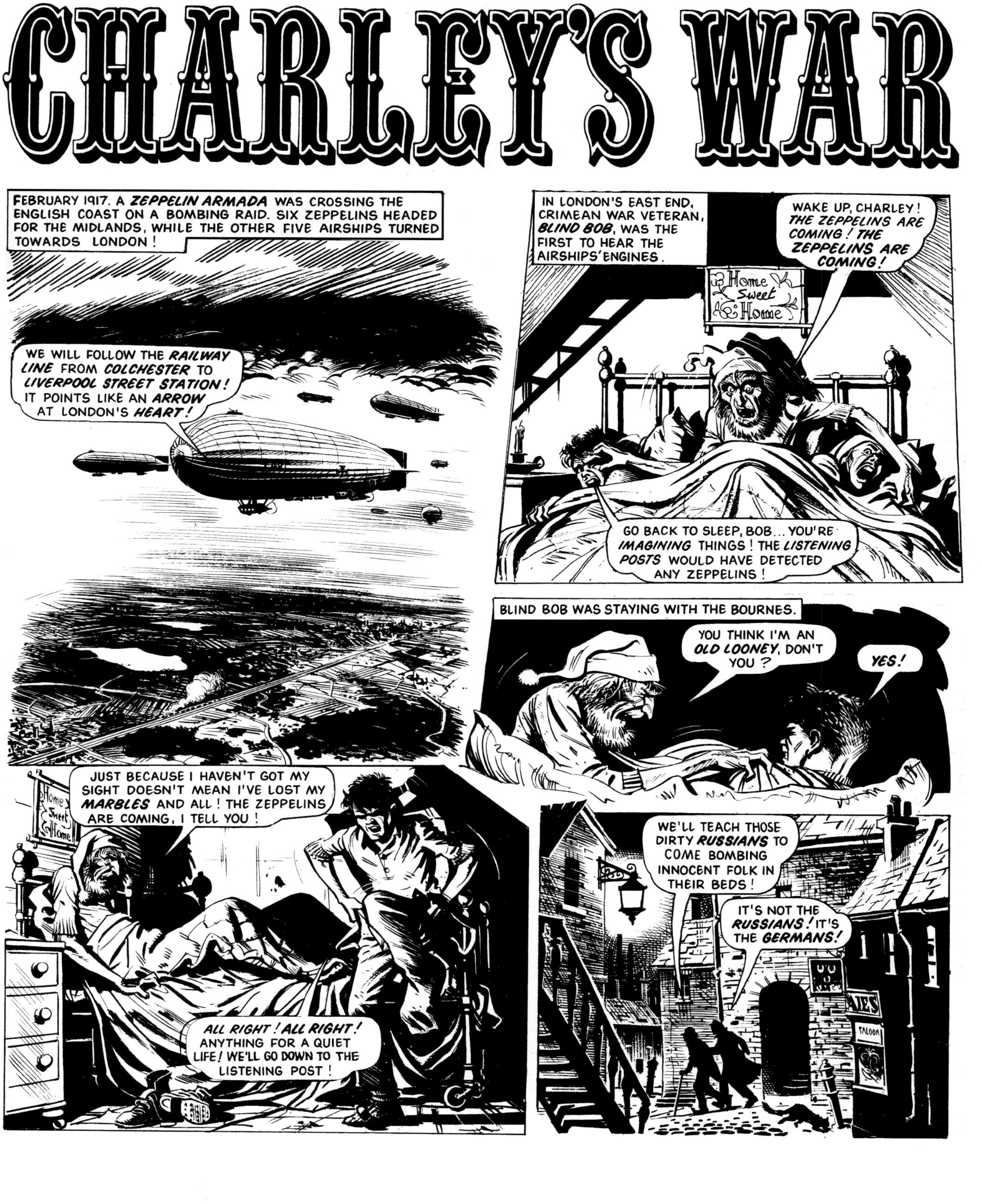
CHARLEY'S WAR
FEBRUARY 1917. A ZEPPELIN ARMADA WAS CROSSING THE ENGLISH COAST ON A BOMBING RAID. SIX ZEPPELINS HEADED FOR THE MIDLANDS, WHILE THE OTHER FIVE AIRSHIPS TURNED TOWARDS LONDON!
WE WILL FOLLOW THE RAILWAY LINE FROM COLCHESTER TO LIVERPOOL STREET STATION! IT POINTS LIKE AN ARROW AT LONDON'S HEART!
IN LONDON'S EAST END, CRIMEAN WAR VETERAN, BLIND BOB, WAS THE FIRST TO HEAR THE AIRSHIPS' ENGINES.
WAKE UP, CHARLEY! THE ZEPPELINS ARE COMING! THE ZEPPELINS ARE COMING!
Home Sweet Home
GO BACK TO SLEEP, BOB... YOU'RE IMAGINING THINGS! THE LISTENING POSTS WOULD HAVE DETECTED ANY ZEPPELINS!
BLIND BOB WAS STAYING WITH THE BOURNES.
YOU THINK I'M AN OLD LOONEY, DON'T YOU?
YES!
JUST BECAUSE I HAVEN'T GOT MY SIGHT DOESN'T MEAN I'VE LOST MY MARBLES AND ALL! THE ZEPPELINS ARE COMING, I TELL YOU!
ALL RIGHT! ALL RIGHT! ANYTHING FOR A QUIET LIFE! WE'LL GO DOWN TO THE LISTENING POST!
WE'LL TEACH THOSE DIRTY RUSSIANS TO COME BOMBING INNOCENT FOLK IN THEIR BEDS!
IT'S NOT THE RUSSIANS! IT'S THE GERMANS!
SALOON

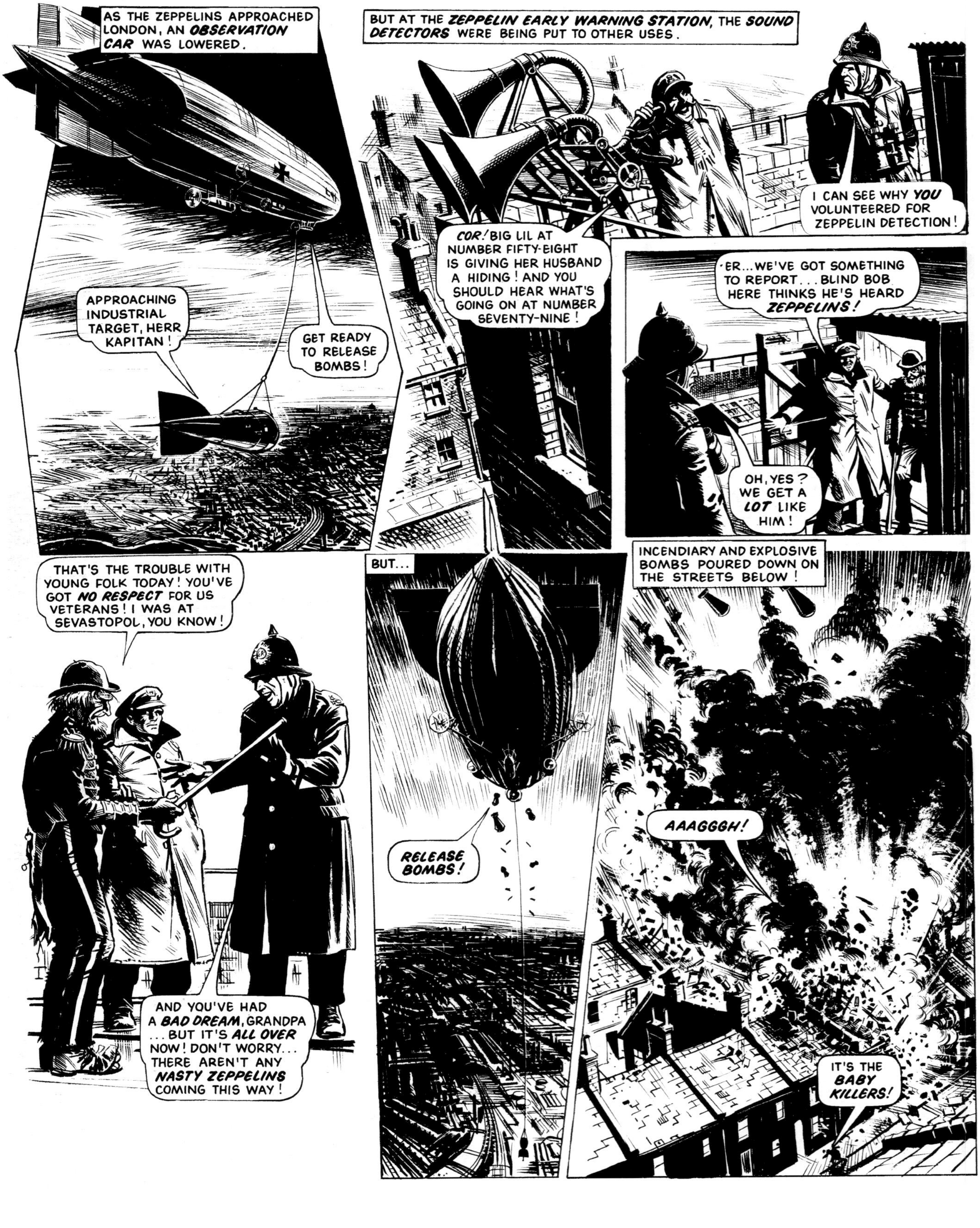

AS THE ZEPPELINS APPROACHED LONDON, AN OBSERVATION CAR WAS LOWERED.
APPROACHING INDUSTRIAL TARGET, HERR KAPITAN!
GET READY TO RELEASE BOMBS!
BUT AT THE ZEPPELIN EARLY WARNING STATION, THE SOUND DETECTORS WERE BEING PUT TO OTHER USES.
COR! BIG LIL AT NUMBER FIFTY-EIGHT IS GIVING HER HUSBAND A HIDING! AND YOU SHOULD HEAR WHAT'S GOING ON AT NUMBER SEVENTY-NINE!
I CAN SEE WHY YOU VOLUNTEERED FOR ZEPPELIN DETECTION!
ER... WE'VE GOT SOMETHING TO REPORT... BLIND BOB HERE THINKS HE'S HEARD ZEPPELINS!
OH, YES? WE GET A LOT LIKE HIM!
THAT'S THE TROUBLE WITH YOUNG FOLK TODAY! YOU'VE GOT NO RESPECT FOR US VETERANS! I WAS AT SEVASTOPOL, YOU KNOW!
AND YOU'VE HAD A BAD DREAM, GRANDPA ... BUT IT'S ALL OVER NOW! DON'T WORRY... THERE AREN'T ANY NASTY ZEPPELINS COMING THIS WAY!
BUT...
RELEASE BOMBS!
INCENDIARY AND EXPLOSIVE BOMBS POURED DOWN ON THE STREETS BELOW!
AAAGGGH!
IT'S THE BABY KILLERS!

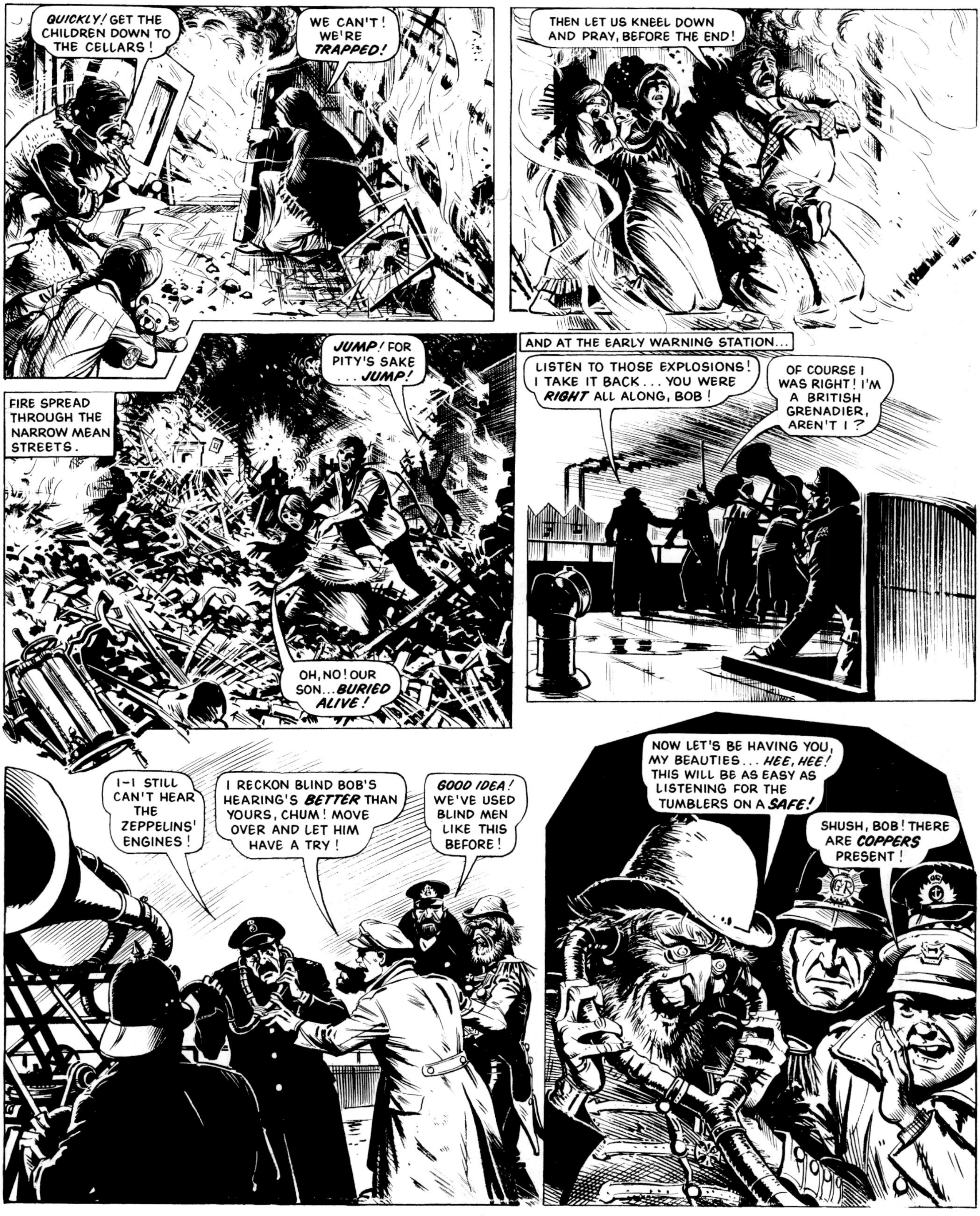

QUICKLY! GET THE CHILDREN DOWN TO THE CELLARS!
WE CAN'T! WE'RE TRAPPED!
THEN LET US KNEEL DOWN AND PRAY, BEFORE THE END!
FIRE SPREAD THROUGH THE NARROW MEAN STREETS.
JUMP! FOR PITY'S SAKE ... JUMP!
OH, NO! OUR SON... BURIED ALIVE!
AND AT THE EARLY WARNING STATION...
LISTEN TO THOSE EXPLOSIONS! I TAKE IT BACK... YOU WERE RIGHT ALL ALONG, BOB!
OF COURSE I WAS RIGHT! I'M A BRITISH GRENADIER, AREN'T I?
I-I STILL CAN'T HEAR THE ZEPPELINS' ENGINES!
I RECKON BLIND BOB'S HEARING'S BETTER THAN YOURS, CHUM! MOVE OVER AND LET HIM HAVE A TRY!
GOOD IDEA! WE'VE USED BLIND MEN LIKE THIS BEFORE!
NOW LET'S BE HAVING YOU, MY BEAUTIES... HEE, HEE! THIS WILL BE AS EASY AS LISTENING FOR THE TUMBLERS ON A SAFE!
SHUSH, BOB! THERE ARE COPPERS PRESENT!

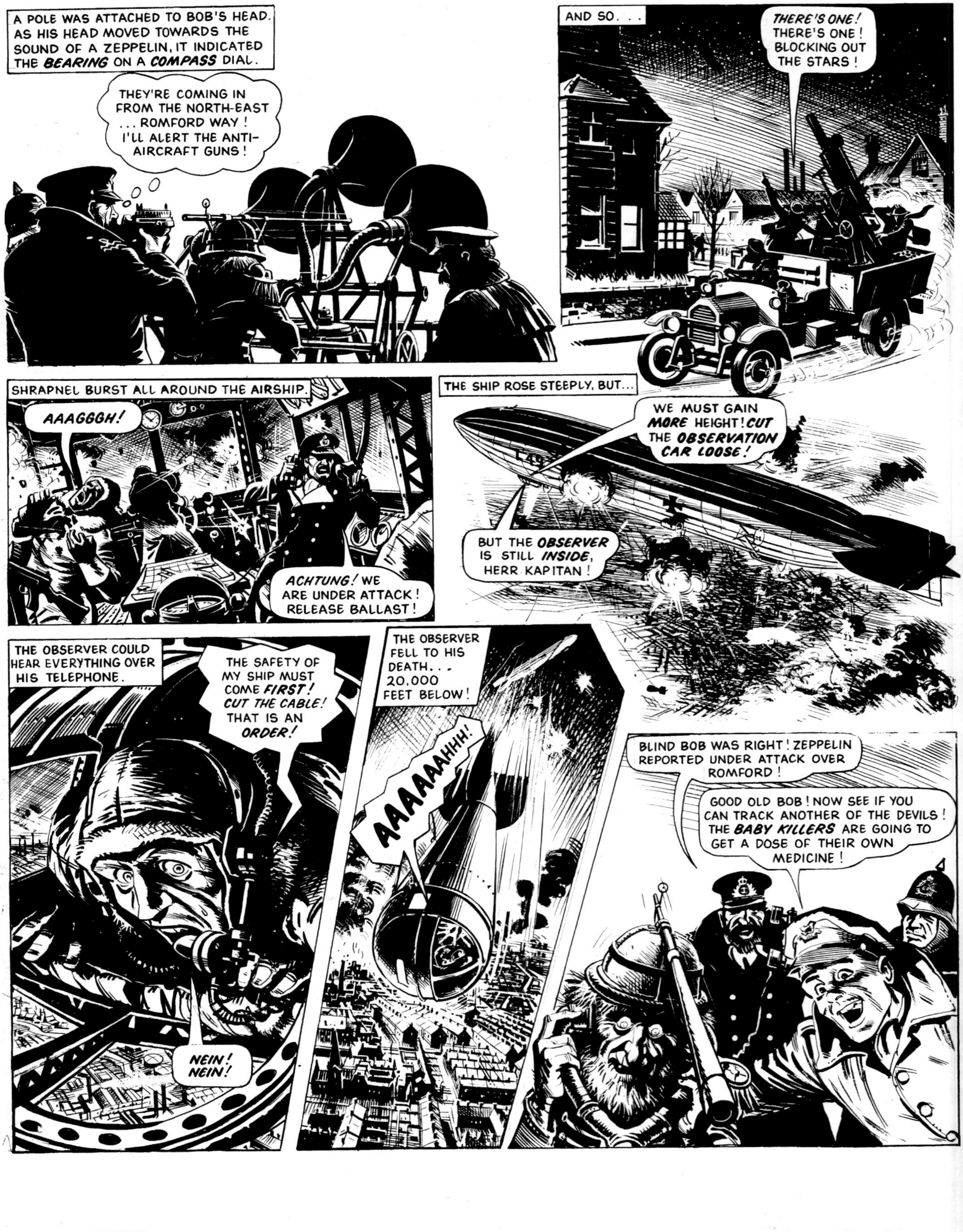

A POLE WAS ATTACHED TO BOB'S HEAD. AS HIS HEAD MOVED TOWARDS THE SOUND OF A ZEPPELIN, IT INDICATED THE BEARING ON A COMPASS DIAL.
THEY'RE COMING IN FROM THE NORTH-EAST ... ROMFORD WAY! I'LL ALERT THE ANTI-AIRCRAFT GUNS!
AND SO...
THERE'S ONE! THERE'S ONE! BLOCKING OUT THE STARS!
SHRAPNEL BURST ALL AROUND THE AIRSHIP.
AAAGGGH!
ACHTUNG! WE ARE UNDER ATTACK! RELEASE BALLAST!
THE SHIP ROSE STEEPLY, BUT...
WE MUST GAIN MORE HEIGHT! CUT THE OBSERVATION CAR LOOSE!
BUT THE OBSERVER IS STILL INSIDE, HERR KAPITAN!
THE OBSERVER COULD HEAR EVERYTHING OVER HIS TELEPHONE.
THE SAFETY OF MY SHIP MUST COME FIRST! CUT THE CABLE! THAT IS AN ORDER!
NEIN! NEIN!
THE OBSERVER FELL TO HIS DEATH... 20,000 FEET BELOW!
AAAAAAAHHH!
BLIND BOB WAS RIGHT! ZEPPELIN REPORTED UNDER ATTACK OVER ROMFORD!
GOOD OLD BOB! NOW SEE IF YOU CAN TRACK ANOTHER OF THE DEVILS! THE BABY KILLERS ARE GOING TO GET A DOSE OF THEIR OWN MEDICINE!

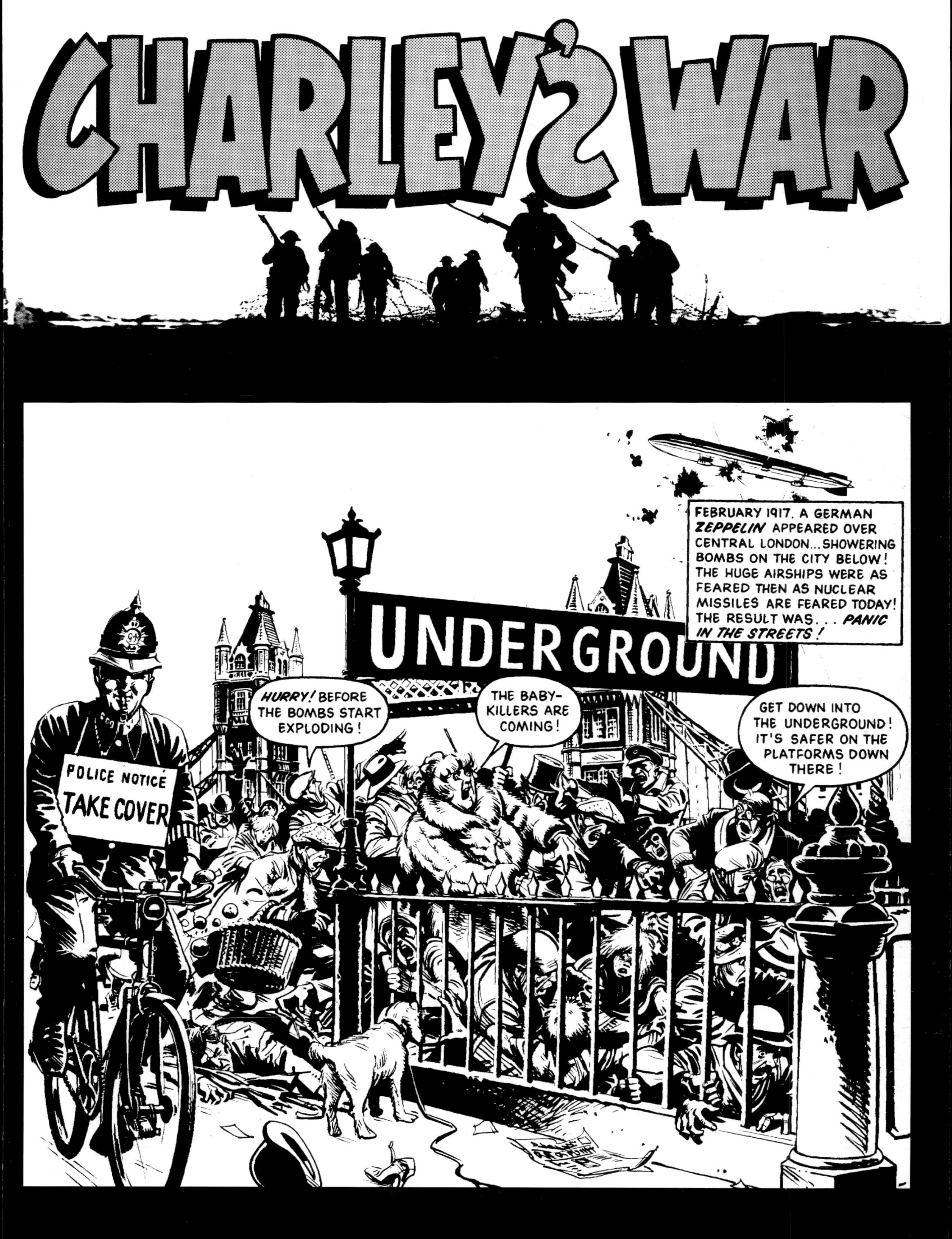
CHARLEY'S WAR
FEBRUARY 1917. A GERMAN ZEPPELIN APPEARED OVER CENTRAL LONDON... SHOWERING BOMBS ON THE CITY BELOW! THE HUGE AIRSHIPS WERE AS FEARED THEN AS NUCLEAR MISSILES ARE FEARED TODAY! THE RESULT WAS. . . PANIC IN THE STREETS!
UNDERGROUND
POLICE NOTICE
TAKE COVER
HURRY! BEFORE THE BOMBS START EXPLODING!
THE BABY-KILLERS ARE COMING!
GET DOWN INTO THE UNDERGROUND! IT'S SAFER ON THE PLATFORMS DOWN THERE!

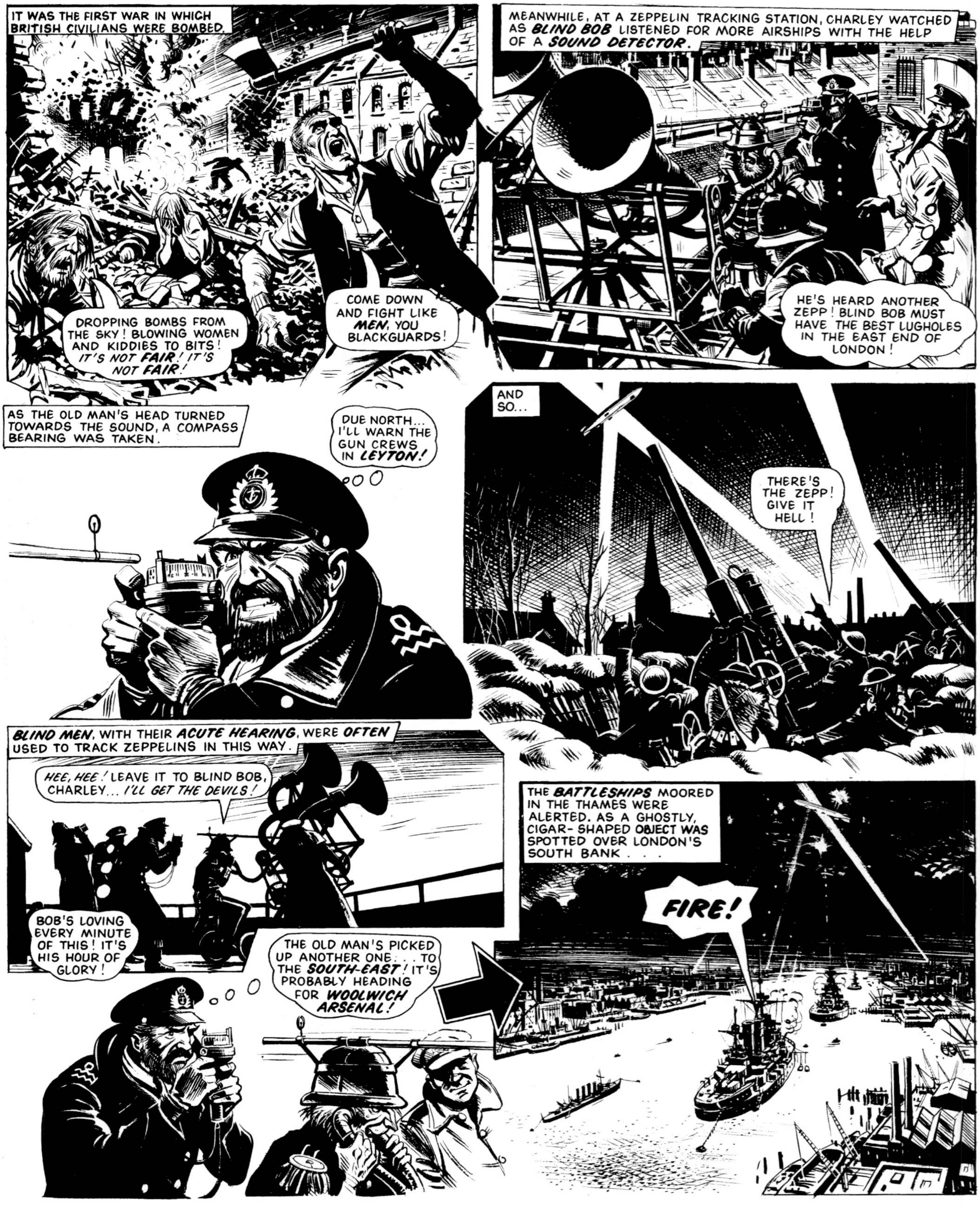
IT WAS THE FIRST WAR IN WHICH BRITISH CIVILIANS WERE BOMBED.
DROPPING BOMBS FROM THE SKY! BLOWING WOMEN AND KIDDIES TO BITS! IT'S NOT FAIR! IT'S NOT FAIR!
COME DOWN AND FIGHT LIKE MEN, YOU BLACKGUARDS!
MEANWHILE, AT A ZEPPELIN TRACKING STATION, CHARLEY WATCHED AS BLIND BOB LISTENED FOR MORE AIRSHIPS WITH THE HELP OF A SOUND DETECTOR.
HE'S HEARD ANOTHER ZEPP! BLIND BOB MUST HAVE THE BEST LUGHOLES IN THE EAST END OF LONDON!
AS THE OLD MAN'S HEAD TURNED TOWARDS THE SOUND, A COMPASS BEARING WAS TAKEN.
DUE NORTH... I'LL WARN THE GUN CREWS IN LEYTON!
AND SO...
THERE'S THE ZEPP! GIVE IT HELL!
BLIND MEN, WITH THEIR ACUTE HEARING, WERE OFTEN USED TO TRACK ZEPPELINS IN THIS WAY.
HEE, HEE! LEAVE IT TO BLIND BOB, CHARLEY... I'LL GET THE DEVILS!
BOB'S LOVING EVERY MINUTE OF THIS! IT'S HIS HOUR OF GLORY!
THE OLD MAN'S PICKED UP ANOTHER ONE... TO THE SOUTH-EAST! IT'S PROBABLY HEADING FOR WOOLWICH ARSENAL!
THE BATTLESHIPS MOORED IN THE THAMES WERE ALERTED. AS A GHOSTLY, CIGAR-SHAPED OBJECT WAS SPOTTED OVER LONDON'S SOUTH BANK...
FIRE!

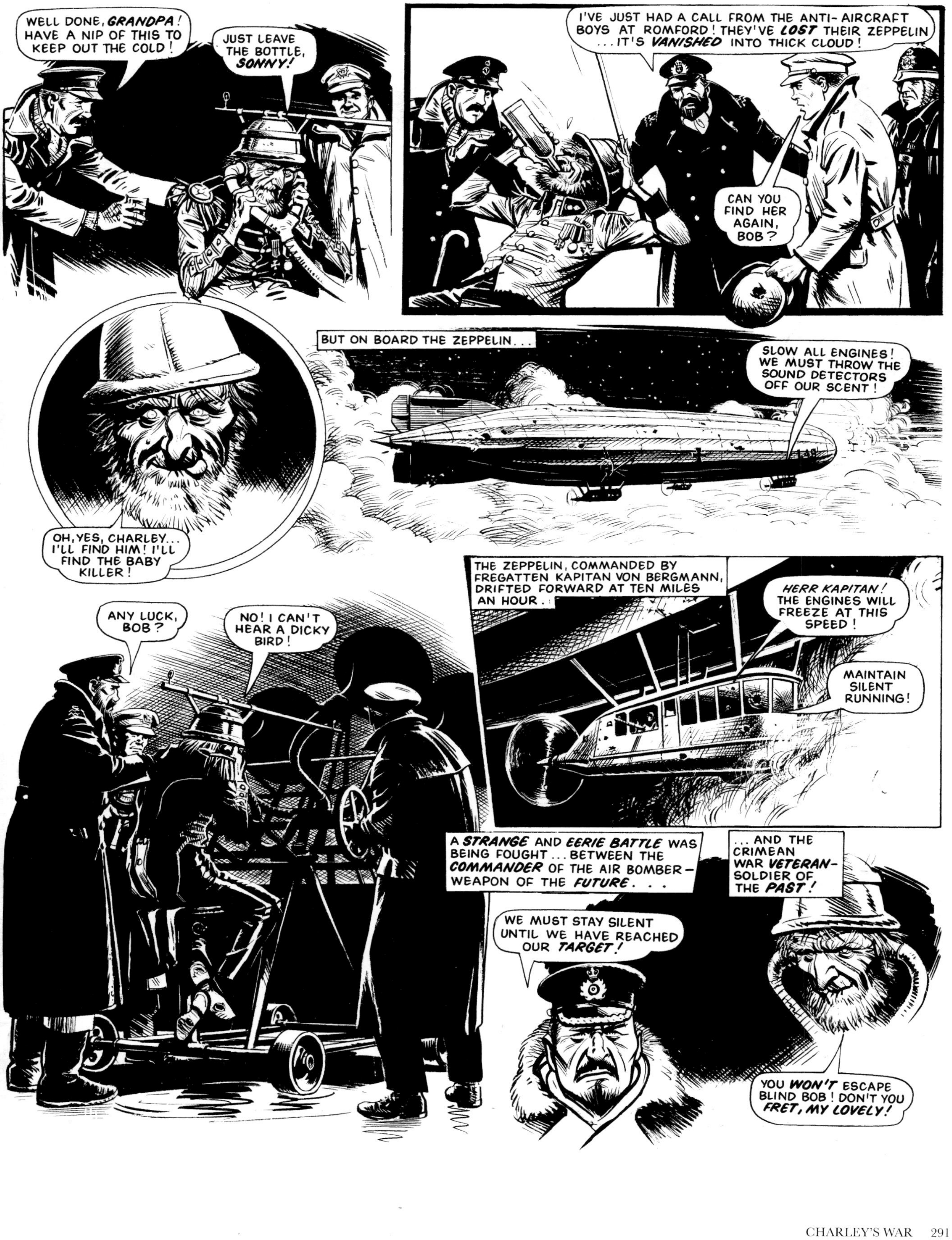

WELL DONE, GRANDPA! HAVE A NIP OF THIS TO KEEP OUT THE COLD!
JUST LEAVE THE BOTTLE, SONNY!
I'VE JUST HAD A CALL FROM THE ANTI-AIRCRAFT BOYS AT ROMFORD! THEY'VE LOST THEIR ZEPPELIN ... IT'S VANISHED INTO THICK CLOUD!
CAN YOU FIND HER AGAIN, BOB?
OH, YES, CHARLEY... I'LL FIND HIM! I'LL FIND THE BABY KILLER!
BUT ON BOARD THE ZEPPELIN...
SLOW ALL ENGINES! WE MUST THROW THE SOUND DETECTORS OFF OUR SCENT!
ANY LUCK, BOB?
NO! I CAN'T HEAR A DICKY BIRD!
THE ZEPPELIN, COMMANDED BY FREGATTEN KAPITAN VON BERGMANN, DRIFTED FORWARD AT TEN MILES AN HOUR.
HERR KAPITAN! THE ENGINES WILL FREEZE AT THIS SPEED!
MAINTAIN SILENT RUNNING!
A STRANGE AND EERIE BATTLE WAS BEING FOUGHT... BETWEEN THE COMMANDER OF THE AIR BOMBER – WEAPON OF THE FUTURE...
... AND THE CRIMEAN WAR VETERAN – SOLDIER OF THE PAST!
WE MUST STAY SILENT UNTIL WE HAVE REACHED OUR TARGET!
YOU WON'T ESCAPE BLIND BOB! DON'T YOU FRET, MY LOVELY!

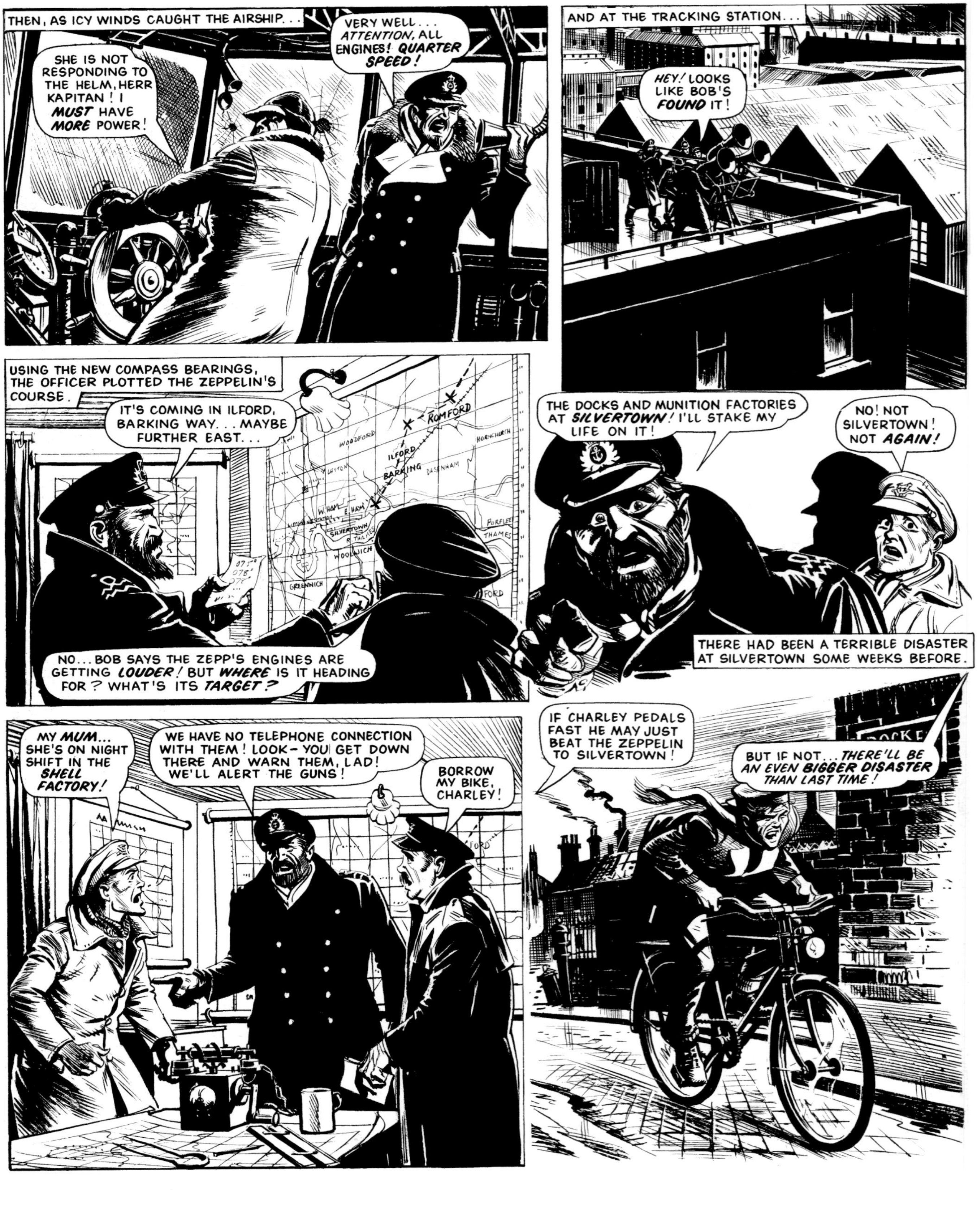
THEN, AS ICY WINDS CAUGHT THE AIRSHIP...
SHE IS NOT RESPONDING TO THE HELM, HERR KAPITAN! I MUST HAVE MORE POWER!
VERY WELL... ATTENTION, ALL ENGINES! QUARTER SPEED!
AND AT THE TRACKING STATION...
HEY! LOOKS LIKE BOB'S FOUND IT!
USING THE NEW COMPASS BEARINGS, THE OFFICER PLOTTED THE ZEPPELIN'S COURSE.
IT'S COMING IN ILFORD, BARKING WAY... MAYBE FURTHER EAST...
ROMFORD
WOODFORD
ILFORD
BARKING
DAGENHAM
HORNCHURCH
W. HAM
E. HAM
SILVERTOWN
PURFLEET
THAMES
WOOLWICH
GREENWICH
NO... BOB SAYS THE ZEPP'S ENGINES ARE GETTING LOUDER! BUT WHERE IS IT HEADING FOR? WHAT'S ITS TARGET?
THE DOCKS AND MUNITION FACTORIES AT SILVERTOWN! I'LL STAKE MY LIFE ON IT!
NO! NOT SILVERTOWN! NOT AGAIN!
THERE HAD BEEN A TERRIBLE DISASTER AT SILVERTOWN SOME WEEKS BEFORE.
MY MUM... SHE'S ON NIGHT SHIFT IN THE SHELL FACTORY!
WE HAVE NO TELEPHONE CONNECTION WITH THEM! LOOK- YOU GET DOWN THERE AND WARN THEM, LAD! WE'LL ALERT THE GUNS!
BORROW MY BIKE, CHARLEY!
IF CHARLEY PEDALS FAST HE MAY JUST BEAT THE ZEPPELIN TO SILVERTOWN!
BUT IF NOT... THERE'LL BE AN EVEN BIGGER DISASTER THAN LAST TIME!

Charley's War

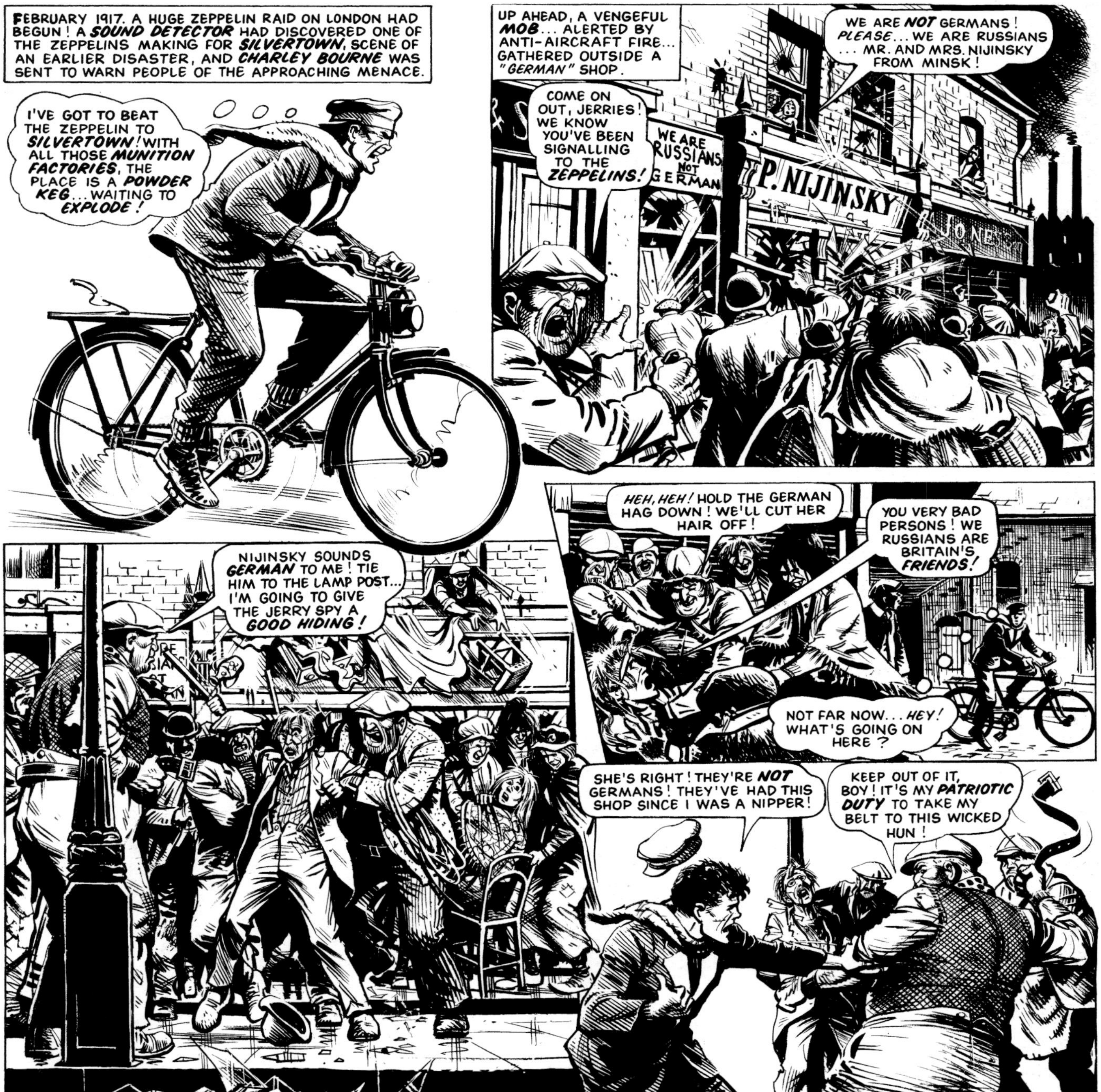
FEBRUARY 1917. A HUGE ZEPPELIN RAID ON LONDON HAD BEGUN! A SOUND DETECTOR HAD DISCOVERED ONE OF THE ZEPPELINS MAKING FOR SILVERTOWN, SCENE OF AN EARLIER DISASTER, AND CHARLEY BOURNE WAS SENT TO WARN PEOPLE OF THE APPROACHING MENACE.
I'VE GOT TO BEAT THE ZEPPELIN TO SILVERTOWN! WITH ALL THOSE MUNITION FACTORIES, THE PLACE IS A POWDER KEG... WAITING TO EXPLODE!
UP AHEAD, A VENGEFUL MOB... ALERTED BY ANTI-AIRCRAFT FIRE... GATHERED OUTSIDE A "GERMAN" SHOP.
WE ARE NOT GERMANS! PLEASE... WE ARE RUSSIANS ... MR. AND MRS. NIJINSKY FROM MINSK!
COME ON OUT, JERRIES! WE KNOW YOU'VE BEEN SIGNALLING TO THE ZEPPELINS!
WE ARE RUSSIANS NOT GERMAN
P. NIJINSKY
NIJINSKY SOUNDS GERMAN TO ME! TIE HIM TO THE LAMP POST... I'M GOING TO GIVE THE JERRY SPY A GOOD HIDING!
HEH, HEH! HOLD THE GERMAN HAG DOWN! WE'LL CUT HER HAIR OFF!
YOU VERY BAD PERSONS! WE RUSSIANS ARE BRITAIN'S FRIENDS!
NOT FAR NOW... HEY! WHAT'S GOING ON HERE?
SHE'S RIGHT! THEY'RE NOT GERMANS! THEY'VE HAD THIS SHOP SINCE I WAS A NIPPER!
KEEP OUT OF IT, BOY! IT'S MY PATRIOTIC DUTY TO TAKE MY BELT TO THIS WICKED HUN!

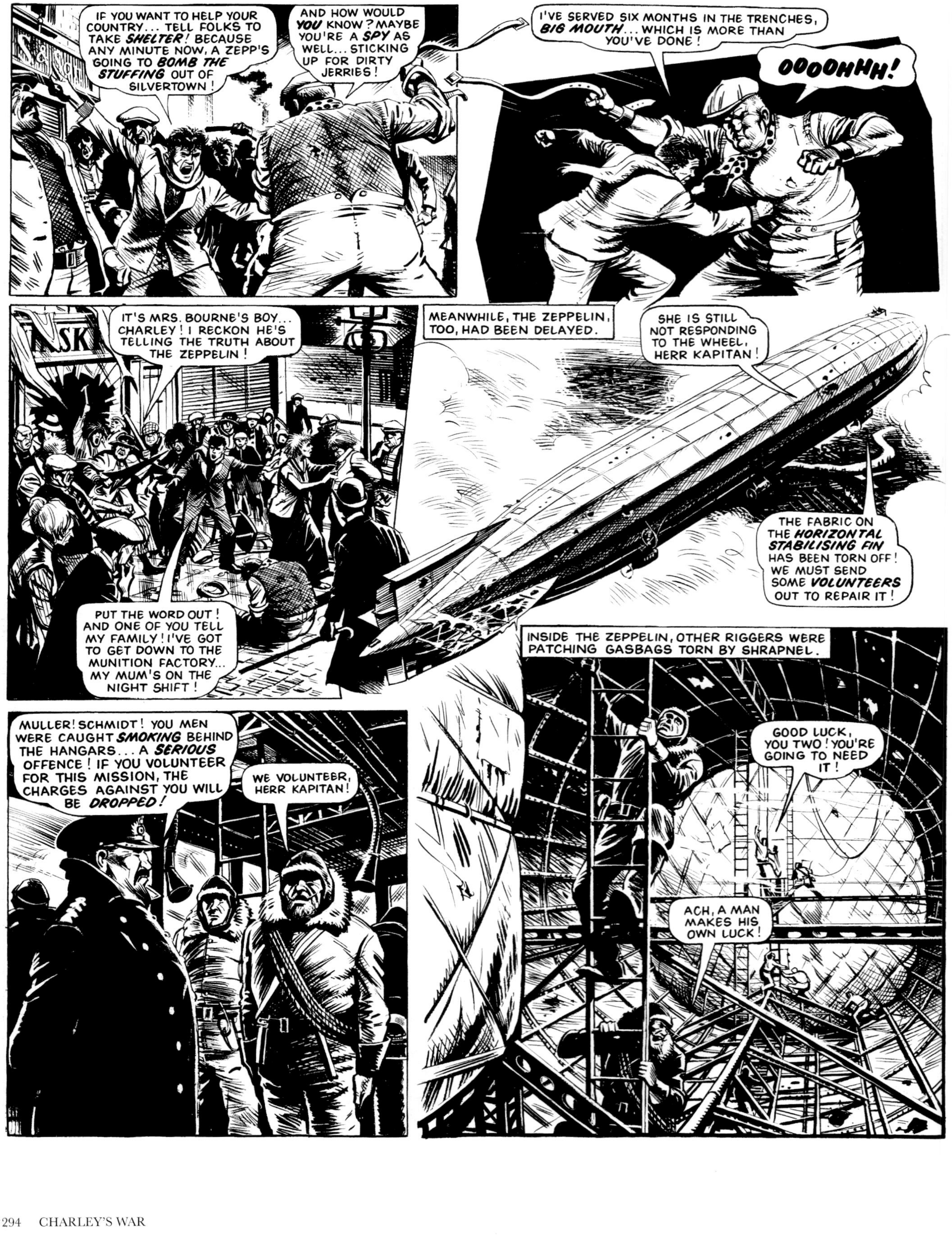
IF YOU WANT TO HELP YOUR COUNTRY... TELL FOLKS TO TAKE SHELTER! BECAUSE ANY MINUTE NOW, A ZEPP'S GOING TO BOMB THE STUFFING OUT OF SILVERTOWN!
AND HOW WOULD YOU KNOW? MAYBE YOU'RE A SPY AS WELL... STICKING UP FOR DIRTY JERRIES!
I'VE SERVED SIX MONTHS IN THE TRENCHES, BIG MOUTH... WHICH IS MORE THAN YOU'VE DONE!
OOOOHHH!
IT'S MRS. BOURNE'S BOY... CHARLEY! I RECKON HE'S TELLING THE TRUTH ABOUT THE ZEPPELIN!
PUT THE WORD OUT! AND ONE OF YOU TELL MY FAMILY! I'VE GOT TO GET DOWN TO THE MUNITION FACTORY... MY MUM'S ON THE NIGHT SHIFT!
MEANWHILE, THE ZEPPELIN, TOO, HAD BEEN DELAYED.
SHE IS STILL NOT RESPONDING TO THE WHEEL, HERR KAPITAN!
THE FABRIC ON THE HORIZONTAL STABILISING FIN HAS BEEN TORN OFF! WE MUST SEND SOME VOLUNTEERS OUT TO REPAIR IT!
MULLER! SCHMIDT! YOU MEN WERE CAUGHT SMOKING BEHIND THE HANGARS... A SERIOUS OFFENCE! IF YOU VOLUNTEER FOR THIS MISSION, THE CHARGES AGAINST YOU WILL BE DROPPED!
WE VOLUNTEER, HERR KAPITAN!
INSIDE THE ZEPPELIN, OTHER RIGGERS WERE PATCHING GASBAGS TORN BY SHRAPNEL.
GOOD LUCK, YOU TWO! YOU'RE GOING TO NEED IT!
ACH, A MAN MAKES HIS OWN LUCK!

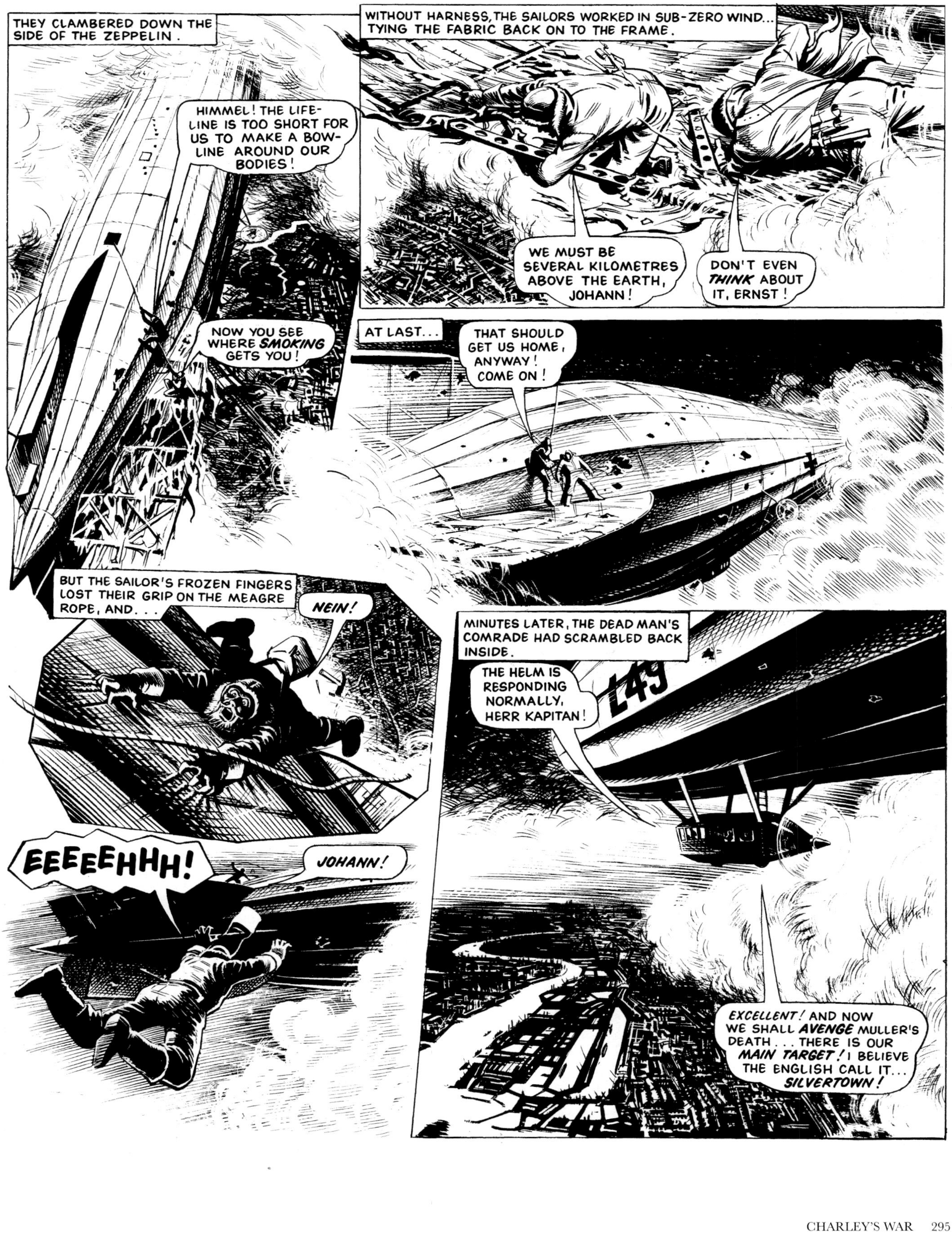

THEY CLAMBERED DOWN THE SIDE OF THE ZEPPELIN.
HIMMEL! THE LIFE-LINE IS TOO SHORT FOR US TO MAKE A BOWLINE AROUND OUR BODIES!
NOW YOU SEE WHERE SMOKING GETS YOU!
WITHOUT HARNESS, THE SAILORS WORKED IN SUB-ZERO WIND... TYING THE FABRIC BACK ON TO THE FRAME.
WE MUST BE SEVERAL KILOMETRES ABOVE THE EARTH, JOHANN!
DON'T EVEN THINK ABOUT IT, ERNST!
AT LAST...
THAT SHOULD GET US HOME, ANYWAY! COME ON!
BUT THE SAILOR'S FROZEN FINGERS LOST THEIR GRIP ON THE MEAGRE ROPE, AND...
NEIN!
EEEEEHHH!
JOHANN!
MINUTES LATER, THE DEAD MAN'S COMRADE HAD SCRAMBLED BACK INSIDE.
THE HELM IS RESPONDING NORMALLY, HERR KAPITAN!
L49
EXCELLENT! AND NOW WE SHALL AVENGE MULLER'S DEATH... THERE IS OUR MAIN TARGET! I BELIEVE THE ENGLISH CALL IT... SILVERTOWN!

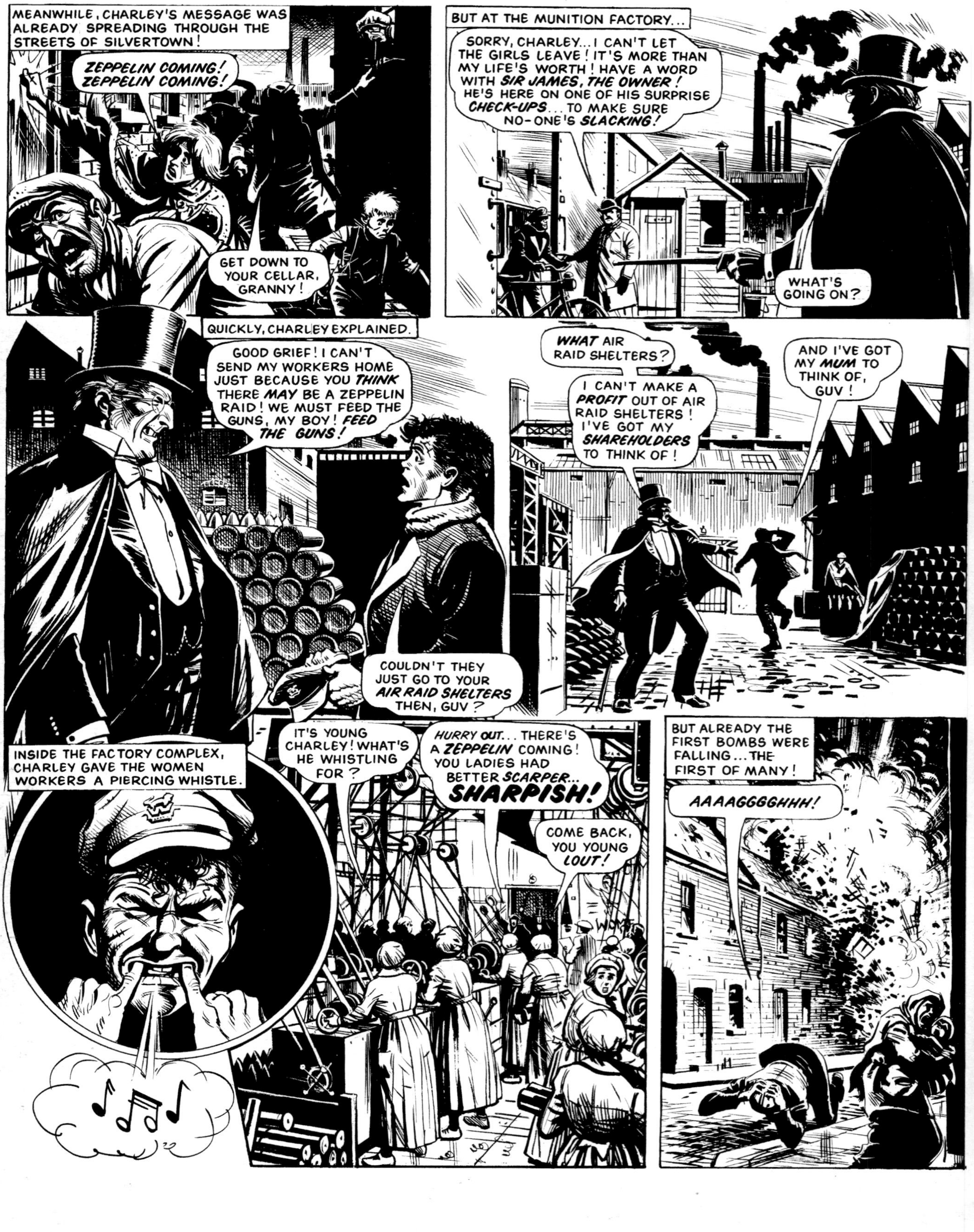
MEANWHILE, CHARLEY'S MESSAGE WAS ALREADY SPREADING THROUGH THE STREETS OF SILVERTOWN!
ZEPPELIN COMING! ZEPPELIN COMING!
GET DOWN TO YOUR CELLAR, GRANNY!
BUT AT THE MUNITION FACTORY...
SORRY, CHARLEY... I CAN'T LET THE GIRLS LEAVE! IT'S MORE THAN MY LIFE'S WORTH! HAVE A WORD WITH SIR JAMES, THE OWNER! HE'S HERE ON ONE OF HIS SURPRISE CHECK-UPS... TO MAKE SURE NO-ONE'S SLACKING!
WHAT'S GOING ON?
QUICKLY, CHARLEY EXPLAINED.
GOOD GRIEF! I CAN'T SEND MY WORKERS HOME JUST BECAUSE YOU THINK THERE MAY BE A ZEPPELIN RAID! WE MUST FEED THE GUNS, MY BOY! FEED THE GUNS!
COULDN'T THEY JUST GO TO YOUR AIR RAID SHELTERS THEN, GUV?
WHAT AIR RAID SHELTERS?
I CAN'T MAKE A PROFIT OUT OF AIR RAID SHELTERS! I'VE GOT MY SHAREHOLDERS TO THINK OF!
AND I'VE GOT MY MUM TO THINK OF, GUV!
INSIDE THE FACTORY COMPLEX, CHARLEY GAVE THE WOMEN WORKERS A PIERCING WHISTLE.
IT'S YOUNG CHARLEY! WHAT'S HE WHISTLING FOR?
HURRY OUT... THERE'S A ZEPPELIN COMING! YOU LADIES HAD BETTER SCARPER... SHARPISH!
COME BACK, YOU YOUNG LOUT!
BUT ALREADY THE FIRST BOMBS WERE FALLING... THE FIRST OF MANY!
AAAAGGGGHHH!

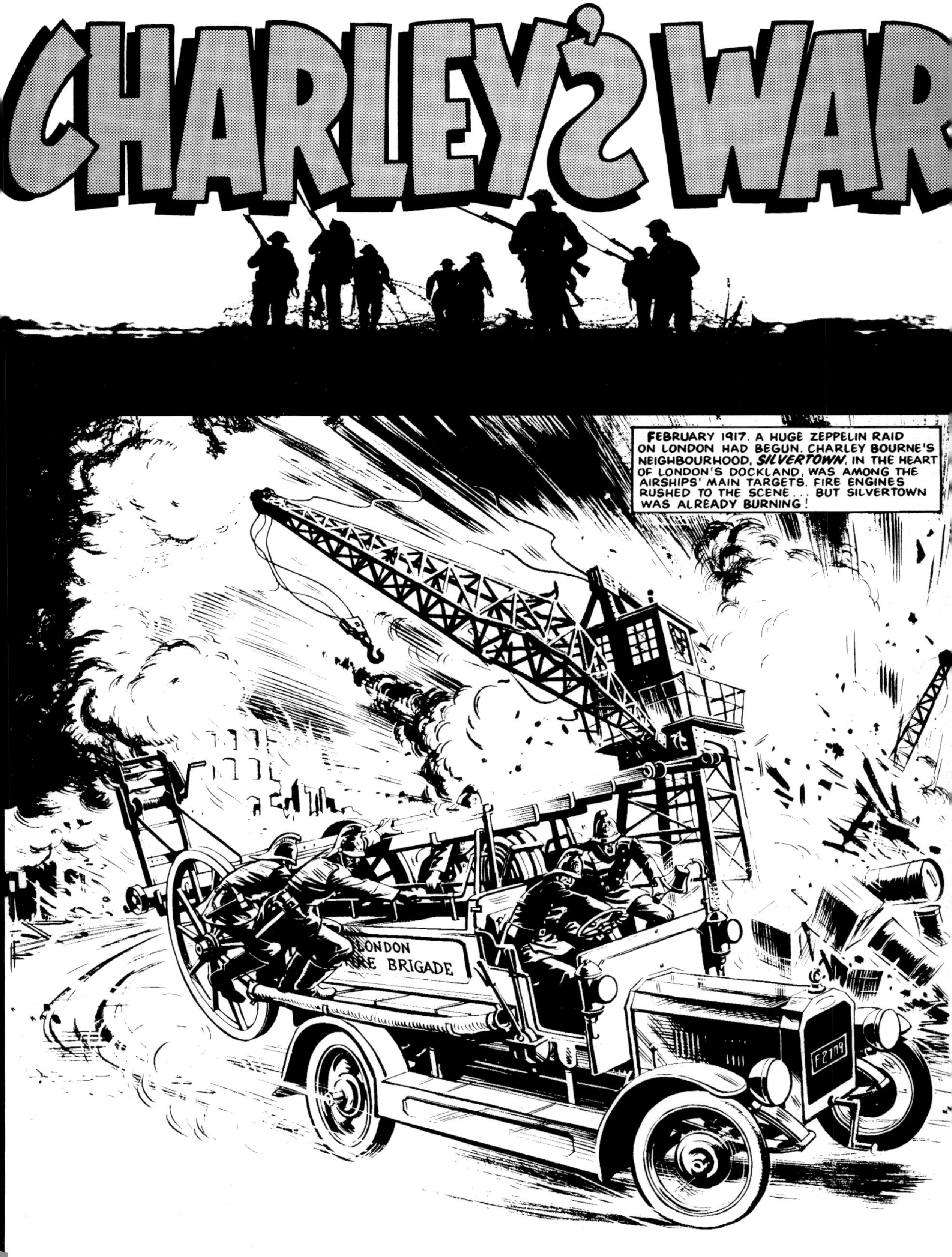
CHARLEY'S WAR
FEBRUARY 1917. A HUGE ZEPPELIN RAID ON LONDON HAD BEGUN. CHARLEY BOURNE'S NEIGHBOURHOOD, SILVERTOWN, IN THE HEART OF LONDON'S DOCKLAND, WAS AMONG THE AIRSHIPS' MAIN TARGETS. FIRE ENGINES RUSHED TO THE SCENE... BUT SILVERTOWN WAS ALREADY BURNING!
LONDON
FIRE BRIGADE

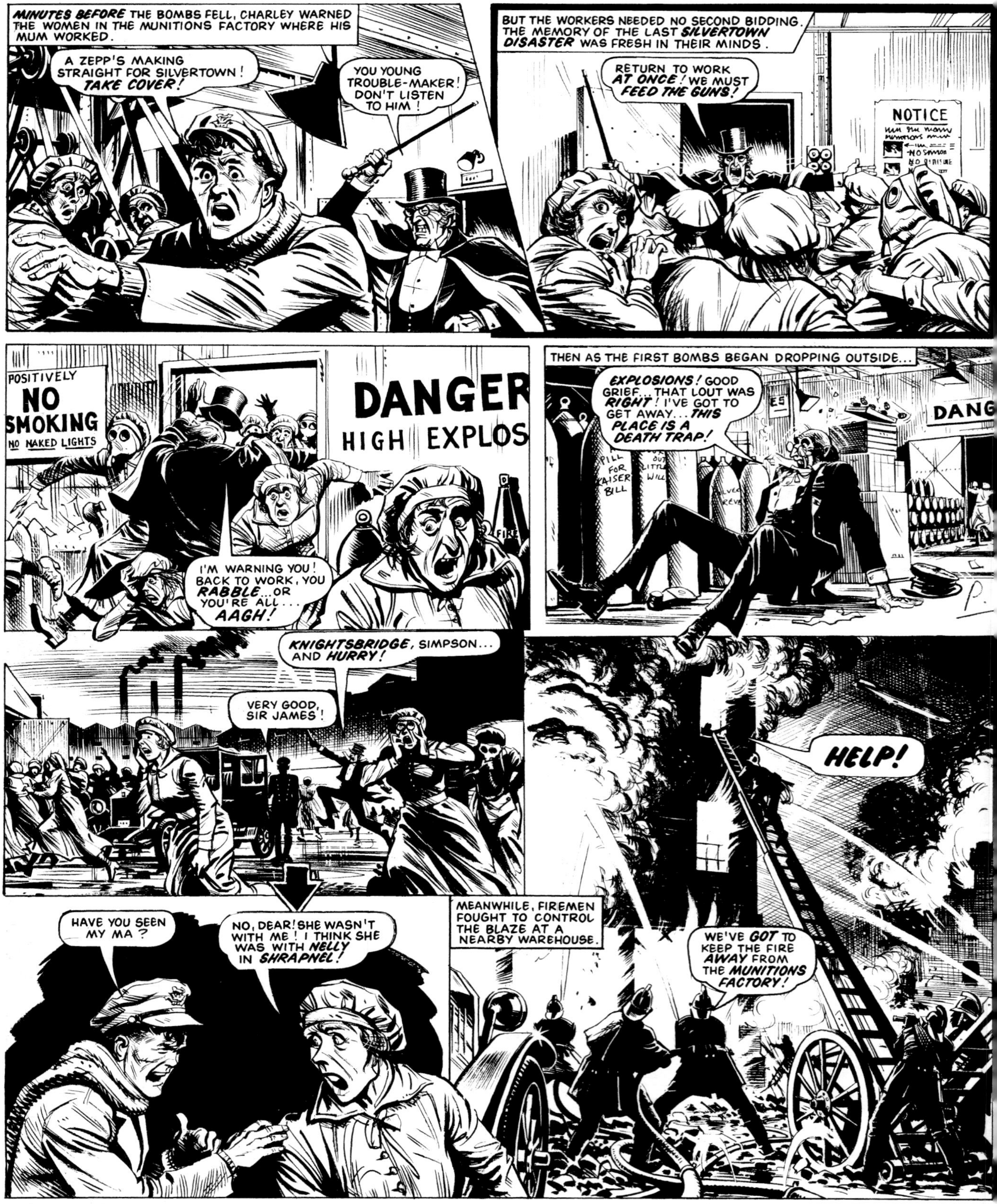
MINUTES BEFORE THE BOMBS FELL, CHARLEY WARNED THE WOMEN IN THE MUNITIONS FACTORY WHERE HIS MUM WORKED.
A ZEPP'S MAKING STRAIGHT FOR SILVERTOWN! TAKE COVER!
YOU YOUNG TROUBLE-MAKER! DON'T LISTEN TO HIM!
BUT THE WORKERS NEEDED NO SECOND BIDDING. THE MEMORY OF THE LAST SILVERTOWN DISASTER WAS FRESH IN THEIR MINDS.
RETURN TO WORK AT ONCE! WE MUST FEED THE GUNS!
NOTICE
POSITIVELY NO SMOKING
NO NAKED LIGHTS
DANGER
HIGH EXPLOS
I'M WARNING YOU! BACK TO WORK, YOU RABBLE... OR YOU'RE ALL... AAGH!
THEN AS THE FIRST BOMBS BEGAN DROPPING OUTSIDE...
EXPLOSIONS! GOOD GRIEF... THAT LOUT WAS RIGHT! I'VE GOT TO GET AWAY... THIS PLACE IS A DEATH TRAP!
DANG
KNIGHTSBRIDGE, SIMPSON... AND HURRY!
VERY GOOD, SIR JAMES!
HELP!
HAVE YOU SEEN MY MA?
NO, DEAR! SHE WASN'T WITH ME! I THINK SHE WAS WITH NELLY IN SHRAPNEL!
MEANWHILE, FIREMEN FOUGHT TO CONTROL THE BLAZE AT A NEARBY WAREHOUSE.
WE'VE GOT TO KEEP THE FIRE AWAY FROM THE MUNITIONS FACTORY!

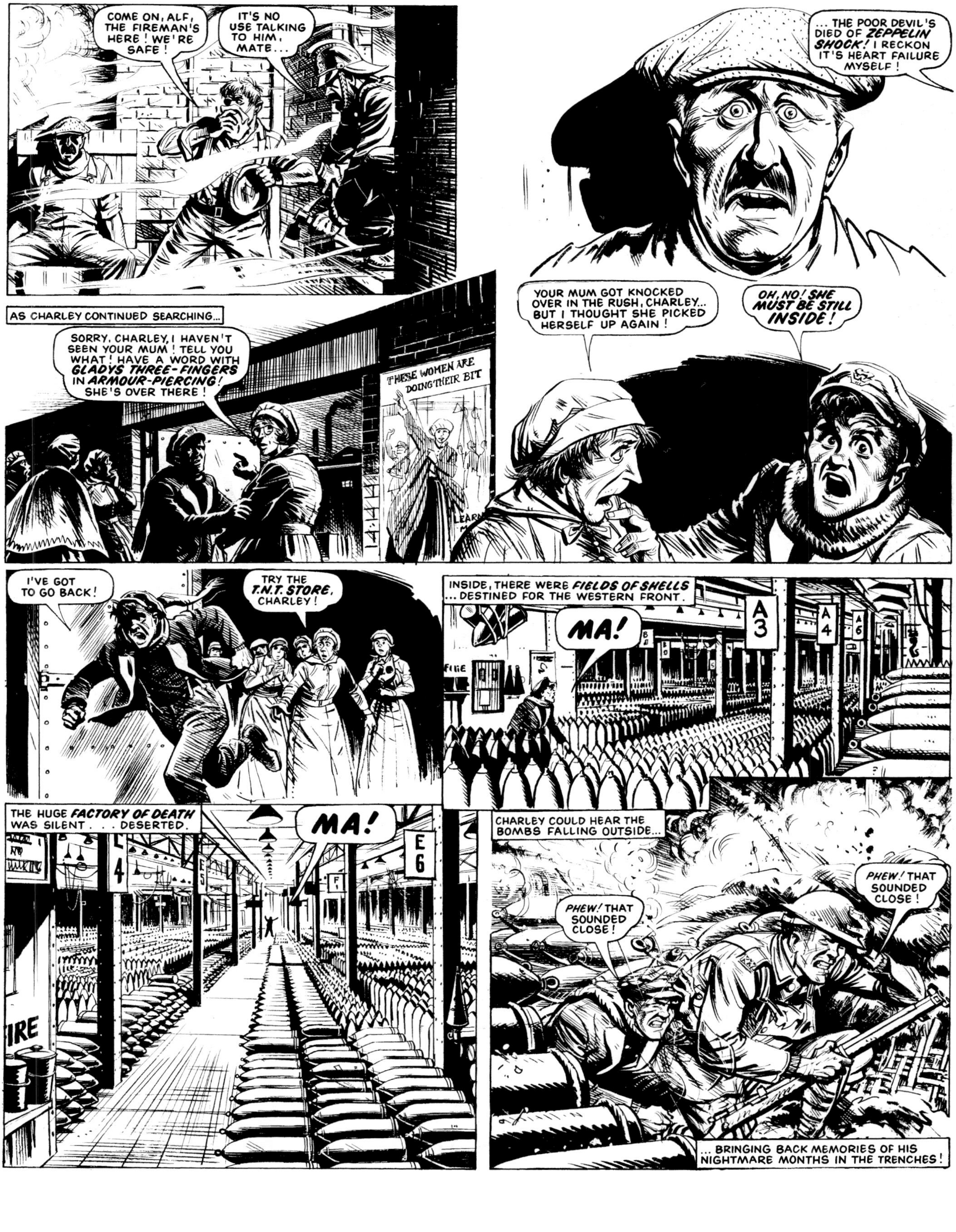

COME ON, ALF, THE FIREMAN'S HERE! WE'RE SAFE!
IT'S NO USE TALKING TO HIM, MATE...
... THE POOR DEVIL'S DIED OF ZEPPELIN SHOCK! I RECKON IT'S HEART FAILURE MYSELF!
AS CHARLEY CONTINUED SEARCHING...
SORRY, CHARLEY, I HAVEN'T SEEN YOUR MUM! TELL YOU WHAT! HAVE A WORD WITH GLADYS THREE-FINGERS IN ARMOUR-PIERCING! SHE'S OVER THERE!
THESE WOMEN ARE DOING THEIR BIT
YOUR MUM GOT KNOCKED OVER IN THE RUSH, CHARLEY... BUT I THOUGHT SHE PICKED HERSELF UP AGAIN!
OH, NO! SHE MUST BE STILL INSIDE!
I'VE GOT TO GO BACK!
TRY THE T.N.T. STORE, CHARLEY!
INSIDE, THERE WERE FIELDS OF SHELLS ... DESTINED FOR THE WESTERN FRONT.
MA!
THE HUGE FACTORY OF DEATH WAS SILENT . . . DESERTED.
MA!
CHARLEY COULD HEAR THE BOMBS FALLING OUTSIDE...
PHEW! THAT SOUNDED CLOSE!
PHEW! THAT SOUNDED CLOSE!
... BRINGING BACK MEMORIES OF HIS NIGHTMARE MONTHS IN THE TRENCHES!

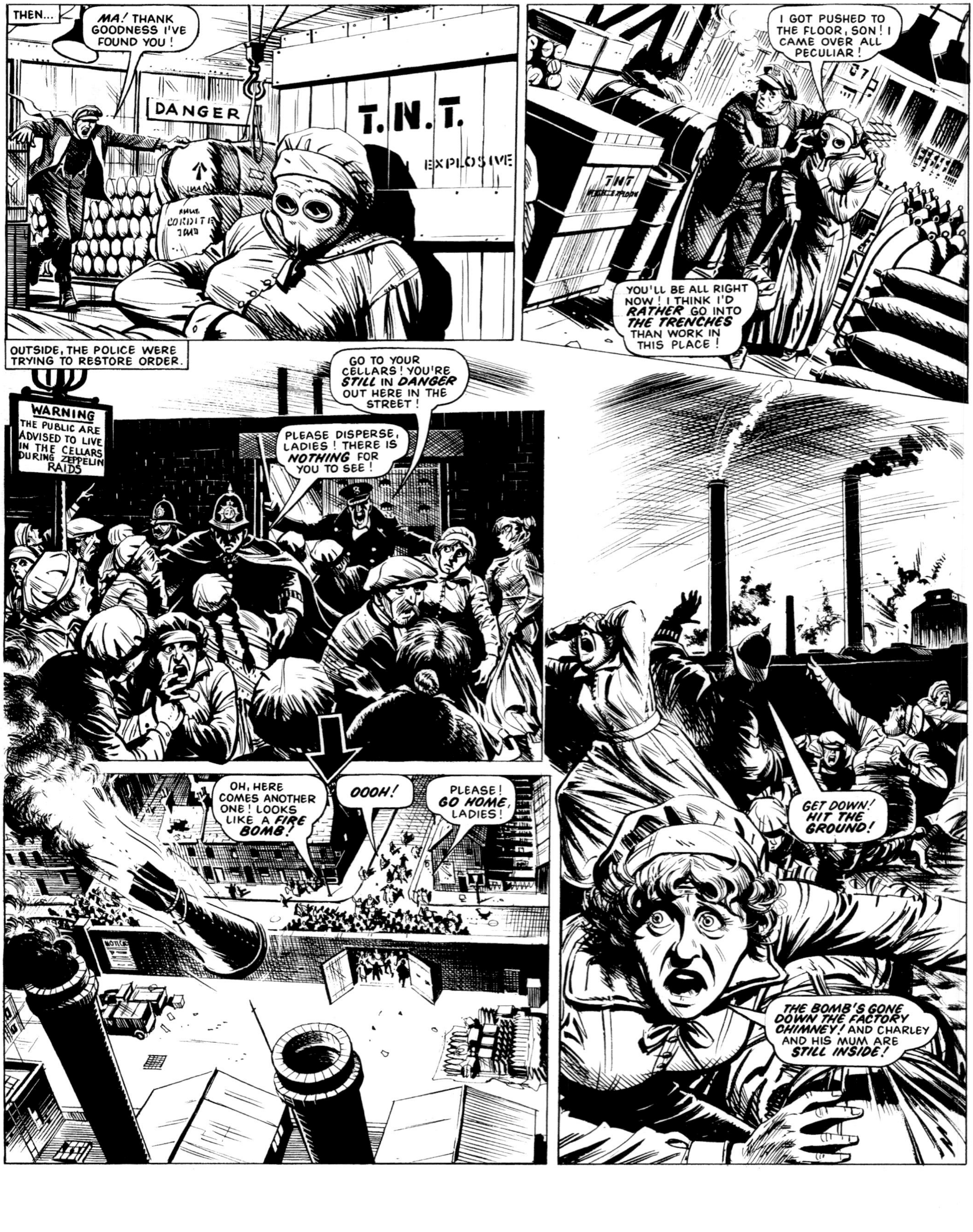
THEN...
MA! THANK GOODNESS I'VE FOUND YOU!
DANGER
T.N.T.
EXPLOSIVE
CORDITE
I GOT PUSHED TO THE FLOOR, SON! I CAME OVER ALL PECULIAR!
YOU'LL BE ALL RIGHT NOW! I THINK I'D RATHER GO INTO THE TRENCHES THAN WORK IN THIS PLACE!
OUTSIDE, THE POLICE WERE TRYING TO RESTORE ORDER.
WARNING THE PUBLIC ARE ADVISED TO LIVE IN THE CELLARS DURING ZEPPELIN RAIDS
GO TO YOUR CELLARS! YOU'RE STILL IN DANGER OUT HERE IN THE STREET!
PLEASE DISPERSE, LADIES! THERE IS NOTHING FOR YOU TO SEE!
OH, HERE COMES ANOTHER ONE! LOOKS LIKE A FIRE BOMB!
OOOH!
PLEASE! GO HOME, LADIES!
GET DOWN! HIT THE GROUND!
THE BOMB'S GONE DOWN THE FACTORY CHIMNEY! AND CHARLEY AND HIS MUM ARE STILL INSIDE!

Charley's War

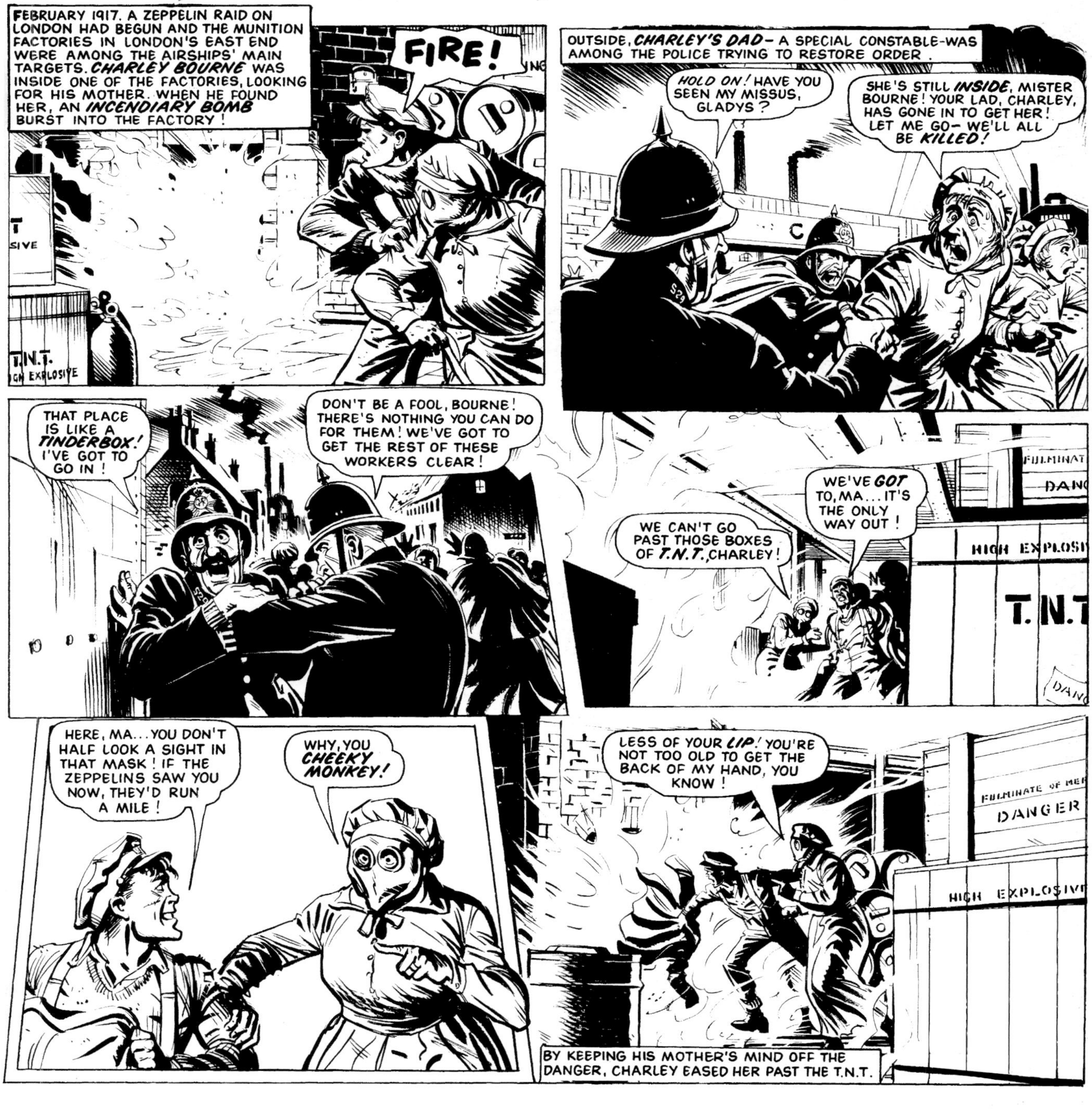

FEBRUARY 1917. A ZEPPELIN RAID ON LONDON HAD BEGUN AND THE MUNITION FACTORIES IN LONDON'S EAST END WERE AMONG THE AIRSHIPS' MAIN TARGETS. CHARLEY BOURNE WAS INSIDE ONE OF THE FACTORIES, LOOKING FOR HIS MOTHER. WHEN HE FOUND HER, AN INCENDIARY BOMB BURST INTO THE FACTORY!
FIRE!
T.N.T.
OUTSIDE, CHARLEY'S DAD – A SPECIAL CONSTABLE – WAS AMONG THE POLICE TRYING TO RESTORE ORDER.
HOLD ON! HAVE YOU SEEN MY MISSUS, GLADYS?
SHE'S STILL INSIDE, MISTER BOURNE! YOUR LAD, CHARLEY, HAS GONE IN TO GET HER! LET ME GO – WE'LL ALL BE KILLED!
THAT PLACE IS LIKE A TINDERBOX! I'VE GOT TO GO IN!
DON'T BE A FOOL, BOURNE! THERE'S NOTHING YOU CAN DO FOR THEM! WE'VE GOT TO GET THE REST OF THESE WORKERS CLEAR!
WE CAN'T GO PAST THOSE BOXES OF T.N.T., CHARLEY!
WE'VE GOT TO, MA... IT'S THE ONLY WAY OUT!
T.N.T
HERE, MA... YOU DON'T HALF LOOK A SIGHT IN THAT MASK! IF THE ZEPPELINS SAW YOU NOW, THEY'D RUN A MILE!
WHY, YOU CHEEKY MONKEY!
LESS OF YOUR LIP! YOU'RE NOT TOO OLD TO GET THE BACK OF MY HAND, YOU KNOW!
DANGER
BY KEEPING HIS MOTHER'S MIND OFF THE DANGER, CHARLEY EASED HER PAST THE T.N.T.

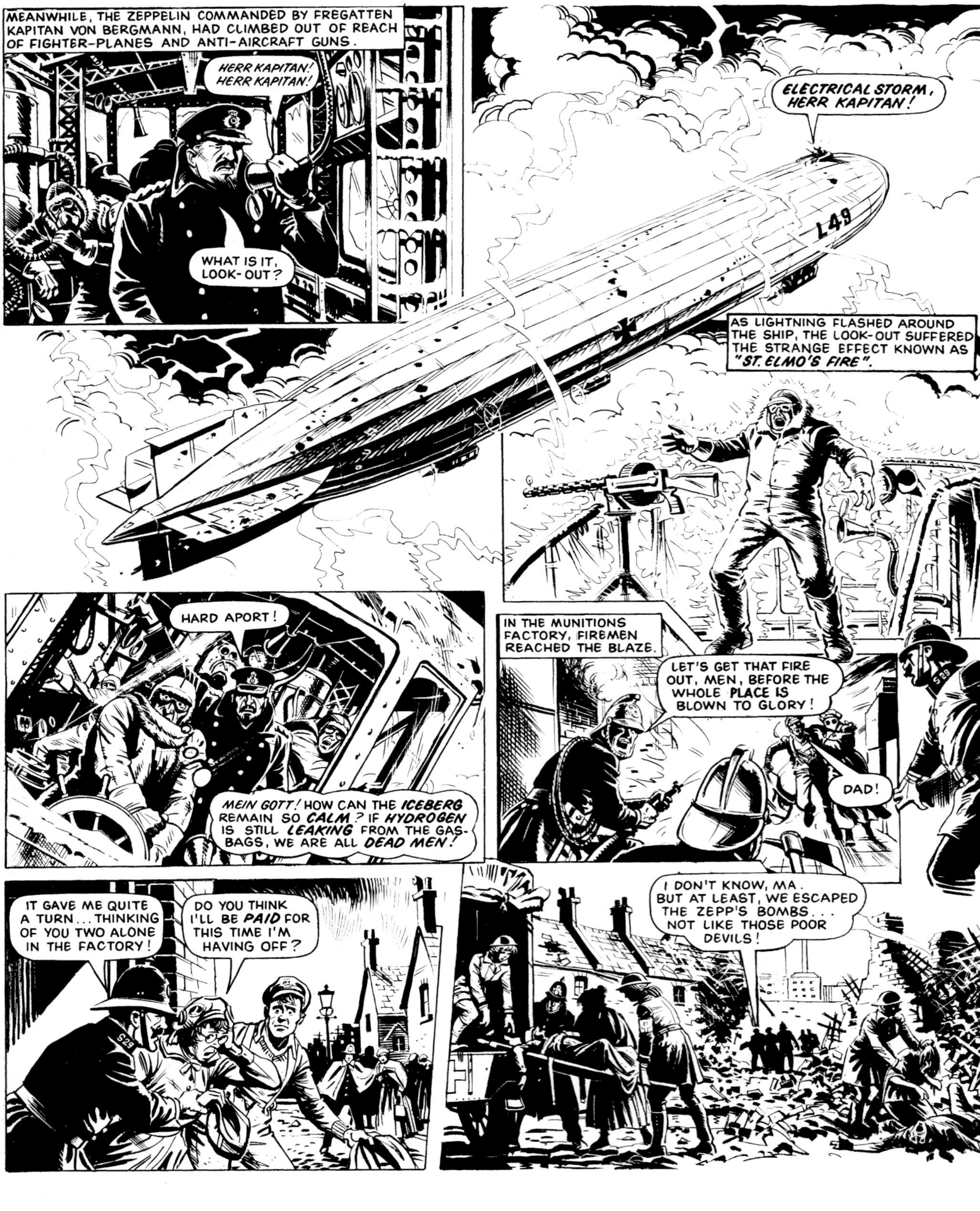
MEANWHILE, THE ZEPPELIN COMMANDED BY FREGATTEN KAPITAN VON BERGMANN, HAD CLIMBED OUT OF REACH OF FIGHTER-PLANES AND ANTI-AIRCRAFT GUNS.
HERR KAPITAN! HERR KAPITAN!
WHAT IS IT, LOOK-OUT?
ELECTRICAL STORM, HERR KAPITAN!
L49
AS LIGHTNING FLASHED AROUND THE SHIP, THE LOOK-OUT SUFFERED THE STRANGE EFFECT KNOWN AS "ST. ELMO'S FIRE".
HARD APORT!
MEIN GOTT! HOW CAN THE ICEBERG REMAIN SO CALM? IF HYDROGEN IS STILL LEAKING FROM THE GAS-BAGS, WE ARE ALL DEAD MEN!
IN THE MUNITIONS FACTORY, FIREMEN REACHED THE BLAZE.
LET'S GET THAT FIRE OUT, MEN, BEFORE THE WHOLE PLACE IS BLOWN TO GLORY!
DAD!
IT GAVE ME QUITE A TURN... THINKING OF YOU TWO ALONE IN THE FACTORY!
DO YOU THINK I'LL BE PAID FOR THIS TIME I'M HAVING OFF?
I DON'T KNOW, MA. BUT AT LEAST, WE ESCAPED THE ZEPP'S BOMBS... NOT LIKE THOSE POOR DEVILS!

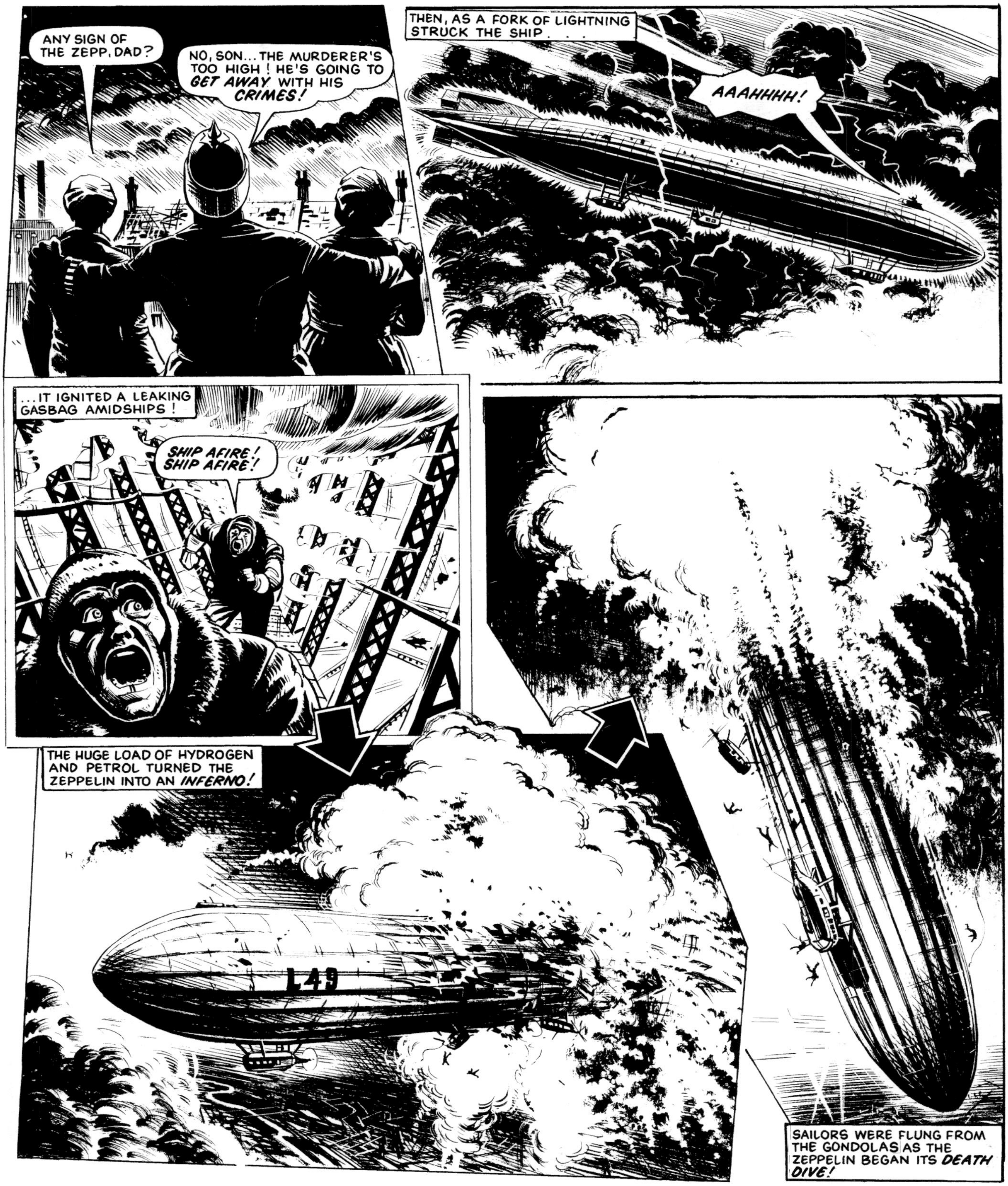
ANY SIGN OF THE ZEPP, DAD?
NO, SON... THE MURDERER'S TOO HIGH! HE'S GOING TO GET AWAY WITH HIS CRIMES!
THEN, AS A FORK OF LIGHTNING STRUCK THE SHIP . . .
AAAHHHH!
...IT IGNITED A LEAKING GASBAG AMIDSHIPS!
SHIP AFIRE! SHIP AFIRE!
THE HUGE LOAD OF HYDROGEN AND PETROL TURNED THE ZEPPELIN INTO AN INFERNO!
L49
SAILORS WERE FLUNG FROM THE GONDOLAS AS THE ZEPPELIN BEGAN ITS DEATH DIVE!

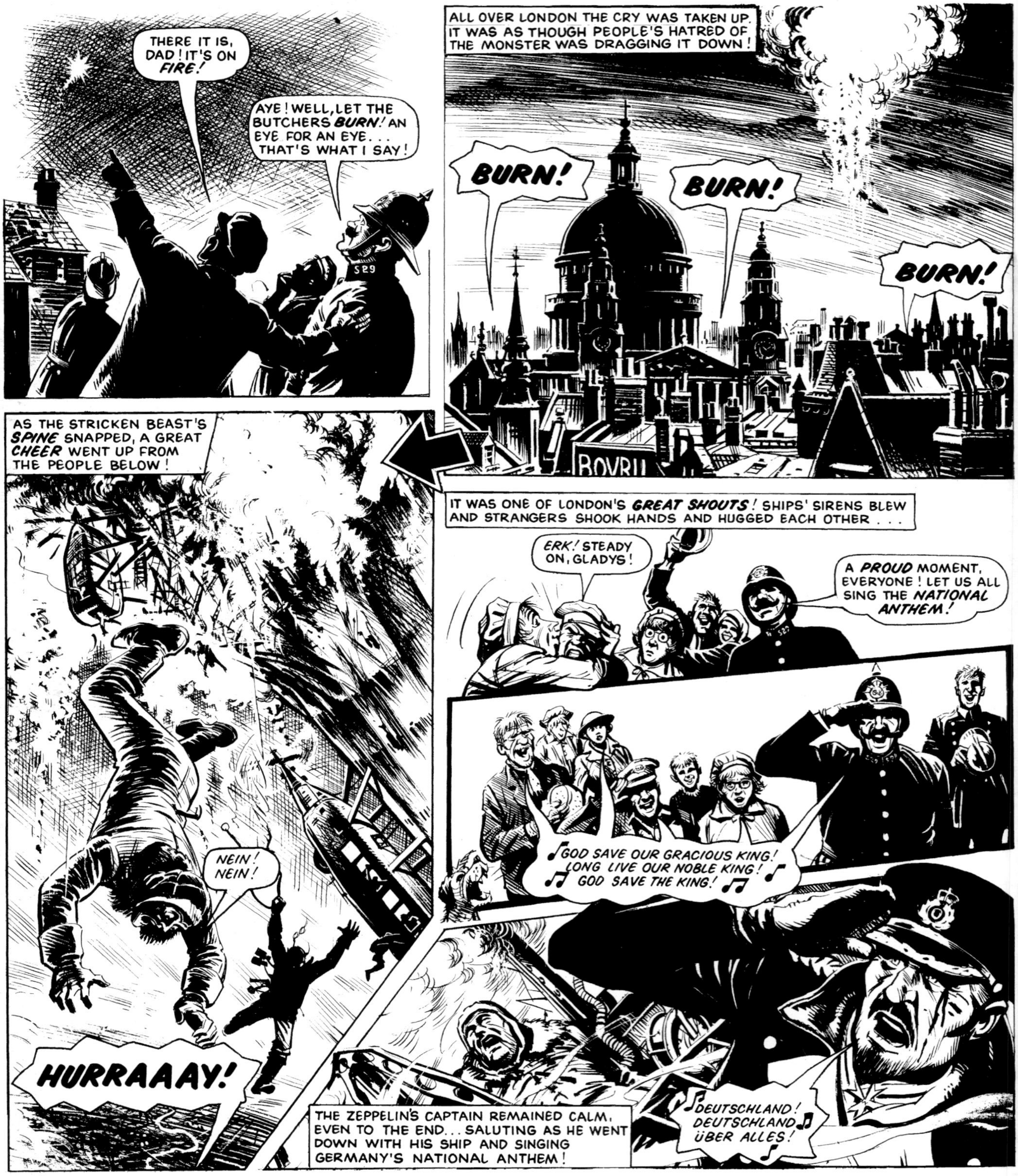
THERE IT IS, DAD! IT'S ON FIRE!
AYE! WELL, LET THE BUTCHERS BURN! AN EYE FOR AN EYE... THAT'S WHAT I SAY!
S29
ALL OVER LONDON THE CRY WAS TAKEN UP. IT WAS AS THOUGH PEOPLE'S HATRED OF THE MONSTER WAS DRAGGING IT DOWN!
BURN!
BURN!
BURN!
BOVRIL
AS THE STRICKEN BEAST'S SPINE SNAPPED, A GREAT CHEER WENT UP FROM THE PEOPLE BELOW!
NEIN! NEIN!
HURRAAAY!
IT WAS ONE OF LONDON'S GREAT SHOUTS! SHIPS' SIRENS BLEW AND STRANGERS SHOOK HANDS AND HUGGED EACH OTHER...
ERK! STEADY ON, GLADYS!
A PROUD MOMENT, EVERYONE! LET US ALL SING THE NATIONAL ANTHEM!
GOD SAVE OUR GRACIOUS KING! LONG LIVE OUR NOBLE KING! GOD SAVE THE KING!
THE ZEPPELIN'S CAPTAIN REMAINED CALM, EVEN TO THE END... SALUTING AS HE WENT DOWN WITH HIS SHIP AND SINGING GERMANY'S NATIONAL ANTHEM!
DEUTSCHLAND! DEUTSCHLAND ÜBER ALLES!

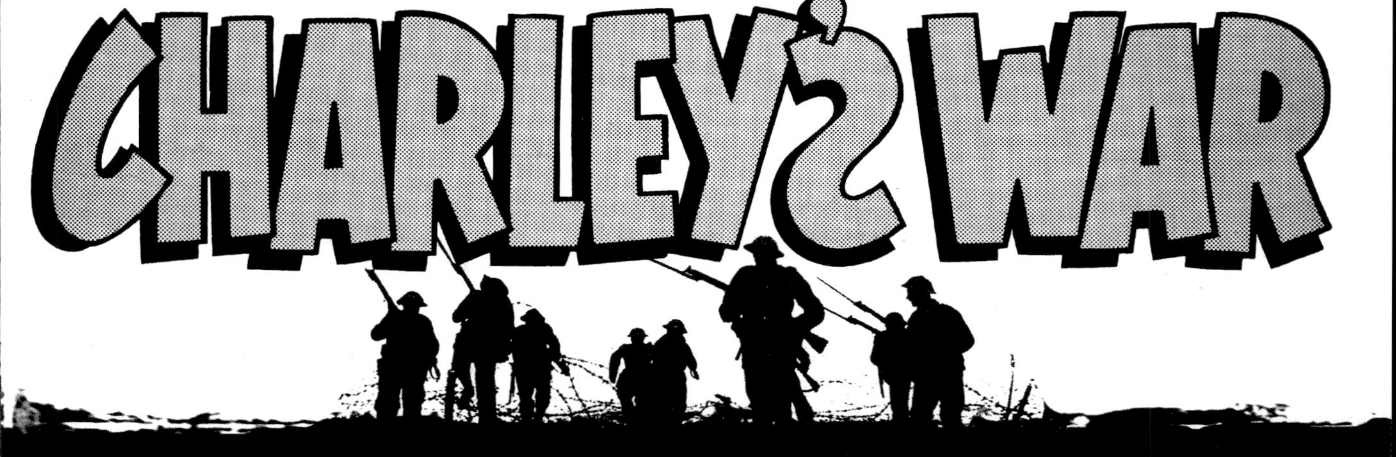
CHARLEY'S WAR

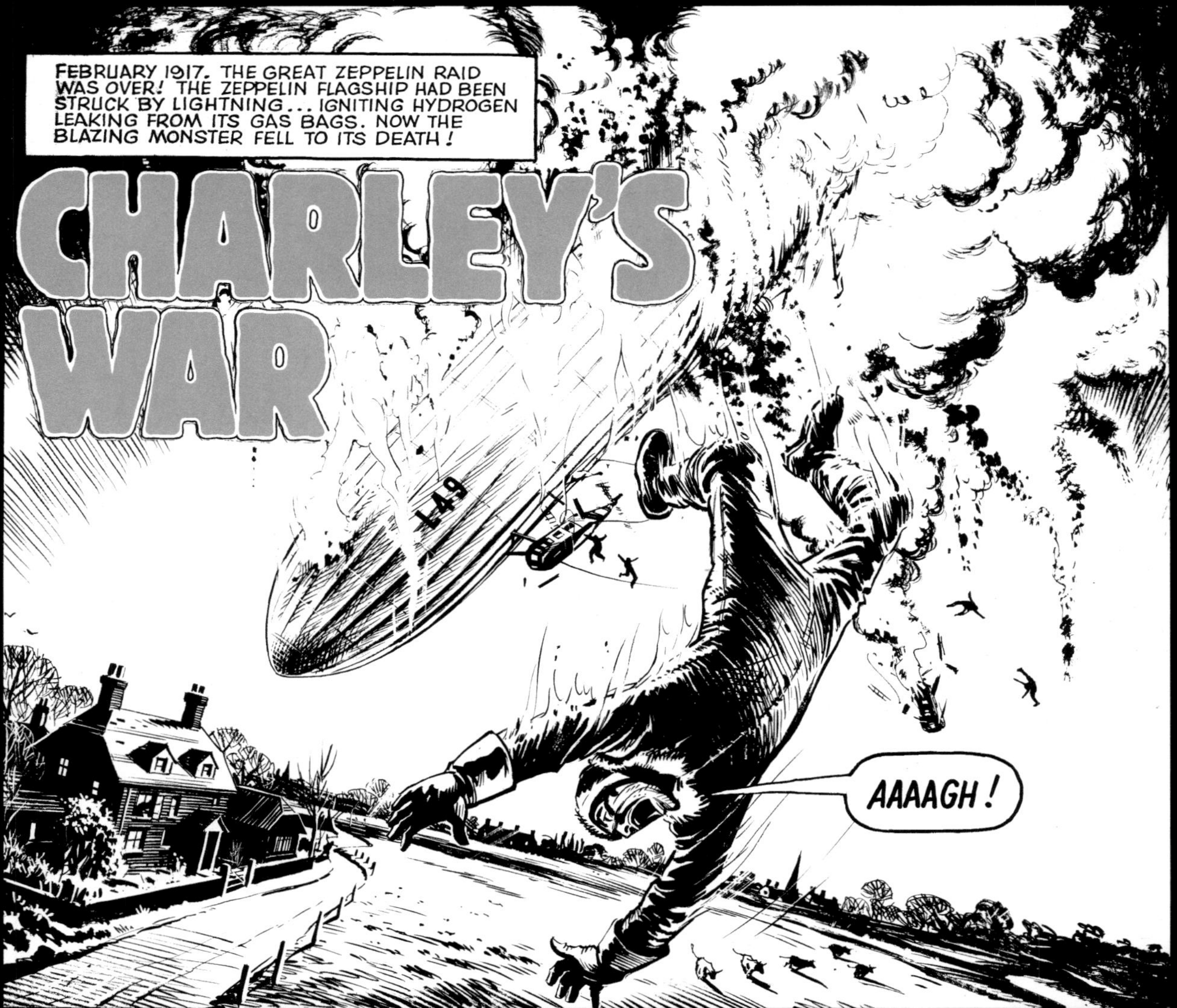
FEBRUARY 1917. THE GREAT ZEPPELIN RAID WAS OVER! THE ZEPPELIN FLAGSHIP HAD BEEN STRUCK BY LIGHTNING... IGNITING HYDROGEN LEAKING FROM ITS GAS BAGS. NOW THE BLAZING MONSTER FELL TO ITS DEATH!
CHARLEY'S WAR
L49
AAAAGH!

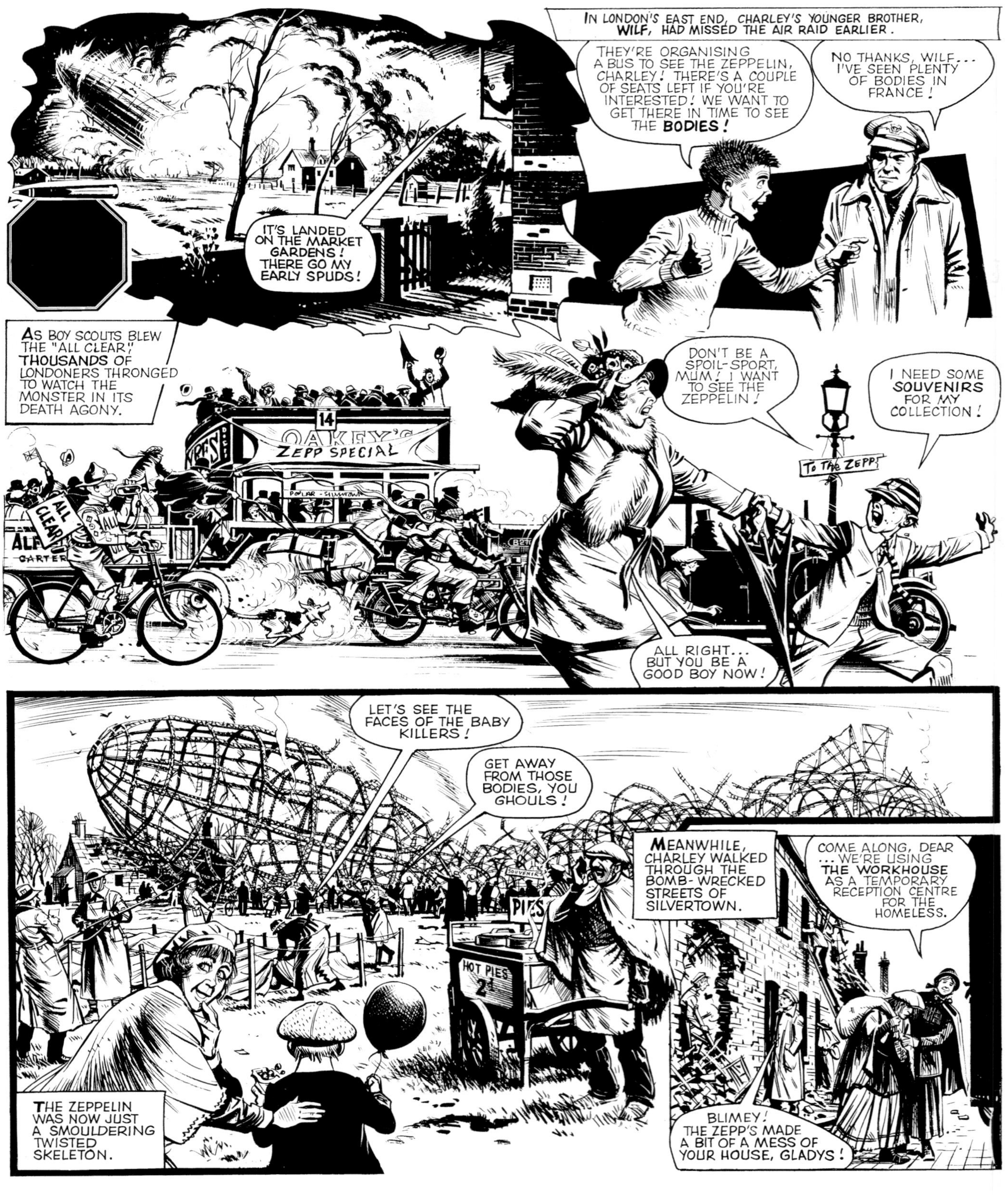
IT'S LANDED ON THE MARKET GARDENS! THERE GO MY EARLY SPUDS!
IN LONDON'S EAST END, CHARLEY'S YOUNGER BROTHER, WILF, HAD MISSED THE AIR RAID EARLIER.
THEY'RE ORGANISING A BUS TO SEE THE ZEPPELIN, CHARLEY! THERE'S A COUPLE OF SEATS LEFT IF YOU'RE INTERESTED! WE WANT TO GET THERE IN TIME TO SEE THE BODIES!
NO THANKS, WILF... I'VE SEEN PLENTY OF BODIES IN FRANCE!
AS BOY SCOUTS BLEW THE "ALL CLEAR," THOUSANDS OF LONDONERS THRONGED TO WATCH THE MONSTER IN ITS DEATH AGONY.
14
ZEPP SPECIAL
ALL CLEAR
DON'T BE A SPOIL-SPORT, MUM! I WANT TO SEE THE ZEPPELIN!
TO THE ZEPP
I NEED SOME SOUVENIRS FOR MY COLLECTION!
ALL RIGHT... BUT YOU BE A GOOD BOY NOW!
LET'S SEE THE FACES OF THE BABY KILLERS!
GET AWAY FROM THOSE BODIES, YOU GHOULS!
PIES
HOT PIES 2d
THE ZEPPELIN WAS NOW JUST A SMOULDERING TWISTED SKELETON.
MEANWHILE, CHARLEY WALKED THROUGH THE BOMB-WRECKED STREETS OF SILVERTOWN.
COME ALONG, DEAR ... WE'RE USING THE WORKHOUSE AS A TEMPORARY RECEPTION CENTRE FOR THE HOMELESS.
BLIMEY! THE ZEPP'S MADE A BIT OF A MESS OF YOUR HOUSE, GLADYS!

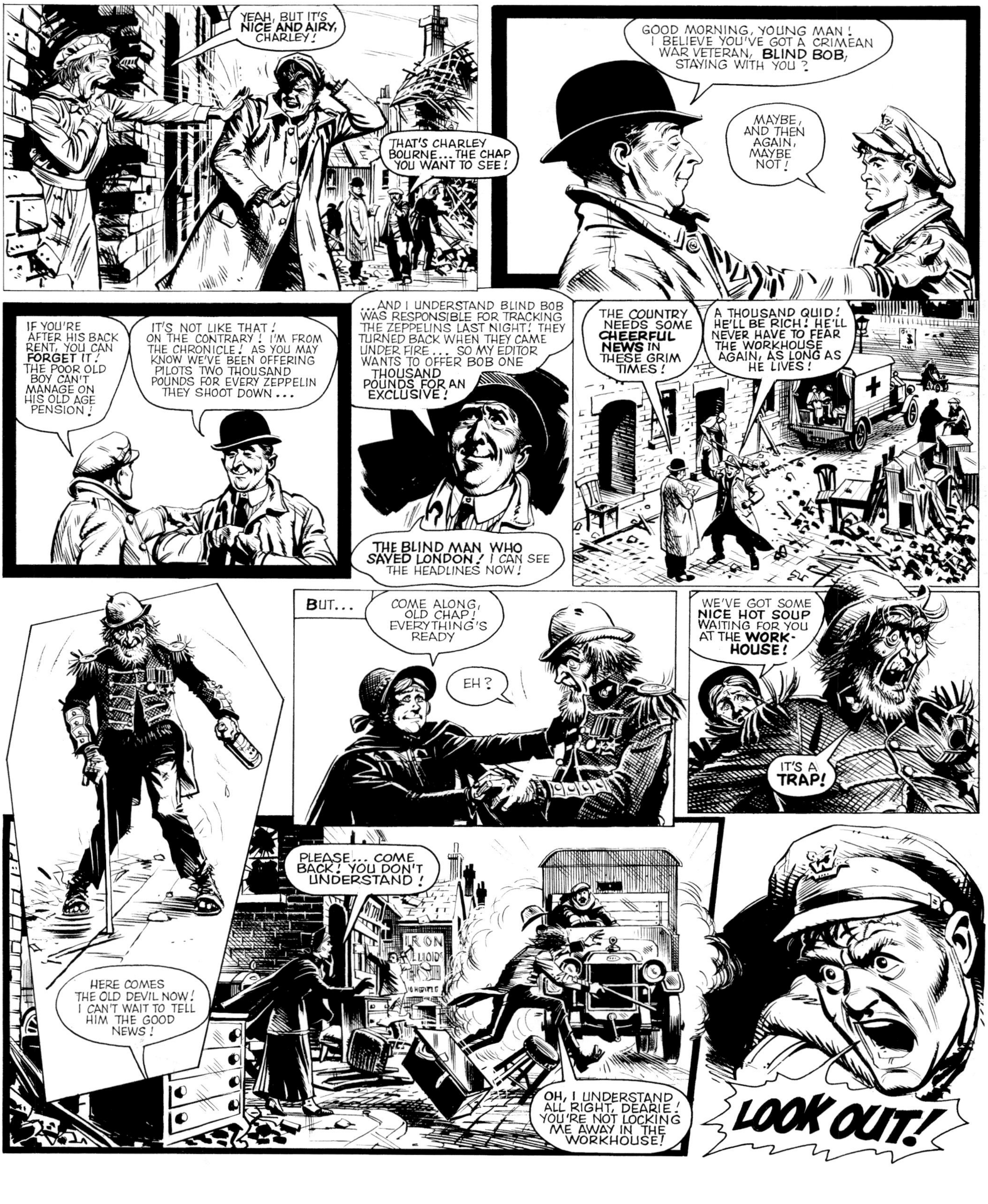

YEAH, BUT IT'S NICE AND AIRY, CHARLEY!
THAT'S CHARLEY BOURNE... THE CHAP YOU WANT TO SEE!
GOOD MORNING, YOUNG MAN! I BELIEVE YOU'VE GOT A CRIMEAN WAR VETERAN, BLIND BOB, STAYING WITH YOU?
MAYBE, AND THEN AGAIN, MAYBE NOT!
IF YOU'RE AFTER HIS BACK RENT, YOU CAN FORGET IT! THE POOR OLD BOY CAN'T MANAGE ON HIS OLD AGE PENSION!
IT'S NOT LIKE THAT! ON THE CONTRARY! I'M FROM THE CHRONICLE! AS YOU MAY KNOW WE'VE BEEN OFFERING PILOTS TWO THOUSAND POUNDS FOR EVERY ZEPPELIN THEY SHOOT DOWN...
...AND I UNDERSTAND BLIND BOB WAS RESPONSIBLE FOR TRACKING THE ZEPPELINS LAST NIGHT! THEY TURNED BACK WHEN THEY CAME UNDER FIRE... SO MY EDITOR WANTS TO OFFER BOB ONE THOUSAND POUNDS FOR AN EXCLUSIVE!
THE BLIND MAN WHO SAVED LONDON! I CAN SEE THE HEADLINES NOW!
THE COUNTRY NEEDS SOME CHEERFUL NEWS IN THESE GRIM TIMES!
A THOUSAND QUID! HE'LL BE RICH! HE'LL NEVER HAVE TO FEAR THE WORKHOUSE AGAIN, AS LONG AS HE LIVES!
HERE COMES THE OLD DEVIL NOW! I CAN'T WAIT TO TELL HIM THE GOOD NEWS!
BUT...
COME ALONG, OLD CHAP! EVERYTHING'S READY
EH?
WE'VE GOT SOME NICE HOT SOUP WAITING FOR YOU AT THE WORK-HOUSE!
IT'S A TRAP!
PLEASE... COME BACK! YOU DON'T UNDERSTAND!
IRON
OH, I UNDERSTAND ALL RIGHT, DEARIE! YOU'RE NOT LOCKING ME AWAY IN THE WORKHOUSE!
LOOK OUT!

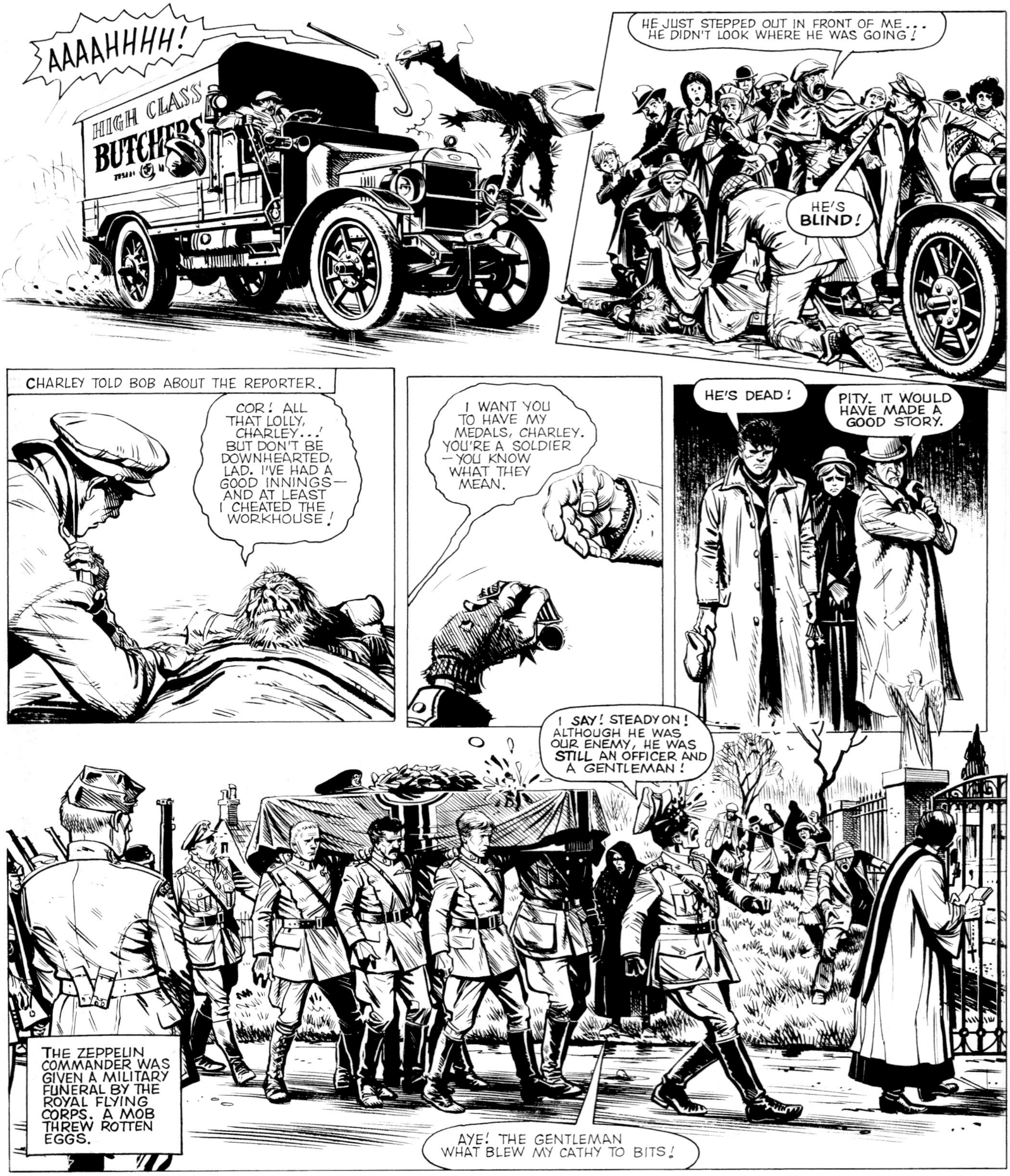

AAAAHHHH!
HIGH CLASS BUTCHERS
HE JUST STEPPED OUT IN FRONT OF ME... HE DIDN'T LOOK WHERE HE WAS GOING!
HE'S BLIND!
CHARLEY TOLD BOB ABOUT THE REPORTER.
COR! ALL THAT LOLLY, CHARLEY...! BUT DON'T BE DOWNHEARTED, LAD. I'VE HAD A GOOD INNINGS— AND AT LEAST I CHEATED THE WORKHOUSE!
I WANT YOU TO HAVE MY MEDALS, CHARLEY. YOU'RE A SOLDIER —YOU KNOW WHAT THEY MEAN.
HE'S DEAD!
PITY. IT WOULD HAVE MADE A GOOD STORY.
THE ZEPPELIN COMMANDER WAS GIVEN A MILITARY FUNERAL BY THE ROYAL FLYING CORPS. A MOB THREW ROTTEN EGGS.
I SAY! STEADY ON! ALTHOUGH HE WAS OUR ENEMY, HE WAS STILL AN OFFICER AND A GENTLEMAN!
AYE! THE GENTLEMAN WHAT BLEW MY CATHY TO BITS!

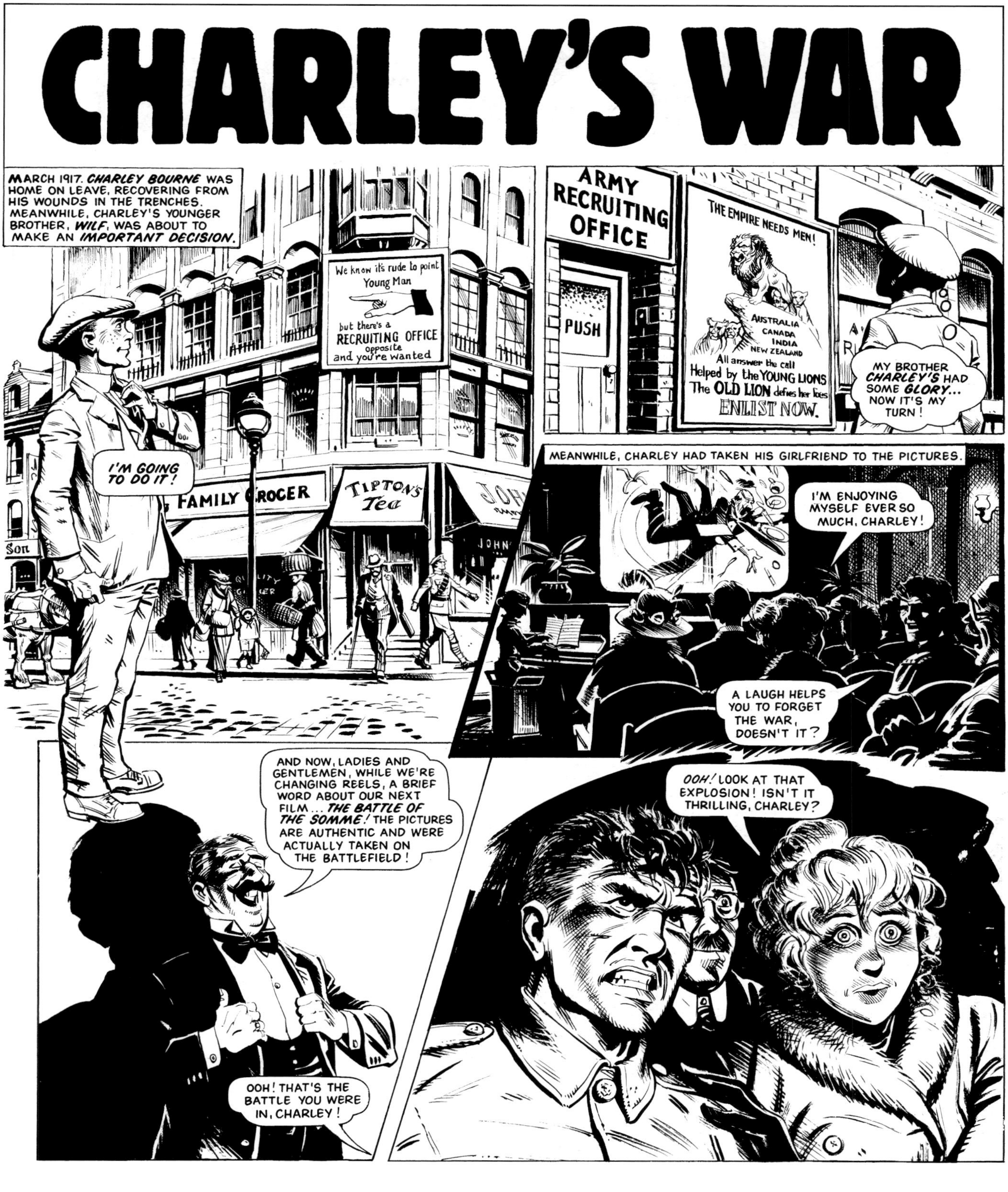
CHARLEY'S WAR
MARCH 1917. CHARLEY BOURNE WAS HOME ON LEAVE, RECOVERING FROM HIS WOUNDS IN THE TRENCHES. MEANWHILE, CHARLEY'S YOUNGER BROTHER, WILF, WAS ABOUT TO MAKE AN IMPORTANT DECISION.
We know it's rude to point Young Man but there's a RECRUITING OFFICE opposite and you're wanted
ARMY RECRUITING OFFICE
PUSH
THE EMPIRE NEEDS MEN! AUSTRALIA CANADA INDIA NEW ZEALAND All answer the call Helped by the YOUNG LIONS The OLD LION defies her foes ENLIST NOW.
MY BROTHER CHARLEY'S HAD SOME GLORY... NOW IT'S MY TURN!
I'M GOING TO DO IT!
FAMILY GROCER
TIPTON'S Tea
MEANWHILE, CHARLEY HAD TAKEN HIS GIRLFRIEND TO THE PICTURES.
I'M ENJOYING MYSELF EVER SO MUCH, CHARLEY!
A LAUGH HELPS YOU TO FORGET THE WAR, DOESN'T IT?
AND NOW, LADIES AND GENTLEMEN, WHILE WE'RE CHANGING REELS, A BRIEF WORD ABOUT OUR NEXT FILM... THE BATTLE OF THE SOMME! THE PICTURES ARE AUTHENTIC AND WERE ACTUALLY TAKEN ON THE BATTLEFIELD!
OOH! THAT'S THE BATTLE YOU WERE IN, CHARLEY!
OOH! LOOK AT THAT EXPLOSION! ISN'T IT THRILLING, CHARLEY?

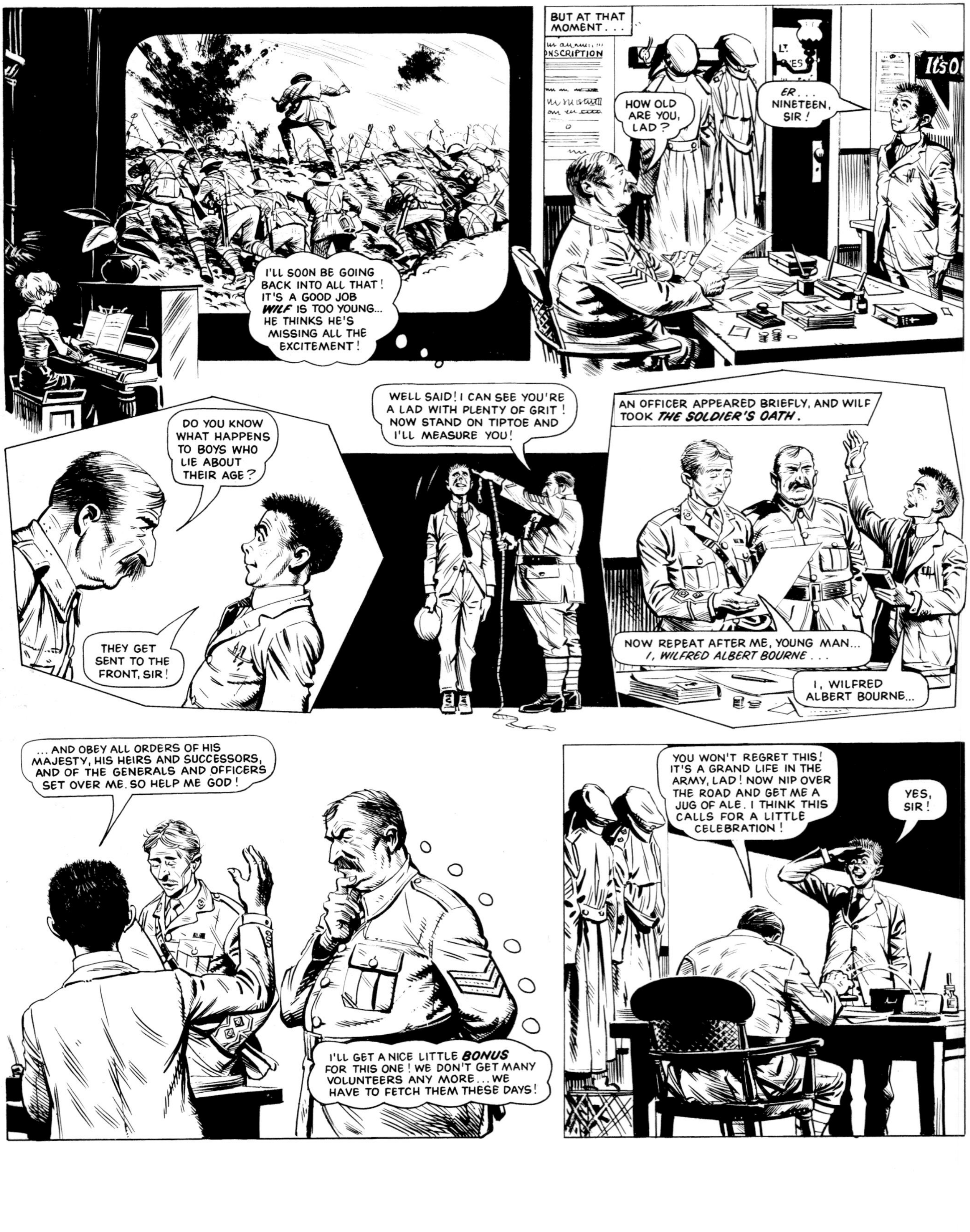
I'LL SOON BE GOING BACK INTO ALL THAT! IT'S A GOOD JOB WILF IS TOO YOUNG... HE THINKS HE'S MISSING ALL THE EXCITEMENT!
BUT AT THAT MOMENT...
HOW OLD ARE YOU, LAD?
ER... NINETEEN, SIR!
DO YOU KNOW WHAT HAPPENS TO BOYS WHO LIE ABOUT THEIR AGE?
THEY GET SENT TO THE FRONT, SIR!
WELL SAID! I CAN SEE YOU'RE A LAD WITH PLENTY OF GRIT! NOW STAND ON TIPTOE AND I'LL MEASURE YOU!
AN OFFICER APPEARED BRIEFLY, AND WILF TOOK THE SOLDIER'S OATH.
NOW REPEAT AFTER ME, YOUNG MAN... I, WILFRED ALBERT BOURNE...
I, WILFRED ALBERT BOURNE...
... AND OBEY ALL ORDERS OF HIS MAJESTY, HIS HEIRS AND SUCCESSORS, AND OF THE GENERALS AND OFFICERS SET OVER ME. SO HELP ME GOD!
I'LL GET A NICE LITTLE BONUS FOR THIS ONE! WE DON'T GET MANY VOLUNTEERS ANY MORE... WE HAVE TO FETCH THEM THESE DAYS!
YOU WON'T REGRET THIS! IT'S A GRAND LIFE IN THE ARMY, LAD! NOW NIP OVER THE ROAD AND GET ME A JUG OF ALE. I THINK THIS CALLS FOR A LITTLE CELEBRATION!
YES, SIR!

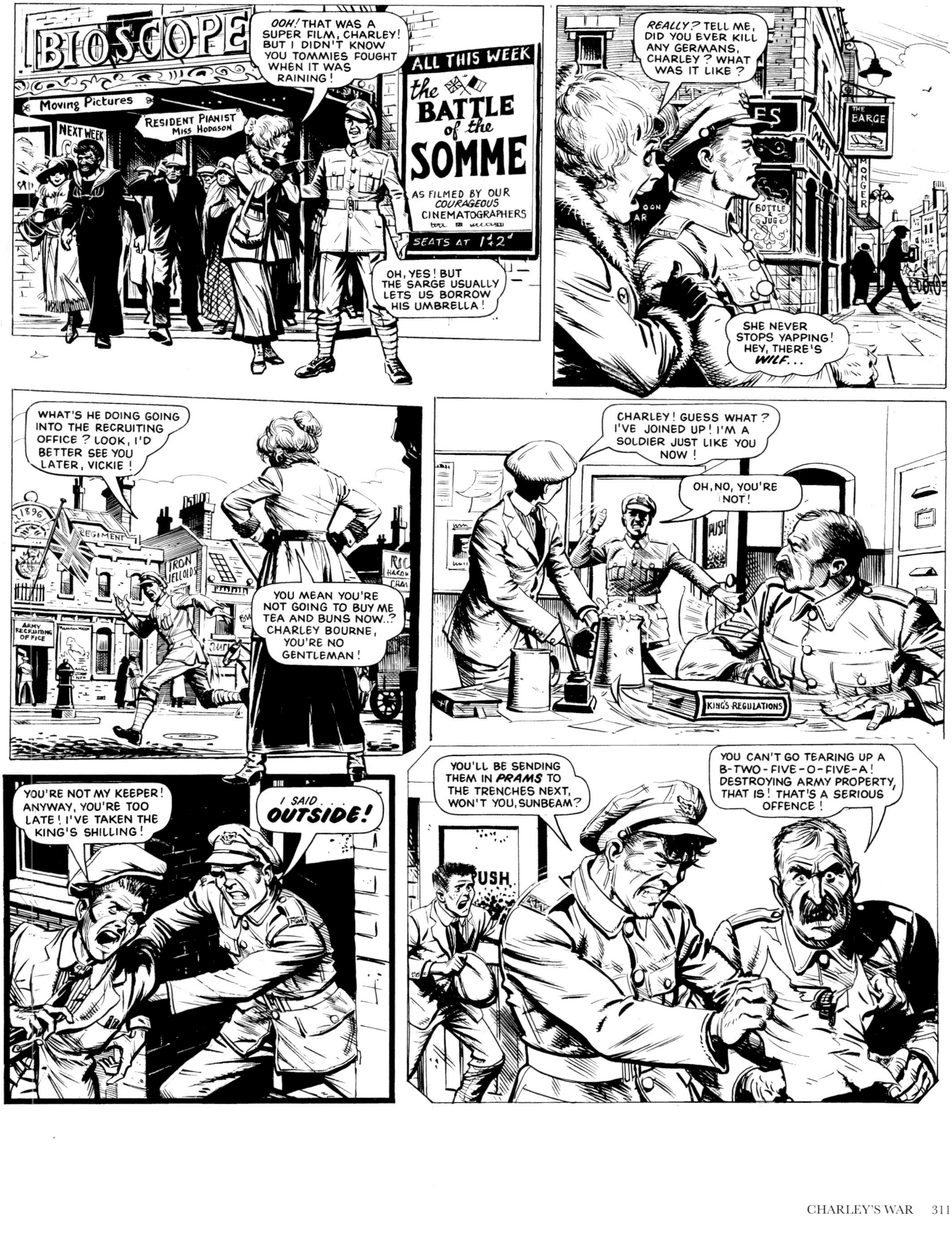
BIOSCOPE
Moving Pictures
RESIDENT PIANIST Miss HODGSON
NEXT WEEK
OOH! THAT WAS A SUPER FILM, CHARLEY! BUT I DIDN'T KNOW YOU TOMMIES FOUGHT WHEN IT WAS RAINING!
ALL THIS WEEK
the BATTLE of the SOMME
AS FILMED BY OUR COURAGEOUS CINEMATOGRAPHERS
SEATS AT 1 1/2 d
OH, YES! BUT THE SARGE USUALLY LETS US BORROW HIS UMBRELLA!
REALLY? TELL ME, DID YOU EVER KILL ANY GERMANS, CHARLEY? WHAT WAS IT LIKE?
THE BARGE
BOTTLE & JUG
SHE NEVER STOPS YAPPING! HEY, THERE'S WILF...
WHAT'S HE DOING GOING INTO THE RECRUITING OFFICE? LOOK, I'D BETTER SEE YOU LATER, VICKIE!
REGIMENT
IRON JELLOIDS
ARMY RECRUITING OFFICE
YOU MEAN YOU'RE NOT GOING TO BUY ME TEA AND BUNS NOW..? CHARLEY BOURNE, YOU'RE NO GENTLEMAN!
CHARLEY! GUESS WHAT? I'VE JOINED UP! I'M A SOLDIER JUST LIKE YOU NOW!
OH, NO, YOU'RE NOT!
PUSH
KING'S REGULATIONS
YOU'RE NOT MY KEEPER! ANYWAY, YOU'RE TOO LATE! I'VE TAKEN THE KING'S SHILLING!
I SAID OUTSIDE!
YOU'LL BE SENDING THEM IN PRAMS TO THE TRENCHES NEXT, WON'T YOU, SUNBEAM?
YOU CAN'T GO TEARING UP A B-TWO-FIVE-O-FIVE-A! DESTROYING ARMY PROPERTY, THAT IS! THAT'S A SERIOUS OFFENCE!
PUSH

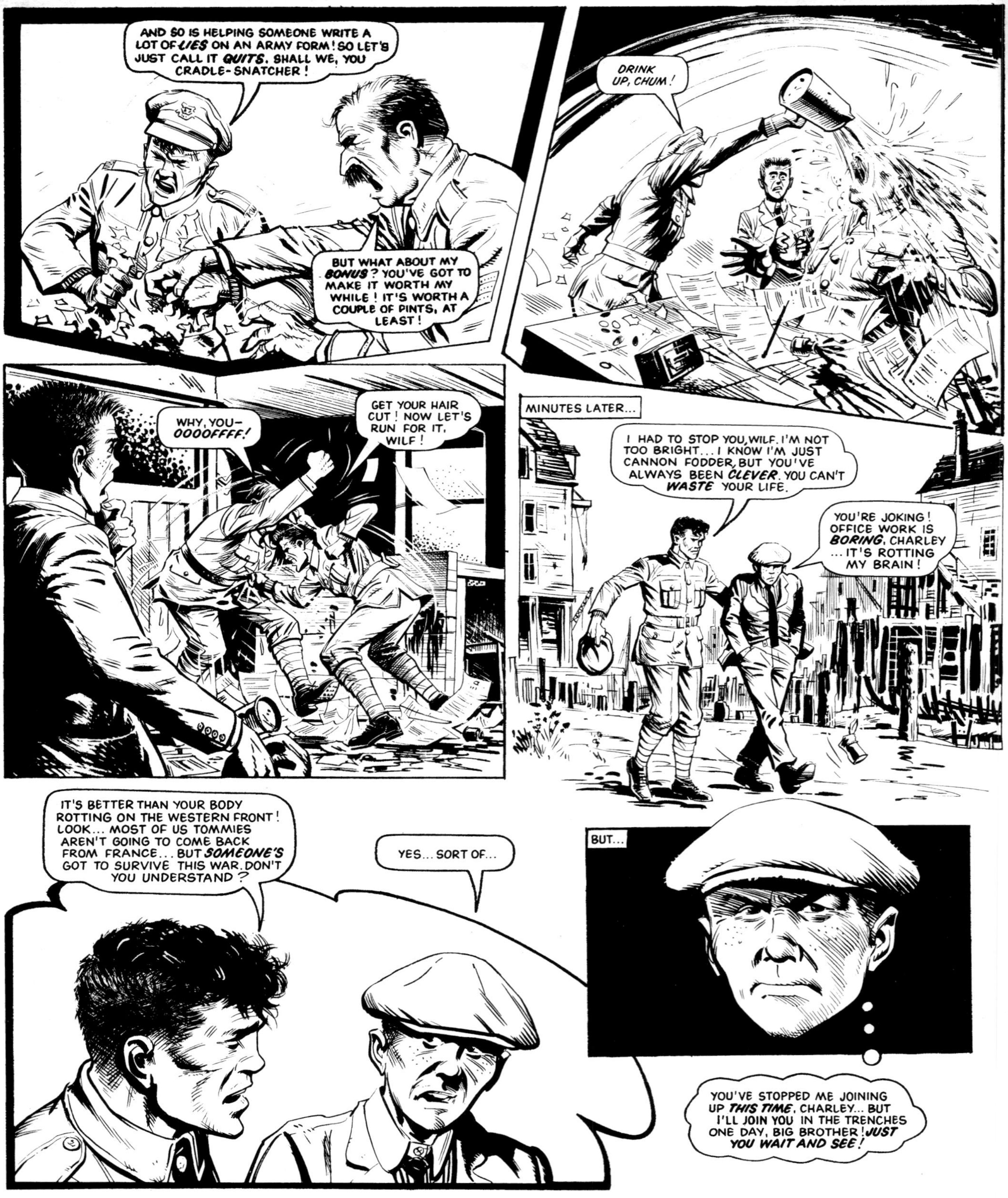
AND SO IS HELPING SOMEONE WRITE A LOT OF LIES ON AN ARMY FORM! SO LET'S JUST CALL IT QUITS, SHALL WE, YOU CRADLE-SNATCHER!
BUT WHAT ABOUT MY BONUS? YOU'VE GOT TO MAKE IT WORTH MY WHILE! IT'S WORTH A COUPLE OF PINTS, AT LEAST!
DRINK UP, CHUM!
WHY, YOU- OOOOFFFF!
GET YOUR HAIR CUT! NOW LET'S RUN FOR IT, WILF!
MINUTES LATER...
I HAD TO STOP YOU, WILF. I'M NOT TOO BRIGHT... I KNOW I'M JUST CANNON FODDER, BUT YOU'VE ALWAYS BEEN CLEVER. YOU CAN'T WASTE YOUR LIFE.
YOU'RE JOKING! OFFICE WORK IS BORING, CHARLEY ... IT'S ROTTING MY BRAIN!
IT'S BETTER THAN YOUR BODY ROTTING ON THE WESTERN FRONT! LOOK... MOST OF US TOMMIES AREN'T GOING TO COME BACK FROM FRANCE... BUT SOMEONE'S GOT TO SURVIVE THIS WAR. DON'T YOU UNDERSTAND?
YES... SORT OF...
BUT...
YOU'VE STOPPED ME JOINING UP THIS TIME, CHARLEY... BUT I'LL JOIN YOU IN THE TRENCHES ONE DAY, BIG BROTHER! JUST YOU WAIT AND SEE!

STRIP COMMENTARY

by Pat Mills

EPISODE 1 (pp. 14–17)

The letters home in the strip were inspired by real correspondence from World War One. I found the genuine letters as emotional as World War One poems. Their limited, terse vocabulary is actually an asset that creates a powerful response in the reader. Therefore, to me, they qualify as poetry. For example, one soldier wrote home:

'There are times out here when we would rather be gone than put up with conditions… when the Germans are bombarding and the boys get knocked over one by one and can't hit back… The boys come along crying like children and shaking like old men still the shells burst in the air… and is a man is not thinking then 'bing' go a bullet and maybe catch that man. And when you are not fighting you are working and it just seems you will get the dirt. But never mind, dear girlie, you are far braver than us, for you have to take what is given… If we go under we are gone… Don't let it spoil your Christmas for Bert would not like it if he was there.'

My neighbour, a Cambridge Don, disagreed with me. 'The letters from the trenches can't be categorised as poetry because they weren't intended as poems,' he loftily informed me. A *Punch* cartoon by Reading put the issue another way. As two 'Tommies' go over the top into an artillery barrage, one says to the other: 'I shouldn't really be here. I don't write poetry.' However, a national poet commented recently that I should actually be pleased the letters home haven't been categorised as poems because then they might end up in some sterile 'A' Level literature curriculum.

EPISODE 2 (pp. 18–21)

The sniper appears at the end of this episode, dressed in medieval armour. Some readers questioned the credibility of this, and even World War Two veterans were sceptical and thought I'd made it up. Of course it was authentic, alongside other strange images in future episodes like gas masks on horses and dogs, and the bizarre early tanks. These images give World War One the feeling of a nightmarish science fiction war. And this is a scary point. We tend to think of apocalyptic war as happening 'manana' — at some terrible and distant time in the future. It's chastening to think we are now living nearly a century after a science fiction war.

EPISODE 3 (pp. 19–24)

The detail on the photo of Charley's family is remarkable. Every one of the Bournes looks a warm and wonderful character. This photo inspired me to develop the family in future episodes. Thus Charley's mother becomes a 'canary' — her skin turned yellow by the shells she was making in an armaments factory. Because of this skin condition, she was socially ostracised and treated as if she were a leper. This was often the fate of the 'canaries' in World War One.

EPISODES 4 – 6 (pp. 25–34)

As Lieutenant Thomas suggests here, the British High Command must have known the impregnable state of the German trenches. Therefore to send soldiers over the top to attack them was a war crime — a clear act of mass murder. Recently, there is a trend amongst historians to justify the actions of the World War One generals. No doubt they would dismiss as naïve the view best expressed in the American post-World War One classic, *War is a Racket* by Brigadier General Smedley D. Butler: 'Only those who would be called upon to risk their lives for their country should have the privilege of voting to determine whether the nation should go to war.'

That sounds rather sensible to me. After all, if General Haig and politicians like Lloyd George actually had to go 'over the top' themselves would they have made more effort to minimise casualties; or even declared war in the first place? The answer is obvious and as relevant to our leaders today as it was then.

EPISODE 7 (pp. 35–37)

The tension continues to mount in preparation for the most shameful day in British military history when 60,000 of the 'Best of British' would be sacrificed. I tried wherever I could to use authentic postcards from the period and the Bruce Bairnsfather card, 'If you knows of a better 'ole', is a classic. His other cartoons and cards also honour the ordinary soldier.

The presentation of the letters was inspired by a story in a romantic teenage paper called *Romeo*, entitled 'The Private War of Nicola Brown'. Despite its unlikely home, this story was actually rather superb. It was drawn by the legendary Estaban Maroto and written by John Cornforth. In stark blacks and whites it showed the horrors of the Crimean War, with diary entries from nurse Nicola Brown. In fact, I think the diary entries worked better graphically on Nicola Brown than the letters on *Charley's War*. Eventually I stopped using them because I felt, as a dramatic device, they were running out of steam. However, I'm not sure everyone would agree with me.

My writing partner at the time, John Wagner, the writer/creator of *Judge Dredd*, was equally impressed by 'The Private War of Nicola Brown' and used similar diary entries in his *Battle* story 'Darkie's Mob' in a very powerful way.

EPISODE 8 (pp. 38–41)

A soldier is about to shoot himself in the foot in Episode 8. Self-inflicted wounds, desertions and executions were commonplace on the frontline. My grandfather was a policeman at the beginning of World War One and was called upon to spend much of his time arresting deserters. He objected strongly to such hateful work and so he joined the army and served as a cook in the trenches. When the war was over, he returned to his job in the police force. I only learnt of this in more recent years, long after he was dead. It's an example of how the 'Tommies' in the trenches were true to the emotive words of the World War One song, 'We'll Never Tell Them.' How many other unsung heroes there must have been whose stories have never been recorded.

EPISODES 9 – 12 (pp. 42–54)

Finally Charley and his mates go 'over the top'. The script still works for me, but I should have given Joe far more space to draw it. There are too many pictures on the page and such a battle needs really large images. Joe did a truly fantastic job here, but really I asked too much of him. I think I was overwhelmed by the horror of it all and I didn't have the skills to pace this better and expand the whole sequence. The bright sunshine of July 1st also makes the pages very white, so we don't get the powerful black and white contrasts of early night scenes.

Turning to the subject matter, I know Joe was sad drawing such a terrible event. He cautiously told me he 'shed a tear or two'. It's a tribute to his artistic genius and temperament that he could depict this relentless conflict for so many years.

EPISODES 13 – 14 (pp. 55–60)

Once again postcards are used to good effect. This military 'form' postcard is one of my favourites. I used it as a satirical device in the style of *Oh, What a Lovely War*. This film had a deep effect on me as a teenager. I saw it at least six times in one year and also watched the stage play. I was impressed by the use of visual metaphors and I tried to use the postcards in a similar way.

Oh, What a Lovely War is a true anti-war film, unlike some of the 'war is hell' variety. So I tried to ensure *Charley's War* was in the same ilk and could never glorify war. This was an important point to me. I once interviewed a soldier who fought in Northern Ireland about his experiences there and in a military prison — before writing about them in another radical comic series I created entitled *Third World War*, centred on the USA and UK's control of the Third World. He told me he joined the army for two reasons; firstly, because he loved the outdoor life; and secondly, because he read war comics as a kid. As I was one of the two creators of *Battle*, I felt some sense of responsibility here. It was one of the reasons why I needed to write *Charley's War*.

EPISODES 15 – 16 (pp. 61–67)

Finally the first day of the Somme is over. Everything that needed to be said is said in that final text panel.

EPISODES 17 – 19 (pp. 68–77)

A new sequence begins, setting the scene for the last great cavalry charge. It also features a Christmas truce. The famous truce of 1914 is well known, but there were others that have barely been recorded because the Generals fiercely opposed the truces and laid down artillery barrages whenever the British and German soldiers were likely to fraternise.

EPISODE 20 (pp. 78–80)

Lonely goes home to a hero's welcome. Joe's detail on the home front is mesmerising as ever. We really feel we are there. When I look at Joe's artwork, it is like going to the movies. You can hear and almost smell the scenes. Because I was familiar with most of the reference source material available, I'm pretty certain Joe actually drew many of these scenes out of his head. This means he had an almost magical artistic gift.

You might imagine that Joe and I spent hours on the phone talking over such scenes. Surprisingly, this is not the case. I never met him and we talked on the phone maybe five times in all the years we worked together. This was the traditional way comics were produced and, on this occasion, it worked.

It's a measure of Joe's professionalism that he never once asked for script changes; he drew everything that was put in front of him without comment or complaint. Yet, by the very nature of the creative process, there must have been occasions when he was less happy with certain stories. He was also drawing before fandom became a significant force in

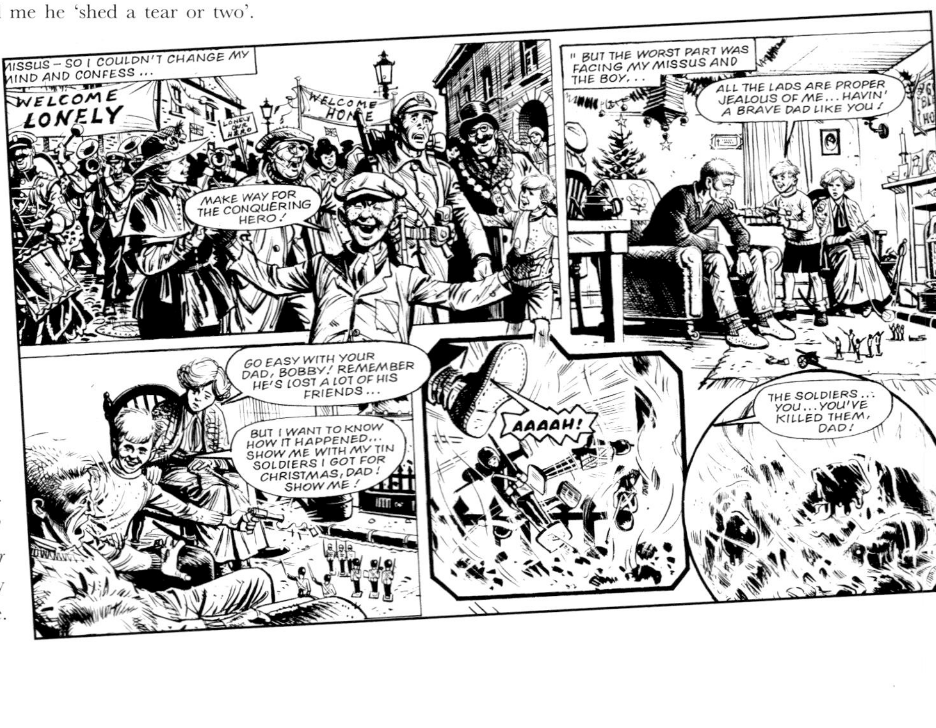
ISSUS – SO I COULDN'T CHANGE MY
IND AND CONFESS ...
WELCOME LONELY
LONELY OUR HERO
WELCOME HOME
MAKE WAY FOR THE CONQUERING HERO!
" BUT THE WORST PART WAS FACING MY MISSUS AND THE BOY...
ALL THE LADS ARE PROPER JEALOUS OF ME... HAVIN' A BRAVE DAD LIKE YOU!
GO EASY WITH YOUR DAD, BOBBY! REMEMBER HE'S LOST A LOT OF HIS FRIENDS...
BUT I WANT TO KNOW HOW IT HAPPENED... SHOW ME WITH MY TIN SOLDIERS I GOT FOR CHRISTMAS, DAD! SHOW ME!
AAAAH!
THE SOLDIERS... YOU... YOU'VE KILLED THEM, DAD!

UK comics; he never received any awards for his work, and the fees he received were barely adequate. So I reached the conclusion that he was drawing not for the fans, not for the money, but purely for the pleasure of it. I decided to use him as my role model in my own approach to my work and it's fair to say he had a significant affect on my life.

EPISODE 21 (pp. 81–84)

Ginger and Charley are under the duckboards at the bottom of a trench. I think this is an interesting example of exploring inner space in comics, rather than outer space. Too often in our medium, we feature vast and meaningless galactic empires, whereas a claustrophobic small space can be far more dramatic, as in this example. Colourful and fantastic science fiction terrains can lead to bad writing habits and quick fix, easy dramatic solutions. The limited possibilities in the trenches forced me to write to a higher standard.

EPISODES 22 – 24 (pp. 85–93)

It was a little uncomfortable having Charley and Ginger out of their usual bitter trench environment. There was a danger of it becoming a ripping yarn, like the first World War One novel I read as a boy, which rejoiced in the title *Dick Daring in the Dardanelles*. But it was absolutely essential so they could be present at the last great cavalry charge. I also feel the plotting pays off when we see at the end of Episode 24 the nightmarish figure of a gas masked horse and rider appear — surely a scene straight from Hell.

I would also feature poison gas later in *Charley's War*, notably at Verdun (a tale told by Charley's French Foreign Legion friend, Blue). Although the Germans used gas first, our record is by no means as clean as some would have us believe. Thus the British used poison gas against the Bolshevik Russians during their invasion of Russia in 1919 but the wind was wrong, so the weapon was ineffective.

I also discovered that, during the 1920s, the British RAF bombed Iraq with poison gas, wiping out several villages. Britain had occupied Iraq in order to obtain its oil and the Kurds were being 'difficult tribesmen'. Our use of poison gas was in contravention of a League of Nations treaty banning such weapons of mass destruction. Churchill was in favour of gas, regarding it as a 'scientific weapon'. My intention was to have Wilf, Charley's younger brother who served as a gunner in the RFC, fight in that conflict. Unfortunately, details were minimal so, with considerable regret, I shelved those plans.

EPISODES 25 – 27 (pp. 94–102)

There was very little information I could find on the physical aspects of the cavalry charge. And I think it shows a little in this sequence. With the benefit of hindsight, I should have researched an earlier cavalry charge, e.g. the Franco-Prussian War or the American Civil War, to dramatise this more effectively.

Research was always a problem on *Charley*. I enjoyed the process, but I had to set myself some time and financial limits, otherwise I'd have gone broke writing it. Ultimately, this problem of research would lead to me ending the serial.

Originally I intended to continue the saga into World War Two, with Charley's son, also named Charley. This was because it's become convenient to isolate World War One and see it as a 'bad' war, and World War Two or later wars as 'good' wars, a viewpoint I strongly disagree with. But, again, research difficulties made it impossible.

EPISODE 28 (pp. 103–105)

Charley is about to shoot Warrior here, but the horse makes a recovery, which was actually just as well. Editorial weren't keen on mercy

killings, no matter the justification. Thus, in a later sequence, a soldier is drowning in mud and begs Charley to shoot him. Charley does so. Although it was authentic, editorial changed it to Charley rescuing the soldier, which was far too convenient for my taste.

The only other censorship changes I can recall were the deletion of a reference to Charley using barbed wire to fish for rats. This was seen as a bit 'offensive'. And later, in 1918, when the Americans join the war, some white US soldiers behave in a racist way towards black US soldiers and threaten them with the justice of the Ku Klux Klan. This was deleted on the grounds that 'it might offend people', presumably the KKK?

Given some of the content of *Charley's War*, I think I got off lightly. It's why I let all these minor changes go because I was also writing about such controversial subjects as the British army mutiny at Etaples. This was a tragic and shocking event which even today little is known about apart from its dramatisation in the BBC TV series, *The Monocled Mutineer*.

EPISODE 29 (pp. 106–108)

Looking back on the opening picture of the soldiers singing in gas masks, it's visually extremely effective. But I doubt it was authentic and I don't think I would write such a scene today.

This book concludes with Charley becoming the 'Thirteenth Runner'. Messengers in war had a high mortality rate and things really don't look good for our hero as he heads off down the trench.

EPISODE 30 (pp. 109–111)

Re-reading this episode after so long, what comes across is a strong story idea, written far too heavily by today's standards. I felt a real desire to edit it after it was drawn; something that wasn't possible in those days, but which I usually insist on now, because a scene that works one way at script stage may come over entirely different once it's drawn. And over-writing becomes glaringly obvious, as it does here.

Heavily editing the final drawn version isn't something artists always approve of, because the writer may alter the story interpretation, and it's by no means common practice even today. You can often tell when a story hasn't been properly edited – the words and the art don't match too well. I think it is necessary to achieve the highest possible standards and I only wish I'd done it here.

But, despite this, the overall sense of trench drama is as powerful as ever and the complexities of the front line are depicted with startling clarity.

EPISODES 31 – 32 (pp. 112–117)

The recreation of the class system in the trenches is authentic and the detail with which Joe depicts it is superb. The image of the dead men lying in the trench on the final page is also powerful.

This episode, too, has some problems from a scripting point of view. The story shows signs of being too influenced by traditional comic writing which can result in unlikely dialogue, for example: 'Noooo! Everyone's dead! Lying in the dirt!' Today, I feel, a silent panel would be far more effective. However, you may disagree and if so, it highlights the changing fashions and often subjective nature of writing and editing.

EPISODES 33 – 36 (pp. 118–129)

The execution of British soldiers by our own side is one of the most tragic aspects of World War One. If anyone regards its depiction in *Charley's War* as being over-emotive or pure 'comic book', then consider the following: bandleader Victor Sylvester had lied about his age, like Charley, and was serving on the Western Front aged seventeen. He was caught reading a document marked, 'For the eyes of officers only', which was a list of soldiers condemned to be shot. As punishment, he was ordered to serve in a firing squad and had to shoot men from his own regiment. During the execution, he shut his eyes, but when he opened them he saw his target was still alive and struggling. An officer finished the man off with a revolver. Sylvester suffered a nervous breakdown as a result.

Robert Graves claimed to have seen a secret order that cases of cowardice should *always* be punished by death, no medical evidence being allowed. The doctors, in any event, supported the authorities. As a result, a soldier who was certified mentally defective was executed. Another who was found behind the lines, choking from poison gas, was also shot. Other victims included a seventeen-year-old, a tramp who had been conscripted and went on his travels again, and a nineteen-year-old volunteer who refused to put his cap on. He was shot two days before Christmas. Sometimes if there was a delay, deserters would be sent back into the trenches until the trial could be arranged and then they would be removed from the front, tried, sentenced and shot.

307 British soldiers were executed. This figure was far higher than the number of French, Germans or Americans shot for desertion.

EPISODES 37 – 38 (pp. 130–135)

Field Punishment Number One was the barbaric punishment used behind the lines, and was a key factor in inciting the explosive British mutiny at the Bull Ring in Etaples. This involved 100,000 British soldiers, and the full truth about it is still unclear. The mutiny inspired the book and TV series *The Monocled Mutineer*, which today's revisionist World War One historians and Tory MPs have heavily criticised as being inaccurate and unsourced. In fact, the book was very accurate and does quote its sources, even including the full name and address of a mutineer.

EPISODE 39 (pp. 136–138)

The horrors of Field Punishment Number One continue and are graphically drawn by Joe. He was from a wartime generation and had seen action in the Navy, so there was nothing '1970s' in his attitudes. The fact that a writer and artist from two very different generations and backgrounds could combine together so effectively strongly suggests we were depicting an objective truth about World War One.

EPISODE 40 (pp. 139–141)

The execution of his commanding officer is still on Charley's mind in this episode – as it is on mine.

Disturbingly, we live in a society where there is a trend by today's historians to rehabilitate the generals responsible for such crimes. For example, *Haig: A Reappraisal 70 Years On*, eds. Brian Bond and Nigel Cave (Leo Cooper, 1999), dispels the 'myths' that Haig was callous, cold and indifferent to the horrors his troops were undergoing.

But it's this same Haig who could not visit seriously injured soldiers because it made him physically sick. And who did not just want to execute British soldiers for desertion; he wanted to shoot Australians, too. He promised he would use the death penalty on them 'very sparingly'.

Similarly, a book on General Kitchener, the originator of concentration camps, has the retro-imperialist title *Kitchener: Architect of Victory, Artisan of Peace* (Carroll & Graf, 2001), which I think tells you all you need to know.

It's worth remembering that, in this same year, the British had just brutally crushed the Easter Rising in Ireland. In May 1916, the Bishop of Limerick wrote to one of these warlords, a General Maxwell, referring to him as the 'military dictator' of Ireland. He went on to say to Maxwell, 'You took great care that no plea for mercy should interpose on behalf of the poor young fellows who surrendered to you in Dublin.

The first announcement we got of their fate was the announcement that they had been shot in cold blood. Personally I regard your action with horror and I believe that it has outraged the conscience of the country. Then the deporting of hundreds and even thousands of poor fellows without a trial of any kind, seems to me an abuse of power as fatuous as it is arbitrary.'

There was nothing unique about General Maxwell – he was part of a military class and breed that deserves our condemnation, not approval, and it's shaming for all of us that historians should now attempt to approve or exonerate these individuals of their appalling misdeeds.

EPISODE 41 (pp. 142–144)

This is the episode where Charley's popular friend Ginger dies suddenly and without warning, which shocked many readers. I did this deliberately, because I loathe works of fiction where a character is 'set up' for death and you can see it coming. I think it's good to challenge the readers' assumptions that a popular sidekick will always be around. We need to maintain a sense of real drama, that anything could happen next.

EPISODE 42 (pp. 145–147)

We see Charley walking along with the remains of his friend in a bag. I often wonder what would have happened if we had actually showed soldiers torn apart by bombs in comics. I am sure we would have been criticised as being disgusting and horrific and such a comic would be promptly banned. But isn't that the point? The real nature of war would be exposed.

EPISODES 43 – 45 (pp. 148–156)

The tanks go into action. They were viewed at the time as 'atrocity' weapons: true weapons of mass destruction. I believe our government and media decide what is an atrocity weapon and what isn't and condition the population accordingly. So a World War One tank is rather an amusing ancient contraption, and a modern tank is an impressive military expression of our industrial might. But, basically, a tank is a 'good' weapon.

Poison gas, however, is an 'atrocity' weapon used by wicked dictators – even though it was used in the 1930s by the RAF on tribesmen in Iraq.

In the recent rehabilitation of General Haig, he is presented as being pro-tank, which is at odds with past accounts. Previously he was presented as a cavalryman who only saw a limited role for the tank. This seems more likely as tanks were only used in a limited way on the Somme.

EPISODES 46 – 47 (pp. 157–162)

Joe had a special gift – to be able to look at a photo and bring it to life from every angle. This he does with the tanks. The scene where the German soldiers are climbing all over the tank is totally convincing. And the tank interior is amazing. It must have come out of his head because there are no references available, and you can almost smell the oil and grease!

By comparison, an image of German soldiers moving a field gun round to shoot the tanks is taken directly from a reference I sent him. Although Joe has done a superb job on it, I still prefer his own vivid imagination.

EPISODES 48 – 49 (pp. 163–168)

Steampunk is very popular these days in comics, but to me World War One was the original steampunk war. And the images here would strongly compete with any steampunk comic strip. What could be more fantastic than wearing medieval masks in landships which communicate with each other by semaphore flags? This is pure H. G. Wells!

EPISODES 50 – 52 (pp. 169–177)

The sequence where Charley's tank smashes into the church is one of my all-time favourites. There is no such record that it happened so dramatically, but it might have done. And that has always been my criterion.

EPISODES 53 – 54 (pp. 178–184)

Episode 54 begins the four-page episodes. These give Joe's work the space it deserves. Three pages a week could look a little cramped on occasion. The extra space gives his art comparable stature to French artists who have drawn similar stories about Verdun and the Russian Front. But it was a real strain for him because of his meticulous detail.

Most British artists can produce around six pages a week as it's the only way to economically survive. It's one reason why British artists work for America where backgrounds aren't so important. In fact one American interviewer commented to me recently that, 'You really make use of the space behind the characters in your stories'.

I understand both points of view, but Joe could never take such short-cuts and I believe it's why he is one of our country's greatest comic artists.

This episode was censored by the new *Battle* editor, Terry Magee. Originally Titch was being sucked down in the mud and Charley had no choice but to agree to Titch's request to shoot him. Instead, the editor wrote in new dialogue with Charley using the rifle to haul him out. And then he arranges for Titch to be sent home. I had to let it go. After all, I was getting away with a lot more…

EPISODE 55 (pp. 185–188)

The Judgement Troopers arrive! This was one of the most popular *Charley's War* stories ever. Not least because Joe now had those four pages to do his art justice. And it's a story I've been asked a lot about. So to answer those queries: the German offensive involving the Judgement Troopers was fictitious, as is the character of Zeiss. But there were lesser German counter-attacks on the Somme and I collected together all the details and combined them into this one powerful assault on the British lines. So the individual incidents are authentic.

Doctor 'No' appears here. Needless to say, the dialogue is authentic. It still makes me angry reading his lines. But what a superb visual rendering of him and how well observed. That arrogant and contemptuous attitude towards lesser mortals. The boozer's red nose. His armoured body language. This is the kind of guy who spends most of his time on the golf course, when he isn't in the pub, and has a five-second attention span when we're telling him our health concerns. Only a handful of comic artists – like Kevin O'Neill, Brian Bolland, Dave Gibbons and Charlie Adlard – could draw such a definitive character today.

EPISODE 56 (pp. 189–192)

A bit more censorship here. Originally they were casting that line out into No Man's Land to fish for rats. The editor thought it was too offensive. But British soldiers did it…

EPISODES 57 – 58 (pp. 193–200)

Another of my favourite scenes is this one, where Colonel Zeiss addresses a parade of pioneer troops. Each one is beautifully characterised. Joe really understood human nature and frailty. To do so, must have made him a very warm and special human being. I could stare at scenes like this for hours and have done.

The episode ends with the Judgement Troopers attacking the British lines.

EPISODE 59 (pp. 201–204)

The most spectacular sequence ever in *Charley's War* begins. This volume began with an episode which I was less than happy with from a scripting point of view. But it ends with one where I am really pleased with my dialogue and pacing. It feels good to me and I doubt, if I was writing it today, whether I would make any changes. The aristocratic officer might be a little stereotypical and effete for some tastes, but I met a similar character only the other day and I was struck by how little some members of the aristocracy have changed in nearly a century. And there's a reason for this. As actor Peter Cushing once said on television, 'I based my life on Tom Merry' – the *Boys' Own* hero. So people do tend to use role models to inspire them, including comic book heroes, a theme Kevin O'Neill and I pursue in our superhero series *Marshal Law*. And they often behave like archetypes they admire or, in this case, a stereotype.

It would be interesting to know which comic book characters today's thirty-somethings may have based their lives on. Charley? Judge Dredd? Slàine? I know of at least one reader who based his life on Judge Dredd…

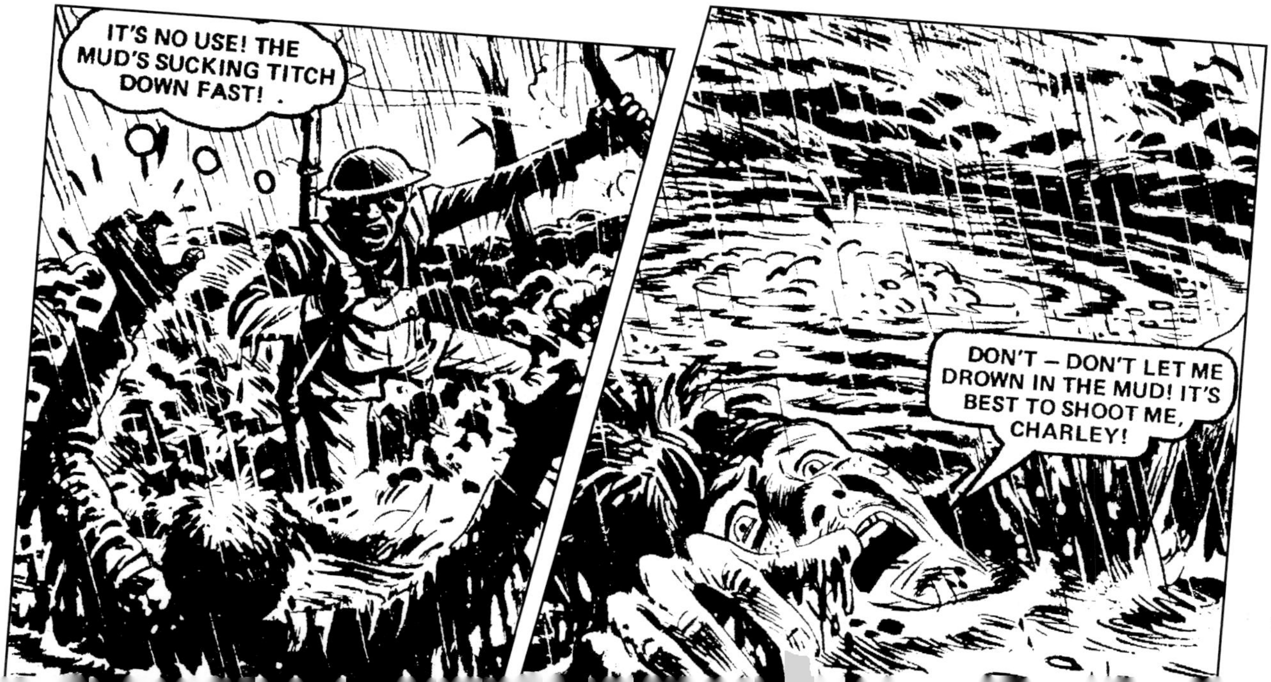
IT'S NO USE! THE MUD'S SUCKING TITCH DOWN FAST!
DON'T – DON'T LET ME DROWN IN THE MUD! IT'S BEST TO SHOOT ME, CHARLEY!

...AS SOON AS MRS. BRUIN'S BACK WAS TURNED, HER NAUGHTY BOYS ESCAPED THROUGH THE WINDOW... HURR! HURR! THAT'S GOOD, THAT IS!

EPISODE 60 (pp. 205–208)

The Donkey Men seem – like so many aspects of World War One – totally bizarre, yet they were authentic. I don't have the imagination to dream them up. Joe's artwork continues to bring the trench war totally alive. I'm often asked whether I'd consider doing something with *Charley's War* today – whether in comic strip, film or prose novel. Looking at these pages, it's hard to see how, because Joe's art is 50% of *Charley's War* and without his contribution, it would be an entirely different story.

EPISODE 61 (pp. 209–212)

Although this battle with the Judgement Troopers is fictional, it is still a combination of a number of genuine separate action incidents. The heroism and non-stop action may seem a little *Ripping Yarns* for some and the serial has been criticised for showing such supposedly 'unlikely' scenes. However, it is taken from a number of sources, including some upbeat and dramatic accounts of life in the trenches written and published during the Great War. One of the authors was Patrick MacGill, I recall. It's unlikely books that showed such 'derring-do' would be reprinted today, because the accepted wisdom for our generation is that the conflict was unrelentingly boring, grim and nightmarish, with little room for more than just the very rare act of personal heroism. This has the unfortunate – and , I believe, entirely calculated – effect of diminishing the efforts of the individual. It makes the ordinary soldier (and we, the readers) seem powerless in the face of Armageddon.

EPISODE 62 (pp. 213–216)

The conversation between the German Major and Colonel Zeiss, during which they discuss the inhumanity of poison gas and shrapnel, seems a little naïve now; yet it is worth remembering that the Germans saw the tank as an inhumane weapon of mass destruction. Today, we have been conditioned to accept it as an entirely legitimate weapon.

EPISODES 63 – 64 (pp. 217–224)

The humour in *Charley's War* has aged well, because we can all relate to its cynicism. Thus a soldier tells Charley to shut the door of a destroyed building: 'You're letting the cold in.' While I was writing the serial, I submitted a proposal for a TV comedy called *Over the Top* about World War One. Loosely based on *Charley's War*, it was an *Upstairs, Downstairs* in the trenches with an officer like Lieutenant Snell ringing a bell in his dug-out for his servant to bring him tea. It never got beyond proposal stage, but I was delighted to see – many years later – *Blackadder Goes Forth* bringing out the dark humour of the trenches. It's one of my favourite comedies. Today, cruel characters like Doctor 'No' and the Officer who sends Charley and his mates back to the trenches would not be out of place in *League of Gentlemen* or *Little Britain*.

EPISODE 65 (pp. 225–228)

'Sandbag Pud' — what a wonderful idea! Only the British Tommy could dream that up.

EPISODES 66 – 67 (pp. 229–236)

The 'Queue of Death' sequence is very powerful and valid, although the Germans feel a bit arch for my taste today. If I was writing this now, I would still have them executing the Tommies – but in a less sadistic, even matter-of-fact way.

Editorial added that panel on page four: 'The young soldier saw sorrow in his comrades' eyes, but also a grim resolve.' I suppose they thought they had to further justify the soldiers' actions. It's unnecessary. Please ignore it.

EPISODE 68 (pp. 237–240)

A brilliant opening pic from Joe. And the *Rainbow* comic is featured here! The look on Charley and co.'s faces as the soldier reads about Mrs. Bruin's naughty boys is sublime!

EPISODE 69 (pp. 241–244)

The evil of the minds that dreamt up combining two gases so the Tommies would take off their masks is unspeakable. It was pointed out to me recently that the two-pronged gas attack is something echoed in modern terror tactics, whereby an initial bomb is then followed up with a second, activated a short time later, designed to maximise casualties and fatalities to the 'first responders' — police, fire, medical etc.

EPISODE 70 (pp. 245–248)

Champagne in the machine gun?!! I can hear some young establishment historian saying now, 'Nonsense! That never happened.' But, like the claim that the Tommies never brewed tea with the machine-gun's boiling water, he would be wrong.

EPISODE 71 (pp. 249–252)

The character of Smith 70 was based on Doug Church, the art editor of *2000 AD*, who designed the visual look of the 'galaxy's greatest comic'.

EPISODE 72 (pp. 253–256)

Editorial introduced this terrible *Charley's War* logo. How awful and inappropriate. It's like something out of a circus.

The Battle Police shoot deserters on the spot. This will possibly be disputed by a reader who wrote me a well-researched 'hate' letter a few months ago. He objected to the anti-war stance of the series and questioned the number of executions of deserters, challenging minor details for their authenticity. He particularly objected to a scene I showed – reprinted in Volume Two – where Tommies were tied by their wrists and feet to gun wheels during 'Field Punishment Number One'. He said they were only tied by their wrists. Therefore I was a liar and also a fascist whom the Kaiser would be proud of.

EPISODE 73 (pp. 257–260)

Colonel Zeiss seems a bit arch today and his neo-Nazi characterisation clearly shows the benefit of hindsight. Despite that, he still works for me. I think he was a good villain.

EPISODE 74 (pp. 261–264)

The final picture on the last page of this episode is worth lingering on. I'm 99% certain that the poignancy of this scene was created by Joe. I certainly don't recall writing it. It shows one train with wounded leaving in one direction, while fresh cannon fodder head off in the opposite direction. Left behind, on a platform positioned strategically between them, is a dead soldier going only to his grave. This is poetic and truly moving. The detail is astonishing and the movie-style down-shot is fabulous. Many a film director would envy it. And it's depicted in just a quarter of a page, too. This could explain why it has been overlooked as an iconic image. I'd like to see it much larger. Congratulations again, Joe. You remain my all-time favourite artist.

EPISODE 75 (pp. 265–268)

By now *Charley's War* was so popular that editorial wanted it to appear on the cover every week, so they asked me to write the story in such a way as to generate strong cover images. Given the anti-war nature of the story, this was rather demanding and, inevitably, we would not always agree on what would make a good comic cover. So when editorial didn't like my ideas, they were relegated to ordinary-sized pictures in the story. This is what happened to my first abortive cover, which is seen here squashed into panel one. Based closely on a dramatic *Stern* magazine cover I found, it shows Charley drowning in mud in his hospital bed. I suspect editorial thought it too horrific or 'lacking in action'.

The ludicrous machine designed to cure post-traumatic stress disorder is taken from a reference I sent Joe. Even today PTSD is still not fully acknowledged or understood and its symptoms are often confused with conventional mental illness. Perhaps traumatic amnesia had something to do with why the soldiers declared in their song, 'We'll never tell them'. Many Tommies must have mercifully forgot the horrors of the trenches.

EPISODE 76 (pp. 269–272)

The funeral hearse was another cover idea of mine, again relegated to the opening picture of the story by editorial. I think an Edwardian hearse is a great cover image, but presumably it 'lacked action'.

The final page, a summary of the disaster of the Battle of the Somme, is a personal favourite of mine. It's hard to see why today's historians legitimise the 'achievements' of General Haig when one reads the chilling statistics on this page. One small change was made by editorial: they placed exclamation marks on the text, notably on 'The Battle of the Somme wiped them out!', which seems so unnecessary. It would have been far more effective without an exclamation mark.

EPISODE 77 (pp. 273–276)

The need to start the stories on the front cover meant the stories would sometimes be rather jerky in order to devise a suitably powerful visual to begin each episode. This is a case in point. But at least it had action, which is why editorial approved it as a cover. The appalling, arch dialogue on the cover makes me cringe. It was added by editorial. It is really dreadful. Please ignore it.

This is where Charley's 'Home Front' story begins. It's worth stressing how risky this was as a concept. Until *Charley's War*, the idea of a hero having a home life and not being in front-line action against the enemy every week was unheard of. Later in the serial I even had Charley marry. But, traditionally, comic-book heroes never had mums, sex lives

or home lives – they seemed to live for action and nothing else. It's understandable why this is so; after all, it's what the readers primarily want. Sometimes, however, you have to ignore the readers and do what is right for the story and yourself. When I made it work – as in this story – it was very satisfying. When I didn't make it work, in some other stories, there would be howls of complaint from the readers, and baying for more blood.

EPISODE 78 (pp. 277–280)

Again, there's a bit of a jerk between episodes here, because of the need for strong cover images. It's a pity, especially as my cover idea was turned down. This time I intended to show the Silvertown disaster as the cover; a truly apocalyptic event in the history of London. Editorial didn't think a scene of total desolation would make a good visual and relegated it to the story proper. I disagree; it just required more effort and design – street signs amidst the debris, the ruined interior of a terraced house, a discarded child's toy and so forth. But action covers are always 'safer'. This ongoing disparity of views emphasises what a maverick story *Charley's War* was in mainstream British comics. And still is. Why is there that ludicrous Teutonic-styled logo on page one? How inappropriate. The exquisitely drawn children singing 'The Hymn of Hate' at the end of the episode seems the stuff of fantasy, but children would sing patriotic songs as their fathers went off to war in their Zeppelins. And I recall in the 1970s, when the warships returned home from the Falklands, naval families greeted them singing Rod Stewart's 'Sailing'.

EPISODE 79 (pp. 281–284)

A nice, safe, action cover here – editorial must have liked this one. The dialogue was added by them. Please ignore it. The Super Zeppelins may seem archaic now but they were the equivalent of the invisible stealth bombers of today. Zeppelins were known as the 'Baby Killers'; an appropriate name for modern bombers, too. Then, as now, governments like to present their super weapons – planes, tanks and missiles – as totally invulnerable, to terrorise and intimidate civilian populations. It reminds me of when the Serbs shot down a stealth bomber attacking Belgrade; they waved a banner for the CNN cameras saying, 'We're sorry, America – we didn't know your planes were invisible.'

EPISODE 80 (pp. 285–288)

The opening picture was once again designed to be a cover, but clearly editorial thought it was too passive. Colchester is my home town so it's often featured in my stories.

The observation car and sound detectors featured in this episode put the 'steampunk' fantasies of science fiction writers in the shade.

EPISODE 81 (pp. 289–292)

Finally, a cover that both the writer and the editor liked! Although the colouring on it was fairly average, so it's just as well you are seeing it in black and white. This episode was reprinted recently in the *Judge Dredd Megazine,* just after the recent London Underground bombings.

It's chilling how at that time even the Underground wasn't safe. Often the Underground is presented in films as a welcoming 'Spirit of the Blitz' shelter, but it was certainly not the intention of the authorities that it should be. During the Great War, people had to *force* their way down into the subway.

EPISODE 82 (pp. 293–296)

I think Charley cycling on his bike must have been another cover that never happened. If so, editorial were absolutely right; it would have looked pretty flat. Now the next scene, with people rioting, would have made a strong cover, but there's no way I'd have got away with it. The ugly scenes of racism against Russians mistaken for Germans have their parallels in recent times. Then – as now – the popular press whipped up hatred against 'the enemy within.'

EPISODE 83 (pp. 297–300)

I went to great lengths to find the correct fire engine reference for the cover. In retrospect, this cover is too traditional for my taste and I wish I had thought of something more in keeping with the anti-war mood of the story. But it had action, so editorial were happy. Thankfully they didn't add any embarrassing dialogue from the firemen!

I particularly like the scene of Sir James scuttling off for Knightsbridge. The traditional propaganda image of the upper classes and the working classes all suffering together in wartime is open to question. No; the working classes suffered far more. As they lived around the munitions factories, they were a prime target and there is some evidence that wealthier parts of London were deliberately not bombed by the Germans. It is something I intended to explore in detail if I had ever written Charley into World War Two. I recall reading that in 1939 the authorities' first move – after the declaration of war – was not to make air-raid shelters for the East End, but to order an enormous quantity of coffins.

I sent Joe references of the factory of death and he has done an excellent job in depicting the fields of shells. Look at the letters on the sides of the posts – it gives you some idea of the vastness of the place. It must have been bigger than an airport car park. I think the scene where Charley runs through the empty factory shouting out 'Ma!' would make a great cover. These 'fields of shells' scenes really are classics and would benefit from enlarging or recreating by a suitable artist to fully appreciate their power.

The penultimate picture where a bomb is about to drop down a factory chimney is a masterpiece. The intricate detail of the streets below and the angle the bomb is falling are magnificent. A movie-maker could not have done better. We are left wondering… Is there is going to be a second Silvertown disaster?

EPISODE 84 (pp. 301–304)

The death of the Zeppelin. These machines seem so bizarre – the stuff of science fiction – that it's easy to forget they were the weapons of mass destruction of their day, shortly followed by the aptly-named, giant 'Gotha' bombers.

It's hard to imagine the 'shock and awe' they must have created. One East End woman at the time exclaimed of the Zeppelins, 'I don't think they ought to be allowed to make them things and go up there, prying into the Almighty's affairs.'

EPISODE 85 (pp. 305–308)

This is one of my all-time favourite episodes. Page 2, panel 3 is fabulous: Joe had a truly British sense of humour and this picture reminds me of the immortal *Just William* illustrations by Thomas Henry. As always, I am mesmerised by Joe's detailing. Take the scene that follows with the skeleton of the Zeppelin and the chap selling hot pies. It is one thing for me to write that in a script, the work of minutes; it is another for Joe to draw it with such engrossing precision.

EPISODE 86 (pp. 309–312)

Because *Charley's War* was the most popular story in *Battle*, editorial wanted to run it on the cover to boost sales, but my ideas about what would make a good cover and theirs rarely coincided. So when they didn't like my idea, it would become the first picture of the episode inside. This is the case here. That image of Wilf outside the recruiting office is superb.

I wanted to establish Charley's brother Wilf as a character, ready for him to feature a year or so later in the serial. This was rather optimistic of me, given the state of British comics, because you never knew whether they would be around long enough; most were not. Many comics were merged into each other within months of their launch in order to artificially boost sales. It annoyed readers but their views were always ignored. This consciously ephemeral attitude greatly harmed British comics. It was summed up by the publisher's merger philosophy of 'hatch, match and despatch'. ✢

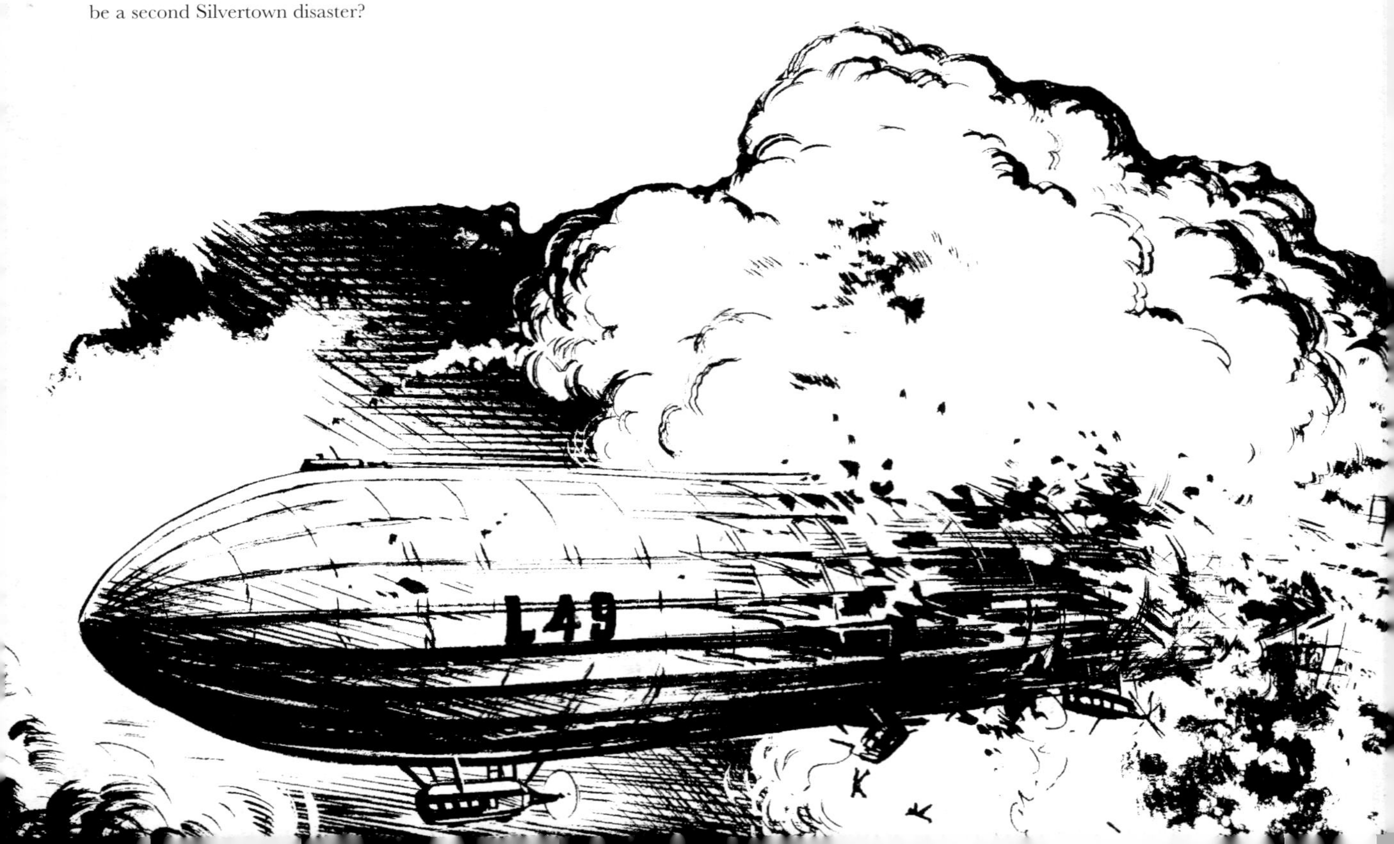
L49